D1746063

CHRONICLES OF THE BIBLE LANDS

Editor Graham Speake
Art Editor Andrew Lawson
Map Editors Nicola Harris,
Zoë Goodwin
Picture Editor Linda Proud
Index Jennifer Drake-Brockman
Design Adrian Hodgkins
Production Clive Sparling

This edition published in 2003
by Angus Books Ltd
12 Ravensbury Terrace
London SW18 4RL

ISBN 1-904594-05-0

AN ANDROMEDA BOOK

Originally published in 1985
by Macdonald & Co
(Publishers) Ltd as
The New Atlas of the Bible

Copyright © 1985 Equinox
(Oxford) Ltd 1985

Planned and produced by Andromeda
Kimber House, 1 Kimber Road
Abingdon, Oxfordshire
OX14 1BZ

All rights reserved, No part of this
publication may be reproduced, stored in
a retrieval system, or transmitted, in any
form or by any means, electronic,
mechanical, photocopying, recording or
otherwise, without prior permission
of the publisher and copyright holder.

Production by Omnipress,
Eastbourne, UK

Printed and bound in Singapore

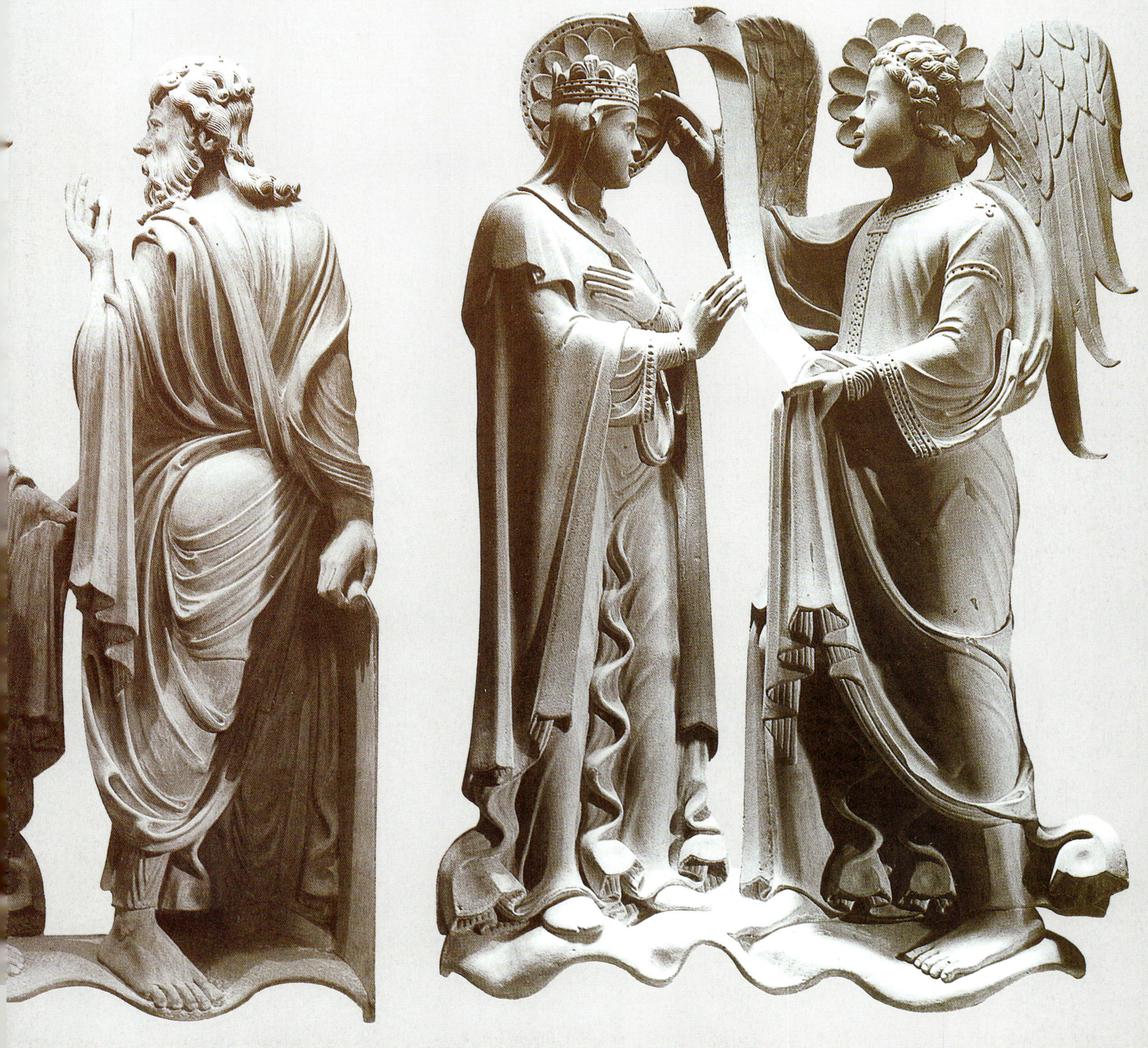

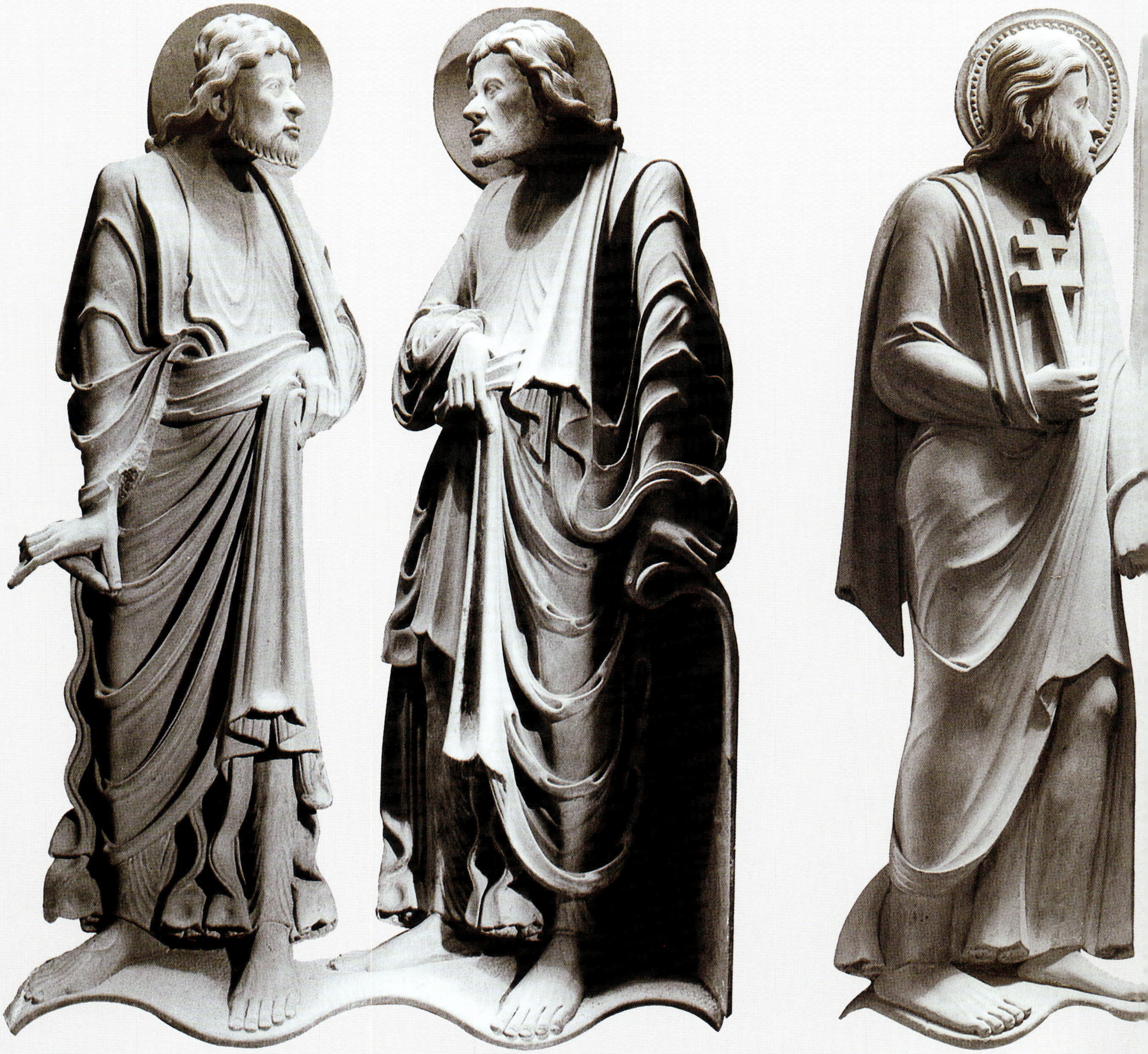

CHRONICLES
OF THE
BIBLE LANDS

JOHN ROGERSON

angus

CONTENTS

8 Chronological Table
12 Preface

Part One: The Bible and its Literature

14 The Composition and Transmission of the Bible

Part Two: The Bible and History

24 An Outline of Biblical History
43 The Bible in Art

Part Three: The Bible and Geography

58 The Geography of Ancient Israel
72 The Coastal Plain North of Mount Carmel
76 The Coastal Plain South of Mount Carmel
84 The Shephelah
94 The Hill Country of Judea
104 The Judean Desert
114 The Negev and Sinai
128 Galilee
146 Bethel, Samaria, Carmel and Jezreel
162 The Jerusalem Hills
192 The Jordan Valley and the Dead Sea
202 Transjordan
214 The Empires Surrounding Israel

225 List of Illustrations
227 Bibliography
229 Gazetteer
233 Index

Special Features

- 16 Writing in the Ancient World
- 18 The Codex Sinaiticus
- 22 Martin Luther: Reformer and Translator
- 64 The Mapping of the Holy Land
- 66 Animals of the Bible
- 68 Plants of the Bible
- 92 Biblical Warfare
- 142 Everyday Life in Biblical Times
- 160 Other Contemporary Religions
- 174 Old Testament Jerusalem
- 182 Herod's Temple at Jerusalem
- 186 Jerusalem as Jesus knew it
- 190 The Topography of the Passion

Site Features

- 74 Tyre and Sidon
- 82 Caesarea
- 88 Lachish
- 100 Bethlehem
- 110 Masada
- 113 Qumran
- 118 Arad
- 120 Beer-sheba
- 125 Timna
- 134 Hazor
- 138 Capernaum
- 157 Megiddo
- 196 Jericho

List of Maps

- 10 Lands of the Bible
- 24 The fertile crescent
- 25 The wanderings of Abraham, Isaac and Jacob
- 26 The routes of the Exodus
- 28 The conquests of Joshua
- 29 Tribal divisions according to the book of Joshua
- 30 The main incidents of the period of the Judges
- 31 The encounters between Saul, David and the Philistines
- 32 David's empire
- 32 Solomon's administrative districts
- 33 The main incidents of the divided monarchy
- 34 The Assyrian empire and its effects on Judah and Israel
- 35 The Babylonian empire and its effects on Judah
- 35 The Persian empire and its significance for Judah
- 36 The conquests of Alexander
- 37 The Maccabean revolt and its aftermath
- 38 The conquests of Herod the Great
- 38 The division of Palestine among Herod's sons
- 40 The missionary journeys of Paul and the expansion of the early Church
- 59 The geography of Israel
- 60 The climate of Israel
- 61 The geology of Israel
- 63 The vegetation of ancient Israel
- 63 Land use in modern Israel
- 71 Key to the regional maps
- 73 The coastal plain north of Mount Carmel
- 77 The coastal plain south of Mount Carmel: northern section
- 79 The coastal plain south of Mount Carmel: southern section
- 84 The Shephelah
- 95 The hill country of Judea
- 105 The Judean desert
- 114 The Negev
- 115 The Sinai peninsula
- 129 Galilee
- 147 The heartland of Israel: Carmel and the valley of Jezreel
- 148 The heartland of Israel: Bethel and the Samaria hills
- 162 The Jerusalem hills
- 192 The Jordan valley and the Dead Sea
- 202 Transjordan: Ammon, Edom, Gilead, Moab, Damascus
- 214 The empires surrounding Israel

CHRONOLOGICAL TABLE

	3000 BC	2000 BC	1000 BC	900 BC
SYRIA/ PALESTINE/ TRANSJORDAN	Early Bronze I 3150–2850 EB II 2850–2650 EB III 2650–2350 EB IV 2350–2200 Middle Bronze I 2200–2000 Region characterized by small city-states, e.g. at Arad, Jericho, Megiddo	MB IIA 2000–1750 MB IIB 1750–1550 Late Bronze I 1550–1400 LB IIA 1400–1300 LB IIB 1300—1200 Iron Age IA 1200–1150 IA IB 1150–1000 1750–1550 Abraham, Isaac and Jacob; descent to Egypt c.1390–1340 Letters to Egypt (Amarna letters) describe disruptive activity of "Habiru" c.1190 Philistines settle in southern coastal plain 1220–1020 Period of Israelite settlement and period of the Judges Saul c.1020–1000	David subdues the Philistines, captures Jerusalem. Solomon builds temple Kingdom divides at death of Solomon c.924 Shoshenq invades Judah and Israel David c.1000–965 Solomon c.967–928 *Judah* Rehoboam 928–911 Asa 908–867 *Israel* Jeroboam 928–907 Baasha 906–883	Omri dominates Judah and Moab Elijah opposes Ahab and Jezebel Elisha has Jehu anointed *Judah* Jehoshaphat 870–846 Jehoram 851–843 Ahaziah 843–842 Athaliah 842–836 Joash 836–798 *Israel* Omri 882–871 Ahab 873–852 Joram 851–842 Jehu 842–814

A cuneiform tablet of about 2900 BC from Mesopotamia.

Clay mask from Hazor, 14th century BC.

Solomon's temple, 10th century BC.

EGYPT	2920 Dynastic period begins. *1st Dynasty* 2920–2770 2360 First step pyramid built, at Saqqara	*15th Dynasty* (Hyksos) 1640–1532 *Amarna Period* 1352–1333 *19th Dynasty* Sethos I (1306–1290) Ramesses II (1290–1224) Mernepbah (1224–1214) c.1300–c.1220 oppression of Hebrews. Exodus from Egypt	Shoshenq I (945–924)	Battle of Qarqar 853 Ahab joins coalition against Shalmaneser
MESOPOTAMIA	2900–2340 Early Dynastic period, characterized by city-states, e.g. Ur Sargon of Akkad (2340–2198) extends Semitic influence 2160–2000 revival of Sumerian influence in Lagash and Ur	Hammurabi (1792–1750) extends power of Babylon to much of Mesopotamia Tiglath-Pileser I (1112–1074) founds neo-Assyrian empire which lasts until 609		Shalmaneser III 859–824 Adad-nirari III 810–782
AEGEAN/ ANATOLIA/ IRAN		c.1600–1450 Old Hittite kingdom gains some ascendancy also in Mesopotamia and Syria c.1450–1200 Great Hittite kingdom		

800 BC	600 BC	200 BC	100 BC	0	AD 100
Adad-nirari's defeat of Damascus ushers in period of prosperity for Judah and Israel	Judah subject to Assyria for much of reign of Manasseh	198 Palestine passes from Ptolemaic to Seleucid rule	63 Pompey enters Jerusalem. Roman period begins	28/9 Public ministry of Jesus	
c. 760 Amos prophesies against religious and social abuses	Necho kills Josiah (609) and controls Judah until 605	167 Jerusalem defiled by Antiochus IV Maccabean revolt begins	? 6/4 Birth of Jesus of Nazareth	30 Crucifixion and Resurrection of Jesus	
c. 750 Hosea c. 735 Isaiah 722/1 Fall of Samaria (Israel) 701 Sennacherib invades Judah	Nebuchadnezzar captures Jerusalem in 597, 587 Temple destroyed in 587 540 return from exile 516 rebuilt temple is dedicated 332 beginning of Hellenistic rule and of Ptolemaic Judah	Greek rulers of Syria/ Palestine (Seleucids) Antiochus III 223–187 Seleucus IV 187–175 Antiochus IV 175–164	Hasmoneans Alexander Jannaeus 103–76 Alexandra 76–67 Aristobulus II 67–63 Herod the Great 37–4	66–73 Jewish revolt against Rome and destruction of temple (70) Herod's sons Philip 4BC–34AD Herod Antipas 4BC–39AD Agrippa I 4BC–44AD	
Judah Uzziah 785–733 Jotham 758–743 Ahaz 743–727 Hezekiah 727–698	Judah Manasseh 698–642 Amon 642–640 Josiah 640–609 Jehoahaz 609–608 Jehoiakim 608–598 Jehoiachin 597–?560 Zedekiah 596–587	Hasmoneans Judas Maccabeus 165–161 Jonathan 161–142 Simon 142–134 John Hyrcanus 134–104 Aristobulus I 104–103		Roman governors of Judea Valerius Gratus 15–26 Pontius Pilate 26–36	
Israel Jehoash 800–784 Jeroboam II 789–748 Menachem 747–737 Pekah 735–733 Hoshea 733–723					

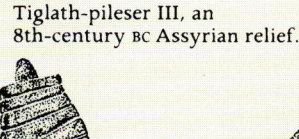

Tiglath-pileser III, an 8th-century BC Assyrian relief.

Alexander the Great at the battle of Issus, detail of a mosaic.

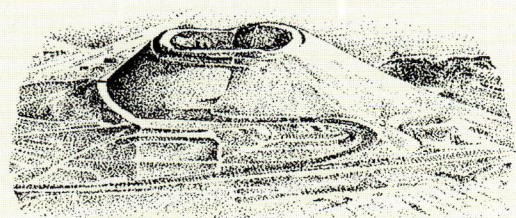

The citadel of Herodium, built by Herod the Great.

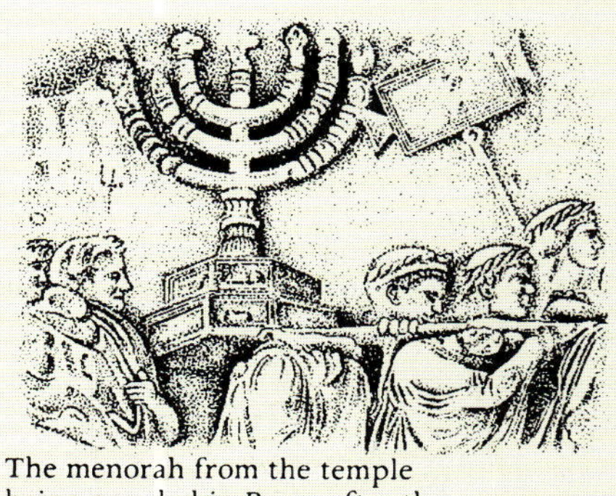

The menorah from the temple being paraded in Rome after the fall of Jerusalem in 70 AD, detail from the arch of Titus.

Teharqa (690–664) Necho II (610–595)	Egypt under Persian rule 525–404, 343–332 Egypt ruled by Alexander the Great 332–323 and the *Ptolemies* Alexandria founded 332 Ptolemy I 304–284		Cleopatra VII 51–30, assists Mark Antony in struggle against Augustus (Octavian)		
Tiglath-Pileser III 745–727 Shalmaneser V 727–722 Sargon II 722–705 Sennacherib 705–681 Fall of Nineveh 612 Nebuchadnezzar II 605–562	Fall of Babylon to Cyrus 540				
c. 650 Median kingdom established	Cyrus (559–529) founds empire of Persians and Medes Alexander's defeat of Persia at Issus (333) opens up to him Syria, Palestine and Egypt		52 Pompey becomes dictator 45 Defeat of Pompey by Julius Caesar 44 Assassination of Caesar Augustus 30BC–14AD	Tiberius 14–37 Caligula 37–41 Claudius 41–54 Nero 54–69 Vespasian 69–79 Titus 79–81 Domitian 81–96	

Bucharest
YUGOSLAVIA
Corsica
ITALY
Gran Sasso
Rome
Adriatic Sea
Danube
Varna
BLACK SEA
BALKAN MOUNTAINS
Sofia
BULGARIA
Skopje
Plovdiv
RHODOPE MTS
Tirane
ALBANIA
Sardinia
Naples
Tyrrhenian Sea
Istanbul
Sea of Marmara
Thessaloniki
Bursa
Ankara
TURKEY
Strait of Otranto
C Sta Maria di Leuca
Corfu
Ionian Sea
PINDUS MTS
Lemnos
Lesbos
Aegean Sea
Palermo
Cephalonia
GREECE
Euboea
Chios
Izmir
Tuz
Kizil Irmak
Erciyas 3960
C Bon
Tunis
Sicily
Ionian Islands
Zacynthos
Athens
Samos
Egridir
Beysehir
TAURUS MOUNTAINS
Adana
TUNISIA
MALTA
Valletta
Naxos
Cyclades
Cos
Dodecanese
Sfax
C Matapan
Rhodes
Djerba
Crete
Nicosia
CYPRUS
Homs
Tripoli
MEDITERRANEAN SEA
LEBANON
Beirut
Dama
Gulf of Sirte
Benghazi
TARABULUS
ISRAEL
Tel Aviv-Yafo
Jerusalem
Jordan
Amma
Dead Sea
CYRENAICA
Alexandria
Libyan Plateau
Qattara Depression
Cairo
LOWER EGYPT
SINAI
LIBYA
Nile
Western Desert
Gulf of Suez
Gulf of Aqaba
FEZZAN
EGYPT
Asyut
Eastern Desert
Idehan Marzuq
Libyan Desert
UPPER EGYPT
Aswan
Ras Banas
Lake Nasser
TIBESTI
Nubian Desert
NIGER
2000m
1000m
500m
0
below sea level
international boundary
disputed boundary
capital city
other important city
mountain peak (in metres)
scale 1:12 000 000
0
400 km
0
300 miles
CHAD
Omdurman
Khartoum
Atbara
SUDAN
White Nile
Blue Nile

Elbrus 5633
CAUCASUS MOUNTAINS
Tbilisi
Kura
Sevan
Baku
CASPIAN SEA
Kara Kum
Amu Darya
KOPPEH MOUNTAINS
Atrak
Ararat 5164
Araks
Murat
Van
Tabriz
Rezaiyeh
Mashhad
ALBORZ MOUNTAINS
Damavand 5604
Tehran
PAROPAMISUS
Hari
AFGHANISTAN
Tigris
Mosul
Zab al Kabir
Zab as Saghir
Khabur
Qom
Dasht-e Kavir
MESOPOTAMIA
Diyala
Baghdad
IRAQ
Tigris
Euphrates
ZAGROS MOUNTAINS
Zard Kuh 4547
Isfahan
IRAN
Harut
Farah
Khash
Dasht-e Lut
Shur
Dasht-i-Margo
Helmand
CHAGAI HILLS
Dasht-i-Tahlab
PAKISTAN
Syrian Desert
Ahvaz
Khersan
Abadan
Basra
Shiraz
Kuh-e-Hazaran 4420
KUWAIT
Al-Kuwayt
Mand
An Nafud
Qeshm
Strait of Hormuz
Persian Gulf
Dasht
to OMAN
BAHRAIN
Manama
QATAR
Doha
Gulf of Oman
Ad Dahna
Riyadh
Abu Dhabi
UNITED ARAB EMIRATES
Muscat
SAUDI ARABIA
OMAN
Nafud ad Dahy
Jiddah
Rub al Khali
ARABIAN SEA
Dahlak Archipelago
Asmera
Sana
HADRAMAWT
YEMEN
SOUTHERN YEMEN
ETHIOPIA
Kobar Sink
Aden
Socotra
INDIAN OCEAN

PREFACE

One may reasonably ask what is the need for another Bible atlas. There exist many atlases of the Bible, but the justification for the present one is that it is different from all the others. Their orientation is historical rather than geographical. They are based upon the history of Israel and the rise of Christianity, and provide maps and illustrations suited to each historical phase. The present Atlas has a primarily geographical orientation. In the main section, Part Three, the land of the Bible is considered region by region, and so the main events of the Bible are treated according to their regional location.

Because of its primarily geographical orientation, the present Atlas has a different aim from more conventional Bible atlases. They are rightly concerned to reconstruct biblical history in a critical way, using all the resources of modern scholarship, including archaeology. The present Atlas does not attempt to reconstruct biblical history, but tries instead to elucidate the geographical conventions that were shared by the biblical writers and their first readers. For example, the story of Samson carrying the gates of Gaza to Hebron in Judges 16:1-3 has a definite geographical setting that was in the mind of the writer, whether or not we are prepared to accept that Samson actually performed the feat.

The aim of the present Atlas, to illumine the geographical setting of biblical narratives, reflects a current trend in biblical studies towards an appreciation of these narratives as stories in their own right. At the same time, it should not be thought that the Atlas will be of no interest to those who wish to study history. In Part Two a brief, and deliberately traditional, outline of biblical history is given, integrated with a series of more conventional historical maps. This is followed by a selection of illustrations of biblical episodes by medieval and modern artists to be contrasted with the more accurate (if less inspired) topographical context provided in Part Three. Careful attention has also been paid to trying to describe what the land looked like in biblical, as opposed to modern, times.

Three main types of user of the Atlas have been envisaged: those general readers who have not been to Israel and who want to know what its main regions looked like in biblical times, so that they may understand the biblical narratives more vividly; those who are visiting Israel and who want a description of each region plus an account of the biblical narratives that are set there; and scholars and students concerned with the literary, historical, topographical and environmental aspects of biblical studies.

The use of the name Israel to denote the land of the Bible as a whole is a convenient and non-political use, if not entirely accurate. Where Israel is used in its modern sense, it refers to Israel as recognized internationally according to the 1949 armistice. As far as possible, Hebrew names are used for modern places in Israel, and Arabic names are used for modern places in Arab territory within the 1949 demarcation. An important exception is that for places named in the Bible the biblical forms of the names are used, as found in the standard English translations of the Bible. This causes some anomalies. On the Hebrew side, the official transliteration of Hebrew names into English often differs from the form familiar in the English Bible; for example, "Yafo" (official transliteration) is the same as English Bible "Joppa". On the Arabic side, the use of forms from the English Bible entails the substitution of Hebrew for Arabic names. Thus El-Khalil becomes Hebron, Beitin becomes Bethel, Seilun becomes Shiloh. It must be stressed that this is done simply for the sake of convenience and has no political implications. Where purely Arabic names are used, they conform to the conventions adopted in the *Student Map Manual*.

In thanking those who have contributed, even if only indirectly, to the production of the present work, I must mention members of various communities – Jewish, Arab, Armenian and expatriate British – whose acquaintance and friendship I have valued. My first visit to Jerusalem 30 years ago was led by the Rt Revd L.J. Ashton, now Anglican bishop in Cyprus and the Gulf, but then senior R.A.F. Chaplain at Habbaniya, Iraq; it engendered a lasting interest in the historical geography of the Bible and led to many subsequent visits. In the past five years my students in the Department of Biblical Studies at Sheffield University have regularly accompanied me on study visits to Israel, and have provided much stimulus for my research and reading. I should also like to acknowledge the many helpful suggestions I have received from my advisory editor and former teacher Professor F.F. Bruce. The members of the editorial team in Oxford have been unfailingly understanding, friendly and hospitable, and it has been a pleasure to work with them.

PART ONE

THE BIBLE AND ITS LITERATURE

THE COMPOSITION AND TRANSMISSION OF THE BIBLE

The Bible has been described as the world's least-read best seller. It has probably been translated into more languages than any other book, and its annual rate of distribution worldwide by the Bible Societies averages something like 11 million complete Bibles, 12 million New Testaments and over 400 million booklets or leaflets containing part of the biblical text. These enormous figures are made possible, of course, by modern methods of printing and distribution; but even before the invention of printing in the west in the 15th century, Bible circulation was on a scale which vastly outstripped that of other books. Further, the communities that produced the Bible had such a concern for their written sacred traditions that the ancient Hebrew people have been called the people of the book. To this description we must add another, which is at the heart of the present publication, that they were also the people of the land, the land of the Bible. These two factors, the book and the land, go closely together, and one of the main aims of this Atlas is to try to make the book more understandable by enabling readers to become more familiar with the land.

The composition of the Bible

Writing was invented and in use in the ancient world by at least the 4th millennium BC. It was initially based upon crude pictures, which eventually formalized into symbols which, when read out, represented syllables, not the sounds of what we know as individual letters of the alphabet. Because syllabic systems of writing needed between 300 and 600 signs, literacy was confined to

Right Divine inspiration comes to St John. This 12th-century French manuscript shows the evangelist writing his gospel, inspired by the Holy Spirit. The corner medallions depict scenes from his life, and his inkhorn is held by Wedric, abbot of Liessies in Hainault.

Below The Old and New Testaments form a library of 66 books containing many different types of writings: creation stories, legal texts, manuals for priests, histories, psalms, proverbs, love poems, prophetic books, gospels, letters. In the New Testament, although the gospels come first, many of the letters were written earlier.

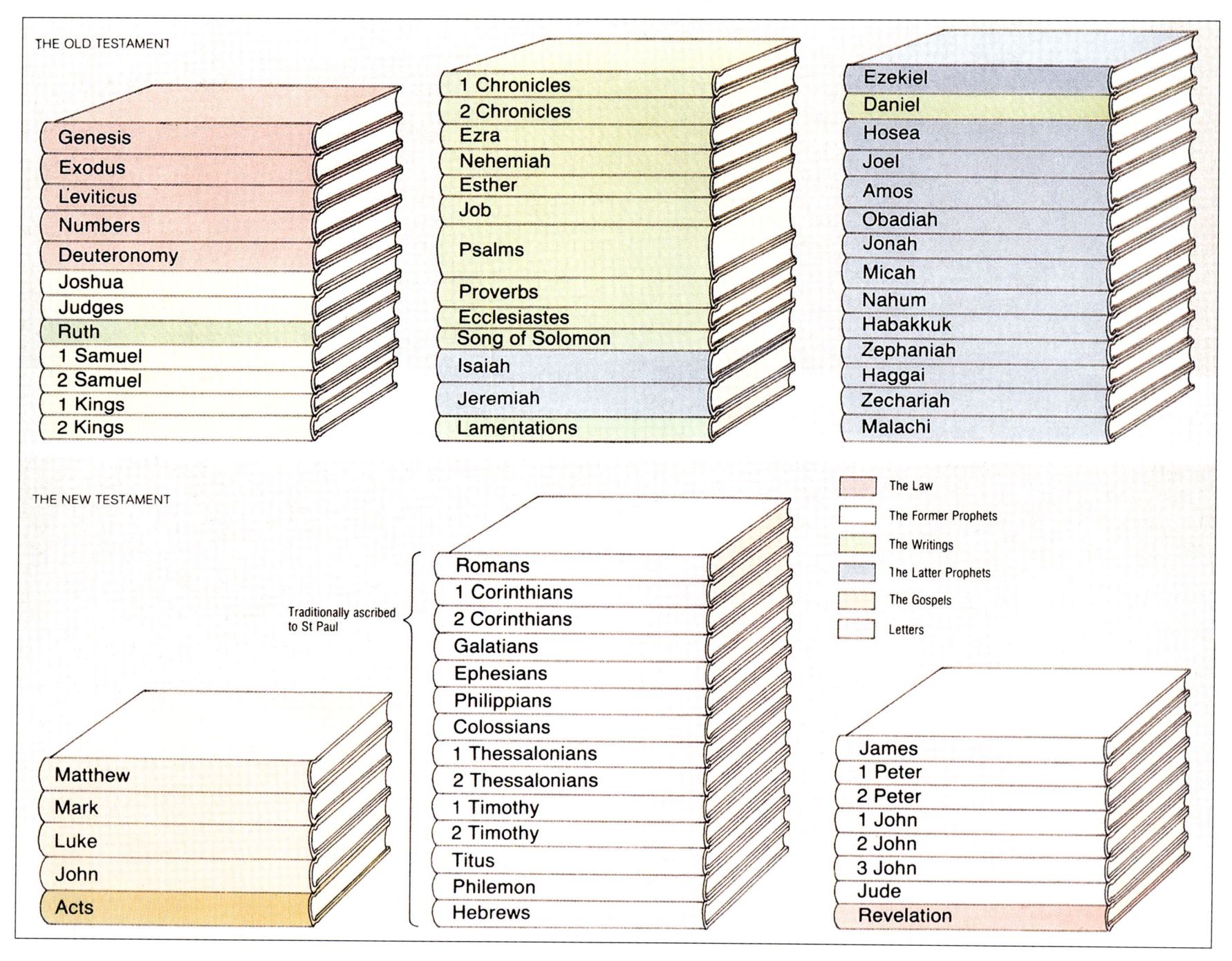

THE OLD TESTAMENT

- Genesis
- Exodus
- Leviticus
- Numbers
- Deuteronomy
- Joshua
- Judges
- Ruth
- 1 Samuel
- 2 Samuel
- 1 Kings
- 2 Kings

- 1 Chronicles
- 2 Chronicles
- Ezra
- Nehemiah
- Esther
- Job
- Psalms
- Proverbs
- Ecclesiastes
- Song of Solomon
- Isaiah
- Jeremiah
- Lamentations

- Ezekiel
- Daniel
- Hosea
- Joel
- Amos
- Obadiah
- Jonah
- Micah
- Nahum
- Habakkuk
- Zephaniah
- Haggai
- Zechariah
- Malachi

THE NEW TESTAMENT

- Matthew
- Mark
- Luke
- John
- Acts

Traditionally ascribed to St Paul:
- Romans
- 1 Corinthians
- 2 Corinthians
- Galatians
- Ephesians
- Philippians
- Colossians
- 1 Thessalonians
- 2 Thessalonians
- 1 Timothy
- 2 Timothy
- Titus
- Philemon
- Hebrews

- James
- 1 Peter
- 2 Peter
- 1 John
- 2 John
- 3 John
- Jude
- Revelation

Legend:
- The Law
- The Former Prophets
- The Writings
- The Latter Prophets
- The Gospels
- Letters

THE COMPOSITION AND TRANSMISSION OF THE BIBLE

Writing in the Ancient World

The invention of writing is one of the major cultural achievements of mankind, similar to the revolution that is now taking place in making data instantly available all over the world by means of computer technologies. The earliest forms of writing, from the 4th millennium BC, were syllabic, that is to say they represented the syllables we hear when we pronounce words. The signs for the syllables themselves had their origins in pictorial representations of natural objects, although the pictures soon became conventional signs. Let us assume that for writing down English words we have a sign that represents a bee and thus the sound "bee", and a sign that represents a leaf and thus the sound "leaf". We could put the two signs together to represent the word "be-lief". Fortunately for the Hebrews, by the time that they came to write down their scriptures, the syllabic system of writing, requiring at least 300 different signs, had been replaced by an alphabet, requiring only 24 to 32 signs. The invention of the alphabet in the second half of the 2nd millennium BC greatly increased the possibility of literacy. It is sometimes a surprise to non-specialists to learn that Hebrew writes down mainly consonants, and that most of the vowels are not represented. In fact it is quite easy to learn to read a script that omits most of the vowels. The Hebrew Bible, however, does have the vowels represented, by a system of lines and dots that were added to the consonantal text in the early Christian centuries. This aided pronunciation of the sacred texts when Hebrew ceased to be a spoken language and become a language used only in the liturgy or by scholars.

Below left The biblical Hebrew script is a distant ancestor of our own Roman alphabet by way of Phoenician, Aramaic and Greek. This table, comparing early Aramaic with early Greek forms, illustrates an intermediate stage in the development.

Right In this tablet from Jamdat Nasr of c.2900 BC hints of the pictorial origin of syllabic script can be seen.

Below Sennacherib's scribes listing booty and prisoners during a battle, from a frieze dating from 704–681 BC. The scribes would be using the syllabic script formed of wedge-shaped strokes known as cuneiform. Theirs was a learned and important profession.

Phonetic value	Early Aramaic	Early Greek
ʾ		
b		
g		
d		
h		
w		
z		
h		
t		
y		
k		
l		
m		
n		
s		
ʿ		
p		
s		
q		
r		
sh		
t		

THE COMPOSITION AND TRANSMISSION OF THE BIBLE

Below Inkwell from the Roman period. In antiquity ink was made from vegetable matter and could also be iron-based. It was not necessarily liquid, but could be a "lump" into which was dipped a stylus that had been wetted.

Above The Cyrus Cylinder relates how Cyrus, king of the Medes and Persians, defeated Babylon in 540 BC. Of great interest for biblical studies is the phrase "May all the gods whom I have resettled in their sacred cities ask Bel and Nebo daily for a long life for me..." This accords with the decree of Cyrus in Ezra 1:1ff, allowing the Jews to return to Jerusalem to rebuild the temple.

Left The Rylands fragment (III.458) of the Greek translation of Deuteronomy 25:1–3, from the first half of the 2nd century AD, is evidence for the existence of a Greek version of at least the Torah by that date.

Below An inscription from the temple mount in Jerusalem which reads "[belonging] to the house of the trumpeting".

a few professionals. The alphabet, as we know it, was not invented until the second half of the 2nd millennium BC, round about the time that Moses is usually thought to have led the Israelites out of Egypt.

Exactly when Abraham, Isaac and Jacob lived is a matter for debate (a traditional view, mentioned in Part Three, is 1750 to 1500 BC). The stories about these founding fathers were no doubt initially preserved and handed down by word of mouth (oral tradition). The same is probably true of most of the stories about the Israelites down to the time of the kingship of David (1000 BC). This is not to say that nothing was written down before this time among the Israelites, but that the stories that we find in the books of, say, Genesis, Exodus, Judges and 1 Samuel give every indication of having been oral traditions that have been written down at a later date. On the other hand, some collections of laws known to us from the ancient world are very much older than the Old Testament, and because of the importance of law in the life of a community, it is not impossible that laws were among the earliest of Israel's written traditions.

The reigns of David and Solomon provided the social conditions for writing activity to flourish in ancient Israel, and from the 10th century onwards written and oral materials began to be collected towards the formation of those parts of the Old Testament that we call the Law (Genesis to Deuteronomy) and the Former Prophets (Joshua to 2 Kings). The rise of the "classical" Prophets in the 8th century BC provided another impetus to the formation of the Bible. Recent research suggests that words spoken by the Prophets were collected, written down and preserved by disciples of the Prophets, who formed prophetic schools, and who were responsible for much literary activity. According to Jeremiah 36, Baruch the scribe wrote down Jeremiah's words from the Prophet's dictation.

With the fall of Jerusalem and the exiles to Babylon in 597 and 587 BC (the temple was destroyed in 587), there was much heart-searching in Israel about the causes of the catastrophe. Israel moved much more decisively towards being the people of the book, and it was probably during the period of the exile (587–539) that the Former Prophets (Joshua to 2 Kings—basically the history of Israel from the conquest under Joshua to the time of the exile) reached something like their present form, and that the Law (Genesis to Deuteronomy) was well on the way to completion. The section known as the Latter Prophets (Isaiah, Jeremiah, Ezekiel and the 12 minor Prophets) was also nearing completion by the end of the 6th century. The third section of the Hebrew Bible, the Writings, contains material some of which is quite old, for example some of the Psalms and some of the Proverbs; it also contains the youngest parts of the Old Testament, such as the books of Chronicles, and the books of Esther and Daniel, as well as the love poems of the Song of Songs, and the wrestlings with doubt and uncertainty in Job and Ecclesiastes.

By the end of the 2nd century BC the Old Testament as we know it from our English Bibles (although with the books in a different order) was substantially complete. Its books were written on scrolls of parchment. Indeed, the word translated as "book" in modern Hebrew meant "roll" in biblical Hebrew. By the time of the rise of Christianity, the Old Testament existed not only in Hebrew, but in a Greek version provided initially for the Jews living in Egypt, and in a Samaritan version for the Samaritan community that lived in the northern hill country of Israel. The Samaritan version, which was confined to the first five books of the Old Testament, was also written in Hebrew. However, it contained interesting textual variants, most of which reinforced the Samaritan claim that Mount Gerizim was the place chosen by God, not Jerusalem. Likewise the Greek version contained variants from what has come down to us as the standard Hebrew text of the Old Testament. For example, the Greek version of Jeremiah was noticeably shorter than the version that we know from our English Bibles, which are based upon the traditional Hebrew text. The discoveries of Hebrew manuscripts from Qumran, the so-called Dead Sea Scrolls, have indicated that at the beginning of the Christian era a number of different versions of the text of the Old Testament existed—a fact borne out by certain quotations of the Old Testament in the New Testament that do not correspond to any known version of the former. There seems to have been, at least in the Qumran community, a lack of concern for having one and only one form of the text. Today, accustomed to the reproduction of thousands of identical texts by the technologies of printing, we may find it difficult to imagine what it must have been like to live in a society or community where everything had to be copied, and in which variations in the text may have been regarded as authoritative rather than as mistakes. At the same time, it must be emphasized that the archetype on which all printed Hebrew Bibles are based is also very well represented among the finds at Qumran.

For the early Church, the Bible was initially the Old Testament in its Greek version, including some writings which have not survived in Hebrew, and which are today classified as the Apocrypha by the Protestant churches. As in the case of the Old Testament, the earliest traditions that were later to form the New Testament consisted of oral accounts, for example of the story of the Passion, or the words and deeds of Jesus. From about 50 AD churches began to preserve letters written to them by leading Christians, notably Paul. These began to be collected together to form a corpus, to be added to the gospels and the Acts which were written somewhere between 70 and 90 AD, although based upon earlier oral and written material. The New Testament, as we know it, was substantially complete by the end of the 1st century.

Manuscripts of the Bible
One of the remarkable things about the Bible is the fact that we have so many ancient manuscripts of it. Whereas our knowledge of Greek plays, histories or philosophical writings sometimes depends upon only a handful of manuscripts dated many hundreds of years after the deaths of their authors (although, of course, they are copies of earlier manuscripts), in the case of the Bible, and particularly the New Testament, we have several thousand manuscripts. The earliest known fragment of

The Codex Sinaiticus

This 4th-century Greek papyrus written in "biblical uncial" (capital letters) contains a few passages of the Old Testament, the whole of the New Testament, and two other writings – the Epistle of Barnabas and parts of the "Shepherd" of Hermas. It was discovered at St Catherine's monastery on Mount Sinai in 1844 by the German scholar Constantin Tischendorf, but he was not able to obtain possession of it until 15 years later. After first being presented to Alexander II of Russia, it was purchased by Britain in the 1930s and placed in the British Museum.

Probably copied in Egypt, the Codex Sinaiticus is written in four columns, and contains corrections by later scribes of the 4th, 6th and 7th centuries. Together with its contemporary, the Codex Vaticanus, it has exercised a vital influence upon all subsequent studies and versions of the New Testament text.

Constantin Tischendorf, 1815–74.

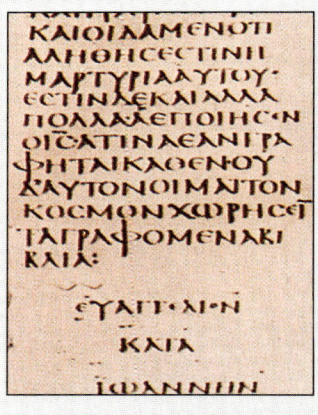

Above With the use of ultraviolet light, it is possible to detect that in the Codex Sinaiticus John's gospel originally ended at 21:24, not at 21:25. A later scribe deleted the non-biblical tailpiece that followed 21:24 in order to add the last verse and a new tailpiece.

Above centre Codex Sinaiticus before binding. The codex (i.e. book) form was typical of Christian as opposed to Jewish methods of writing sacred books. Jews preserved the scroll form.

Above The library at St Catherine's monastery.

Aerial view of the monastery of St Catherine on Mount Sinai. The monastery stands at an altitude of about 1660m (5452ft). Built at the request of Greek hermit monks by the emperor Justinian in the 6th century AD, it is still lived in by Greek monks, although many of the surrounding refuges once occupied by hermits and others are now deserted.

THE COMPOSITION AND TRANSMISSION OF THE BIBLE

the New Testament is the Rylands fragment of St John's gospel, usually dated about 150 AD, but there also exist substantial portions of that gospel and the letters of Paul that are dated in the late 2nd century. These are written on papyrus, and were discovered in Egypt where conditions are suitable for the preservation of ancient papyrus. From the 4th century date the great uncial (written in capital letters) manuscripts which contain most of the Old and New Testaments in Greek. Of these, the most famous are Codex Sinaiticus and Codex Vaticanus. As the names suggest, Vaticanus is in the Vatican Library in Rome, while Sinaiticus was discovered in the 19th century at the monastery of St Catherine on Mount Sinai in the Sinai peninsula, and is now in the British Museum in London. All such manuscripts are in book form ("codex" means book), and the Christian Church seems to have preferred this form of binding the separate leaves together, while the Jewish community preferred to

Below left The Rylands fragment (457) of St John (18:31-33, 37-38) dates from about 150 AD, and indicates that this gospel was in circulation in Egypt early in the 2nd century. The contrast between the Rylands fragment and the magnificent opening of St Matthew in the Lindisfarne Gospels (*right*) eloquently marks the progress of Bible production during six or seven hundred years.

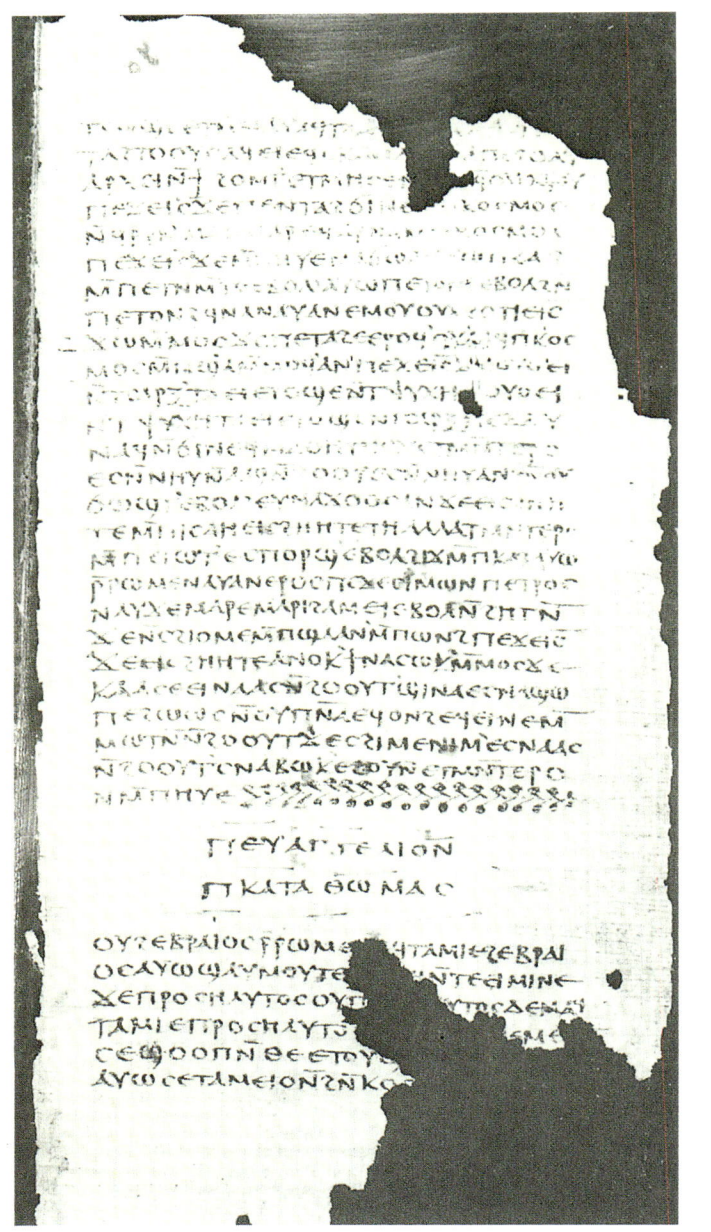

The discovery of the gospel of Thomas in 1945 at Nag Hammadi provides evidence that written collections of sayings of Jesus circulated independently of the other gospels in the first two Christian centuries. Although Thomas does not represent the main stream familiar from the New Testament, it sheds light on the origins of the gospels. *Above* The first page of Thomas's gospel. *Left* The Nag Hammadi library, including the gospel of Thomas.

keep them together in rolls.

Because versions of the New Testament could only be made by copying them by hand, mistakes of many kinds inevitably crept into the manuscripts. The many types of mistake cannot be listed here, but a good example concerns the Lord's Prayer. In its Lucan version (Luke 11:2–4) it is shorter than in its Matthean version (Matthew 6:9–13). Because the prayer was (and still is) recited in its longer Matthean version, it was tempting for scribes to make the Lucan version conform with the Matthean version, either deliberately, or through carelessness. Another example that can be cited concerns the longer and shorter versions of the words of Jesus at the Last Supper as related by Luke. In the shorter version (Luke 22:17–19) Jesus blesses the cup before he blesses the bread. The longer version adds verses 19b–20, a blessing over the cup, perhaps in an attempt to bring the words of Jesus into line with the traditions in Mark and Matthew, as well as into line with the practice of the Church when it celebrated the Lord's Supper. With the establishment of important centres of Christian scholarship such as Alexandria, Caesarea and Antioch, attempts were probably made in those areas to standardize the text of the New Testament, with the result that regional text types began to emerge, although this last statement is a gross oversimplification of a complex matter. Among the important manuscripts that have survived is Codex Bezae, in the Cambridge University Library, which has some unusual readings in Luke and Acts, as well as some significant omissions.

Whatever the divergences among Greek manuscripts of the New Testament, the translation of the Bible into Latin by Jerome in the early 5th century gave to the western Church a version of the Old and New Testaments that became standard (though not unaltered) for centuries. The monasteries became the places where Bibles were copied, and some famous manuscripts can be seen today in the Cathedral Library in Durham and in the library of Trinity College, Dublin. The invention of printing revolutionized the availability of the Bible. Not only did it become possible for scholars to possess printed Hebrew and Greek Bibles; the Reformation in the early 16th century aimed to make the Bible available to ordinary people in their own language. So far as Bibles in English were concerned, Tyndale's New Testament was published in 1526, and his translation of the first five books of the Old Testament in 1530. In 1535 Coverdale's Bible was published, to be followed by "Matthew's" Bible in 1537, the Great Bible of 1539, the Geneva Bible of 1560 and the Bishops' Bible of 1568. The publication of the King James, or Authorized, Version in 1611 was a landmark in the history of the Bible in English. Based on the Bishops' Bible and drawing on other earlier English versions, it was a revision rather than a totally new translation. It is still used in many parts of the English-speaking world, in spite of the large number of translations that have been produced since World War II. The Revised Standard Version, used in the present Atlas, is a revision of a revision of the King James Version. While retaining the dignity of the language of the latter, it incorporates the many discoveries of biblical scholarship since 1611.

Martin Luther: Reformer and Translator

At the end of April 1521 Luther was "kidnapped" on his way back to Wittenberg from Worms, where he had argued his cause before the emperor. The purpose of the "kidnapping" was to enable him to disappear and thus to be safe from his enemies. He grew a beard, wore lay dress (he was a monk) and became Junker (knight) Georg, living at the Wartburg Castle near Eisenach. Here, in December 1521, he began to translate the Greek New Testament into German, so that it could be read by anyone who was literate. He completed the work in the amazingly short period of 11 weeks, and it was published in September 1522 with illustrations by Lukas Cranach and his assistants. In spite of being expensive, it quickly sold out and a new edition was published in December 1522. In 1523 it was reprinted no fewer than 12 times in several different places.

The translation of the whole of the Old Testament took somewhat longer – 12 years from 1522 to 1534. However, the first five books (the Pentateuch) were published in 1523, and from then on a new section was published each year or two. The complete Bible in German appeared in 1534, although it was to undergo many revisions before Luther's death in 1546. Luther's undertaking ensured that the provision of the Bible for all who wished to read it was a fundamental part of the Reformation. The Reformation stress on the Bible and its availability for those who could read meant that Reformation theology expounded the biblical text as a ground for faith and hope, rather than dwelling on the lives of saints as examples to be followed. Luther was followed, in Britain, by Tyndale, Coverdale, Rogers and many others. The 16th century was the great century of Bible translation and publication.

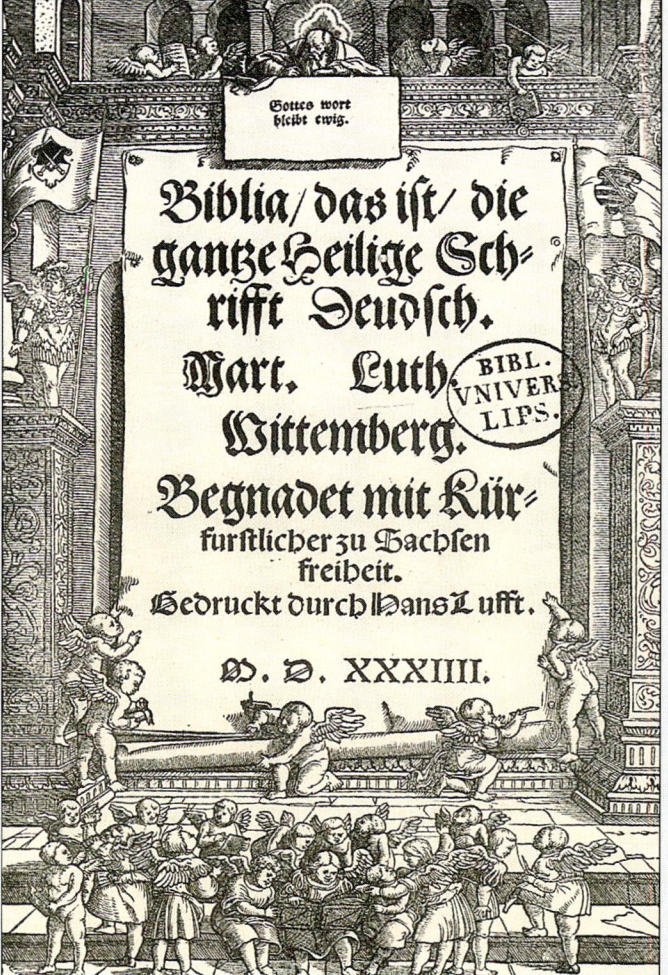

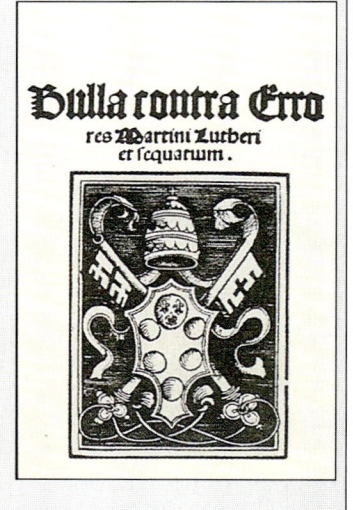

Left Title-page of the first complete German Bible, 1534.

Far left The "Great Bible" of 1539 was based upon the earlier work of Tyndale, Coverdale and Rogers. Tyndale had worked on his translation of the New Testament in Wittenberg, Luther's city, in 1524-25. The woodcut of the title-page shows Henry VIII delivering the word of God to Archbishop Thomas Cranmer and Secretary Thomas Cromwell, who pass it on to the clergy and laity.

PART TWO
THE BIBLE AND HISTORY

AN OUTLINE OF BIBLICAL HISTORY

The Patriarchs: Abraham, Isaac and Jacob
The story of the Hebrews begins at Genesis 12:1–3 with the call of Abraham to leave his country, and to journey to a land that God will show him. Genesis 11:31–32 makes it clear that Abraham's family had moved from Ur in southern Mesopotamia (although a different northern Ur is advocated by some) and had settled in Haran. Genesis 12 envisages a long journey from Haran to Egypt, with Abraham pausing in Shechem and Bethel, and returning (in Genesis 13:3) to Bethel.

The date of Abraham is still a matter for considerable disagreement among scholars. Opinions range from placing him with some confidence in the period around 1750 BC to the view that as a historical personage he is lost in the mists of antiquity and that the stories about him reflect the time of the Israelite monarchy (10th century onwards) or even the post-exilic period (6th century onwards).

Apart from Abraham's expedition against the coalition of the five kings (Genesis 14), the narratives about Abraham and Isaac place these Patriarchs in Bethel, Shechem, Hebron and Beersheba. The narrative of Abraham sending his servant Eliezer to seek a wife (Genesis 24) reintroduces northern Mesopotamia, and provides a link with the story of Jacob's flight to Haran to escape the wrath of Esau. The story of Jacob ends with the episode of Joseph being sold into Egypt and the ensuing famine that eventually caused Jacob and his family to settle in Egypt, after the reconciliation between Joseph and his brothers.

In their final form the Patriarchal traditions contain several important theological themes: the promise of the land of Canaan to Abraham and his

The fertile crescent
A striking feature of the land which constituted ancient Babylonia, Assyria, Syria, Israel and the kingdoms east of the Jordan valley is the distinction between fertile land and desert. In Babylonia and Assyria fertility was mainly dependent on the rivers Euphrates and Tigris and their tributaries. In Israel and Syria it depended upon rainfall and springs. Because patterns of human settlement were dependent upon fertility, Israel became a bridge between the powerful empires of Egypt to the southwest, and Assyria and Babylonia to the north and east.

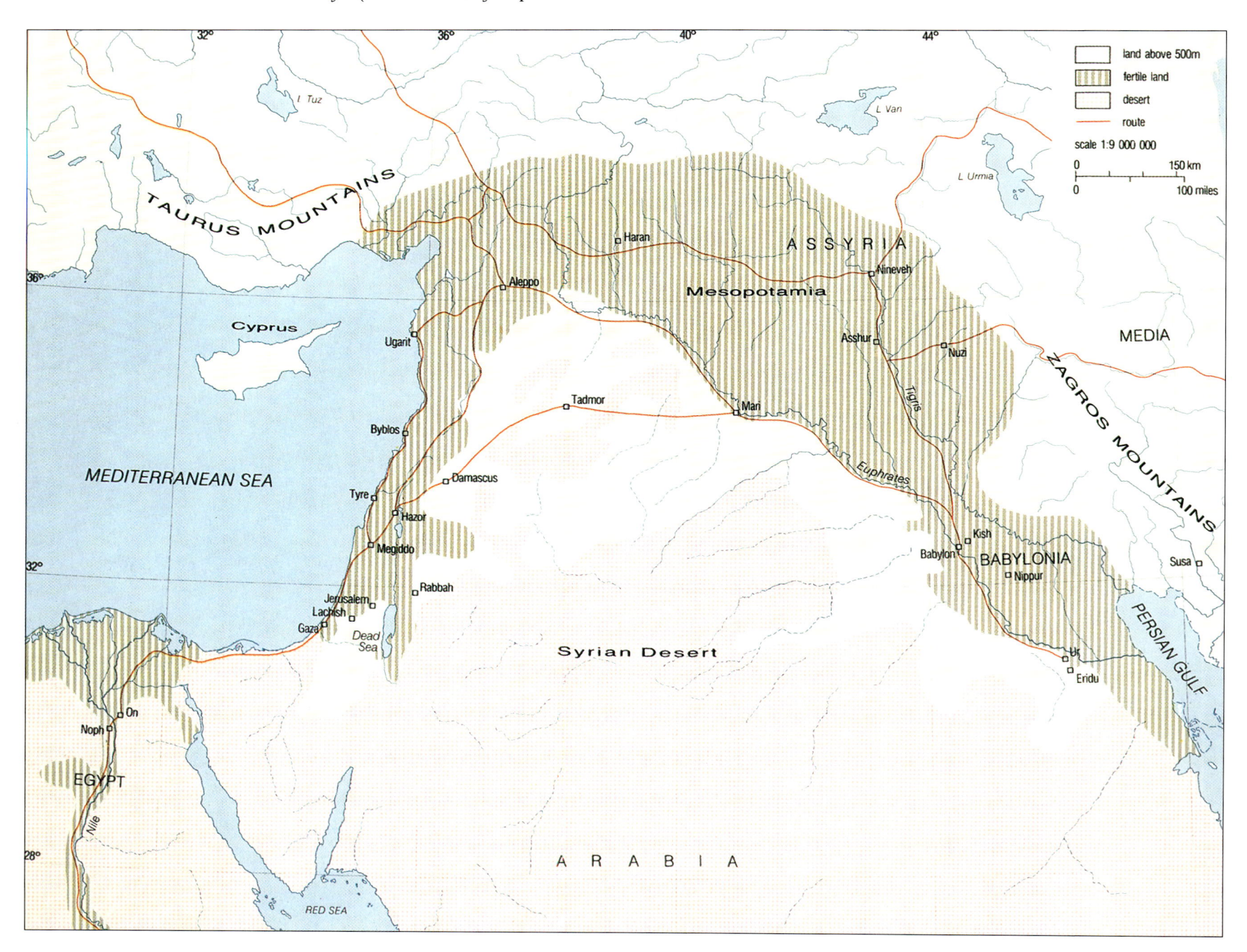

descendants; the miraculous provision of an heir to Abraham; and the providential safeguarding of Sarah, Rebekah and Joseph. The narratives also indicate the relatedness but separateness of the later Israel and its immediate neighbours. Ammon and Moab are the sons of Lot (Genesis 19:37–38); Edom is founded by Esau. As the story unfolds, and characters such as Lot and Esau fall away to the periphery, so the main path of God's purpose becomes clear, running through Abraham, Isaac and Jacob.

The Patriarchs are often described as "semi-nomads", or are compared with modern bedouin. Such comparisons are precarious. Unless our opinion is that the Patriarchal narratives contain no authentic information, we should take seriously the fact that Abraham is portrayed as a city dweller who left his home. Naturally he would have adapted his life to the conditions that prevailed while he was on the move—and the land of Canaan probably looked somewhat different in the 2nd millennium BC compared with today. Moreover the bedouin have their own history, and have not been isolated from the world in the "timeless desert". It is better to say that we know little about the life of the Patriarchs than to make unwise comparisons.

From the Exodus to the settlement in Canaan (?1300–1100 BC)

This series of events (the Exodus—wilderness—Sinai—settlement) is here taken as one because the various parts are interlocked. It is not possible to say that the biblical narrative presents a picture of this period that is free from difficulty. At the surface level of reading, it does appear that 12 sons of Jacob (later to found the 12 tribes) went down into Egypt, were later forced into slavery, left Egypt *en bloc* and wandered through the wilderness, receiving the Law at Mount Sinai on the way, and eventually settled by force of arms in Ammon and Gilead in Transjordan (see p.204 on these regions) and in much of the land on the western bank.

However, looking beneath the surface, evidence can be found to suggest a more complex picture, even if it is difficult to assemble this picture in any way that will carry a consensus of scholarly opinion. The following points have been urged against the straightforward picture outlined in the paragraph above. In some cases they may be contradictory, and the listing of them does not imply that we should approve or reject them. (1) Genesis 34 describes the Israelite conquest of Shechem in the Patriarchal period *before* the Exodus. There is no

The wanderings of Abraham, Isaac and Jacob
The stories of Abraham, Isaac and Jacob are tales of large families moving from place to place with their herds and possessions. The tradition asserts on several occasions that they were natives of northern Mesopotamia, and that their roots may have been in southern Mesopotamia. Their connection with the land of Canaan (later Israel) is not permanent, and they move finally to Egypt. Yet the building of altars at Shechem and Bethel, and the purchase of a burial place at Hebron, are claims upon the land. Modern scholarship suggests that parts of the Patriarchal family remained in Canaan when Jacob went down to live in Egypt.

AN OUTLINE OF BIBLICAL HISTORY

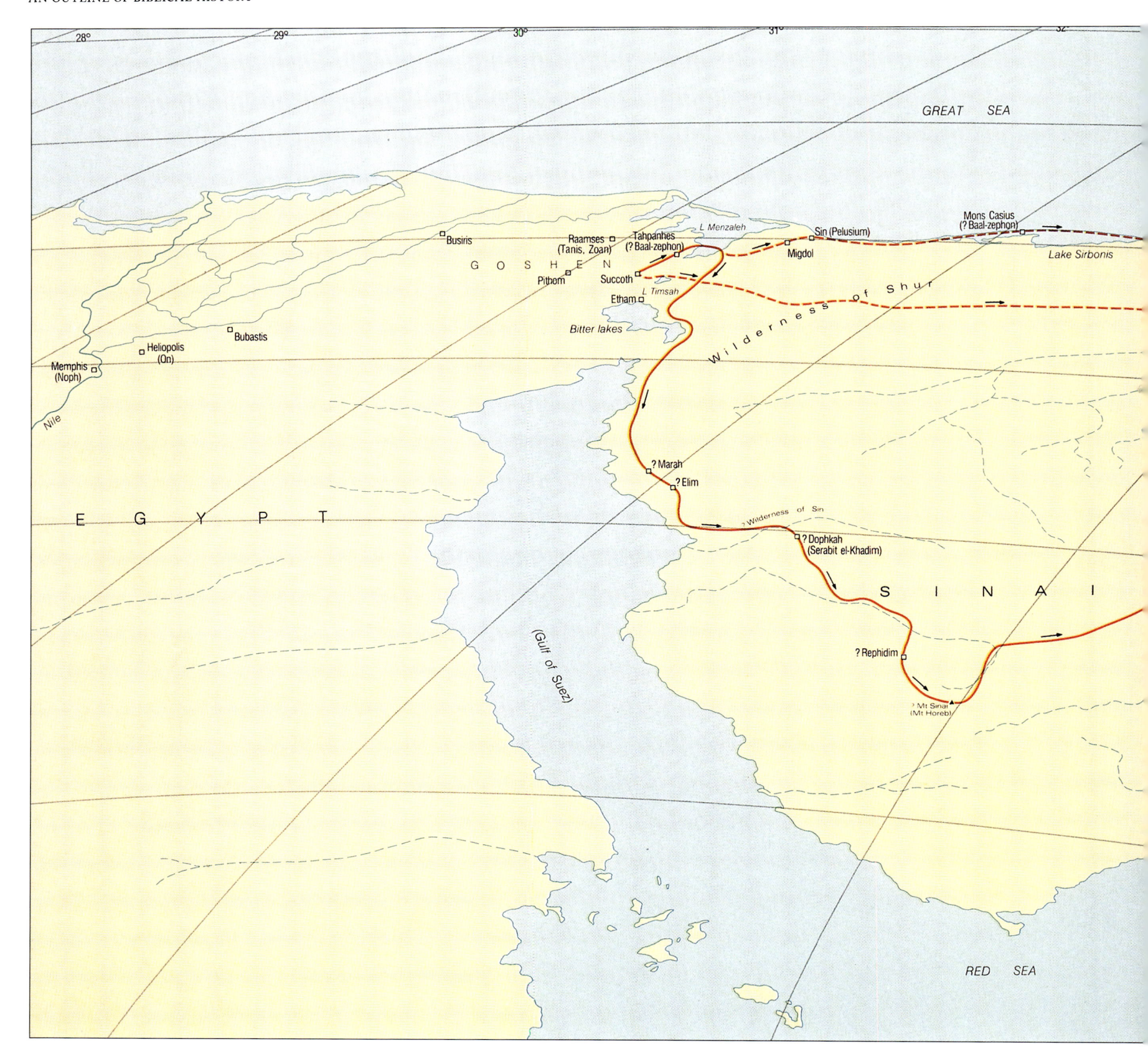

explicit account of the conquest of this area in the book of Joshua. (2) Genesis 38 implies that Judah did not go down into Egypt but remained in Canaan. (3) Numbers 21:1–3 suggests an Israelite invasion of Canaan from the south, not from the east across the Jordan. (4) Numbers 33:41–49 suggests that an earlier "wave" of Israelites journeyed to Canaan through Edom and Moab in the 14th century, before the Exodus. (5) Lists of tribes vary. For example, Simeon is absent from Deuteronomy 33, and the number is made up to 12 by dividing the house of Joseph between Ephraim and Manasseh. These points could be added to, and readers who want to pursue the matter further are advised to consult a standard critical history of Israel.

If we follow the surface picture indicated in the opening paragraph, the Hebrews settled in Egypt in the land of Goshen (Genesis 47:27), and some time after the death of Joseph were conscripted into slave gangs and forced to rebuild the cities of Pithom and Raamses (Exodus 1:11). The slavery is usually dated either in the reign of Sethos I (1306–1290 BC), who is known for his building projects, or in that of Ramesses II (1290–1224), if the Raamses of Exodus 1:11 is to be identified with Pi-Ri'amsese in the eastern Nile delta. Ramesses II was responsible for removing his capital to this location. The Pharaoh of the Exodus was the successor of the Pharaoh of the Oppression (Exodus 2:23), either Ramesses II or Merneptah

The routes of the Exodus
The exact route of the Exodus is unknown. The biblical narratives can even be interpreted to allow the view that the Hebrews left Egypt in two or more waves. However, this suggestion is not meant to rule out the decisive departure which is still commemorated in the Jewish Passover. The present map seeks to identify the possibilities, and thus to indicate the uncertainties.

AN OUTLINE OF BIBLICAL HISTORY

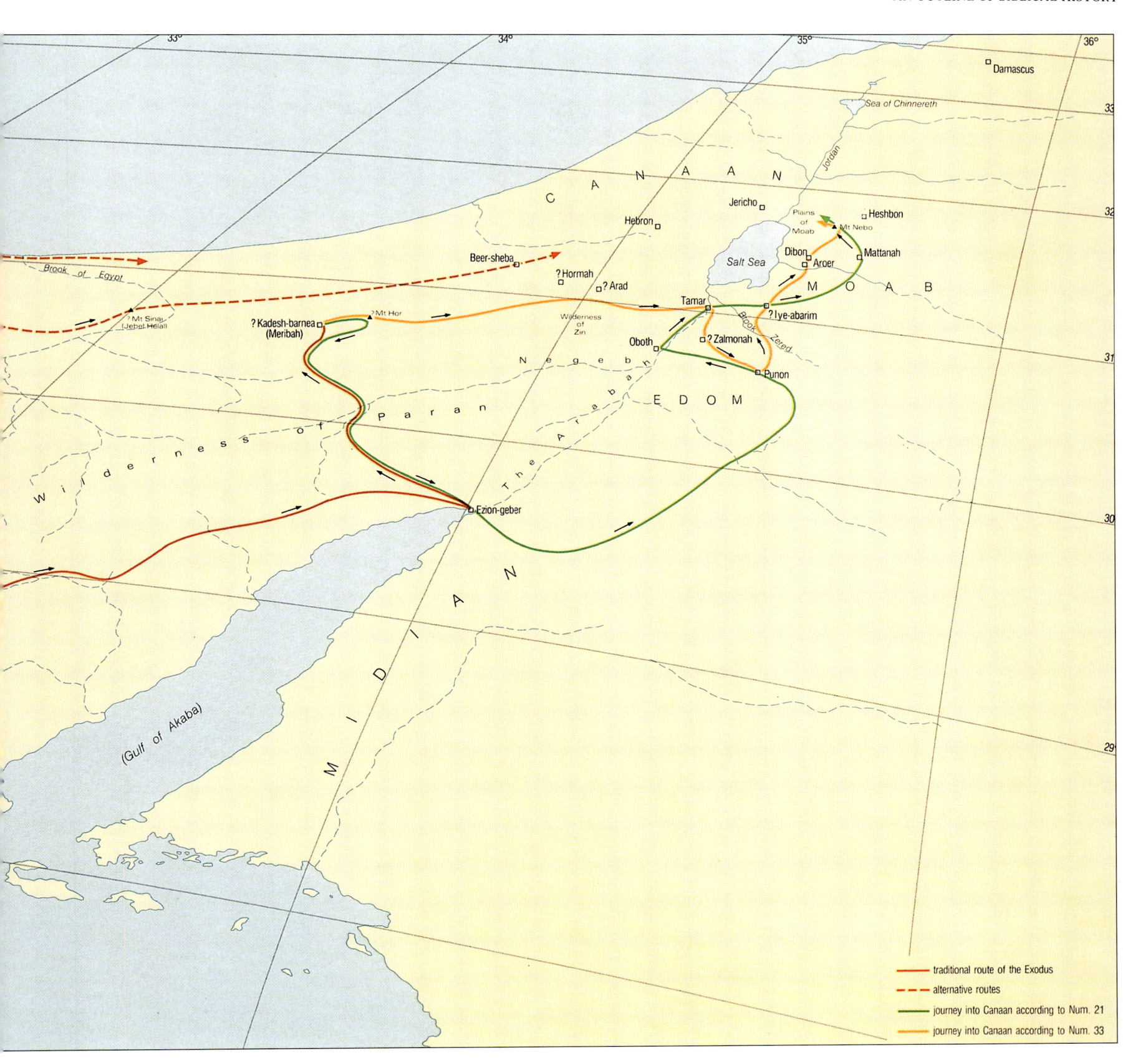

—— traditional route of the Exodus
--- alternative routes
—— journey into Canaan according to Num. 21
—— journey into Canaan according to Num. 33

(1224–1214). The route taken by the Hebrews from Goshen to the Red Sea (or Sea of Reeds, as some prefer) is a matter of opinion. The traditional route assumes that the Hebrews crossed a southern extension of Lake Menzaleh before making for the Bitter Lakes, and then went along a route a little to the east of the eastern coast of the Gulf of Suez before moving inland to the traditional site of Mount Sinai at Jebel Musa. A second reconstruction has the Hebrews turning due east opposite Lake Timsah, and making for the alternative site of Mount Sinai at Jebel Helal. A third approach suggests that the Hebrews journeyed along the strip of land that separated the Mediterranean Sea from Lake Sirbonis and that the deliverance from Pharaoh at the Red Sea took place there.

The route taken in the Exodus and wilderness wanderings is difficult to reconstruct because so many of the places mentioned cannot be identified with any degree of certainty. It is also the case that some experts believe that the itineraries derive from the practices of later pilgrimages rather than from reminiscences of the time of the wanderings.

Geographically speaking, the conquest of Canaan presents few problems, but when the actual areas attacked and conquered according to the book of Joshua are plotted, the gaps in the picture are quite surprising. After the initial attack against Jericho, and the advance to the Bethel hills to attack Ai, Joshua proceeded to the northern

AN OUTLINE OF BIBLICAL HISTORY

plain of the Jerusalem saddle. There he defeated a coalition of kings from the Judean hills and the Shephelah who had gone to punish the city of Gibeon for making an alliance with Joshua. He followed up his victory with attacks on other cities in the Judean hills and Shephelah (Joshua 6–10). The next attack was not, as one would expect, on the hill country north of Jerusalem, but on Hazor in upper Galilee (Joshua 11). This is the last explicit account of an Israelite campaign led by Joshua, although a list of kings defeated by Joshua in Joshua 12 fills in one or two, but by no means all, of the gaps. Thus, in its details, the book of Joshua does not describe the conquest of the entire land, although several general summaries in Joshua assert that the whole land was conquered, with certain exceptions.

The manner of the Israelite occupation of Canaan is at present a major area of debate in Old Testament scholarship. Opinions vary from the view that the conquest is confirmed by archaeology, through the theory that the Israelites under Joshua were assisted by kinsfolk who had settled before the Exodus, to the suggestion that Israel was born as an egalitarian reaction on the part of people living in Canaan to the oppressive policies of the Canaanite city-states. Although it is not the purpose of this Atlas to provide a full-scale history of Israel, the following observations can be made. (1) Some archaeological findings appear to support claims made in the book of Joshua that certain cities were destroyed by the Israelites. To reject such evidence out of hand is to exhibit a degree of caution that would probably not be exercised if we were dealing with a text other than the Bible. (2) Some archaeological facts do not support the accounts in Joshua, indicating that some caution is necessary. (3) The view that proto-Israelite groups in Canaan joined in with a newly arrived group of Israelites can be accepted cautiously. (4) The intensive research into agricultural methods and patterns of life in the period of the settlement and early Iron Age is to be welcomed. It is certain that many more things were taking place in Canaan between the 13th and 11th centuries BC than are indicated in the book of Joshua.

The conquests of Joshua
The amount of the land conquered by the Israelites, according to what we are told in the book of Joshua, is surprisingly small, for all that summary verses (e.g. 10:40) make much greater claims. There are several possible explanations, including the view that Joshua contains only a small portion of the original story of the conquest, or that the occupation of Canaan took much longer and was more complex than a superficial reading of Joshua might suggest. It is also possible that some parts of the land were already occupied by groups closely related to the Israelites, and therefore did not need to be conquered.

- ● city attacked and burned by Joshua
- ○ city whose king was defeated by Joshua (Josh. 12:9-24)
- ● city not conquered by Joshua
- ■ city of the coalition of Adonizedek
- ◆ city of the coalition of Jabin
- — campaigns of Joshua
- ▨ "the land that yet remains" (Josh. 13:2)
- × site of important battle

scale 1:1 250 000
0 — 40 km
0 — 30 miles

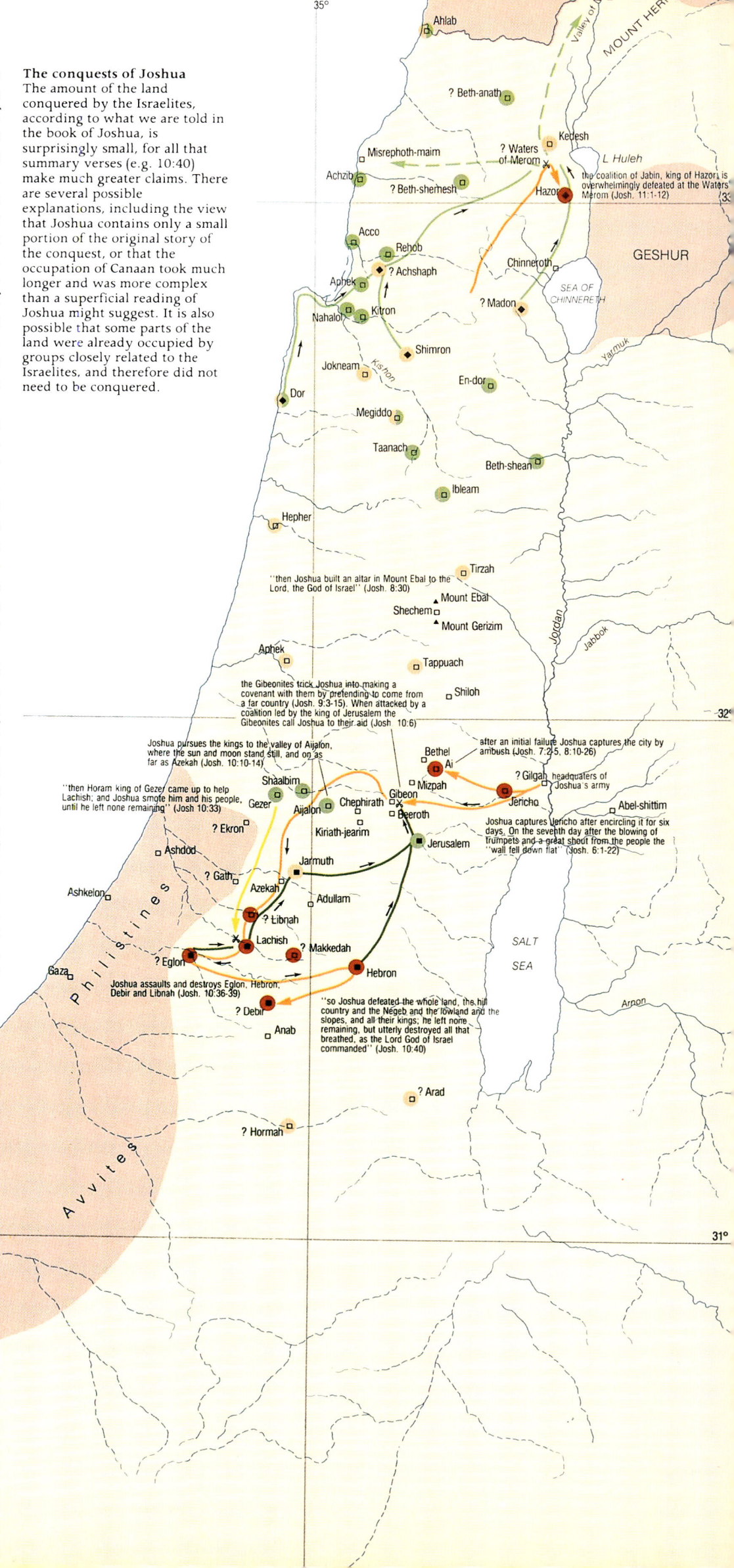

The period of the Judges and the rise of the monarchy (1100–1000 BC)

The period of the Judges, as presented in the book of Judges, was dominated by invasions by neighbouring peoples, seen by the narrative as God's punishment on Israel for turning to other gods. The deliverers who were raised up to save Israel are presented as rulers of the whole nation, although the oppressions from which they delivered the people were probably local in character. Only one major threat to Israel from inside the land is described, that of Sisera and the Canaanite coalition defeated by Deborah and Barak (Judges 4–5).

Towards the end of the period of the Judges, pressure was put on the tribe of Dan by the Philistines, a non-Semitic people who had arrived by land and sea in the 12th century and who had settled in the southern coastal plain. After forcing Dan to migrate to the far north, the Philistines probably turned their attention to Judah, their immediate neighbours to the east, although there is no mention of this in the biblical narrative unless the encounter between David and Goliath took place at this time rather than in the reign of Saul. If it is correct to assume that they made no real headway against Judah, they now turned their attention to the tribes of Benjamin and Ephraim. At the battle of Aphek (1 Samuel 4:1–11) the Philistines defeated the Israelites, and probably occupied at least the Bethel hills, later destroying Shiloh. It was during the period of Philistine ascendancy that Saul rose to the kingship.

In 1 Samuel 8–11 possibly three traditions about the origin of the kingship have been woven together. Whereas the modern historian would reconstruct one account from his sources and refer to these in footnotes, the biblical writers tried to preserve the various traditions, even if it was not easy to fashion a coherent narrative: at 1 Samuel 8 the people request a king of Samuel, who replies that they are rejecting God as their king; at 1 Samuel 9:1–10:16 God takes the initiative and directs Samuel to anoint Saul as a prince over Israel; 1 Samuel 11 describes how Saul delivered the men of Jabesh-gilead from the Ammonites, after which the kingship was "renewed". Much

Tribal divisions according to the book of Joshua
The tribal boundaries are not as clear as might be supposed. In the cases of Issachar, Dan, Simeon, Reuben, Gad and Manasseh east of the Jordan, the source material (Joshua 13–19) names only the cities allocated to these tribes without defining the borders in any detail. It is probable that some boundaries fluctuated. Dan was forced by Philistine pressure from its position to the west and south of Ephraim; Kiriath-jearim is allocated to both Judah and Benjamin. There are also indications from tribal lists (e.g. Genesis 49, Deuteronomy 33) that the power of one tribe over another varied. Such variations may have led to territorial adjustments.

AN OUTLINE OF BIBLICAL HISTORY

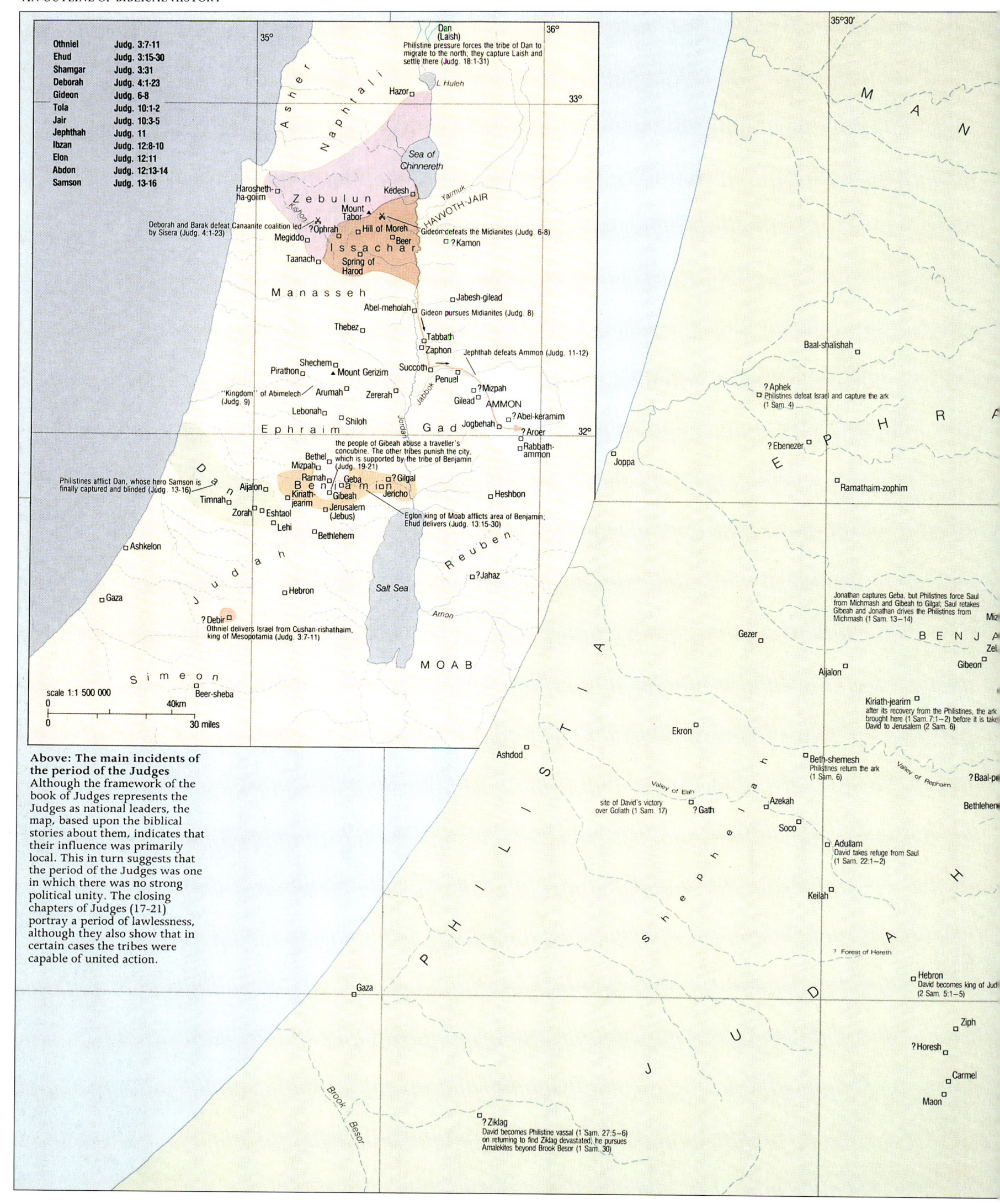

Othniel	Judg. 3:7-11
Ehud	Judg. 3:15-30
Shamgar	Judg. 3:31
Deborah	Judg. 4:1-23
Gideon	Judg. 6-8
Tola	Judg. 10:1-2
Jair	Judg. 10:3-5
Jephthah	Judg. 11
Ibzan	Judg. 12:8-10
Elon	Judg. 12:11
Abdon	Judg. 12:13-14
Samson	Judg. 13-16

Above: The main incidents of the period of the Judges
Although the framework of the book of Judges represents the Judges as national leaders, the map, based upon the biblical stories about them, indicates that their influence was primarily local. This in turn suggests that the period of the Judges was one in which there was no strong political unity. The closing chapters of Judges (17-21) portray a period of lawlessness, although they also show that in certain cases the tribes were capable of united action.

AN OUTLINE OF BIBLICAL HISTORY

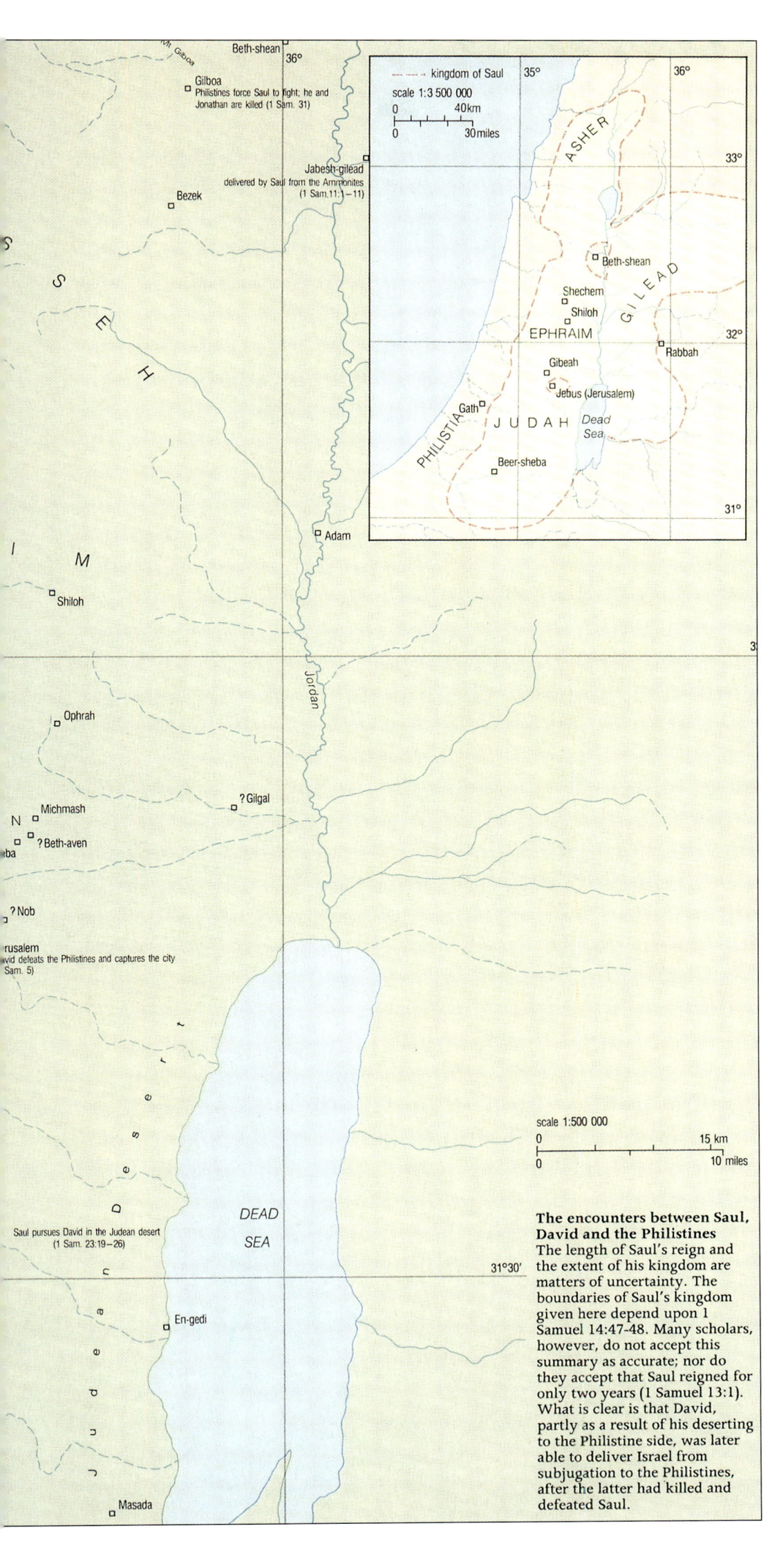

about the beginning and course of Saul's reign is unknown. We do not know how long he reigned (estimates vary from two years to 32), nor whether his rule achieved peace for Israel (cf. 1 Samuel 14:47–48) or was merely a brief episode in which the Israelites, led by Saul, offered some resistance to the Philistines.

Recent research has rightly questioned whether Saul was strictly speaking a king, and has suggested chief (of a chiefdom) as a more appropriate label. Also it has been argued that many more factors were involved in the rise of the monarchy than the Philistine threat. While we can accept this general point, it has to be admitted that we are still far from able to see the Philistine threat in the context of sociological and other factors.

Saul and his sons were killed in battle by the Philistines on or near Mount Gilboa on the edge of the valley of Jezreel, and it was left to David to convert failure into success, to the point where Israel controlled a small empire. David was an enigmatic figure with strong Moabite and Ammonite connections. After Saul had forced him from the court, partly because Saul suspected that he had designs on the throne, David lived the life of an outlaw followed by a band of discontented men (1 Samuel 22:1–2). When Saul's pursuit of him became intolerable, David deserted to the Philistines and became a vassal of Achish, king of Gath. From the southern city of Ziklag David secretly set about re-establishing good relations with the people of Judah. At the time of Saul's death David was spared from having to fight against the Israelites, and in the period that followed Saul's death he became king of Judah, ruling from Hebron presumably with Philistine approval. After the deaths of Abner, Saul's commander, and Ish-baal, Saul's successor, David was invited to become king over all Israel. The exact sequence of subsequent events is unclear, but in sum they involved removing the capital to Jerusalem which David captured from the Jebusites, defeating the Philistines decisively, and extending Israelite rule to Damascus, Ammon, Moab and Edom. David seems to have been less successful as a king than as a soldier. During his reign there were two revolts against him, one led by his son Absalom. Whatever his failings, David's greatness cannot be denied. He completely reversed the military and political fortunes of his people, and in choosing Jerusalem as his political and religious capital he determined the importance of that city for all time.

From Solomon to the fall of Jerusalem (c. 970–587 BC)

David's successor Solomon, building on the foundations laid by his father, brought Israel to the peak of success in many spheres. Jerusalem was extended, and the temple was built on the northeastern hill overlooking the city of David. Many cities were rebuilt. Solomon traded with surrounding countries, and established a great reputation as an author of proverbs and songs. The life of the court was sumptuous. Against this, parts of David's empire began to split away, and Solomon even ceded to Tyre Israelite cities in the coastal plain north of Acco to pay for his building works. There were slave gangs conscripted from Israelites living north of Judah.

The encounters between Saul, David and the Philistines
The length of Saul's reign and the extent of his kingdom are matters of uncertainty. The boundaries of Saul's kingdom given here depend upon 1 Samuel 14:47-48. Many scholars, however, do not accept this summary as accurate; nor do they accept that Saul reigned for only two years (1 Samuel 13:1). What is clear is that David, partly as a result of his deserting to the Philistine side, was later able to deliver Israel from subjugation to the Philistines, after the latter had killed and defeated Saul.

AN OUTLINE OF BIBLICAL HISTORY

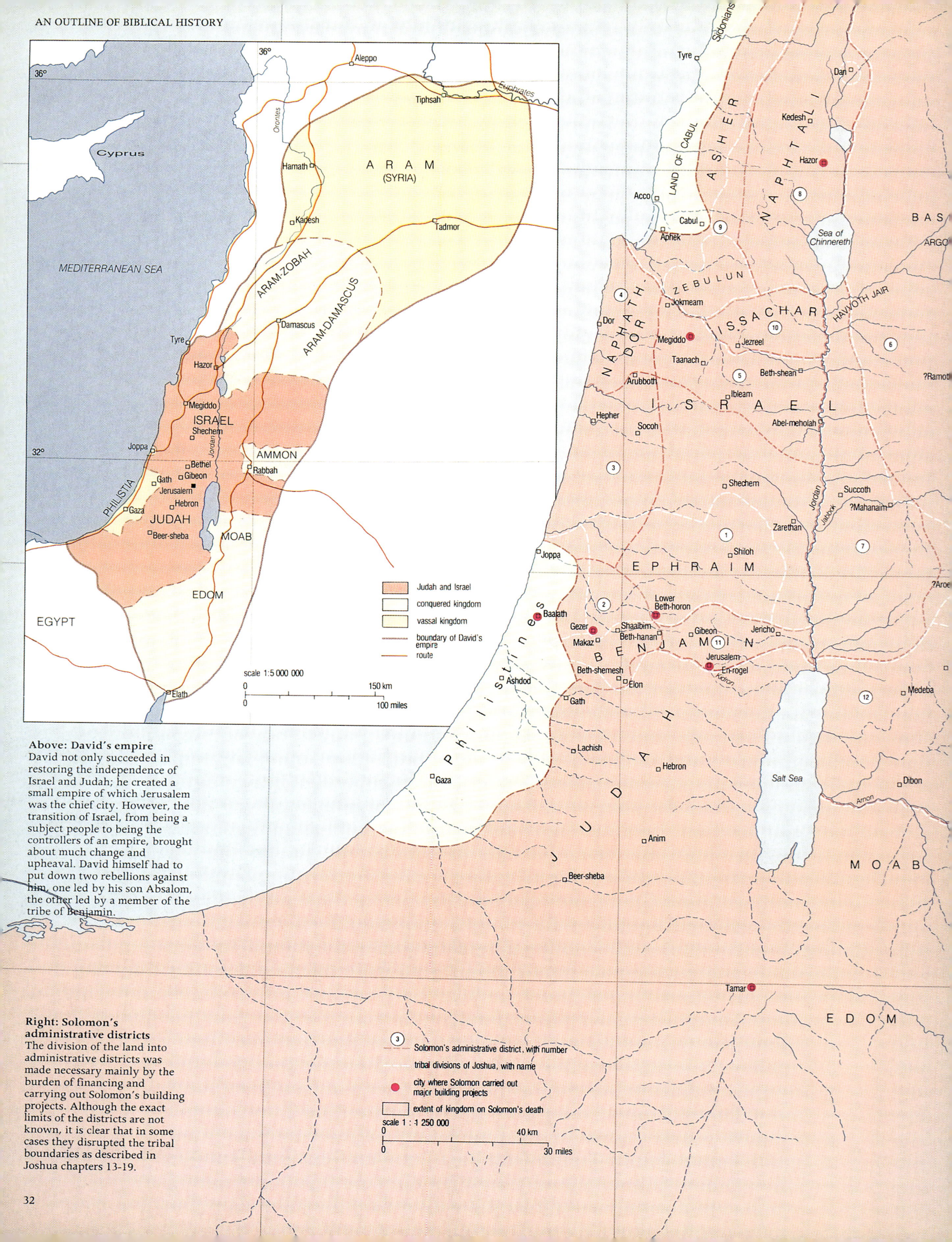

Above: David's empire
David not only succeeded in restoring the independence of Israel and Judah; he created a small empire of which Jerusalem was the chief city. However, the transition of Israel, from being a subject people to being the controllers of an empire, brought about much change and upheaval. David himself had to put down two rebellions against him, one led by his son Absalom, the other led by a member of the tribe of Benjamin.

Right: Solomon's administrative districts
The division of the land into administrative districts was made necessary mainly by the burden of financing and carrying out Solomon's building projects. Although the exact limits of the districts are not known, it is clear that in some cases they disrupted the tribal boundaries as described in Joshua chapters 13-19.

When Solomon died in about 928 BC, the northern tribes insisted on putting their grievances to Solomon's son Rehoboam before accepting him as king. Rehoboam heeded the advice of those who urged him not to be conciliatory, with the result that 10 northern tribes rebelled under the leadership of Jeroboam and established a kingdom called Israel with its capital initially at Shechem. The immediate cause of the division of the kingdom was the hardship which Solomon's reign produced for the northern tribes. However, it must not be forgotten that the political unity of the tribes had never been strong. They had united in the face of the Philistine threat, but even David had experienced two revolts, the second being a revolt in the north. The view of the writer of 1 Kings 11 is that the division was caused by Solomon's apostasy, when he turned from the God of Israel to the gods of his many foreign wives. Such apostasy would certainly have blinded Solomon to the demands for social justice implicit in Israel's relationship with God.

The new northern kingdom was probably set up not only in the name of social justice, but in the name of religion. Jeroboam set up two shrines, one in Bethel and one in Dan, with golden calves as the throne of the invisible God. He proclaimed to his people: "Behold your Elohim, O Israel, who brought you up out of the land of Egypt" (1 Kings 12:28). The Hebrew "*Elohim*" can be translated as either God or gods. For the writer of 1 Kings, "gods" was intended, because the northern kingdom, from a southern perspective, was an experiment in apostasy. For Jeroboam himself, who had been encouraged by the prophet Ahijah to rebel, the new kingdom was probably an attempt to reassert the older Exodus faith, which seemed to have been lost sight of with the shift to Jerusalem, its new temple and its royal ideology.

The boundary between the southern kingdom of Judah (plus Benjamin) and Israel seems to have been roughly the division between the Jerusalem saddle and the Bethel hills, although it fluctuated for several decades as the two kingdoms fought each other. An event that affected both kingdoms deeply was the campaign of the Egyptian king Shishak (Shoshenq I, 945—924 BC) in about 924 BC. This was apparently directed against the main fortified cities in both Judah and Israel, and was designed to weaken them. Shishak exacted heavy tribute from Jerusalem, and his campaign may have been the reason for Jeroboam removing his capital from Shechem to Penuel in Transjordan.

The opening years of the 9th century saw Judah, in alliance with Damascus, in the ascendancy over Israel. Judah was able to consolidate its border with Israel, while Damascus threatened Israel's cities in north upper Galilee. In about 882/1 civil war broke out in the northern kingdom. The eventual victor, Omri (c. 882/1–871), set about transforming Israel into the most powerful small nation in the region. He transferred his capital to the new site of Samaria, he subdued the territory of Moab and he made Judah subordinate to his policies. In his reign and that of his son Ahab (c. 873–852) a determined attempt was made to supplant the religion of the God of Israel with that of the Tyrian Baal, whose ardent advocate was Ahab's wife Jezebel. This official policy brought fierce opposition from the prophetic groups led by Elijah and Elisha. Ahab's reign was also marked by the strength of Assyria, and of Damascus with whom Ahab fought several bitter battles before being killed at Ramoth-gilead. In the reign of Ahab's son Joram (Jehoram), Elisha inspired a rebellion against the house of Omri and Ahab, by having an army commander Jehu anointed king. Jehu (842–814) succeeded in killing all those related to Omri and Ahab, and in removing the Baal religion from official worship. He was forced, however, to pay heavy tribute to Assyria, and he and his son Johoahaz suffered greatly at the hand of the Syrian king Hazael. A revolution in Judah against the queen mother

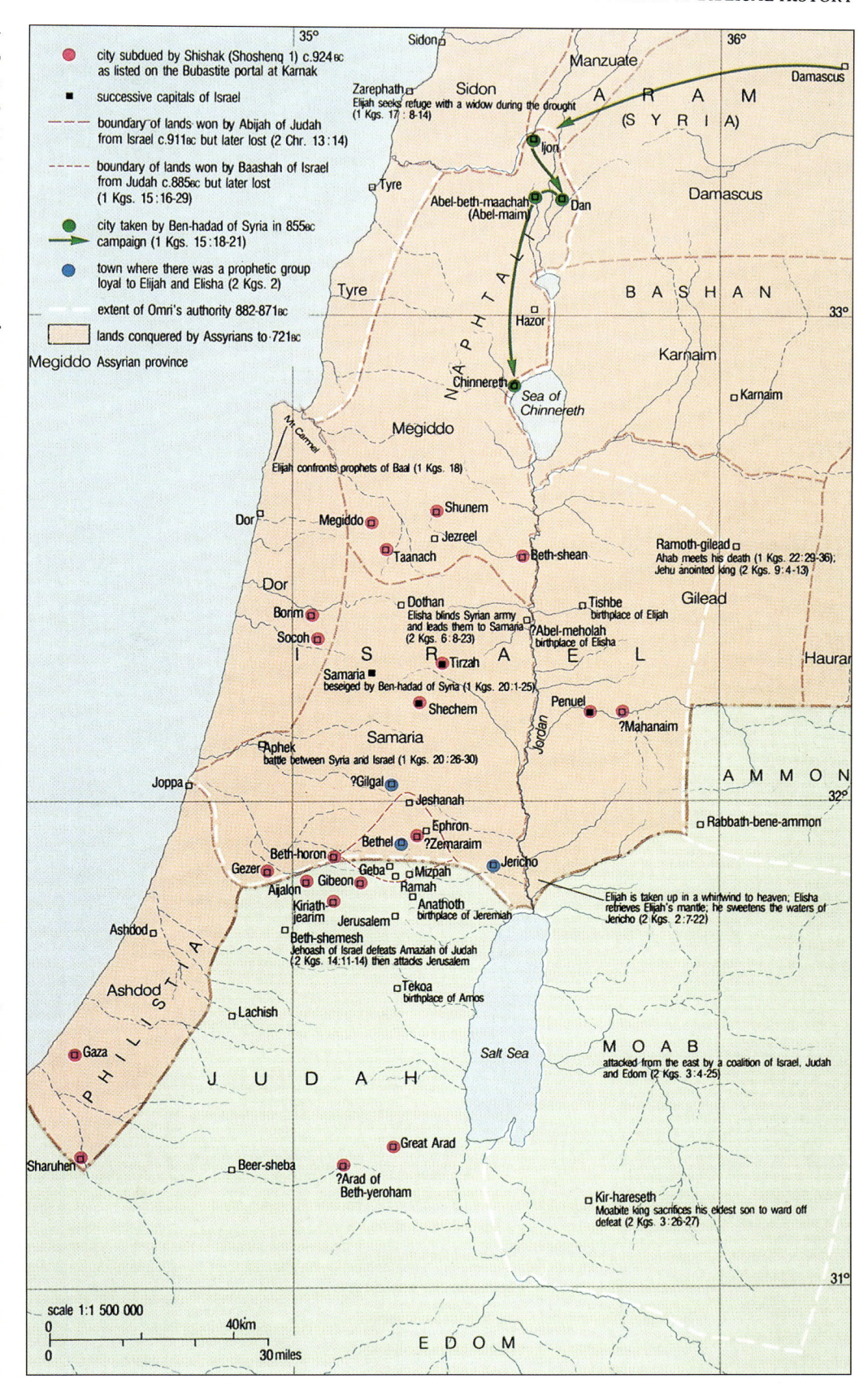

The main incidents of the divided monarchy
The period of the divided monarchy (c. 928-721 BC) saw many ups and downs. The northern kingdom (Israel) was threatened from the north by Damascus and Assyria, before being absorbed into the Assyrian empire in 721 BC. However, for a brief spell in the 9th century, Omri and Ahab controlled a small empire, and shortly before its collapse Jeroboam II restored some of its former glory. From the south the Egyptian Shishak raided Judah and Israel in c. 924 BC and destroyed many cities.

An Outline of Biblical History

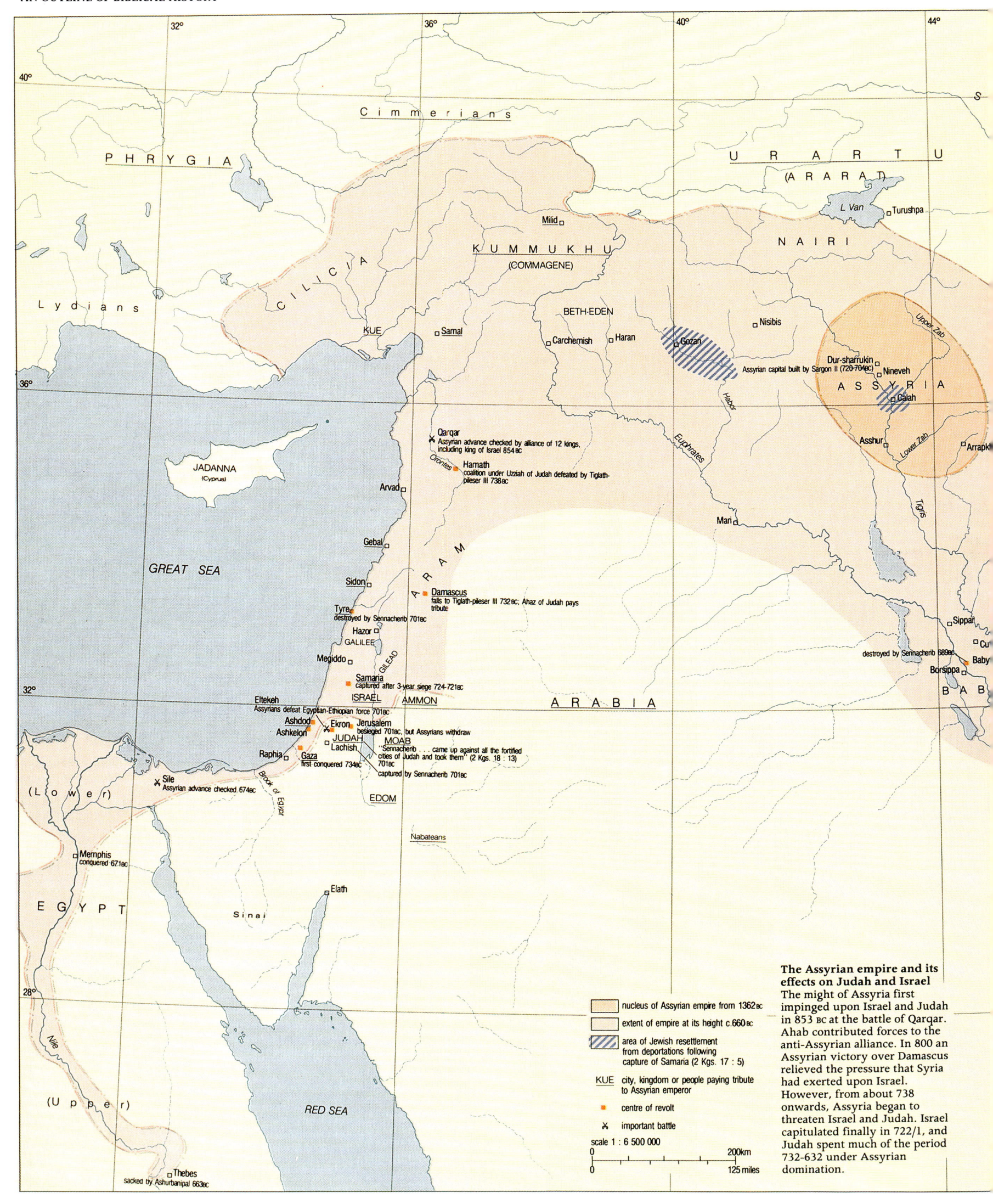

The Assyrian empire and its effects on Judah and Israel

The might of Assyria first impinged upon Israel and Judah in 853 BC at the battle of Qarqar. Ahab contributed forces to the anti-Assyrian alliance. In 800 an Assyrian victory over Damascus relieved the pressure that Syria had exerted upon Israel. However, from about 738 onwards, Assyria began to threaten Israel and Judah. Israel capitulated finally in 722/1, and Judah spent much of the period 732–632 under Assyrian domination.

Legend:
- nucleus of Assyrian empire from 1362 BC
- extent of empire at its height c.660 BC
- area of Jewish resettlement from deportations following capture of Samaria (2 Kgs. 17:5)
- KUE city, kingdom or people paying tribute to Assyrian emperor
- centre of revolt
- important battle

scale 1 : 6 500 000

Map annotations:
- Qarqar: Assyrian advance checked by alliance of 12 kings, including king of Israel 854 BC
- Hamath: coalition under Uzziah of Judah defeated by Tiglath-pileser III 738 BC
- Dur-sharrukin: Assyrian capital built by Sargon II (720–704 BC)
- Damascus: falls to Tiglath-pileser III 732 BC; Ahaz of Judah pays tribute
- Tyre: destroyed by Sennacherib 701 BC
- Samaria: captured after 3-year siege 724–721 BC
- Eltekeh: Assyrians defeat Egyptian-Ethiopian force 701 BC
- Jerusalem: besieged 701 BC, but Assyrians withdraw
- Lachish: "Sennacherib ... came up against all the fortified cities of Judah and took them" (2 Kgs. 18:13) 701 BC; captured by Sennacherib 701 BC
- Gaza: first conquered 734 BC
- Sile: Assyrian advance checked 674 BC
- Memphis: conquered 671 BC
- Thebes: sacked by Ashurbanipal 663 BC
- Babylon: destroyed by Sennacherib 689 BC

AN OUTLINE OF BIBLICAL HISTORY

Athaliah, who was of the house of Omri, brought Jehoash (Joash) to the throne. His reign (836–798) was also one in which Hazael pressed him sorely and exacted tribute.

Some relief came to both kingdoms at the turn of the century when the Assyrians crushed Damascus. In Judah Uzziah (c. 785–733) and in Israel Jeroboam II (c. 789–748) enjoyed long and prosperous reigns. However, especially in the northern kingdom, social justice was ignored, and the end of this period saw the activity of the first "classical" Prophets, Amos and Hosea, and heard their message of impending judgment if there was no reformation. With the accession of Tiglath-pileser III to the Assyrian throne in 745, a threat from the north once more hung over the two kingdoms. The small nations failed to repel the Assyrian king, and in about 733 he conquered Damascus, Galilee and Israelite Transjordan. The king of Judah, Ahaz, who had appealed to him for help against Israel and Damascus (against the advice of Isaiah), became his vassal. In 724 Hoshea king of Israel rebelled against Assyria, and after a siege of three years Samaria fell, and the independent life of the northern kingdom ended. Many people were deported and replaced by peoples from elsewhere in the Assyrian empire. Under Hezekiah (c. 727–698) Judah tried to throw off Assyrian domination, and this led to an invasion of Judah in 701 BC, and a siege of Jerusalem, in which the city managed to hold out. However, Assyrian dominance could not be resisted, and for much of the

Left: The Babylonian empire and its effects on Judah
The opposition of Judah to Assyria, focused especially in the reign of Josiah (c. 640-609 BC), played a small part in Assyria's defeat by Babylon. Babylon in turn became a threat to Judah, capturing Jerusalem in 597 BC and deporting 10 000 of Judah's most important people. In 587, following Zedekiah's rebellion, Jerusalem and its temple were destroyed.

Below: The Persian empire and its significance for Judah
The defeat of Babylon by Cyrus, king of Persia, in 540 BC enabled some of the Jewish exiles to return to Jerusalem. The Jewish community was greatly strengthened by the work of Ezra and Nehemiah who reorganized the religious and civil life of the community with Persian royal support.

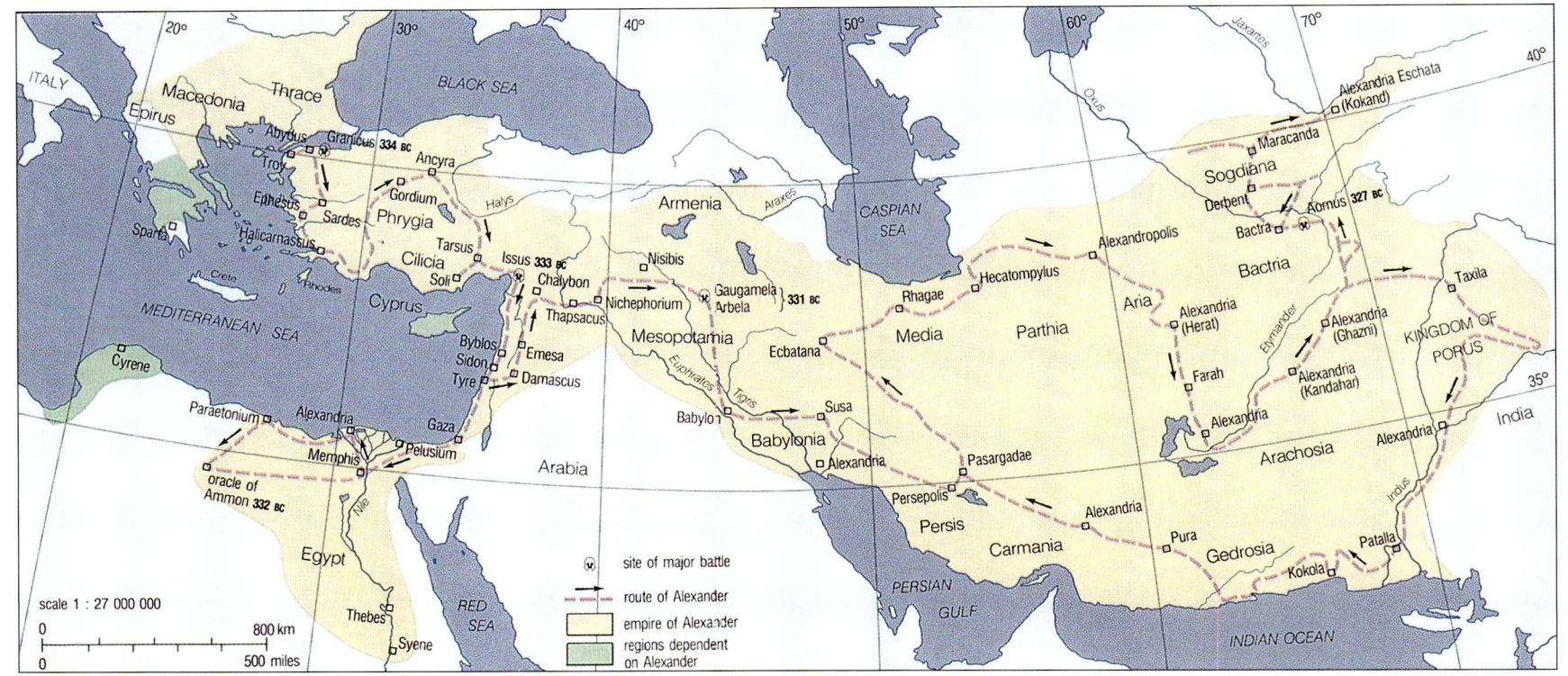

reign of Manasseh (698–642) Judah was subject to Assyria. At this time pagan religious practices reasserted themselves, and the biblical writers saw this as one of the blackest periods for Judah.

The death of Manasseh coincided with the decline of Assyrian power. His son was assassinated two years later, and Josiah (640–609) acceded at the age of eight, backed by anti-Assyrian citizens. His reign saw a religious reformation, in which all cult centres other than Jerusalem were abolished, and the temple itself was purged of elements of foreign religion. Josiah also extended his sphere of influence into parts of the former northern kingdom. His reign ended tragically when he was killed in battle at Megiddo, trying to prevent the Egyptian Neco (Necho II, 610–595) from taking part in the battle of Haran at which the Assyrian army was finally crushed by the Babylonians.

With Josiah's death his reforms were soon forgotten, and the prophet Jeremiah, whose ministry had begun in 627 BC, once again began to warn the people of impending judgment. In 597 the Babylonian king Nebuchadnezzar captured Jerusalem, and there occurred the most significant of the three deportations of 597, 587 and 582. King Jehoiachin and Ezekiel were among those deported on this occasion. In 589 Jehoiachin's uncle, Zedekiah, who had ruled since 597, rebelled against Nebuchadnezzar. Jerusalem was besieged and, in spite of Jeremiah's advice that surrender was the proper response, the city held out for 18 months and finally fell in 587. There was then another (smaller) deportation, and this time the city and the temple were destroyed. A new administration at Mizpah under the rule of Gedaliah lasted until Gedaliah was assassinated by a member of the royal family, Ishmael. Judahites loyal to Gedaliah, fearing Babylonian reprisals, fled to Tahpanes in Egypt (possibly Tell Dafana in the northeast part of the Nile delta), taking with them an unwilling Jeremiah.

From the exile to the beginning of Roman rule (587–63 BC)

The deported Jews were resettled in the region between Babylon and Erech, beside the canal between these two cities called in Ezekiel 1:1 the river Chebar. The king (Jehoiachin) and the other notables were taken to Babylon itself, and imprisoned. Those exiles who established themselves in Babylon found themselves surrounded by sights that must have been astounding. With its canals, gardens and great buildings Babylon must have seemed to many to epitomize a civilization and religion superior to that known in Judah. However, the exile, if a disaster, was a creative period. It led to much religious reflection on the part of faithful Israelites, and was probably the period in which much Old Testament material began to assume the form in which we know it. The exile was also the real beginning of the dispersion of the Jews (as they are usually called from the exile onwards) to many parts of the world. When Babylon fell in 540 to the Persian king Cyrus, and permission was granted to the Jews to return to Jerusalem, many remained where they were. We also know of a Jewish colony in Egypt at Elephantine, north of the first cataract of the Nile, in the late 5th century. The Jews here were mercenary soldiers employed by the Persians during the period of Persian rule in Egypt, and they had their own temple.

Those who returned to Judah in about 539 had a hard time, and they did not succeed in rebuilding the temple until 516 BC. In the mid-5th century Nehemiah found Jerusalem in a parlous state with broken-down walls, a small population and many social and religious abuses. In association with, or later followed by, Ezra, he reordered the social and religious life of Judah, and laid the foundations for its survival.

The next major change was brought about by the conquests of Alexander the Great following his victory over the Persians at the battle of Issus in 333 BC. He incorporated into his empire Syria, Palestine and Egypt, and opened the way for the spread of Greek culture and language in those areas. After his death in 323 BC, Judah came under the rule of the Ptolemies in Egypt, a dynasty established by one of Alexander's generals. Greek cities

The conquests of Alexander
The conquests of Alexander the Great opened a new chapter in the history of Israel. Not only did the Jews pass from Persian rule to that of Alexander, and then to that of his generals and their descendants, first in Egypt and later in Syria; the spread of Greek language, literature and culture was to have a profound effect upon the religious life of the Jews, and would assist in the rise and spread of Christianity. That the New Testament was written in Greek and not in Hebrew or Aramaic resulted ultimately from the changes produced by Alexander's conquests.

began to be founded, especially in Transjordan. Between 200 and 198 BC, Judah was wrested from Egypt by the Greek rulers of Syria, the Seleucids. Hostility in Jerusalem between those who welcomed and those who rejected Greek culture became acute, and the high priesthood was put up to the highest bidder, the financial beneficiary being the Seleucid king. In the reign of Antiochus IV (175–164) an attempt was made to proscribe the Jewish religion, and the temple was defiled when the cult of Zeus Olympios was inaugurated in December 167 BC.

Antiochus' act provoked the Maccabean revolt, initiated by the priest Mattathias of Modein, and carried out by his sons Judas (167–160), Jonathan (160–143) and Simon (142–135/4). It is possible that a revolt had begun before Judaism was proscribed, and that its prohibition was a response to this revolt. However, the house of Mattathias (known as the Hasmonean dynasty) took over the leading role. The course of the revolt was complex, and the fortunes of the Jews fluctuated greatly. The following landmarks can be indicated. In 164 the temple was recaptured and rededicated. The annual commemoration of this event is the festival of Hanukkah. In 152 Jonathan became high priest, and in 142 Jewish autonomy was recognized by Demetrius II. This granting of autonomy was not the end of troubles for the Jews, however, and it was not until 128 BC in the rule of John Hyrcanus (135/4–104) that anything like real peace was experienced.

John Hyrcanus and his successor Aristobulus I (104–103) set about creating the conditions that

Right: The Maccabean revolt and its aftermath
The Maccabean revolt, which began in 167 BC, was initially a struggle to preserve the Jewish faith against Hellenistic opposition. The revolt later became a movement for Jewish independence, which saw the Jewish area of control enlarged by successive rulers. The event of major significance for biblical history was the reconquest of Galilee, which had remained outside the main Jewish sphere of influence since the 8th century BC. Galilee would be the birthplace of the Christian movement.

AN OUTLINE OF BIBLICAL HISTORY

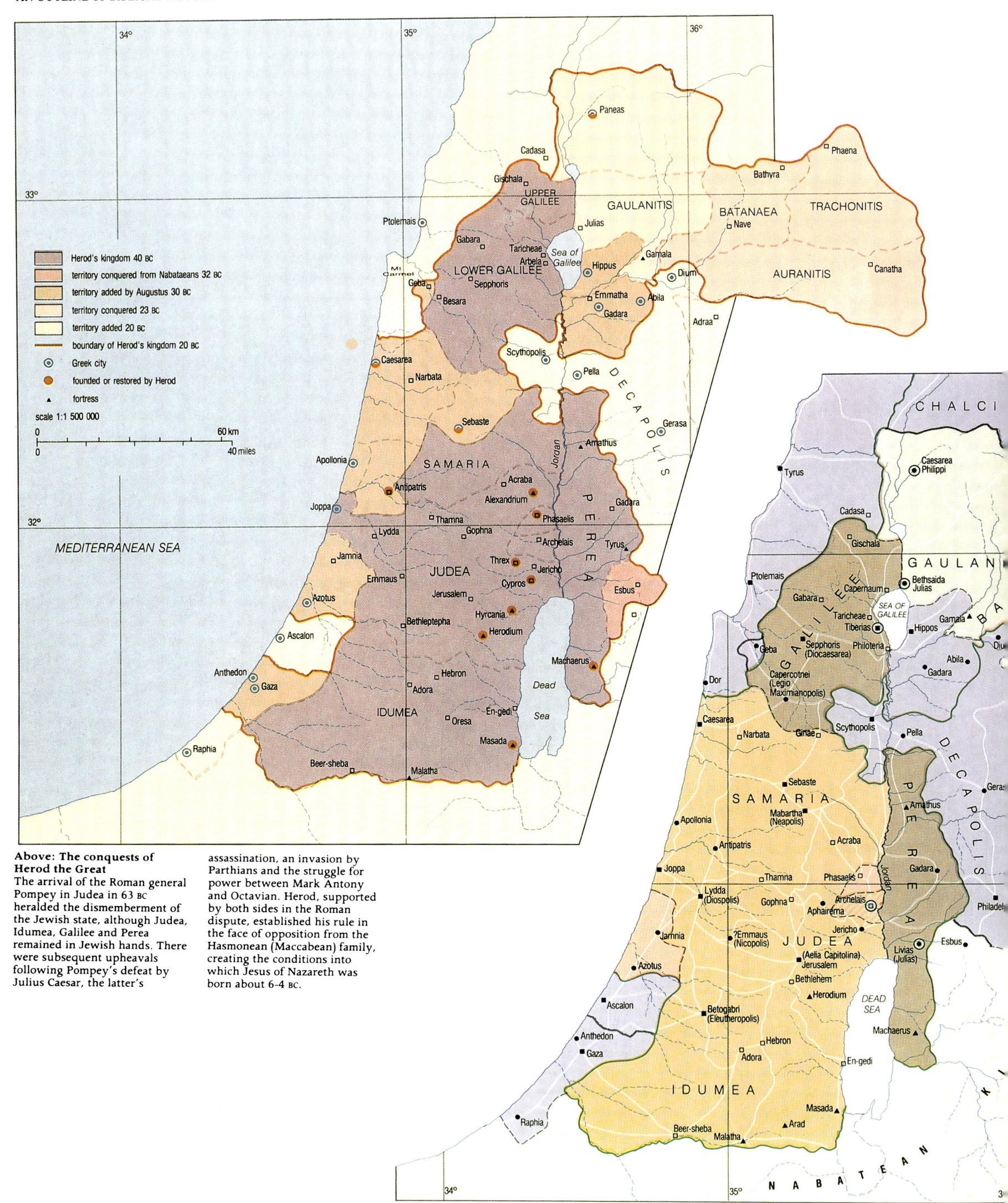

Legend:
- Herod's kingdom 40 BC
- territory conquered from Nabataeans 32 BC
- territory added by Augustus 30 BC
- territory conquered 23 BC
- territory added 20 BC
- boundary of Herod's kingdom 20 BC
- ⊙ Greek city
- ● founded or restored by Herod
- ▲ fortress

scale 1:1 500 000

Above: The conquests of Herod the Great

The arrival of the Roman general Pompey in Judea in 63 BC heralded the dismemberment of the Jewish state, although Judea, Idumea, Galilee and Perea remained in Jewish hands. There were subsequent upheavals following Pompey's defeat by Julius Caesar, the latter's assassination, an invasion by Parthians and the struggle for power between Mark Antony and Octavian. Herod, supported by both sides in the Roman dispute, established his rule in the face of opposition from the Hasmonean (Maccabean) family, creating the conditions into which Jesus of Nazareth was born about 6–4 BC.

Below: The division of Palestine among Herod's sons
The Palestine in which Jesus grew up and pursued his ministry was very different from that into which he was born. On Herod's death the land was divided among his three surviving sons. However, the son who ruled Judea, Idumea and Samaria was replaced by a Roman procurator in 6 AD. The Herod mentioned in the gospels, Herod Antipas, ruled Galilee and Perea.

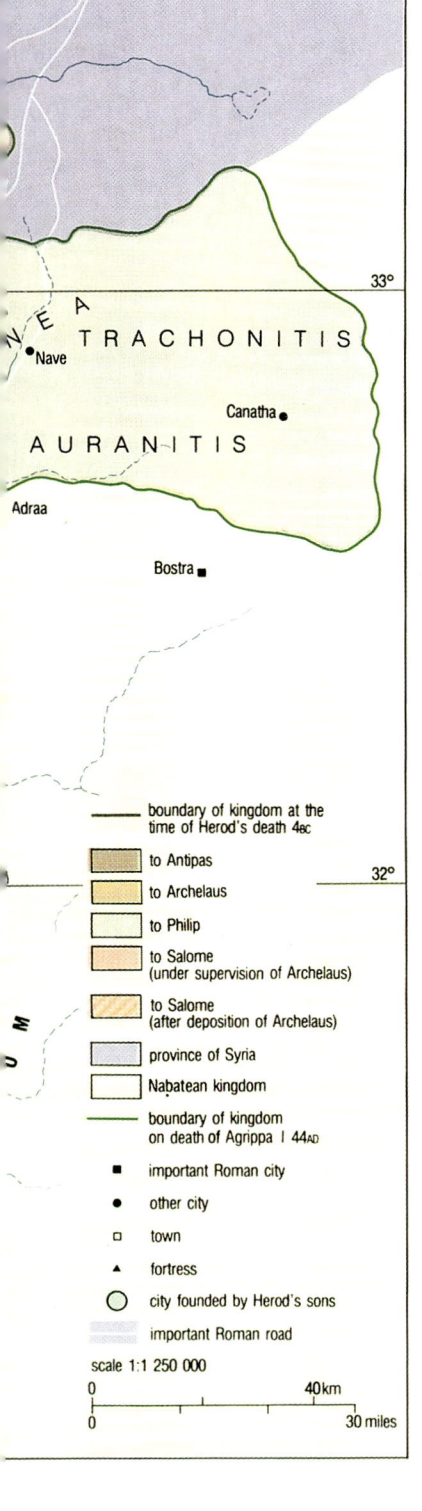

existed in the time of Jesus. Idumea (the Edomite kingdom established in southern Judah after the exile) was forcibly converted to Judaism, Galilee was made into a predominantly Jewish area, and the Jewish presence in Perea in Transjordan was consolidated. Following the reigns of Alexander Jannaeus (103–76) and his wife Salome Alexandra (76–67), rivalry within the ruling family brought the downfall of the Hasmoneans and the arrival in 63 BC of the Roman general Pompey.

Roman rule to the close of the apostolic age (63 BC–c. 100 AD)

The first decades of Roman rule in Judea were complicated by the struggle for supremacy in Rome itself (Pompey was defeated by Julius Caesar, after whose assassination there was a struggle between Mark Antony and Octavian) and by the attempt of the Hasmoneans to regain power. In 40 BC Herod, an Idumean, was appointed king of Judea by the Romans, and ruled from 37 to 4 BC. His reign was a time of peace, and of massive building projects, which established Caesarea as the principal city of the province, and which transformed Jerusalem into the city that Jesus knew. The temple was also enlarged and virtually rebuilt. On Herod's death the kingdom was divided between three of his sons. Herod Antipas (the Herod of the gospels who imprisoned and executed John the Baptist) ruled over Galilee and Perea until he was deposed in 39 AD, Philip ruled over the northeastern territories, while Archelaus was given Judea, Idumea and Samaria. Archelaus was deposed in 6 AD, and his territories were ruled by Roman procurators, including Pontius Pilate (26–36 AD). The rule by procurators was broken briefly when Herod Agrippa I, who had succeeded Herod Antipas in 39 AD as ruler of Galilee and Perea, was made king over Judea, Idumea and Samaria. He ruled thus from 41 AD to his death in 44, after which the government reverted to that of Roman procurators. As the rule of the latter was often corrupt and tyrannical, growing unrest led to the outbreak of the First Jewish Revolt in 66 AD. In the campaign that the Romans mounted in response, Jerusalem and its temple were destroyed in 70 AD, and the last survivors of the rebels committed suicide at Masada in 73 AD rather than surrender.

The ministry of Jesus

Into the general outline of the history of 1st-century Palestine it is now necessary to fit the origin and earliest expansion of Christianity. Jesus of Nazareth was born in the reign of Herod the Great. A date that is commonly given is 4 BC, the year of Herod's death. The account in Matthew 2:1–23, although it gives no figure, implies that Jesus was born towards the end of Herod's reign. Matthew explains that the parents of Jesus took him to Egypt to escape from Herod's massacre of children in Bethlehem, and that when they received news of Herod's death they returned, not to Judea, which was ruled by Archelaus, but to Galilee (Matthew 2:22–23). Matthew's account would suggest a date of between 6 and 4 BC for the birth. The information that the family returned not to Judea but to Galilee could indicate that they had lived in Bethlehem all along.

In Luke's account (2:1–7) the birth of Jesus is dated to the time of a census which took place when Quirinius was governor of Syria (although there are several possible ways of rendering the Greek). Quirinius became governor of Syria in 6 AD, and there has been much debate about the translation and historical accuracy of the passage. Luke's account implies that the family lived in Nazareth all along, and that the visit to Bethlehem was for the purposes of the census, after which, having performed the necessary sacrificial duties in Jerusalem, they returned to Nazareth. The accounts in Matthew and Luke can be conflated by assuming that, after the visit to Bethlehem from Nazareth for the census, Joseph and Mary and their newly born son obtained more permanent lodgings in Bethlehem, visited Jerusalem, and were still in Bethlehem when the kings from the east arrived. The flight to Egypt then followed, and the return to Nazareth took place after Herod's death.

The gospel narrative proper begins with the ministry of John the Baptist, which Luke (3:1–2) dates to the fifteenth year of the reign of Tiberius, that is 28/9 AD (another suggestion, following Jewish methods of calculating reigns, is 27 AD). The scene of John's activity was probably the area of the Jordan near to Jericho. Jesus came from Galilee to be baptized by John, and according to John's gospel (1:35–51) Jesus made contact with some of the men he was later to call to discipleship. Prior to the arrest of John (John 3:24), Jesus had already gathered some disciples around him (John 2:1–2, 11), had visited Jerusalem (John 2:13–3:21) and had spent time in Judea.

The imprisonment of John the Baptist, possibly in 28 AD, was the signal for the beginning of the public ministry of Jesus in Galilee (Mark 1:14). This ministry lasted for perhaps a year, but its actual course is impossible to reconstruct because the material for this period in the gospels is arranged thematically rather than chronologically. With reasonable certainty it can be said that Jesus made Capernaum the base for his ministry (Matthew 4:13), that he appointed 12 followers and sent them out in twos to preach and to heal (Mark 6:7–13), that he taught a good deal by the Sea of Galilee and crossed it on various occasions, and that he was supported by a group of women, some of whom were well connected (Luke 8:2–3).

Towards the end of the period of the Galilean ministry Jesus withdrew, first to the region of Tyre and Sidon (Mark 7:24–30), then to the Decapolis (Mark 7:31–37), and finally to the region of Caesarea Philippi, where Peter made his declaration of belief that Jesus was the Messiah (Mark 8:27–30). The Transfiguration followed some days later, presumably somewhere in the Hermon range close to Caesarea Philippi (Mark 9:1–8).

Leaving Galilee, Jesus and his disciples went to Judea and to Perea (Mark 10:1), and they may have visited Jerusalem from time to time for important festivals. How long Jesus remained in Judea and Perea is not known; some authorities suggest the six months before Holy Week.

Holy Week itself is usually dated to April of 30 AD, and it began for Jesus and his disciples with the triumphal entry into Jerusalem on Palm Sunday. The next few days were devoted to preaching and disputing in the temple, the nights being spent at Bethany. On the Thursday evening

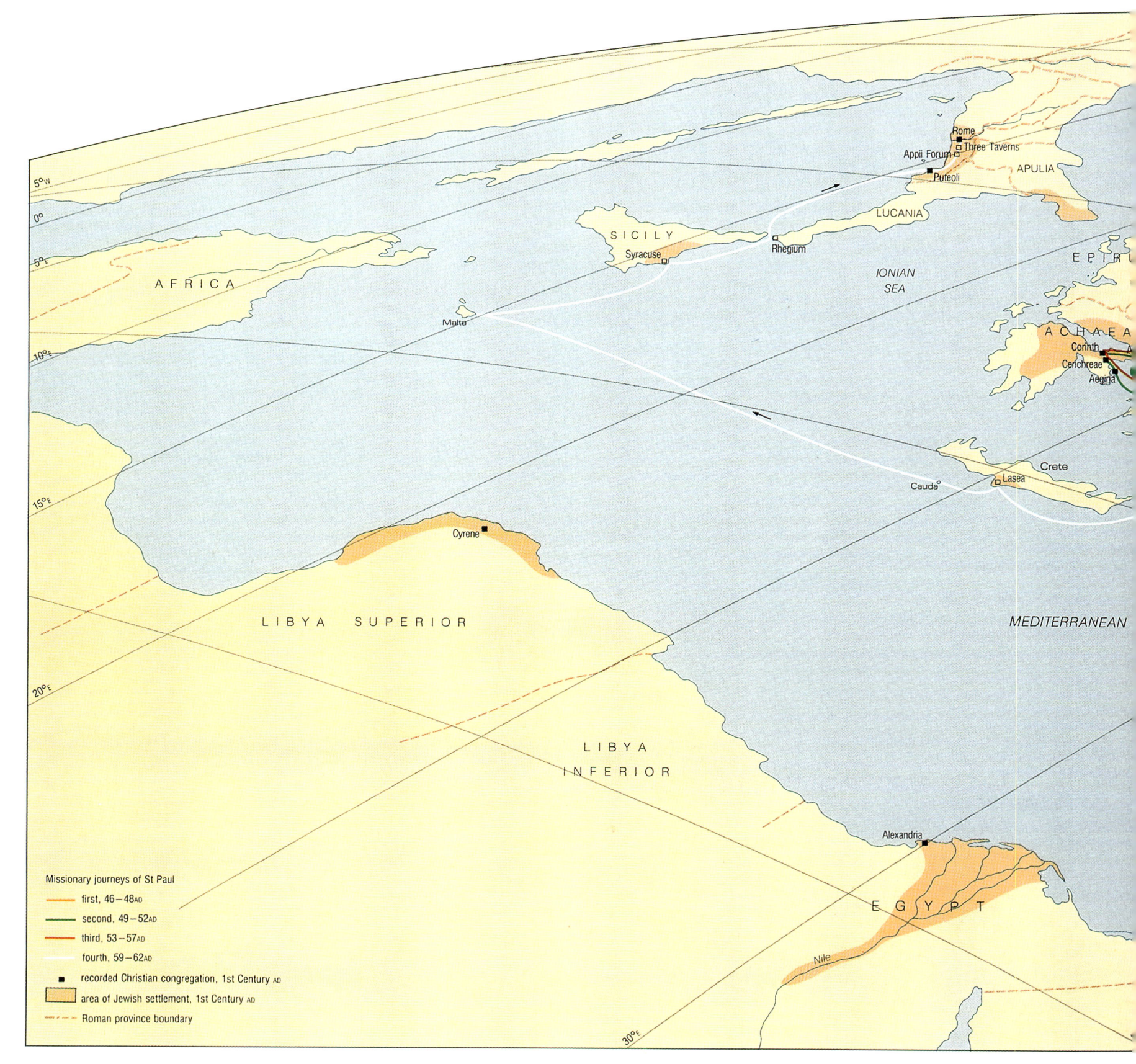

Jesus arranged to eat the Passover meal with his disciples (Mark 14:12–16). Whether or not this was the night of the official Passover is debatable. John (18:28) is clear that it was at least the night before the official Passover evening. The issue is not that of the day on which Jesus ate the Last Supper with his disciples; the gospels seem to be agreed that this was a Thursday. The question concerns the date, and whether or not the Thursday was also the date of the official Passover. If it was not, we must assume that Jesus, knowing that he would be executed before the official Passover, arranged a substitute meal on the last night of his life. After the meal he was arrested in the Garden of Gethsemane, and was tried and condemned by both Jewish and Roman authorities so that he could be executed before the beginning of the festival.

Two days after his death his disciples found the tomb empty, and were convinced that Jesus was alive when he appeared to them on various occasions (1 Corinthians 15:3–11). The appearances took place both in Jerusalem and in Galilee and did not last indefinitely, but ended with a commissioning of the disciples, placed in Galilee by Matthew (28:16–20) and near Jerusalem by Luke (24:44–53; Acts 1:1–11).

The missionary journeys of Paul and the expansion of the early Church
Christianity spread from Palestine to many parts of the Roman empire by various means. However, the Pauline missions were important not only because of the ground that they covered, but because they raised the issue of the relationship of the Jewish law to non-Jews who had become Christians. The decision to make minimal demands upon Gentile Christians was an important factor in the spread of Christianity to non-Jews.

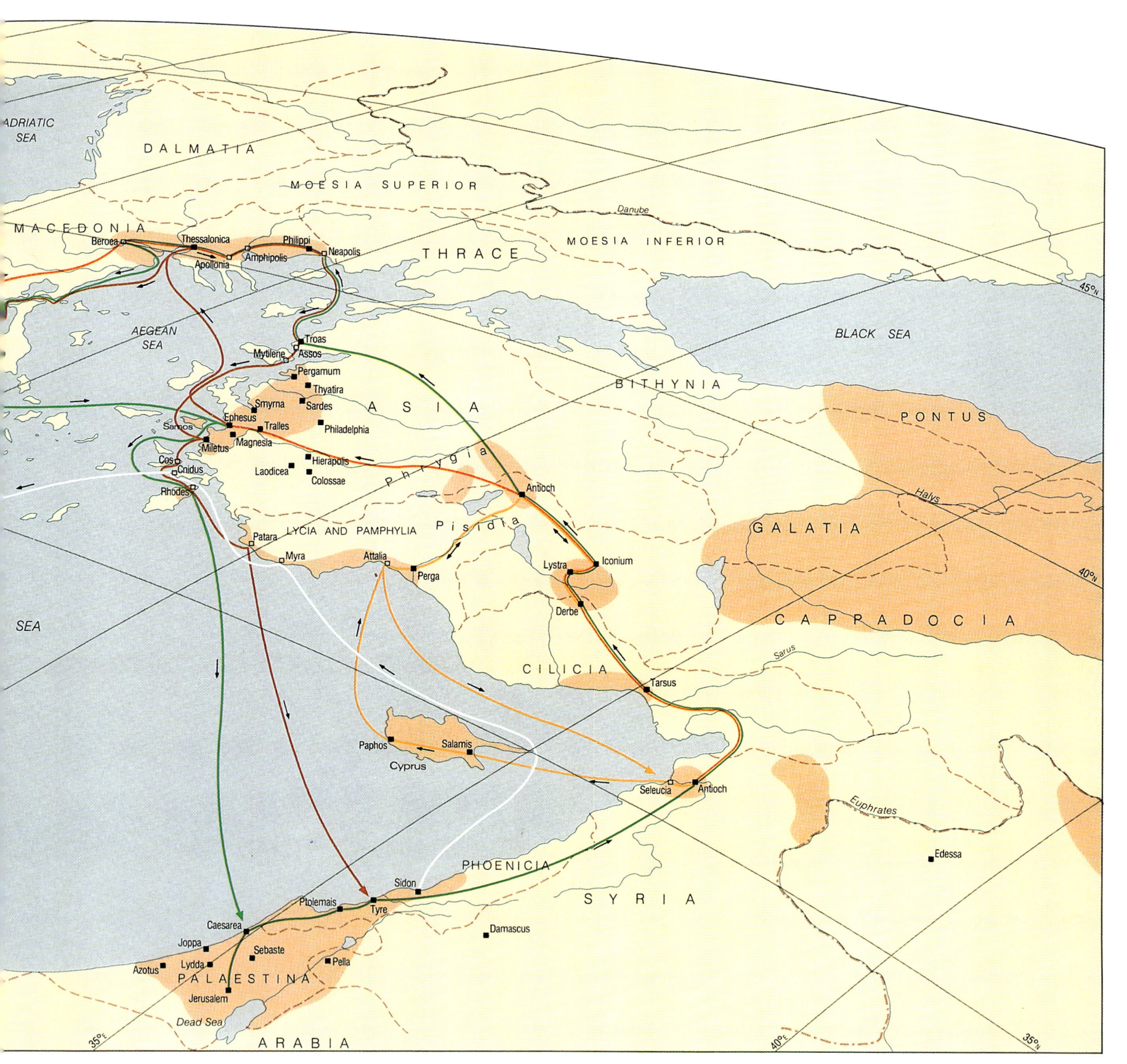

The expansion of the Church to the time of Paul's missionary journeys (30–46 AD)

The earliest Christian community was located in Jerusalem. Its members worshipped regularly in the temple, and practised a type of community life in which possessions were held in common (Acts 4:32–36). They included both Aramaic- and Greek-speaking Jews. Prominent among the latter was Stephen, whose bold preaching soon led to his martyrdom.

The persecution which followed the martyrdom scattered the Jerusalem Church, and Philip, a leading Hellenist, went to Samaria, where his preaching met with a success that the Jerusalem leaders endorsed (Acts 8:4–17). The Christian mission was further extended when Peter, now resident in Joppa, preached in Caesarea to the centurion Cornelius and his household (Acts 10). By 44 AD Peter had returned to Jerusalem, the year in which Herod Agrippa I killed the apostle James and imprisoned Peter (Acts 12:1–19). By this time Christianity had spread to the extent that the Church in Antioch began to take the initiative in preaching to non-Jews as well as Jews.

The person who was foremost in this mission was Saul of Tarsus, better known as Paul. Initially he was an ardent persecutor of the Church, but in about 32/3 AD he became a follower of Christ as the result of a vision while he was on his way to apprehend Christians in Damascus. After escaping from Damascus, Paul went to Arabia, probably to the Nabatean kingdom, where he may have preached, and may have provoked the hostility of its ruler to the point where he was not welcome when he returned to Damascus (2 Corinthians 11:32–33). Three years after his conversion he visited Jerusalem for a fortnight where he saw Peter and James the brother of Jesus (Galatians 1:18–19). Nothing is known about his movements for the next eight or nine years, until he again visited Jerusalem (Galatians 2:1ff.) either at the onset or in the course of his missionary journeys.

Paul's missionary journeys

One of the main themes of the Acts of the Apostles is the evangelization of non-Jews. Two problems evidently confronted the earliest Christians: first, whether Jesus was the anointed servant of God for non-Jews as well as Jews; and second, whether non-Jews who became Christians should observe all or part of the Mosaic Law. As presented in Acts, force of circumstances brought these questions to a head. First, Peter preached the gospel at Caesarea to the Roman centurion Cornelius, in obedience to a divine vision. Second, some believers, who were forced to leave Jerusalem following the stoning of Stephen (Acts 6–7), reached Antioch and there preached the gospel to non-Jews (Acts 11:20–21). This marked Antioch as a mixed congregation of Jewish and non-Jewish Christians. Paul became a member of this congregation upon the initiative of Barnabas (Acts 11:25–26). The position of Antioch in relation to Asia Minor, as well as the cosmopolitan character of its Christian community, made it the ideal base for further Christian outreach (Acts 13:1–3).

Since Barnabas was a native of Cyprus (Acts 4:36), it was natural that the missionaries should go first to that island before making their way to Pisidian Antioch, Iconium, Lystra and Derbe in Asia Minor (47–48 AD). In every case they preached first to the Jews in the synagogues of those towns, but the result was that not only Jews, but Gentiles too accepted the gospel. In some cases these were Gentiles who were sympathetic to Judaism and attached to, but not full members of, synagogues (cf. Acts 14:1). In other cases, as with Sergius Paulus, the gospel was preached directly to Gentiles (Acts 13:7–12). Upon reaching Derbe, Paul and Barnabas retraced their steps, visiting their converts and providing for them a framework of church organization (Acts 14:23). They sailed directly from Attalia to Antioch, but did not revisit the island of Cyprus.

The response of non-Jews to the preaching of the gospel answered the question of whether Jesus was the anointed servant of God for Gentiles as well as Jews. The problem of the extent to which non-Jewish Christians should observe the Mosaic Law now came to a head, and was dealt with at the Council of Jerusalem (Acts 15). This meeting laid upon Gentile Christians the obligations of avoiding meat offered to idols or from which the blood had not been drained, and of avoiding fornication (Acts 15:20, 29). The mission of Paul and Barnabas was endorsed. The way was open for the second missionary journey (49–52 AD).

The aim of this journey was to revisit the churches of the first journey, but from the outset there was a disagreement between Paul and Barnabas over whether they should take with them John Mark, who had failed to complete the first missionary journey (cf. Acts 13:13; 15:37–38). Thus Barnabas and John Mark sailed to Cyprus (Acts 15:39), and Paul and Silas journeyed overland, presumably via Paul's native Tarsus, to Derbe, Lystra and Iconium.

Of their movements from Iconium we know only that they had "gone throughout Phrygia and the region of Galatia" and that the Holy Spirit forbade them to preach either in Asia or in Bithynia (Acts 16:6–8). We next find Paul and his companions at Troas, where Paul's vision of a man of Macedonia asking him for help is the occasion for the voyage across the Aegean Sea to Neapolis, Philippi, Thessalonica, Beroea, Athens and Corinth. In Philippi Paul and Silas were imprisoned, and were able to effect the conversion of their gaoler (Acts 16:25–32); in Thessalonica the house of their host was attacked (Acts 17:5); and in Athens Paul preached to the philosophers on the Areopagus. Paul seems to have spent some time in Corinth (Acts 18:18), in company with Aquila and Priscilla, who had been forced to leave Rome under the prescript of Claudius in 49 AD (Acts 18:2). While Paul was at Corinth, the Christian mission was unofficially regarded as "not unlawful". The Roman proconsul Gallio refused to take action against Paul when he was accused of persuading men to worship God contrary to the (Mosaic) Law (Acts 18:12–17). After his stay in Corinth Paul moved on via Ephesus and Caesarea to Antioch.

Paul began his third journey (53–57 AD) by retracing the route he had taken on the second journey, visiting the churches in Galatia and Phrygia in order to strengthen and encourage them (Acts 18:23). However, on his second journey he had promised to revisit the city of Ephesus (Acts 18:19–21), and this he now did, staying there for two years (Acts 19:10). Paul found at Ephesus some partial believers who had been taught by Apollos, but who did not know of the Holy Spirit or of baptism in the name of Jesus (Acts 18:24–19:7). Acts tells us of his stay in Ephesus only that it was a time of intensive preaching and healing, and that Paul's success brought a violent reaction from craftsmen whose livelihood depended upon the worship of the goddess Diana. At 1 Corinthians 15:32 there is a verse that suggests that Paul may have been subjected to a fight with wild animals in the arena at Ephesus, although it could well be that he is speaking figuratively.

Paul's movements from Ephesus are not certain, and their reconstruction is bound up with the problem of how the letters to the Corinthians fit in with the journeys. It is usually assumed that Paul sailed from Ephesus to Thessalonica, went down to Corinth, retraced his steps to Thessalonica and then proceeded to Philippi, from where he sailed to Tyre, making brief calls along the way. For obvious reasons he did not stop at Ephesus, but spoke to the elders of the Ephesus Church at Miletus (see Acts 20:1–21:17). From Tyre he went via Caesarea to Jerusalem.

THE BIBLE IN ART

The Ascension: detail of stained glass in Le Mans cathedral, c. 1145.

It is not difficult to appreciate why incidents from the Bible have inspired so much art – from obscure as well as famous artists. Quite apart from the power which the Church exercised for many centuries, and the hold that it had over the thinking of men and women, biblical stories have an inherent fascination and constitute a major challenge for any artist. Obvious examples are the contrast between the armed giant Goliath and the shepherd boy David, or the wretchedness of the returned prodigal son and the unspeakable joy of his father. In the period before the Bible was readily available to ordinary people, the depiction of these stories played an important part in the Church's teaching and preaching.

The reason for our including in an Atlas of the Bible what can only be an unrepresentative fragment of artistic portrayals of biblical episodes is that it provides a contrast with Part Three. There, these episodes are set in their proper geographical context, in some cases with the help of aerial photography. For most of the period of the Church's existence no such facility has been available. Most of the artists had little idea of what the Holy Land looked like, and usually presented it in the context of the landscapes and manner of dress with which they were themselves familiar. We have a great advantage in being able to imagine biblical incidents against their authentic geographical settings. On the other hand, the advantage is not entirely ours. We do not know where the return of the Prodigal Son took place (if indeed it is an actual incident and not just a marvellous illustrative story), and even if we did, that knowledge would not help us to understand what the parable teaches us. Thus the artistic representations that follow are not just a foil to Part Three. They are a reminder that knowledge of the geography of the Holy Land is a means to better understanding of the Bible; and few have expressed more powerfully the meaning of its stories than the great artists whose work has been inspired by the Bible.

THE BIBLE IN ART

"They set taskmasters over them to afflict them with heavy burdens; and they built for Pharaoh store-cities"
(EXODUS 1:11) ▷

Moses on Mount Sinai: medieval manuscript.

"The Lord said to Moses, 'Go down; for your people, whom you brought up out of the land of Egypt, have corrupted themselves . . . they have made for themselves a molten calf, and have worshipped it and sacrificed to it'"
△ (EXODUS 32:7-8)

Israel in Egypt: Edward Poynter (1836-1919).

"Lot's wife behind him looked back, and she became a pillar of salt"
◁ (GENESIS 19:26)

Lot's Wife Turned into a Pillar of Salt: 14th-century Hebrew manuscript.

THE BIBLE IN ART

"The angel of the Lord called to him from heaven . . . 'do not lay your hand on the lad or do anything to him; for now I know that you fear God'"
(GENESIS 22:11-12) ▷

"Then Joseph could not control himself before all those who stood by him; and he cried, 'Make every one go out from me' . . . and he wept aloud"
◁ (GENESIS 45:1-2)

Joseph Receives his Brethren: 6th-century manuscript.

The Sacrifice of Isaac: etching by Rembrandt (1606-69).

45

THE BIBLE IN ART

"She made him sleep upon her knees; and she called a man, and had him shave off the seven locks of his head. Then she began to torment him, and his strength left him"
(JUDGES 16:19)

"Then Samson went down with his father and mother to Timnah, and he came to the vineyards of Timnah. And behold, a young lion roared against him"
(JUDGES 14:5)

"He found a fresh jawbone of an ass, and put out his hand and seized it, and with it he slew a thousand men"
(JUDGES 15:15)

"But Samson lay till midnight, and at midnight he arose and took hold of the doors of the gate of the city and the two posts, and pulled them up, bar and all, and put them on his shoulders and carried them to the top of the hill that is before Hebron"
(JUDGES 16:3)

Scenes from the Story of Samson: 13th-century French manuscript.

THE BIBLE IN ART

"And Samson grasped the two middle pillars upon which the house rested, and he leaned his weight upon them"
(JUDGES 16:29)

THE BIBLE IN ART

"And David took the head of the Philistine and brought it to Jerusalem"
(1 SAMUEL 17:54) ▷

David with the Head of Goliath, detail: bronze relief by Lorenzo Ghiberti (1378-1455).

"He asked water and she gave him milk, she brought him curds in a lordly bowl. She put her hand to the tent peg and her right hand to the workmen's mallet; she struck Sisera a blow"
▽ (JUDGES 5:25-26)

Jael and Sisera: drawing after the Master of Flémalle (c. 1430).

"She came to Jerusalem with a very great retinue, with camels bearing spices, and very much gold, and precious stones; and when she came to Solomon, she told him all that was on her mind"
(1 KINGS 10:2) ▷

The Queen of Sheba's Visit to Solomon: Piero della Francesca (c. 1410-92).

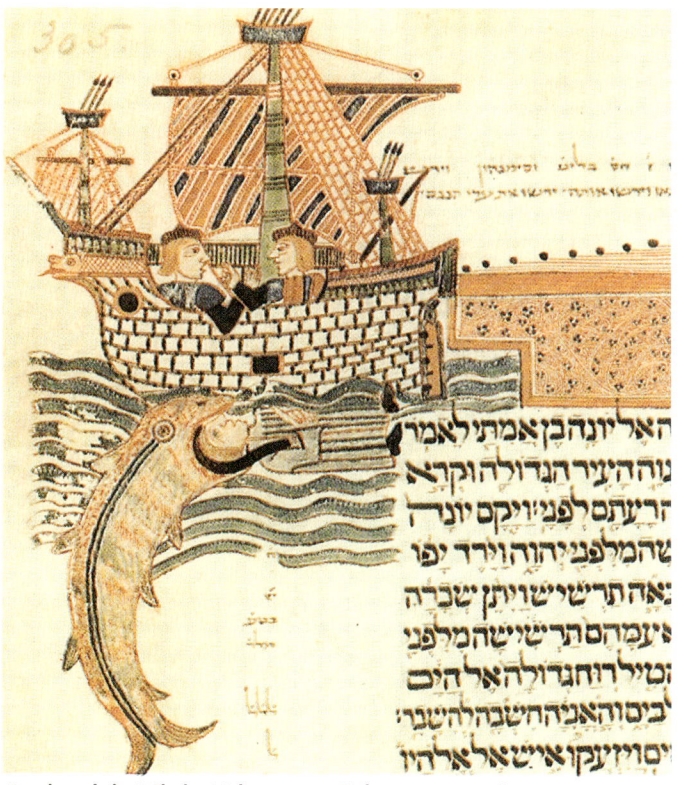

THE BIBLE IN ART

"And the Lord appointed a great fish to swallow up Jonah"
◁ (JONAH 1:17)

"She struck his neck twice with all her might, and severed his head from his body . . . and gave Holofernes' head to her maid, who placed it in her food bag. Then the two of them went out together, as they were accustomed to go for prayer"
(JUDITH 13:8-10) ▷

Jonah and the Whale: 15th-century Hebrew manuscript.

Judith: Botticelli (1445-1510).

49

THE BIBLE IN ART

"This my son was dead, and is alive again; he was lost, and is found"
(LUKE 15:24)

"The angel said to her . . . 'you will conceive in your womb and bear a son, and you shall call his name Jesus'"
(LUKE 1:30-31)

"He set him on his own beast and brought him to an inn, and took care of him"
(LUKE 10:34)

The Prodigal Son: etching by Rembrandt (1606-69).

The Annunciation: wood relief by the Ottobeuren Master (c. 1520).

The Good Samaritan: etching by Rembrandt (1606-69).

THE BIBLE IN ART

Christ's Entry into Jerusalem: Pietro Lorenzetti (active 1320-48).

"Most of the crowd spread their garments on the road, and others cut branches from the trees and spread them on the road. And the crowds that went before him and that followed him shouted, 'Hosanna to the Son of David!'"
(MATTHEW 21:8-9) △

"They spat upon him, and took the reed and struck him on the head"
(MATTHEW 27:30) ▷

The Mocking of Christ: Fra Angelico (1387-1455).

Overleaf: The Maestà, detail: Duccio (active 1278-1319).

"Jesus of Nazareth, a man attested to you by God with mighty works and wonders and signs . . . this Jesus . . . you crucified and killed by the hands of lawless men. But God raised him up, having loosed the pangs of death, because it was not possible for him to be held by it"
(ACTS 2:22-24) ▷

51

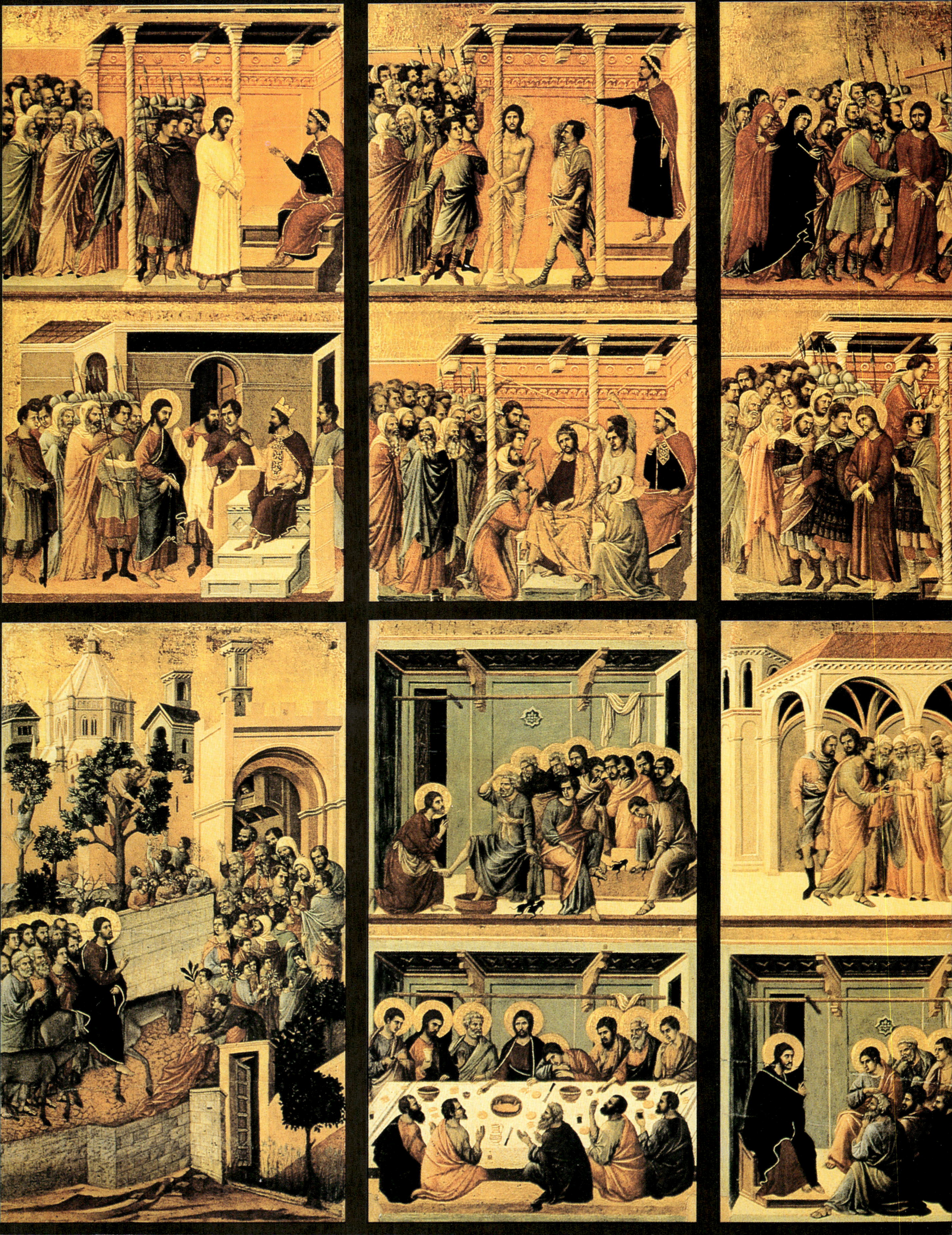

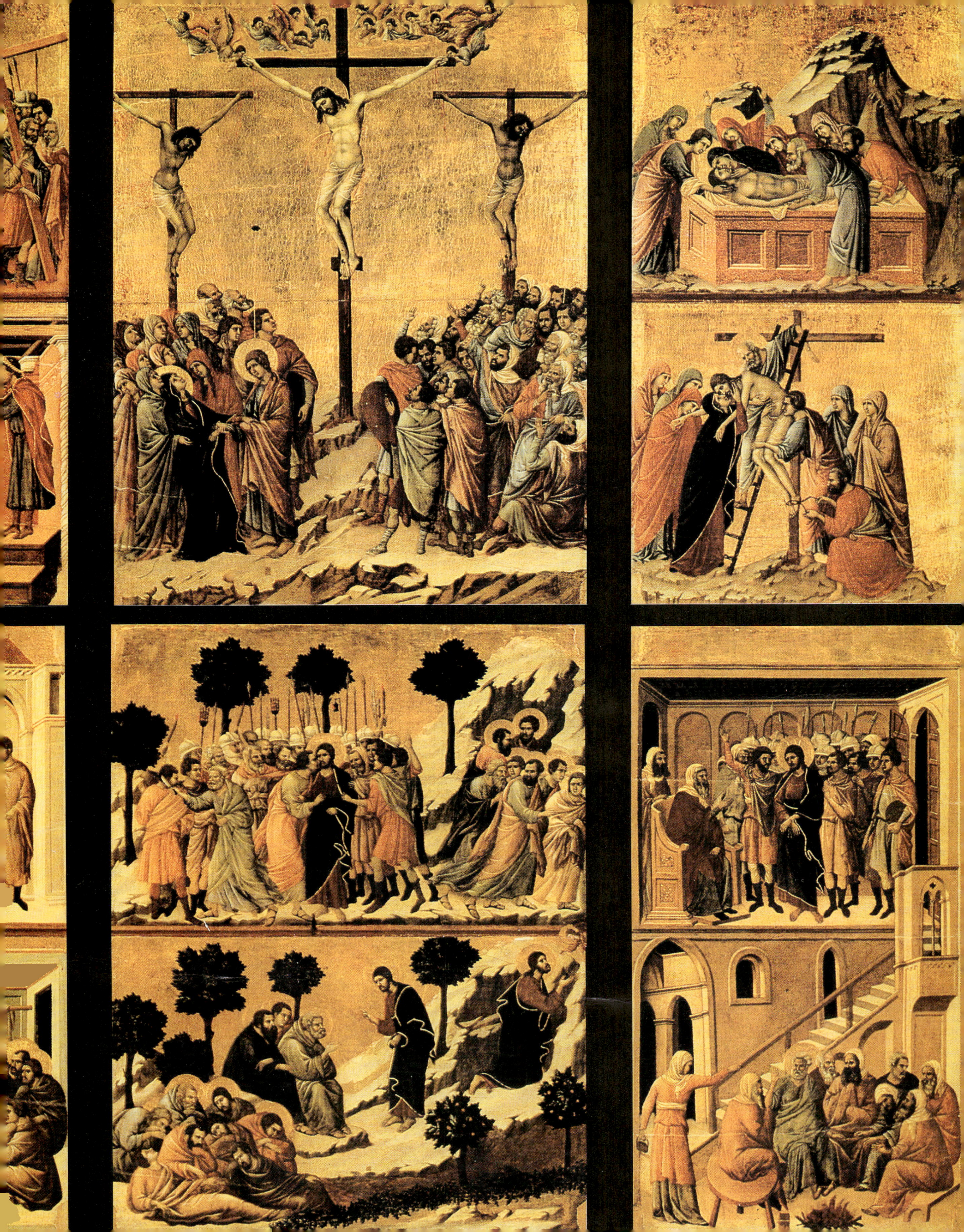

THE BIBLE IN ART

> "They took the body of Jesus, and bound it in linen cloths with the spices, as is the burial custom of the Jews"
> (JOHN 19:40)

The Deposition: Rogier van der Weyden (c. 1400-64).

THE BIBLE IN ART

"Mary stood weeping outside the tomb"
(JOHN 20:11) ▷

The Penitent Magdalene: woodcarving by Donatello (1386-1466).

THE BIBLE IN ART

"And there appeared to them tongues as of fire ... And they were all filled with the Holy Spirit and began to speak in other tongues, as the Spirit gave them utterance"

(ACTS 2:3-4) ▷

Peter's Sorrow: 17th-century Ethiopian manuscript.

"Peter remembered how Jesus had said to him, 'Before the cock crows twice, you will deny me three times.' And he broke down and wept"

(MARK 14:72) △

The Conversion of St Paul: 9th-century manuscript.

"I journeyed to Damascus ... At midday, O king, I saw on the way a light from heaven, brighter than the sun, shining round me and those who journeyed with me ... I heard a voice saying to me in the Hebrew language, 'Saul, Saul, why do you persecute me?' ... And I said, 'Who are you, Lord?' And the Lord said, 'I am Jesus whom you are persecuting. But rise and stand upon your feet; for I have appeared to you for this purpose, to appoint you to serve and bear witness to the things in which you have seen me and to those in which I will appear to you'"

(ACTS 26:12-16) △

The Descent of the Holy Ghost: El Greco (1541-1614).

PART THREE
THE BIBLE AND GEOGRAPHY

THE GEOGRAPHY OF ANCIENT ISRAEL

The land of the Bible, it has been suggested, can best be thought of in terms of six strips placed side by side, each running from north to south. The first strip is the coastal plain. Starting in the north, it begins 20km (12.4 miles) north of Acco at the northern tip of the bay of Haifa. Initially it is some 5km (3.1 miles) wide, but it broadens as it approaches the bay of Haifa to nearly 13km (8 miles). The Carmel range cuts it off completely at the southern tip of the bay of Haifa, and it begins again south of Carmel, where for a distance of 30km (18.6 miles) it is only 4km (2.5 miles) wide, or less. South of Nahal (stream) Tanninim it begins to broaden out until it is over 20km 12.4 miles) wide at the point where the valley of Aijalon offers a route to the central hill country. South of this point the plain merges on its eastern side with the second strip (which is, in fact, only half a strip)—the Shephelah or lowlands. South of Gaza the coastal plain begins to merge into the Negev.

In biblical times the coastline of the bay of Haifa was to the east of the present coastline, and there were swamps at both northern and southern ends of the bay. To the south of Carmel the region close to the coast consisted of either sands or swamps, but settlement was possible, especially at the mouths of the rivers and winter streams. There were woodlands south of Nahal Tanninim consisting of deciduous oak or carob, with settlements on the eastern edge of the plain, at the foot of the central hills.

The second strip (or half strip), the Shephelah, is a series of round hills and broad valleys which form a transition between the coastal plain and the central hill country, providing a number of routes from the plain eastwards. Valleys running north to south provide important routes in these directions, and divide the Shephelah into a western and an eastern section.

The third strip is the central hill country. Beginning in the north in upper Galilee, it consists of a high central block of hills reaching heights of over 1000m (3280ft) with complicated outcrops on the eastern side. The hills here provide no easy passage in any direction, and ancient routes avoided them. In lower Galilee the central hills are broken by several very broad valleys running roughly west to east, providing routes from the coastal plain to the Sea of Galilee region.

The central hills are broken by the triangular valley of Jezreel, a broad plain which runs roughly northwest to southeast from the coastal plain to the Jordan valley, and which is 25km (15.5 miles) wide at its broadest point (north to south). South of the valley of Jezreel the hills begin to increase in height, punctuated by broad valleys, until the central core of the Samarian hills is reached with heights in the region of 900m (2953ft). South of Nablus a long narrow valley running roughly north to south leads further into the central core of the hills, until a region is reached known as the Bethel hills. Here there are few valleys, and the main road takes a very serpentine course. The next section of the central hills is the Jerusalem saddle, characterized in the north by a small plateau and to east and west by valleys that facilitate west-to-east travel. South of Bethlehem the hills increase in height to over 1000m (3280ft) until they begin to descend towards the Negev.

The fourth strip is the rift valley, which is part of a fault that extends to East Africa. At the Sea of Galilee it is already 210m (689ft) *below* sea level at the surface of the sea. From this point it descends until it reaches minus 400m (1312ft) at the surface of the Dead Sea, the bottom of the sea at its deepest point being a further 400m (1312ft) lower. The conditions in the rift valley range from semi-arid to arid and desert, except for the area immediately bordering the river Jordan itself.

The fifth strip is the hills rising to the east of the rift valley. To the northeast of the Sea of Galilee they rise to 1100m (3609ft) before forming a plateau that reaches to Damascus. South of the Sea of Galilee is a hilly region which resembles the central hills of the western bank. Further to the south there are high plateaux of 800–900m (2625–2953ft). A feature of these eastern hills is the fact that they are divided along an east–west line by several rivers, which cut deep valleys. Further east the fifth strip shades into the sixth strip—the Syrian desert.

As briefly described, the land of the Bible is one of great contrasts. The "strips" each have their own particular characteristics, and as one follows them from west to east some remarkable differences in altitude are apparent. The coastal plain is largely at sea level, after which the central hills rise to 1000m (3280ft), the rise being modulated in the

Right: The geography of Israel The cross-section (*below*) by itself does not indicate the complexity of the land as a whole. On the physical map it is possible to see some correlation between the "strips" described in the text and the underlying physical structure of the land. For example, the Shephelah is well defined, as are the small valleys that are so characteristic of the northern central hill country.

Below The cross-section from west to east shows up clearly the remarkable variations in height of the different regions. Most striking is the rift valley, flanked by high ranges of hills on both sides.

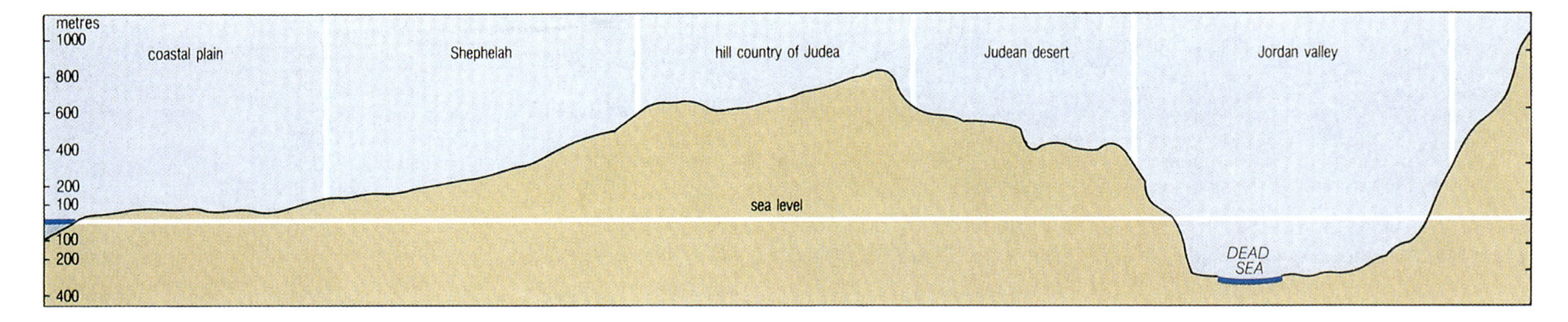

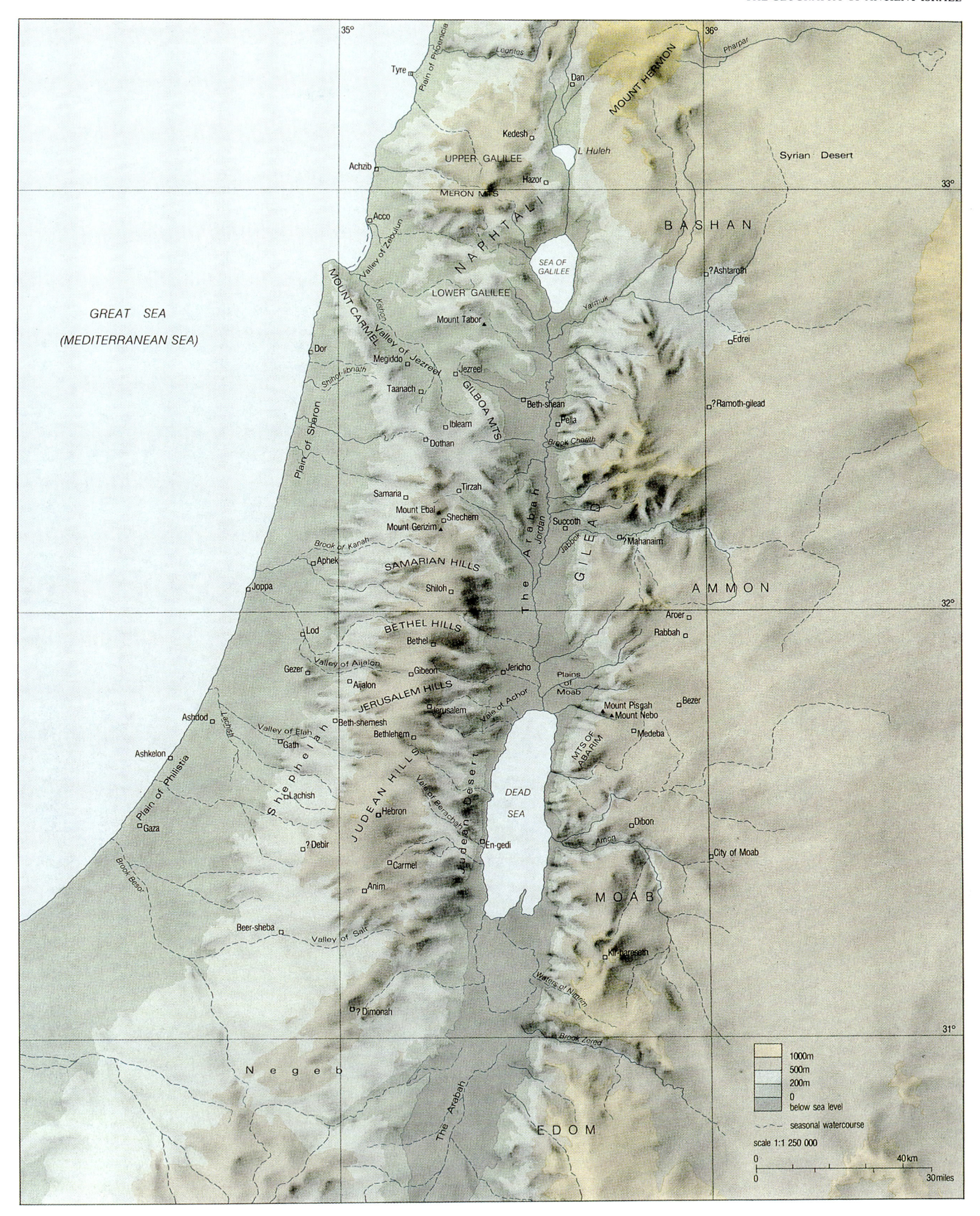

THE GEOGRAPHY OF ANCIENT ISRAEL

THE GEOGRAPHY OF ANCIENT ISRAEL

south by the Shephelah. From 1000m (3280ft) there is a steep plunge into the rift valley, which is 400m (1312ft) *below* sea level at its deepest surface point, after which the eastern hills rise to 1100m (3609ft) or more, before shading into the desert. Other outstanding features include the way in which the Carmel range cuts the coastal plain into two, and the way in which the valley of Jezreel interrupts the central mountain ridge.

There are considerable variations in temperature, with the most striking contrast on the western side of the Jordan being between the Judean hills and the shore of the Dead Sea. It is no wonder that at all documented periods those who were powerful or wealthy enough to afford a summer and a winter residence spent winters near the Dead Sea and summers on the central hills. On the eastern hills of Transjordan the climate differs again, with cooling breezes in summer, and colder winters than on the western hills.

Again, even within a particular strip such as the western central hill country, there can be variations that profoundly affect the possibility of travel or of settlement. The most noticeable differences are between the Jerusalem saddle, the Bethel hills and the Samarian hills where, going northwards, one passes from a small plateau with a straight road into an area where progress is possible only by seemingly endless winding around the sides of hills, to an area where all of a sudden spectacular small valleys begin to separate the round hills.

The biblical landscape

Visitors to Israel and the West Bank today will readily appreciate that in some areas the past 60 years or so have produced enormous changes in the landscape. These changes are most obvious in the coastal plain, in the region immediately south of the Sea of Galilee and in the environs of Jerusalem. But once visitors get away from this obvious urbanization, industrialization and recently introduced intensive agriculture, do they see the land as it was in biblical times? If, for example, they wind their way through the Bethel hills, or get out into the Judean hills south of Bethlehem, or into the hills of upper Galilee, do they see biblical landscapes?

In the first place it has to be said that the biblical period lasted a long time—1300 years from the settlement of the Israelites in Canaan to the end of the first Christian century, and longer if one goes back to a conservative historical dating of the Patriarchs (Abraham, Isaac and Jacob) around 1750 to 1500 BC. In such a long period, especially with the urbanization that occurred from the time of David and Solomon, there were bound to be changes in the landscape. However, the view is commonly expressed that at the beginning of the biblical period (for the sake of convenience, from 1200 BC) the land resembled what we see today when we encounter hills that are bare of soil, or terraced for the purposes of agriculture, or covered with bushes and scrub.

That the land of the Bible does not appear today as it did in ancient times (say, 4000 BC) is common ground. At that period its hills, from south of Hebron northwards on the west of the Jordan, were covered with evergreen oak forest and its associates, while in areas such as the coastal plain and part of the Carmel range the deciduous oak (Tabor oak) and its associates were to be found. It is also commonly accepted that the loss of these forests is the reason for the chronic erosion of soil that is apparent today (where it has not been rectified in recent years). The rainy season, roughly from October to April, can produce very heavy downpours. Where there are evergreen trees, the force of the rain is broken, and the roots of the trees and the associated undergrowth allow the moisture to be retained. With the loss of the trees, there is little to prevent the soil being washed from the hills to the valleys. There has been no fundamental change in climate since biblical times, merely erosion caused by the loss of trees.

If all this is common ground, what is disputed is the extent to which trees had been lost and the soil had been eroded by the beginning of the biblical period (say, 1200 BC). Before an attempt is made to answer the question (in fact, only informed guesses can be made), it will be useful to consider

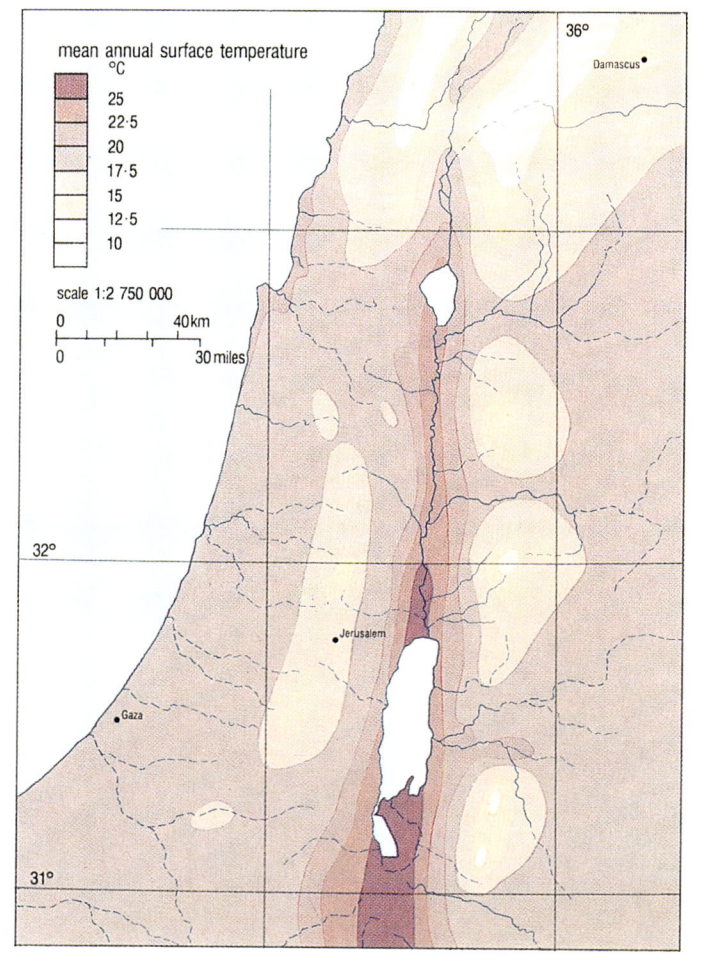

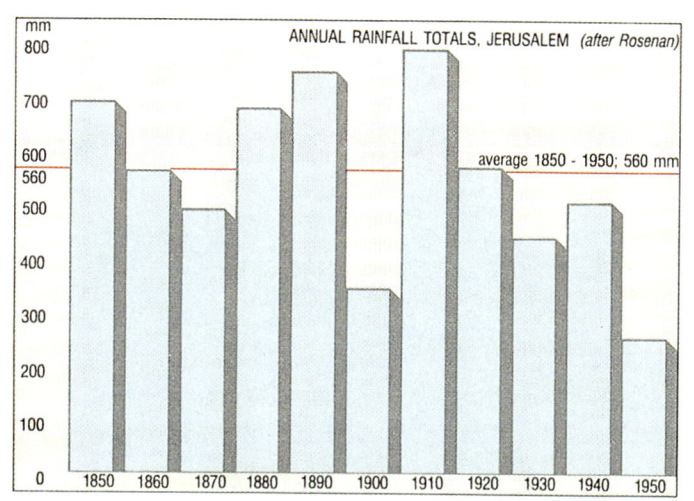

Far right: The geology of Israel
The underlying geological features of the land largely support and illumine the physical features described on pages 58-59.

Right and left: The climate of Israel
The rainfall and temperature maps add a further dimension to the complex physical environment of life in the land of the Bible. Rainfall is at its highest in the northern part of the land, and is lower in the south. It also decreases close to the rift valley. The rainy season (roughly October to March) corresponds to the colder part of the year, as indicated by the temperature charts. Thus, generally speaking, there is a warm dry season, and a colder wet season. However, there are sometimes significant deviations from the general picture, the cycles of drought being of especial concern for both ancient and modern inhabitants of the land.

former rains (Oct)

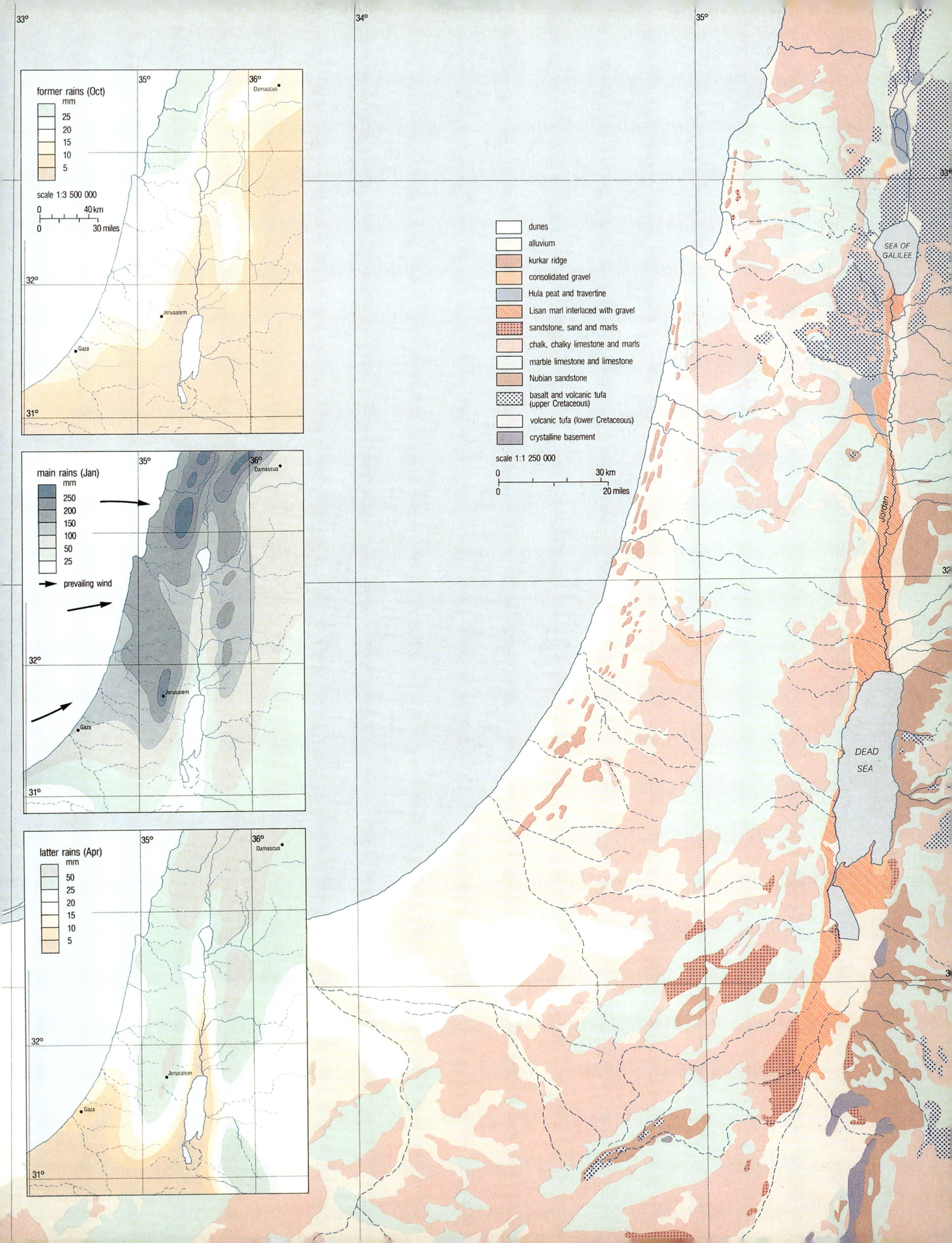

mm
- 25
- 20
- 15
- 10
- 5

scale 1:3 500 000

0 — 40 km
0 — 30 miles

main rains (Jan)

mm
- 250
- 200
- 150
- 100
- 50
- 25

→ prevailing wind

latter rains (Apr)

mm
- 50
- 25
- 20
- 15
- 10
- 5

Legend

- dunes
- alluvium
- kurkar ridge
- consolidated gravel
- Hula peat and travertine
- Lisan marl interlaced with gravel
- sandstone, sand and marls
- chalk, chalky limestone and marls
- marble limestone and limestone
- Nubian sandstone
- basalt and volcanic tufa (upper Cretaceous)
- volcanic tufa (lower Cretaceous)
- crystalline basement

scale 1:1 250 000

0 — 30 km
0 — 20 miles

SEA OF GALILEE

Jordan

DEAD SEA

Damascus
Jerusalem
Gaza

THE GEOGRAPHY OF ANCIENT ISRAEL

what is at issue. The question is at its most acute when the settlement in Canaan and the structure of Israelite society at this period are considered. Putting the matter rather simplistically, it would be easier to settle in a land where large-scale erosion provided easy access to hilly areas well away from the sites of powerful city-states than it would be to settle in a land still largely wooded where settlement would require systematic burning and clearing. Furthermore, if settlement was accompanied by the need for organized communal working, this would certainly call for more complex social organization than if groups were moving into "empty" hilly areas grazing their flocks. Much writing in the present century about the Israelite settlement has assumed that the settlers were primarily shepherds, organized socially in such a way that power was shared among the leaders of the families, moving about a land which looked essentially like the land we see today where it has escaped the modernizations of the present century. But arguably a completely different picture is required. The settlers were, or needed to become, by virtue of the landscape, agriculturalists, settling in wooded areas, and organized socially in ways that gave considerable power to individuals to plan and organize the communal working. At the time of writing, the questions of the ecology, methods of food production, social organization, population size and patterns of settlement in the early Iron Age (from 1200 BC) are matters for intensive research and discussion, and look like being a major growing point in biblical studies for some years to come. At this preliminary stage in the discussion the present Atlas, in addition to its wider aims, seeks to make only one contribution to the matter, and that concerns what we can guess about the extent of the woods and forests in about 1200 BC.

In preparing the maps for the Atlas, all the known major settlements for what is loosely called the 2nd millennium BC have been plotted. The definition "2nd millennium" is loose, because many of the settlements go back into the early 3rd millennium. It is also the case that the settlements marked were not necessarily occupied continuously or even for very long periods; and there were important general changes in patterns of settlement in the 2nd millennium. The point about plotting the settlements, however, is that they indicate where it was *possible* to settle in the 2nd millennium, even if only for limited periods. When plotted, the overall pattern shows that with few exceptions, and those always notable, settlement was on the fringes of hill country, on hills overlooking valleys or on plains at the foot of hills. The central cores of hilly regions, and in many cases very wide ranges of hills, remained without settlements. Part of the reason was that they lacked water supplies, and were in any case difficult for agriculture. But it is a reasonable guess that they were also wooded or forested. This point is expanded in the detailed treatments of the regions that follow, where literary evidence for the existence of woods and forests in biblical times is also cited.

Visitors to the land of the Bible today are faced with many exciting surprises as they encounter the different types of landscape in a comparatively small country. They should, however, also bear in mind that the people whose lives are recorded in the narratives of the Bible lived in a land with many more woods and forests than today. These areas were the homes of wild beasts—lions, leopards and bears, to name the most frightening. The woods and forests may also have been areas of terror and mystery to the ordinary people, places representing the forces of chaos and uncertainty that surrounded the attempts to impose order and regularity upon life. Although what is attempted in the Atlas in this matter can be no more than carefully prepared guesswork, readers of the Bible can test for themselves, by sensitive and alert reading, the extent to which wooded landscapes and the presence of dangerous animals affected the life and literary symbolism of biblical times.

A false-colour satellite image can reveal the character of a landscape from a viewpoint hundreds of miles above the earth's surface. In this photograph, of the lands surrounding the Dead Sea, plantations appear as patches of red amid scorching hills and valleys almost totally denuded of forests since biblical times.

Below: The vegetation of ancient Israel
This map shows the areas of vegetation as they probably were before human settlement began to affect the landscape significantly. Before this time, the land was extensively wooded or forested with evergreen oak and its associates. One of the contentions of the present Atlas is that much more of this ancient tree cover existed in 1200 BC than is often supposed.

Right: Land use in modern Israel
This map shows how great the contrast is between the land in ancient times and the land as it is today. Apart from the urbanization and industrialization of parts of the country, modern methods of irrigation and agriculture make cultivation possible in areas where it was not before. Visitors to Israel today need to be reminded that, although the basic contours of the land remain unchanged, the modern cover and land use differ considerably from those in biblical times.

Vegetation of ancient Israel
- oases
- cultivated land
- marsh and salines
- mixed dwarf shrub
- grassland and shrubs with remnants of Tabor oak and carob forest
- forest and maquis
- sand dunes
- semi-desert
- desert
- cereal crops (barley, wheat)
- fruit (dates, figs, olives, persimmon, pomegranates)
- vines
- flax
- grazing land (cattle, goats, sheep)
- fishing
- Tyrian purple
- I iron
- S salt
- important route

Modern land use legend
- arable land
- irrigated arable land
- fruit-growing area
- irrigated fruit-growing area
- citrus grove
- olive grove
- vineyard
- fishpond
- urban area
- forest
- sand dunes
- uncultivated semi-arid land
- uncultivated arid land
- major road
- major railway

scale 1:1 500 000
scale 1:1 250 000

The Mapping of the Holy Land

The Holy Land has probably been mapped more often than any other part of the world. From the triumph of Christianity in the Roman empire early in the 4th century to the Muslim conquest in 638 AD, the Holy Land was a place of pilgrimage. The Crusades in the 10th to 12th centuries put the land back under the control of western Christendom for a century or so, and in the 19th century the number of travellers from the west increased dramatically. Throughout the whole period the Jewish community retained a deep interest in the study of the land. Many pilgrims and visitors left accounts of their travels, and, in any case, the study of the topography of the Holy Land was always an integral part of biblical studies. Dating from the 15th century onwards there exist many attempts to portray the land or important parts of it, such as Jerusalem; but we must remember that no scientific surveys of it were made until the 19th century. How the Holy Land was presented to readers of the Bible prior to the modern period is outlined here.

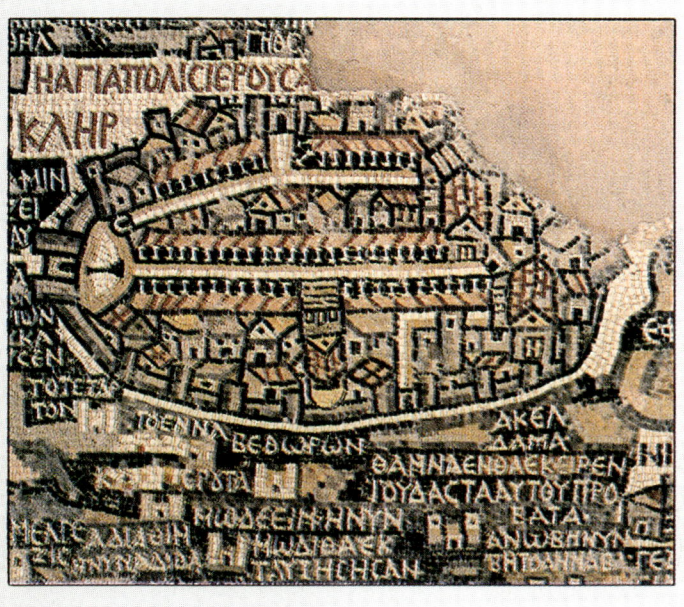

THE MAPPING OF THE HOLY LAND

Below A 13th-century map of the world with Jerusalem at the centre. An attempt is made not only to represent the geographical relationship of the countries, but to portray their characteristic animals, landscapes and peoples. At this time, the account of the dispersion of the peoples in Genesis 10 was a primary source for information about the geography of the world and its peoples.

The 13th-century English monk Matthew Paris included a map of the pilgrims'- and crusaders' route from Britain to the Holy Land in his historical compilation, the *Chronica maiora*. A detail from this map *(below)* shows the ports along the Palestine coast, with the walled city of Jerusalem beyond. Within the walls are – curiously – the temple of God and the temple of Solomon. The circular object in the lower right-hand angle of the walls indicates the Holy Sepulchre.

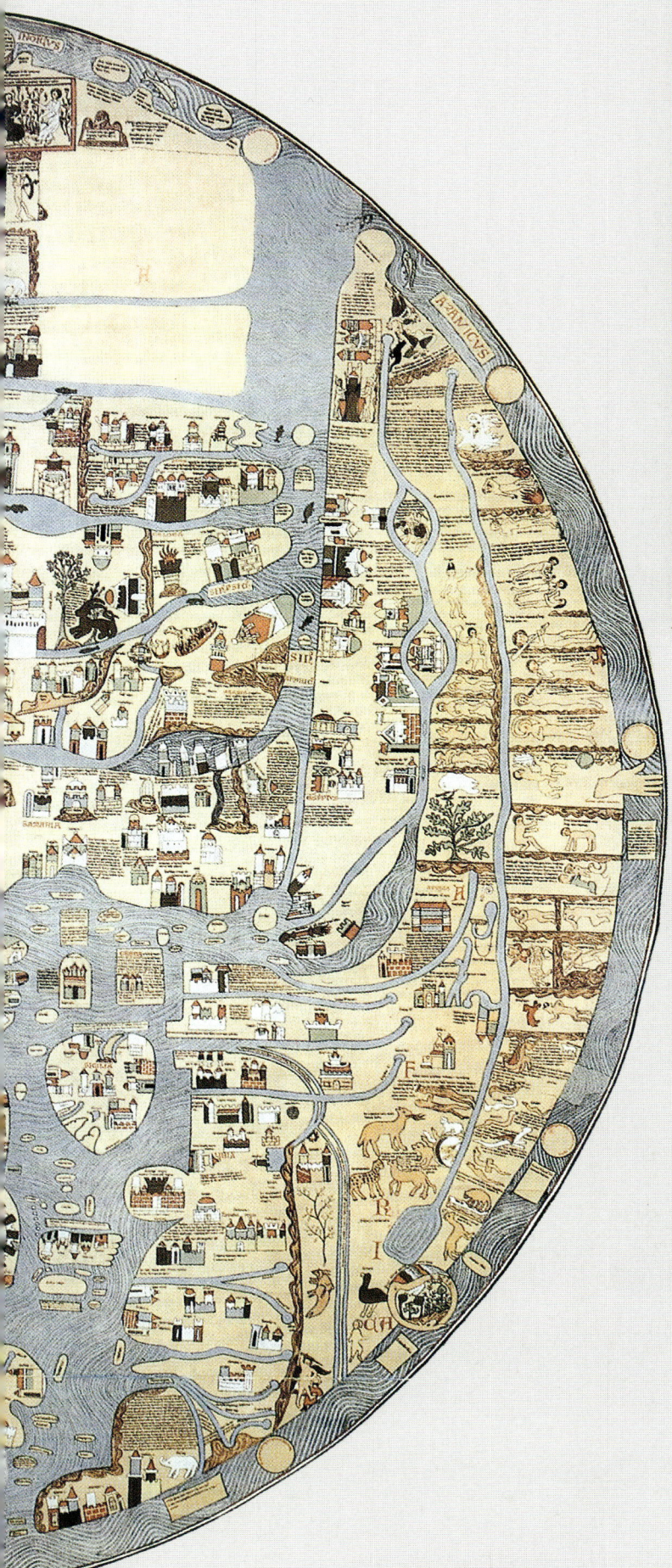

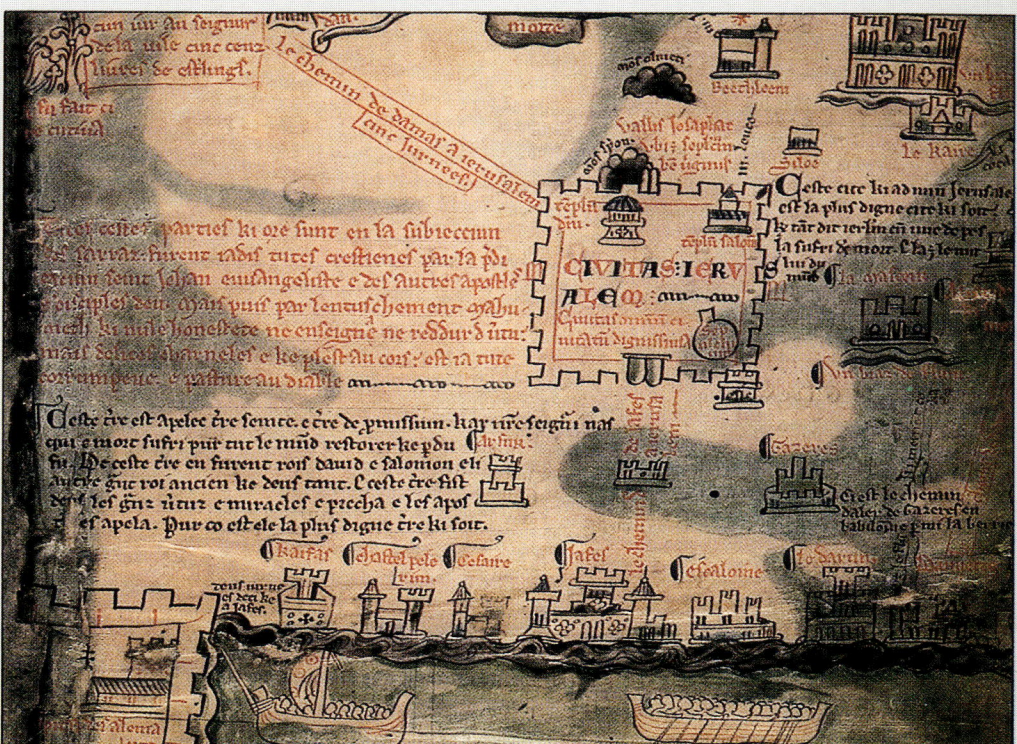

Far left top Not a map of the Holy Land, but of Babylon and its empire drawn in c. 600 BC. The idea that the capital is the centre of the world reappears in the medieval example *(left)*.

Far left bottom Discovered in 1884 in a church in Madaba on the eastern side of the Dead Sea, this mosaic portrays the Holy Land and Egypt at about 600 AD. It has an east–west orientation, so that north is on the left-hand side. Although it is much damaged in parts, the portrayal of Jerusalem as it then was is well preserved and enables holy sites to be identified. The church marking the traditional site of the Resurrection of Jesus can be seen in the middle of the lower half of the city.

Right The maps published by the Palestine Exploration Fund in 1880 laid the basis for all subsequent scientific cartography of the Holy Land. The work was undertaken by members of the Royal Engineers from 1873. One of the leaders of the project was Lt H. H. Kitchener, later Lord Kitchener of Khartoum.

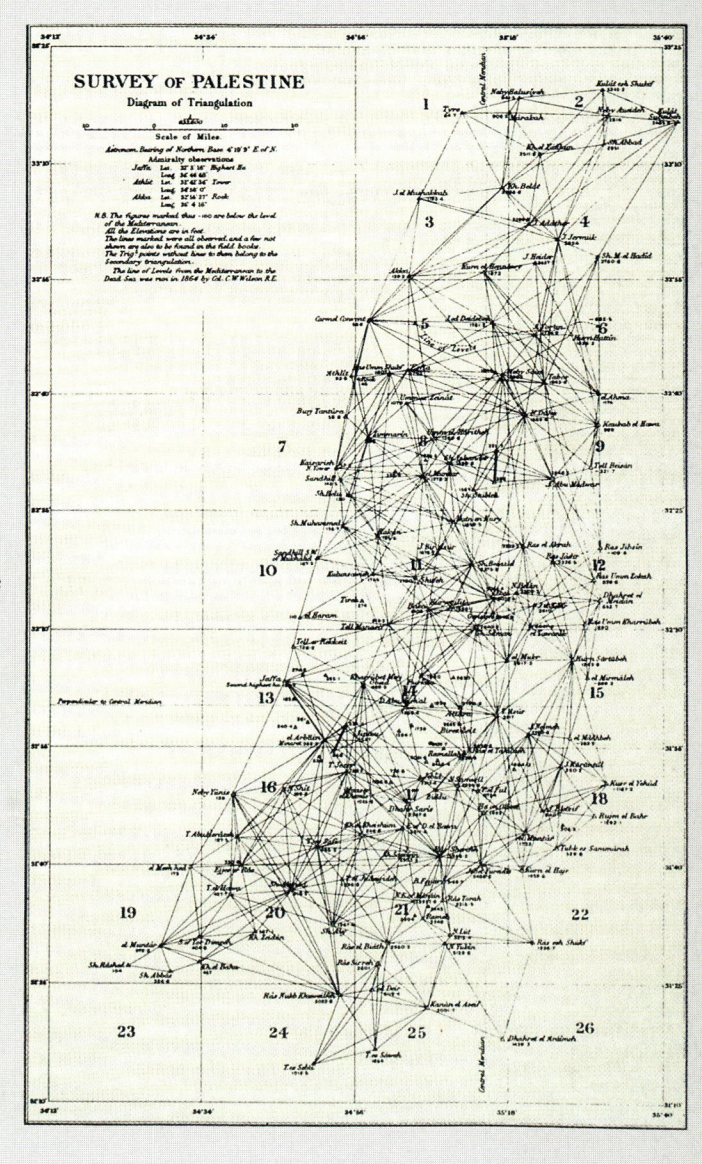

Animals of the Bible

Many animals and birds are mentioned in the Bible, and many lessons are drawn from their behaviour. Isaiah contrasts the faithfulness of animals to their masters with Israel's unfaithfulness to God. "The ox knows its owner, and the ass its master's crib; but Israel does not know, my people does not understand" (Isaiah 1:3). Proverbs exhorts the sluggard to "Go to the ant, consider her ways, and be wise" (Proverbs 6:6). Domesticated animals, such as sheep, goats, oxen and asses were important for daily life in biblical times. Wild animals on the other hand, including lions, bears, boars and herds of bulls, constituted a danger. The shepherd was especially vulnerable when he was pasturing his flocks in lonely places.

It is not always easy to know exactly which animals the biblical writers are referring to. Modern translations of the Bible often differ from older versions in this regard. Thus, in what follows, the Authorized Version has been used to provide a reference to badgers, while the R.S.V. footnote to the passage mentioning peacocks suggests, as an alternative translation, baboons! The animals on these pages are illustrated not by modern photography, but by medieval art, as a reminder of the uncertainties that surround the identification of biblical animals and their relation to modern species.

Peacock.

"Once every three years the fleet of ships of Tarshish used to come bringing gold, silver, ivory, apes, and peacocks" (1 KINGS 10:22) △

Dogs.

"Even the dogs under the table eat the children's crumbs" △ (MARK 7:28)

"Flee from the midst of Babylon, and go out of the land of the Chaldeans, and be as he-goats before the flock" ▽ (JEREMIAH 50:8)

Owl.

"I am like an owl of the waste places" △ (PSALM 102:6)

Lions.

"The young lions roar for their prey, seeking their food from God" (PSALM 104:21) ▷

He-goat.

ANIMALS OF THE BIBLE

"And God said, 'Let the earth bring forth living creatures according to their kinds'"
(GENESIS 1:24)

"You know that your father and his men are mighty men, and that they are enraged, like a bear robbed of her cubs"
(2 SAMUEL 17:18)

"I clothed thee also with broidered work, and shod thee with badgers' skin"
(EZEKIEL 16:10)

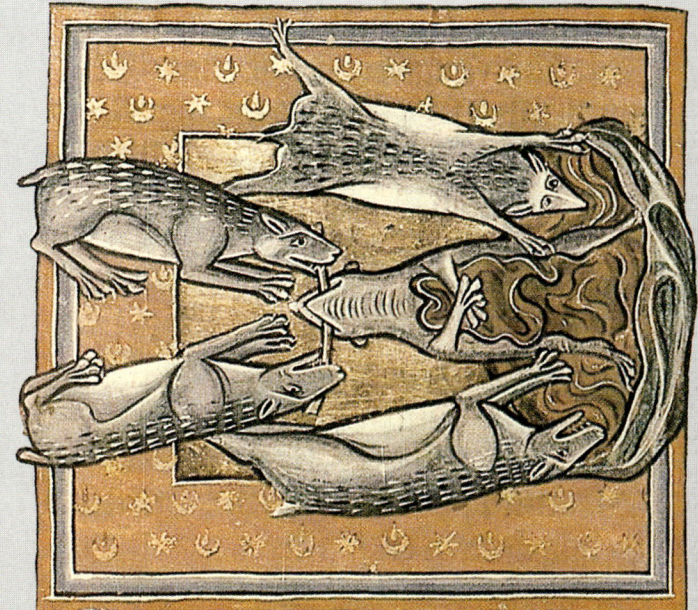

The creation of the animals.

Badgers.

"Samson turned aside to see the carcass of the lion, and behold, there was a swarm of bees in the body of the lion, and honey"
(JUDGES 14:8)

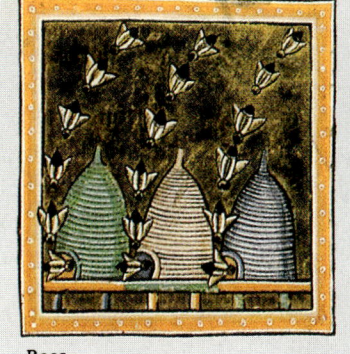

Bees.

"Many bulls encompass me, strong bulls of Bashan surround me; they open wide their mouths at me, like a ravening and roaring lion"
(PSALM 22:12-13)

Bull.

67

Plants of the Bible

The identification of plants in the Bible is not always easy. For example, the tradition that Adam and Eve ate an apple (although the fruit itself is not named) has provoked discussion as to whether apples were in fact known in Israel in biblical times. Again, the "lily of the field" is usually identified today as an anemone. Over a hundred plants are mentioned in the Bible, and they had many uses. Trees provided fruit, gum, timber for building and fuel for burning. Vines produced wine, olives produced oil. From a plant such as *Boswellia sacra* were made incense and perfume. Balm (*Commiphora gileadensis*) was used for healing, and henna (*Lawsonia inermis*) produced dye. Those who lived in biblical times had a much wider knowledge of plants and their properties than the average person today.

> "Consider the lilies of the field, how they grow . . . even Solomon in all his glory was not arrayed like one of these"
> ▽ (MATTHEW 6:28–29)

Lilies of the field.

Fig.

PLANTS OF THE BIBLE

"He cuts down cedars; or he chooses a holm tree or an oak and lets it grow strong among the trees of the forest"
(ISAIAH 44:14) ▽

"Pomegranate, palm, and apple, all the trees of the field are withered"
(JOEL 1:12) ▽

Oak.

Pomegranate.

"From the fig tree learn its lesson: as soon as its branch becomes tender and puts forth its leaves, you know that summer is near"
◁ (MATTHEW 24:32)

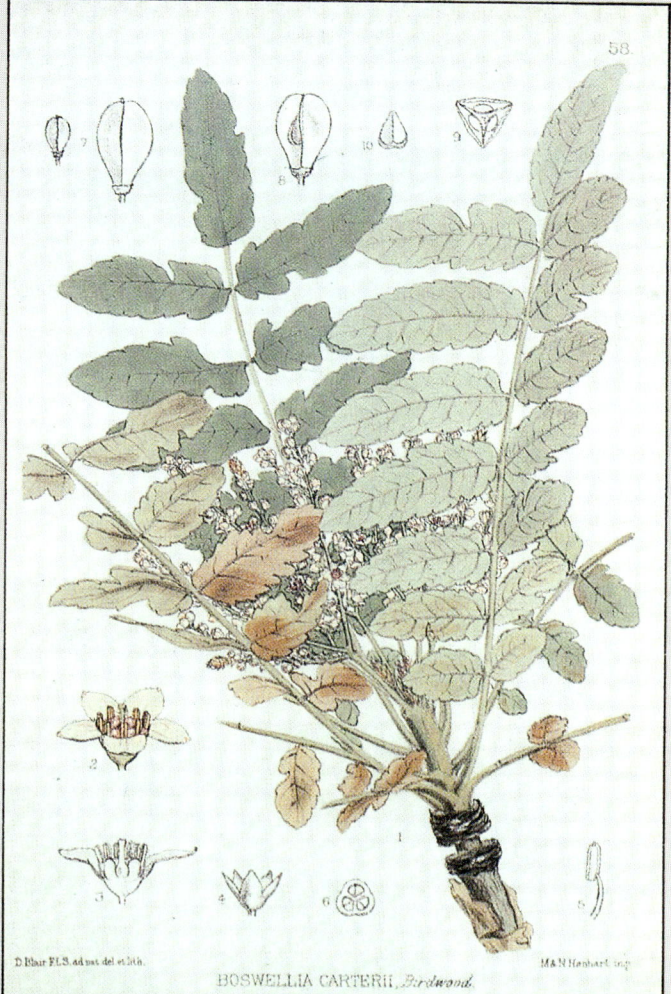

Thistle.

"Are grapes gathered from thorns, or figs from thistles?"
(MATTHEW 7:16) △

"They offered him gifts, gold and frankincense and myrrh"
(MATTHEW 2:11) ▷

Frankincense.

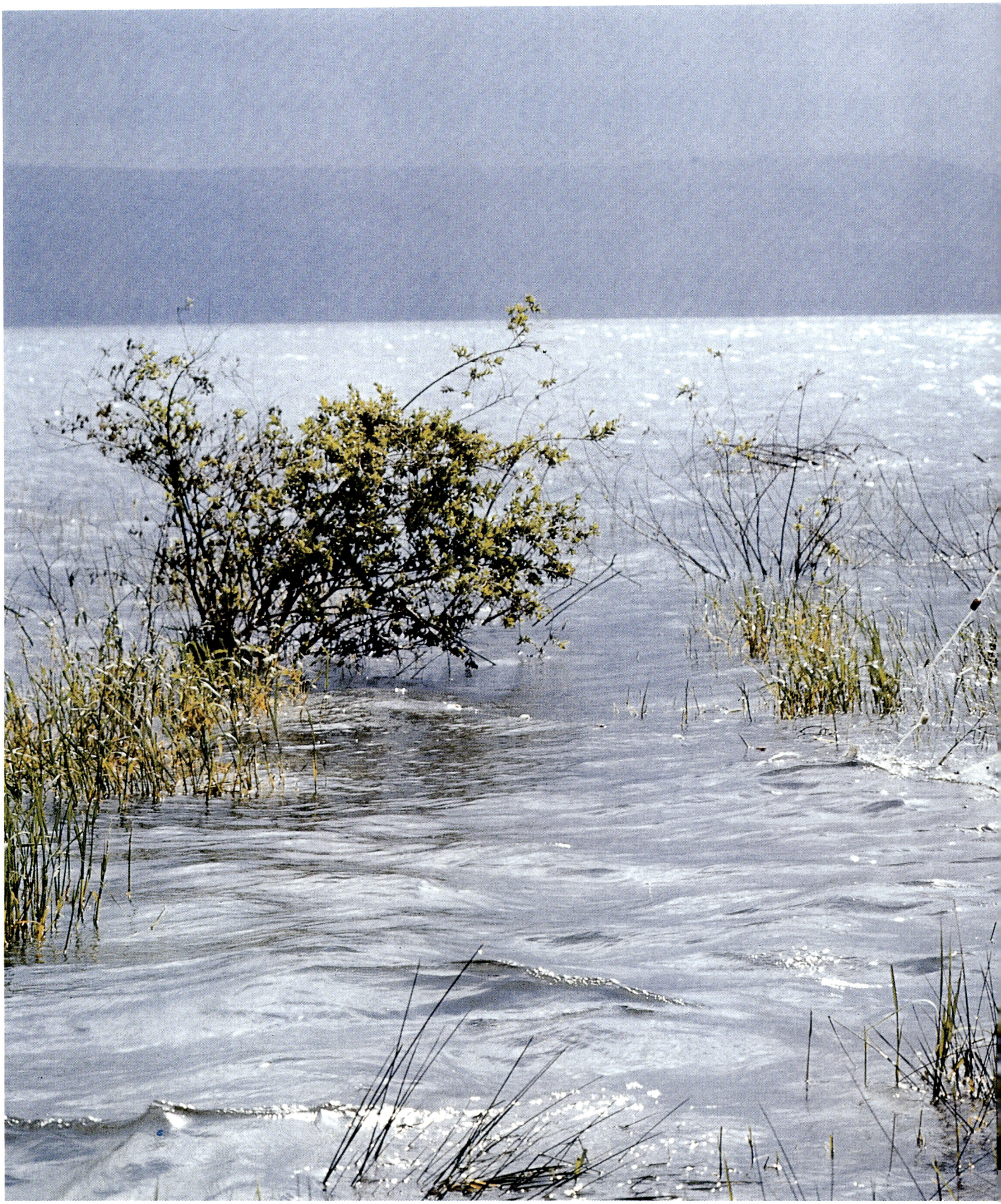

In the following pages the lands of the Bible are divided into 12 regions. Each section begins with a map describing that region in biblical times. The principal events of the Bible are then treated according to their regional location.

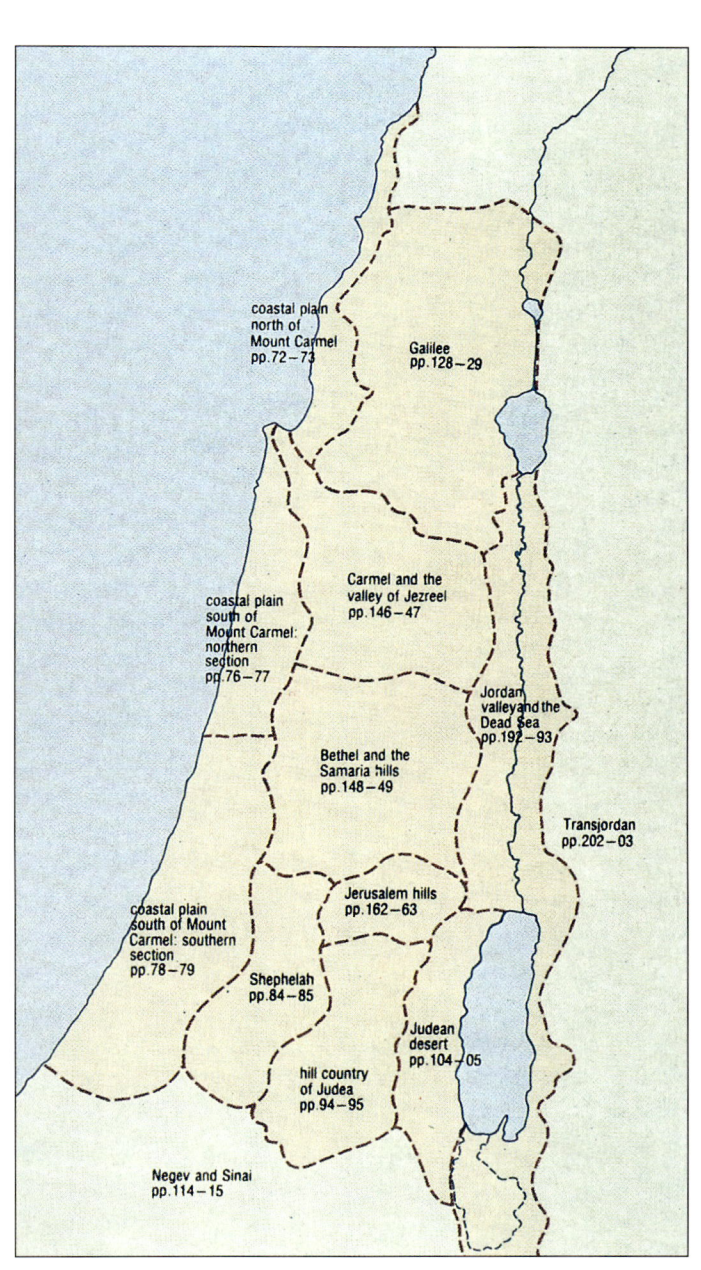

"The kingdom of heaven is like a net which was thrown into the sea and gathered fish of every kind"

(MATTHEW 13:47)

THE COASTAL PLAIN NORTH OF MOUNT CARMEL

Description of the region
The modern visitor to the area between Mount Carmel and Rosh ha-Niqra sees industrial developments, a seaside resort and the intensive cultivation of fruit, especially bananas. To the immediate north of the Carmel range is Haifa's industrial area, including the oil refinery. The main road that links Haifa with Acco is flanked for the first half of the journey by small factories, with considerable development to the west as far as the sea. For the second half of the journey from Haifa to Acco the most notable feature to the east is the series of pools, used for intensive fish farming. To the north of Acco lies the town of Nahariyya, which began in 1934 as an agricultural settlement, and which has become an important seaside resort.

To visitors to the same region in the 19th century, the countryside looked somewhat different. To the northeast of Acco were gardens in which were cultivated oranges, pomegranates, lemons and figs, as well as various vegetables. To the south of Acco was a large swamp, formed by the conjunction of the Nahals Naaman and Hillazon and by the failure of the river to carry the increased volume of water. Much of the sandy bay between Acco and Haifa was ideal for a gallop on horseback, but to the immediate north of the Carmel range the flow of the Nahal Kishon into the sea required the horses to swim and the rider to use a boat. To the south of where the Kishon entered the sea, a delta had formed. Modern changes in the landscape have entailed the draining of the Kishon delta to enable the Haifa industrial area to be built, and the transformation of the Naaman swamp into the ponds for fish farming.

The terrain itself can be divided into the bay of Haifa, stretching from Haifa to Acco, and the coast of Galilee from Acco northwards to Rosh ha-Niqra. At Rosh ha-Niqra the coastal plain, which is about

Right This terracotta figurine (c. 7th century BC) of a pregnant woman from Achzib is evidence of Phoenician influence upon this region. The interest in fertility, which it indicates, was a tendency deplored by the Prophets of Israel.

Below This 19th-century view from near the mouth of the river Kishon is in stark contrast with what the modern visitor sees. Today, the area is occupied by an oil refinery and industrial estate, and the slopes of Mount Carmel in the distance have had apartments and houses built upon them.

Above Acco, drawn by David Roberts in 1839, had always been of importance to the governors of Syria, largely for its position at the northern tip of the bay of Haifa.

Note (U) = unlocated site
Abdon (Ebron) Josh. 21:30; Judg. 12:13,15; 1 Chr. 6:74 **B3**
Acco (Ptolemais) Judg. 1:31; Acts 21:7 **B4**
Achshaph Josh. 11:1; 12:20; 19:25 **B4**
Achzib Josh. 15:44; 19:29; Judg. 1:31; Mic. 1:14 **B3**
Ahlab (Mahalah) Judg. 1:31 **C2**
Aijalon Judg. 12:12 (U)
Allammelech Josh. 19:26 (U)
Amad Josh. 19:26 (U)
Aphek (Aphik) Josh. 19:30; Judg. 1:31 **B4**
Bealoth 1 Kgs. 4:16 (U)
Beth-emek Josh. 19:27 **B4**
Cabul Josh. 19:27; 1 Kgs. 9:13 **C4**
Ebron see Abdon
Hali Josh. 19:25 (U)
Hammon Josh. 19:28; 1 Chr. 6:76 **B3**
Helbah Judg. 1:31 (U)
Hosah (Uzu) Josh. 19:29 **C2**
Kishon, River Judg. 4:7,13; 5:21; 1 Kgs. 18:40 **B5**
Mahalab see Ahlab
Mishal Josh. 19:26; 21:30 **B4**
Misrephoth-maim Josh. 11:8; 13:6 **B3**
Nahalol Josh. 19:15; 21:35; Judg. 1:30 **B5**
Neiel Josh. 19:27 **C4**
Okina Judith 2:28 (U)
Ptolemais see Acco
Rehob Josh. 19:30; 21:31; Judg. 1:31; 1 Chr. 6:75 **B4**
Sarepta see Zarephath
Tyre (Tyrus) 2 Sam. 5:11; 24:7; 1 Kgs. 5:1; 7:13,14; 9:11,12; 1 Chr. 14:1; 22:4; 2 Chr. 2:3,11,14; Ezra 3:7; Neh. 13:16; Ps. 45:12; 83:7; 87:4; Isa. 23:1,5,8,15,17; Jer. 25:22; 27:3; 47:4; Ezek. 26:2–7,15; 27:2,3,32; 28:2,12; 29:18; Joel 3:4; Amos 1:9,10; Zech. 9:2,3; 2 Macc. 4:18; Acts 12:20; 21:3,7; Matt. 11:21,22; 15:21; Mark 3:8; 7:24,31; Luke 6:17; 10:13,14 **C2**
Uzu see Hosah
Zarephath (Sarepta) Lev. 4:26; 1 Kgs. 17:9,10; Obad. 20; Luke 4:26 **C1**

Legend

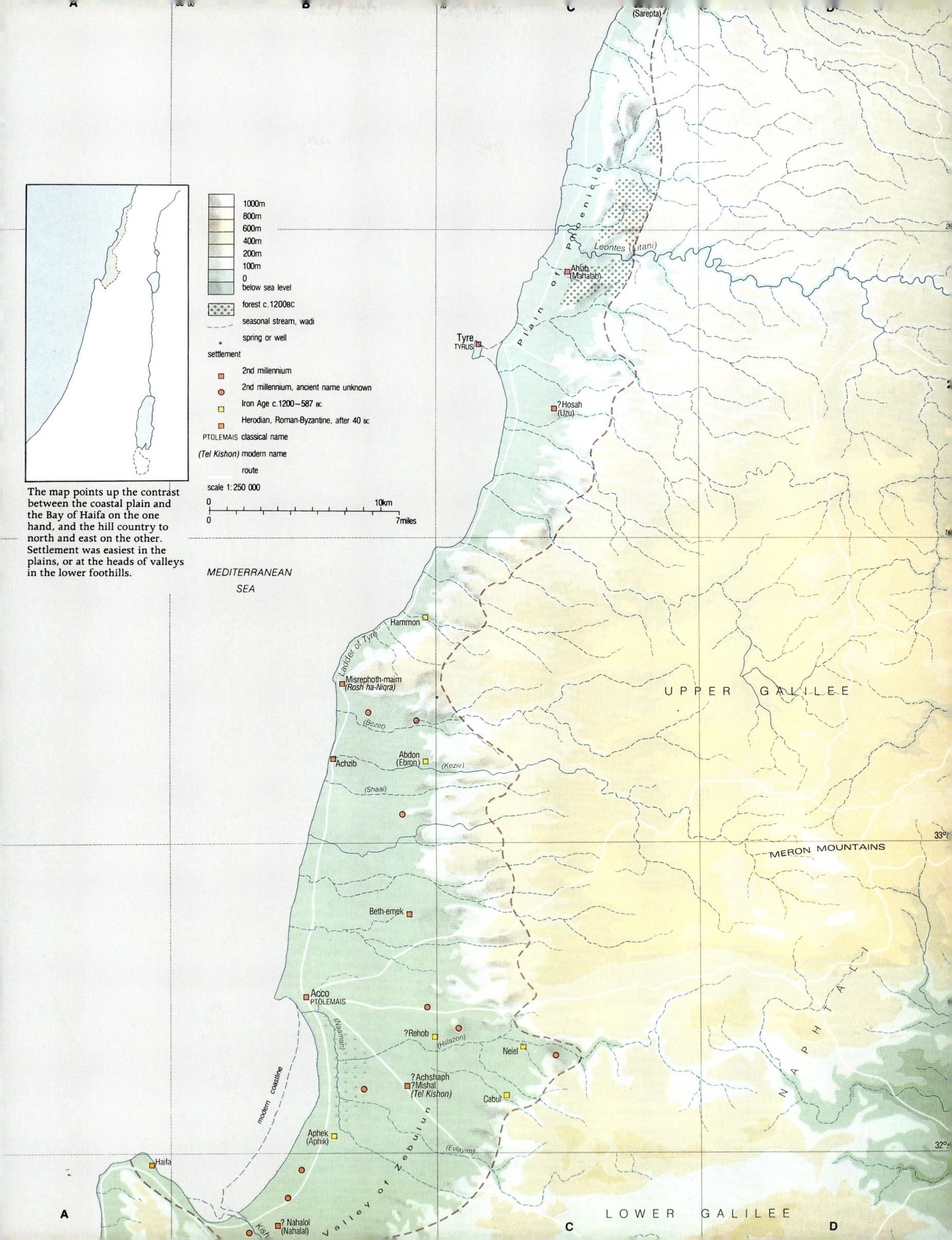

- 1000m
- 800m
- 600m
- 400m
- 200m
- 100m
- 0
- below sea level
- forest c.1200 BC
- seasonal stream, wadi
- spring or well
- settlement
  - 2nd millennium
  - 2nd millennium, ancient name unknown
  - Iron Age c.1200–587 BC
  - Herodian, Roman-Byzantine, after 40 BC
- PTOLEMAIS classical name
- (Tel Kishon) modern name
- route

scale 1:250 000

0 — 10km
0 — 7miles

The map points up the contrast between the coastal plain and the Bay of Haifa on the one hand, and the hill country to north and east on the other. Settlement was easiest in the plains, or at the heads of valleys in the lower foothills.

Map labels

MEDITERRANEAN SEA

Plain of Phoenicia
(Sarepta)
Leontes (Litani)
Ahlab (Mahalab)
Tyre / TYRUS
?Hosah (Uzu)

Hammon
Ladder of Tyre
Misrephoth-maim (Rosh ha-Niqra)
(Bezet)
Achzib
Abdon (Ebron)
(Keziv)
(Shaal)

UPPER GALILEE
MERON MOUNTAINS

Beth-emek

modern coastline
Acco / PTOLEMAIS
(Na'aman)
?Rehob (Hillazon)
Neiel
?Achshaph
?Mishal (Tel Kishon)
Cabul

NAPHTALI

Aphek (Aphik)
(Evlayim)
Haifa
Valley of Nebulun
Kish...
?Nahalol (Nahalal)

LOWER GALILEE

Tyre and Sidon

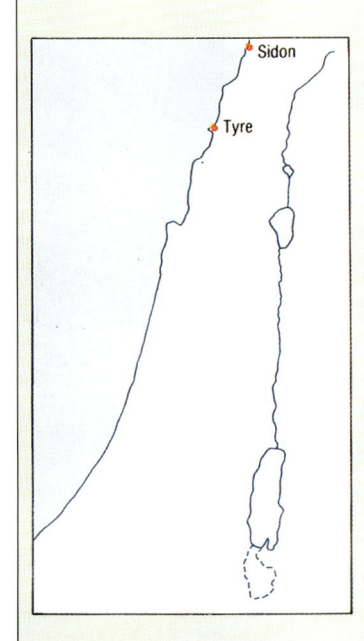

Tyre was a major seaport in biblical times, and was an island until Alexander the Great built a mole to facilitate his siege of the city. It was also a great trading centre, from which Solomon obtained some of his materials for building the temple. Its wealth was famed, and by means of its wealth it became the epitome of art and culture. Together with Sidon, it was the heart of the Phoenician maritime empire that spread right across the Mediterranean with colonies as far away as Spain.

Sidon was a seaport in northern Phoenicia, occupying a well-watered site, and possessing a harbour that was protected by small islands out to sea. During its long and varied history Sidon was sometimes dominated by neighbouring Tyre, and was invariably regarded as a prize by the major conquerors who invaded the area. Unlike Tyre, Sidon welcomed Alexander the Great.

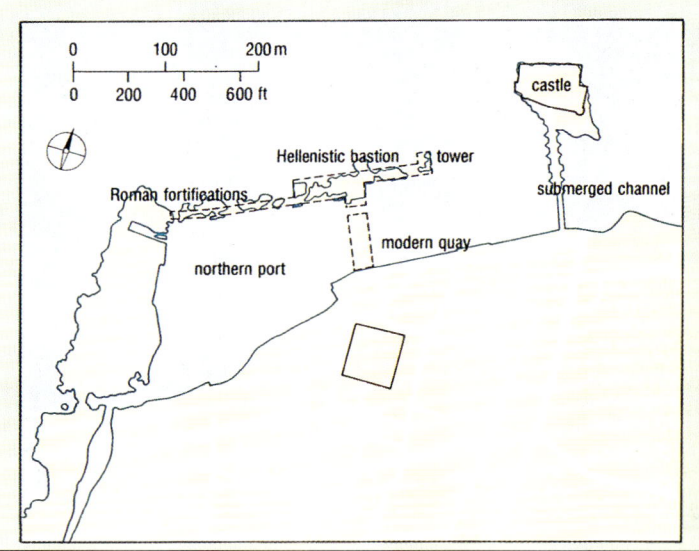

Above Sidon, some 35km (21·7 miles) to the north of Tyre, was similarly famous as a centre of trade and culture. This Phoenician anthropoid sarcophagus was found in a tomb there.

Left Tyre passed through many hands, including the Romans', the remains of some of whose buildings can still be seen. Paul stayed here for a week on his way back to Jerusalem from his third missionary journey.

Far left Plan of ancient Sidon.

5km (3·1 miles) wide, is abruptly cut off by hills running roughly west to east. From this barrier southwards it is about 15km (9·3 miles) to Acco, and much of the soil is deep and fertile and well supplied with water from six watercourses, which water it from east and west, as well as an average rainfall of over 600mm (23·6in). The area from Acco to Haifa, known as the valley of Zebulun, is about 20km (12·4 miles) long and 6 to 9km (3·7 to 5·6 miles) wide.

It is not clear whether in biblical times the coastline between Acco and Haifa was the same as it is today. There is evidence of major settlements in the 2nd millennium BC along a line roughly following the shape of the present coastline, but about 3·75km (2·3 miles) to the east. These settlements were either on the seashore, or separated from the sea by navigable swamps. It is evident that the combined actions of the Nahal Kishon and the sea current have deposited considerable amounts of sand along the bay of Haifa coastline.

In the 2nd millennium the major settlements were either within easy reach of the sea, or close to springs and rivers if further to the east. The settlers presumably lived from fishing and from agriculture. There is no evidence of major settlement east of a line roughly 15km (9·3 miles) east of the coast between Acco and Rosh ha-Niqra. We may presume that the hills to the east of this line were wooded with evergreen forests of the Palestinian oak (*Quercus calliprinos*) and its associates.

The biblical record

The first main reference to this region in the Bible is in Joshua 19:24–31, where the tribe of Asher is allocated a region stretching from Carmel to Tyre, a total of 22 cities and their dependent villages. That this allocation was ideal rather than actual is indicated in Judges 1:31, which states that "Asher did not drive out the inhabitants of Acco, or the inhabitants of Sidon, or of Ahlab, or of Achzib, or of Helbah, or of Aphik, or of Rehob." However, most of these cities seem to have become Israelite by the end of the reign of David. Joab's census journey (2 Samuel 24:4–8) seems to have included the region (see verse 7); and when Solomon needed to make an extra payment to Hiram for the building of the temple in Jerusalem, he ceded to Hiram

Left An incised stone bowl from Sidon, apparently representing a ritual of the god Melkart. If, in the rite, the king played the role of the god, this may explain why Ezekiel 28 criticizes the king of neighbouring Tyre for acting like a deity.

Below This aerial view of Tyre gives us some idea of what the city was like when it was an island. Its isolation from the mainland and its sheltered harbour gave it great natural advantages, enabling it to withstand a 13-year Babylonian siege by Nebuchadnezzar in the 6th century BC.

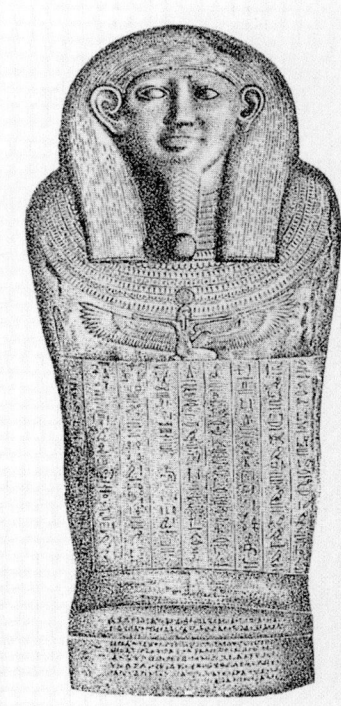

Above This sarcophagus of King Tabnit of Sidon was apparently made originally for the Egyptian general Penptah, and then reused for Tabnit. The Phoenician inscription at its foot, dating from the end of the 6th century BC, warns that the sarcophagus should not be opened.

20 cities in Galilee, which are presumed to have included all the Israelite cities in the coastal region from Mount Carmel northwards to Ahlab.

In modern times Haifa has become the most important seaport in the northern part of Israel. In biblical times the area of Haifa was probably inaccessible from the east because of the swamps of the Kishon delta. In contrast Acco was more accessible, and served as the major northern seaport. It is mentioned in the Bible in Acts 21:7 under its Hellenistic name of Ptolemais. The biblical Acco was nearly 2km (1·2 miles) east of the present coastline.

To the north of Rosh ha-Niqra there is a series of ranges of hills, known as the "ladder of Tyre". There is virtually no coastal strip until about 8km (5 miles) south of Tyre, and then only a small one. From Rosh ha-Niqra northwards it was necessary to ascend hills in order to progress towards Tyre. Tyre itself was in Old Testament times an island some 600 to 750m (656 to 820yd) from the coast, and it was the most important southerly Phoenician city. It was a great entrepôt for trade and commerce, and it was to Hiram king of Tyre (969–936 BC) that Solomon looked when he needed materials for the building of the Jerusalem temple (1 Kings 9:11). A vivid picture of Tyre's wealth and beauty is given in the denunciation of the prince of Tyre in Ezekiel 28. Tyre played a fateful role in the history of the northern kingdom through Jezebel, the wife of Ahab (c.873–852 BC). She worked tirelessly to replace with her own god the worship of the God of Israel. Often mentioned together with Tyre is the Phoenician city of Sidon, some 35km (21·7 miles) up the coast from Tyre. About 15km (9·3 miles) south of Sidon on the coast is Zarephath (Sarepta), the town to which Elijah was commanded to go during the drought that occurred while he was locked in a bitter struggle with Ahab and Jezebel (1 Kings 17:8). Elijah is specifically commanded to go to "Zarephath, which belongs to Sidon", and there is no doubt deliberate irony in the fact that the prophet provided for a non-Israelite widow and her son during the drought when many Israelites went hungry. A similar motif is found in the New Testament. In Matthew 15:21–28 (Mark 7:24–30) Jesus withdraws to the "district of Tyre and Sidon" and performs a miracle for a non-Israelite woman whose daughter is a demoniac.

THE COASTAL PLAIN SOUTH OF MOUNT CARMEL

Description of the region
The coastal plain southwards from the point where the Carmel range meets the sea is normally divided into three main regions. The first, known as the Carmel coast, is roughly 30km (18·6 miles) long, and on average only about 3km (1·9 miles) wide. It is bordered on the east by the Carmel range and the northern hill country. Its southern limit is the Nahal Tanninim.

The second section, known as the Sharon (a Hebrew name found, for example, in Isaiah 35:2), extends from the Nahal Tanninim to the river Yarkon, which enters the sea immediately north of Tel Aviv. (Some authorities prefer to regard the boundary as the Nahals Aijalon and Nahshon.) It is roughly 50km (31 miles) long and on average 15km (9·3 miles) wide. Immediately south of the Nahal Tanninim the plain widens dramatically from 2km (1·2 miles) to 12km (7·5 miles). South of the river Yarkon the plain is known as the Judean plain, and is divided into a northern and a southern section. The northern section, about 85km (52·8 miles) long, extends to the Nahal Lachish which enters the sea immediately north of Ashdod. The bounds of the southern are harder to determine, because it is bordered by a semi-arid zone whose limits can vary. Normally the Nahal Shiqma, entering the sea midway between Ashkelon and Gaza, is taken to mark the boundary with the Negev coast.

Visitors to this region in the 19th century would hardly recognize it today. Of the section from Haifa to Caesarea, Thomson wrote in 1857, "it is about as profitable, and far more pleasant to traverse this

Arbatta (region) 1 Macc. 5:23 **B2 C2**
Arubboth 1 Kgs. 4:10 **C3**
Caesarea (Strato's Tower) Matt. 16:13; Mark 8:27; Acts 10:1,24; 11:11; 12:19; 18:22; 21:8,16; 23:23,33; 25:1,4,6,13 **B3**
Dor (Tantura) Josh. 11:2; 12:23; 17:11; Judg. 1:27; 1 Kgs. 4:11; 1 Chr. 7:29 **B2**
Hepher Josh. 12:17; 1 Kgs. 4:10 **B3**
Jashub Num. 26:24 **C3**
Naphath-dor (region) Josh. 11:12; 1 Kgs. 4:11 **C2**
Ophrah Judg. 6:11,24; 8:27,32; 9:5 **C4**
Sharon, plain of Chr. 5:16; 27:29; S. of S. 2:1; Isa. 33:9; 35:2; Acts 9:35 **B3 B4**
Shihor-libnath, River Josh. 19:26 **B2**
Soco (Socoh) 1 Kgs. 4:10 **C3**
Strato's Tower see Caesarea
Tantura see Dor

Left The kurkar ridges that characterize the western edges of the coastal plain form a drainage barrier against the waters that run to the sea. The marsh effect that results at some points is visible here.

Right The most striking feature of this map is the narrowness of the strip immediately to the south of the Carmel range. Its broadening is quite dramatic. The patterns of settlement generally follow the widening of the plain.

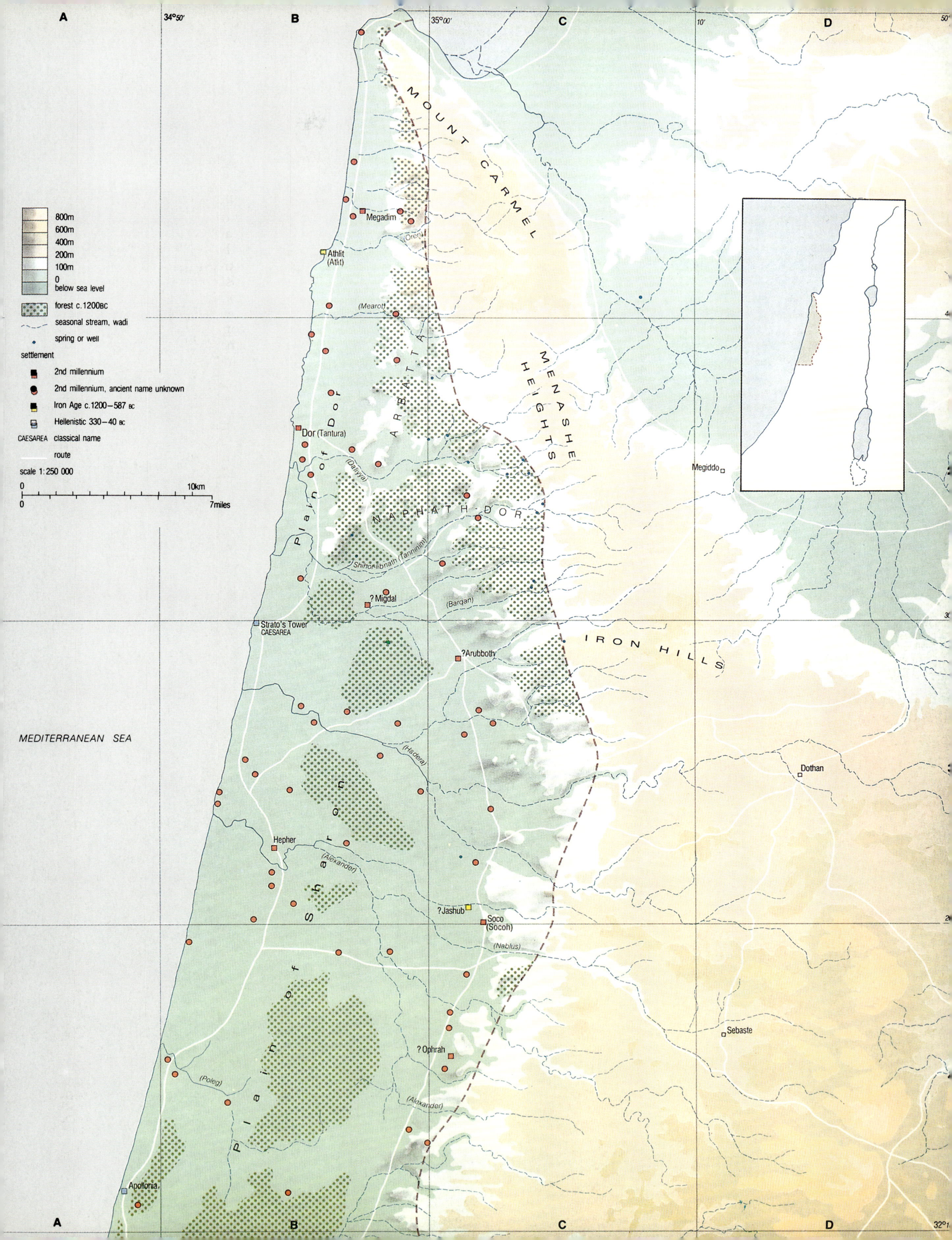

A
34°50′
B
35°00′
C
10′
D
50′
MOUNT CARMEL
MENASHE HEIGHTS
IRON HILLS
NAPHATH-DOR
ARABATTA
Plain of Dor
Plain of Sharon
MEDITERRANEAN SEA
Megadim
(Oren)
Athlit
(Atlit)
(Mearot)
Dor (Tantura)
(Dalyya)
Shihor-libnath (Tanninim)
? Migdal
(Barqan)
Strato's Tower
CAESAREA
?Arubboth
(Hadera)
Hepher
(Alexander)
?Jashub
Soco
(Socoh)
(Nablus)
? Ophrah
(Poleg)
(Alexander)
Apollonia
Megiddo
Dothan
Sebaste
800m
600m
400m
200m
100m
0
below sea level
forest c.1200BC
seasonal stream, wadi
spring or well
settlement
2nd millennium
2nd millennium, ancient name unknown
Iron Age c.1200–587 BC
Hellenistic 330–40 BC
CAESAREA classical name
route
scale 1:250 000
0
10km
0
7miles

nine hours in imagination than to ride them on horseback." Down as far as Athlit he saw no important villages or ruins. However, G.A. Smith observed oak woods and remains of forests in this area, as did many earlier authorities quoted by Smith. Tantura (Dor) appeared to Thomson as a "sad and sickly hamlet. . . on a naked sea beach, with a marshy flat between it and the base of the eastern hills". From Caesarea down to Gaza he was struck by the large sand dunes, in some places 5km (3·1 miles) wide, and to the east of what is today Netanya he saw pine forests growing on the sandy soil: "the finest specimens we have seen in Palestine". South of the river Yarkon, especially in the "Lod basin" (on which see below), G. A. Smith reported "far more cultivation—fields of corn and melons, gardens, orange groves, and groves of palms". Today the area is still one of intensive agricultural activity. This, however, is shared with an international airport at Lod, major road and rail links, especially at Tel Aviv.

Far left Dor was a seaport founded probably in the Late Bronze Age. It passed into Israelite hands in the reign of David, and was the centre of one of Solomon's administrative districts. In Persian times (after 540 BC) a Greek colony was founded there. Although the Jewish Hasmonean rulers ended its independence, Pompey restored its autonomy in 63 BC. The stone head of a man (*left*) from Dor is of Hellenistic date.

Note (U) = unlocated site

Accaron see Ekron
Adida see Hadid
Aphek (Antipatris) Josh. 12:8; 1 Sam. 4:1; 29:1; Acts 23:31 **D1**
Ashdod (Azotus) Josh. 11:22; 15:46,47; 1 Sam. 5:1,3,5–7; 6:17; 2 Chr. 26:6; Neh. 13:23–24; Isa. 20:1; Jer. 25:20; Amos 1:8; 3:4; Zeph. 2:4; 9:6; Acts 8:40 **B3**
Ashkelon (Ascalon) Judg. 1:18; 14:19; 1 Sam. 6:17; 2 Sam. 1:20; Jer. 25:20; 47:5–7; Amos 1:8; Zeph. 2:4,7 **B4**
Asor (Azor) Josh. 19:45 **C1**
Azotus see Ashdod
Baalah, Mount Josh. 15:11 **C2**
Baalath Josh. 19:44; 1 Kgs. 9:18; 2 Chr. 8:6 **C2**
Belus, River see Kedron, River
Bene-berak Josh. 19:45 **C1**
Beth-dagon Josh. 15:41 **C2**
Eben-ezer (Aphek) 1 Sam. 4:1; 5:1 **D1**
Ekron (Accaron) Josh. 13:3; 15:11,45–46; 19:43; Judg. 1:18; 1 Sam. 5:10; 6:16–17; 2 Kgs. 1:2,3,6,16; Jer. 25:20; Amos 1:8; Zeph. 2:4; Zech. 9:5,7 **D3**
Elah, valley of 1 Sam. 17:2,19; 21:9 **C3 D3**
Elon Josh. 19:43 (U)
Eltekeh (Elteke) Josh. 19:44; 21:23 **D2**
Gath (Metheg-ammah) Josh. 11:22; 13:3; 1 Sam. 5:8; 6:17; 17:4, 23; 21:10,12; 27:2–4; 2 Sam. 1:20; 8:1; 21:20,22; 1 Chr. 20:6,8; 1 Kgs. 2:39–40; 2 Kgs. 12:17; 1 Chr. 8:13; 18:1; 2 Chr. 26:6; Amos 6:2; Mic. 1:10 **D3**
Gath-rimmon Josh. 19:45; 21:24; 1 Chr. 6:69 **C1**
Gaza Deut. 2:23; Josh. 13:3; 15:47; Judg. 1:18; 6:4; 16:1,21; 1 Sam. 6:17; Jer. 25:20; 47:1,5; Amos 1:6,7; Zeph. 2:4; Zech. 9:5; Acts 8:26 **B4**
Gibbethon Josh. 19:44; 21:23; 1 Kgs. 15:27,28; 16:15,17 **C2**
Gilgal Josh. 12:23 **D1**
Gimzo 2 Chr. 28:18 **D2**
Gittaim (Gath) 2 Sam. 4:3; Neh. 11:33 **D2**
Hadid (Adida) Ezra 2:33; Neh. 7:37; 11:34; 1 Macc. 12:38; 13:13 **D2**
Jabneel (Jamnia) Josh. 15:11; 2 Chr. 26:6 **C2**
Jamnia 1 Macc. 12:8,9 **C2**
Jehud Josh. 19:45 **D1**
Joppa Josh. 19:46; 2 Chr. 2:16; Ezra 3:7; Jonah 1:3; Acts 9:36,38,42,43; 10:5,8,23,32; 11:5,13 **C1**
Kedron 1 Macc. 15:39,41; 16:5–10 **C3**
Kedron (Belus), River 1 Macc. 16:5–10 **C2**
Lod (Lydda, Diospolis) 1 Chr. 8:12; Ezra 2:33; Neh. 7:37; 11:35; Acts 9:32,35 **D2**
Me-jarkon Josh. 19:46 **C1**
Metheg-ammah see Gath
Neballat Neh. 11:34 **D2**
Ono 1 Chr. 8:12; Ezra 2:33; Neh. 6:2; 7:37; 11:35 **D1**
Rakkon Josh. 19:46 **C1**
Shikkeron Josh. 15:11 **C3**
Zeboim 1 Sam. 13:18; Neh. 11:34 (U)
Zephathah, vale of 2 Chr. 14:10 **C3 C4**

Map Legend

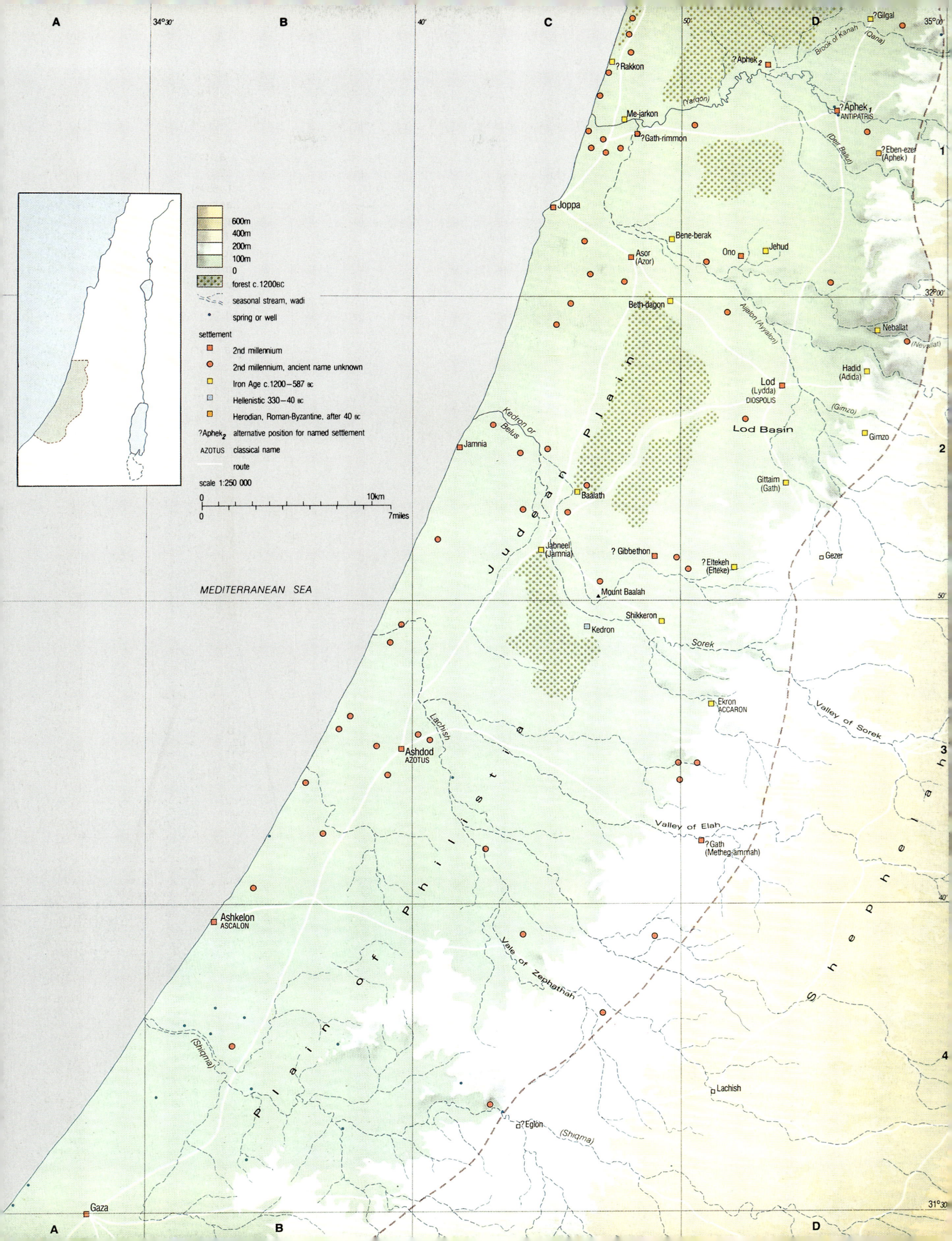

- 600m
- 400m
- 200m
- 100m
- 0

- forest c.1200 BC
- seasonal stream, wadi
- spring or well

settlement
- ■ 2nd millennium
- ● 2nd millennium, ancient name unknown
- ▪ Iron Age c.1200–587 BC
- ▪ Hellenistic 330–40 BC
- ▪ Herodian, Roman-Byzantine, after 40 BC

?Aphek₂ alternative position for named settlement
AZOTUS classical name
— — — route
scale 1:250 000

0 — 10km
0 — 7 miles

Map Labels

MEDITERRANEAN SEA

?Gilgal
?Rakkon
?Aphek₂
Me-jarkon (Yarqon)
?Gath-rimmon
?Aphek / ANTIPATRIS
?Eben-ezer (Aphek)
Joppa
Bene-berak
Asor (Azor)
Ono
Jehud
Beth-dagon
Neballat (Nevallat)
Aijalon (Ayyalon)
Lod (Lydda) DIOSPOLIS
Hadid (Adida)
Lod Basin
Gimzo (Gimzo)
Kedron or Belus
Jamnia
Baalath
Gittaim (Gath)
Jabneel (Jamnia)
?Gibbethon
?Eltekeh (Elteke)
Gezer
Mount Baalah
Shikkeron
Kedron
Sorek
Ekron ACCARON
Valley of Sorek
Lachish
Ashdod AZOTUS
Valley of Elah
?Gath (Metheg-ammah)
Ashkelon ASCALON
Vale of Zephathah
(Shiqma)
Lachish
?Eglon
(Shiqma)
Gaza

Plain of Judah
Plain of Philistia
Shephelah

THE COASTAL PLAIN SOUTH OF MOUNT CARMEL

In order to understand what the region looked like in biblical times it is necessary to consider aspects of its geology, ecology and patterns of settlement. During geological time, the sea advanced and retreated several times, on each occasion returning to a lower level. This had the effect of forming three parallel coastlines of kurkar ridges (a type of sandstone hardened by water and other elements). The most westerly of these ridges is the present coastline, except that it has been almost entirely eroded by the sea from Athlit northwards. South of the river Yarkon the kurkar ridge is protected from the sea by extensive sand dunes. Between the river Yarkon and the Nahal Hadera the ridge appears as a continuous range of cliffs rising to 50 to 60m (164 to 197ft) at their highest point near Netanya. The range is broken where the main rivers and Nahals (Alexander, Poleg, Yarkon) enter the sea. There is also a stretch of the ridge immediately south of the Yarkon. From the Nahal Hadera to Athlit the cliffs are in various stages of erosion.

About 1km (0·6 miles) to the east of the first kurkar ridge is the second ridge, on average 300m (328yd) wide, and rising to a height of 20 to 30m (66 to 98ft) in the northern part of the Sharon, and 40 to 50m (131 to 164ft) in the southern part. The third ridge is about 3km (1·9 miles) east of the second, and is covered by 10 to 20m (33 to 66ft) of red sand, which reaches heights of 50 and 80m (164 and 262ft) in the north and south of the Sharon respectively. In some areas the third ridge and its sands are some 8km (5 miles) wide. The ridge is broken by the rivers and Nahals that cross it to enter the sea, and extensively by the "Lod basin". It is not found with its associated sands south of the Nahal Sorek, but is covered by the rich soils that are typical of the plain south of the "Lod basin" before the semi-arid zone intervenes.

The effect of these three ridges in ancient times was as follows. Between the first ridge (the coastline) and the second was a sandy strip where settlement was possible on or near the banks of the rivers and Nahals. Between the second and third ridges was an area of swamps, caused by the failure of the rivers and Nahals to drain completely into the sea. The third ridge, the "red ridge", was covered with deciduous oak forests, as well as the pines which Thomson observed. Remains of a deciduous oak forest (Tabor oak—*Quercus ithaburensis*) survived until World War I when it was used by the Turks as fuel for steam locomotives. To the east of the "red ridge" and its forests was a plain of rich soil, reaching to the foothills. This plain was ideal for agriculture.

Patterns of settlement in the 2nd millennium show that nowhere was the "red ridge" occupied except at the very edge. This strongly supports the presence of woodlands, and shows that the "red ridge" formed a barrier between settlements on the coast and those at the edge of the foothills, except where valleys cut through the ridge. The settlements at the edge of the foothills, usually close to water sources, were agricultural settlements, working the rich soil of the plain between the "red ridge" and the foothills. The settlements on the coast were also probably primarily agricultural, cultivating the soil between the first and second ridges with the help of irrigation from the rivers

Joppa, Ashdod and Gaza were three of the most important towns on or near the sea in the southern part of the coastal plain. Joppa (*below right*) was the main natural harbour in the region, and is mentioned in Egyptian sources as early as the 15th century BC. In spite of occupation for over 3000 years and much rebuilding, a modern view still highlights its natural advantages.

Ashdod and Gaza became Philistine cities with the invasion of the "sea peoples" in the 12th-11th centuries BC. The figurine shown here (*left*), recovered from excavations over the past 20 years, is of a seated woman, and probably dates from the 12th century BC.

As the most southerly of the cities of the coastal plain, Gaza (*above*) had strategic importance, and was a gateway to Egypt along the coast. Egypt controlled it whenever possible. In the biblical record it appears as the centre of the Philistine power, and is where Samson met his death.

entering the sea. However, some fishing and trading also took place. In the "Lod basin", a small triangular plain with rich soil, settlements were established in all parts of the plain. It should be emphasized that most of the settlements marked on the map existed for only part of the 2nd millennium. Their function in this Atlas is to indicate possible areas of settlement in conjunction with the local geology and ecology. The settlements should also be considered in relation to the main lines of communication in the 2nd millennium. The main route from Egypt to the north went northwards along the coast through Gaza and Ashdod to Joppa, where it turned northeast along the Yarkon valley to Aphek, and then proceeded along the edge of the foothills (see p.26). However, there were other routes along the entire coastal area, and this fact also affected the patterns of settlement.

The biblical record

In the Old Testament the region under consideration is allocated to the tribes of Judah, Ephraim and Manasseh. It is not possible to determine the exact boundaries, but to Judah is allocated the land roughly south of the Nahal Sorek (Joshua 15:11–12), to Ephraim the land between Nahal Sorek and the river Yarkon (Joshua 16:8, assuming that the brook Kanah is the Wadi Qana and joins the Yarkon), and to Manasseh the remainder of the coastal plain northwards to Mount Carmel. It is also possible that Dan was given the port of Joppa and a "corridor" to it, if this is the meaning of Joshua 19:46.

In practice the tribes concerned probably exercised little control over these areas. Judges 1:18–19 states that, although Judah defeated Gaza, Ashkelon and Ekron, it "could not drive out the inhabitants of the plain, because they had chariots of iron". Judges 1:29 also states that "Ephraim did not drive out the Canaanites who dwelt in Gezer", while Manasseh could not conquer Dor (Judges 1:27). Indeed, Ephraim and Manasseh can hardly be expected to have done more than control the eastern part of the coastal plain between the foothills and the wooded "red ridge"; and since this strip contained the main international route from Egypt northwards, Egypt most likely controlled the area up to the rise of Assyrian power in the 8th century BC. The northern part of the strip allocated to Judah was occupied by the Philistines in the 12th century BC. Although under David and Solomon the Philistines were subdued, it is unlikely that Judah exercised any effective control over the area after the death of Solomon. Exceptions were in the reigns of Uzziah (c. 785–733 BC), who breached the walls of Gath, Jabneh and Ashdod, and who built cities in Philistine territory (2 Chronicles 26:6), and Hezekiah (c. 727–698 BC), who "smote the Philistines as far as Gaza" (2 Kings 18:8).

By far the greatest number of Old Testament references to the coastal region occur in the stories of the struggle between the Philistines and Samson, the hero of the tribe of Dan. Thus, Samson killed 30 men in Ashkelon in order to get the 30 sets of garments, which he lost when his Philistine wife betrayed the meaning of the riddle about the beehive in the dead lion's carcass (Judges 14:5–20, especially verse 19). Gaza suffered the loss of its gates when Samson took them to Hebron (Judges 16:1–3), and it was to Gaza that the blinded Samson was taken, and where he pulled down the pillars of the great building, killing himself and some 3000 Philistines (Judges 16:23–30). In the wars between the Philistines and the Israelites before the reign of Saul the Philistines forced a battle at Aphek. They were able to use the main route in order to concentrate their forces, and victory gave them access to the hill country via the Wadi Qana (1 Samuel 4:1–11). The Ark of the Covenant, which was captured in this battle, was taken first to Ashdod, then to Gath, then to Ekron, before it was returned to the Israelites (1 Samuel 5:1–12). Gath was also the home city of the Philistine giant Goliath, and the city to whose king David fled when Saul was seeking to kill him (1 Samuel 27:1–12). Of the towns to the north of the Philistine cities, Joppa is mentioned as the seaport from which Jonah set sail in the opposite direction to that in which God had commanded him to go (Jonah 1:3), and as the port to which were shipped the materials for both the first and second Jerusalem temples (2 Chronicles 2:16, Ezra 3:7).

The New Testament reflects the important changes that took place in the area following the Roman occupation in 63 BC. By far the most important change was the building of Caesarea. Although there had been a naval station near the site since the end of the Persian period (c. 340 BC), the city as known in New Testament times was begun by Herod the Great in 22 BC and inaugurated in 10–9 BC. In 6 AD Caesarea became the capital of the Roman province of Judea and the residence of the Roman governors. The most remarkable building achievements at Caesarea were the harbour and the water system. There was apparently a southern breakwater some 600m (656yd) long in the shape of a large arc. Together with a northern breakwater of some 250m (273yd), the harbour area was about 3·5 acres. The water supply consisted of two aqueducts, the higher of which was constructed in the reign of Herod. It was 9km (5·6 miles) long, and brought water from springs on the southern slopes of Mount Carmel.

When Peter went to preach in Caesarea to the Roman centurion Cornelius (Acts 10:1–48), he was, in effect, going to the most prestigious Gentile city in the province. Thereafter, the Christian community in Caesarea is mentioned several times in Acts. On arriving back from his last missionary journey, Paul sailed (or went by road) from Tyre to Caesarea (Acts 21:8) and stayed with Philip the evangelist. It was in Caesarea that Paul was imprisoned for two years (Acts 24:27—but see the commentaries) and where he defended himself before Festus and before Herod Agrippa II and his sister Bernice (Acts 25–26).

Caesarea

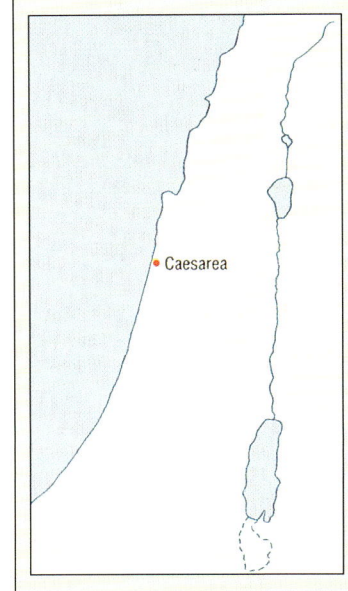

The building of Caesarea bore witness to the great technological advances that had been made by the end of the 1st century BC. Ancient towns such as Joppa and Dor depended for their livelihood upon their location on the coast and the availability of fresh water. Caesarea is a triumph of technology at a part of the coast not naturally suited to becoming the site of a provincial capital. Although there was a small coastal station there several hundred years earlier, it was Herod the Great who built Caesarea in the years 22-9 BC, making it into the major port of the region, and the main residence of the Jewish kings and Roman procurators who ruled Judea. The latter included Pontius Pilate who was governor at the time of Jesus' Crucifixion and lived here from 26 to 36 AD, and Felix who imprisoned Paul in the city for two years and who lived here from 52 to 50 AD. From New Testament times until the period of the Crusades, Caesarea retained its strategic importance. Its ancient remains, continually being uncovered by archaeologists, are impressive to modern visitors, and are eloquent testimony to its former greatness.

THE COASTAL PLAIN SOUTH OF MOUNT CARMEL

Below centre A coin minted at Caesarea by Trajanus Decius bearing the inscription "Colonia Prima Flavia Augusta Caesarea".

Below A tessera (or token) found in the sea at Caesarea depicting the ancient harbour there.

Below Beside the port ancient columns protrude from the sea-washed wall at the point where the Phoenician naval station once stood.

Below centre Inside the Crusader city a passage with pointed arches dating from the 13th century AD leads to the southeast corner.

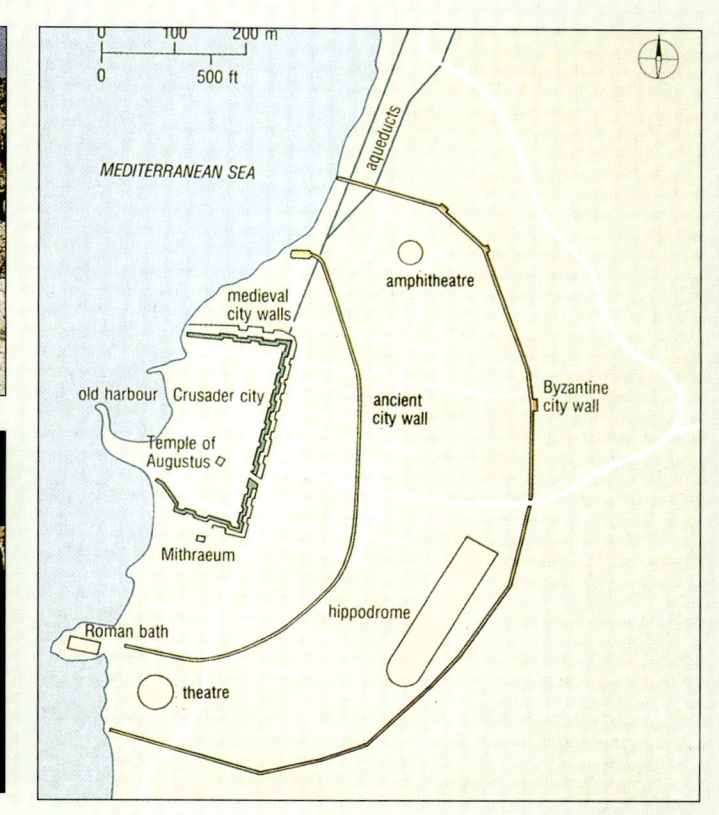

Left Caesarea's greatest need, apart from protection from the sea, was a water supply. This was provided by two aqueducts, the higher of which, shown here, brought water from the southern slopes of Mount Carmel 9km (5.6 miles) from the city. This aqueduct was built in Herod's reign.

Above This aerial view of Caesarea shows remains dating mostly from the medieval city (11th-13th centuries AD). By this time, the city had shrunk considerably in size. The area in the foreground would have been part of the city in its heyday.

THE SHEPHELAH

Description of the region

"Shephelah" is a Hebrew word meaning lowlands, and is found in both Old and New Testaments. In Joshua 15:20–63 it designates an area different from "the extreme South" (Hebrew *negev*, verse 21) and "the hill country" (Hebrew *har*, verse 48).

The precise area indicated by "Shephelah" is not easy to define. Its northern boundary is usually held to be the valley of Aijalon, which is probably part of a geological fault which continues into the "Lod basin". On the eastern side the Shephelah is separated by a series of valleys running roughly north to south as far as Tarqumiya (Iphtah), and running roughly to the southwest thereafter. These valleys and the boundary that they form with the higher eastern hills are vividly described by G. A. Smith. The southern limits are probably best put at the Nahal Shiqma, while the western limit is where the hills meet the coastal plain. However, this latter boundary is not clearly discernible, as broad valleys from the coastal plain at some points penetrate the hills and give the hills the impression of belonging to the plain. The whole area thus defined is a strip about 45km (28 miles) long and about 15km (9·3 miles) wide.

In the western half of the Shephelah, at heights of roughly 120 to 350m (394 to 1148ft), the hills are of soft limestones and chalk. A series of short valleys running from north to south roughly down the middle of the Shephelah divides the western from the higher eastern hills of the area. These hills are covered by a hard layer of lime, from 1 to 2m (3·3 to 6·6ft) thick. They are more rounded than in the western sector, and less suited to agriculture.

As one moves from north to south, the rainfall decreases. At its northern margin the Shephelah receives 500mm (19·7in) of rainfall on average, at its middle 350mm (13·8in), and on the south margin

Note (U) = unlocated site

Achzib (Chezib) Gen. 38:5; Josh. 15:44; 19:29; Judg. 1:31; Mic. 1:14 **C3**
Adithaim Josh. 15:36 (U)
Adullam Gen. 38:1,12–20; Josh. 12:15; 15:35; 1 Sam. 22:1; 2 Sam. 23:13; 1 Chr. 11:15; 2 Chr. 11:7; Neh. 11:30; Mic. 1:15; 2 Macc. 12:38 **D3**
Aijalon (Elon) Josh. 10:12; 19:42,43; 21:24; Judg. 1:35; 1 Kgs. 4:9; 1 Chr. 6:69; 2 Chr. 11:10 **D1**
Aijalon, valley of Josh. 10:12 **C1 D1**
Anem 1 Chr. 6:73 (U)
Ashan Josh. 15:42 (U)
Ashnah Josh. 15:43 **C3 D2**
Azekah Josh. 10:10,11; 15:35; 1 Sam. 17:1; 2 Chr. 11:9; Neh. 11:30; Jer. 34:7 **C2**
Beer 1 Sam. 15:8; Judg. 9:21 **C2**
Beth-shemesh (Har-heres, Ir-shemesh) Josh. 19:41; 21:6; Judg. 1:35; 1 Sam. 6:9–20; 1 Kgs. 4:9; 2 Kgs. 14:11,13; 1 Chr. 6:59; 2 Chr. 25:21,23; 28:18 **C2**
Bozkath Josh. 15:39 **C3**
Cabbon Josh. 15:40 **C3**
Chezib *see* Achzib
Chitlish Josh. 15:40 **B3**
Debir Josh. 10:38,39; 11:21; 15:7,15–16; 21:15; Judg. 1:11; 1 Chr. 6:58 **C4 D4**
Dilean Josh. 15:38 **B3**
Eglon Josh. 10:3,23,34,37; 12:12; 15:39 **B3 C4**
Elam Ezra 2:31; Neh. 7:34 **C3**
Elon Josh. 19:43 **C2**
Elon-beth-hanan 1 Kgs. 4:9 (U)
Emmaus (Nicopolis) 1 Macc. 3:40,57; 4:3; 9:50; Luke 24:13 **C1**
Enaim Gen. 38:14,21 (U)
Enam Josh. 15:34 (U)
En-gannim Josh. 15:34 **C2**
Ephes-dammim (Pas-dammim) 1 Sam. 17:1; 1 Chr. 11:13 (U)
Eshtaol Josh. 15:33; 19:41; Judg. 16:31; 18:2, 8, 11 **D2**
Ether Josh. 15:42 **C3**
Gazara *see* Gezer
Geder Josh. 12:13 (U)
Gederah (Gederoth) Josh. 15:36; 1 Chr. 4:23; 12:4 **C2**
Gederothaim Josh. 15:36 **C2**
Gedor 1 Chr. 4:18,39 (U)
Gezer (Gazara) Josh. 10:33; 12:12; 16:3,10; 21:21; Judg. 1:29; 2 Sam. 5:25; 1 Kgs. 9:15–17; 1 Chr. 6:67; 7:28; 14:6; 20:4; 1 Macc. 4:15 **C1**
Hadashak Josh. 15:37 (U)
Har-heres *see* Beth-shemesh
Harim Ezra 2:32,39; Neh. 7:35,42 **C3**
Iphtah (Tricomias) Josh. 15:43 **D3**
Irnahash 1 Chr. 4:12 (U)
Ir-shemesh *see* Beth-shemesh
Ithlal Josh. 19:42 (U)
Jarmuth Josh. 10:3,5,23; 12:11; 15:35; Neh. 11:29 **C2**
Joktheel Josh. 15:38 (U)
Keilah Josh. 15:44; 1 Sam. 23:1–13; Neh. 3:17,18 **D3**
Lachish Josh. 10:3,5,23,31–35; 12:11; 15:39; 2 Kgs. 14:19, 18:14,17; 2 Chr. 11:9; 25:27; Neh. 11:30; Isa. 36:2; Jer. 34:7; Mic. 1:13 **C3**
Lahmam Josh. 15:40 **C3**
Libnah Num. 33:20,21; Josh. 10:29,31–32,39; 15:42; 21:13; 2 Kgs. 8:22; 19:8; 23:31; 1 Chr. 6:57; 2 Chr. 21:10; Isa. 37:8 **C3**
Magbish Ezra 2:30 **C3**
Makaz 1 Kgs. 4:9 **C2**
Makkedah Josh. 10:16,17,21,28,29; 15:41 **C3**
Mareshah (Marisa) Josh. 15:44; 2 Chr. 11:8; 14:9–10; 20:37; 1 Macc. 5:66; 2 Macc. 12:35 **C3**
Migdal-gad Josh. 15:37 **C3**
Mizpeh Josh. 15:38 (U)
Moresheth-gath Jer. 26:18; Mic. 1:1, 14 **C3**
Naamah Josh. 15:41 (U)
Nahash 1 Chr. 4:12 **C3**
Nezib Josh. 15:43 **D3**
Nicopolis *see* Emmaus
Pas-dammim *see* Ephes-dammim
Soco (Socoh) Josh. 15:35; 1 Sam. 17:1; 2 Chr. 11:7; 28:18 **C2**
Sorek, valley of Judg. 16:4 **C2**
Tappuah Josh. 15:34 (U)
Timnah Josh. 15:10, 19:43; Judg. 14:1–2,5; 2 Chr. 28:18 **C2**
Tricomias *see* Iphtah
Zanoah Josh. 15:34; Neh. 3:13; 11:30 **D2**
Zenan Josh. 15:37 **B3**
Zorah Josh. 15:33; 19:41; Judg. 13:2,25; 16:31; 18:2,8,11; 2 Chr. 11:10; Neh. 11:29 **C2**

Left The area of Zorah and Eshtaol is the heartland of the early territory of Dan, and of the tribe's hero, Samson. Extensive modern planting of trees helps to convey something of what it would have looked like in Old Testament times.

Right The Shephelah is a transitional area in the south of Israel merging on the west into the coastal plain and on the east into the central hill country. It provided the setting for some of the most important incidents in the Old Testament.

Map Legend

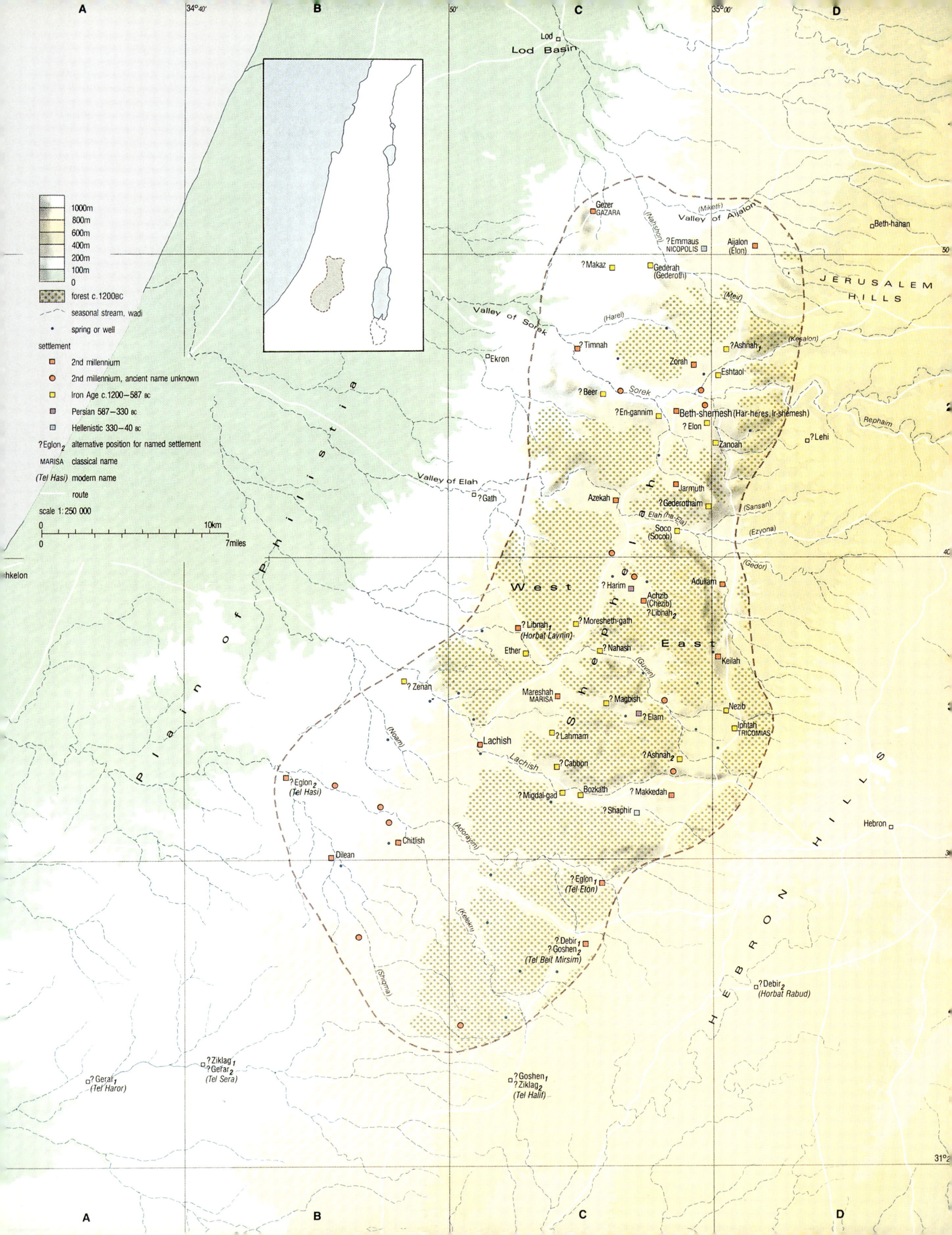

- 1000m / 800m / 600m / 400m / 200m / 100m / 0
- forest c.1200 BC
- seasonal stream, wadi
- spring or well
- settlement
  - ■ 2nd millennium
  - ● 2nd millennium, ancient name unknown
  - ▪ Iron Age c.1200–587 BC
  - ▪ Persian 587–330 BC
  - ▪ Hellenistic 330–40 BC
- ?Eglon₂ alternative position for named settlement
- MARISA classical name
- (Tel Hasi) modern name
- route
- scale 1:250 000
- 0 — 10km / 0 — 7miles

Place Names

Lod
Lod Basin
Gezer / GAZARA
Valley of Aijalon
(Miketh)
(Nahshon)
?Emmaus NICOPOLIS
Aijalon (Elon)
Beth-hanan
?Makaz
Gederah (Gederoth)
Valley of Sorek
JERUSALEM HILLS
(Harel)
(Meiri)
?Timnah
Zorah
?Ashnah₁
(Kesalon)
Ekron
Eshtaol
?Beer
Sorek
?En-gannim
Beth-shemesh (Har-heres, Ir-shemesh)
?Elon
Zanoah
?Lehi
Rephaim
Plain of Philistia
Valley of Elah
?Gath
Azekah
Jarmuth
?Gederothaim
(Sansan)
Elah (ha-Ela)
Soco (Socoh)
(Ezyona)
(Gedor)
West
?Harim
Adullam
Achzib (Chezib)
?Libnah₂
?Libnah₁ (Horbat Lavnin)
Moresheth-gath
Ether
?Nahash
East
Keilah
(Guvrin)
?Zenan
Mareshah MARISA
?Magbish
?Elam
Nezib
Iphtah TRICOMIAS
(Noarn)
Lachish
?Lahmam
?Ashnah₂
Lachish
?Cabbon
?Migdal-gad
Bozkath
?Makkedah
?Shaphir
Hebron
(Adorajim)
?Eglon₁ (Tel Hasi)
Chitlish
Dilean
?Eglon₂ (Tel Eton)
HEBRON HILLS
(Kelah)
?Debir₁
?Goshen₂ (Tel Beit Mirsim)
?Debir₂ (Horbat Rabud)
(Shiqma)
shkelon
?Gerar₁ (Tel Haror)
?Ziklag₁
?Gerar₂ (Tel Sera)
?Goshen₁
?Ziklag₂ (Tel Halif)

250mm (9·8in). This decline in rainfall as one moves to the south is reflected in patterns of settlement, which show a clear preference for the northern section.

The pattern of settlement in the 2nd millennium indicates a line of occupation along the eastern limit of the Shephelah (Adullam, Keilah, Eglon, Debir) and a line along the boundary between the western and eastern sections (Beth-shemesh, Jarmuth, Moresheth-gath, Mareshah, Lachish). There appears to have been little settlement of the eastern Shephelah other than at its eastern and western margins. The exceptions are in major valleys that pierce the hills. It is reasonable to conclude from this that the eastern Shephelah was forested or thickly wooded in the biblical period, on its eastern side with the evergreen oak and its associates, and on its western side with the evergreen carob-lentisk association.

The ancient vegetation of the lower western Shephelah is not known. It contains, in its many valleys, rich soil, and it was extensively cultivated in ancient times. The Old Testament says of Solomon that he made "cedar as plentiful as the sycamore of the Shephelah" (1 Kings 10:27). The sycamore is probably the *Ficus sycomorus* (sycamore fig). In 1 Chronicles 27:28 we read that David put Baal-hanan in charge of the "olive and sycamore trees in the Shephelah". It may well be, then, that parts of the western slopes contained areas of intense cultivation of olives and sycamore figs, and also vineyards (Judges 14:5).

The main routes of the area in biblical times followed the east–west valleys, and the north–south divisions between the eastern margin of the Shephelah and the central hills and the eastern and western Shephelah. Thus, Lachish not only stood on a north–south route running from Beth-shemesh, but at its junction with an east–west route along the Nahal Lachish as far as Hebron. When Samson performed the prodigious feat of carrying the gates of Gaza some 70km (43·5 miles) to Hebron, he most likely took this route (Judges 16:1–3). The strategic position of Lachish, as well as its superb natural site, made it the second most important city in Judah, whose capture by the Assyrian king Sennacherib in 701 BC was commemorated in the famous reliefs now in the British Museum.

The biblical record

The earliest extensive reference to the Shephelah is in Joshua 10. The king of Jerusalem, alarmed that the city of Gibeon has allied itself with the Israelites, calls to his aid the kings of Hebron, Jarmuth, Lachish and Eglon (Joshua 10:3). It is interesting to note the strategic positions of these cities. Hebron controls the route southwards from Jerusalem to the Negev, Lachish and Jarmuth are on the route that divides the eastern from the western Shephelah, while Eglon (if this is the Judean Eglon, Tel Eton(?), as opposed to the Philistine Eglon, Tel Hasi (?)) is on the route that divides the eastern Shephelah from the central hills. Their alliance may well have been part of a treaty of mutual assistance that enabled them to gain revenue from their control of the routes.

In the ensuing battle the five kings were decisively defeated, and Joshua requested God to prolong the daylight so that he could make his victory as complete as possible (Joshua 10:12–14). The defeated enemy fled along the Wadi Miketli (Nahal Beth Horon) into the valley of Aijalon. From there the forces who were probably trying to return to Lachish went along the Nahals Nahshon and Meir into the great valley of the Nahal Sorek at Beth-shemesh, and on to the route that led to Lachish. However, they were battered by a hailstorm all the way to Azekah, which killed more men than had the swords of the Israelites (Joshua 10:11).

With this victory over the kings who controlled the main routes of the area and their armies, Joshua was able to turn his attention to the cities from which the kings had come. After overcoming Libnah (Joshua 10:29–30—if correctly identified with Horbat Lavnin, a city some 7km (4·4 miles) south-southeast of Azekah) Joshua proceeded to Lachish, and overcame this great city in spite of assistance for Lachish from Gezer more than 35km (21·7 miles) to the north (Joshua 10:31–33). Joshua next

A typical landscape in the Shephelah showing broad valleys and gentle hills. Many of Samson's exploits took place in this sort of country.

turned his attention to Eglon (Joshua 10:34–35). If Eglon is correctly identified with Tel Eton, Joshua most likely proceeded southeast along the Nahal Lachish to the route between the eastern Shephelah and the central hills, and then approached Eglon from the east. His flank secured, Joshua was able to move east-northeast against Hebron (Joshua 10:36–37) before "turning back" (Joshua 10:38) to Debir (either Tell Beit Mirsim or Horbat Rabud). The cities of Hebron and Debir are also recorded as having been taken by Caleb (Joshua 15:13–17). This could be the same incident as recorded in Joshua 10:36–39 (in which Joshua overcame Hebron and Debir by setting the Calebites to fight against these cities), or it may imply a later period when Hebron and Debir had been reoccupied. The details are repeated in Judges 1:10–13.

The Shephelah is next mentioned in the story of Samson's struggle with the Philistines. The territory of the tribe of Dan included 17 cities, some of which, if correctly identified (for example Beneberak with Givat ha-Radar, Gath-rimmon with Tel Gerisa (Joshua 19:45)), were on the coast south of where the Nahal Yarkon enters the sea. The others were along the broad valley of the Nahal Sorek or on hills overlooking the valley, and in the "Lod basin". Although this territory makes sense geographically, in practice the Danites were confined to a small area to the west of Beth-shemesh, on the hills overlooking the broad valley of the Nahal Sorek. In this country, at Zorah, Samson was born (Judges 13:2).

The first incident recorded of the adult Samson occurs at Timnah (Judges 14:1) where Samson is attracted to a Philistine woman. This reference to the presence of Philistines in Timnah is significant. It shows that the Philistines had spread up the valley of the Nahal Sorek and were already occupying Danite territory (see Joshua 19:43 for Timnah as a Danite city). Samson's Timnah wife was the woman who enticed from him the secret of the honey in the lion's carcass (Judges 14:5–20). Poor relations between Samson and his Timnah wife's family led to Samson setting fire to the grain crops and the olive orchards in the Timnah area (Judges 15:1–8). Judges 15:9–20 relates a Philistine raid on Judah, in which Samson became involved. The location of the incident, Lehi, is unknown; the incident is important in that it indicates the growing power of the Philistines and the pressure which they exerted on the tribe of Dan. This pressure forced the Danites out of the area allocated to them in Joshua 19:40–46. Judges 18:2 can be taken to mean that Dan was reduced to two cities, Zorah and Eshtaol, before the tribe set out for the far north and established itself near the source of the river Jordan at Laish (Judges 18:27–29). Of the story of Samson and Delilah we are told only that it happened in the "valley of Sorek" (Judges 16:4).

The site of the encounter between David and the Philistine giant Goliath can be established approximately. According to 1 Samuel 17:1, the Philistines encamped between Soco and Azekah at Ephesdammim, a site not identified. However, Soco and Azekah are both on the same side of the Nahal ha-Elah, and it is clear from 17:3 that the contending armies camped on hills on opposite sides of the Nahal ha-Elah, thus making themselves safe from surprise attacks as well as putting themselves in a position from which they could watch the single combat of their champions in the valley below. With the defeat of Goliath, the Israelites pursued the Philistines down the Nahal ha-Elah to Gath and Ekron (17:52).

Cities of the Shephelah are next mentioned in the accounts of David's attempts to escape from Saul when the latter wished to kill him. According to 1 Samuel 22:1, David gathered around him in the "cave of Adullam" a motley group of 400 followers. Adullam was an old Canaanite city (Joshua 12:15) on the route between the eastern Shephelah and the central hills. It was also close to the Nahal ha-Elah, which afforded easy access to both the west and the east. David no doubt chose the spot because it stood at a crossroads, but in country where his band could quickly vanish into the surrounding forests. Towards the end of 2 Samuel (23:13–17) is the account of David sending three warriors from Adullam to Bethlehem, at a time when there was a Philistine garrison in Bethlehem, in order to bring back water from the well. The incident is best dated to the time when David was on the run from Saul, and the Philistines had extended their domination into the heartland of Judah. David's warriors, if they took an obvious route, could have reached Bethlehem easily by going along the Nahal Ezyona and then taking a smaller valley that would bring them close to Bethlehem. However, the obvious route would have been the best guarded, and David's heroes were no doubt masters of the unexpected, who knew the byways far better than the Philistines. On an occasion when the Philistines were plundering in the region of Keilah (1 Samuel 23:2) David went to assist that city. This was a short distance from Adullam along the route separating the eastern Shephelah from the central hills.

There are no important references to the Shephelah after the time of David until the reign of his grandson, Rehoboam (928–911 BC). This king fortified parts of Judah, and so far as this affected the Shephelah his work ranged over names that will by now be familiar: Soco, Adullam, Mareshah, Lachish, Azekah, Zorah and Aijalon (2 Chronicles 11:6–10. Gath is also mentioned, but is in a different position from the other towns named, although its exact location is uncertain). This means that the route dividing the eastern from the western Shephelah became a fortified frontier. However, these preparations did not save Rehoboam from invasion by the Egyptian king Shishak (Shoshenq I, 945–924) in 924 BC. Although 1 Kings 14:25–27 records only Shishak's interest in Jerusalem, Egyptian records suggest that the Pharaoh proceeded up the main south–north route, keeping to the west of Rehoboam's fortified line, and then turned eastwards in a two-pronged attack towards Jerusalem. Shishak probably did not go to Jerusalem itself, but received tribute at Gibeon before turning northwards against fortified cities in Israel.

In the early 8th century (c. 786 BC) a clash between Amaziah, king of Judah, and Joash, king of Israel, occurred in the Shephelah at Beth-shemesh (2 Kings 14:8–14). Amaziah had fought successfully against the Edomites to the southeast of Judah (2 Kings 14:7) and now challenged Joash to a fight for supremacy in the region. Joash warned Amaziah not to be so foolish, in a celebrated fable:

Lachish

"A thistle on Lebanon sent to a cedar on Lebanon, saying, 'Give your daughter to my son for a wife'; and a wild beast of Lebanon passed by and trampled down the thistle" (2 Kings 14:9). Amaziah would not be deterred, and a battle took place at Beth-shemesh.

We may well ask why the Israelite king, whose capital Samaria was to the north of Jerusalem, should fight the Judean king at Beth-shemesh which was west-southwest of Jerusalem. The answer is that the battle was probably fought with horses and chariots, which could be deployed in the broad valley which Beth-shemesh overlooks. The Israelite king would have brought his chariots down the main route running along the foothills of the coastal plain. By assembling his force at Beth-shemesh, he posed a difficult tactical problem for Amaziah. If Amaziah did not engage him at Beth-shemesh, Joash could raid the cities along the route from Beth-shemesh to Lachish. If Amaziah met Joash at Beth-shemesh and lost, Joash could send his forces up the Nahal Refaim to Jerusalem. This is, in fact, what happened. Amaziah was defeated at Beth-shemesh, and Joash proceeded to Jerusalem where he broke down part of the city wall (2 Kings 14:13).

The strategic problem of how to defend the Shephelah against an enemy who approached from the west was to trouble the Jerusalem kings on several occasions. In the reign of Ahaz (c. 743–727 BC) the Philistines raided the Shephelah and took the cities of Beth-shemesh, Aijalon, Gederah, Soco and Timnah (2 Chronicles 28:18). This setback was probably reversed by Ahaz's successor, Hezekiah (c. 727–698 BC), who harried the Philistines as far as Gaza (2 Kings 18:8). However, Hezekiah's success was short-lived. His attack on the Philistines was part of his rebellion against the Assyrians, who had been overlords of the whole area since Ahaz appealed to Tiglath-pileser III for protection (2 Kings 16:7–8). Hezekiah now faced the wrath of Sennacherib.

The Assyrians mounted a two-pronged attack —one against Jerusalem along the central hill country from the north (see Isaiah 10:27b–32), the other down the western side of Judah aimed at Lachish. With the fall of Lachish, represented in the famous reliefs, the way was open for the Assyrian king to take the towns of Mareshah, Moresheth-gath and Adullam, as well as other unidentified towns and villages in the area (Micah 1:10–15). The western route was probably also preferred by Nebuchadnezzar in 587 BC in his second campaign against Jerusalem. Not only do we learn from Jeremiah 34:7 that, apart from Jerusalem, only Azekah and Lachish of the fortified sites remained; letter 4 of the so-called Lachish letters, which were written to Lachish from an unidentified observation point between Azekah and Lachish, chronicles and moment of the fall of Azekah: "We are watching for the [fire or smoke] ... signals of Lachish... for we cannot see Azekah."

After the Babylonian exile (597–540 BC) there remains only one reference in the Old Testament to the Shephelah. Nehemiah 11:29–30 lists Zorah, Jarmuth, Zanoah, Adullam, Lachish and Azekah as villages where the people of Judah lived. In the New Testament the Shephelah is mentioned in Acts 9:35.

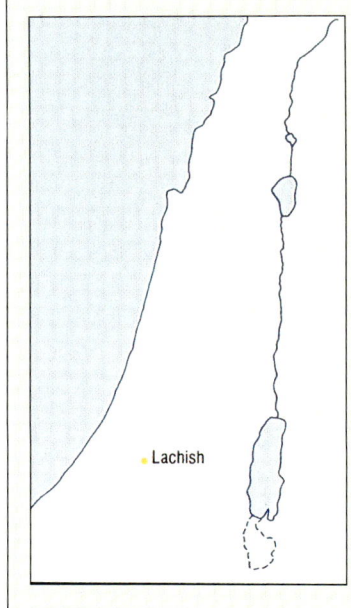

Lachish was the second most important Judean city after Jerusalem. Unlike Hebron, it was never a capital of Judah; but it occupied a strategic position on both north–south and east–west routes. It was first occupied in the latter part of the 3rd millennium BC, and there were many subsequent occupations. Joshua 10:32 claims that Joshua defeated the city. Certainly it became an important fortified Israelite city, whose siege and capture (701 BC) were portrayed in Sennacherib's famous reliefs, which are now in the British Museum. In 587 the city was besieged and captured by the Babylonians, but after the exile Jews returned to live there, and it was also possibly the residence of a Persian administrator for the area. Occupation of the site ceased some time in the 2nd century BC.

Top At the northwest foot of the tell (or mound) are the remains of a temple dating from the period of an Egyptian-dominated city (c. 1450–1250 BC). The ivory duck's head was one of many objects recovered from the temple.

Above Recent excavations at Lachish have included the investigation of the Assyrian ramp built in the siege of 701 BC.

Right This view indicates the size and importance of the tell in relation to the surrounding countryside and its routes. It has commanding views in three directions.

THE SHEPHELAH

Below Pots, lamps, bowls and jars found at Lachish. Other finds here have included an iron fork with three prongs and a 9th-century BC vessel for sacrificial purposes which suggests survival of the Canaanite cult to this late date.

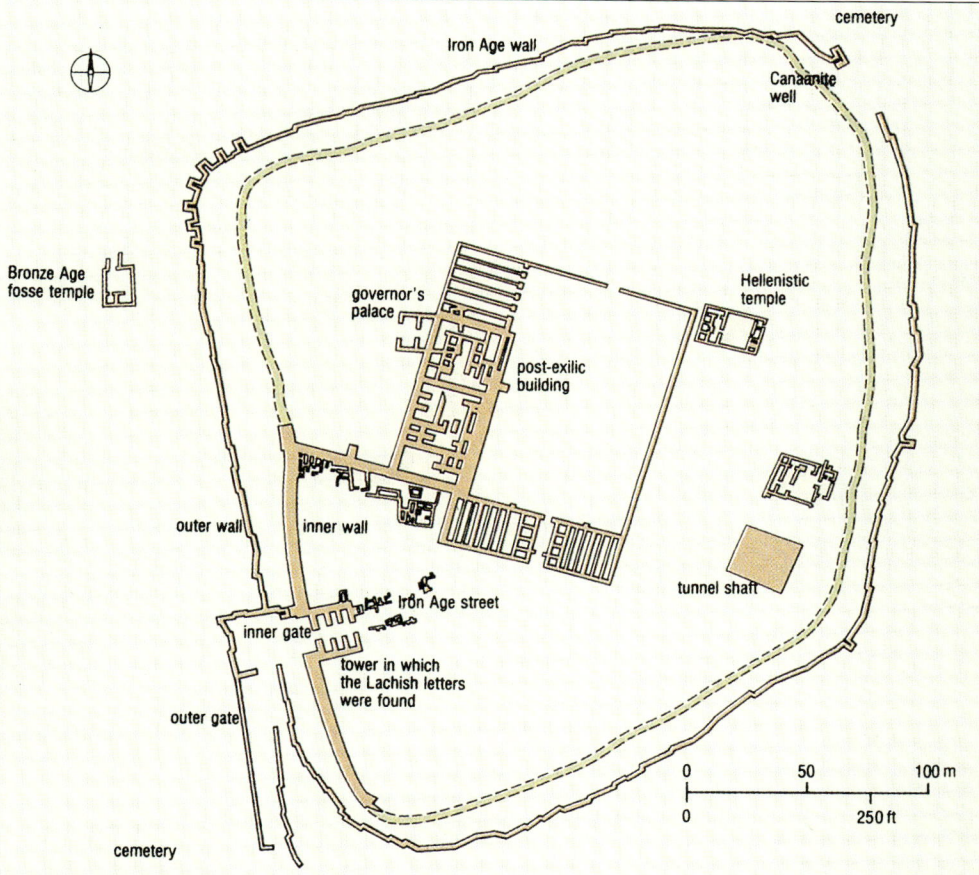

Above The so-called Lachish letters were discovered in the guard room of the entrance to Lachish, in excavations in 1935 and 1938. They were written to the city, probably in 588/7 BC, from an outpost that could see both Lachish and Azekah. The conclusion of letter 4, pictured here, says that the observers can no longer see the (fire) signals of Azekah. Presumably, this was because that city had fallen to the Babylonians.

THE SHEPHELAH

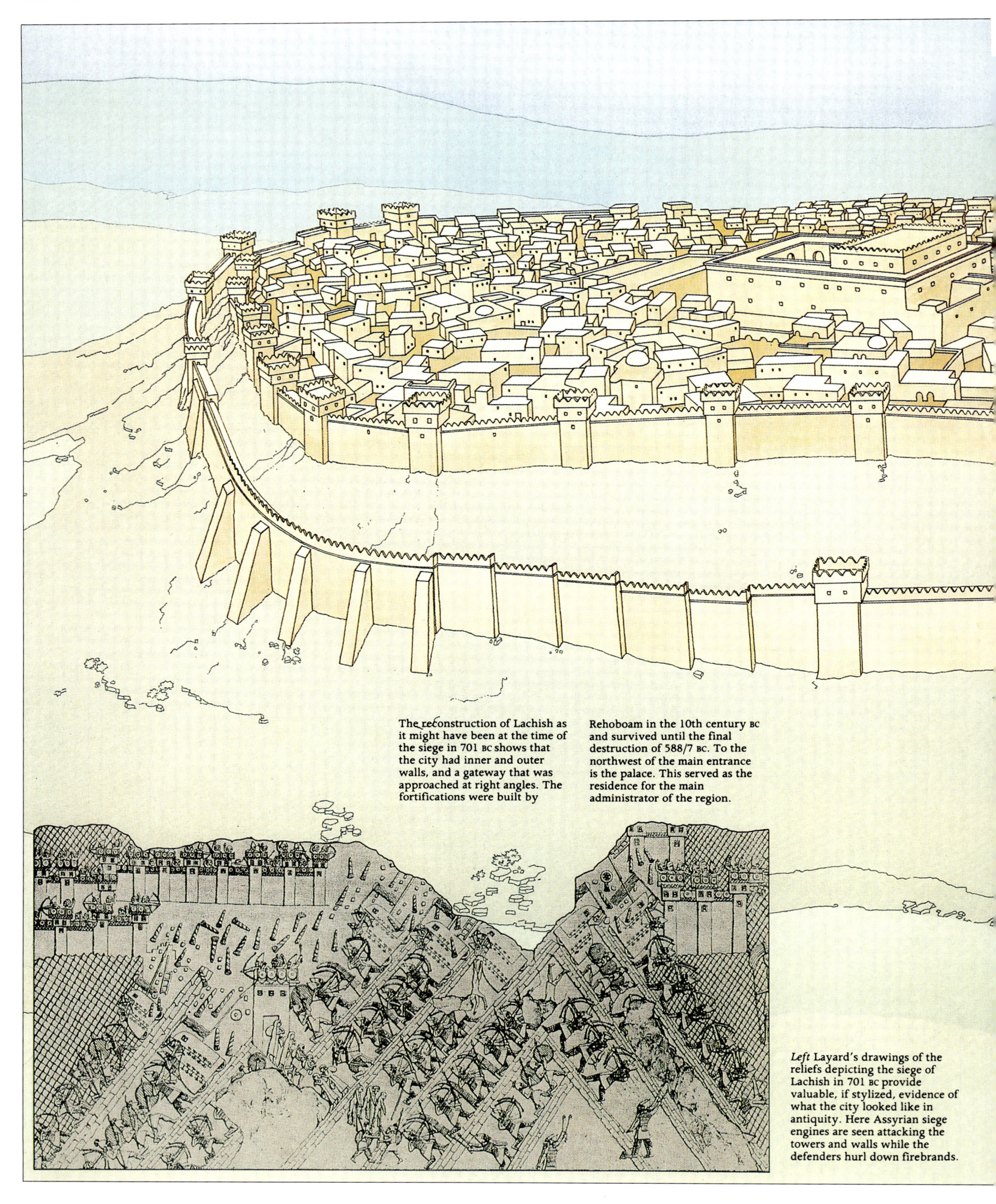

The reconstruction of Lachish as it might have been at the time of the siege in 701 BC shows that the city had inner and outer walls, and a gateway that was approached at right angles. The fortifications were built by Rehoboam in the 10th century BC and survived until the final destruction of 588/7 BC. To the northwest of the main entrance is the palace. This served as the residence for the main administrator of the region.

Left Layard's drawings of the reliefs depicting the siege of Lachish in 701 BC provide valuable, if stylized, evidence of what the city looked like in antiquity. Here Assyrian siege engines are seen attacking the towers and walls while the defenders hurl down firebrands.

THE SHEPHELAH

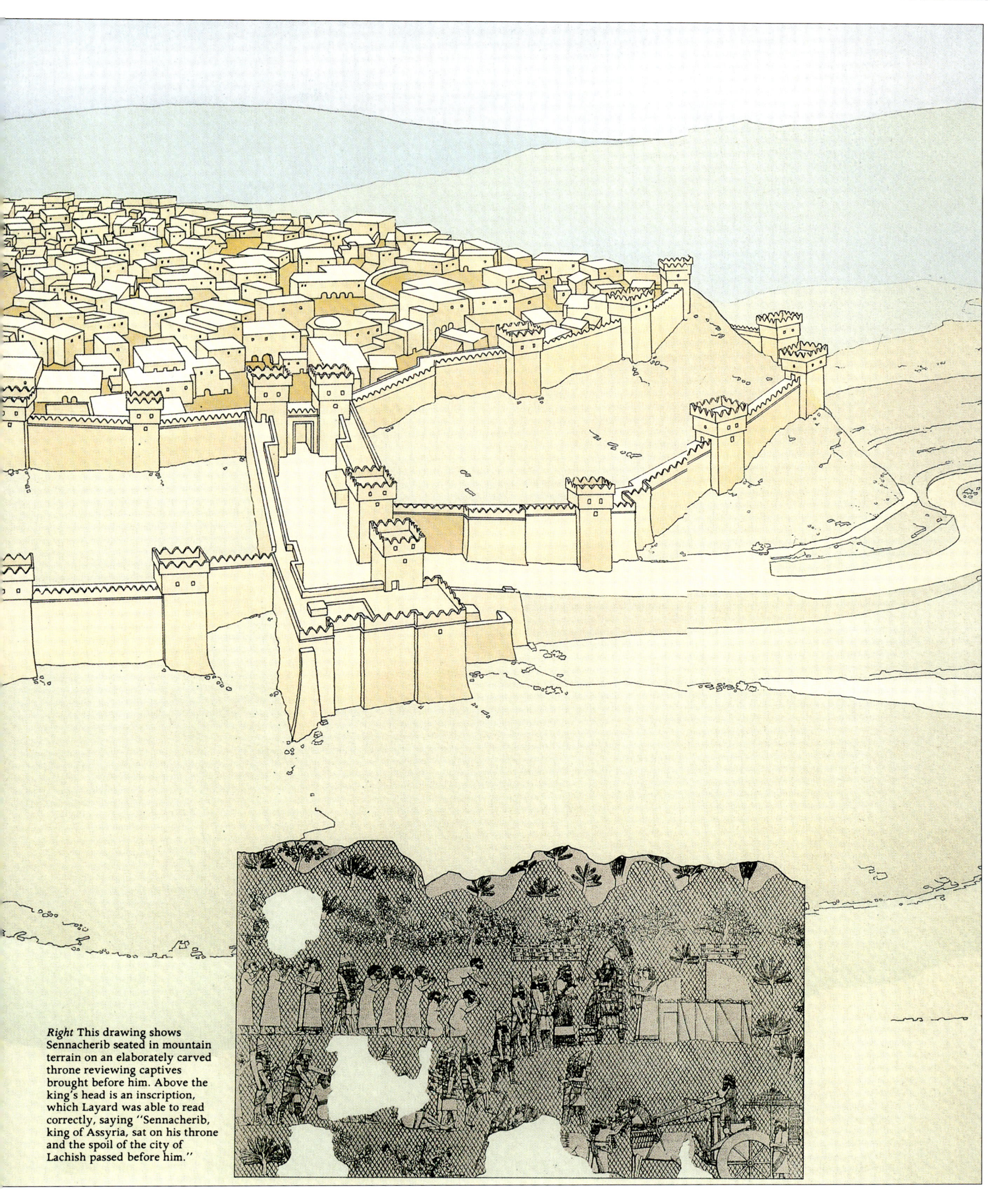

Right This drawing shows Sennacherib seated in mountain terrain on an elaborately carved throne reviewing captives brought before him. Above the king's head is an inscription, which Layard was able to read correctly, saying "Sennacherib, king of Assyria, sat on his throne and the spoil of the city of Lachish passed before him."

Biblical Warfare

Warfare was a prominent, if regrettable, feature of life in biblical times. The book of Joshua ascribes Israel's possession of the land to military conquest, and when Israel was threatened with extermination by the Philistines, it took a great soldier, David, to deliver his people by the art of war. Israel and Judah were constantly threatened by large empires – Egypt, Assyria and Babylon—and by smaller nations such as Syria. At other times the Israelites enlarged their borders by military means. In New Testament times the Jews lived under Roman military occupation, and in 73 and 135 AD Jewish revolts were firmly crushed by the Romans. War was the backcloth against which many people in biblical times lived out their lives, and in the shadow of which they had to try to identify the holy people and the royal priesthood that they believed God had called them to be. The temptation to trust only in the strength of their own arms was often irresistible. The drawings on these pages are all based on Assyrian reliefs depicting the siege of Lachish in 701 BC.

Below The archer was an important figure in ancient warfare, and the quiver contained his deadly ammunition. King Ahab of Israel was killed in battle by an arrow wound (1 Kings 22:34).

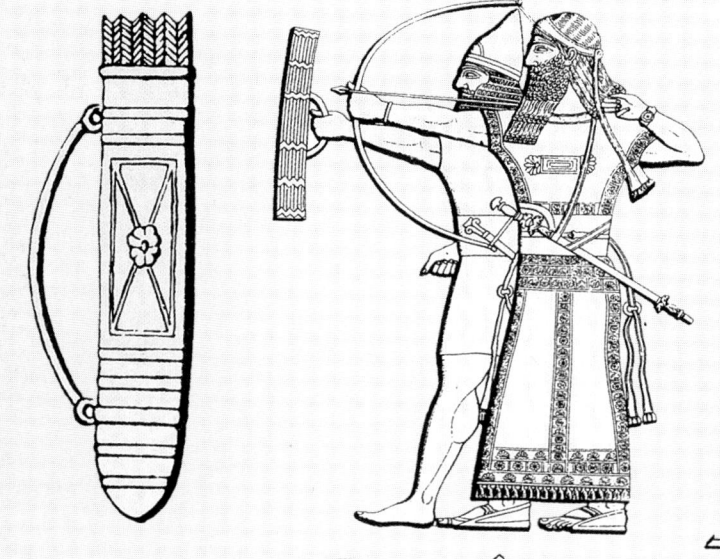

Left When crossing a river, chariots had to be dismantled and transported by boat. Individuals swam with the aid of inflated skin floats.

BIBLICAL WARFARE

Right Individual combat would most likely take place in mopping-up operations, once a city had been broken into or an army's lines in the open field had been breached. Here we see the use of a short sword or dagger.

Below In order to break down the walls of fortified cities, siege engines were developed. They carried battering rams and were constructed so as to protect their operators from the weapons of the defenders. It was also necessary to engage the defenders so as to break their spirit of resistance.

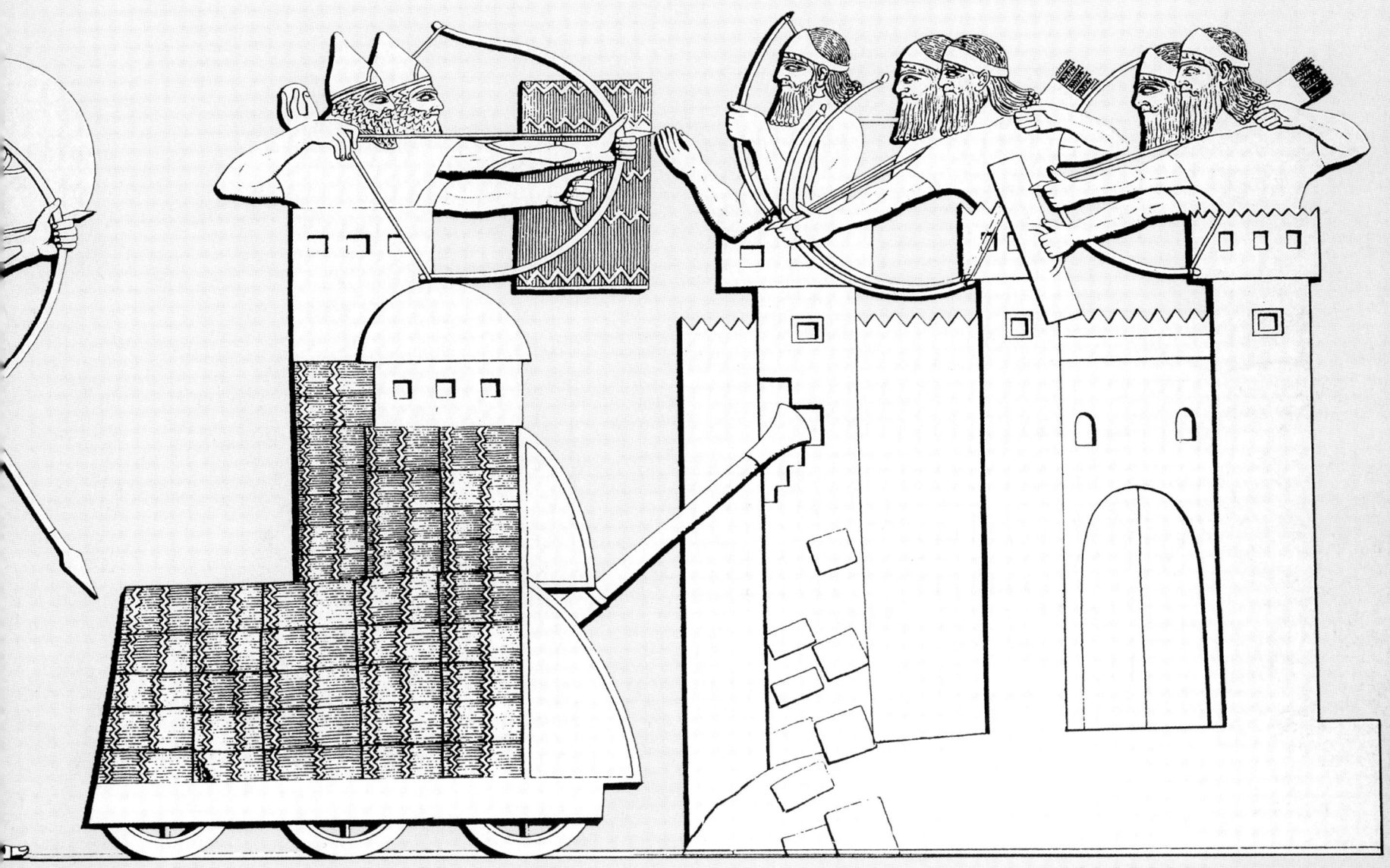

Left The Assyrian army used several techniques when operating in wooded country. Here we see individual scouts and observers as well as troops in line abreast.

Right The cavalry of ancient warfare was composed not of mounted horsemen, but of horse-drawn chariots. These could deploy soldiers rapidly on suitable terrain, and could also accommodate archers.

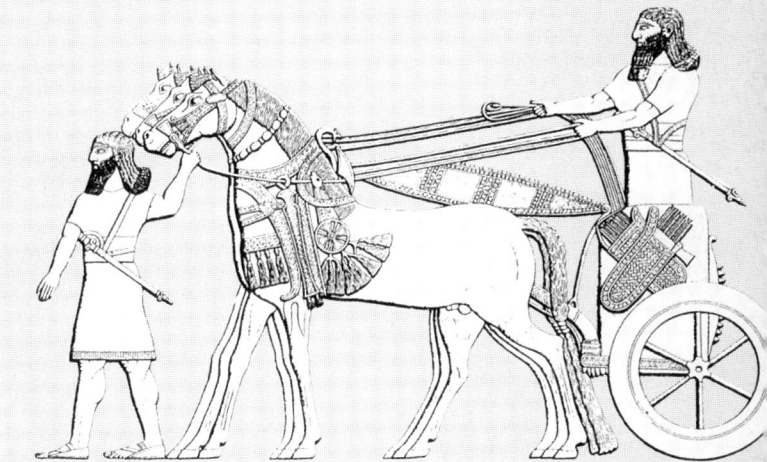

THE HILL COUNTRY OF JUDEA

Above The Judean hills are easily seen to be larger than those of the Shephelah, with the valleys between them very much narrower. In Old Testament times, where there were no settlements, the hills would have been covered with evergreen oak forest.

Description of the region

Geographers divide the Judean hills into three regions—the Hebron hills, which begin at the Nahal Beer Sheva some 40km (25 miles) south of Hebron and extend to just below Bethlehem, the Jerusalem saddle, which goes approximately from Bethlehem to several miles south of Ramallah, and the Bethel hills, which extend as far as the Wadi Sereda. In the present section, only the Hebron hills and Bethlehem will be considered. Jerusalem and the hills to the north are described on pages 162–91.

The Hebron hills are bordered on the west by the valley which separates them from the eastern Shephelah. To the south lie the arid basins of the Jordan valley and the Beer-sheba basin, while to the east the land falls away into the Judean desert and the Jordan valley. However, the geography of the Judean desert is complex (see p.104) and of significance for understanding parts of the Hebron hills and events in the Bible relating to them.

From the point of view of vegetation, the Hebron hills fall into two areas. From Bethlehem to about 10km (6·2 miles) south of Hebron the ancient vegetation probably consisted of evergreen oak forests, possibly with patches of Aleppo pines. To the south of this the ancient vegetation was that of the Mediterranean semisteppe, with shrubs and isolated trees. The average annual rainfall of the Hebron hills, 700mm (28in) at their northern end, diminishes to 450mm (18in) at Hebron itself, and to 300mm (12in) on the hills to Hebron's south.

Note (U) = unlocated site
Adoraim (Adora) 2 Chr. 11:9; 1 Macc. 13:20–22 **C2**
Ain *see* En-rimmon
Ain-rimmon *see* En-rimmon
Anab Josh. 11:21; 15:50 **B3**
Anim Josh. 15:50 **C3**
Aphekah Josh. 15:53 **C2 C3**
Arab Josh. 15:52 **C3**
Atroth-beth-joab 1 Chr. 2:54 (U)
Beth-anoth Josh. 15:59 **C2**
Beth-basi 1 Macc. 9:62,64 **D1**
Beth-ezel Mic. 1:11 **B3**
Bethlehem (Ephrath, Ephrathah) Gen. 35:16,18,19; 48:7; Judg. 12:8,10; Ruth 1:1,2,19,22; 2:4; 4:11; 1 Sam. 16:4; 17:12,15; 20:6,28; 23:14; 1 Chr. 11:16,18; 2 Chr. 11:6; Ezra 2:21; Neh. 7:26; Mic. 5:2; Matt. 2:1,5–6,8,16; Luke 2:4,15; John 7:42 **D1**
Beth-marcaboth *see* Madmannah
Bethsura *see* Beth-zur
Beth-tappuah Josh. 15:53 **C2**
Bethul (Bethuel) Josh. 19:4; 1 Sam. 30:27; 1 Chr. 4:30 **B4 C3**
Beth-zaith (Beth-zita, Bezeth) 1 Macc. 7:19 **C2**
Beth-zechariah 1 Macc. 6:32,33 **C2**
Beth-zita *see* Beth-zaith
Beth-zur (Bethsura) Josh. 15:85; 1 Chr. 2:45; 2 Chr. 11:7; Neh. 3:16; 1 Macc. 4:61; 6:7,31,49; 11:65 **C2**
Bezeth *see* Beth-zaith
Carmel Josh. 15:55; 1 Sam. 15:12, 25:2,5,7,40; 27:3; 30:5; 2 Sam. 2:2; 3:3; 23:35 **C3**
Cozeba 1 Chr. 4:22 **C2**
Dannah Josh. 15:49 **C3**
Debir (Kiriath-sannah, Kiriath-sepher) Josh. 10:38,39; 11:21; 15:7,15–16; 21:15; Judg. 1:11; 1 Chr. 6:58 **B3 C3**
Dumah Josh. 15:52 **B3**
Eltekon Josh. 15:59 (U)
En-rimmon (Ain, Ain-rimmon, Rimmon) Josh. 15:32; 19:7; 1 Chr. 4:32; Neh. 11:29 **B3**
Ephrath, Ephrathah *see* Bethlehem
Eshan Josh. 15:52 **B3**
Eshtemoa Josh. 15:50; 21:14; 1 Sam. 30:28; 1 Chr. 6:57 **C3**
Etam 1 Chr. 4:32; 2 Chr. 11:6 **D1**
Gedor Josh. 15:58 **C2**
Gibe-ah Josh. 15:57 **C1**
Gilo(h) Josh. 15:51; 2 Sam. 15:12; 23:34 (U)
Goshen Josh. 10:41; 11:16; 15:51 **B3**
Gurbaal *see* Jagur
Halhul Josh. 15:58 **C2**
Hebron (Kiriath-arba) Gen. 13:18; 23:2; 35:27; Num. 13:22; Josh. 10:3,5,23,36, 39; 11:21; 12:10; 14:13–15; 15:13,54; 21:13; Judg. 1:10,20; 16:3; 1 Sam. 30:31; 2 Sam. 2:1; 3:11; 15:7–10; 1 Chr. 6:55,57; 11:1,3; 29:27; 2 Chr. 11:10; Neh. 11:25; 1 Macc. 5:65 **C2**
Hereth 1 Sam. 22:5 **C2**
Holon (Hilen) Josh. 15:51; 21:15; 1 Chr. 6:58 **C2**
Horesh 1 Sam. 23:15–19 **C3**
Humtah Josh. 15:54 (U)
Ithnan Josh. 15:23 (U)
Jagur (Gurbaal) Josh. 15:21; 2 Chr. 26:7 **B4**
Janim Josh. 15:53 **C2**
Jattir Josh. 15:48; 21:14; 1 Sam. 30:27; 1 Chr. 6:57 **C3**
Jekabzeel (Kabzeel) Josh. 15:21; 2 Sam. 23:30; 1 Chr. 11:22; Neh. 11:25 **B4**
Jeshua Neh. 11:26 **B4**
Jezreel Josh. 15:56; 1 Sam. 25:43; 27:3; 30:5; 2 Sam. 2:2; 3:2 **C3**
Jokdeam Josh. 15:56 **C3**
Juttah Josh. 15:55; 21:6 **C3**
Kabzeel *see* Jekabzeel
Kain Josh. 15:57 **C3**
Kerioth-hezron Josh. 15:25 **C3**
Kiriath-arba *see* Hebron
Kiriath-sanna *see* Debir
Kiriath-sepher *see* Debir
Maarath (Maroth) Josh. 15:59; Mic. 1:12 **C2**
Madmannah (Beth-marcaboth) Josh. 15:31; 1 Chr. 2:49 **B3**
Mamre (Terebinthus) Gen. 13:18; 14:13; 18:1; 35:27; 49:30; 50:13 **C2**
Maon Josh. 15:55; 1 Sam. 23:24,25; 25:2 **C3**
Maroth *see* Maarath
Nebo Ezra 2:29; Neh. 7:33 **C2**
Netophah 2 Sam. 23:28,29; 2 Kgs. 25:23; 1 Chr. 2:54; 9:16; 11:30; 27:13,15; Neh. 7:26; 12:28; Jer. 40:8; Ezra 2:22 **D1**
Rimmon *see* En-rimmon
Sansannah Josh. 15:31 **B3**
Shamir Josh. 15:48 **B3**
Soco (Socoh) Josh. 15:48 **C3**
Tekoa 2 Sam. 14:2,4,9; 23:26; 1 Chr. 11:28; 27:9; 2 Chr. 11:6; 20:20; Jer. 6:1; Amos 1:1 **D2**
Telem (Telaim) Josh. 15:24; 1 Sam. 15:4 (U)
Zair *see* Zior
Zanoah Josh. 15:56 **C3**
Zior (Zair) Josh. 15:54; 2 Kgs. 8:21 **C2**
Ziph Josh. 15:55; 1 Sam. 23:24; 1 Chr. 4:16; 2 Chr. 11:18 **C3**
Ziph, Wilderness of 1 Sam. 23:14,15; 26:2 **C3**
Zirah 2 Sam. 3:26 (U)

Right That part of the hill country of Judah known as the Hebron hills extends from just south of Bethlehem to 40km (25 miles) beyond Hebron. On the west it is separated from the Shephelah by a series of valleys; on the east it merges into the Judean desert.

Map Legend

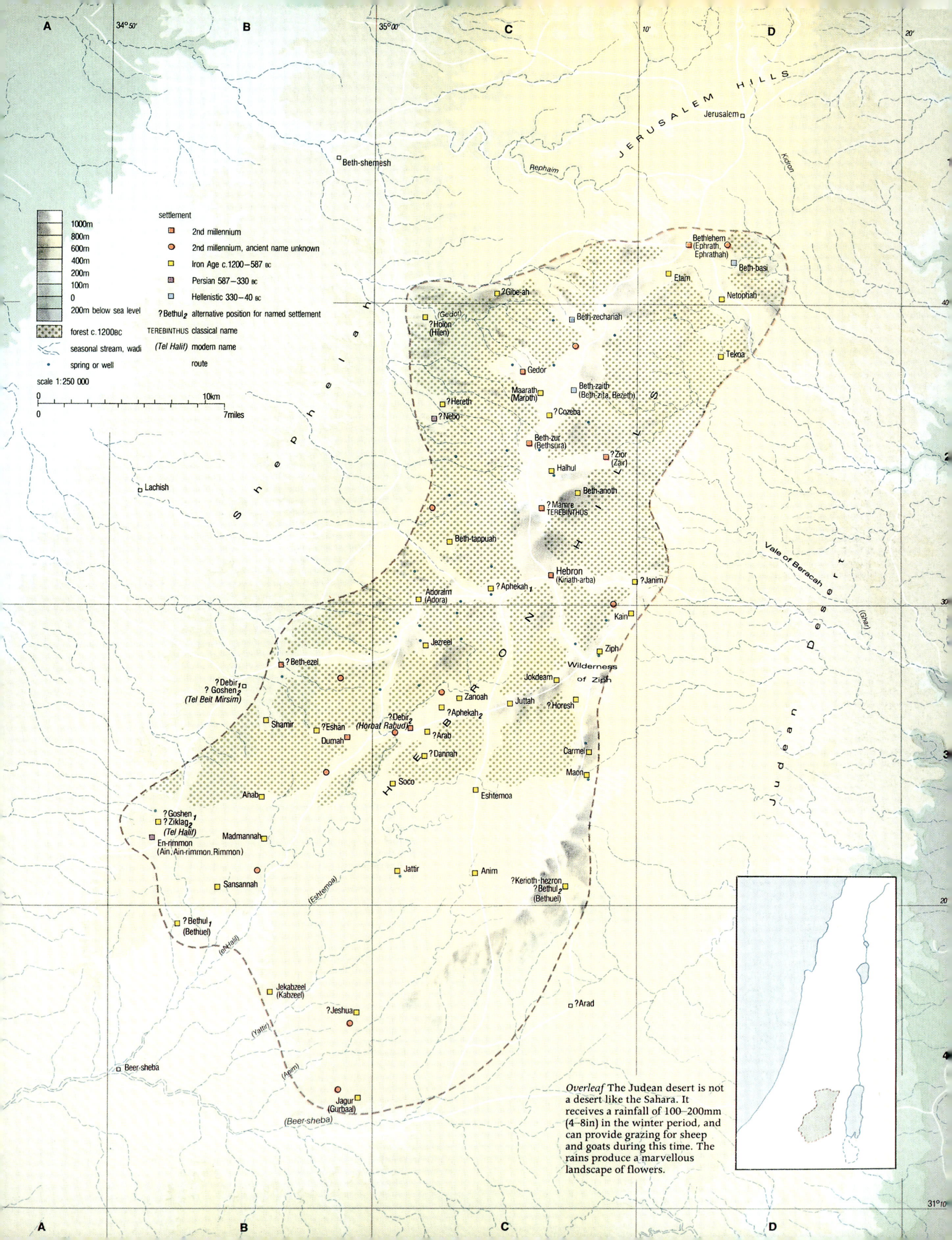

elevation:
- 1000m
- 800m
- 600m
- 400m
- 200m
- 100m
- 0
- 200m below sea level

settlement:
- ▪ 2nd millennium
- ● 2nd millennium, ancient name unknown
- ▫ Iron Age c.1200–587 BC
- ▪ Persian 587–330 BC
- ▫ Hellenistic 330–40 BC
- ?Bethul₂ alternative position for named settlement
- forest c.1200BC
- TEREBINTHUS classical name
- (Tel Halif) modern name
- seasonal stream, wadi
- spring or well
- route

scale 1:250 000
0 — 10km
0 — 7miles

Place names on map

Jerusalem, JERUSALEM HILLS, Rephaim, Kidron, Beth-shemesh, Bethlehem (Ephrath, Ephrathah), Beth-basi, ?Gibeah, Etam, Netophah, (Gedor), ?Holon (Hilen), Beth-zechariah, Tekoa, Gedor, Maarath (Maroth), Beth-zaith (Beth-zita, Bezeth), ?Hereth, ?Cozeba, ?Nebo, Beth-zur (Bethsura), ?Zior (Zair), Halhul, Beth-anoth, ?Mamre TEREBINTHUS, Beth-tappuah, Hebron (Kiriath-arba), Vale of Beracah, Adoraim (Adora), ?Aphekah₁, ?Janim, Kain, Jezreel, Ziph, ?Beth-ezel, Wilderness of Ziph, ?Debir₁, ?Goshen₂ (Tel Beit Mirsim), Zanoah, ?Aphekah₂, Juttah, ?Horesh, Shamir, ?Eshan, Dumah, ?Debir (Horbat Rabud), ?Arab, ?Dannah, Carmel, Maon, Anab, Soco, Eshtemoa, ?Goshen₁, ?Ziklag₁ (Tel Halif), Madmannah, En-rimmon (Ain, Ain-rimmon, Rimmon), Jattir, Anim, ?Kerioth-hezron ?Bethuel (Bethuel), Sansannah, (Eshtemoa), Judean, ?Bethul₁ (Bethuel), (eshHalil), Jekabzeel (Kabzeel), ?Jeshua, ?Arad, Beer-sheba, (Anim), (Yattir), Jagur (Gurbaal), (Beer-sheba), Shephelah, HEBRON HILLS

Overleaf The Judean desert is not a desert like the Sahara. It receives a rainfall of 100–200mm (4–8in) in the winter period, and can provide grazing for sheep and goats during this time. The rains produce a marvellous landscape of flowers.

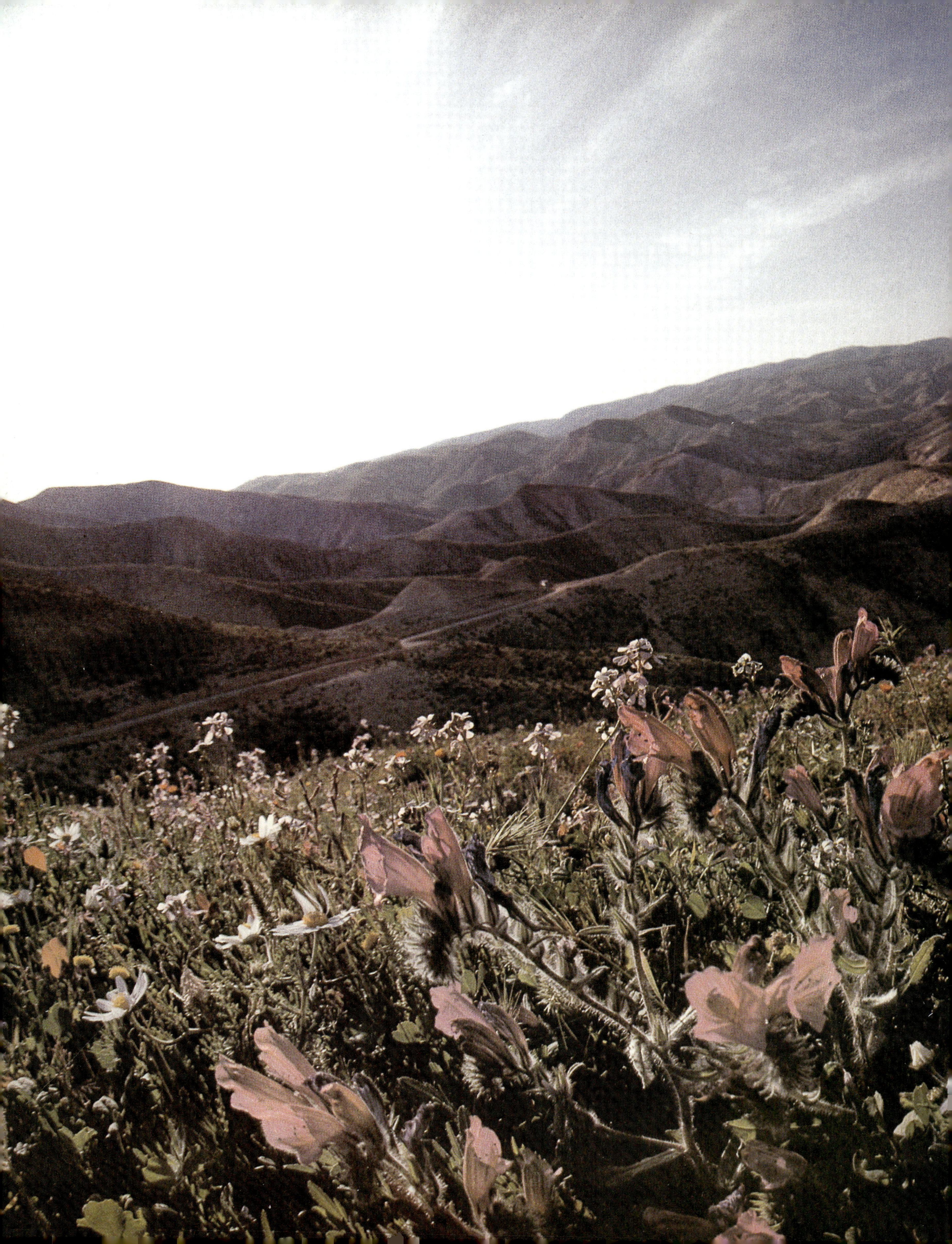

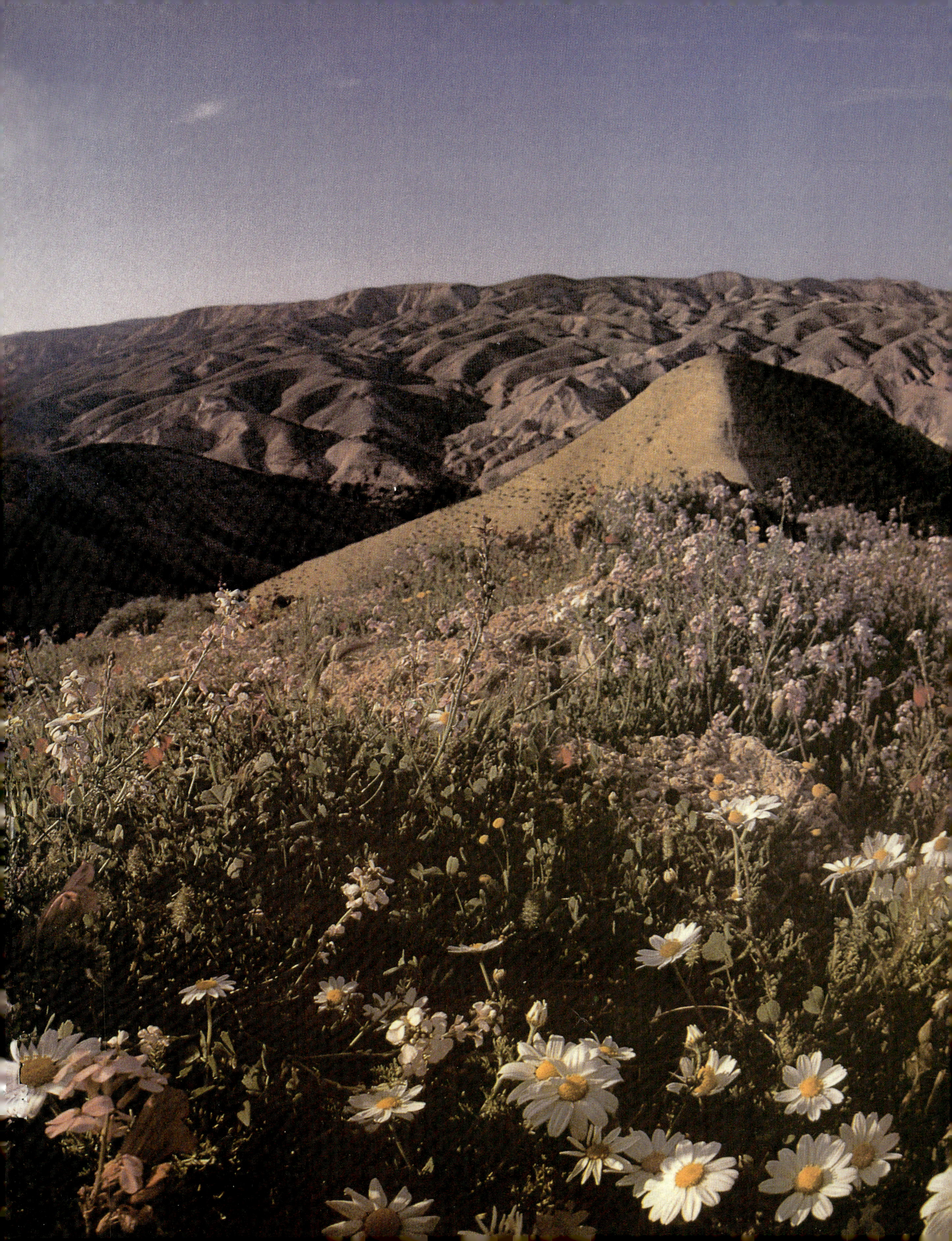

THE HILL COUNTRY OF JUDEA

The patterns of settlement are quite revealing. In the 2nd millennium the settlements were either on the main route from Bethlehem to Beer-sheba via Hebron, or on the western or eastern fringes of the hills. The exceptions, such as Eshtemoa or Anim in the south, were at the heads of valleys. Of the settlements along the main north–south route, all were either where there were springs, or were along the Wadi el-Halil. Additional settlements established by the tribe of Judah, in so far as they can be identified, did not change the picture fundamentally. Probably we should envisage the area in biblical times as forested at least as far as 10km (6·2 miles) south of Hebron. Where there were settlements, the forests would be cleared, and it is likely that the hills were terraced so as to allow the cultivation of vines in particular. The picture of Judah, given in Genesis 49:11, emphasizes its vineyards:

> Binding his foal to the vine
> and his ass's colt to the choice vine,
> he washes his garments in wine
> and his vesture in the blood of grapes;

There is also the tradition that the spies who spied out the land brought back a cluster of grapes from the Hebron region (Numbers 13:21–24).

In addition to its agriculture, Judah depended upon the rearing of sheep. Amos, whose home village was Tekoa on the eastern fringe of the hills several miles south of Bethlehem, is described as a shepherd (and a tender of sycamore figs, Amos 7:14); and in 1 Samuel 25 we read of the rich man Nabal (if that was his real name—the Hebrew means "fool", and that is how Nabal behaved, see 1 Samuel 25:25) who possessed 3000 sheep and 1000 goats. Nabal came from Maon and operated his sheep business in Carmel, southeast of Hebron on the eastern fringe of the hills. Sheep husbandry on the eastern fringes of the Hebron hills was made possible by the way in which the Judean desert moves down to the Dead Sea in a series of steps, providing rough terraces. It is possible, depending on rainfall, to graze flocks on the lower steps in winter, moving to the higher ones (which have a higher rainfall) as summer approaches. In the story of Joseph (Genesis 37:12–17), Jacob's sons had taken the flocks from Hebron all the way to Shechem (a distance of 75km (46·6 miles) as the crow flies) and then from Shechem to Dothan (another 35km (21·7 miles)). Presumably the rainfall had made it impossible to graze the flocks in the Judean desert east of Hebron, and the brothers had been forced to go to the generally more fertile northern hills. Lack of rainfall may explain why the pit in which Joseph was put by his brothers was dry (Genesis 37:24).

Because the Hebron hills form a continuous and self-contained area, it is easy to understand why they were the domain of one tribe—Judah—whereas the northern territories were divided among numerous tribes. In the same way we can understand why Judah (together with Benjamin, who shared with Judah the "Jerusalem saddle") remained a separate entity when the united kingdom split into the two kingdoms of Judah and Israel.

That Hebron should be capital of this area was a natural consequence of its position. The town stands in a small vale, and is at a sort of crossroads. It commands the north–south route from Jerusalem to Beer-sheba, and to the west has easy access to the Shephelah and coastal plain via the Nahal Lachish. On the eastern side, small wadis which link with the Wadi el-Ghar lead into the Judean desert and ultimately to the Dead Sea coast at En-gedi.

The biblical record

It was at Hebron that Abraham established himself after he had returned from Egypt, and had divided the land between himself and Lot (Genesis 13:18, and verses 8–10). It was also here that Abraham mounted his expedition against the four kings (Genesis 14:1, 13), received the three mysterious visitors who promised him the birth of a son, and pleaded with God not to destroy Sodom and Gomorrah (Genesis 18:1–15, 22–33). Sarah, Abraham's wife, died at Hebron, and Abraham purchased a cave for her burial in the vicinity from Ephron (Genesis 23:1–20). This was to become the

Right In the 2nd century BC the site of the cave of Machpelah, which Abraham had purchased as his burial place, and where he and other Patriarchs were buried, was located in Hebron. Herod the Great enclosed it, and laid the foundations for the massive buildings that today cover the site. The objects in the foreground are a reminder that the manufacture of glassware is a feature of Hebron.

Near Hebron both ploughing *(left)* and domestic architecture *(below left)* still follow traditional lines.

burial place of Abraham himself (Genesis 25:7–10), and later of Isaac (Genesis 35:27–29) and Jacob (Genesis 49:29–33). Hebron also seems to have become Jacob's main place of residence after the death of Isaac, the place from which he sent Joseph to follow his brothers (Genesis 37:14), and where he dwelt when Joseph's brothers went to Egypt to buy grain during the famine (Genesis 42–44), although in the Joseph story Jacob's residence is usually described as "the land of Canaan" (for example Genesis 42:29).

We next hear of Hebron during the wilderness wanderings when the spies came to Hebron and brought back from the area a cluster of grapes (Numbers 13:21–24). In the account of the Israelite conquest the king of Hebron was one of the four kings who joined with the king of Jerusalem in opposing Joshua (Joshua 10:3–5. As has been pointed out above (p.87), the triple account of the conquest of Hebron by Joshua (Joshua 10:36–37) and by Caleb (Joshua 15:14 and Judges 1:9–10) may be varying descriptions of the same event. In Joshua 21:12 we are told that Hebron "and its villages" were given to Caleb. The mention of villages is interesting in the light of Y. Karmon's description of the ordering of economic life in that region. He indicates that because only large villages in easily defended positions could offer security, and because the unproductive nature of large parts of the land meant that cultivation had to be spread over a wide area, large settlements were surrounded by a considerable number of temporary or seasonal settlements. This observation throws light on the mention of Hebron's "villages" in Joshua 21:12, and has implications for social organization.

After the Philistines had defeated and killed Saul (1 Samuel 31), and while David was still a Philistine vassal, he moved to Hebron, where he was anointed king over Judah (2 Samuel 2:1–4). From Hebron he sent out his forces, presumably with Philistine approval, to fight against the remnants of Saul's army led by Abner (2 Samuel 2:8ff.). Abner himself was killed treacherously by Jaob at Hebron, in satisfaction of a blood feud between them (2 Samuel 2:18–23, 3:22–30). The death of Abner hastened the collapse of the support of the northern tribes for the house of Saul, and the

Bethlehem

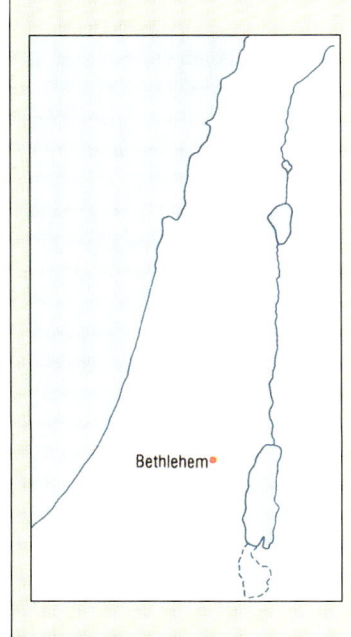

Although Bethlehem was not in itself an important place in biblical times, it owes its fame to its associations with David and with the birth of Jesus. The village is on the western edge of the Judean wilderness, and in all ages it has been a place of welcome for people coming from the wilderness. The story of Ruth (Ruth 1:1), however, indicates that Bethlehem itself could suffer from lack of water if the rains failed. The books of Ruth and I Samuel contain evidence of the mixed pastoral and agricultural economy of ancient Bethlehem: Ruth gleaning grain after the harvesters in the fields of Boaz (Ruth 2) and her great-grandson David minding his father's sheep (1 Samuel 16:11). Although David spent most of his adult life in Hebron and Jerusalem, his association with Bethlehem through his birth gave rise to a prophetic hope that a future ruler would be born there (Micah 5:2). That hope was taken up in the New Testament tradition of the birth of Jesus at Bethlehem, although he too spent not only the bulk of his adult life elsewhere, but all of his childhood also. Nonetheless, Bethlehem soon featured on pilgrims' itineraries, with the basilica founded in 330 by the emperor Constantine as the focal point for their visit.

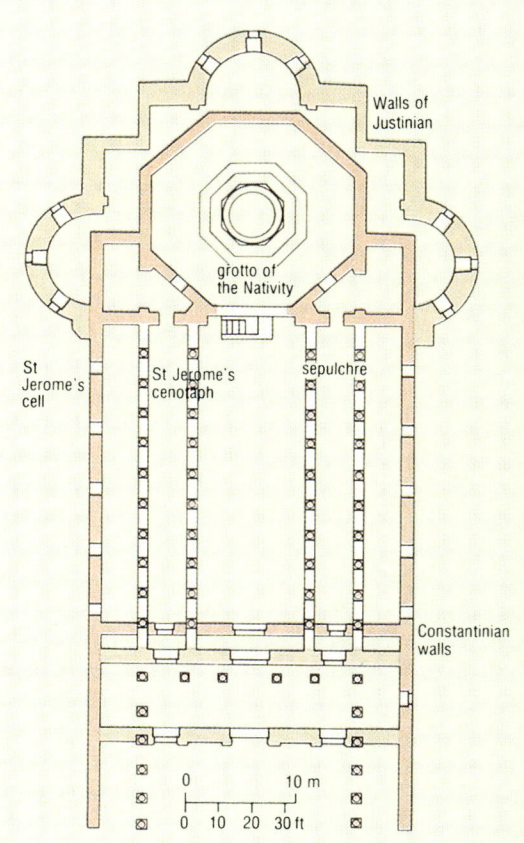

Above The present church of the Nativity, built over the 4th-century church of which there are considerable remains, dates from the 6th century. Its single low entrance requires all who enter to bend or stoop.

Right Holman Hunt's 19th-century view of Bethlehem from the north shows the village dominated by the convents that flank the church of the Nativity which contains the traditional birthplace of Jesus. Today the fields in the foreground have been mostly built upon.

THE HILL COUNTRY OF JUDEA

Right Bethlehem is seen framed against the hills of the wilderness of Judea.

Above A typical scene in the heart of Bethlehem today, with high stone walls, narrow streets and arches.

Left Ground plan of the church of the Nativity.

THE HILL COUNTRY OF JUDEA

elders of Israel came to Hebron to appoint David king over Israel as well as Judah (2 Samuel 5:1–5). According to 2 Samuel 5:5, David spent seven and a half years as king in Hebron. However, the assumption of authority over north and south necessitated a new headquarters. Hebron was too far to the south for sovereignty to be exercised over the northern tribes, and accordingly David conquered Jerusalem and it became the capital, not only of the united kingdom, but of Judah also, after the kingdom divided at the death of Solomon (2 Samuel 5:6–10).

With the transfer of authority from Hebron to Jerusalem, the city all but disappears from the biblical record. The exception is the revolt of David's son Absalom, related in 2 Samuel 15:1–12. By choosing Hebron as the city in which to raise the standard of revolt, Absalom was no doubt appealing powerfully to sentiment. The citizens of Hebron would approve the restoration to their city of the prestige that Jerusalem had stolen, while others would think fondly of the supposedly better days when David ruled the north and the south from Hebron, and before he conquered adjacent countries with all the social and economic ramifications that this created for the ordinary citizens of Judah and the north.

When Judah succumbed to the might of Babylon in 587, it is likely that the southern part of the Hebron hills, including Hebron, was given over to the Edomites. Although some Jews settled in Hebron after the exile (Nehemiah 11:25 gives Hebron its ancient name of Kiriath-arba), the city belonged to the province of Idumea during the Maccabean period, when Judas Maccabeus attacked it in 163 BC, demolishing its fortifications and burning down its forts on all sides (1 Maccabees 5:65). In 125 BC John Hyrcanus restored to the Jewish kingdom the southern part of the Hebron hills, forcing the inhabitants to become Jews. Herod the Great in 20 BC enclosed the traditional site of the burial of the Patriarchs in Hebron. The city is not mentioned in the New Testament.

Left The citadel of Herodium, built by Herod the Great 12km (7·5 miles) from Jerusalem and clearly visible from there, was the focal point of a large settlement. The aerial photograph (*above*) shows the four towers. After his death in 4 BC Herod is thought to have been buried in the north tower (to the right in the picture) which is still unexcavated.

From the point of view of the text of the Bible, the next most famous town in Judea after Hebron was Bethlehem (see p.100). It was never a large settlement, possibly because water was not abundantly provided by springs in the vicinity. Its two main means of livelihood were sheep and grain; yet the story of Ruth envisages a situation in which famine had so affected Bethlehem that Elimelech and Naomi left the village in order to travel to Moab. Bethlehem's most famous son in the Old Testament, David, had encountered both lions and bears while tending his father's flocks (1 Samuel 17:34–36), and we can presume that these animals lived in the forests of the Hebron hills or the caves of the Judean desert. It was in Bethlehem that David was anointed by Samuel (1 Samuel 16:1–13) and from there that he evacuated his parents to Moab while he was on the run from Saul (1 Samuel 22:3–4). After the stories of David, Bethlehem is mentioned in the Old Testament only as a town fortified by Rehoboam (2 Chronicles 11:6), and as the town from which

shall come forth for me
one who is to be ruler in Israel (Micah 5:2).

In the New Testament Bethlehem is famous as the town where Jesus was born (Matthew 2:1, Luke 2:4–7), and to which the wise men journeyed to worship the newly born king (Matthew 2:2–6). Here also male children aged two and under were massacred at the orders of King Herod in his vain attempt to eliminate the newly born king (Matthew 2:16).

Of the remainder of the Hebron hills, it has been noted above that Tekoa was the home of the prophet Amos, and that while he led a marauding band, David had dealings with a wealthy sheep owner in the Maon-Carmel area (1 Samuel 25:2–42). There are also references in the story of David to Ziph and to the wilderness of Ziph (1 Samuel 23:15ff., 26:1ff.). Ziph has been identified as Tell Ziph to the southeast of Hebron, and David seems to have hidden there from Saul at a place called Horesh in the wilderness of Ziph (1 Samuel 23:15–18). Here David and Jonathan made a covenant together. It is not certain whether the name "Horesh" should be taken in its usual sense of "forest". If it meant "forest", then David and his band lived in the forest near Ziph.

The inhabitants of Ziph clearly disliked David's presence. If David behaved towards the Ziphites in the way that he acted towards Nabal (1 Samuel 25:5–8), demanding contributions for his men's rations, it is understandable that the Ziphites tired of David and betrayed him to Saul. On the first occasion that David was betrayed, Saul almost caught him, and David was saved only when news of a Philistine raid forced Saul to call off the pursuit (1 Samuel 23:24–29). On the second occasion (1 Samuel 26:1–25), David gained the advantage over Saul. Accompanied by Abishai, David penetrated the camp of his weary pursuers and had it in his power to kill the man whose suspicion and jealousy would ultimately force David to flee to the Philistines for protection. However, David would not take advantage of the situation, and instead berated Saul's guards for not having protected their king against the man whose life Saul sought.

THE JUDEAN DESERT

Left Bedouin in the Judean desert. The word "desert" is to some extent a misnomer since at certain times of the year the terrain is suitable for grazing sheep.

Below The weird-looking scenery of the Judean desert has been caused by the erosion of rocks by the winter rains. In summer the rocks are mostly bare; in winter they can be covered with flowers.

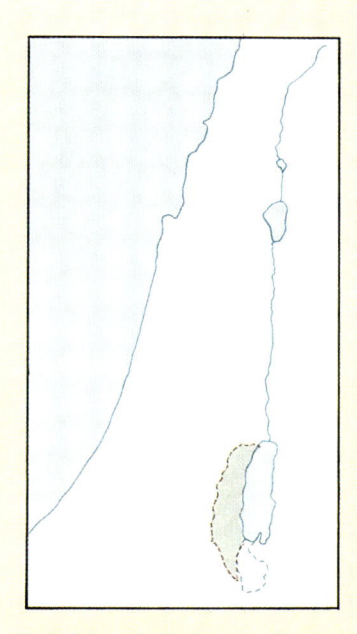

Beracah, vale of 2 Chr. 20:26 **B2 B3**
Beth-arabah Josh. 15:6,61; 18:18,22 **D1**
City of Salt Josh. 15:62 **C1 C2**
En-eglaim Ezek. 47:10 **C1**
En-gedi (Hazazon-tamar) Gen. 14:7; Josh. 15:62; 1 Sam. 23:29; 24:1; 2 Chr. 20:2; S. of S. 1:14; Ezek. 47:10 **C3**
Judah, Wilderness of Josh. 15:61–63; Matt. 3:1 **B2 B3**
Middin Josh. 15:61 **C1**
Nibshan Josh. 15:62 **C1 C2**
Secacah Josh. 15:61 **C1**

Description of the region

The Judean desert is the area from the eastern edge of the Judean hills (that is the Hebron hills, the Jerusalem saddle and the Bethel hills) to the Dead Sea and Jordan valley. In the present section, only that portion which goes to the Dead Sea from Bethlehem southwards will be considered (for the other areas see pp.184 and 194). At the outset it must be stated that "desert" is a misleading word if it carries with it ideas of deserts such as the Sahara, with miles of sand stretching as far as the horizon. It is true that the Judean desert contains semi-arid areas, especially in the regions closest to the Dead Sea. Much of the Judean desert, however, is suitable for grazing sheep at certain times of the year.

At its western edge the Judean desert is 800 to 1000m (2625 to 3280ft) above sea level, from which heights it sinks to 400m (1312ft) *below* sea level in the space of about 20km (12·4 miles). Rainfall diminishes from an average of 700mm (28in) at the western edge to 150mm (6in) at the Dead Sea coast. The descent from west to east is in a series of steps, each of which ends in a fairly level plateau of some 2 to 3km (1·2 to 1·9 miles) in width. At the shore of the Dead Sea are cliffs of some 100 to 200m (328 to 656ft) in height, which at some points reach almost to the waterline. These cliffs, which form the base of the lowest step, are barren, and are in places intersected by canyons which bring the rains east of the watershed into the Dead Sea.

Overleaf This spectacular view of a storm over the Judean desert indicates that rainfall can be heavy when it occurs and can result in flooding. In late Hellenistic and Herodian times, channels and cisterns to trap flood water were built at such places as Qumran and Masada.

1000m
800m
600m
400m
200m
100m
0
200m below sea level

seasonal stream, wadi
• spring or well

settlement
▢ Iron Age c.1200–587 BC
▢ Hellenistic 330–40 BC

?Middin₂ alternative position for named settlement
(Qumran) modern name
route

scale 1:250 000
0   10km
0 7miles

Right The region shown here at its western edge is 800 to 1000m (2625 to 3280ft) above sea level. Where it reaches the Dead Sea it is 400m (1312ft) *below* sea level. It is a semi-arid region, but in winter is able to provide grazing for sheep and goats. Where there were springs, especially on the shore of the Dead Sea, settlement was possible in ancient times.

JERUSALEM HILLS
Jerusalem
Kidron
Bethlehem
Valley of Achor
?Middin₁ ?Middin₃
?City of Salt₁
?Secacah₂ (Qumran)
?Secacah₁ ?Secacah₃
En-eglaim
?Nibshan₁
?Nibshan₃
?Middin₂
Beth-arabah (Rujm et-Bahr)
Jordan

Wilderness of Jeruel

?Nibshan₂ (Ein el-Ghuweir)
?City of Salt₂ (Ein et-Turaba)

(el-Murabba'at)
Ascent of Ziz (Hasasa)

HEBRON HILLS
Hebron
Vale of Beracah

DEAD SEA
SALT SEA
SEA OF THE ARABAH

(Ghar)
(David)
En-gedi (?Hazazon-tamar)

Wilderness of Judah

Masada

?Arad

modern coastline

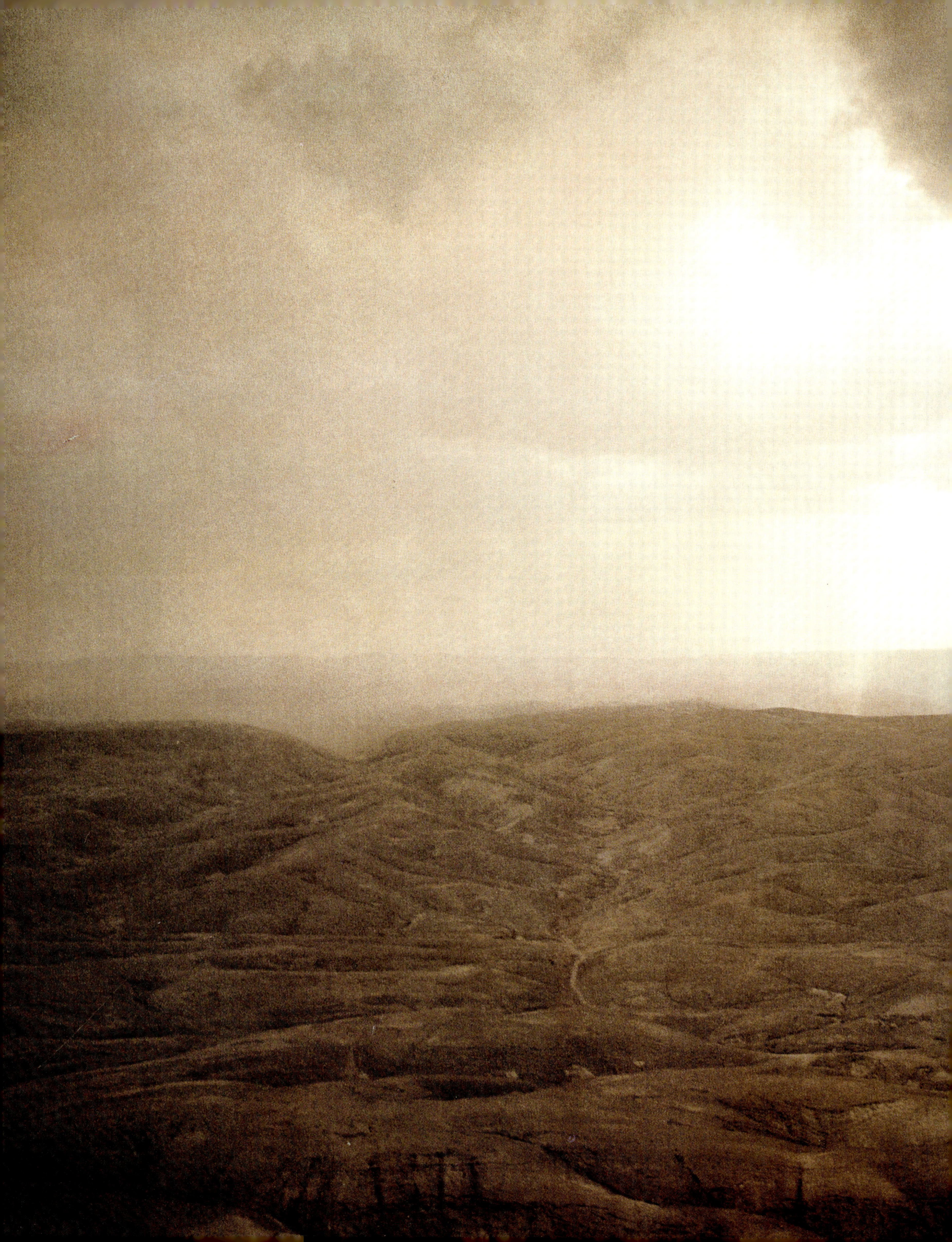

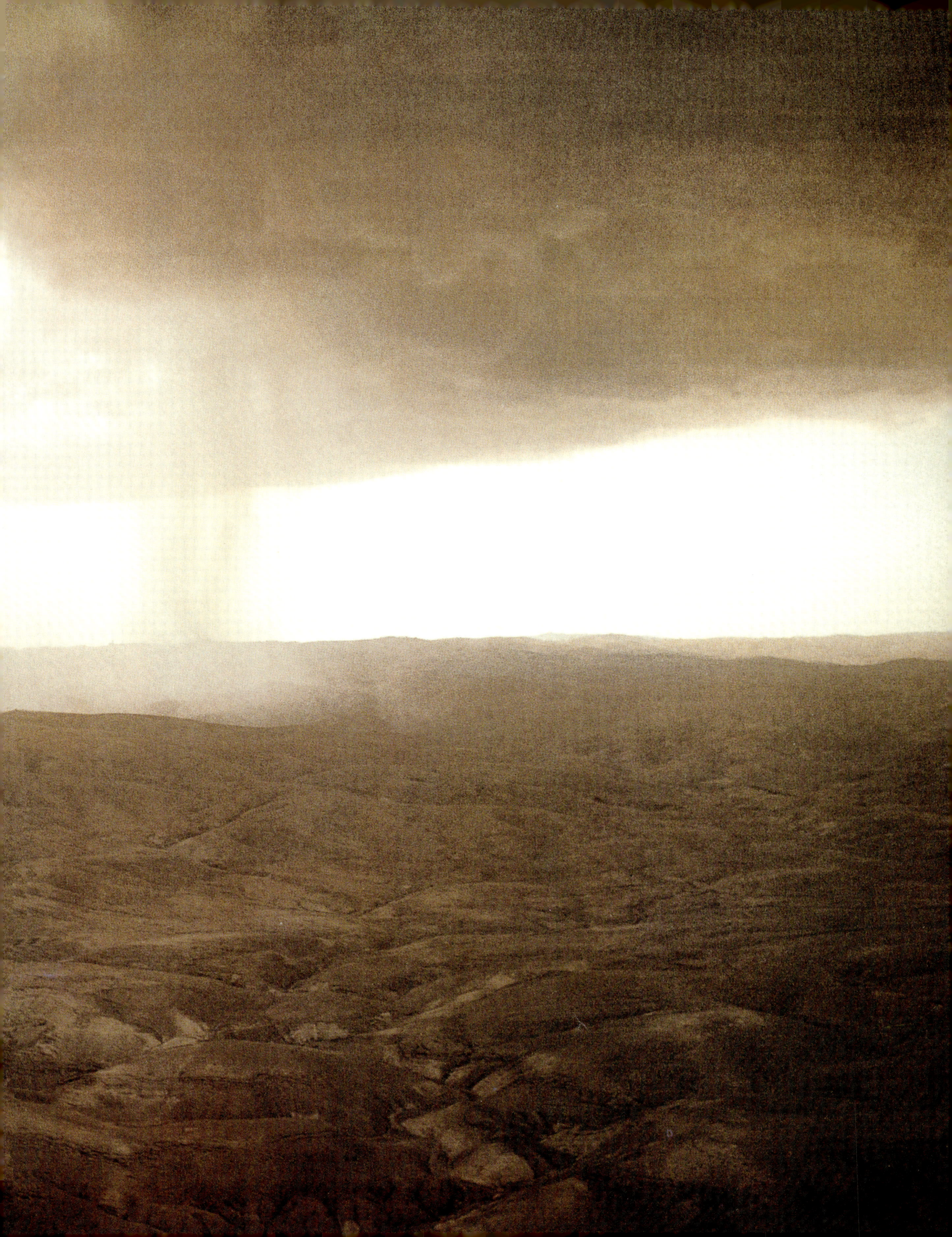

Depending on the annual rainfall, flocks can be grazed in winter first on the lower slopes, then on the higher.

In the 2nd millennium there do not appear to have been any settlements in this region, in spite of the promising conditions at En-gedi and the fact that there was a temple there in the 4th millennium BC. Joshua 15:61 allocates to Judah six cities and their villages in the Judean desert, of which En-gedi can be identified with confidence, and the remainder with a slightly lesser degree of certainty (see p.112 below).

En-gedi (Tell Goren), at the foot of the Nahal David, is situated in an oasis watered by several springs. G. A. Smith's language abounds with superlatives as he contrasts "one of the driest and most poisoned regions of our planet" with the oasis as he approached it, riding down the slopes of the Judean desert towards the Dead Sea: suddenly, over the edge of a precipice, 400 feet below him he sees "a river of verdure burst from the rock, and scatter, reeds, bush, trees, and grass, down other 300 feet to a mile of gardens by the beach of the blue sea." In the Old Testament En-gedi was famed for its palm trees (which is the point of the identification of Hazazon-tamar (Hazazon of the palms) with En-gedi in 2 Chronicles 20:2), and for its henna blossom and vineyards (Song of Solomon 1:14).

The biblical record

While David was on the run from Saul, he sought refuge in the "strongholds of En-gedi" and in the "wilderness of En-gedi" (1 Samuel 23:29, 24:1). Presumably we are to understand by "strongholds" the sort of cave into which Saul went to relieve himself, and in the innermost parts of which David and his men were hiding (1 Samuel 24:3). This incident, in which David crept up on Saul from the depths of a cave and cut off a piece of his robe while Saul was relieving himself, was the first occasion on which David spared Saul when he could easily have killed him (1 Samuel) 24:1–7). The mention of the sheepfolds in verse 3 indicates that during the winter shepherds grazing their flocks on the lower steps of the Judean desert would come down at night to the warmer temperatures of the En-gedi area, and would quarter the flocks in sheepfolds whose walls were of rough stones.

To the south of En-gedi along the Dead Sea coast is the famous fortress of Masada. This remarkable site is an isolated plateau some 410m (1345ft) above the Dead Sea with steep slopes on every side. The plateau itself is about 600m (656yds) long and 320m (350yds) wide at its longest and widest. It is therefore virtually impregnable to attack, but highly vulnerable to siege, possessing no natural water supply.

Masada is not explicitly mentioned in the Bible, but it is worth considering whether it was visited by David during his flights from Saul. The Hebrew name *Mesada* means "stronghold", and although the earliest reference to Masada by this name occurs in about 50 BC, it is quite likely that anyone hiding in the Judean desert in ancient times who came across Masada would call it *Mesada*—a stronghold. In the story of David's flights from Saul the Hebrew words *Mesad* and *Mesuda*, both

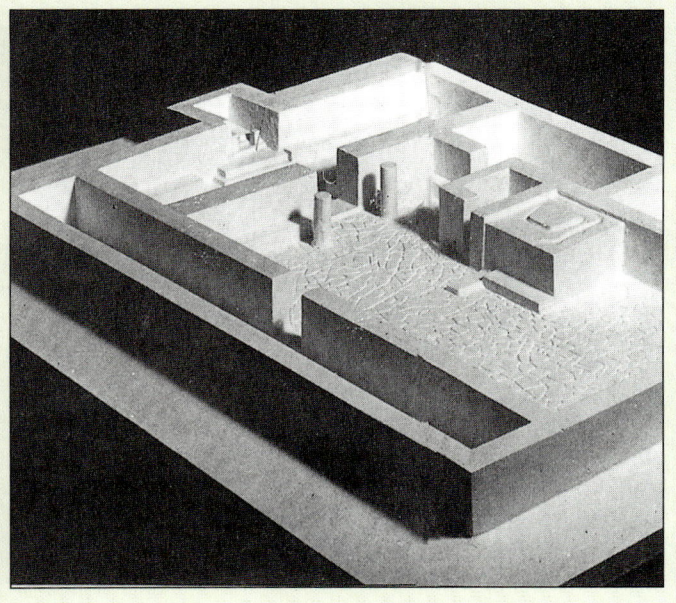

THE NEGEV AND SINAI

narrative tells of the digging of wells by Isaac's men, and that Isaac then proceeded to Beer-sheba.

In Genesis 20 there are fewer details, but the incident very closely parallels that in Genesis 26. Abraham journeys to Gerar from somewhere near Kadesh, but no famine is mentioned. The king of Gerar is again Abimelech, but there is no mention of Philistines, except at the conclusion of chapter 21, where it is stated that "Abraham sojourned many days in the land of the Philistines." That Abraham went from Gerar to Beer-sheba can be inferred from 21:25–33. In 2 Chronicles 14:9–15 there is a brief account of a victory of Asa, king of Judah (908–867 BC), over Zerah the Ethiopian, and how Asa pursued the foe as far as Gerar and then attacked the cities in close proximity to Gerar.

One of these nearby cities was Ziklag, if the latter is to be identified with Tel Sera (another opinion locates Ziklag at Tel Halif 15km (9·3 miles) north-northeast of Beer-sheba). This was the city given to David by Achish, king of Gath, when David became a Philistine vassal (1 Samuel 27:6), and in which David prepared the way for his rise to power should Saul be defeated by the Philistines. From Ziklag David made pitiless raids against the Amalekites and other non-Judahites who inhabited the Negev, sparing no man or woman alive, lest anyone should live to inform Achish of what David was really doing and contradict his claim that he was raiding peoples associated with Judah (1 Samuel 27:8–12). When the Philistines forced Saul into what would be for him the tragic final battle and David was obliged to make the long journey to the area of Mount Gilboa, it is not surprising that the Amalekites used his absence from Ziklag to strike back at David. On his return from the battle with Saul in which his troops were not allowed to fight (1 Samuel 29:3–11), David found Ziklag in flames and the women and children taken away. David now pursued the enemy with 600 men, 200 of whom had to drop out of the chase after some 25km (15·5 miles) at the Nahal Besor (Brook Besor). Presumably they were exhausted after the long journey from the Mount Gilboa area. Helped by a captured informer, David was able to surprise the Amalekites while they were celebrating their victory (1 Samuel 30:9–20). In an act of solidarity with the 200 men too exhausted to go further than the Nahal Besor, David shared the booty with them also, against the advice of those who said that only the actual combatants should share the spoils (1 Samuel 30:21–24).

The second main section of the northern Negev is the plateau and basins, with Beer-sheba the main place of settlement. By far the largest part of the section, to the southwest of Beer-sheba, consists of the greatest concentration of sand dunes in present-day Israel. This sand is crossed, and thus divided into two sections, by the Nahal Besor. On the southeast fringes the sands give way to chalk hills. These chalk hills are in turn divided along a line running roughly east–west by the Nahal Beer-sheba. The hills to the north of the Nahal merge into the Hebron hills. Beer-sheba itself stands on the Nahal Beer-sheba in a gap of some 5km (3·1 miles) between the chalk hills. To the east of the town are two broad basins, the Beer-sheba basin and the (higher) Arad basin. In ancient times there was a series of fortified settlements from Beer

who is also called the king of the Philistines. (The latter reference can be understood to mean that Abimelech was king in a place where the Philistines were later to settle, some time in the 12th century BC.) According to Genesis 25:11, Isaac was at Beer-lahai-roi, an unidentified place near Kadesh (Genesis 16:14; on Kadesh see below). If it is permissible to take Genesis 25:11 with Genesis 26, we can suppose that the famine necessitated a move either south to Egypt or to the north. While Abraham had gone to Egypt when there was famine (Genesis 12:10–19), Isaac is commanded to stay in the promised land and so goes northwards to Gerar, situated near a line of springs. The

Sheva eastwards along the basins as far as Arad. Two of them, Tel Masos and Tel Malhata, have not been identified for certain with particular towns named in the Old Testament.

That Beer-sheba should have become an important place in the northern Negev is clear from its location. It stood on routes from the Negev to the coastal plain, the Shephelah, the Hebron hills and the rift valley, and although the rainfall of the Beer-sheba and Arad basins is only 200mm (8in) per annum, these basins were always capable of being cultivated.

As has been mentioned above, Beer-sheba first appears in the Bible as a place of residence of Abraham (Genesis 21:31–34, 22:19) and Isaac (Genesis 26:23). We can also infer from Genesis 26:33 and 28:10 that Isaac was living at Beer-sheba when he asked Esau to hunt game for him, an occasion on which Jacob tricked Esau out of his blessing (Genesis 27:1–29). It is not easy to guess where Esau might have gone from Beer-sheba with his bow and arrows to hunt game for Isaac's meal. As part of the trickery, Rebekah told Jacob to take two goats from the flock so that she could prepare the food for Isaac (Genesis 27:9), so presumably Esau was hunting wild goats. If the incident is set in the winter (rainy) season, wild goats would come to where there was temporary vegetation in the Negev; otherwise Esau would have had to go north towards the Hebron hills, or down into the rift valley near a spring.

It is interesting to compare the blessings which Isaac gives to his two sons, when we bear in mind the contrast between the well-watered land north of Beer-sheba and the poorly watered land to its south. Isaac's blessing, stolen by Jacob from Esau, is:

> May God give you of the dew of heaven,
> and of the fatness of the earth,
> and plenty of grain and wine. (Genesis 27:28)

Esau's consolation blessing, if it can be called that, is:

> Behold, away from the fatness of the earth shall your dwelling be,
> and away from the dew of heaven on high.

Jacob was now forced to flee from Esau, setting out from Beer-sheba to go to Haran (Genesis 28:10). He was next to visit Beer-sheba on his way down to Egypt where he would be reunited with his long-lost son Joseph, now lord of Egypt (Genesis 46:1). While at Beer-sheba, on the journey to Egypt, Jacob is assured by God that he will bring the people back from Egypt as a great nation. This promise is, perhaps, a reflection of the fact that Beer-sheba came to be recognized as the southernmost part of the promised land, as in the phrase "from Dan to Beer-sheba" (1 Samuel 3:20).

Outside the stories about Abraham, Isaac and Jacob, Beer-sheba is mentioned little in the Bible; but such references as there are witness to its importance. Samuel appointed his sons to be judges there (1 Samuel 8:2), the town provided the mother of Jehoash, king of Judah (2 Kings 12:1), the priests of its "high place" were deposed by Josiah (2 Kings 23:8) and it was resettled by return-

Beer-sheba

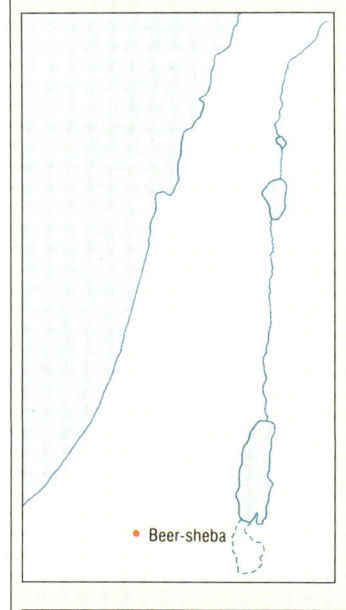

The name Beer-sheba most naturally reminds us of the stories of Abraham, Isaac and Jacob. However, that site is probably under the modern town of Beer Sheva. The magnificent Tell Beer-sheba was first built as a city at the end of the 11th century BC, and under Solomon it was later fortified by a massive wall. Although it was destroyed in the 10th century, possibly by the Egyptian Shishak, it was restored, and endured as the fortified southern border town of Judah until its destruction by Sennacherib in 701/700 BC. The most notable feature of the layout of this town was the road that ran the whole way round it, just inside the defensive walls. The chief public buildings occupied slightly higher ground in the centre of the city, with storehouses and a small shrine near the city gate. After the Assyrian onslaught the city never recovered its former glory.

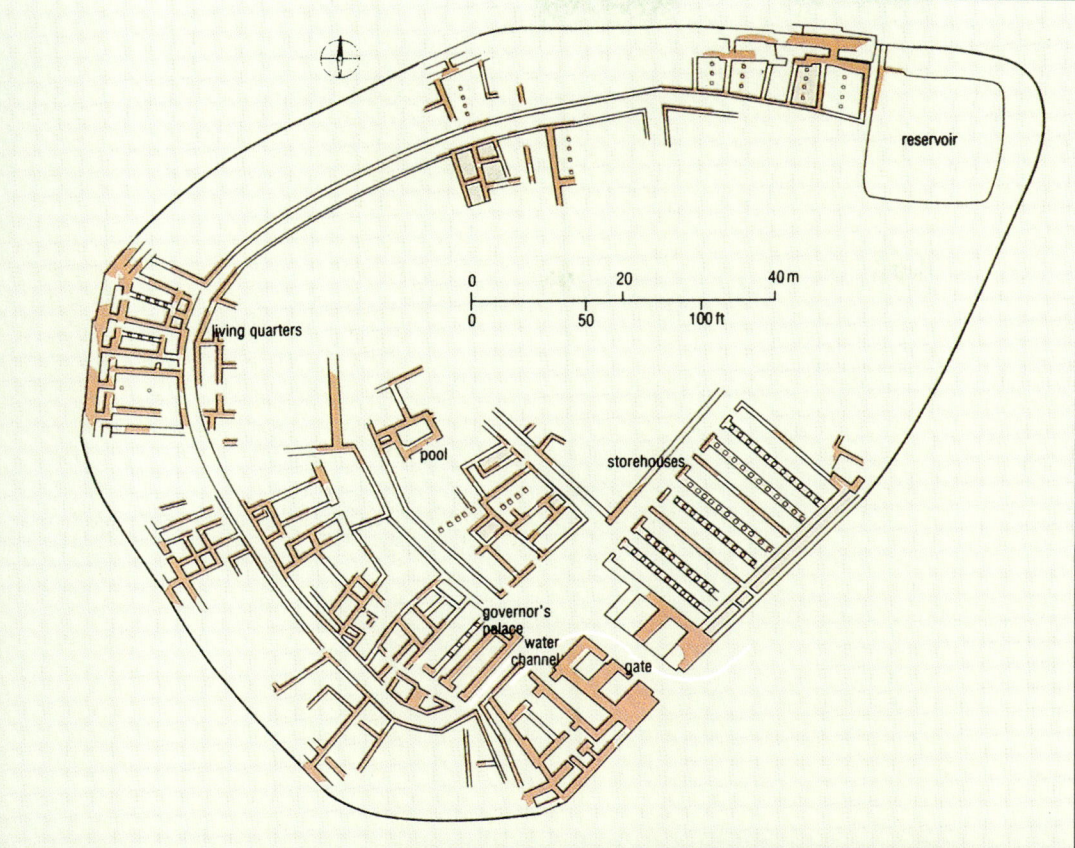

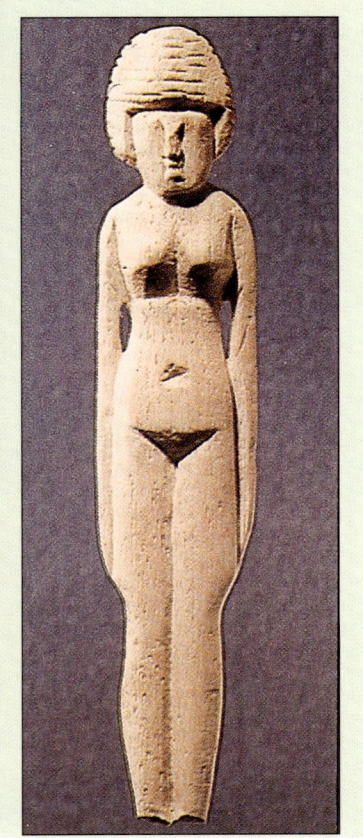

THE NEGEV AND SINAI

ing Jews after the exile (Nehemiah 11:27). Excavations at Beer-sheba suggest that the Patriarchs and the post-exilic Jews settled or stayed in an area today covered by the town of Beer-sheba. The mound of Tel Sheba, outside the present town, was built during the early period of the Israelite monarchy, and destroyed in the 8th century.

To the southeast of Beer-sheba is Tel Masos, a site tentatively identified with the biblical Hormah. In Numbers 14:45 is an account of an Israelite defeat at Hormah at the hands of the Amalekites and the Canaanites "who dwelt in that hill country". The occasion is that of the Israelites trying to go up into the promised land without God's sanction. Tel Masos is very close to the point where the Hebron hills separate the Beer-sheba and Arad basins at Mount Ira. The incident of Numbers 21:1–4 (see a reference to the same incident at Numbers 33:40) also fits well into this area if Tel Masos is Hormah. The king of Arad learns that the Israelites are approaching, and takes some of them prisoner. The Israelites strike back and destroy the cities in the area. Arad itself, a site whose excavation has revealed a temple and ostraca (inscribed potsherds), is mentioned only at Joshua 12:14 in addition to the passages in Numbers. In the Joshua passage the king of Arad is listed as one of those defeated by the Israelites.

Another strategically located settlement was Aroer, to the southeast of Hormah. This town is mentioned as belonging to Judah (Joshua 15:22, reading Aroer for Adadah), and was a town to which David sent some of the spoil after he had avenged himself against the Amalekites (1 Samuel 30:28).

Of the third main section of the Negev, little can be said in regard to the biblical narrative. In form and structure it is a remarkable area, consisting of a series of fold mountains running from northeast to southwest. In two cases severe erosion of upfolded mountains (mountains pushed upwards by pressure beneath) has left spectacular craters. In biblical times a route went from Aroer along the Nahal Aroer to the site of the present-day Dimona and from there in a southwesterly direction along a trough between two ridges to the present-day Sede Boqer. Surveys suggest that in the reign of Solomon this route was protected by forts and outposts, probably as the main route to Ezion-geber on the Gulf of Akaba. These forts may, however, have been destroyed in Shishak's operations against Judah and Israel in the reign of Rehoboam (1 Kings 14:25–28).

The central Negev

The central Negev is usually divided into two areas, the high Negev and the central basins. As the name suggests, the high Negev is characterized by the highest mountains to be found in the whole of the Negev region. The area is dominated by a range of mountains running along an axis of east-northeast to west-southwest, reaching at their highest point a height of 1033m (3389ft). However, the principal range is characterized by a massive piece of erosion which forms a kind of crater nearly 40km (25 miles) long, 8km (5 miles) wide at its widest point and 500m (1640ft) deep. West of this central range the country is mountainous, with several descending plateaux. To the east the

Above A famous feature of life at Beer Sheva is the camel market, a reminder of the fact that the town serves as a centre for the bedouin of the area.

Top Site plan of Beer-sheba in the 8th century BC.

Far left Aerial view of Tell Beer-sheba from the south. In the foreground is visible the bed of the Nahal Beer Sheva. The entrance to the city gate can be seen just to the right of the bottom edge of the Tell. The modern city is out of the picture to the left. In the distance is the small settlement of Omer.

Left A female figurine from Beer-sheba.

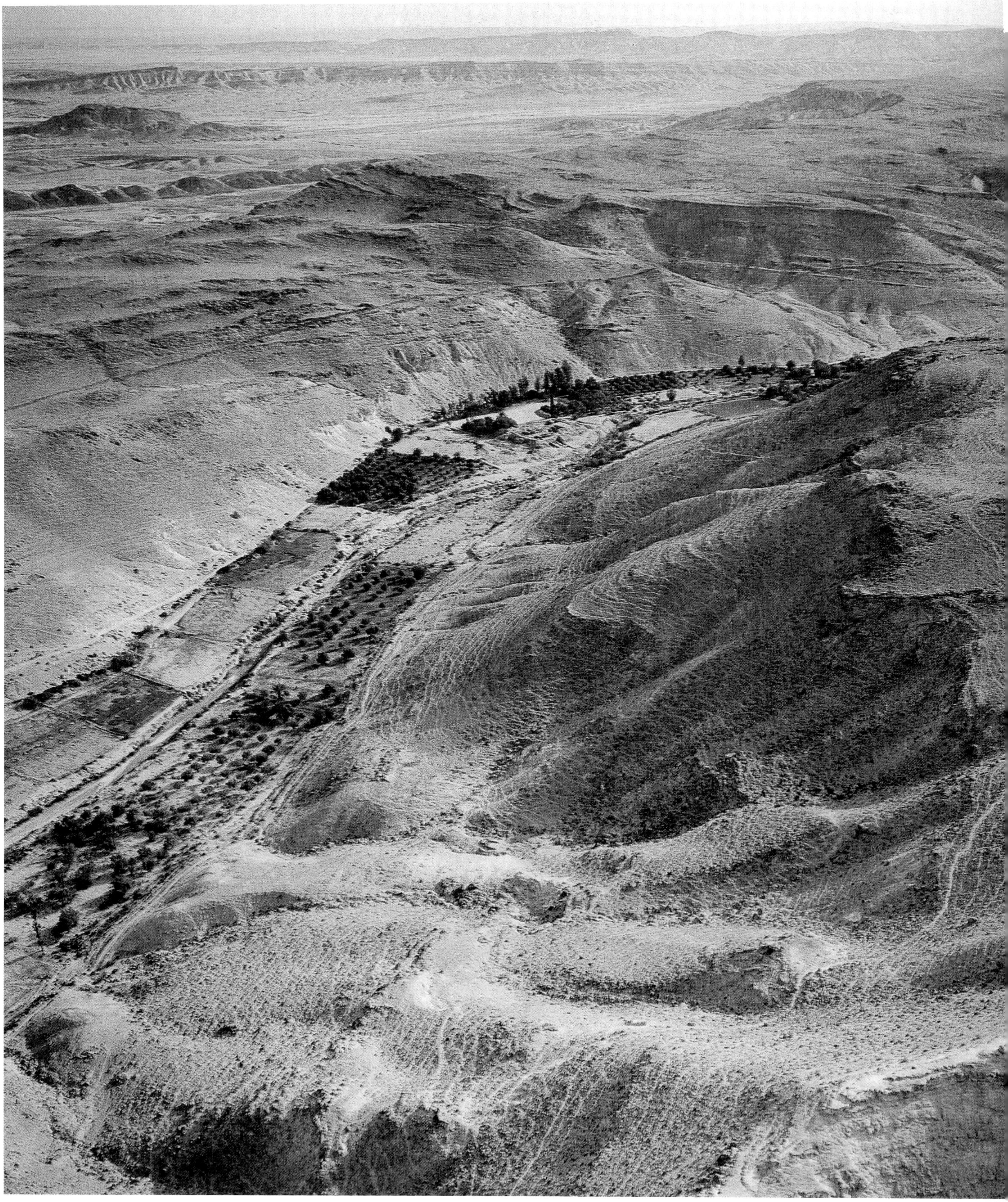

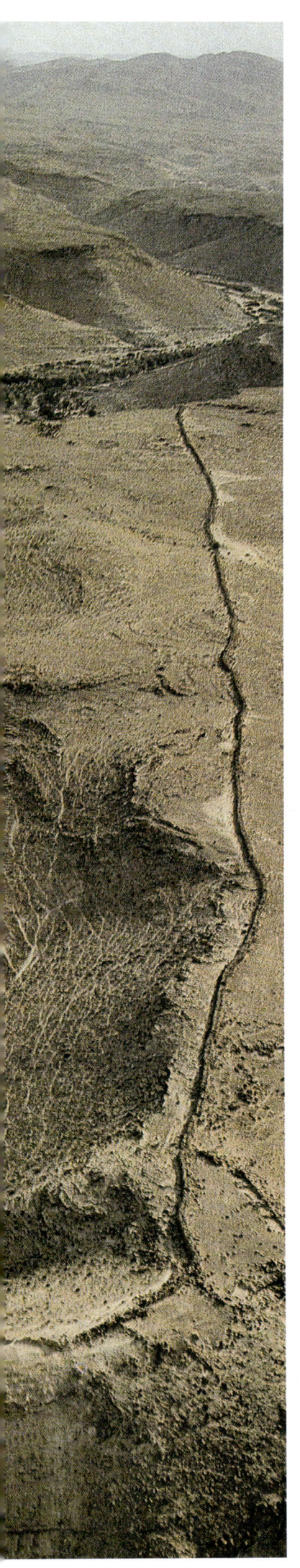

country is lower with large wide plains.

From the Old Testament point of view, the most important site of the high Negev is Kadesh-barnea, on the western edge of the high Negev and on the border between the Negev and Sinai. There is a difference of opinion about the identification of Kadesh-barnea. Many scholars place it at Ein el-Qudeirat, while others locate it some 10km (6·2 miles) southeast of Ein el-Qudeirat at Ein Qedeis. The physical difference between the two sites is neatly summarized by C.H.J. de Geus: "'Ain Qdeis is an open place with not much water and, as it seems now, with few other natural resources. 'Ain el Qudeirat has plenty of water and grazing possibilities for goats and sheep, but is situated in a deep and narrow valley." This is not the place to argue the merits of the rival identifications. Although Ein el-Qudeirat looks the more attractive because of its abundant water, de Geus writes that there is no convincing reason against Ein Qedeis (which may have preserved the ancient name) being Kadesh.

Wherever it was located, Kadesh was, according to the Old Testament, one of the most important sites in the formative days of ancient Israel. The first mention of Kadesh, other than as a kind of signpost (e.g. Genesis 16:14), is at Numbers 13:26. The spies return from spying out the land and they come back to "Moses and Aaron and to all the congregation of the people of Israel in the wilderness of Paran, at Kadesh". Previously (Numbers 12:16, 13:3) the Israelites are described as being in the wilderness of Paran. The identification of Kadesh as the place from which the spies were sent out is confirmed by Deuteronomy 1:19–25.

When the 12 spies returned to Kadesh, 10 of them brought back a bad report of the promised land. As a result of this act of faithlessness God condemned all those present at Kadesh aged 20 and upwards, except for Joshua and Caleb, not to set foot in the promised land. The ban extended to Moses himself.

If we are to assume that the incidents of Numbers 16–19 happened at Kadesh (no change of location is mentioned, but Numbers 20:1 implies an arrival in Kadesh), we may note the following sequence of events. A rebellion against Moses was led by Korah, Dathan, Abiram and On (Numbers 16:1ff.). Their complaint was that Moses had not brought them to the promised land and that Moses and Aaron should not have exclusive priestly authority. In an ensuing contest an earthquake swallowed up the principal leaders of the revolt and their families, and fire from heaven destroyed their supporters (Numbers 16:31–35). A protest on the part of the rest of the Israelites at the fate of Korah and the others resulted in a divine plague, which abated only when Aaron made atonement for the dissentients.

In Numbers 20:1–13 Kadesh was a place where Moses produced water by striking a rock, when the people complained of lack of water. It was also from Kadesh that Moses sent out messengers to the king of Edom requesting a passage through the land of Edom (Numbers 20:14–21).

The incidents at Kadesh made a considerable impression upon later traditions of the Old Testament. The murmuring against Moses for the lack of water is recalled in Psalm 95:8, when the worshippers in the temple are warned:

Harden not your hearts, as at Meribah,
as on the day at Massah in the wilderness,
when your fathers tested me. . .

(For the identification of Meribah with Kadesh, see Numbers 20:13, 27:14.) The incidents of the destruction of Abiram and the provoking of God at Meribah are also mentioned in Psalm 106:16–17, 32–33.

Deuteronomy 1:46 states that the Israelites stayed at Kadesh "many days", and this has caused scholars to surmise that it was at Kadesh that Israel consolidated its faith and attained a unity of purpose before moving on to possess the promised land. The Old Testament itself provides no evidence for such guesses, correct though they may be. For the Old Testament writers Kadesh remains a symbol of warning to Israel not to put God to the test by doubting his power and goodwill towards his people. The New Testament also picks up the symbols, without mentioning Kadesh, and warns believers: "Take care, brethren, lest there be in any of you an evil, unbelieving heart, leading you to fall away from the living God" (Hebrews 3:12, and cf. verses 16–19).

When the Israelites left Kadesh, they journeyed to Mount Hor, where Aaron died. The location of Mount Hor is uncertain, but recent opinion seems to be agreed that it is to be found on the route from Kadesh that skirts the northern edge of the high Negev and reaches the rift valley plain along the Nahal Zin. Some locate Mount Hor at Jebel es-Sabha, an isolated set of hills reaching to 451m (1480ft), while others find it at Imaret el-Khoreisha. Modern maps of Israel often locate it at Mount Zin, an isolated hill reaching to 268m (880ft) by the Nahal Zin, 50km (31·1 miles) further to the east than the other two locations. If Oboth (Numbers 21:10) is to be located at Mesad Rahel, the famous incident of Moses setting up the brazen serpent is probably to be located in the region of the Nahal Zin (Numbers 21:4–9).

The rift valley

Two more places in the Negev remain for discussion, both in that section of the Negev which lies in the rift valley. The first is Ezion-geber, today identified as Tell el-Kheleifa, on the Jordanian side of the border on the northern coast of the Gulf of Akaba. Although Ezion-geber is mentioned in the wilderness itineraries of Numbers 33:36 and Deuteronomy 2:8, its first important reference is in connection with Solomon's building works in 1 Kings 9:26. This passage informs us that Solomon built a fleet of ships at Ezion-geber. Their purpose was to trade with those parts of the Near East that could be reached by sea from the Gulf of Akaba. In 1 Kings 9:26 Ezion-geber is said to belong to Edom —an indication of Solomon's control of Edom, or

Left Aerial view of Wadi el-Qudeirat from the west. A notable feature is the wall on the right of the picture, whose purpose is not known. Suggestions are that it enclosed a sanctuary, kept out animals or prevented erosion. To the left of centre in the upper half of the picture a small tell is visible, where a fort from the 8th to 6th century has been found. At the top right corner of the picture is Ein el-Qudeirat, a possible site of biblical Kadesh-barnea.

THE NEGEV AND SINAI

Left The wilderness of Zin. In this region of the Negev spectacular erosion of those rocks that were originally forced up by pressure from beneath has taken place.

Below Ezion-geber on the north coast of the Gulf of Akaba where Solomon built a fleet.

part of it, at that time. Excavations at Tell el-Kheleifa indicate that after Solomon's death Ezion-geber was destroyed by fire. In the region of Jehoshaphat (870–846 BC) the king of Judah was again in control of a rebuilt and enlarged Ezion-geber, suffering the misfortune of the wreck of his ships there (1 Kings 22:47–49). After the reign of Jehoshaphat there is no further mention in the Old Testament of Ezion-geber. It is stated at 2 Kings 14:22, however, that Uzziah (785–733) built Elath and restored it to Judah. The exact site of Elath is not known, but it is presumed to be close to Ezion-geber in the light of texts such as Deuteronomy 2:8. The loss of Elath to the Edomites in the reign of Uzziah's grandson Ahaz (733–727) is related at 2 Kings 16:6.

When Tell el-Kheleifa was first excavated shortly before World War II, the excavators found the site to be an inhospitable spot. It was subjected to strong winds coming down the rift valley from the north, and frequent sandstorms hindered the digging. The excavators found that the tell (or mound) was at the extreme western limit of the sweet-water springs. No doubt the Israelite builders of Ezion-geber could go no further east because this would have taken them even further into Edomite territory. The strong winds from the north may have been responsible for the wrecking of the fleet of Jehoshaphat, which was perhaps blown from its moorings.

Timna, some 20km (12.4 miles) north of Tell el-Kheleifa, is not mentioned in the Bible (the Timnah that is mentioned is in the Shephelah—see p.87). However, it has become of interest to Old Testament scholars as a result of the discovery of the Hathor temple in the excavations of 1969 and 1974. Timna itself is today, and was in ancient times, known for the production of copper, which is found within the Nubian sandstone on the site.

Timna

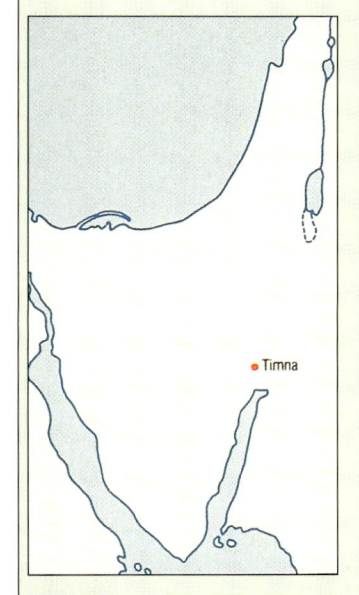

Copper was mined in the region of Timna as early as the 4th millennium BC. After a gap of over a thousand years mining and smelting resumed in the 13th century BC. In the 12th century BC the Egyptians took a keen interest in Timna, but the site soon came to be dominated by the Midianites who are connected in the biblical tradition to the Israelites by Moses' marriage to Jethro's daughter (cf. Exodus 3:1). The Egyptians built at Timna a temple to the goddess Hathor. The Midianites turned it into a Midianite shrine, which has been found to have striking similarities with the Israelite tent shrine of the wilderness wanderings period.

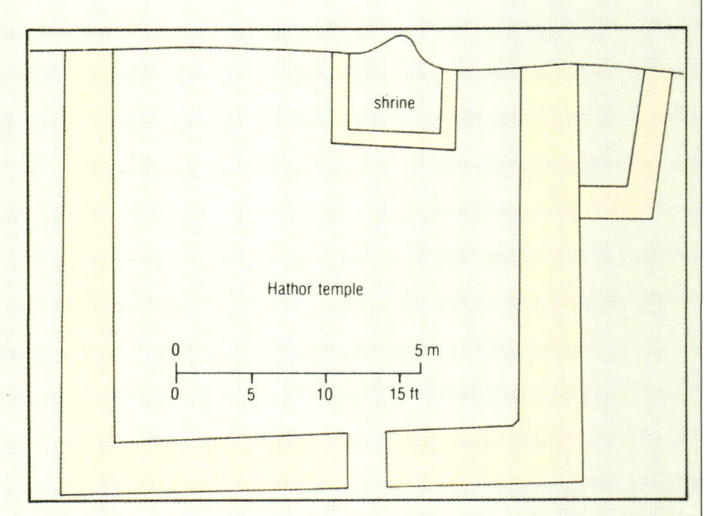

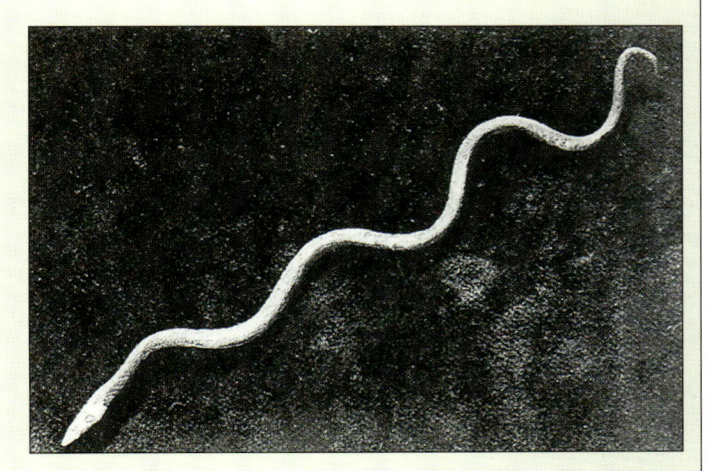

Right Various fragmentary representations of the Egyptian goddess Hathor have been recovered from the site. She was the goddess of dance, music, love and joy.

Far right The discovery of a copper snake in the Midianite shrine is interesting in view of the biblical narrative of the brazen serpent which was set up on a pole (Numbers 21:6-9).

Above and right Some of the rocks and shafts from which the copper was mined.

THE NEGEV AND SINAI

The Hathor temple enjoyed several phases of existence, of which the Midianite period (12th century BC) is the most interesting for our purposes. During the Midianite period the sanctuary took the form of a tent shrine, in the most holy part of which was a 12cm (4·7in) long copper snake with a gold-gilded head. The possible connections between this Midianite tent shrine and early Israel are striking.

The biblical tradition is clear that Moses had Midianite connections. After his flight from Egypt (Exodus 2:11–15) Moses came "to the land of Midian" where he married the daughter of the Midianite priest Jethro. After Moses had led the Israelites out of slavery in Egypt, his father-in-law came to him and acknowledged his faith in the God of Israel (Exodus 18:10–12). When Moses had received the 10 commandments, these were placed in the Ark of the Covenant which in turn was placed within a tent shrine (see Exodus 40:16–21). We have also noticed that Moses set up a bronze snake on an occasion when the people were attacked by snakes. It is impossible to trace the exact relationship between the Midianite and Israelite tent shrines and snakes, but it can hardly be accidental in view of the Old Testament's linking of Moses and the Midianite priest Jethro.

Sinai

As we turn from the Negev to the Sinai peninsula, we are concerned only with one principal site —Mount Sinai. It is true that the Israelites spent many years in the Sinai/Negev region, but we are better able to locate Old Testament sites in the Negev than in Sinai. Even the route of the Exodus itself is a matter of debate (see p.27), with at least two main theories about the location of the Red Sea which the Israelites miraculously crossed, and which route they took to get there.

The first main question is whether Mount Sinai is to be located in the far south of the peninsula, or whether it is to be sought much further north, near Kadesh. Thus, there are those who identify Mount Sinai with Jebel Helal some 60km (37·3 miles) west of Kadesh. A strong argument against this identification is the insistence of the Old Testament that Mount Sinai (also called Horeb) was a considerable distance from Kadesh. Thus Deuteronomy 1:2 explains "It is eleven days' journey from Horeb by the way of Mount Seir to Kadesh-barnea." This would be more than ample time to cover 60km. Again, when Elijah fled in terror from the threat of Jezebel (1 Kings 19:1–8), he needed "forty days and forty nights" to take him from one day's journey beyond Beer-sheba to Mount Horeb. While it may be granted that "forty days and forty nights" is a biblical way of denoting a long period of time, Elijah did not need more than a few days to travel about 130km (80·8 miles) from south of Beer-sheba to Jebel Helal.

Granted that Mount Sinai/Horeb is to be located in the far south of the Sinai peninsula, the site cannot be identified with certainty. Ancient tradition places Mount Sinai at Jebel Musa. Visitors have suggested alternative sites, for example Jebel Serbal some 35km (21·7 miles) northwest of Jebel Musa. The famous German Egyptologist, Richard Lepsius (1810–84), who visited the region in 1845, described the advantages, as he saw them, of Jebel Serbal over Jebel

Above Jebel Musa, the traditional site of Mount Sinai, is part of a cluster of mountains whose highest peak reaches about 2644m (8672ft). Jebel Musa itself is 2273m (7455ft) high.

Left The name Sinai desert is a misnomer if it suggests vast expanses of sand. In fact there is only one notable area of sand, which separates the great plateau extending northwards from Jebel et-Tih from the mountain ranges that are in the bottom of the triangle formed by the gulfs of Suez and Akaba.

Musa as follows: "Gebel Musa, invisible from every quarter, almost concealed and buried, neither distinguished by height, form, position, nor any other peculiarity, presented nothing which could have induced the native tribes, or the Egyptians who had settled there, to give it the peculiar designation of the 'Mount of (the wilderness of) Sin', while Serbal, attracting the eye to itself from all sides, and from a great distance, unequivocally commanding the whole of the northern portion of the primitive range, has always been the central point for the widely-scattered inhabitants of the country, and the goal of travellers..." The debate cannot be resolved here, and strong arguments against Jebel Serbal have been advanced. What is indisputable is the supreme importance of Mount Sinai/Horeb for the religion of the Bible. At Horeb Moses received his call to lead God's people out of slavery (Exodus 3:1–12) and it was to the same mountain that Moses led the people after the Exodus (Exodus 19, cf. Exodus 3:12). While Moses was receiving the Law on Mount Sinai, the people grew weary of waiting and denied their God by making the Golden Calf (Exodus 32:1–6). Thus the mountain was at one and the same time a symbol for God's graciousness and his people's disobedience:

> They exchanged the glory of God
> for the image of an ox that eats the grass
> (Psalm 106:20).

In other traditions of the Old Testament, Sinai was a mountain that trembled like the other mountains when God passed through Edom and the wilderness (Judges 5:4–5, Psalm 68:7–8). It was to Horeb that Elijah fled in the reign of Ahab (873–851/2) and where God spoke to him, not in the thunder and lightning that had accompanied the lawgiving at Sinai (Exodus 19:16), but in the "still small voice" (1 Kings 19:12). The strands Horeb, Moses, Elijah are drawn together not only in Malachi 4:4–5, but in the New Testament story of the Transfiguration (Mark 9:2–8) when, on another mountain, Jesus was joined by Moses and Elijah and they spoke together of his departure (exodus) "which he was to accomplish at Jerusalem" (Luke 9:31).

GALILEE

Left Near the site of the biblical city of Dan is one of the sources of the river Jordan. Today the area is a park and nature reserve, through which the stream runs.

Right The region is divided between upper Galilee to the north and lower Galilee in the south. The two regions had no natural centre in ancient times, and the geological structure of upper Galilee made settlement and travel very difficult. Lower Galilee is characterized by long valleys running approximately west to east. The area of western upper Galilee has remained difficult to settle right up to today, and it preserves some of the best examples of the original oak forest.

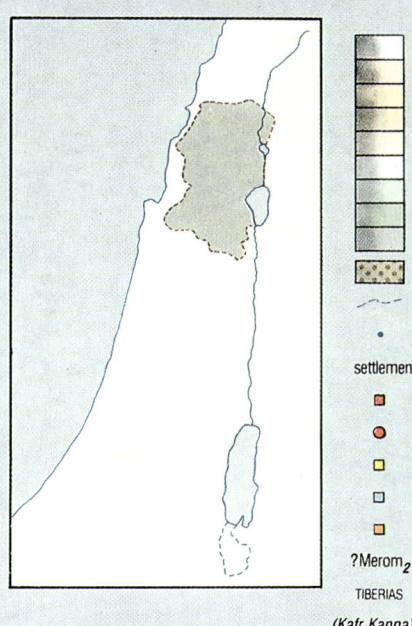

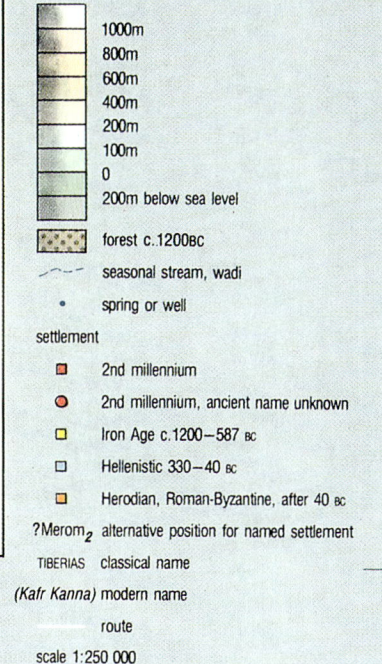

Note (U) = unlocated site

Abel-beth-maacah 2 Sam. 20:14,15,18; 1 Kgs. 15:20; 2 Kgs. 15:29; 2 Chr. 16:4 D1
Achshaph Josh. 11:1; 12:20; 19:25 A3 A4
Adamah Josh. 19:36 D3
Adami-nekeb Josh. 19:33 C4
Ammathus *see* Hammath
Anaharath Josh. 19:19 C5
Arbela 1 Macc. 9:2 C4
Aznoth-tabor Josh. 19:34 C4
Beer Judg. 9:21 D5
Beten Josh. 19:25 A4
Beth-anath Josh. 19:38 B3 C1 C4
Beth-dagon Josh. 19:27 C3
Bethlehem Josh. 19:15 B4
Beth-pazzez Josh. 19:21 (U)
Beth-rehob Judg. 18:28 (U)
Bethsaida (Julias) Matt. 11:21; Mark 6:45; 8:22; Luke 9:10; 10:13; John 1:44; 12:21 D3
Beth-shemesh Josh. 19:38; Judg. 1:33 B2 D4
Cana John 2:1,11; 4:46; 21:2 B4 C4
Capernaum Matt. 4:13; 8:5; 11:23; 17:24; Mark 1:21; 2:1; 9:33; Luke 4:23,31; 7:1; 10:15; John 2:12; 4:46; 6:17,24,59 D3
Chesulloth (Chisloth-tabor) Josh. 19:12,18 B4
Chinnereth (Chinneroth, Gennesaret) Josh. 11:2; 19:35; 1 Kgs. 15:20; Matt. 14:34; Mark 6:53 D3
Chinneroth, Sea of *see* Galilee, Sea of
Chisloth-tabor *see* Chesulloth
Chorazin Matt. 11:21; Luke 10:13 D3
Daberath Josh. 19:12; 21:28; 1 Chr. 6:72 C4
Dalmanutha *see* Tarichaeae
Dan (Laish, Leshem) Gen. 14:14; Deut. 34:1; Josh. 18:29; 19:47; Judg. 18:7,14,27,29; 20:1; 2 Sam. 3:10; 17:11; 24:2,15; 1 Kgs. 4:25; 12:29–30; 15:20; 2 Kgs. 10:29; 1 Chr. 21:2; 2 Chr. 16:4; 30:5; Jer. 4:15; 8:16; Amos 8:14 D1
Dimnah *see* Rimmon
Edrei Josh. 19:37 (U)
En-dor Josh. 17:11; 1 Sam. 28:7; Ps. 83:10 C5
En-haddah Josh. 19:21 C4
En-hazor Josh. 19:37 C2
Eth-kazim Josh. 19:13 (U)
Gabatha Josh. 19:13 B4
Galilee, Sea of (Kinneret, Lake of Gennesaret, Sea of Chinnereth, Sea of Tiberias) Num. 34:11; Josh. 13:27; Matt. 4:18, 15:29; Mark 1:16; 7:31; Luke 5:1; John 6:1 D4
Gath-hepher Josh. 19:13; 2 Kgs. 14:25 B4
Gennesaret *see* Chinnereth
Gennesaret, Lake of *see* Galilee, Sea of
Hammath (Ammathus) Josh. 19:35; 21:32 D4
Hannathon Josh. 19:14 B4
Hazor Josh. 11:1, 10–13; 12:19; 19:36; Judg. 4:2,17; 1 Kgs. 9:15; 2 Kgs. 15:29 D2
Heleph Josh. 19:33 C4
Helkath Josh. 19:25; 21:31; 1 Chr. 6:75 A4
Horem Josh. 19:38 C2
Hukkok Josh. 19:34 C3
Idalah Josh. 19:14,27 B4
Iphtah-el Josh. 19:14,27 B4
Jabneel Josh. 19:33 D4
Janoah 2 Kgs. 15:29 B1 B3 D1
Japhia Josh. 19:13 B4
Jotbah (Jotapata) 2 Kgs. 21:19 B4
Kanah Josh. 19:28 B1
Kartah Josh. 19:35 (U)
Kartan (Kiriathaim) Josh. 21:32; 1 Chr. 6:76 C2
Kattath *see* Kitron
Kedesh (Cadasa) Josh. 12:22; 19:37; 20:7; 21:32; Judg. 4:6,9,10; 2 Kgs. 15:29 D2
Kedesh (Ziddim) Josh. 19:35; Judg. 4:6 D4
Kinneret *see* Galilee, Sea of
Kiriathaim *see* Kartan
Kishion Josh. 19:20; 21:28 C5
Kitron (Kattath) Josh. 19:15; Judg. 1:30 A4
Laish *see* Dan
Lakkum Josh. 19:33 D4
Leshem *see* Dan
Madon (Adamah) Josh. 11:1; 12:19; 19:36 C4
Magdala *see* Tarichaeae
Mareal Josh. 19:11 (U)
Merom Josh. 11:5–7
Merom, Waters of Josh. 11:5–7 C3 D2
Mesiloth 1 Macc. 9:2 (U)
Migdal-el Josh. 19:38 D2
Moreh, Hill of Judg. 7:1 C5
Nahalloth Josh. 19:15; 21:35; Judg. 1:30 A4 B4
Nain Luke 7:11 C5
Naphath Josh. 17:11 (U)
Naphtali (region) Judg. 7:23; 1 Chr. 27:19; 2 Chr. 34:6; Ps. 68:27; Isa. 9:1; Ezek. 48:3,34; Matt. 4:13,15 C3
Nazareth Matt. 2:23; 21:11; Mark. 1:24; 14:67; 16:6; Luke 1:26; 2:51; 4:16; 4:34; 18:37; 24:19; John 1:45,46; 18:5,7; 19:19; Acts 2:22; 3:6; 10:38; 26:9 B4
Neah Josh. 19:13 (U)
Ophrah Judg. 6:11,24; 8:27,32; 9:5 B5 C5
Rakkath Josh. 19:35 D4
Rama Matt. 2:18 C3
Ramah Josh. 19:29 B2
Rehob Josh. 19:28 B2
Rimmon (Dimnah, Rimmono) Josh. 19:13; 21:35; 1 Chr. 6:77 B4
Rumah 2 Kgs. 23:36 B4
Sarid Josh. 19:10,12 B5
Shahazumah Josh. 19:22 C5
Shimron (Simonias) Josh. 11:1; 12:20; 19:15 B4
Shion Josh. 19:19 C4
Shunem Josh. 19:18; 1 Sam. 28:4; 1 Kgs. 4:8 C5
Simonias *see* Shimron
Tabor, Mount Josh. 19:22; Judg. 4:6,12,14; Ps. 89:12; Jer. 46:18; Hos. 5:1 C4
Tarichaeae (Dalmanutha, Magdala) Matt. 27:56,61; 28:1; Mark 15:40,47; 16:1,9; Luke 8:2; 24:10; John 19:25; 20:1,18 D4
Tiberias John 6:1; 23; 21:1 D4
Tiberias, Sea of *see* Galilee, Sea of
Yiron Josh. 19:38 C2
Zaanannim Josh. 19:33; Judg. 4:11 C4
Zer Josh. 19:35 (U)
Ziddim *see* Kedesh

A
B
C
D
35°10'
20'
30'
40'
33°00'
50'
32°40'
?Janoah2
?Shimron-meron
?Achshaph
Abel-beth-maacah
Dan
(Laish, Leshem)
Daphne
(Dan)
(Hermon)
Kanah
?Beth-anath3
(Dubbe)
?Janoah1
Jordan
Yattir
(Ain Aazziye)
?Migdal-el
?Kartan
(Kirjathaim)
?Rehob
?Ramah
?En-hazor
?Meroth
Kedesh
CADASA
UPPER GALILEE
Yiron
?Merom1
(Horbat Sevi)
LAKE HULEH
?Horem
Waters of Merom
?Beth-shemesh2
Admon
820m
(Dishon)
Sasa
Gischala
(Kezib)
(Hazor)
Hazor
(Daron)
Plain of Hazor
MERON MOUNTAINS
?Merom2
?Janoah3
Kenaan
955m
Gath
Rosh Pinna
Beth-dagon
Jordan
Adamah
Rama
?Beth-anath1
NAPHTALI
Acco
Beth-haccherem
(Shazor)
Chorazin
Waters of Merom (Amud)
?Bethsaida1
JULIAS
(Korazim)
?Bethsaida2
Hukkok
Capernaum
?Achshaph1
Heptapegon (Tabgha)
(Zalmon)
Chinnereth
(Chinneroth, Gennesaret)
Valley of Nebulun
Gabara
SEA OF GALILEE
Jotbah
(Jotapata)
Cana1
(Horbat Qana)
TARICHEAE
(Dalmanutha, Magdala)
Arbela
KINNERET
LAKE OF GENNESARET
SEA OF CHINNERETH
SEA OF TIBERIAS
?Beth-anath2
Rakkath
?Madon
(Adamah)
Hannathon
Rumah
Rimmon
(Dimnah, Rimmono)
TIBERIAS
LOWER GALILEE
?Kitron (Kattath)
?Beten
(Yiftahel)
Hammath
(Ammathus)
?Helkath
?Achshaph2
(Tel Regev)
(Zippori)
?Iphtah-el
Iphtah-el
Sepphoris
DIOCAESAREA
Adami-nekeb
Cana2
(Kafr Kanna)
Bethlehem
Gath-hepher
?Idalah
?Harosheth-ha-goiim
?Aznoth-tabor
?Heleph
Kedesh
(Ziddim)
Zaanannim
Tibon
?Shion
(Yavneel)
?Lakkum
Kishon
?Shimron
(Simonias)
Nazareth
Jabneel
Daberath
Japhia
Mount Tabor
TABYRIUM
?Beth-shemesh1
?Nahalol2
Chesulloth
(Chisloth-tabor)
En-haddah
Gabatha
Sarid
Valley of Jezreel
?Kishion
?Shahazumah
En-dor
Nain
Hill of Moreh
HAMORE HILL
?Anaharath
(Tabor)
Jordan
?Ophrah1
Shunem
?Ophrah2
?Beer
A
B
C
D

Description of the region

The name "Galilee" comes from the Hebrew word *galil* meaning a circuit or district. In Joshua 20:7 and 21:32 the town of Kedesh is said to be in Galilee (or *the* Galilee as the Hebrew always puts it). In 1 Kings 9:11 Solomon gives to Hiram 20 cities in Galilee, while in 2 Kings 15:29 Galilee is mentioned along with towns in the far north (Abel-beth-maacah, Janoah, Kedesh and Hazor) as constituting "all the land of Naphtali" which was captured by the Assyrian king Tiglath-pileser III in about 734 BC. A famous passage in Isaiah 9:1 has the phrase "Galilee of the nations".

Scholarly opinion is divided about the history of the name. One view is that the ancient name was "Galilee of the nations", that is the district where peoples of many nations lived, with Galilee (the district) being a shortened form. Another view is that the ancient name was simply Galilee (the district). By New Testament times Galilee was understood to cover the region from the plain of Jezreel northwards to the Litani river, the eastern border being the rift valley.

In the present treatment the coastal section from Mount Carmel northwards will be omitted (see p.72) as will be the plain of Jezreel (see p.151). Included are the Sea of Galilee and the rift valley northwards to Dan, and the border country between modern Israel and Lebanon.

As thus defined, Galilee falls into two main regions (apart from the Sea of Galilee and the rift valley), known in ancient times as upper and lower Galilee. These designations reflect the fact that the mountains of upper Galilee are considerably higher than those of lower Galilee. In upper Galilee mountain summits reach heights of 1208m (3963ft), 1071m (3514ft) and 1048m (3438ft), whereas the highest points in lower Galilee are 598m (1962ft) and 588m (1929ft). However, the two regions have very different physical characteristics.

Upper Galilee is dominated by the Meron mountains, which in ancient and modern times alike formed a barrier against east-to-west travel some 10km (6.2 miles) in length north to south. The mountains were also a place of refuge for fugitives. To the east of the Meron range is another range of hills, dominated by the Kenaan (995m, 3264ft) and Admon (or Ben Zimrah, 820m, 2690ft) summits. This range is divided from the Meron range by the deep gorge of the Nahal Ammud, which presented another obstacle to east–west travel. Although the rainfall in upper Galilee is the highest in Israel, averaging 800 and 600mm (31 and 24in) on higher and lower ground respectively, the area was not an easy one for settlement in ancient times. The upper hills were covered with evergreen oak forest, remnants of which remain between Meron and Sasa, and the western and eastern slopes were also wooded. Settlement was largely limited to suitable sites along main routes, and to sites on the edge of hills where springs were to be found. In many cases, springs were located at points where the soil was unsuitable for agriculture. Because of the natural conditions, no one site was able to establish itself in Old Testament times as dominant in upper Galilee.

Lower Galilee is best divided into three strips running north to south. The western strip is a range of chalk hills some 15 to 20km (9.3 to 12.4 miles) wide, the Allonim hills. It is bordered roughly (though not completely) on its eastern side by the route running from Gevat to Tel Hannaton. The chalk is covered by a layer of hard lime up to 5m (16.4ft) thick which prevents soil from forming and springs from occurring, and has preserved the largest expanse of deciduous oak forest in the area. The middle strip, which funnels outwards to west and east at its northern end, is a series of limestone blocks running roughly southwest to northeast, each about 20km (12.4 miles) long. Their width varies from 3 to 10km (1.9 to 6.2 miles). The limestone blocks are separated by chalk plateaux and by basins. Mount Tabor is an isolated hill at the southeast edge of this second strip, reaching to 588m (1929ft). The third strip is about 34km by 14km (21.1 by 8.7 miles), and covered by basalt. The Nahal Tabor and subsidiary watercourses have cut a deep and irregular valley trough across it in a northwest-to-southeast direction.

The rainfall of lower Galilee is 600 to 500mm (24 to 20in) for the western and central strips but lower in the eastern part. This lower rainfall and the basaltic soil in the east have always made agriculture difficult in this area. Indeed, of the three strips, settlement has always been concentrated in the central one.

Together with upper and lower Galilee, we shall also consider the Sea of Galilee and the rift valley to the north of the sea as far as Dan. The Sea of Galilee has many names. It was possibly Kinneret before the Israelite settlement, and is referred to in the Old Testament as the Sea of Chinnereth (Numbers 34:11, Joshua 12:3 (Chinneroth), Joshua 13:27). In the New Testament it is called the Lake of Gennesaret (Luke 5:1), the Sea of Tiberias (John 6:1) and, simply, the sea (Mark 4:1, 5:1). It is roughly pear-shaped, about 20km (12.4 miles) long and 13km (8.1 miles) wide at its longest and widest. It mainly occupies a depression in the rift valley, and is thus some 210m (689ft) below sea level at the surface; it is 44m (144ft) deep at its deepest, in the northern part. With the exceptions of the south and the northeast, it is bordered by steep slopes which rise to about 200m (656ft) above sea level on the western side and 300m (984ft) above sea level on the eastern side. The river Jordan enters and leaves the sea at its northern and southern extremities. Because of its low altitude, the sea enjoys very warm temperatures in both summer and winter.

To the north of the Sea of Galilee the rift valley runs for about 17km (10.6 miles) before it broadens out into the Huleh valley, an area some 25km (15.5 miles) long and 7km (4.4 miles) wide at the points of greatest distance. Of all the areas discussed in the present section, it has changed the most drastically in recent times from what it would have looked like in biblical times. Prior to the draining of the valley in 1951–58, a third of the area was occupied by the Huleh lake and the Huleh swamps to the north of the lake. In ancient times these presented an impassable barrier, and the main east–west routes had to skirt them to south and north.

Right A view of lower Galilee looking east. In the background is the Jordan valley and on the skyline are the mountains of Transjordan.
Overleaf This early 19th-century view of the Sea of Galilee overlooking Tiberias suggests a very small population in the area. Today Tiberias is a small town. Even so, the Sea of Galilee area is probably less populated now than it was in the time of Jesus.

GALILEE

GALILEE

City of Tiberias on the Sea of Galilee
April 22nd 1839

GALILEE

Thomson has left a vivid picture of the swamps and lake in the mid-19th century. Of the Huleh marsh, he wrote: "The infant Jordan seems in danger of suffocation in this tangled jungle of cane and bushes... It is an utterly impassable slough, worse than Bunyan ever dreamed of." Thomson goes on to relate how he approached the verge in order to shoot ducks: "suddenly I was in oozy mud that seemed to have no bottom. Flinging the gun back and struggling desperately, I regained the bank, and ever after kept a sharp and suspicious eye upon its treacherous depths." Of the lake, Thomson wrote that the shore was as well defined as that of any other lake, but only accessible at two main points. At its southern end he saw a triangular marsh, an impenetrable jungle of cane. The whole area—plain, marsh, lake and surrounding mountain—was "the finest hunting ground in Syria...Panthers and leopards, bears and wolves, jackals, hyenas and foxes, and many other animals, are found, great and small, while it is the very paradise of the wild boar and the fleet gazelle." Today draining and modern agricultural methods have made the valley one of Israel's most prosperous agricultural regions, with fruit growing and fish farming on a large scale.

The biblical record

Before Galilee and its sea and the Huleh valley are described in relation to specific passages of the Bible, a word must be said about the overall history of the region in relation to the Bible. In the Old Testament it is mentioned on only a few occasions. The seat of government of the northern kingdom, Israel, was located in the hill country of Samaria, and was naturally the focus of interest of the northern kingdom. In about 734 the Assyrian king Tiglath-pileser III overran probably the whole of Galilee, limiting the northern kingdom to the rump of the Samaria hill country. For the next 600 years or so, such Jewish communities as remained in the area lived under foreign rule. At the beginning of the 2nd century BC there were Jewish communities in Galilee living in religious communion with Jerusalem, and the Maccabean rulers went to their help. Thus 1 Maccabees 5:21–23 states that Simon (142–134 BC) "went to Galilee and fought many battles against the Gentiles, and the Gentiles were crushed before him... Then he took the Jews of Galilee and Arbatta, with their wives and children, and all they possessed, and led them to Judea with great rejoicing." Presumably, this means that all those Jews who wished to go to Judea with Simon went, rather than that all Jews in Galilee went. Until the time of Aristobulus I (104–103 BC) Galilee was more non-Jewish than Jewish. Aristobulus conquered Galilee, united it with Judea and forcibly converted its population to Judaism. Jesus, then, grew up and conducted most of his ministry in an area that does not figure greatly in the Old Testament, and that came under Jewish control and attained a majority Jewish population only 100 years before his birth.

The earliest reference to a town in Galilee in the Bible occurs in Genesis 14:14, where Abraham is said to have pursued the alliance of kings to Dan and beyond in order to rescue his nephew Lot. Recent excavations at Dan have uncovered the entrance to the gate of the city that would have

Hazor

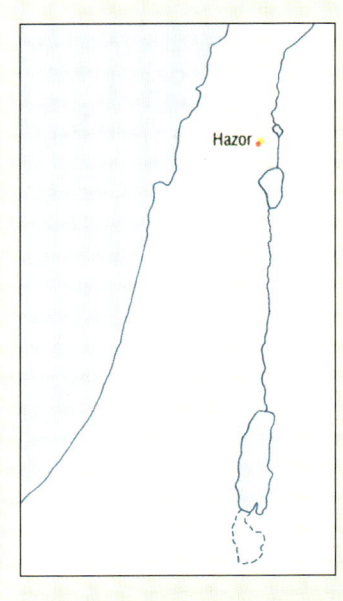

Hazor was in fact two cities, not one, in the period from the 18th to the 13th century BC. The so-called upper city on the tell dates from the first half of the 3rd millennium, and was inhabited as late as the 2nd century BC. The lower city lasted from the 18th to the 13th century. Both cities were destroyed in the 13th century (cf. Joshua 11:10). Only the upper city was rebuilt, and under Solomon, and later under Omri and Ahab, it was strongly fortified. Its water system was one of the many notable features of this city strategically placed on north–south and east–west routes. Hazor's international significance is attested by its appearance in 2nd-millennium texts from both Egypt and the northern Mesopotamian kingdom of Mari. Although the Assyrians destroyed the city in 732 BC, a citadel remained on the tell and was sporadically occupied by later invaders seeking to control this key area.

Below At the northern edge of the lower city an area was excavated in which there had been temples at four different periods. The temple of the 13th century BC is distinguished by its basalt orthostats, of which this lion is one.

Below This cult mask of the 14th century BC was possibly attached to the face of a sculpture in one of the temples in the lower city. Since its mouth and nostrils are not pierced, and in any case are small, it was presumably not worn by humans.

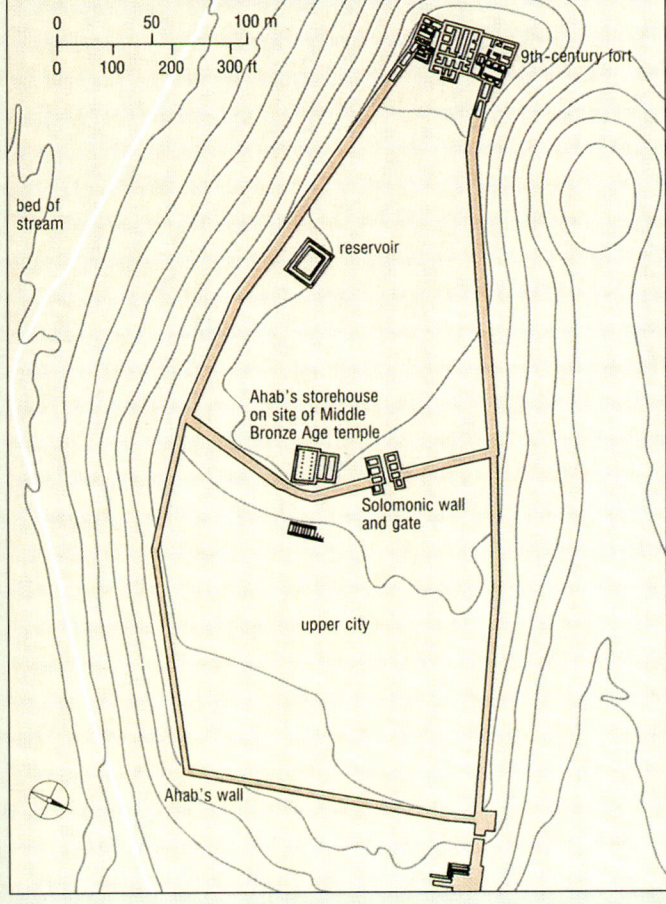

Left Aerial view of Hazor looking towards the southeast. Two excavated sections of the upper city can be seen. In the lower one is the great shaft of the water system. In the upper section the famous "pillared building" can be made out. The lower city is in the bottom left of the picture.

Above Site plan of the upper city.

Right A potter's workshop from the 14th century BC was found in the lower city. The mask (*above*) was among the objects in the workshop.

been there in Abraham's time. At this period, of course, the city was not called Dan but Laish, the name being changed after the Danites moved from their original settlement in the Shephelah (see p.87) and established themselves in the far north (Judges 19).

The book of Joshua records a decisive battle fought by the Israelites against a Canaanite coalition at the "waters of Merom", the coalition being led by Jabin, king of Hazor (Joshua 11:1–9). Hazor (see p.134) has been identified and excavated, and is an important site at a crossroads of routes going north–south and east–west. Merom has not been identified for certain; nor have Madon and Shimron, other cities of the coalition (if their names in the Hebrew textual tradition are correct—the Greek tradition has slightly different names). If Merom is to be located at Horbat Sevi (Khirbet el-Hureibeh), the battle at the "waters of Merom" could have taken place in the valley where the Nahal Dishon emerges from its narrow course into the Huleh valley. With their horses and chariots the Canaanites could not ascend the hills, and Joshua and his men, who came "suddenly" upon the Canaanites (Joshua 11:7), probably out of wooded hills, defeated the enemy before the horses and chariots could be put to use. The Canaanites fled in various directions, using the routes that were close to the scene of the battle. Joshua now turned back and captured Hazor and burned it. A destruction of the city at the end of the 13th century is indicated by archaeological findings.

In the apportionment of Galilee among the tribes, the lion's share of the area went to Naphtali. Asher took the coastal strip and part of the Allonim hills (see above, p.130), while Zebulun took the southwestern part of the Allonim hills and part of the valley of Jezreel as far as the bed of the Nahal Kishon (Joshua 19:10–16, 24–39). Judges 1:33 records that Naphtali did not drive out the inhabitants of Beth-shemesh and Beth-anath, but (later?) subjected them to forced working.

In Judges 4–5 an account is given of a second Israelite confrontation with a coalition of Canaanite cities led by Jabin, king of Hazor. The coincidences between the two confrontations—the two-fold occurrence of Jabin and Hazor and the fact of the Canaanite coalition using chariots and horses—have led some commentators to argue that the traditions in Joshua 11:1–9 and Judges 4–5 derive from one and the same event. From the geographical point of view, the two incidents are probably quite distinct. If the incident of Joshua 11:1–9 is correctly located to the north of Hazor, it took place many miles north of the Judges 4–5 battle. The latter took place in the valley of Jezreel, the Israelite tribes having gathered together at Mount Tabor (Judges 4:6, 14). Further, although Jabin is mentioned as the Canaanite king who oppressed Israel, the central villain is not Jabin but Sisera, his commander, who was killed by Jael the Kenite woman. The Kedesh mentioned in verses 6 and 9–10 is probably Kedesh-naphtali, close to the Sea of Galilee, not the Kedesh north of Hazor. In both the prose (Judges 4) and the poetic (Judges 5) accounts the Israelite victory is ascribed to God. The famous verses at Judges 5:20–21

From heaven fought the stars,
from their courses they fought against Sisera.
The torrent Kishon swept them away,
the onrushing torrent, the torrent Kishon

may indicate that a cloudburst swelled the Nahal Kishon until it flooded the valley of Jezreel, disabling the Canaanites' chariots. The difficulty of its drainage into the sea in ancient times has already been noted (p.72). The verses also express an Old Testament belief that God commands heavenly armies to fight for his people. The Old Testament writers would have seen the cloudburst (if that is what it was) as a demonstration of God's control of the natural order. It is possible that the place where Sisera lived, Harosheth-ha-goiim (Judges 4:2), is to be understood as "the forest inhabited by the Gentiles".

Galilee is next mentioned in 2 Samuel 20:14–22. During the reign of David there was a revolt of the northern tribes led by Sheba, son of Bichri. Sheba was pursued by Joab and a crack group of soldiers (2 Samuel 20:7) to Abel-beth-maacah in the very northern part of Israel. The city was saved when a wise woman persuaded the inhabitants of the city to execute Sheba and to throw his head to the besieging army. Her words to Joab constituted a powerful plea: "I am one of those who are peaceable and faithful in Israel; you seek to destroy a city which is a mother in Israel; why will you swallow up the heritage of the Lord?" (2 Samuel 20:19). In the face of such a plea, Joab could not but agree that Sheba's execution would save the city and the woman more than justified her claim that "They were wont to say in old time 'Let them but ask counsel at Abel'; and so they settled a matter."

The next important reference to a town in Galilee is in 1 Kings 12:29, when Jeroboam, the leader of the revolt of the northern tribes against Solomon's son Rehoboam, set up in Dan (as well as in Bethel) a rival shrine to that in Jerusalem. Not many years later the third king of Israel, Baasha, who had become king in a coup d'état (1 Kings 15:25–30), lost the whole of Galilee to Ben-hadad, king of Syria (1 Kings 15:16–20). Asa, king of Judah, bribed Ben-hadad to form an alliance against Baasha, and the Syrians conquered "Ijon, Dan, Abel-beth-maacah, and all Chinneroth with all the land of Naphtali". How long Galilee remained lost to Israel is not known, but if the region was not reconquered before the reign of Omri (882–871), it must have been during that monarch's rule. Omri greatly extended the boundaries of Israel, so that he dominated Transjordan as far as Moab. He also made treaties with Tyre and Sidon, and his son Ahab fought many battles with the Syrians. It would be surprising if Omri did not restore Galilee to his kingdom, if this had not already been done.

The political power established by Omri and his son Ahab was achieved at the expense of the traditional religion of Israel. Indeed, Ahab's wife Jezebel was an ardent propagator of Melkart, the god of her native Tyre. Bitter opposition to the house of Omri came from the prophetic groups led by Elijah and Elisha, and they succeeded in overthrowing the house of Omri through what is known as the prophetic revolution. Jehu, anointed king by a servant of Elisha, purged the descendants of Omri in a series of bloody acts (2 Kings

This view of Nazareth gives a good impression of how the town nestles into its hilly surroundings. Today the scene is dominated by the Franciscan church which commemorates the Annunciation of the birth of Jesus. In New Testament times Nazareth was a small village of no importance.

9–10). There was a price to be paid for this blood letting. The internal feuding weakened Israel and allowed the Syrians under King Hazael to inflict serious damage on the land. The implication of 2 Kings 10:32–33 is that Hazael captured Israelite territory east of the river Jordan; but things became much worse if 2 Kings 13:7 is to be understood literally. Jehoahaz, son of Jehu, is said to have had just "fifty horsemen and ten chariots and ten thousand footmen; for the king of Syria had destroyed them and made them like the dust at threshing."

The possibility must not be ruled out that Galilee was again lost at this time until just before the turn of the 9th century BC when Adad-nirari III crushed Damascus, and so weakened it that Jehu's grandson Jehoash was able to reverse Israel's fortunes (2 Kings 13:24–25, and cf. 13:5). Under Jeroboam II (789–748) Israel's borders were enlarged to the north far beyond their traditional limits. The period of Jeroboam's rule was to be an Indian summer for Galilee. On his death the kingdom quickly fell into chaos, and in about 734 the Assyrian king Tiglath-pileser III overran Galilee and took the people into exile (2 Kings 15:29). The area became the Assyrian province of Megiddo, but Isaiah still refers to it as "Galilee of the nations" as he looks forward to the time when God will "make glorious" the "contempt" of the lost territories (Isaiah 9:1, Hebrews 8:23).

As already remarked, the foundation for the Galilee of the New Testament was laid by the conquests of Aristobulus I (104–103 BC). Under Herod the Great, who ruled with the consent and support of Rome, the areas separating Galilee from Judea were conquered, so that Galilee was not an isolated Jewish enclave in the north. At Herod's death, however, the emperor Augustus divided the kingdom among Herod's sons. Galilee fell to Herod Antipas, which explains the reference to Pilate's attempt to get Antipas to deal with Jesus before the Crucifixion, when Pilate learned that Jesus was a Galilean (Luke 23:6–12). Antipas built Tiberias in commemoration of the Roman emperor.

The Galilee in which Jesus spent most of his life was a prosperous region. On the shores of the Sea of Galilee, and to within 5km (3·1 miles) of it, the ruins of 12 towns have been discovered. Karmon says that, judging from these ruins and the remains of synagogues and other public buildings, the population of the area must have been "much larger than the present [1971] population of about 35 000". In Galilee olives, figs, dates, flax and vines were grown, and pottery was made. Near the Sea of Galilee the preservation of fish by salting and its export were major occupations. In the basaltic areas agricultural grinders and presses were made from the basalt, while dyeing is also reported.

Nazareth, in which Jesus grew up, was an unimportant small town. The main centre was Sepphoris. Nathaniel's exclamation "can anything good come out of Nazareth?" (John 1:46) is quite understandable. Such a thought may also have been in the minds of the people of Nazareth when they rejected Jesus (Mark 6:1–6; cf. Luke 4:16–30). Not only did Nazareth seem to be unimportant, but its citizens could not find it conceivable that one who had grown up in their midst should himself embody the passage from Isaiah 61:1–2:

> The Spirit of the Lord God is upon me,
> because the Lord has anointed me
> to bring good tidings to the afflicted;
> he has sent me to bind up the brokenhearted,
> to proclaim liberty to the captives,
> and the opening of the prison to those who are bound.

Capernaum

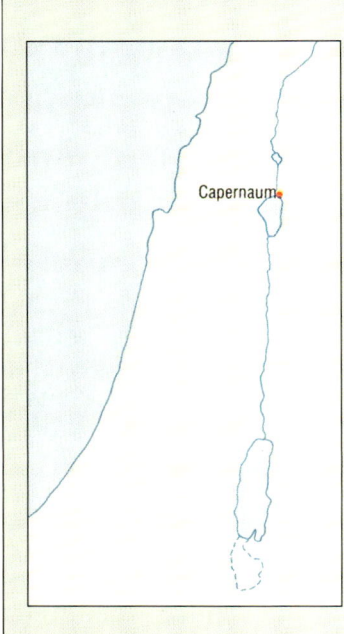

Capernaum, situated on the northwest coast of the Sea of Galilee, was one of the most important towns in the ministry of Jesus. After leaving his home in Nazareth, Jesus made Capernaum his principal residence, influenced, no doubt, by the fact that his earliest followers such as Peter lived there. It was a border town between Galilee and the territory of Philip on the eastern side of the river Jordan. Jesus performed several miracles in Capernaum, but he said that it would be more tolerable for the wicked city of Sodom on the day of judgment than for Capernaum (Matthew 11:23–24). Despite this uncompromising repudiation, evidence has been found there of a continuous Christian tradition dating from as early as the late 1st century. From at least the 4th century it was a destination for pilgrims and the house identified as belonging to Peter had already been incorporated into a church.

Right The houses at Capernaum were built from the black basalt stones that are typical of the area, the result of volcanic activity. The stones were not cut or shaped, and the gaps between them were filled with smaller stones and perhaps a primitive mortar. The floors were also made of basalt stone blocks laid closely together, with gaps that would permit such objects as coins to slip between them (see Luke 15:8). The roofs were made from light beams laid across the walls and covered with branches, straw and earth. The complex of dwellings pictured here was in use from the 1st century BC and illumines the incident of the healing of the paralysed man let down through the roof at Capernaum (Mark 2:1–12). Jesus probably sat where people gathering in the courtyards could hear him. Access to where he sat was barred, and one of the flimsy roofs was easily stripped off sufficiently to allow the paralysed man to be lowered on his mattress.

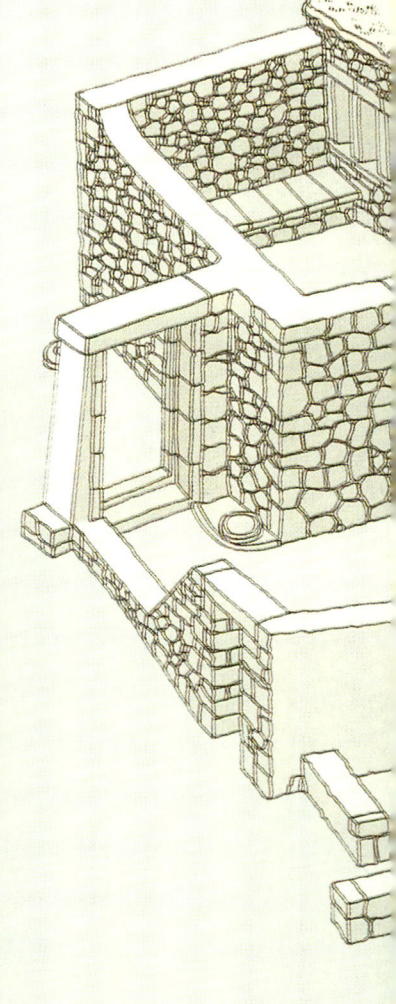

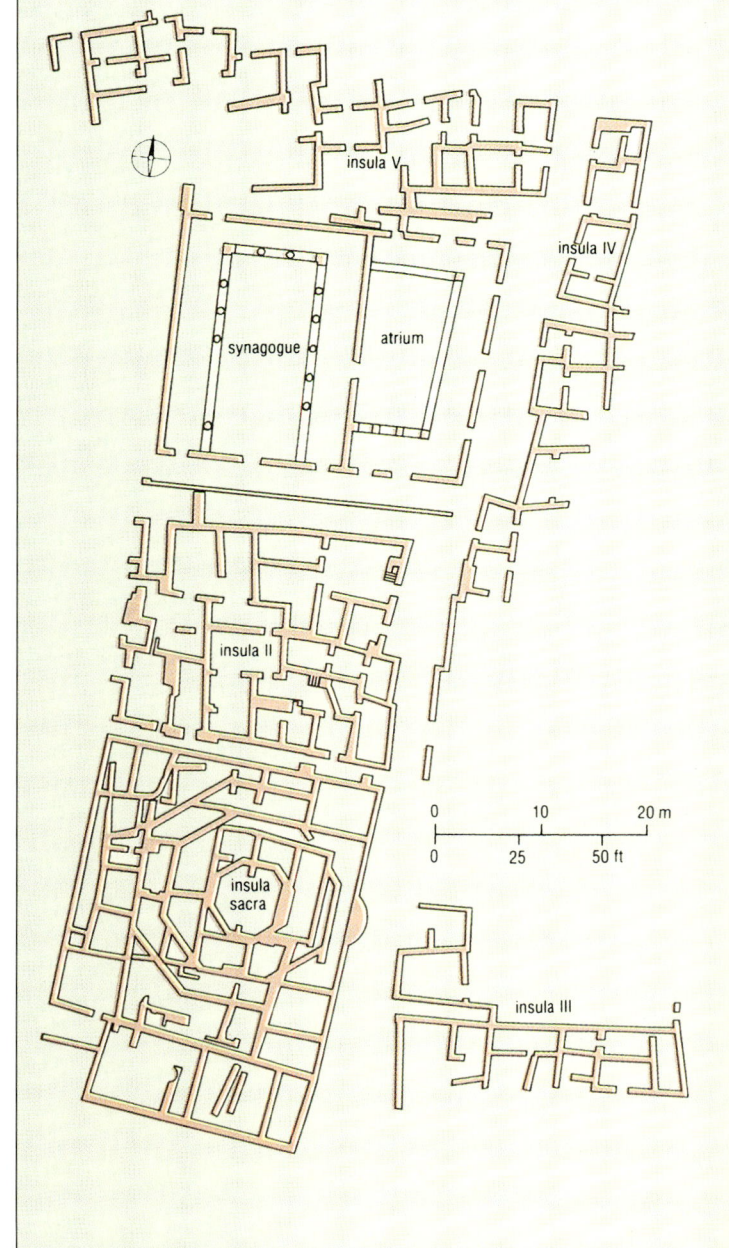

Above left Aerial view of Capernaum from the southeast. The synagogue is clearly visible on the right, while to the left of centre the large roof covers the site of Peter's house and the subsequent churches built there. From the height of the land in the background it is possible to see how the levels have risen, and why Capernaum was just a mound for centuries before the modern excavations.

Left The Ark of the Covenant being brought to Jerusalem by David, depicted on a monumental stone preserved at Capernaum.

Far left Site plan showing the synagogue, Insula II (see *above*) and the complex of Peter's house at Insula I (insula sacra).

GALILEE

The ministry of Jesus

The actual ministry of Jesus in Galilee was concentrated around the Sea of Galilee. After his rejection by Nazareth he moved to Capernaum (Matthew 4:13) and it was here that he called the first disciples (Matthew 4:18–22), although John 1:35–42 implies that Jesus had previously met Andrew and Peter in the Jericho region where John the Baptist was preaching and baptizing. The Capernaum of the time of Jesus had been founded probably in the 2nd century BC. Its inhabitants lived from fishing, farming and trading. Their houses were built from the undressed black basalt stones with which the region abounds. Capernaum was also a boundary town between Galilee, which was ruled by Herod Antipas, and the territory of Philip, which began on the eastern side of the Jordan where it entered the northern end of the Sea of Galilee; the major city of that area was Bethsaida, about 4km (2·4 miles) from Capernaum. In fact Peter was a native of Bethsaida (John 1:44), but he resided in Capernaum either because of marriage (Mark 1:29–30) or because he preferred to live in a more predominantly Jewish region. Even if Capernaum was more Jewish than Bethsaida (cf. John 12:20–21), it had a Roman centurion (Matthew 8:5–13) and border and customs trade, from which Matthew was called to be a disciple (Matthew 9:9).

Capernaum was the scene of several healing miracles. In its synagogue Jesus healed on the Sabbath a man possessed by a demon (Mark 1:21–28). This is not the synagogue that visitors to Capernaum see today, which dates from the late 4th to early 5th century AD. The site of the synagogue in the time of Jesus is unknown. It is not impossible that it was beneath the present synagogue, although it was probably a much more modest structure. Its builder was the Roman centurion whose slave Jesus healed in Capernaum (Luke 7:1–10).

Two miracles are recorded at Peter's house: the healing of his mother-in-law (Mark 1:29–30) and the healing of the man let down through the roof (Mark 2:1–12). Excavations at Capernaum have disclosed a house which contains evidence, in the form of graffiti, that Christian worship took place there in the late 1st century AD. Later Christian tradition also identified this as Peter's house, and in the 5th century an octagonal church was built there. The friends of the sick man let him down through the roof, which reminds us that, because the houses were built of basalt blocks with little or no mortar, the roofs were not substantial, otherwise the walls would not bear their weight. In spite of being the focus for the ministry of Jesus, and the place of several miracles, Capernaum's rejection of Jesus and his message was such that Jesus declared

Mount Tabor is the traditional site of the Transfiguration of Jesus. A church which commemorates this event can be seen slightly to the left of the summit. The picture shows vividly how Mount Tabor stands out from its surroundings, making it a natural rallying point (Judges 4:6) as well as a site likely to attract religious attention.

Right The famous Byzantine mosaic of the loaves and fishes found at Tabgha indicates an early association of the feeding of the five thousand with the spot. The mosaic has recently been relocated before the high altar of the restored church there.

The synagogue at Chorazin dates possibly from the 3rd century AD. It is built of basalt, a stone common in the area, and is in the classical style.

that Sodom would fare better than Capernaum on the day of judgment (Matthew 11:24).

If certain incidents can be located with confidence in Capernaum, it must be noted that the remainder of the Galilean ministry cannot be so placed. It is evident from the condemnations of cities (Matthew 11:20–24) that Jesus visited Bethsaida and Chorazin, but we know nothing of what he did in Chorazin, and for Bethsaida we have only one account of a healing, that of a blind man (Mark 8:22–26). Christian tradition has, of course, supplied locations for some of the most famous incidents. Visitors today will find sites for the feeding of the five thousand at Tabgha, for the miraculous draught of fishes (Luke 5:1–11; John 21:1–14) a little to the south of Tabgha, and for the giving of the Sermon on the Mount at the hill on which stands the Mount Beatitudes monastery. Of these incidents, nothing can be said for certain about the location of "the mountain" from which the Beatitudes were spoken (Matthew 5:1), and Luke 6:17 states that Jesus "came down" from the hills and stood "on a level place" to speak the Beatitudes. For the draught of fishes, it can be guessed that the disciples most likely kept their boats near Capernaum, and that this miracle should be placed near there. The feeding of the five thousand, although placed by Luke 9:10 at Bethsaida, seems to demand a site on the eastern side of the Sea of Galilee, perhaps opposite Tiberias. John 6:16–25 implies that after the feeding of the five thousand Jesus crossed to the opposite side of the sea, to Capernaum. This makes it difficult to think of Bethsaida, 4km (2.5 miles) from Capernaum, as the site. It is also stated in John that boats from Tiberias came near to the place of the miracle. The location of the miracle of the healing of "Legion" (Mark 5:1–13) is dealt with in the section on Transjordan.

One of the few places in Galilee actually named in connection with an incident in the life of Jesus is Nain, a town well to the south of the Sea of Galilee, on the northern side of the hills known today as Givat Ha-more that border the valley of Jezreel. Here Jesus restored to life the only son of a widow of that place (Luke 7:11–17). It is interesting that on the southern side of that same range of hills is Shunem, where Elisha also restored a son to life, that of the Shunammite woman (2 Kings 4:8–37). Another named site is Cana of Galilee, where Jesus turned water into wine (John 2:1–11). This was also the village where Jesus received a request from an official in Capernaum to heal his ailing son (John 4:46–54). There is some uncertainty about the location of Cana, although Christian tradition identifies it with Kafr Kanna, on the route from Nazareth to Tiberias.

Another traditional Christian location is Mount Tabor for the site of the Transfiguration (Mark 9:2–8). Mount Tabor is certainly a most imposing hill. It can properly be described as "high" in relation to its surroundings, and it makes topographical sense to say that Jesus passed through Galilee on his way from the mountain to Capernaum (Mark 9:30–33) if Mount Tabor is the site of the Transfiguration. On the other hand, the gospel tradition is agreed that the Transfiguration took place after Peter's confession at Caesarea Philippi (Mark 8:27–33), which is 70km (43.5 miles) from Mount Tabor as the crow flies. It is true that the gospels speak of six to eight days as elapsing between the confession of Peter and the Transfiguration (Mark 9:2, Luke 9:28), but the narrative does not give the impression that these days were spent making the journey from Caesarea Philippi to Mount Tabor. The possibility cannot be ruled out that the Transfiguration took place to the north of Caesarea Philippi, perhaps in the Hermon region.

The comment has been made that a striking feature of the gospel narratives is the absence of reference to the major centres of population in Galilee. We have already seen that the gospels presuppose that Jesus visited Chorazin but do not record what he did or said there, from which it is clear that the record of his Galilean ministry is not complete. However, there is no indication that he ever visited during his public ministry the chief city of Sepphoris, only 6km (3.7 miles) from Nazareth, nor Tiberias only 10km (6.2 miles) from Capernaum, nor other regional centres such as Gabara or Taricheae (probably Magdala, the home of Mary Magdalene). This Atlas is not the place to discuss the reasons for Jesus' avoidance of important towns in Galilee (if he did avoid them). However, a regional approach is able to show that there are some interesting implications arising from the record of the places where Jesus was and was not active.

Everyday Life in Biblical Times

Over 3000 years separate us from the Israelites who lived in the empire ruled by David, and 1900 years separate us from the New Testament era. Unlike Egypt, where everyday life is richly portrayed in contemporary illustrated texts, no such illustrations survive from ancient Israel and reconstructions of scenes on the evidence of artefacts unearthed by the archaeologists inevitably contain an element of artistic fancy. It has therefore long been the practice that everyday life in ancient Israel is illustrated from the customs of present-day dwellers in the Holy Land. This is what is done here; but a word of warning is necessary. The villagers and the bedouin of the Holy Land today are the product of many factors that make them unlike the biblical Israelites and Jews. For example, the camel nomadism of the bedouin became possible only with the invention of the saddle in the 1st millennium AD. The peasant stock of Palestine has sometimes intermarried with the lower classes of their foreign rulers: Greeks and Romans, Crusaders, Turks. However, some of the basic technologies of food production have probably remained unchanged for centuries, although the Muslim conquest in the 7th century and the quranic prohibition of the drinking of alcohol have meant that vineyards are today tended only in the few Christian areas of the land. The paramount importance of collection and storage of water in a region of scanty rainfall has remained a constant factor and rainwater cisterns feature on both inhabited and archaeological sites.

Using the wind to separate chaff from wheat.

"The wicked . . . are like chaff which the wind drives away"
(PSALM 1:4)

Threshing with a sledge pulled over the grain by a horse.

"I will make of you a threshing sledge, new, sharp, and having teeth"
(ISAIAH 41:15)

EVERYDAY LIFE IN BIBLICAL TIMES

"I will seek the lost, and I will bring back the strayed"
(EZEKIEL 34:16) ▷

"The ploughman should plough in hope . . . of a share in the crop"
(1 CORINTHIANS 9:10) ▽

A shepherd.

"The kingdom of heaven is like leaven which a woman took and hid in three measures of flour, till it was all leavened"
(MATTHEW 13:33) ▷

Ploughing.

Baking bread.

143

EVERYDAY LIFE IN BIBLICAL TIMES

"Will the Lord be pleased . . . with ten thousands of rivers of oil?"
(MICAH 6:7) ▷

Oil press.

Oil lamp.

A tomb. Ossuaries.

"They cast lots to divide his garments"
(LUKE 23:34) ▷

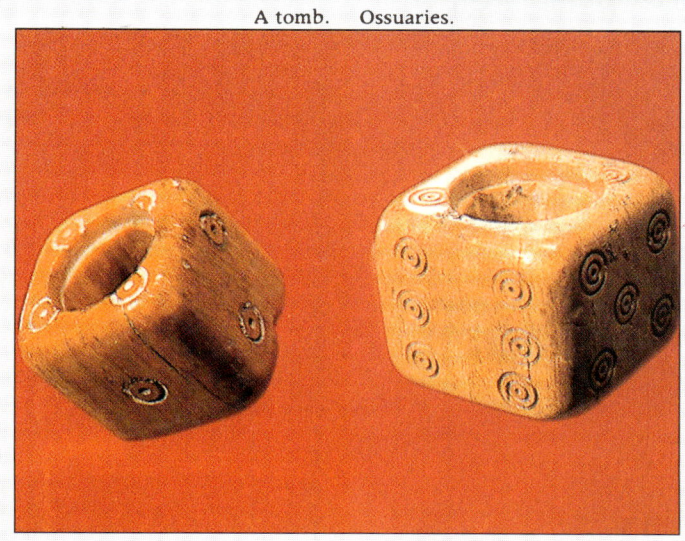

"He sent and took the bones out of the tombs"
△ (2 KINGS 23:16)

Dice.

EVERYDAY LIFE IN BIBLICAL TIMES

"Whose likeness and inscription is this?"
(MATTHEW 22:20) ▽

Coin mould.

Coin of Tyre.

"Jezebel . . . painted her eyes, and adorned her head"
(2 KINGS 9:30) ▽

Cosmetics.

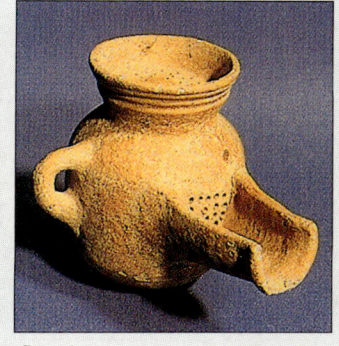

Beer jug.

"'Come', they say . . . 'let us fill ourselves with strong drink; and tomorrow will be like this day, great beyond measure'"
(ISAIAH 56:12) △

A frying pan.

"David . . . saw from the roof a woman bathing"
(2 SAMUEL 11:2) ▽

Stone weights.

"You shall not have in your bag two kinds of weights, a large and a small"
(DEUTERONOMY 25:13) △

"She took the pan and emptied it out before him"
(2 SAMUEL 13:9) △

Woman bathing.

BETHEL, SAMARIA, CARMEL AND JEZREEL

Left The valley of Jezreel, seen here from the north, is a major feature of the northern part of Israel, dividing lower Galilee from the Samaria hills.

Right The Jezreel valley provided a major route from west to east, from the coastal plain to the Jordan valley. During the dry season it was ideal terrain for the deployment of chariots in warfare. It also constituted a natural boundary between Galilee and the Samaria hills. The Carmel range presented an obstacle to access to the valley of Jezreel from the southern coastal plain, and passes through Carmel were of strategic importance. The geological difference of the Menashe hills not only allowed much more settlement there than elsewhere; these hills contained one of the major passes, guarded at the northern end by Megiddo.

Note (U) = unlocated site
Ataroth Num. 32:3,34; Josh. 16:2,7 **B5**
Balamon (Balbalim, Bebai, Belmain) Judith 4:4; 7:3; 8:3; 15:4 (U)
Beth-eked 2 Kgs. 10:12,14 **B4**
Beth-haggan (En-gannim) 2 Kgs. 9:27; Josh. 19:21; 21:29 **C4**
Beth-millo Judg. 9:20 (U)
Beth-shittah Judg. 7:22 **D3**
Bezek 1 Sam. 11:8 **D4**
Bileam *see* Ibleam
Dabbesheth Josh. 19:11 **B3**
Dothan Gen. 37:17; 2 Kgs. 6:13 **C4**
Ebez Josh. 19:20 (U)
En-gannim *see* Beth-haggan
Esdraelon, plain of *see* Jezreel, valley of
Geba Judith 3:10 **C5**
Gilboa 1 Sam. 28:4; 31:1; 2 Sam. 21:12 **D4**
Great Plain *see* Jezreel, valley of
Hapharaim Josh. 19:19 **B3**
Harod Judg. 7:1; 2 Sam. 23:25; 1 Chr. 11:27 **D3**
Harosheth-ha-goiim Judg. 4:2,13,16 **B2**
Ibleam (Bileam) Josh. 17:11; Judg. 1:27; 2 Kgs. 9:27; 1 Chr. 6:70 **C4**
Jezreel Josh. 19:18; 1 Sam. 25:43; 29:1,11; 1 Kgs. 4:12; 18:45,46; 21:1,3; 2 Kgs. 8:29; 9:10,15,16,36; 10:6,7; 2 Chr. 9:30, 36; 10:6–7,11; 22:6 **C3**
Jezreel, valley of (Great Plain, plain of Esdraelon, plain of Megiddo) Josh. 17:16; Judg. 6:33; 2 Chr. 35:22; Hos. 1:5; Zech. 12:11 **C3**
Jokneam (Jokmeam) Josh. 12:22; 19:11; 21:34; 1 Kgs. 4:12; 1 Chr. 6:68 **B3**
Kattath *see* Kitron
Kishon, river Judg. 4:7,13; 5:21; 1 Kgs. 18:40 **C3**
Kitron (Kattath) Josh. 19:15; Judg. 1:30 **B1 B3**
Megiddo Josh. 12:21; 17:11; Judg. 1:27; 5:29; 1 Kgs. 4:12; 9:15; 2 Kgs. 9:27; 23:29–30; 1 Chr. 7:29; 2 Chr. 35:22; Zech. 12:11; Rev. 16:16 **C3**
Megiddo, plain of *see* Jezreel, valley of
Ophrah Judg. 6:11,24; 8:27,32; 9:5 **C3 D3**
Rabbith Josh. 19:20 **D4**
Samaria 1 Kgs. 13:32; 16:24,28; 20:1,10,17; 22:37–39,51; 2 Kgs. 1:2; 6:24; 7:1,18; 10:1; 16:6; 18:10,34; 21:13,18; 2 Chr. 18:2; 25:13; 28:15; Ezra 4:10; Neh. 4:2; Isa. 9:9; 10:9–11; Jer. 23:13; 31:5; Hos. 7:1; 8:5,6; 10:5,7; 13:16; Amos 3:9; 4:1; 6:1; 8:14; Obad. 19; Mic. 1:1,5,6; Luke 17:11; John 4:4,9; Acts 8:1,5,14 **C5**
Taanach Josh. 12:21; 17:11; 21:25; Judg. 1:27; 5:19; 1 Kgs. 4:12; 1 Chr. 7:29 **C3**
Thebez Judg. 9:50 **D5**
Tirzah Josh. 12:24; 1 Kgs. 14:17; 15:21,23; 16:6,8,9,15,17,23; 2 Kgs. 14:14,16; S. of S. 6:4 **D5**

Map Legend

scale 600m / 400m / 200m / 100m / 0 / 200m below sea level

settlement
- ■ 2nd millennium
- ● 2nd millennium, ancient name unknown
- □ Iron Age c.1200–587 BC
- □ Hellenistic 330–40 BC
- □ Herodian, Roman-Byzantine, after 40 BC

forest c.1200BC
seasonal stream, wadi
• spring or well

SEBASTE classical name
(Muhraqa) modern name
route

scale 1:250 000
0 — 10km
0 — 7miles

Map Labels

MOUNT CARMEL
?Harosheth-ha-goiim
(Oren)
Horn of Carmel (Muhraqa)
Jokneam (Jokmeam)
?Dabbesheth
(Yoqneam)
Kishon
Valley of Jezreel
Great Plain
Plain of Esdraelon
Plain of Megiddo
(Adashim)
Mount Tabor
?Kitron (Kattath)
Hapharaim
MENASHE HEIGHTS
?Ophrah 1
Hill of Moreh
HAMORE HILL
?Ophrah 2
Megiddo
Jezreel
Harod
Spring of Harod
Beth-shittah
Taanach
GILBOA MOUNTAINS
IRON HILLS
(Zadon)
(Harod)
Beth-shean
Beth-haggan (En-gannim) GINAE
Ibleam (Bileam)
Gilboa
(Hadera)
Valley of Dothan (Arrabeh Plain)
Dothan
(Bezeq)
Jordan
Beth-eked
Rabbith
Bezek
Sanur Plain
Attara-Rama Basin
(Nablus)
Ataroth
Thebez
Geba
Yazith
?Beth-amri
Tirzah
?Siphtan
Sharaf Basin
Samaria SEBASTE

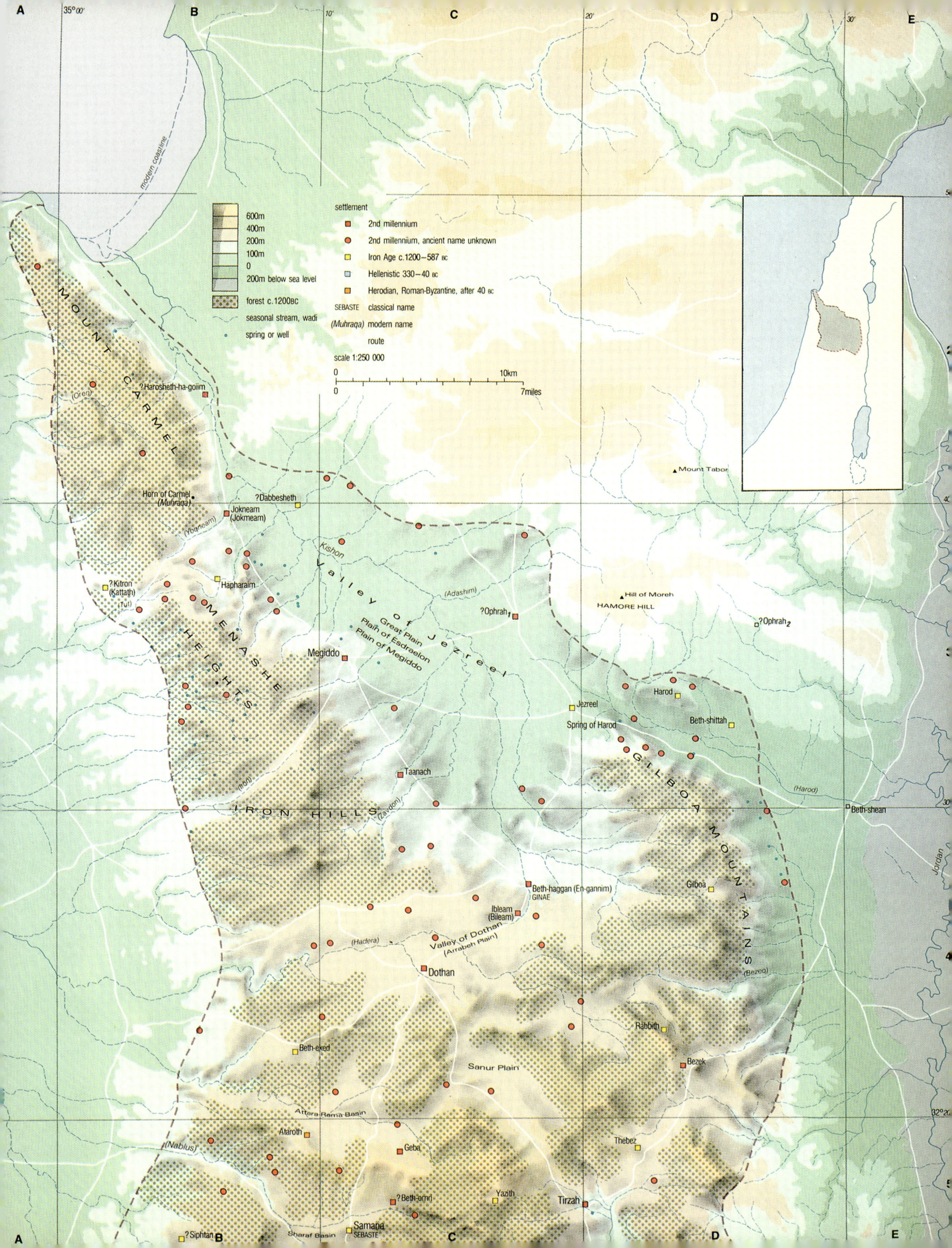

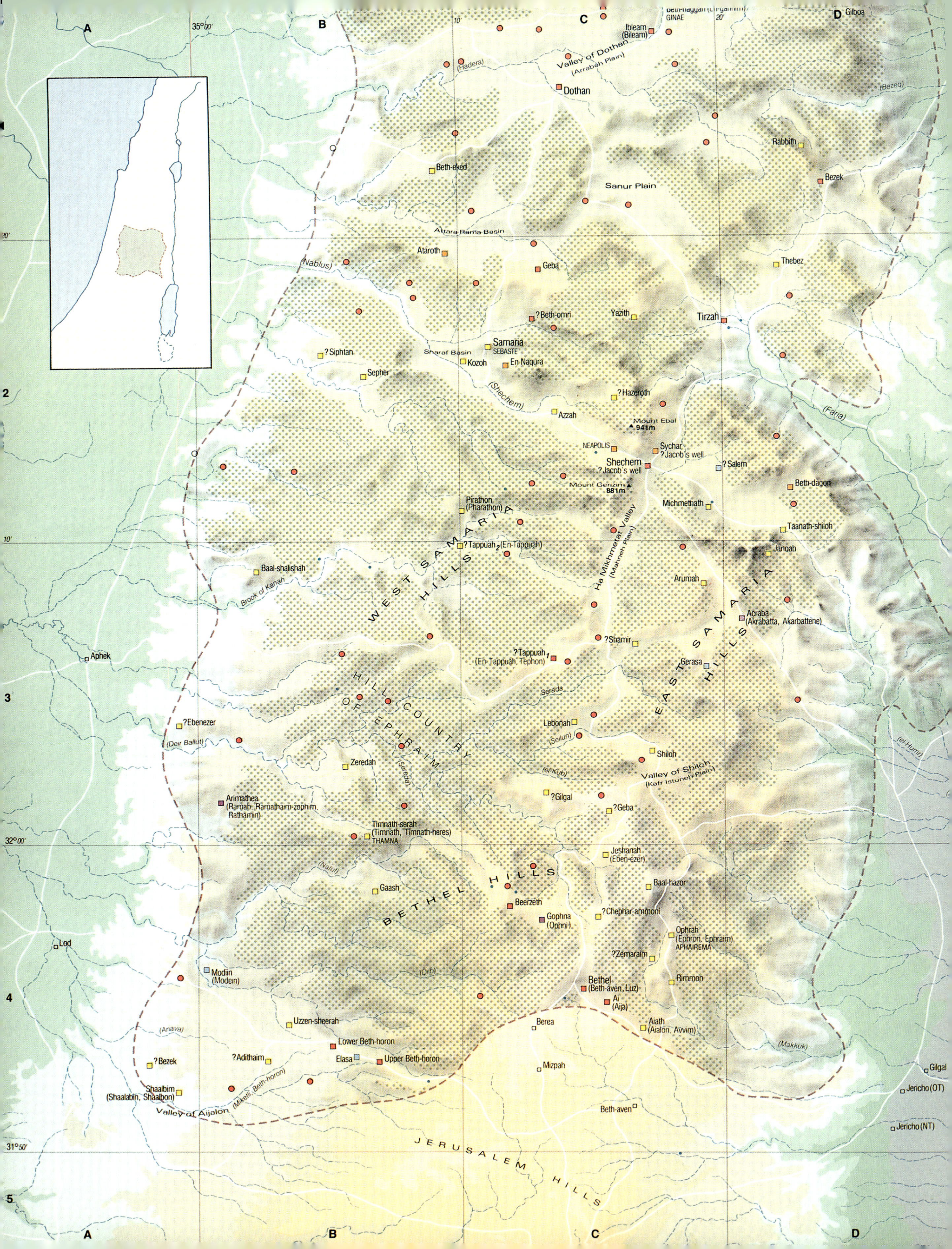
A
B
C
D
35°00'
10'
20'
Gilboa
Ibleam
(Bileam)
GINAE
Valley of Dothan
(Arrabah Plain)
(Hadera)
Dothan
(Bezeq)
Rabbith
Beth-eked
Bezek
Sanur Plain
Attara-Rama Basin
20'
Ataroth
Geba
Thebez
(Nablus)
?Beth-omri
Yazith
Tirzah
Samaria
SEBASTE
Sharaf Basin
?Siphtan
Kozoh
En-Naqura
Sepher
2
(Shechem)
?Hazeroth
(Far'a)
Azzah
Mount Ebal
941m
NEAPOLIS
Sychar
?Jacob's well
Shechem
?Jacob's well
?Salem
Mount Gerizim
881m
Beth-dagon
Pirathon
(Pharathon)
Michmethath
Ha Mikhmetat Valley
(Mahneh Plain)
Taanath-shiloh
10'
?Tappuah2 (En-Tappuah)
Janoah
Baal-shalishah
WEST SAMARIA HILLS
Brook of Kanah
Arumah
Acraba
(Akrabatta, Akarbattene)
?Shamir
EAST SAMARIA HILLS
Aphek
?Tappuah1
(En-Tappuah, Tephon)
Gerasa
HILL COUNTRY OF EPHRAIM
Serada
3
?Ebenezer
Lebonah
(Deir Ballut)
(Seilun)
(el-Humr)
Shiloh
Zeredah
(el-Kub)
Valley of Shiloh
(Kafr Istuneh Plain)
?Gilgal
?Geba
Arimathea
(Ramah, Ramathaim-zophim, Rathamin)
Timnath-serah
(Timnath, Timnath-heres)
THAMNA
32°00'
Jeshanah
(Eben-ezer)
(Natuf)
Baal-hazor
BETHEL HILLS
Gaash
Beerzeth
?Chephar-ammoni
Gophna
(Ophni)
Ophrah
(Ephron, Ephraim)
APHAIREMA
Lod
?Zemaraim
Modiin
(Modein)
(Dilb)
Bethel
(Beth-aven, Luz)
Rimmon
4
Ai
(Aija)
Uzzen-sheerah
Berea
Aiath
(Aialon, Avvim)
(Anava)
Lower Beth-horon
(Makkuk)
?Adithaim
Elasa
Upper Beth-horon
?Bezek
Mizpah
Gilgal
Shaalbim
(Shaalabin, Shaalbon)
Jericho (OT)
Valley of Aijalon
(Mikeh Beth-horon)
Beth-aven
Jericho (NT)
31°50'
JERUSALEM HILLS
5
A
B
C
D

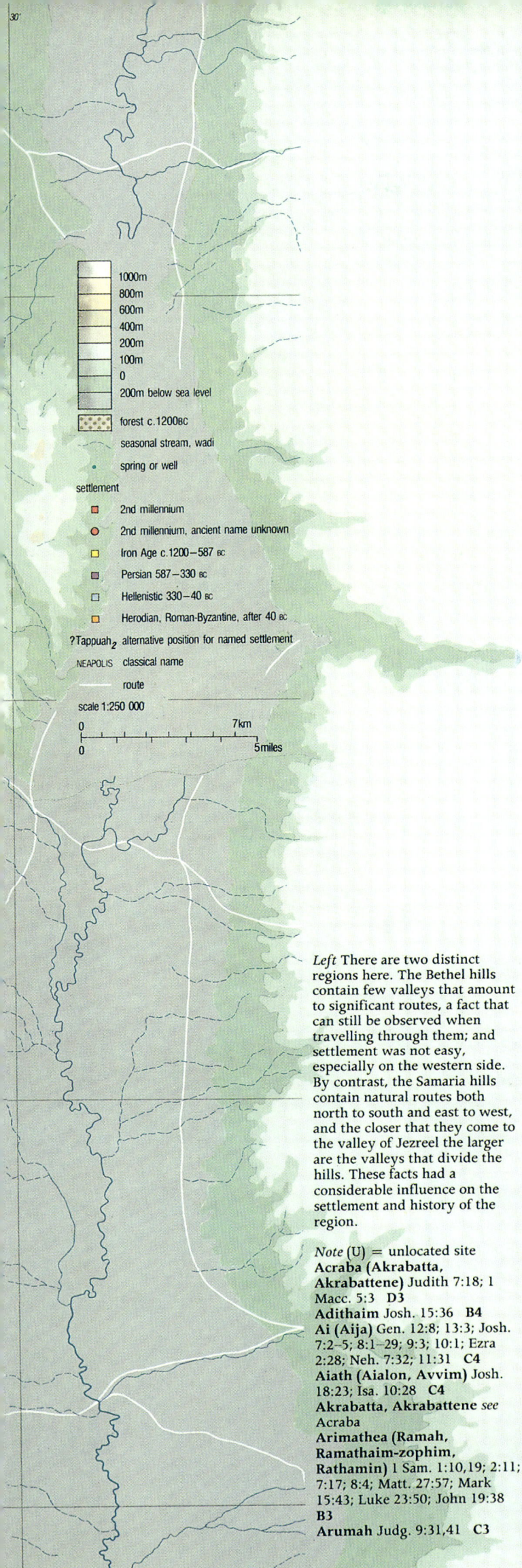

BETHEL, SAMARIA, CARMEL AND JEZREEL

Map legend:
- 1000m, 800m, 600m, 400m, 200m, 100m, 0, 200m below sea level
- forest c.1200 BC
- seasonal stream, wadi
- spring or well
- settlement
  - 2nd millennium
  - 2nd millennium, ancient name unknown
  - Iron Age c.1200–587 BC
  - Persian 587–330 BC
  - Hellenistic 330–40 BC
  - Herodian, Roman-Byzantine, after 40 BC
- ?Tappuah₂ alternative position for named settlement
- NEAPOLIS classical name
- route
- scale 1:250 000
- 0 — 7km
- 0 — 5miles

Left There are two distinct regions here. The Bethel hills contain few valleys that amount to significant routes, a fact that can still be observed when travelling through them; and settlement was not easy, especially on the western side. By contrast, the Samaria hills contain natural routes both north to south and east to west, and the closer that they come to the valley of Jezreel the larger are the valleys that divide the hills. These facts had a considerable influence on the settlement and history of the region.

Note (U) = unlocated site
Acraba (Akrabatta, Akrabattene) Judith 7:18; 1 Macc. 5:3 D3
Adithaim Josh. 15:36 B4
Ai (Aija) Gen. 12:8; 13:3; Josh. 7:2–5; 8:1–29; 9:3; 10:1; Ezra 2:28; Neh. 7:32; 11:31 C4
Aiath (Aialon, Avvim) Josh. 18:23; Isa. 10:28 C4
Akrabatta, Akrabattene see Acraba
Arimathea (Ramah, Ramathaim-zophim, Rathamin) 1 Sam. 1:10,19; 2:11; 7:17; 8:4; Matt. 27:57; Mark 15:43; Luke 23:50; John 19:38 B3
Arumah Judg. 9:31,41 C3
Avvim see Aiath
Ayyah 1 Chr. 7:28 (U)
Azzah Deut. 2:23; 1 Kgs. 4:24; Jer. 25:20 C2
Baal-hazor 2 Sam. 13:23 C4
Baal-shalishah 2 Kgs. 4:42 B3
Beerzeth 1 Macc. 9:4 C4
Bethel (Beth-aven, Luz) Gen. 12:8; 13:3; 28:19; 31:13; 35:1; 36:8,15–16; Josh. 8:9,12,17; 12:16; 16:1,2; 18:13,22; Judg. 4:5; 1 Sam. 7:6; 13:2; 1 Kgs. 12:29–33; 13:1,4,32; 2 Kgs. 2:2,3,23; 10:29; 1 Chr. 7:28; 2 Chr. 13:19; Jer. 48:13; Hos. 12:4; Amos 3:14; 5:5,6; 7:10,13 C4
Beth-horon (lower) Josh. 16:3; 18:13; 1 Kgs. 9:17; 2 Chr. 8:5; (upper) Josh. 16:5; 2 Chr. 8:5; (both together) Josh. 18:14; 21:22; 1 Chr. 6:68; 7:24; B4
Bethulia Judith 4:6; 6:10,11,14; 7:1,3,6,13,20 (U)
Bezek Judg. 1:4–5 A4
Bochim Judg. 2:1,5 (U)
Chephar-ammoni Josh. 18:24 C4
Ebal, Mount Deut. 11:29; Josh. 8:30,33 C2
Eben-ezer see Jeshanah
Elasa 1 Macc. 9:5 B4
En-tappuah Josh. 17:17 (U)
Gaash Josh. 24:30; Judg. 2:9; 2 Sam. 23:30; 1 Chr. 11:32 B4
Geba Josh. 21:17 C3
Gedor 1 Chr. 12:7 (U)
Gerizim, Mount Deut. 11:29; 27:12; Josh. 8:33; Judg. 9:7 C2
Gilgal Deut. 11:30; 2 Kgs. 2:1; 4:38 C3
Gophna (Ophni) Josh. 18:24 C4
Hazeroth Deut. 1:1; Num. 11:35; 33:17 C2
Jacob's Well John 4:5 C2
Janoah Josh. 16:6,7 D3
Jeshanah (Eben-ezer) 1 Sam. 7:12; 2 Chr. 13:19 C4
Lebonah Judg. 21:19 C3
Luz see Bethel
Michmethath Josh. 16:6; 17:7 C2
Modin (Modein) 1 Macc. 2:1,15,23,70; 9:19; 13:25,30; 2 Macc. 13:14 B4
Ophni see Gophna
Ophra (Aphairema, Ephron, Ephraim) Josh. 18:15,23; 1 Sam. 13:17,23; 2 Chr. 13:9; John 11:54 C4
Pirathon (Pharathon) Judg. 12:15; 2 Sam. 23:30; 1 Chr. 11:31; 1 Macc. 9:50 C2
Ramah, Ramathaim-zophim, Rathamin see Arimathea
Salem Gen. 14:18 C2
Shaalbim (Shalabian, Shallbon) Josh. 19:42; Judg. 1:35; 2 Sam. 23:32; 1 Kgs. 4:9; 1 Chr. 11:33 B4
Shamir Judg. 10:1,2 C3
Shechem Gen. 12:6; 33:18; 34:26; 35:4; 37:12–14; Num. 26:31; Josh. 17:2,7; 20:7; 21:21; 24:1,25,32; Judg. 8:31; 9:1–41,46,47,49,59; 21:19; 1 Kgs. 12:1; 25:1; 1 Chr. 6:67; 7:28; 2 Chr. 10:1; Ps. 60:6; 108:7; Jer. 41:5; Acts 7:16 C2
Shiloh Josh. 18:1,8,9,10; 21:2,19,21; 22:9,12; Judg. 18:31; 21:19; 1 Sam. 1:24; 3:21; 4:3,4; 1 Kgs. 2:27; 14:2,4; Ps. 78:60; Jer. 7:12,14; 26:6,9; 41:5 C3
Taanath-shiloh Josh. 16:6 D2
Tappuah (Tephon) Josh. 12:17; 16:8; 17:7,8; 2 Sam. 2:9; 1 Macc. 9:50 B3
Timnath-serah (Thamna, Timnath, Timnath-heres) Josh. 19:50; 24:30; Judg. 2:9; 1 Macc. 9:50 B3
Uzzen-sheerah 1 Chr. 7:24 B4
Zemaraim Josh. 18:22 C4
Zeredah 1 Kgs. 11:26 B3

Description of the region

This section combines areas which geographers normally treat separately. The Bethel hills are regarded as a continuation of the Hebron hills, separated from them by the Jerusalem saddle. The valley of Jezreel is usually treated together with Galilee, while the Carmel range is taken together with the Gilboa mountains. The reason for treating in one section the areas named in the title is that they constitute the heartland of what became the northern kingdom after the division of the kingdom at Solomon's death. As has been pointed out in the section on Galilee (p.134), Israel's hold on the area to the north of the valley of Jezreel was at times tenuous. However, until the final destruction of the northern kingdom by the Assyrians in 721 BC, the kingdom even in its weakest moments was able to hold on to most of the Bethel and Samaria hills. The treatment of these areas together also enables a contrast to be drawn between the main territory of Judah and that of the heartland of Israel.

We have seen that Judah occupied quite exacting country. The Judean desert afforded only grazing for sheep, and agriculture was limited on the Hebron hills and the eastern Shephelah. The western Shephelah was better provided, yet even here the rainfall diminished the further south one went. The Bethel hills resemble the Hebron hills, except that they are much wider because they extend to the coastal plain on the west without an intervening Shephelah. Also, on their east side the Bethel hills descend more abruptly into the rift valley. The Samaria hills, on the other hand, have broader valleys between the hills, and the further north one goes the more small plains one sees, until the quite substantial plains of the Marj Sanur and the Sahel Arrabeh (valley of Dothan) are reached. Several miles from the Sahel Arrabeh is the town of Jenin (Beth-haggan) on the edge of the valley of Jezreel which forms a great plain between the Samarian hills and lower Galilee and at its broadest point is nearly 20km (12·4 miles) wide.

Turning now to describe the areas in a little more detail, we can see that the Bethel hills provided little encouragement in ancient times either for settlement or for travel. The limestones which cover most of the hills formed only shallow, uncultivable soils, and such settlement as there was tended to be on slopes overlooking watercourses. The patterns of settlement in the 2nd millennium also suggest that the area was forested. On the central core of the Bethel hills, for example, it is noticeable that the settlements are on the eastern or western fringes of the mountains. Travel in the Bethel hills was made difficult by the deep valleys which the watercourses cut into the hills, and by the fact that these did not combine together in such a way as to provide natural routes in either a west–east or a north–south direction. The geographical divide between the Bethel hills and the Jerusalem saddle was roughly the boundary in Old Testament times between Benjamin to the south and Ephraim to the north.

The hills of Samaria begin at a line running roughly west–east along the courses of the wadis Deir Ballut, el-Kub and Seilun to the Sahel Kafr Istuneh (valley of Shiloh). Their northern boundary is the Sahel Arrabeh (valley of Dothan), the valley of Jezreel and the Gilboa range. Further, the Samaria hills are divided into eastern and western halves by a line running south-southwest to north-northeast through the Sahel Mahneh (Emek ha-Mikhmetat) to Tubas. The dominating feature of the western Samarian hills is the high central core of mountains whose most famous summits are Jebel et-Tur (Mount Gerizim, 881m, 2890ft) and Jebel Islamiyeh (Mount Ebal, 941m, 3087ft). These two summits are divided by the valley of the Wadi Nablus (Nahal Shechem). To the south of the central core the western hills are at their widest. The rocks are hard, and the valleys are deeply cut. Not only is there little cultivable land, but some of the limestone, especially towards the coastal plain, is unsuitable for cultivation. Patterns of settlement in the 2nd millennium BC indicate only sparse occupation of these southerly western hills, mostly on slopes above or at the head of watercourses.

Above the Wadi Nablus the hills are predominantly of chalk and there are several basins, notably the Deir Sharaf and Attara-Rama basins, the Marj Sanur and the Sahel Arrabeh (valley of Dothan). There is a noticeable increase of 2nd-millennium settlements in the northerly western hills, both around the basins and along the wider valleys cut by watercourses into the chalk hills. To the north of the Sahel Arrabeh (valley of Dothan) begins the Carmel range (see below).

The eastern Samarian hills also have a mountainous core, which attains heights almost comparable to those of the western core, before sloping steeply to the rift valley. As a result of the steep slopes, and their deeply cut watercourses, settlement in the 2nd millennium was very much more sparse than in the western sector. In the northern part of the eastern hills there was virtually no settlement at all. In the southern part settlement was concentrated along the Wadi Faria and on the extreme eastern or western slopes of the mountainous core, at the head of watercourses or where there were springs.

The Carmel range is usually divided into three parts. The northern part, roughly north of the Nahals Tut and Jokneam, rises steeply from the valley of the Nahal Kishon to a ridge whose height increases the further south it goes, until it reaches a maximum height of 548m (1798ft). To the west of the ridge is a basin along part of which flows the Nahal Oren. To the west of this basin hills slope more gently down to the coastal plain, being cut by watercourses that conduct the waters from the west of the watershed to the Mediterranean. At the southeastern edge of this first area of the Carmel range is the horn of Carmel, the traditional site of Elijah's confrontation with the prophets of Baal (1 Kings 18). The site, also called Muhraqa, is at a height of 482m (1581ft) and has a commanding view in several directions.

The second portion of the Carmel range is called the Menashe heights. It is roughly 18 by 12km (11·2 by 7·4 miles), formed of soft limestone and chalk, rising in height as it goes south. Agriculturally it is in a quite different class from those sections of Carmel to its north and south. The patterns of settlement in the 2nd millennium show how suitable it was for subsistence compared with the other parts of Carmel. At its southern boundary, mainly along the valley of the Nahal Iron, went one of the principal international routes in biblical times—the "Way of the Sea" from the coastal plain to the valley of Jezreel. Guarding this route on the edge of the valley of Jezreel was the magnificent mound of the city of Megiddo. South of the Nahal Iron and to the northern edge of the Sahel Arrabeh (valley of Dothan) are the Iron hills. In the 2nd millennium settlement here was principally on the northern edges of the Sahel Arrabeh.

Usually considered together with the Carmel range is the Gilboa range which juts out into the southeastern edge of the valley of Jezreel. Its core of highest mountains, which reach a maximum of 538m (1765ft), is shaped roughly in an arc. On the northern and eastern sides of the core there are steep slopes into the valleys of Harod and Bethshean. These valleys are about 100m (328ft) below sea level, thus accentuating the height of the central core if viewed from the east. On the western side the Gilboa range slopes to the Jezreel valley and the Samaria hills by way of a terrace about 300m (984ft) high and terraced slopes. In ancient times settlement was confined to the side that overlooks the valleys of Harod and Bethshean, this side being by far the better provided with springs.

The valley of Jezreel is a triangular plain of about 365sq km (141sq miles) which connects the coastal plain north of Haifa with the rift valley by way of smaller valleys at its northwestern and southeastern extremities. It is a vast catchment area for the Nahal Kishon, which was liable to flooding before the construction of a modern drainage system. As will be noted later, the valley was the scene of important battles in biblical times; but patterns of settlement suggest that the swamps that were known at least from Roman times were also present in biblical times. Settlement was principally on the edges of the valley, and was particularly concentrated at the point where the Menashe heights bordered it.

Taking together the regions treated in the present section, we may presume that, apart from the valley of Jezreel and the basins of western Samaria, the whole area was forested in ancient times. Examples of pine and evergreen oak forests survive on the northern part of the Carmel range, while the Menashe heights were suitable for the deciduous Tabor oak. Thomson, probably wrongly identifying the "forest of Ephraim" in which the forces of David and Absalom fought (2 Samuel 18:6–7) with the woods on the western bank of the Jordan, nonetheless provides useful information. He commented that "the region where the battle was fought is still covered with such forests—that 'wood of Ephraim', with thick oaks, and tangled bushes, and thorny creepers growing over rugged rocks..."

The biblical record
The earliest mention of the region in the Bible is in Genesis 12:6 where it is reported that Abraham stopped at Shechem at the "oak of Moreh". The importance of Shechem (Tell Balata) derived from its location. It is flanked by the mountains Ebal and Gerizim, and it stands in the valley of the Wadi Nablus where the wadi joins the Sahel Mahneh. It is at a crossroads of north–south and east–west routes, in a part of the land where such routes were few and far between in biblical times. While at Shechem, Abraham received the promise that his descendants would be given the land of Canaan (Genesis 12:7). Shechem was an apt place for such a promise, being a centre of communications and giving commanding views of the land from the mountains flanking it. Jacob too paused at Shechem on his return from his Aramean exile (Genesis 33:18–20). It is recorded that he purchased land there and erected an altar to God, the God of Israel.

Genesis 34 relates a distasteful incident in which two of Jacob's sons, Simeon and Levi, play a trick on the men of Shechem in retaliation for the humiliation of Dinah, Jacob's daughter, by Shechem, the son of the prince of the city. Shechem's lust for Dinah having turned to tender love, he wishes to marry Dinah formally. Jacob's sons demanded that before Dinah or any other of their family could be married to a Shechemite, it would be necessary for the men of Shechem to be circumcised. When the men of Shechem agreed and were circumcised, Simeon and Levi, against their father's wish, killed the men of Shechem while they were still weak from the effects of the circumcision. Some scholars have seen in this story an early stage of the Israelite conquest before the Exodus. It has been pointed out that the book of Joshua contains no explicit account of the conquest of the Shechem area, yet the tribes gather there at the close of the book (chapter 24). One possible explanation would be that Shechem did not need to be conquered by Joshua because it was already in the hands of Israelites who had not gone down to Egypt.

In Deuteronomy 27 is recorded a command of Moses to the Israelites to set up an altar on Mount Ebal when they occupy the land of Canaan, and to set up stones on which God's Law is to be written. A ceremony is also to be performed in which six tribes stand on Mount Gerizim and six on Mount Ebal, after which the Levites rehearse 12 commandments expressed in the form of prohibitions (the so-called Shechemite Dodecalogue). Joshua 8:30–35 records the fulfilment of this command.

In the apportionment of the land among the tribes, the whole of the area under discussion in the present section was allocated to Ephraim and Manasseh, with Manasseh having the lion's share (Joshua 17:7–18; Ephraim and Manasseh had other possessions as well). It is interesting to note Joshua's response to the dissatisfaction of Ephraim and Manasseh with their portion. The tribes complained: "The hill country is not enough for us; yet all the Canaanites who dwell in the plain have chariots of iron, both those in Beth-shean and its villages and those in the Valley of Jezreel" (Joshua 17:16). Joshua replied: "You are a numerous people, and have great power... but the hill country shall be yours, for though it is a forest, you shall clear it and possess it to its farthest borders; for you shall drive out the Canaanites, though they have chariots of iron, and though they are strong" (Joshua 17:17–18). The final chapter of Joshua (chapter 24) records the address of Joshua at Shechem to all the tribes and their leaders, including the challenge to the tribes to have sole allegiance to the God of Israel: "choose this day whom you will serve... but as for me and my house, we will serve the Lord" (Joshua 24:15).

Above The Wadi Faria is one of the most important valleys of the eastern Samarian hills. From a little north of Nablus it runs in a southeasterly direction to the Jordan valley, thus providing the major west–east route in that part of the range.

Left The entrance to Nablus, drawn by David Roberts in 1839. The town lies in a narrow valley, famous for its beauty and fertility.

The period of the Judges

During the period of the Judges two important battles were fought in the valley of Jezreel. The first, recorded in Judges 4–5, was against a coalition of Canaanite cities, and has been dealt with in the section on Galilee (p.136), since the Israelite forces met at Mount Tabor. Judges 4 suggests that the main combatants on the Israelite side were from the Galilee tribes of Zebulun and Naphtali. However, the poetic account of the battle in Judges 5 suggests that there were also contingents present from Manasseh (Machir), Ephraim and Benjamin (Judges 5:14).

The victory of Deborah and Barak over the Canaanite cities in the north possibly created a power vacuum that was exploited by the enemies who oppressed Israel in Judges 6. These were the Midianites and Amalekites, roving peoples who were usually located in the Negev (see pp.119, 126). It is possible that poor rainfall in the Negev forced them to travel to the more fertile north. Some groups may have passed along the coastal plain to Gaza (Judges 6:4), while others came along the Jordan valley and into the valley of Jezreel along the Beth-shean and Harod valleys, or kept to the east of Edom and Moab and crossed Jordan south of the Sea of Galilee.

The hero of the Israelite battle against the Midianites and Amalekites was Gideon of the tribe of Manasseh, whose home town of Ophrah has been tentatively located at Afula in the valley of Jezreel. If this identification is correct, Gideon will have summoned to his aid the tribes geographically closest to him—Manasseh, Asher, Zebulun and Naphtali (Judges 6:35), although Issachar is not mentioned. The opposing forces gathered in the valley of Jezreel—the Midianites near Givat Ha-more (the hill of Moreh, Judges 7:1), while Gideon was at the important spring of Harod (En Harod) in the Harod valley, where he reduced his army to a mere 300. The reduction was partly based on observing whether his men maintained an alert position while drinking water (Judges 7:4–7). The battle was won by a ruse in which Gideon approached the enemy camp at night with flaring torches concealed under pitchers. At the agreed signal the torches were uncovered and the enemy panicked, supposing themselves to be surrounded by a mighty force (Judges 7:15–23).

In the rout that followed, the Midianites fled down the Jordan valley and across to the eastern hills. Gideon countered by following them across the Jordan, and by calling out the men of Ephraim to hold the fords of the river, so that the enemy could not cross back. We may presume that the Ephraimites went down to the Jordan from the Sahel Kafr Istuneh (valley of Shiloh). Gideon's victory was such that it is mentioned in other Old Testament traditions. Psalm 83:9–11 appeals to this victory as well as to that of Deborah and Barak:

> Do to them as thou didst to Midian,
> as to Sisera and Jabin at the river Kishon...
> Make their nobles like Oreb and Zeeb,
> all their princes like Zebah and Zalmunna (cf. Judges 7:25, 8:15).

Further, in the prophecy of the birth or coronation of the prince in Isaiah 9:4, it is said:

> For the yoke of his burden,
> and the staff for his shoulder,
> the rod of his oppressor,
> thou hast broken as on the day of Midian.

At Gideon's death his son Abimelech set himself up as a king in Shechem, and enjoyed a stormy rule that lasted for three years (Judges 9). The fact that Gideon had a concubine in Shechem (Judges 8:31) puts a question mark against the identification of Ophrah with Afula. While this location is ideal for the battle of Gideon against the Midianites, Afula is a long way from Shechem for Gideon to have a concubine there. Perhaps, in spite of his refusal of the offer of kingship (Judges 8:23, which some scholars understand as a polite acceptance), Gideon enjoyed a sufficient reputation for him to be fêted far beyond his own town, and for him to have a sort of scattered harem.

Abimelech himself appears to have come from Arumah (Khirbet el-Urma) to the southeast of Shechem. Judges 9:31 mentions him being at Arumah, and at Judges 9:1 he "goes to" Shechem. After Abimelech had persuaded the people of Shechem to make him king (Judges 9:6), Jotham, the one surviving son of Gideon in Shechem who had not been killed by Abimelech's hired assassins (Judges 9:4–5), climbed Mount Gerizim and from there spoke his famous fable (Judges 9:7–20). After a short period, relations between Abimelech and Shechem turned sour, some of the Shechemites rebelled, and Abimelech finally destroyed the city that had made him king and sowed it with salt (Judges 9:45). He also burned the city's tower and all that were sheltering in it (Judges 9:46–49). He met his death while besieging Thebez, identified by some as Tubas and others as Tirzah (Tell el-Farah) (Judges 9:50–56).

Shechem, as we shall see shortly, continued to play an important role in the history of Israel long after the period of the Judges. For the moment, we turn to a city that was important as Israel's religious sanctuary in the premonarchic period. Shiloh (modern Seilun) is at the northern edge of a small plain from which it is possible to go down to the Jordan valley via Wadi Fasail or Wadi el-Humr. Joshua 18:1ff. tells us that the Israelites assembled there and that seven of the tribes received there their share of the land. Shiloh would be an obvious place to assemble for any group that had formerly established its base at Gilgal near Jericho, which is what is envisaged in Joshua 4:19–20. Joshua 18:1 also says that the Israelites set up the tent of meeting at Shiloh, and Judges 21:19 mentions an annual festival at Shiloh. Curiously, according to Judges 20:27, the Ark of the Covenant at this time was not at Shiloh but at Bethel, another important sanctuary to be discussed later. The annual festival at Shiloh provided the opportunity for the men of the tribe of Benjamin, who were short of potential wives (see p.168), to capture some of the maidens of Shiloh when they came to dance at the festival (Judges 21:16–24).

Shiloh is also the setting for the opening of 1 Samuel, the famous story of Hannah's prayer at the sanctuary that God would reverse her childlessness and grant her a son, whom she in turn would dedicate to God's service (1 Samuel 1). The boy who was born to Hannah was Samuel, who served at the sanctuary, and who heard one evening a voice calling him, which was the voice of God, though Samuel mistook it for the voice of Eli the priest (1 Samuel 3). The sombre message that God gave to Samuel was that because of the wickedness of the sons of Eli (1 Samuel 2:12–17) God would punish Eli's house (1 Samuel 3:10–14). The fulfilment of this threat came about when the Philistines defeated Israel at the battle of Aphek, captured the Ark of the Covenant, which had been carried into battle, and killed the two sons of Eli who accompanied the Ark. The text of 1 Samuel 4 gives no hint that Shiloh was destroyed on that occasion. Indeed, a straight reading of 1 Samuel 4:17ff. indicates that Shiloh was not destroyed, because Eli was at Shiloh when news was brought to him that his sons had been killed and the Ark lost. However, in the time of Jeremiah (late 7th century) there was a tradition that God had destroyed Shiloh (Jeremiah 7:12). Perhaps the Philistines destroyed the city and its sanctuary in the follow-up to their initial victory. Aphek, the site of the battle, guarded one of the few west–east routes across the Samarian hills, and was almost level with Shiloh. The detail that the Ark was brought from Shiloh to Aphek (1 Samuel 4:1–4), and the supposition that the Philistines followed up their victory by destroying Shiloh, fit the geographical situation perfectly. The presumed destruction of Shiloh by the Philistines ended the city's importance as far as the Old Testament tradition is concerned. In Jeremiah 41:5 it is recorded that after the destruction of Jerusalem (587 BC) and the murder of the governor Gedaliah (about 582 BC) men came to the temporary seat of administration at Mizpah (see p.180) from Shiloh, as well as from Samaria and Shechem, to present offerings at the temple. These unfortunate men were killed by Gedaliah's assassins, presumably in order to keep the crime a secret (Jeremiah 41:4–8).

With the rise of David to the kingship, and the capture of Jerusalem, that city eclipsed the cities that had hitherto been prominent in the tradition: Beer-sheba, Hebron, Shechem, Bethel. At the death of Solomon, however, the northern tribes were determined to do something to alleviate the hardships they had suffered under Solomon. They gathered at Shechem, and put their demands to Solomon's son Rehoboam that he should ease their burdens (1 Kings 12:1–11). It is interesting that Rehoboam had gone to Shechem to be made king there over Israel (1 Kings 12:1), since David had become king over Israel while still at Hebron, and Solomon was crowned in somewhat rushed circumstances at Jerusalem (1 Kings 1:38–40). Shechem, even though overshadowed by Jerusalem, still retained importance and prestige. In the event Rehoboam refused to accede to the requests for the easing of burdens, and the northern tribes revolted under the leadership of Jeroboam (1 Kings 12:16–24). Jeroboam was encouraged in his rebellion by the prophet Ahijah from Shiloh, who had previously torn his garment into 12 pieces, 10 of which he had given to Jeroboam, signifying that he would rule over 10 tribes (1 Kings 11:26–32). Initially, Jeroboam built Shechem to be the capital of the new northern kingdom Israel (1 Kings 12:25), but he seems to have moved his capital to Penuel in the Jordan valley, possibly as a result of the invasion of the Egyptian Pharaoh Shishak in 924 BC. This is the last substantial reference in the Old Testament to Shechem, apart from the passage already mentioned above from Jeremiah 41:5.

This Egyptian head from Jokneam reminds us of the campaign of Thutmose III in 1468 BC in which he won a decisive victory over the Canaanites in a battle near Megiddo.

The sanctuary at Bethel

One of Jeroboam's most important acts was his establishment of Bethel as one of the main religious sanctuaries of his kingdom (1 Kings 12:29). Bethel (modern Beitin) was situated at the southern end of the Bethel hills, on a crossroads of routes that went north–south and west–east. It was well supplied with water through springs, although its defensive position was not strong. It is mentioned first in Genesis 12:8 as a place near which Abraham built an altar on his way from Shechem to the Negev and Egypt, and then as the place to which he returned after his brief sojourn in Egypt (Genesis 13:1–4). Bethel was also the place where Abraham and Lot parted company. It is not surprising that the wooded Bethel hills could not support the flocks and herds of both of them. From Bethel it is possible to see down into the Jordan valley, and Lot chose to go to that part of the land which was "well watered everywhere like the garden of the Lord" (Genesis 13:10). Bethel next appears in the story of Jacob, as the scene of Jacob's famous dream in which a ladder is set up from earth to heaven (Genesis 28:10–22), with angels ascending and descending upon it. A vivid description of the site of Bethel, and of the remarkable stones to the north of the village that may underlie the dream, has been provided by the American scholar J.P. Peters in 1904: "You are far above Jerusalem, which is visible away to the south. You look over a succession of hills and then across the huge, deep cleft of the Jordan valley to Gilead and Moab beyond. . .just here, occurs a freak of nature so singular that it is difficult to convince oneself that nature and not man is the author. Huge stones seem to be piled one upon another to make columns nine or ten feet or more in height. . . Whoever stands on the hillside above Bethel, especially toward evening, understands with a new understanding the fascinating story of Jacob's flight when night overtook him near Bethel, and there on the height, which was so much nearer to heaven than all the country round about him, he saw the 'ladder'." This description accords well with the story that Jacob, on the morrow, set up a pillar and anointed it with oil.

The king of Bethel is named in Joshua 12:16 as one of those defeated by Joshua, although it is in Judges 1:22–25 that an account of an Israelite conquest of the city itself is found. Not far from Bethel is the town of Ai (modern Khirbet et-Tell), the town which Joshua initially failed to capture after his triumph at Jericho (Joshua 7:2-5). Ai has become a *cause célèbre* in Old Testament studies because archaeological evidence suggests that the site was abandoned from about 2400 BC to 1220 BC, and was therefore not occupied at the time of the Israelite conquest. Attempts to vindicate the biblical narrative in the face of this negative archaeological evidence include the suggestion that Ai was an outpost of Bethel at the time (cf. Joshua 8:17). Since "Ai" means "ruin" in Hebrew, there may be deliberate irony intended in the story—that the Israelites should attempt to capture a ruin, and fail.

The prestige of Bethel as a sanctuary was responsible for the Ark of the Covenant being there in the period of the Judges (Judges 20:27), and for it being chosen by Jeroboam as a major shrine in his new kingdom. The establishment of the shrine in Bethel, in deliberate rivalry to Jerusalem, was to be a source of anguish to the writers of the books of Kings as they traced the history of the people over the following 300 years. Immediately after they noted the setting up of the sanctuary, the writers of Kings recorded a prophecy of an unnamed man of God coming to Bethel and saying to the altar of incense: "O altar, altar, thus says the Lord: 'Behold, a son shall be born to the house of David, Josiah by name; and he shall sacrifice upon you the priests of the high places who burn incense upon you, and men's bones shall be burned upon you'" (1 Kings 13:2–3). Until the fulfilment of this word in the reign of Josiah (2 Kings 23:15–20), and while the northern kingdom lasted, the writers of Kings condemned every king of Israel as evil, because of following in the steps of Jeroboam.

For apparently different reasons, the Prophet Amos strongly condemned Bethel. The writers of Kings regarded the shrine as a breach of the law of the book of Deuteronomy, that only in the place that God chose should sacrifice be offered to him (Deuteronomy 12:13–14). Amos' complaint was that the worship at Bethel was offensive to God because it was not matched by righteous action on the part of the pious, especially in the area of social justice. "On the day I punish Israel for his transgressions", declared the Prophet in God's name, "I will punish the altars of Bethel, and the horns of the altar shall be cut off and fall to the ground" (Amos 3:14). In an ironic address to the pious, Amos (4:4) urged them to "come to Bethel, and transgress", and he declared in a later passage (5:5) "Bethel shall come to nought." There the Hebrew, "Bethel shall come to *Aven* [nought]", is possibly a reference to Beth-aven, implying that Bethel will become as insignificant and unimportant as Beth-aven (cf. Hosea 5:8). These and other sayings against Bethel and the northern kingdom drew a response from Amaziah the priest of Bethel. "O seer, go, flee away to the land of Judah, and eat bread there, and prophesy there; but never again prophesy at Bethel, for it is the king's sanctuary, and it is a temple of the kingdom" (Amos 7:12–13). Amos was not to be easily put off. Bethel might well be a royal sanctuary with hallowed traditions connecting it with Abraham and Jacob. One thing only mattered for the Prophet, and that was that he should speak the words God gave him: "I am a herdsman, and a dresser of sycamore trees, and the Lord took me from following the flock, and the Lord said to me, 'Go, prophesy to my people Israel'" (Amos 7:14–15).

The capital at Samaria

Amos lived in the middle of the 8th century. Although Bethel was still a significant shrine in his day, the capital city of the northern kingdom had been for over 100 years the city of Samaria. The king responsible for building the capital at Samaria was Omri (c. 882–871), an army commander who took the throne after a coup d'état and civil war (1 Kings 16:15–22). Perhaps Omri realized the need for a new capital because he overcame one of his rivals by besieging Tirzah, which had become the capital in succession to Shechem and Penuel as early as the reign of Jeroboam. Tirzah is usually identified provisionally with Tell el-Farah.

Samaria is to the northwest of Shechem, close to the Deir Sharaf plain within the Samarian hills, and on a route to the coastal plain along the Wadi Nablus. It is a magnificent site, being a large rounded hill reaching to 463m (1519ft), and attached to other ground only on its eastern side. The shrewdness of Omri's choice of a capital is shown by the fact that, when it finally capitulated to the Assyrians in 722/1, this was only after a siege lasting three years (2 Kings 17:5). From the time of Omri to its fall in 722/1 Samaria remained the northern capital.

In spite of the undoubted political and economic achievements of Omri, the biblical narrative devotes only 14 verses to him in all. Much more space is devoted to his son Ahab, and his daughter-in-law Jezebel, in whose reign Elijah and the prophetic groups waged a bitter struggle on the issue of who was to be the God of Israel. Elijah began by proclaiming a drought in the land. The effect of this was such that after three years Ahab was forced to scour the land in order to save his horses and mules. "Go through the land to all the springs of water and to all the valleys", were his instructions to his chief steward. "Perhaps we may find grass and save the horses and mules alive, and not lose some of the animals" (1 Kings 18:5).

There next followed the confrontation between Elijah and the prophets of Baal on Mount Carmel. The traditional site for this confrontation is the "horn of Carmel", a point at the southern end of the Carmel hills (see above, p.150) where two main ridges meet. There is now a Carmelite monastery at the site, and a well a little way down the slope from the summit of 482m (1581ft). Although it cannot be proved that the contest took place here, the site is sufficiently imposing in itself for it to be likely that there was an altar here which was used for the contest.

The terms of the contest were that each side should pray to its god for fire to come down from heaven and consume a sacrifice. There were ranged against Elijah 450 prophets of Baal, but in spite of their entreaties, their cutting themselves with swords and lances and their limping dances, no fire fell. When Elijah called upon the God of Israel, fire, possibly lightning, fell from heaven upon the altar he had prepared and consumed not only the sacrifice but the water in the trench about the altar. The prophets of Baal were taken down to the Kishon and there killed. If the traditional site is the correct one, there is a path from the horn of Carmel to the Jezreel valley and the course of the Kishon. After the contest Elijah's servant perceived a tiny cloud over the sea, and as the sky grew black, Elijah advised Ahab to ride with all haste to Jezreel lest the rains should prevent him. Jezreel, probably Ahab's winter residence, was at the eastern end of the valley of Jezreel, where it joins the Harod and Beth-shean valleys. It was about 30km (18·6 miles) from the traditional site of Elijah's contest, and if there was to be a severe storm, Ahab was in real danger of the valley of Jezreel flooding when the Kishon overflowed. Ahab set off back to Jezreel, but was outrun by Elijah who greeted him at the

Above Samaria, rebuilt by Herod the Great and renamed Sebaste, contains many vestiges of its Roman past. Here an Arab herdsman drives his sheep along a former Roman road.

Above right Discoveries from Israelite Samaria of the 9th century BC include the famous ivories which adorned the royal palace. Here a sphinx is shown in a lotus thicket.

Right Beitin is the modern Arab village that stands near the site of ancient Bethel. According to the Old Testament, Abraham built an altar and Jacob set up a sacred pillar here. Later Bethel became one of the chief shrines of the northern kingdom.

city gate (1 Kings 18:41–46). Mount Carmel seems to have been also one of the haunts of Elisha. It was to Elisha at Mount Carmel that the Shunammite woman went when her son died (2 Kings 4:25), and Elisha visited Mount Carmel on his way from Bethel to Samaria (2 Kings 2:25).

For the period of the Prophets Elijah and Elisha and their enemies the house of Omri and Ahab, there are several interesting narratives in which Samaria features. At 1 Kings 20 we read that Ben-hadad, the Syrian king, besieged Samaria, bringing many horses and chariots. Presumably Ben-hadad's best route was to come down to the valley of Jezreel, through to the coastal plain via the vale of Dothan, and then east to Samaria. By this route he would avoid going near Megiddo where Ahab had considerable forces of horses and chariots. Presumably Ben-hadad camped in the Deir Sharaf plain with his forces.

The Syrians were defeated (1 Kings 20:16–21) and rationalized their defeat in the following words: "Their [Israel's] gods are gods of the hills, and so they were stronger than we; but let us fight against them in the plain, and surely we shall be stronger than they" (1 Kings 20:23). The following spring the battle was renewed (1 Kings 20:26). Spring would see the end of the rains, and thus routes would be more firm, but the countryside would have plenty of grass cover for the animals and crops for the men. This time the battle was at Aphek in the coastal plain, the site chosen by the Philistines for one of their decisive actions against Israel (see p.82). Syria was defeated, but Ben-hadad was spared by Ahab. It is interesting that a prophet, who wished to demonstrate visibly to Ahab the king's disobedience to God in sparing Ben-hadad, predicted that a lion would kill another prophet who refused to wound the first prophet when he requested that he be struck (1 Kings 20:35–43). Presumably the lion was in the forests of the western Samarian or Bethel hills.

It was in Samaria that Ahab held the council of war with Jehoshaphat, king of Judah, which was to lead to his death in battle at Ramoth-gilead (1 Kings 22). On the occasion of the council of war, one prophet, Micaiah ben Imlah, stood out against 400 other prophets who predicted a resounding victory for Ahab. Micaiah, however, related his vision of God surrounded by the heavenly council, from which came forth a spirit who said that he would lure Ahab to his death by being a lying spirit in the mouth of the other prophets. Ahab's subsequent death in battle was seen by the biblical writers as a punishment for his seizure of Naboth's vineyard (1 Kings 21). Naboth had a vineyard near Ahab's palace in Jezreel, and when he refused to sell it to the king, Jezebel arranged for Naboth to be falsely accused of blasphemy and to be stoned to death. However, Ahab's use of this stratagem to obtain Naboth's vineyard brought Elijah's condemnation and the prophecy that dogs would lick up Ahab's blood where they had licked up Naboth's. We should note that there is an apparent discrepancy, geographically speaking, between this prophecy and its fulfilment. Naboth was stoned outside Jezreel (1 Kings 21:13), while Ahab's blood was licked up by the dogs at Samaria (1 Kings 22:38) when the dead king was brought back there for burial.

In the reign of Ahab's second son, Joram, the Syrians besieged Samaria and succeeded in reducing the city to the point of capitulation (2 Kings 6:24–7:20). The famine in the city reached the point where children were being boiled and eaten. Elisha predicted the speedy end of the siege and the resumption of normal trading in the city gate. This is the famous occasion on which the besiegers departed in a panic because they heard reports that they were to be attacked by foreign kings coming to Samaria's relief. Four lepers, who were barred from the city, decided to visit the Syrian camp, found it deserted, and then had a splendid time eating and drinking and helping themselves to the spoil. Their revelry was checked when one of them said, "We are not doing right. This day is a day of good news; if we are silent and wait until the morning light, punishment will overtake us; now therefore come, let us go and tell the king's household" (2 Kings 7:9). When the good news was brought to the city, and two mounted men rode after the enemy, all the way as far as the Jordan was littered with clothes and equipment thrown away in haste by the Syrians. Presumably their route to the Jordan valley was via the Wadi Faria.

The final outcome of the opposition of Elijah and Elisha to the house of Omri and Ahab was that one of Elisha's prophets went to Ramoth-gilead and anointed Jehu king over Israel, with instructions to destroy the family of Omri and Ahab (2 Kings 9:1–10). The king of Israel, Joram, was recovering at Jezreel from wounds sustained while fighting at Ramoth-gilead. Driving his chariot furiously so that he would get to Jezreel before the news that he had been anointed and proclaimed king, Jehu came upon an unsuspecting Joram as well as Ahaziah, king of Judah, who was also at Jezreel. Joram and Ahaziah went out to meet Jehu. Jehu shot Joram dead with an arrow, and then pursued Ahaziah who made off towards Beth-haggan (Jenin). Ahaziah was shot trying to escape into the Samarian hills. It now remained for Jehu to kill Ahab's wife, Queen Jezebel, who was at Jezreel, and the remainder of the sons of Ahab, 70 in all in Samaria, whose severed heads were brought by the elders and rulers of Samaria to Jezreel. There they were put in two heaps at the entrance to the gate of the city.

The triumph of the prophetic revolution, inspired by Elijah and Elisha and executed by Jehu, did not have the permanent effect of bringing the people of Israel back to their God. In the 8th century the Prophets denounced the idolatry and injustice of Samaria. Hosea spoke of "the wicked deeds of Samaria" (7:1), and prophesied that "the calf of Samaria shall be broken to pieces" (8:6) and that "Samaria's king shall perish" (10:7). Amos denounced the

> cows of Bashan
> who are in the mountain of Samaria,
> who oppress the poor, who crush the needy,
> who say to their husbands,
> 'Bring, that we may drink' (4:1).

Micah regarded Samaria as the main source of the northern kingdom's corruption.

> What is the transgression of Jacob?
> Is it not Samaria? . . .
> Therefore I will make Samaria
> a heap in the open country,
> a place for planting vineyards;
> and I will pour down her stones into the valley,
> and uncover her foundations (1:5–6).

The destruction of Samaria in 722/1 BC completed these prophecies, although, as we shall see, this did not end the importance of Samaria in Old Testament history. There is, however, one other, delightful tradition that includes Samaria that should be mentioned.

In the story of Elisha (2 Kings 6:8–23) it is related that, while Elisha was in Dothan, the king of Syria sent an army to capture him, because his prophetic powers enabled him to tell in advance to the king of Israel all the plans of the king of Syria. Elisha's servant rose in the morning, saw the horses and chariots surrounding the city, and in some distress brought the news to his master. Elisha spoke the memorable words, "Fear not, for those who are with us are more than those who are with them" (2 Kings 6:16), and then prayed that the servant should be able to see what he could see—that the mountain was full of horses and chariots of fire around about Elisha. The Prophet next asked God to make the army temporarily blind, after which he led them to Samaria, delivered them into the power of the king of Israel, but would not let the king kill them.

After the fall of Samaria in 722/1 BC, the population of the province was deported and replaced with people from other parts of the Assyrian empire (2 Kings 17:24). This encouraged paganism, and the narrative records that God punished the people by sending lions against them (2 Kings 17:25). Presumably in the upheavals caused by war and the deportations, agriculture suffered, lions were not hunted, and these animals increased in numbers in the woods and forests. Samaria retained its importance as the capital of the Assyrian province.

The reign of Josiah (640–609), or rather his death, brings to our notice one of the most

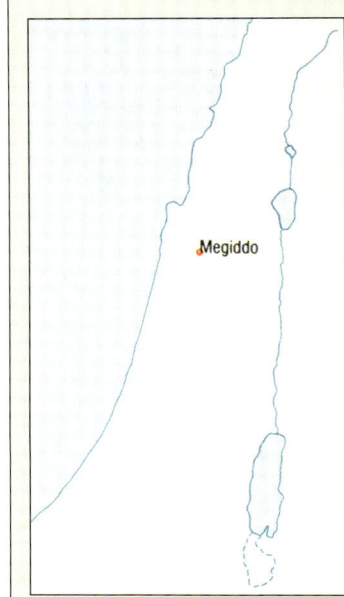

Right This ivory showing a king seated on his throne before his victorious soldiers and their prisoners dates from the 14th or 13th century BC and indicates the Egyptian influence prevalent at that time.

Far right The famous jasper seal from the 8th century BC reads "Belonging to Shema, servant of Jeroboam".

Above A horned altar from the Solomonic period, 10th–9th century BC.

Right Aerial view of Megiddo looking north. The Israelite grain silo is identifiable as a round pit in the centre. To the bottom left of the silo is the site of the stables that are now usually dated to the 9th century BC. Beyond the tell is the valley of Jezreel.

Megiddo

Megiddo is not only a magnificent mound in its own right; it is situated strategically at the northern end of the Iron valley, down which passed one of the most important routes through the Carmel range. Although rarely mentioned in the Old Testament, excavations have indicated Megiddo's importance throughout its history from the 4th millennium to the 6th century BC. During the 2nd millennium BC the original Canaanite city passed through Egyptian, Israelite and Philistine hands, but early in the 10th century David recaptured it and it attained a new splendour when Solomon made it the capital of an administrative district, fortifying it strongly and building a royal residence there. The 9th-century stables with accommodation for 450 horses and chariots show that the kings of Israel recognized the importance of cavalry in maintaining active control of the international route through the valley of Jezreel.

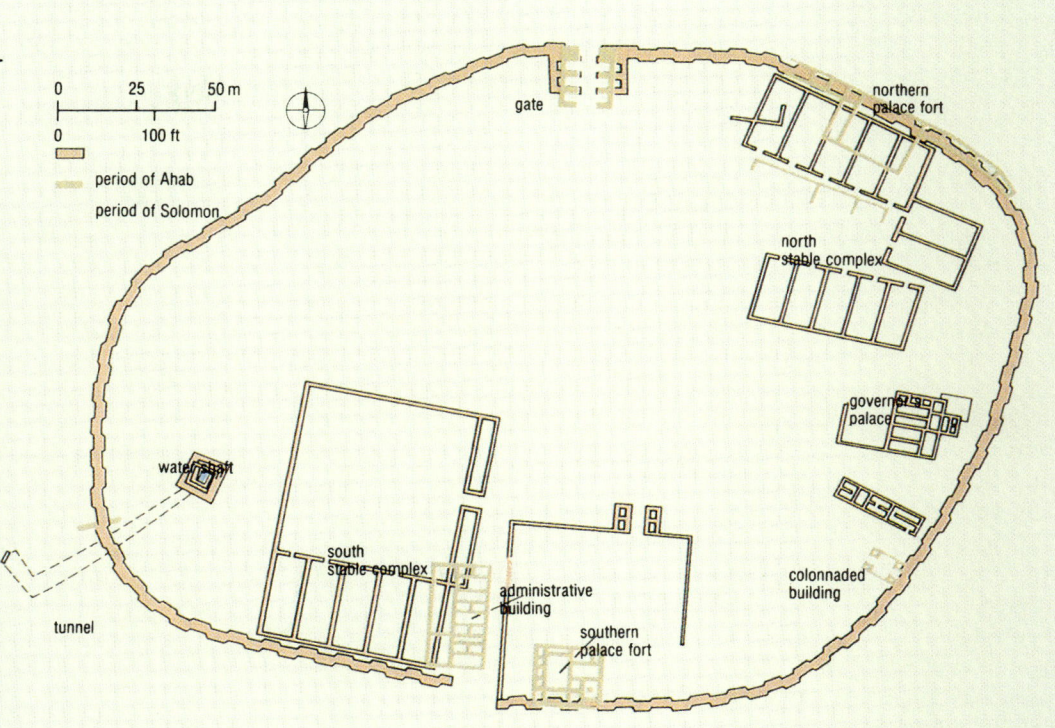

Below Part of the water tunnel that enabled water to be drawn inside the city from the natural supply at the northwest foot of the tell. The tunnel was probably constructed in the reign of Ahab (873–852 BC).

Bottom Figurines of a ram and a monkey found at Megiddo.

important cities of ancient Israel, but one rarely mentioned in the biblical text, Megiddo. This magnificent city stood at a most strategic site, on a slope overlooking the valley of Jezreel at the northeastern corner of the Menashe heights, commanding the road through the heights from the coastal plain to the Jezreel valley. Joshua 12:21 claims that its king was killed, but Judges 1:27 records that the tribe Manasseh did not drive out the inhabitants of Megiddo or its villages. By the reign of Solomon, Megiddo was in Israelite hands (1 Kings 4:12), and excavations have revealed extensive stables from the time of Omri and Ahab. The only substantial biblical reference to Megiddo after the time of Solomon concerns Josiah's death in 609. Josiah met in battle near Megiddo the Egyptian king Necho II. Apparently Josiah was trying to stop Necho from going to the assistance of the king of Assyria who was making a last stand at Haran (the Hebrew text of 2 Kings 23:29 says that Necho was going *against* the king of Assyria). Josiah was bitterly hostile to Assyria, and thus wanted to oppose any Assyrian ally. He paid for his convictions with his life. Megiddo, incidentally, was the city where Ahaziah died (see above, p.156) after Jehu's men had shot him near Ibleam (2 Kings 9:27).

In spite of the repopulation of the northern kingdom with non-Israelites after the fall of Samaria, there remained in the northern kingdom Israelites loyal to the God of Israel. Attention has already been drawn to Jeremiah 41:5, which records that 80 men came from Samaria, Shechem and Shiloh in about 582 BC to the seat of Judean administration at Mizpah. Ezra 4:1–3 claims that when the temple in Jerusalem was being rebuilt under Zerubbabel (c. 520 BC), people from the north, described as "adversaries of Judah and Benjamin", asked to help with the building on the grounds that "we worship your God as you do, and we have been sacrificing to him ever since the days of Esar-haddon king of Assyria who brought us here." Zerubbabel rejected this request. In the governorship of Nehemiah (c. 445 BC) the rebuilding of the wall of Jerusalem was opposed by Sanballat, governor of Samaria. It is usually held that Judea at this time came under the aegis of Samaria, and that the governor of Samaria resented, and therefore attempted to hinder, the rebuilding of the ancient rival city of Jerusalem by someone who was thus diminishing Sanballat's authority and prestige.

These and one or two similar passages are a reminder that, even after the fall of Samaria, there continued to live in the former northern kingdom people who regarded themselves as devotees of the God of Israel and as heirs to the traditions and promises of ancient Israel. Exactly how and when the religious community known as the Samaritans came into being, we cannot say. Probably, by the end of the 4th century BC, the old rivalries between north and south had formalized themselves into the existence of the Samaritans, with a temple on Mount Gerizim overlooking Shechem, and a priesthood and rituals. Although John Hyrcanus destroyed Shechem and the Mount Gerizim temple (suggested dates for this range from 128 to 107 BC), and annexed the area of Samaria to Judea, the Samaritans retained their distinctive beliefs.

The New Testament record

The situation that existed in New Testament times can be sketched as follows. From 6 AD Samaria together with Judea was under the control of Roman governors. The chief city of the area was Sebaste—the city of Samaria rebuilt and renamed by Herod the Great in commemoration of Augustus. Shechem was apparently abandoned as a major settlement between its destruction by John Hyrcanus and its rebuilding in 72 AD by Vespasian under the name of Neapolis, from which is derived its present-day name of Nablus. However, there existed between Judea and Galilee a religious community called the Samaritans, who used as scripture the first five books of the Old Testament, and who believed, among other things, that Mount Gerizim was the place that God had chosen for his people to worship him.

The existence of Samaritans was an important element in the ministry of Jesus and the earliest expansion of Christianity. Relationships between Jews and Samaritans in the 1st century AD generally were at best cool, and at worst hostile. Jews going from Galilee to Judea and back usually avoided Samaria by taking the Jordan valley route, unless they were moving in large numbers in connection with a major festival. In the story of the visit of Jesus and his parents to Jerusalem when Jesus was aged 12 (Luke 2:41–51), it is assumed that the parents went one day's journey towards Galilee before discovering that Jesus was not with them. The traditional site for one day's caravan journey from Jerusalem is the village of el-Bireh close to Ramallah, with its abundant water. Luke 9:51–56 records an incident in which a Samaritan village would not give shelter to Jesus and his disciples when they were journeying from Galilee to Jerusalem "because his face was set towards Jerusalem". James and John may have been expressing typical Jewish resentment against Samaritans when they responded: "Lord, do you want us to bid fire come down from heaven and consume them?" Other expressions in the New Testament of contempt for Samaritans can be found at John 8:48 where the opponents of Jesus accuse him in the words: "Are we not right in saying that you are a Samaritan and have a demon?" Luke 17:11 records that Jesus was "passing along between Samaria and Galilee" when he met 10 lepers near a village. "Passing along between" may well mean that he was going along the Harod and Beth-shean valleys so as to reach the Jordan valley. He was thus, on this occasion, avoiding going through Samaria on his way to Jerusalem. One of the lepers healed by Jesus was a Samaritan, and he alone came back to thank Jesus. Commenting, Jesus exclaimed: "Were not ten cleansed? Where are the nine? Was no one found to return and give praise to God except this foreigner?" (Luke 17:17–18).

Jesus may well have described the Samaritan leper as a foreigner on this occasion, but in the parable of the good Samaritan he held up as the model of the one who acted as a neighbour, not a Jew, but a Samaritan. That must have grated terribly on the ears of Jesus' listeners and offended them deeply, in a way that we cannot appreciate if we know nothing of Jewish–Samaritan relations at that time.

The New Testament incident that gains most from being set in its Samaritan context is the encounter between Jesus and the Samaritan woman at Jacob's well (John 4:1–42). There is no Old Testament record of Jacob establishing a well in this area. Jesus, on his way from Judea to Galilee, "had to pass through" Samaria. If the narrative of John 4 is meant, geographically, to carry on from the end of the preceding chapter, it is odd that Jesus, who was already in the Jordan valley, should go to Galilee not along the Jordan valley but via the central hill country. It entailed a detour whose necessity is difficult to appreciate. The site of the encounter was Jacob's well, said to be close to a town called Sychar. If Sychar is to be identified with Askar to the northeast of Shechem, further questions have to be answered. The traditional location of Jacob's well is at Balata, the site of ancient Shechem. Askar is about a mile distant from the traditional Jacob's well, and has its own well. Why did the woman not use that well, but go to one a mile distant, assuming that the traditional location of Jacob's well at Balata is correct? One reasonable guess is that the woman, whose reputation was doubtful, feared to use the local well at Askar and went a mile distant. Jesus, too, may have used this well, not wishing to encounter Samaritan hostility in Askar itself.

If this guess is anywhere near the truth, then two very different people, shunning the well closest to Sychar for very different reasons, met and had a momentous conversation. Partly it was a discussion of the merits of the Samaritan mountain, Mount Gerizim, versus Jerusalem, as the place chosen supremely by God; but it moved also on to a deeper level at which the woman found herself confronted by someone who made discussions about the relative merits of holy sites irrelevant, and who made new hope and faith possible at the place where she found herself.

In this story, set under the shadow of Mount Gerizim, many of the paradoxes of the Christian gospel are expressed. Jesus breaks down divisions not only by speaking with a Samaritan woman but by being ready to use her vessels. Modern commentaries incline to the view that the words rendered "Jews have no dealings with Samaritans" (John 4:9) mean that Jews will not share vessels with Samaritans for fear of becoming unclean. Further, Jesus, knowing her to be of dubious morals, not only spoke with her but promised to give her the water of eternal life. Next, the woman, on the basis of a no doubt imperfect understanding of who Jesus was, became a missionary to her own people. The scene closes with the Samaritans of the town expressing a faith and hope in Jesus that was hardly possible for many of his fellow countrymen: "They said to the woman, 'It is no longer because of your words that we believe, for we have heard for ourselves, and we know that this is indeed the Saviour of the world'" (John 4:42).

Samaria appears last in the Bible as the place of the first expansion of Christianity beyond Jerusalem. Following the stoning of Stephen (Acts 7:54–60), a persecution against the Church in Jerusalem scattered its members "throughout the region of Judea and Samaria" (Acts 8:1). Philip went to an unnamed city in Samaria, where his preaching and miracle working led to many being baptized as followers of Jesus Christ. Peter and John then visited the city in order to lay hands on the newly baptized so that they might receive the Holy Spirit. The attempt of Simon Magus to buy from the apostles the means of becoming a channel of the Holy Spirit was strongly resisted, after which Peter and John returned to Jerusalem, taking the opportunity to preach to many Samaritan villages as they went.

The Samaritan community today numbers only 500 or 600 in all and is centred in Nablus. They kill the Passover lambs every year at a sacred site on Mount Gerizim overlooking Nablus.

Other Contemporary Religions

One of the constant themes of the Old Testament is that the people of Israel are unfaithful to God and that they turn to other gods. This unfaithfulness is sometimes expressed by the image of Israel as a bride that has become a harlot and has deserted her husband (Jeremiah 3:1-10). Three particular features of other, local, religions that are illustrated here, and which are condemned in the Old Testament, are fertility cults, the cult of the departed, and resort to witchcraft and sorcery. These three activities represented attempts by ordinary people to come to terms with those aspects of their daily lives over which they had little or no control: rainfall or lack of it, death, and unexplainable things such as illness or fatal accidents. By simulating fertility, for example, by means of sacred prostitution, popular religion hoped to establish harmony with the forces of nature and thus encourage fertility among the crops and domesticated animals. The cult of the departed enabled them to cope with the grief and personal loss that death brought to the community. Witchcraft and sorcery gave hope that disaster could be warded off and demons, thought to be responsible for illness, expelled. In opposition to the popular religion, the Prophets of Israel insisted that material prosperity depended upon Israel's obedience to the Law of God, backed up by social justice especially in defending the rights of the weak and the poor. The characterization of faithless Israel as a harlot was based upon the use of sacred prostitution in the fertility rites. However, many ordinary Israelites seem to have found the religion of their neighbours more attractive than the moral demands of the Law and the Prophets.

Below left Incense stands, like this Canaanite example, were in common use. The serpent motif suggested fertility because of the reptile's ability to renew its skin.

Below The bull calf was a common fertility symbol in the ancient Near East. The Old Testament records that while Moses was receiving the Law on Mount Sinai, the Israelites were making a Golden Calf (Exodus 32, see p.44). Jeroboam set up bull images at Bethel and Dan when he formed the breakaway

The setting up of sacred stones was something done all over the ancient Near East. It is recorded that Jacob set up a sacred stone at Bethel (Genesis 28:18). The stones had many religious uses. They could represent the deity, they could mark the spot at which sacred offerings were to be made, or they could be memorial stones for the departed. Their size varied. Those found at Gezer (*below*) reached a height of 3·25m (10ft 8in) while at the "stelae temple" at Hazor (*below right*) they were no higher than 65cm (2ft 2in). They are all thought to be memorial stones for the departed.

OTHER CONTEMPORARY RELIGIONS

kingdom of Israel (1 Kings 12:28). It is usually assumed that in the early religion of Israel (12th to 10th centuries BC) bull figures were regarded as the throne of the invisible deity. However, because the bull was connected with fertility religion, it was likely to corrupt the religion of ordinary Israelites.

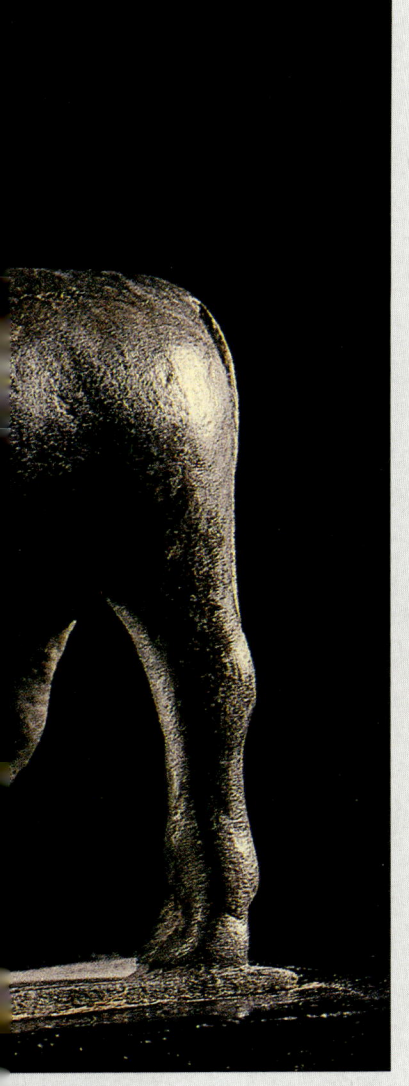

Below This collection of female clay figurines representing the goddess Astarte emphasizes the fertility theme. The breasts are enlarged and prominent, and the objects served to focus the hopes of the people that they would be blessed with fertility on the land, in their cattle and in their families. Dating from the 8th century BC, they were found in the coastal region inhabited by the Philistines.

Left This gold dagger from Gezer was no doubt more of a cult object than a weapon. It portrays a female figure, probably a goddess.

Above An anthropoid Philistine sarcophagus. Certain features of Philistine burials indicate a connection with the Aegean region from which the Philistines came to Syria, Israel and Egypt in the 12th century BC. Little is known about the distinctive features of their religion.

Above A demon figure, common in Mesopotamian witchcraft. The Old Testament view of Babylon was that it was a land of sorcerers and enchantments (Isaiah 47:12). However, witchcraft was practised in Israel, and is condemned in Deuteronomy 18:10-14.

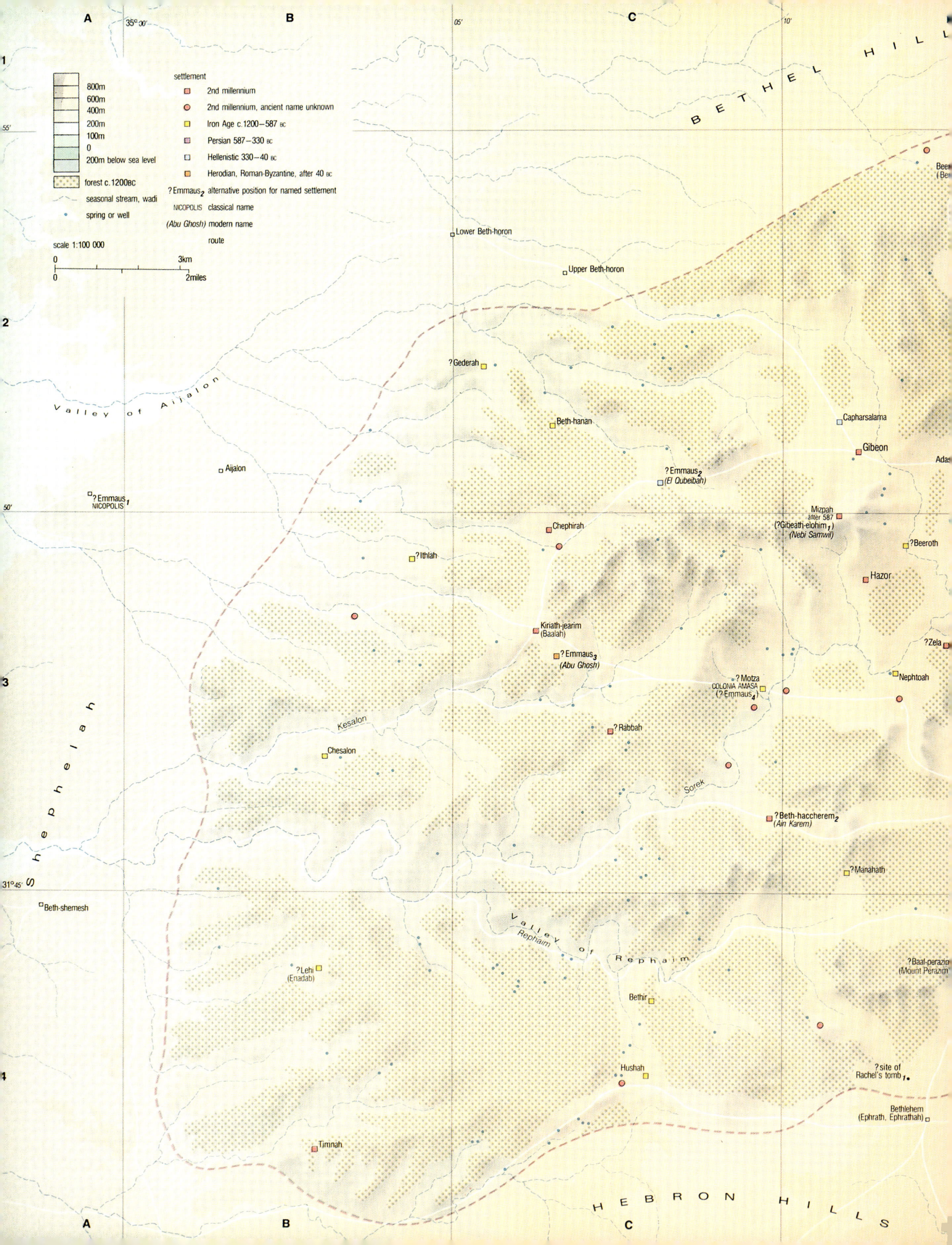

Map: Region around Jerusalem (Bethel Hills to Hebron Hills)

Legend

- scale 1:100 000 — 0 to 3km / 0 to 2miles
- Elevation: 800m, 600m, 400m, 200m, 100m, 0, 200m below sea level
- forest c.1200BC
- seasonal stream, wadi
- spring or well

settlement
- 2nd millennium
- 2nd millennium, ancient name unknown
- Iron Age c.1200–587 BC
- Persian 587–330 BC
- Hellenistic 330–40 BC
- Herodian, Roman-Byzantine, after 40 BC
- ?Emmaus₂ alternative position for named settlement
- NICOPOLIS classical name
- (Abu Ghosh) modern name
- route

Labeled features and settlements:

- BETHEL HILLS (upper right)
- HEBRON HILLS (lower right)
- Shephelah (left side)
- Valley of Aijalon
- Valley of Rephaim
- Kesalon (stream)
- Sorek (stream)

Settlements:
- Lower Beth-horon
- Upper Beth-horon
- Beeroth (Be...) (far right, top)
- ?Gederah
- Beth-hanan
- Capharsalama
- Gibeon
- Adasa
- Aijalon
- ?Emmaus₁ / NICOPOLIS
- ?Emmaus₂ (El Qubeibah)
- Mizpah after 587 / ?Gibeath-elohim₁ (Nebi Samwil)
- ?Beeroth
- Chephirah
- ?Ithlah
- Hazor
- Kiriath-jearim (Baalah)
- ?Emmaus₃ (Abu Ghosh)
- ?Motza / COLONIA AMASA / ?Emmaus₄
- ?Zela
- Nephtoah
- Chesalon
- ?Rabbah
- ?Beth-haccherem₂ (Ain Karem)
- ?Manahath
- Beth-shemesh
- ?Lehi (Enadab)
- ?Baal-perazim (Mount Perazim)
- Bethir
- Hushah
- ?site of Rachel's tomb
- Bethlehem (Ephrath, Ephrathah)
- Timnah

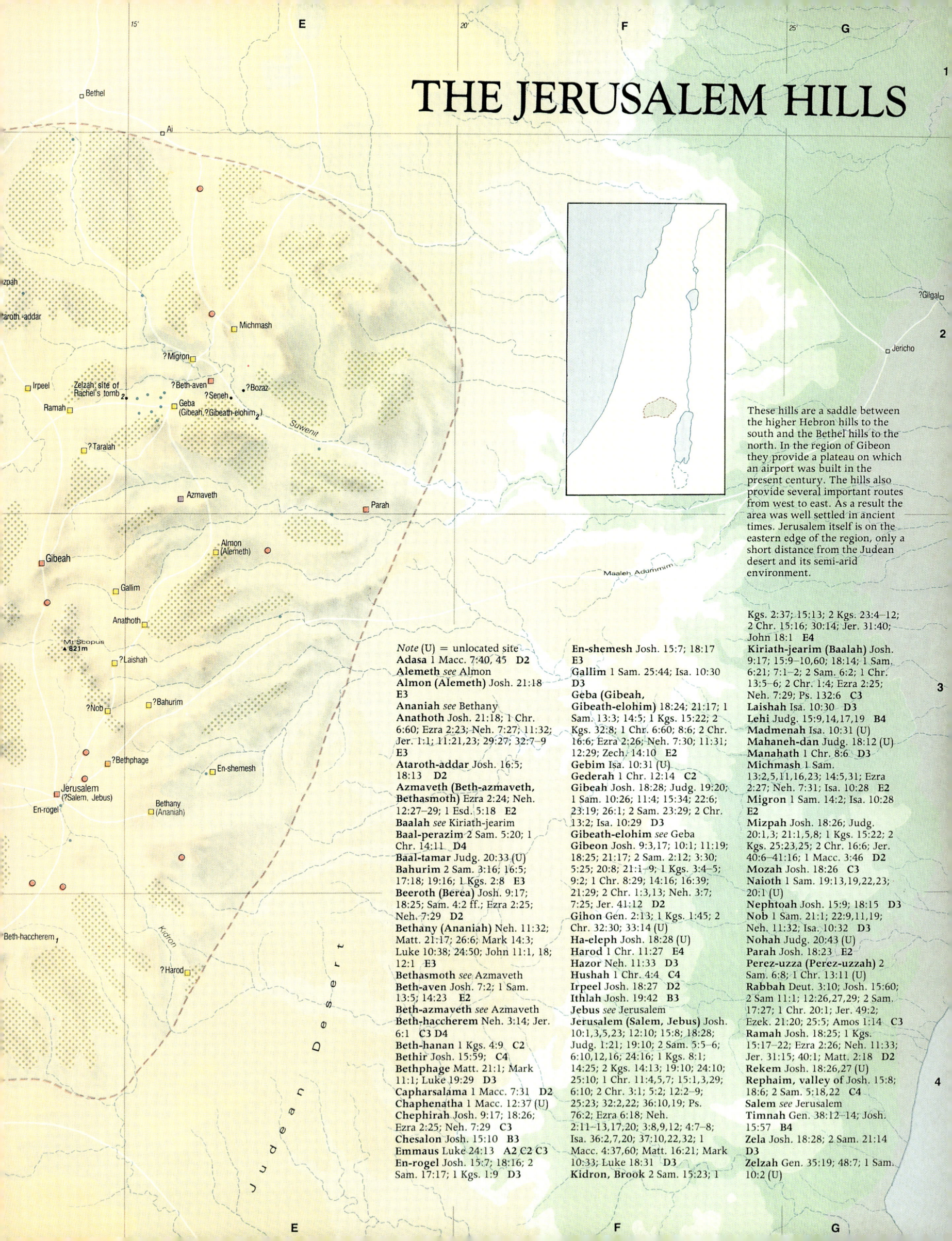

THE JERUSALEM HILLS

These hills are a saddle between the higher Hebron hills to the south and the Bethel hills to the north. In the region of Gibeon they provide a plateau on which an airport was built in the present century. The hills also provide several important routes from west to east. As a result the area was well settled in ancient times. Jerusalem itself is on the eastern edge of the region, only a short distance from the Judean desert and its semi-arid environment.

Note (U) = unlocated site
Adasa 1 Macc. 7:40, 45 D2
Alemeth see Almon
Almon (Alemeth) Josh. 21:18 E3
Ananiah see Bethany
Anathoth Josh. 21:18; 1 Chr. 6:60; Ezra 2:23; Neh. 7:27; 11:32; Jer. 1:1; 11:21,23; 29:27; 32:7–9 E3
Ataroth-addar Josh. 16:5; 18:13 D2
Azmaveth (Beth-azmaveth, Bethasmoth) Ezra 2:24; Neh. 12:27–29; 1 Esd. 5:18 E2
Baalah see Kiriath-jearim
Baal-perazim 2 Sam. 5:20; 1 Chr. 14:11 D4
Baal-tamar Judg. 20:33 (U)
Bahurim 2 Sam. 3:16; 16:5; 17:18; 19:16; 1 Kgs. 2:8 E3
Beeroth (Berea) Josh. 9:17; 18:25; Sam. 4:2 ff.; Ezra 2:25; Neh. 7:29 D2
Bethany (Ananiah) Neh. 11:32; Matt. 21:17; 26:6; Mark 14:3; Luke 10:38; 24:50; John 11:1, 18; 12:1 E3
Bethasmoth see Azmaveth
Beth-aven Josh. 7:2; 1 Sam. 13:5; 14:23 E2
Beth-azmaveth see Azmaveth
Beth-haccherem Neh. 3:14; Jer. 6:1 C3 D4
Beth-hanan 1 Kgs. 4:9 C2
Bethir Josh. 15:59 C4
Bethphage Matt. 21:1; Mark 11:1; Luke 19:29 D3
Capharsalama 1 Macc. 7:31 D2
Chaphenatha 1 Macc. 12:37 (U)
Chephirah Josh. 9:17; 18:26; Ezra 2:25; Neh. 7:29 C3
Chesalon Josh. 15:10 B3
Emmaus Luke 24:13 A2 C2 C3
En-rogel Josh. 15:7; 18:16; 2 Sam. 17:17; 1 Kgs. 1:9 D3

En-shemesh Josh. 15:7; 18:17 E3
Gallim 1 Sam. 25:44; Isa. 10:30 D3
Geba (Gibeah, Gibeath-elohim) 18:24; 21:17; 1 Sam. 13:3; 14:5; 1 Kgs. 15:22; 2 Kgs. 32:8; 1 Chr. 6:60; 8:6; 2 Chr. 16:6; Ezra 2:26; Neh. 7:30; 11:31; 12:29; Zech. 14:10 E2
Gebim Isa. 10:31 (U)
Gederah 1 Chr. 12:14 C2
Gibeah Josh. 18:28; Judg. 19:20; 1 Sam. 10:26; 11:4; 15:34; 22:6; 23:19; 26:1; 2 Sam. 23:29; 2 Chr. 13:2; Isa. 10:29 D3
Gibeath-elohim see Geba
Gibeon Josh. 9:3,17; 10:1; 11:19; 18:25; 21:17; 2 Sam. 2:12; 3:30; 5:25; 20:8; 21:1–9; 1 Kgs. 3:4–5; 9:2; 1 Chr. 8:29; 14:16; 16:39; 21:29; 2 Chr. 1:3,13; Neh. 3:7; 7:25; Jer. 41:12 D2
Gihon Gen. 2:13; 1 Kgs. 1:45; 2 Chr. 32:30; 33:14 (U)
Ha-eleph Josh. 18:28 (U)
Harod 1 Chr. 11:27 E4
Hazor Neh. 11:33 D3
Hushah 1 Chr. 4:4 C4
Irpeel Josh. 18:27 D2
Ithlah Josh. 19:42 B3
Jebus see Jerusalem
Jerusalem (Salem, Jebus) Josh. 10:1,3,5,23; 12:10; 15:8; 18:28; Judg. 1:21; 19:10; 2 Sam. 5:5–6; 6:10,12,16; 20:4; 24:16; 1 Kgs. 8:1; 14:25; 2 Kgs. 14:13; 19:10; 24:10; 25:10; 1 Chr. 11:4,5,7; 15:1,3,29; 6:10; 2 Chr. 3:1; 5:2; 12:2–9; 25:23; 32:2,22; 36:10,19; Ps. 76:2; Ezra 6:18; Neh. 2:11–13,17,20; 3:8,9,12; 4:7–8; Isa. 36:2,7,20; 37:10,22,32; 1 Macc. 4:37,60; Matt. 16:21; Mark 10:33; Luke 18:31 D3
Kidron, Brook 2 Sam. 15:23; 1 Kgs. 2:37; 15:13; 2 Kgs. 23:4–12; 2 Chr. 15:16; 30:14; Jer. 31:40; John 18:1 E4
Kiriath-jearim (Baalah) Josh. 9:17; 15:9–10,60; 18:14; 1 Sam. 6:21; 7:1–2; 2 Sam. 6:2; 1 Chr. 13:5–6; 2 Chr. 1:4; Ezra 2:25; Neh. 7:29; Ps. 132:6 C3
Laishah Isa. 10:30 D3
Lehi Judg. 15:9,14,17,19 B4
Madmenah Isa. 10:31 (U)
Mahaneh-dan Judg. 18:12 (U)
Manahath 1 Chr. 8:6 D3
Michmash 1 Sam. 13:2,5,11,16,23; 14:5,31; Ezra 2:27; Neh. 7:31; Isa. 10:28 E2
Migron 1 Sam. 14:2; Isa. 10:28 E2
Mizpah Josh. 18:26; Judg. 20:1,3; 21:1,5,8; 1 Kgs. 15:22; 2 Kgs. 25:23,25; 2 Chr. 16:6; Jer. 40:6–41:16; 1 Macc. 3:46 D2
Mozah Josh. 18:26 C3
Naioth 1 Sam. 19:13,19,22,23; 20:1 (U)
Nephtoah Josh. 15:9; 18:15 D3
Nob 1 Sam. 21:1; 22:9,11,19; Neh. 11:32; Isa. 10:32 D3
Nohah Judg. 20:43 (U)
Parah Josh. 18:23 E2
Perez-uzza (Perez-uzzah) 2 Sam. 6:8; 1 Chr. 13:11 (U)
Rabbah Deut. 3:10; Josh. 15:60; 2 Sam 11:1; 12:26,27,29; 2 Sam. 17:27; 1 Chr. 20:1; Jer. 49:2; Ezek. 21:20; 25:5; Amos 1:14 C3
Ramah Josh. 18:25; 1 Kgs. 15:17–22; Ezra 2:26; Neh. 11:33; Jer. 31:15; 40:1; Matt. 2:18 D2
Rekem Josh. 18:26,27 (U)
Rephaim, valley of Josh. 15:8; 18:6; 2 Sam. 5:18,22 C4
Salem see Jerusalem
Timnah Gen. 38:12–14; Josh. 15:57 B4
Zela Josh. 18:28; 2 Sam. 21:14 D3
Zelzah Gen. 35:19; 48:7; 1 Sam. 10:2 (U)

THE JERUSALEM HILLS

Description of the region
As we have already noticed (p.94), the Jerusalem hills form a saddle between the Hebron hills to the south and the Bethel hills to the north. The saddle is about 200m (656ft) lower than the highest points of the Hebron and Bethel hills, and in its northern section has a plateau on which, in modern times, it was possible to construct an airport. To the west the main watercourses that drain towards the Mediterranean Sea meet the coastal plain at points where the plain makes considerable inroads into the Shephelah. The most considerable inroad is the broad valley of Aijalon (see p.84). The result of this pattern of drainage is that there are several comparatively easy west-to-east routes along the watercourses across the Jerusalem saddle. Furthermore, because Jerusalem itself is roughly level with the northern end of the Dead Sea, any west-to-east route which wishes to continue further is bound to pass close to Jerusalem. Passage to the east from Jerusalem to the rift valley is also considerably easier from Jerusalem than it is, for example, from Hebron.

Patterns of settlement in the 2nd millennium indicate that towns and villages were concentrated around Jerusalem and along the watershed route from Jerusalem to Bethel. To the west of Jerusalem settlement was heaviest on the western fringes of the hills, overlooking valleys. It is to be presumed that the Jerusalem hills were forested at least at the beginning of the Old Testament period. The name of the town Kiriath-jearim means city of forests (or woods), and David was instructed by God to come upon the Philistines opposite the balsam trees when he fought them in the valley of Rephaim to the southwest of Jerusalem. Unfortunately it is not known what kind of tree is meant by the word traditionally translated as balsam tree. In the northern part of the Jerusalem hills Saul and his army entered "the forest" while pursuing the Philistines (1 Samuel 14:25), while Elisha, on his way from Jericho to Bethel, cursed the boys who insulted his baldness, with the result that "two she-bears came out of the woods and tore forty-two of the boys" (2 Kings 2:24).

Today the hills of the area are comparatively bare, except where modern planting of trees has been undertaken. This bareness was also apparent in the 11th century, when the Crusaders besieged Jerusalem. Runciman presents the evidence of the sources thus: "it was still necessary to find wood with which to build the machines. Little was to be obtained on the bare hills round Jerusalem; and the Crusaders were obliged to send expeditions for many miles to collect what was required. It was only when Tancred and Robert of Flanders penetrated with their followers as far as the forests round Samaria and came back laden with logs and planks . . . [that] work could start upon the machines." We may understand a little of the way in which the deforestation came about if we remember that much wood was needed to fuel the sacrifices that were consumed on the altar in the Jerusalem temple and elsewhere. If it is true that Solomon offered 1000 burned offerings on the altar at Gibeon (1 Kings 3:4—the Hebrew implies that he did this on more than one occasion), it is instructive to calculate how many trees would have been needed to be consumed in such an operation. We need to remember also that there was an Israelite sacrificial cult at Jerusalem requiring regular burned offerings for over 900 years. This must have made some impression on the forests of the region.

Jerusalem itself is on the eastern edge of the Jerusalem saddle. Only a few miles to the east rainfall decreases dramatically, and the conditions of the Judean desert prevail (see p.104). Although an ancient city, it could not compete for natural advantages with sites such as Lachish or Megiddo or even many lesser sites, and presumably, had not David made it his capital, Jerusalem would have remained a small town on the north–south watershed route and on the west–east route from the coastal plain to the rift valley immediately to the north of the Dead Sea. Jerusalem is overlooked by the hills to its east, and in David's day by the hill to the west of the spur which he captured from the Jebusites. Perhaps something of the comparative insignificance of Jerusalem is expressed in Psalm 68:16, when the mountain of Bashan is asked

> Why look you with envy, O many-peaked mountain,
> at the mount which God desired for his abode,
> yea, where the Lord will dwell for ever?

However, before Jerusalem is considered in the great detail that it demands, the remainder of the region will be considered.

The biblical record
In the first place it is worth recording that, although the Patriarchs Abraham and Jacob must have passed Jerusalem in their journeyings, they never worshipped there. The cities that figure in the Patriarchal narratives are Shechem, Bethel and Hebron, where the Patriarchs were buried. If the Salem mentioned in Genesis 14:18 is to be identified with Jerusalem, then there is one link between the Patriarchs and Jerusalem, but that is all.

The first mention of the Jerusalem hills is found in Joshua 9:3–27, the account of the inhabitants of Gibeon and their cities playing a trick on Joshua so as to avoid destruction. The Gibeonites and their allies dressed as though they had come a long distance, journeyed about 30km (18·6 miles) to the Israelite camp at Gilgal and made with Joshua a covenant of peace. When the Israelite armies reached Gibeon and the other cities, the inhabitants reminded Joshua of the covenant. The continuation of the narrative in Joshua 10 is interesting in the light that it sheds on Gibeon. The king of Jerusalem is alarmed at the report of the Israelites' conquest of Ai and the treaty with the Gibeonites "because Gibeon was a great city, like one of the royal cities, and because it was greater than Ai, and all its men were mighty" (Joshua 10:2). The coalition formed by the king of Jerusalem to punish the Gibeonites was essentially a coalition of cities that controlled routes through the Judean hills and the Shephelah (see p.86). Joshua, however, rescued the Gibeonites and defeated the kings.

In the apportionment of the land among the tribes, the northern boundary of Judah, which basically went from a little to the north of Jerusalem to the Nahal Kesalon and then along the Nahal

Above Jerusalem from the Mount of Olives, a 19th-century painting by Edward Lear. The hills were already bare of trees by the time of the Crusades in the 11th century AD.

Overleaf Aerial view of el-Jib, site of the ancient city of Gibeon, looking north. The modern villagers live on the northern end of the mound, which made it possible to excavate the site during the years 1956–62. The nature of the "plateau" on which el-Jib is located is well seen from the air.

Sorek, bulged to the north so as to take in Kiriath-jearim (Joshua 15:9). In the region of Jerusalem itself the border went to the south of the city, putting Jerusalem outside of Judah. However, Joshua 15:63 implies that Jerusalem was a city of Judah because the people of Judah could not drive out the Jebusites who lived in Jerusalem. The details about the boundary and cities of the tribe of Benjamin at Joshua 18:11–28 confirm the common boundary with Judah, place "Jebus (that is, Jerusalem)" in Benjaminite territory, and also list Kiriath-jearim as a city in Benjamin, having earlier called it "a city belonging to the tribe of Judah". These discrepancies doubtless reflect fluctuating relationships between Benjamin and Judah over the course of time.

Judges 1 (verses 8, 21) records that the men of Judah captured Jerusalem and set it on fire, and that the people of Benjamin did not drive out the Jebusites who lived in Jerusalem, "so the Jebusites have dwelt with the people of Benjamin in Jerusalem to this day". Taken at their face value, these verses imply that the two peoples whose boundary met just to the south of Jerusalem both tried to curb the control of Jerusalem over the main north–south route, the Judahites by sacking but not occupying the city, and the Benjaminites by making an agreement that allowed the inhabitants of Jerusalem to remain where they were.

Judges 3 records a Benjaminite deliverer when Eglon, the king of Moab, defeated Israel, and occupied "the city of palms", probably Jericho. The narrative stresses the fact that the Benjaminite deliverer, Ehud, was left-handed. The Hebrew word for being left-handed bears a similarity to words that usually denote bodily defects. In Ehud's case his left-handedness enabled him to conceal a sword on his right-hand side, with which he struck down Eglon, probably in Jericho. Ehud was further able to rally the Israelites to come down and seize the fords of the river Jordan, so that the Moabites, trapped on the western side, had no hope of escape. An incidental reference to the town of Kiriath-jearim in Judges 18:12 remarks that on their

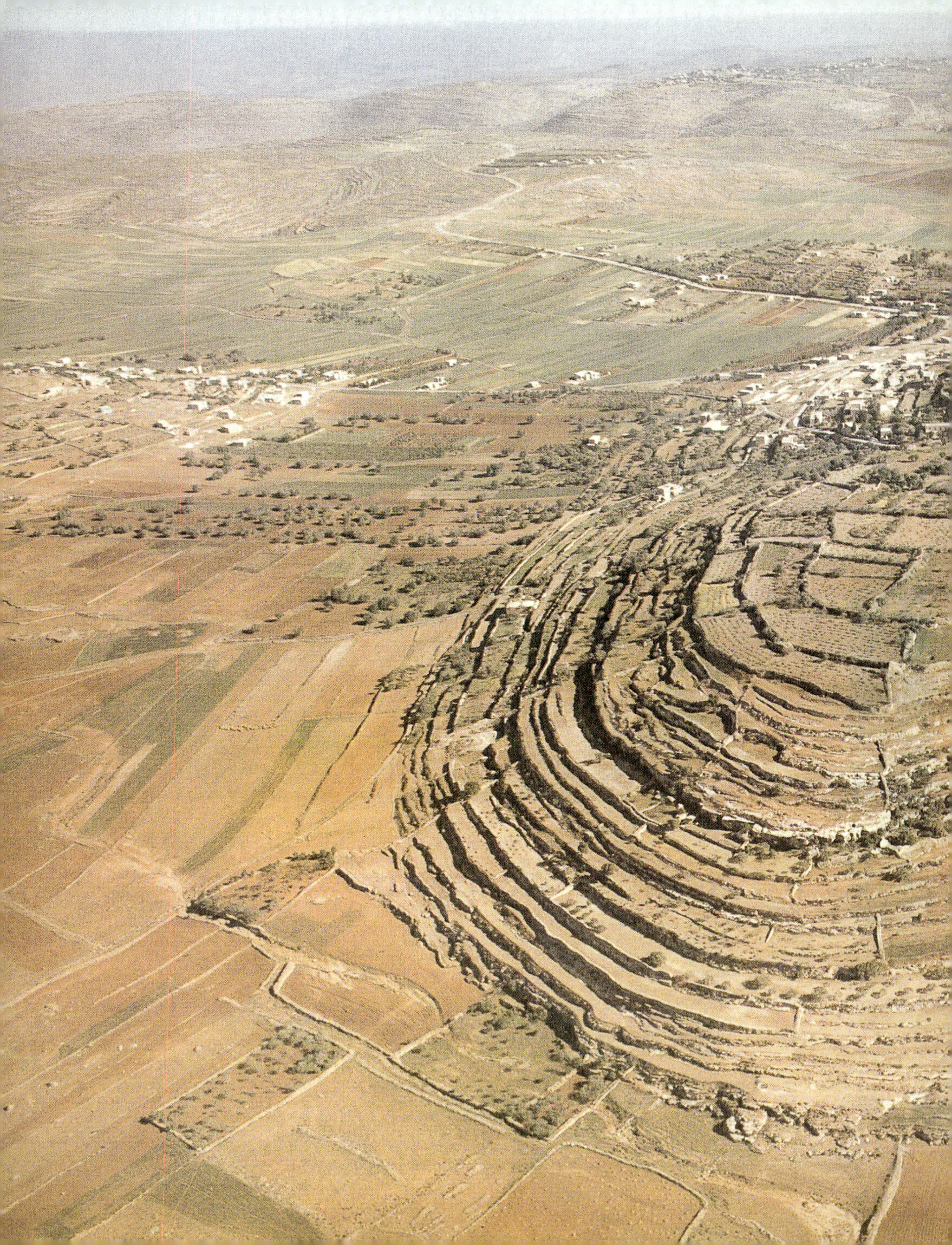

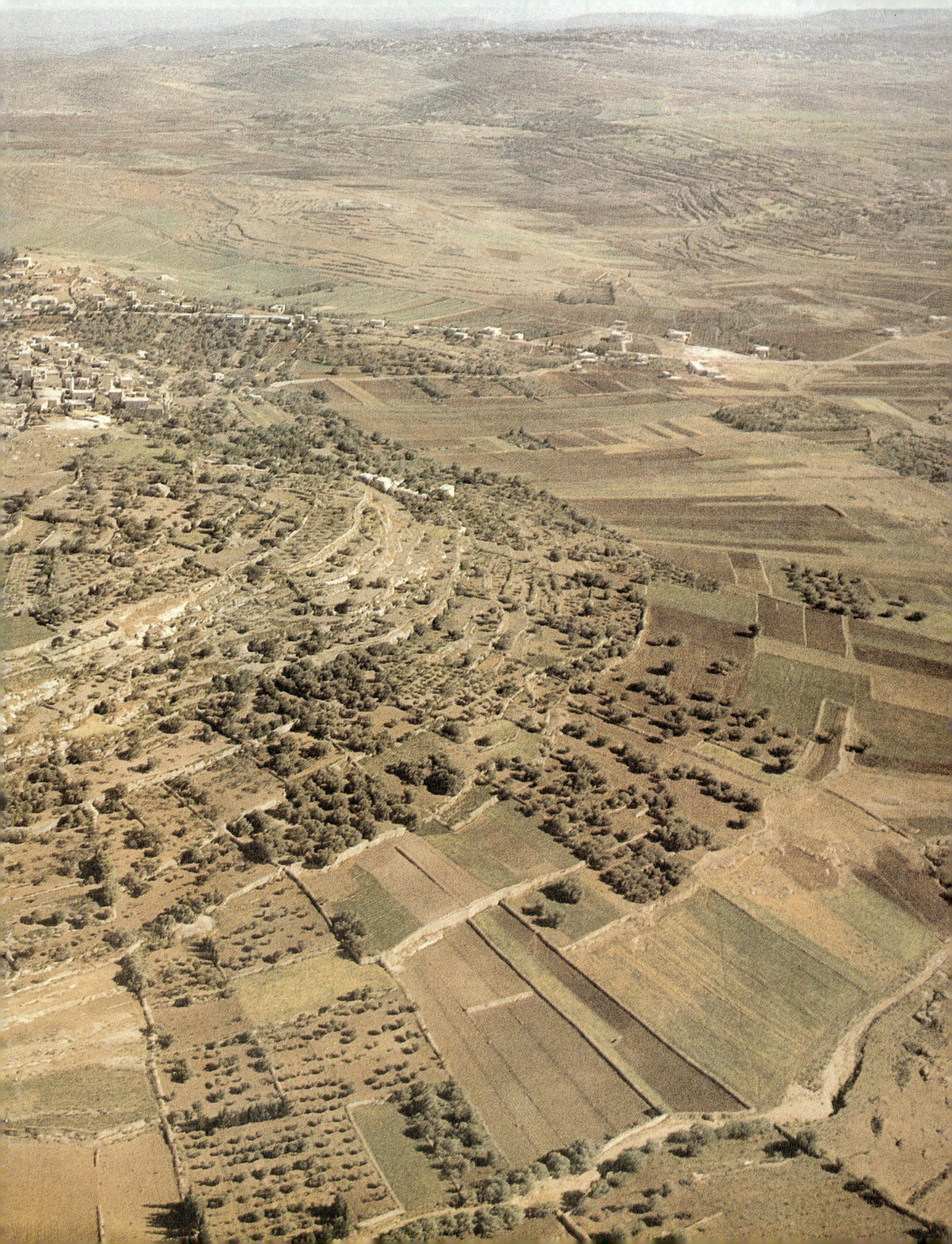

way to the far north the people of Dan camped at "Kiriath-jearim in Judah", thus giving to a spot to the west of the city the name Mahaneh-dan (the camp of Dan).

The closing chapters of Judges relate a major incident, set mostly in the Jerusalem hills, that needs careful consideration. It concerns a Levite who lived in the remote hill country of Ephraim, and who had a concubine whose home was Bethlehem. The concubine having returned to her father's house for four months, the Levite came to fetch her back, eventually setting off with her for Ephraim in the late afternoon. On reaching Jerusalem, the Levite rejected the idea that his party should stay overnight in that city. "We will not turn aside into the city of foreigners, who do not belong to the people of Israel; but we will pass on to Gibeah" (Judges 19:12). Gibeah, if correctly identified with Tell el-Ful, was a few miles to the north of Jerusalem. The party obtained overnight lodgings with a man who, like the Levite, normally lived in Ephraim. During the evening the ironical situation developed that some of the very Israelites, whom the Levite had preferred to the foreigners in Jerusalem, made a strange demand which it is possible to interpret as a request that they should homosexually abuse the Levite. The Levite's host eventually met the demand by pushing out of the house the Levite's concubine, who was subjected to rape, and was found in the morning to be dead. The Levite took the dead concubine back to his home before summoning all Israel to punish the men of Gibeah. The people were summoned by the dismembered body of the concubine being sent to all parts of the country.

The resulting assembly of the Israelites came from every part of Israel with the exception of the town of Jabesh-gilead. The people gathered at Mizpah, from where they went to Bethel in order to seek God's will. When battle was joined, the people of Benjamin, who came as one man to defend Gibeah, inflicted heavy losses on the other Israelites on successive days. On the third day the Israelites pretended to be defeated, drew the Benjaminites away from Gibeah and sent an ambush party to take Gibeah. Thus the Benjaminites were defeated, their towns were set on fire and the slaughter was such that at the end of the battle there remained only 600 men, and the women. So that the tribe would not die out, and because the remainder of the Israelites had vowed not to provide wives for the Benjaminites, the Israelites mounted an expedition to the defaulting town of Jabesh-gilead, and killed everyone except the virgins, who were brought back to be wives for the 600 remaining Benjaminite men. Another 200 women were taken from the maidens who danced at the annual Shiloh festival.

The incident is strange and difficult to evaluate. In view of the unprecedented unity among the tribes that it achieved, some have seen in the incident evidence for the existence of a political and religious institution called the amphictyony, with a central sanctuary and a common law. In current scholarship the amphictyony theory is less popular than it once was. Although the period of the Judges did not establish much common action on the part of the tribes, the enormity of the crime of raping and killing a defenceless girl was, to the Israelites as a whole, so serious that nothing less than concerted action against the wrongdoers and those who supported them could put the matter right.

The period of the monarchy

Action in the Jerusalem hills dominates the first half of 1 Samuel, as it does the end of Judges. Although Samuel, the great figure who brings to an end the line of Judges and inaugurates the kingship, spent his childhood at Shiloh (see p.152), his active ministry was in the territory of Benjamin. His home city is named as Ramah (1 Samuel 7:17) and places where he went on circuit as a judge were Bethel, Gilgal and Mizpah. An act of deliverance from the Philistines, led by Samuel, and recorded in 1 Samuel 7:5–14, sees him sacrificing at Mizpah, with the result that God thunders (from heaven) against the Philistines, who are then routed by the Israelites. In spite of this success, it is recorded that the elders of the Israelites demanded of Samuel a king "to govern us like all the nations" (1 Samuel 8:5). This demand was put to Samuel in Ramah, and after warning the people not to want an earthly king, Samuel dismissed them, recalling them later to Mizpah (1 Samuel 10:17).

There next follows a narrative whose geographical details are obscure. Saul is introduced (only later in 1 Samuel 10:26 is it stated that his home was Gibeah), and his abortive quest for his father's lost asses is narrated. Saul began his search in the hill country of Ephraim, and then passed through the lands of Shalisha, Shaalim and Benjamin, before coming to the land of Zuph. If, as has been suggested, these "lands" are areas belonging to various families in Ephraim, and if Baal-shalishah (2 Kings 4:42) is a site to the east of Kafr Malik, then Saul will have gone some 20km (12·4 miles) northeast from his home of Gibeah, before turning back and coming to Ramah (1 Samuel 9:5–10). The connection between the land of Zuph and Ramah can tentatively be made on the basis of 1 Samuel 1:1, where the home of Samuel's father is named as Ramathaim-zophim, which possibly means Ramah of the Zuphite family. Assuming that this is correct, Saul's journey was in the shape of an ellipse, with the young man finishing about 4km (2·5 miles) north of where he started from. Having arrived at Ramah expressly in order to ask Samuel to use his powers to tell him where the lost asses were, Saul found himself unexpectedly welcomed by the great seer whom he had not previously met. As Samuel sent Saul on his way, he anointed Saul to be "prince" over Israel, in accordance with God's instructions (1 Samuel 10:1).

Samuel also stated that, near to Rachel's tomb, Saul would be met by two men who would tell him that the lost asses had been found. The mention of Rachel's tomb raises an interesting problem. Modern visitors who travel from Jerusalem to Bethlehem will see the traditional site of Rachel's tomb shortly after a branch of the road to the right in the direction of Beit Jala. The location of Rachel's tomb there, well into the territory of Judah, reflects the tradition in Genesis 35:19–20 and Genesis 48:7 that "she was buried on the way to Ephrath (that is, Bethlehem)." The equation of Bethlehem and Ephrath is also to be found in the famous passage in Micah 5:2:

> But you, O Bethlehem Ephrathah
> who are little to be among the clans of Judah,
> from you shall come forth for me
> one who is to be ruler in Israel.

In 1 Samuel 10:2 there is a different tradition about the location of Rachel's tomb, which places it at Zelzah. Unfortunately, the site of Zelzah cannot be identified with any degree of certainty, but the area in which, according 1 Samuel 10:2, it was to be found can be easily defined. Saul is told to go on from Rachel's tomb to Gibeath-elohim, where there is a Philistine garrison (1 Samuel 10:5). If this is the town of Geba, where, according to 1 Samuel 13:3, there was a Philistine garrison, then Rachel's tomb was on a route between Ramah and Geba. Geba will also be meant by the reference to Gibeah in 1 Samuel 10:10. It was to this town that Saul went, and joined the band of ecstatic prophets, thus giving rise to the saying "is Saul also among the prophets?" The narrative of 1 Samuel now resumes the story begun in 1 Samuel 8:4–22. Samuel summons the Israelites to Mizpah, he again warns them against the dangers of an earthly king, and he proceeds to choose a king by lot. Saul is chosen and acclaimed, and returns to his home of Gibeah.

In 1 Samuel 11 Saul is farming peacefully in his home town of Gibeah, when he has a message from men of Jabesh-gilead who have been threatened by Nahash, king of Ammon. A link between Jabesh-gilead and the people of Benjamin has already been noticed. Saul summons the Israelites to his aid by cutting his oxen into 12 pieces and sending them throughout the land. The situation of Judges 19 is reversed. There the concubine was dismembered to summon the Israelites against Benjamin. Now Saul dismembers the oxen to summon them to the aid of his tribe Benjamin against Nahash. After a brilliant victory Saul is proclaimed king in Gilgal. It is not easy to relate this to the facts that Saul had already been made king in Mizpah, and that Samuel had anointed him (to be prince, not king, if a difference is intended) at Ramah.

A formal description of Saul's reign begins in 1 Samuel 13, with several incidents set in the Jerusalem hills. Verses 2-4 of 1 Samuel 13 indicate that Saul and Jonathan chose the best soldiers from among the Israelites, 3000 in all, sent the remainder of the people home, and retained the 3000 as a standing army, 2000 being with Saul in Michmash, and the remaining 1000 being with Jonathan in Gibeah. A successful raid by Jonathan on the Philistine garrison at Geba stirred the Philistines into action (1 Samuel 13:3–7). They mustered 30 000 chariots and supporting troops, and encamped "in Michmash to the east of Beth-aven", while Saul withdrew to Gilgal in the Jordan valley. Although we cannot be certain what all this entailed, it is a reasonable guess that the Philistines mounted such a show of force that Saul was driven out of Michmash into the Jordan valley, from where he could vanish, if need be, into the hills of Transjordan. The Philistines are unlikely to have deployed such large forces (even if the numbers are exaggerated, it is still a very large army) in one spot, assuming that there is the requisite space at Michmash, which is doubtful. Probably, after expelling Saul from Michmash, they strung themselves out along the north-south routes, thus denying Saul any possibility of moving back from the rift valley to the hills of the Michmash region, and preventing him from going to anyone's aid in the hill country. The result of the Philistine deployment was that "the people hid themselves in caves and in holes and in rocks and in tombs and in cisterns, or crossed the fords of the Jordan to the land of Gad and Gilead" (1 Samuel 13:6–7).

It is at this point in the narrative that there is a reference back to the account of Samuel having anointed Saul at Ramah (cf. 1 Samuel 10:8 and 13:8). In the Ramah incident, Samuel had told Saul to wait for him to come to Gilgal after seven days. Now, in 1 Samuel 13, we see Saul waiting for Samuel to come to him at Gilgal, and when Samuel delays and the people scatter from him, Saul presents the burned offering, and earns the condemnation of Samuel for exceeding his office. It is difficult to suppose that the link-up between the two stories is anything other than an editorial device whose purpose is to suggest that Saul reigned for only seven days before he acted foolishly and God rejected him. If we ignore the link-up, we can well sympathize with Saul's dilemma as the people deserted from him and in desperation he presented a burned offering, hoping that this would bring decisive action from God.

The next part of the story is obscure in the Hebrew Bible, since Samuel goes back from Gilgal to Gibeah, while Saul is suddenly to be found in Gibeah (Hebrew text: Geba) without having gone there. We should probably follow the reading of the ancient Greek translation here, which has retained material lost through a copyist's error from the traditional Hebrew text. In the New English Bible 1 Samuel 13:15 reads "Samuel left Gilgal [without more ado and went on his way. The rest of the people followed Saul, as he moved from Gilgal towards the enemy]. At Gibeah of Benjamin he mustered the people who were with him. . ." (The words in brackets represent the additional words in the ancient Greek translation, omitted by the RSV.) We can now hazard the guess that, even though Saul's forces had shrunk to 600, he made his way back to Gibeah. He had suffered a defeat in that the Philistines now controlled Michmash, Saul's former headquarters. From Michmash the Philistines sent out raiding parties in three directions, presumably to plunder the land for food for the Philistine army.

The narrative continues with the assault by Jonathan and his squire on the garrison at Michmash. The details are cryptic, but we may guess that Jonathan went northeast from Gibeah to the canyon-like Wadi Suwenit, entered the Wadi at its southeastern end and proceeded up it towards Michmash, which is a little over 1 km (0·6 miles) from the northwestern exit of the canyon. The location of the two rocky crags, Bozez and Seneh (1 Samuel 14:4–5), has been much discussed. Possibly they were at the entrance to the canyon at the Michmash end. Jonathan and his squire had agreed to attack the Philistines only if the latter challenged them to come up. The two Israelites duly exposed themselves, the Philistines jeered –"Look, Hebrews are coming up out of the holes

THE JERUSALEM HILLS

where they have hid themselves'' (1 Samuel 14:11)—and then challenged Jonathan and his companion to come up. We are not necessarily to presume that Jonathan went up immediately. From the fact that they crawled up the canyon on their hands and knees we may guess that they went back down the canyon, and crawled out of it at a point where they were screened from Michmash, and then came around the back of the hills upon Michmash from a totally unexpected direction. Their fierce onslaught caused such panic that the watchman in Gibeah saw that something was amiss in Michmash, thus giving Saul the chance to mobilize his forces and launch a general attack against the Philistines, who were eventually routed and pursued as far as the valley of Aijalon. In the course of the battle, when Saul had made the people swear not to touch food until the victory was complete, the people entered a forest in which honey was dripping from the hives. They did not eat, but Jonathan, who did not know of the oath, ate some honey, thereby causing God not to speak to Saul by means of the divine oracle until Jonathan's "crime" was discovered (1 Samuel 14:24–30, 36–46). It should be noted that not all authorities see a reference to a forest in 1 Samuel 14:25–26. The Hebrew has a slight difficulty which causes the New English Bible to offer a translation in which there is no mention of a forest.

The remainder of the narrative of Saul that is set in the Jerusalem hills presents him as ruling from his town of Gibeah, where his growing jealousy and suspicion of David impel him to attempt to kill David by striking him down with a spear (1 Samuel 18:11). David is forced to flee to Samuel at Ramah, and when Saul sends his men to capture David and then comes himself to Ramah, he is overcome by the ecstasy of the prophetic group in Ramah over which Samuel presides (1 Samuel 19:18–24). David next flees to the sanctuary at Nob, possibly the modern village El-Isawiya to the southeast of Mount Scopus, where occurs the incident later to be referred to by Jesus. Ahimelech, the priest at Nob, gives David and his men the holy bread to eat, the bread that is placed before God and which is thus no longer common or ordinary bread (1 Samuel 21:3–6). He does this because of the plight of David and his men, and because, according to the rules of war, they have been abstaining from marital intercourse. In Mark 2:23–28, which records a controversy between Jesus and his opponents about the observance of the Sabbath, Jesus used the incident of David eating the holy bread to argue that institutions must serve human needs, not vice versa. The action of Ahimelech was betrayed to Saul, and in his rage the king massacred the priests at Nob and their families except for Abiathar, who escaped to join David.

One other detail about Saul, and significant for a later discussion, comes at the end of 2 Samuel, when a three-year famine in the reign of David is related by God to the fact that "There is bloodguilt on Saul and on his house, because he put the Gibeonites to death"(2 Samuel 21:1). The narrative goes on to explain that in his religious zeal Saul had "sought to slay" the Gibeonites because they were not Israelite. This statement recalls Joshua 9:3–27 and the trick played by the Gibeonites on Joshua in order to avoid destruction (see p.164). Saul, whose association with ecstatic prophets is well attested in the tradition, had disregarded the earlier oath in his zeal for God, although it is not clear how many Gibeonites he killed. Saul's motive may have been purely religious—to remove a non-Israelite enclave from his kingdom. Alternatively, the non-Israelite Gibeonites may readily have gone over to the side of the Philistines when the latter were in the ascendancy. It is also possible that Saul wished to reduce the importance of Gibeon which would be a formidable rival to his own town of Gibeah as a capital. We have already noticed that in Joshua 10:2 Gibeon is described as "a great city, like one of the royal cities", and in 2 Samuel 21:6 and 9 there is present at Gibeon a "mountain of the Lord" (if this is the correct reading). Because Kiriath-jearim was associated with Gibeon (Joshua 9:17), and because the Ark of the Covenant was located at Kiriath-jearim before David took it to Jerusalem (1 Samuel 7:2), it has been suggested that some sort of official worship of the God of Israel was based at Gibeon and Kiriath-jearim. These can be no more than speculations, but the undoubted importance of Gibeon may have caused Saul to cast jealous eyes upon it. In order to atone for whatever crime Saul had committed at Gibeon, David gave seven of Saul's grandsons to the Gibeonites, who hanged them "on the mountain before the Lord". It has been suggested, with great plausibility, that the Gibeonite "mountain of the Lord" and indeed its high place were located at the imposing Nebi Samwil, 2km (1·2 miles) south-southeast of Gibeon.

Gibeon is the setting for a confrontation between the army of David and that of Saul's son Ish-baal in the period immediately after the death of Saul (2 Samuel 2:12–17). It is to be presumed that at this period David was still a Philistine vassal and that his masters allowed him to do some policing of the Jerusalem hills against the forces of Ish-baal, whose base of operations was at Mahanaim in the Jordan valley. The opposing troops, led by Joab and Abner respectively, met at the pool of Gibeon. Whether or not the pool is the great cistern discovered in the 1956–57 excavations at Gibeon, it is noteworthy that Gibeon was the meeting place. As in the story of the combat between David and Goliath, so in this case champions from each side were chosen to engage in initial combat. There were 12 from each side, and they appear to have engaged in a type of fighting involving short swords and a combat position in which they held each other's hair. After the individual combat the armies fought, and Abner was defeated, but during the pursuit he killed Joab's brother Asahel, thus opening the way for Joab to kill him at Hebron when he came later to talk to David (see p.99).

The city of David

Following the deaths of Abner and Ish-baal, David was made king in Hebron over the northern tribes (2 Samuel 5:1–5), and now decided to move his capital from Hebron which was too far to the south. In choosing Jerusalem, a city just beyond the border of Judah, he was going as far to the north as he could without losing touch with his own people of Judah. Jerusalem was at a point which controlled important routes, and it was still inhabited by non-Israelites; he could thus make it his own city with a minimum of resentment.

As has been remarked above, Jerusalem in itself was not the best possible site for a city. The spur on which the Jebusite city stood, though protected by deep valleys to east, south and west, was overlooked by the hill on the northern side to which

Previous page Aerial view of the village of Jeba across the Wadi Suwenit. Jeba is probably the site of biblical Geba which was in the territory of Benjamin. The Wadi Suwenit enters a canyon as it leaves the left-hand side of the picture. Jonathan crawled along this canyon in order to surprise the Philistine garrison at Michmash, the modern village of Mukhmas, which is just below the bottom of the picture.

Jerusalem from the west. The walls were built by the Turks in the 16th century. To the left of centre is the citadel, site of Herod's upper palace. To the far right is the squat tower of the Dormition church. In the background is the Mount of Olives, crowned by the Russian tower of the Ascension (the furthest right of the three towers); the furthest left tower on the skyline is on Mount Scopus.

the spur was joined. Its water supply, from the Gihon spring, was adequate but not outstanding, and it was overlooked by other hills to the west and east. However, its inhabitants had fortified it to the extent that, when David came to take the city, the defenders taunted David by saying "You will not come in here, but the blind and the lame will ward you off" (2 Samuel 5:6). Exactly how David took the city is not known. The text of 2 Samuel 5:8 presents great difficulties of translation, especially the word *sinnor*. In the King James Version it was translated as "gutter", but in the Revised Standard Version it is assumed that the word means "water shaft" and the implication is that David's soldiers climbed up a shaft from near the foot of the spur into the heart of the city. The New English Bible translates the word as "grappling-iron", implying a totally different method of access. It is also possible that the *sinnor* was a type of weapon.

Having captured the city, however this was accomplished, David fortified Jerusalem and built the city "from the Millo inward" (2 Samuel 5:9). Here is another problem, in that the meaning of "Millo" is unknown. One suggestion, since the word may be connected with the Hebrew verb "to fill", is that the surface area of the spur was enlarged by the building of retaining walls part way down the slopes of the spur. The space between the walls and the curve of the slopes was then "filled" and a platform resulted on which buildings could be erected.

Scholars are not agreed about the precise order of the events recorded in 2 Samuel 5. As it stands, the narrative suggests that David first captured Jerusalem and then defeated the Philistines in two battles. Many scholars believe that David captured Jerusalem *after* he had defeated the Philistines. The problem arises because 2 Samuel 5:17 says that "the Philistines went up in search of David; but David heard of it and went down to the stronghold." The questions that have to be answered are where was the stronghold, and from where did David go down to it? The most obvious candidate for the stronghold is Adullam, where he had sheltered during his flight from Saul (see p.87). That the Philistines deployed themselves in the valley of Rephaim suggests that they expected to find David in Jerusalem, since the valley of Rephaim contributes to one of the west–east routes from the coastal plain, and reaches the central hills a little to the south of Jerusalem. If, as many assume, David still had his headquarters in Hebron, the Philistines could surely have had a better plan than to deploy themselves in a valley over 20km (12·4 miles) to the north of Hebron. It seems to make better sense that the Philistines expected to find David in Jerusalem, that he established his quarters to the south of the Philistines and that he defeated them by coming upon them from unexpected directions. At 2 Samuel 5:23 we read the explicit order from God "You shall not go up; go around to their rear, and come upon them opposite the balsam trees." The strange order, "when you hear the sound of marching in the tops of the balsam trees, then bestir yourself" (2 Samuel 5:24), has prompted the suggestion that David and his men made a night detour, and that the noise in the trees heralded the arrival of the land breeze occasioned by the warming up of the land by the sun. Of course, it was also believed that the armies of God included the forces of nature, and David is told to regard the "marching in the tops of the balsam trees" as a sign that God had gone on ahead to defeat the Philistines.

Old Testament Jerusalem

Old Testament Jerusalem differed from most of the other tells or mounds that are featured in this Atlas. The city captured by David was on a spur adjoining a hill to the north, and overlooked by hills to the east and west, although from the time of Solomon onwards it expanded to the north and west. Apart from its strategic position on north–south and east–west routes, it was not an obvious choice for an administrative centre (Gibeon was already an attractive possibility), but with brilliant judgment David made it his capital and began the process by which it became the most famous city in the world. When he selected as his site for an altar a Jebusite threshing-floor on the hill immediately north of his city, he inaugurated the long history that was to make the mount holy ground for Jews, Christians and Muslims alike.

Below At the southern end of the city of David is a necropolis containing what some scholars believe to be the original tomb of David. The depression at the end of the tunnel of this tomb could have housed a sarcophagus 1.2m (4ft) wide. From just inside the present entrance to the tomb is a magnificent view over the Kidron valley.

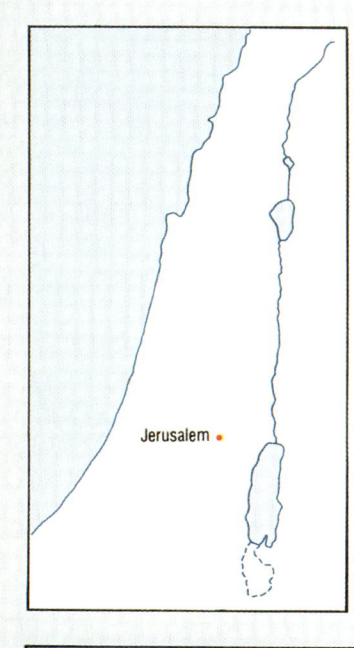

Above Jars and sculpted heads excavated from the city of David.

Right This aerial view of Jerusalem looking northwards shows the spur of the city of David in the lower half of the picture, below and outside the medieval walls. The Kidron valley is to the right of the spur. The central valley dividing the spur from the hill to the left has been considerably filled up with debris over the centuries. In the centre of the walled city is the Dome of the Rock, completed at the end of the 7th century AD, and Islam's third most holy place. Somewhere on the platform which it occupies stood the first and second temples.

Nehemiah's inspection:
(Nehemiah 2:11-16)
1. Valley Gate
2. Jackal's Well
3. Dung Gate
4. Fountain Gate
5. King's Pool

Gates in time of Nehemiah:
(Nehemiah 3:1-12)
6. Sheep Gate
7. Fish Gate
8. Tower of the Hundred
9. Tower of Hananel
10. Old Gate
11. Tower of the Ovens

present area of Haram es-Sharib

temple

palace

8th-century walls

Hasmonean palace

Xystus gymnasium

Seleucid Acra?

additions by Solomon

8th-century enlargement

ancient walls discovered in excavations

Hezekiah's tunnel

Gihon

rebuilding by Nehemiah on the ridge

fragments of ancient walls

walls of Jebusite city

late post-exilic wall

upper pool

conjectural additions by Hezekiah (maximal view); also line of Hellenistic and Hasmonean walls

conjectural addition by Hezekiah (minimal view)

lower pool

late post-exilic wall

THE JERUSALEM HILLS

The religious significance of Jerusalem
After his capture of Jerusalem, David brought the Ark of the Covenant to the city (2 Samuel 6), and it was placed in a special tent. He also set up an altar "on the threshing floor of Araunah the Jebusite" (2 Samuel 24:18–25). However, the great high place of the Jerusalem hills was still located at Gibeon (or Nebi Samwil, if this was Gibeon's high place). Before the building of the temple in Jerusalem, Solomon sacrificed at Gibeon, "for that was the great high place" (1 Kings 3:4), and it was at Gibeon, not Jerusalem, that Solomon had the dream in which he chose wisdom when God promised to give him whatever he asked (1 Kings 3:5–9).

With the building of the temple (c. 955 BC) on the hill immediately to the north of the city, Jerusalem became the religious capital of the Israelites. It had its rivals, for example Bethel (see p.153), but from now on, in the biblical narrative, Jerusalem becomes the focus of all religious and political happenings, and a symbol for the future establishment of God's kingdom.

With Jerusalem, there came into the religion of Israel a cluster of symbols derived from the wider religious ideology of the ancient Near East. These symbols were, however, incorporated into the religion of Israel, and became a source of new ways of expressing Israel's faith. This can be seen especially in some of the Psalms. For example, Psalm 68, in spite of the great problems of interpretation that it presents, describes the coming of God from Mount Sinai to Mount Zion in Jerusalem. This coming is presented as a great series of triumphs of God over his enemies, and the verse "Thou didst ascend the high mount, leading captives in thy train, and receiving gifts among men, even among the rebellious, that the Lord God may dwell there" (Psalm 68:18) is taken up in Ephesians 4:8 in reference to Christ's Ascension. The presence of God in Jerusalem becomes such a ground of hope that Psalm 46 has the confident refrain, "The Lord of hosts is with us, the God of Jacob is our refuge", and the same Psalm refers to a "river whose streams make glad the city of God" (Psalm 46:4). The idea here is probably that the two springs of Jerusalem, Gihon and En-rogel, are manifestations of the river of Paradise, believed in the ancient Near East to flow beneath sacred mountains. We may detect the same imagery in Ezekiel's vision of the river flowing from the restored temple and making fertile the Judean wilderness and the Dead Sea (Ezekiel 47:1–12). When the prophets have a vision of God's future reign of universal justice and peace, this is sometimes expressed in terms of the exaltation of Jerusalem:

> It shall come to pass in the latter days
> that the mountain of the house of the Lord
> shall be established as the highest of the mountains,
> and shall be raised up above the hills;
> and peoples shall flow to it,
> and many nations shall come, and say:
> "Come, let us go up to the mountain of the Lord,
> to the house of the God of Jacob..."
> (Micah 4:1–2, cf. Isaiah 2:2–3).

Furthermore, Jerusalem furnished a royal ideology

which saw the king as adopted or "born" by God on the day of his coronation, to occupy a special position as the guardian of God's people responsible to God for preserving justice and for protecting and supporting the poor and needy. In Psalm 2:7 it is proclaimed to the newly crowned king, "You are my son, today I have begotten you", while in Psalm 110:4, a very difficult Psalm to interpret, the king is declared to be the heir of the ancient rights and privileges of the priest-kings of Jerusalem: "You are a priest for ever after the order of Melchizedek." Both of these passages, deriving from the royal ideology of Jerusalem, are taken up in the New Testament and applied to Jesus. The verse from Psalm 2 appears in the narrative of the baptism of Jesus (Mark 1:11), while the epistle to the Hebrews uses Psalm 110:4 to interpret the work of Christ in high-priestly terms.

It is impossible to say how much of the Zion and royal ideologies was already present in the time of David and Solomon; and a reconstruction of the Solomonic temple will be found on page 182. What needs to be re-emphasized here is that David's removal of his capital from Hebron to Jerusalem is arguably the most significant single event in the Bible in geographical terms.

With the defeat of the Philistines and the capture of Jerusalem, it might be thought that David would henceforth reign in peace and prosperity. This was not to be the case, and a most ironical situation arose when his son Absalom raised the standard of revolt in Hebron (2 Samuel 15). For all that Jerusalem could be easily defended and had been fortified by David, the king's advice on hearing of Absalom's revolt was "Arise, and let us flee; or else there will be no escape for us from Absalom; go in haste, lest he overtake us quickly, and bring down evil upon us, and smite the city with the edge of the sword" (2 Samuel 15:14). Presumably, David did not think that he could hold out indefinitely in Jerusalem, in face of a largely hostile people (if the people was so largely hostile). Absalom in Hebron had further to go to get down to the Dead Sea route than David had to go to get to the river Jordan from Jerusalem, and Absalom would also have to journey northwards to cut off David, since the Dead Sea was a barrier to his west–east progress. Perhaps it was precisely this sort of advantage of Jerusalem over Hebron that had led David to change his capital city.

At 2 Samuel 15:30 we have the sad picture of David fleeing from Jerusalem, crossing the Kidron valley and ascending the Mount of Olives, "weeping as he went, barefoot and with his head covered". There is an interesting reference to the summit of the Mount of Olives "where God was worshipped" (2 Samuel 15:32). When Josiah reformed the cult in 622/1, we are told that he "defiled the high places that were east of Jerusalem" (2 Kings 23:13), and it may well be that while the cult at Jerusalem became primarily a royal and national cult, the ordinary inhabitants of Jerusalem and its surroundings used a holy place on the Mount of Olives for their regular worship. On the far side of the Mount of Olives was Bahurim, where David was cursed by Shimei, a member of Saul's family (2 Samuel 16:5). It served as a hiding place for the two spies, Jonathan and Ahimaaz, who were deputed by David to inform him of Absalom's intentions, and who usually waited at En-rogel for information from a servant girl (2 Samuel 17:17–20).

The revolt of Absalom was crushed, and Absalom was killed. However, David was to face another revolt, this time from the northern tribes, a revolt which ended in the remote northern city of Abel-beth-maacah (see p.136). For present purposes, we note that Gibeon appears in the story. The commander of Absalom's forces against David had been Amasa, but David had pardoned him and put him in command of the army in place of Joab because Joab had killed Absalom against David's orders. When the northern tribes revolted, David ordered Amasa to mobilize the men of Judah and to report in three days' time (2 Samuel 20:4). Amasa delayed; why, we can only guess. Was he still loyal to Absalom? Did he doubt the loyalty to David of the people of Judah? Because he delayed, David sent Abishai and David's personal troops (which were later joined by Joab) to fight the northern tribes. At the great stone at Gibeon, Joab and the other men met Amasa. Gibeon was a strange place for Amasa to be if he was rallying the people of Judah; and if he had already rallied them, why had he not reported with them to David in Jerusalem as ordered? It may be that Joab suspected Amasa's motives and loyalty to David, even though Joab had cause to be envious of the man who had taken over his own job. For whatever reason, Joab played a trick on Amasa and struck him down, after which Joab rallied David's supporters and went after the northern rebels.

With David in old age, his remaining sons, Adonijah and Solomon, vied for the succession (1 Kings 1). In a manner reminiscent of the action of Absalom, Adonijah, who was next to Absalom in precedent of birth, began to demonstrate his claims to the throne by having chariots and horsemen and 50 men to run before him. Adonijah now arranged for a secret ceremony at the spring En-rogel, at which he sacrificed sheep and oxen, and at which the guests cried out "Long live King Adonijah!" (1 Kings 1:25). A rival movement was now set in train, sanctioned by David, focusing attention on Solomon, who was taken to the other spring, Gihon, riding upon David's own mule. There Solomon was anointed king by Zadok the priest and the prophet Nathan, trumpets were blown and the people cried "Long live King Solomon!" (1 Kings 1:39). When news of this was brought to Adonijah, he realized that he was defeated, and he sought sanctuary at the altar. Solomon pardoned him, but later killed him when Adonijah exceeded his position. Anyone who has heard Handel's great coronation anthem "Zadok the Priest" and has not studied the biblical passage from which its words are taken, will be surprised to discover that the anointing of Solomon took place at a spring at the foot of the city, and that the ceremony was hastily arranged in order to counteract Adonijah's pre-emptive move.

Division of the kingdom

During the reign of Solomon the first temple in Jerusalem was built (it is illustrated on p.182). The united kingdom of David and Solomon was not, however, to last. Solomon's building works had extracted a heavy price from the people, and there was much discontent. In order to finance and provide manpower for his projects, Solomon divided the northern tribes among 12 administrative districts. As a young man named Jeroboam, who was in charge of Solomon's forced working, was leaving Jerusalem, he was met by Ahijah, the prophet of Shiloh, who tore his new garment into 12 pieces and gave 10 to Jeroboam, signifying the later division of the kingdom (1 Kings 11:29–39). The fact that Jeroboam received only 10 pieces is significant. Why did he not receive 11? The answer is that, although the southern kingdom that remained loyal to the house of David is always called Judah, it consisted in fact of Judah and Benjamin. Thus, when Solomon's son Rehoboam decided to reconquer the rebelling northern tribes, "he assembled all the house of Judah, and the tribe of Benjamin" (1 Kings 12:21). The alliance of Benjamin with Judah, when, in the reign of David, a Benjaminite had led a revolt against David, had at least a geographical basis. Benjamin occupied the northern part of the Jerusalem hills and there was no natural boundary between Judah and Benjamin, whereas the geographical division between the Jerusalem hills and the Bethel hills (see p.149) provided some natural features towards a defensible border. The northern boundary of the territory of Benjamin, although not identical with this geographical division, had some important common features.

The monarchy had hardly divided into the two kingdoms, north and south, when both were greatly weakened by the invasion of the Egyptian Pharaoh Shishak in about 924 BC. The biblical tradition records the incident thus: "In the fifth year of King Rehoboam, Shishak king of Egypt came up against Jerusalem; he took away the treasures of the house of the Lord and the treasures of the king's house" (1 Kings 14:25–26). This passage is probably an excerpt from temple archives, which recorded the fate of the temple's possessions. This is why it mentions only Jerusalem, and speaks as though Shishak actually came to Jerusalem. From a list of places Shishak claimed to capture, in which Jerusalem is not mentioned, it is possible to reconstruct his campaign, a campaign directed against fortified cities in the Negev, the coastal plain, the Jerusalem and Samarian hills, the Jordan valley and the valley of Jezreel. Of cities close to Jerusalem, Shishak attacked Gezer, Aijalon, Kiriath-jearim, Beth-horon and Gibeon. It is to be presumed that at Gibeon either Shishak demanded tribute from Rehoboam, or Rehoboam brought it unsolicited in order to ensure that Shishak went northwards.

Although the invasion of Shishak weakened both kingdoms, fighting between them, concentrated in the Jerusalem hills, went on for several generations. Rehoboam's son Abijam (911–908) succeeded in pushing his northern frontier to Bethel and beyond (2 Chronicles 13:19–20). Baasha, king of Israel (906–883), reversed the situation, pushed his frontier further to the south, "and built Ramah, that he might permit no one to go out or come in to Asa king of Judah" (1 Kings 15:17). This meant that he controlled the north–south route so firmly that the southern kingdom was denied access to the north by the main route in the hill country. In order to get this blockade lifted, Asa king of Judah (908–867) sent tribute to Ben-hadad king of Syria to persuade him to invade the extreme northern cities of Israel (see p.136). So successful was this alliance that Baasha retreated, Asa fortified Mizpah and Geba, and the frontier between the two kingdoms was stabilized. For the rest of its existence, the southern kingdom of Judah included also most of the territory of Benjamin.

The Assyrian and Babylonian invasions

The next important event set in the Jerusalem hills is the invasion of Judah by Sennacherib in 701 BC. At this time Hezekiah (727–698) was on the throne. He pursued a largely anti-Assyrian policy, which was risky, given that the Assyrians had extinguished the northern kingdom in 721 BC and that Hezekiah's father Ahaz had been an Assyrian vassal. His rebellion in 701 prompted an Assyrian invasion that devastated the land, an event described as follows in Isaiah (1:7):

> Your country lies desolate,
> your cities are burned with fire;
> in your very presence
> aliens devour your land.

This was the occasion on which Sennacherib conquered Lachish and recorded the event in the famous reliefs (p.88). Isaiah interpreted the devastation as just punishment by God against Israel for its sins. A remnant was to be preserved, however, in that Jerusalem was saved, even though it too was deeply affected by corruption. The problem of reconstructing the course of events from the biblical narratives and the Assyrian records is one of the most hotly disputed questions in Old Testament scholarship. The purpose of this Atlas is to illuminate the biblical narrative rather than to reconstruct biblical history. Thus the view will be taken that Sennacherib extracted heavy tribute from Hezekiah (2 Kings 18:13–16) and then demanded the surrender of Jerusalem, which Hezekiah denied him, until the Assyrian king was forced to withdraw. Our main concern is with Hezekiah's fortification of Jerusalem in the face of the siege.

Hezekiah's preparations are described most fully at 2 Chronicles 32:3–5: "he planned with his officers. . .to stop the water of the springs that were outside the city. . .he set to work resolutely and built up all the wall that was broken down, and raised towers upon it, and outside it he built another wall." We also read that "Hezekiah closed the upper outlet of the waters of Gihon and directed them down to the west side of the city of David" (2 Chronicles 32:30). Hezekiah's strategy of securing his own water supply while denying water to his attackers is paralleled by the tactics of the Muslim defenders of Jerusalem against the Crusaders in 1099 AD. Runciman writes, "On the news of the Franks' approach [Iftikhar] took the precaution of blocking or poisoning the wells outside the city. . .the Crusaders. . .were soon in difficulty over their water supply. . .The only source of pure water available to the besiegers came from the (lower) pool of Siloam, below the south walls, which was dangerously exposed to missiles from the city. To supplement their

Above The Siloam inscription, found in the last century at the southwestern end of Hezekiah's tunnel, records the meeting of two parties of workmen working from opposite directions and the flow of water that followed their breakthrough.

Previous page The so-called tomb of Absalom in the Kidron valley is a cube of rock cut from the surrounding cliffs, to which have been added classical columns and a cylindrical top. Whether or not it was itself a tomb is doubtful, and the association with Absalom is a pious legend. It may have marked the entrance to a burial area behind it, known as the tomb of Jehoshaphat. The tombs were certainly built before the time of Jesus and would have been seen by him.

THE JERUSALEM HILLS

supplies of water, they had to travel six miles or more." To defend it in 701 BC, Hezekiah constructed the Siloam tunnel.

The Siloam tunnel is about 535m (1750ft) long and runs beneath Jerusalem from the Gihon spring to the (upper) pool of Siloam, following a snakelike course, the reason for whose shape has not been satisfactorily explained. It was constructed by two parties of workmen starting from opposite ends, who eventually met at a point which today is easily recognizable by the alterations of course immediately before the join-up. The working parties each made small corrections as they worked towards the sounds made by their opposite numbers. The 19th-century surveyors of the tunnel found it silted up, and at some points the height available for a man to crawl through was as little as 56cm (22in) with the waters running at 30cm (11·8in). Today, apart from occasional heights of only 152cm (60in), visitors to the tunnel can wade through without too much discomfort. An important question is that of the position of the city wall in Hezekiah's time. Some investigations of Jerusalem have suggested that the pool of Siloam was itself outside the city on the western side, and that elaborate steps were taken to disguise the outlet. If the "another wall", referred to in the quotation from 2 Chronicles 32:5, enclosed the pool of Siloam and put it within the city, this would make better sense of why Hezekiah constructed the tunnel.

Although Hezekiah's refusal to surrender Jerusalem was heroically vindicated, Judah could not remain free from Assyrian domination. In the long reign of Hezekiah's son Manasseh (698/7–642) there were many years in which Judah was a vassal state. The accession to the throne in 640 of the eight-year-old Josiah coincided with a decline in Assyria's fortunes, thus giving the king and his backers the chance to assert once more the independence of Judah. In 622/1, following the discovery of "the book of the law" in the temple, a religious reformation was begun which entailed removing all places of worship other than Jerusalem. Some of these "high places" were no doubt local shrines used by Israelites; others, according to the writers of 2 Kings, had been built by Solomon to perpetuate the worship of the gods of his foreign wives (2 Kings 23:13). All cult objects used for the worship of other gods were destroyed, and priests who were engaged in idolatry were removed from their positions.

During the reign of Josiah, the prophet Jeremiah began his ministry. He is described as "the son of Hilkiah, of the priests who were in Anathoth in the land of Benjamin" (Jeremiah 1:1). Anathoth, probably the present-day Anata, was some 3km (1·9 miles) northeast of Jerusalem. It is interesting to note its description as being "in the land of Benjamin". Although the village had been part of the kingdom of Judah ever since the division of the monarchy, its identification as being Benjaminite had not altered. The priests in Anathoth were possibly descended from Abiathar, the priest who had served David but who had backed Adonijah and not Solomon in the struggle to succeed David. Because of this support for Adonijah, Abiathar was expelled to Anathoth (1 Kings 2:26–27). The interpretation of the book of Jeremiah presents formidable problems, and many questions cannot

Top A view of the village of Anata, thought to be the site of Anathoth, birthplace of Jeremiah.

Right The entrance to the spring of Gihon, the beginning of Hezekiah's tunnel.

be answered with certainty. We know nothing of Jeremiah's attitude to Josiah's reforms, although it is often assumed that the prophet opposed them because they supposedly altered the external conditions of religion, but did not change people inwardly. We can only guess at whether or not Josiah's reforms affected the livelihood or the status of the Anathoth priests, or whether as a resident in Benjamin Jeremiah had cause to be hostile to the Judahite kings of Jerusalem. However, Jeremiah played a decisive role in the events before and after the destruction of Jerusalem in 587 BC.

In 597 Nebuchadnezzar, king of Babylon, captured Jerusalem, exiled King Jehoiachin to Babylon together with at least 10000 of the nobility, army commanders and craftsmen, and set on the throne Jehoiachin's uncle Zedekiah (2 Kings 24:17). Another prophet, Hananiah, who came from Gibeon, was confident that this exile would last no more than two years (Jeremiah 28:1–4). Jeremiah was convinced that the exile would not be long, and wrote to the exiles in Babylon. "Build houses and live in them; plant gardens and eat their produce. Take wives and have sons and daughters; take wives for your sons, and give your daughters in marriage, that they may bear sons and daughters; multiply there, and do not decrease" (Jeremiah 29:5–6).

In 588 Zedekiah rebelled against Nebuchadnezzar who replied by besieging Jerusalem. Jeremiah proclaimed that the city would fall because God was fighting against it, and that surrender was the proper course of action. Not surprisingly, this was regarded as treason, Jeremiah's life was threatened, and on occasions he was imprisoned. If he believed that the city would fall, he also believed in a renewal of Israelite life. On being asked to perform his duties, as a next-of-kin, to buy from his cousin a field at Anathoth, Jeremiah duly made the purchase, had his act publicly witnessed, and declared "thus says the Lord of hosts, the God of Israel: Houses and fields and vineyards shall again be bought in this land" (Jeremiah 32:15).

With the fall of Jerusalem in 587, the Babylonians set up an administration for Judah under Gedaliah at Mizpah (Jeremiah 40:1–6). The location of this Mizpah raises an interesting question. The usual location of Mizpah is at Tell en-Nasbeh, about 11km (6·8 miles) north of Jerusalem, and it can be accepted that previous references to Mizpah in the present section should be placed there. Several factors point to a different location for the Mizpah mentioned in Jeremiah 40–41. First, when Jeremiah was being taken captive to Babylon, he was released at Ramah (Jeremiah 40:1) and told to "return" to Gedaliah. Ramah is south of Tell en-Nasbeh, so it is odd that Jeremiah was told to "return" to a town that had not yet been reached. Secondly, the day after Ishmael had murdered Gedaliah and his supporters, he set out to escape from the inevitable Babylonian reprisal by crossing the Jordan into the country of the Ammonites (Jeremiah 41:10). However, Israelite forces led by Johanan heard of Ishmael's crime, and decided to head him off. Johanan came upon Ishmael at the great pool at Gibeon (Jeremiah 41:12). But Gibeon is 5km (3·1 miles) south-southwest of Tell en-Nasbeh, an unlikely direction for Ishmael to be moving in if he wanted to go east to the Jordan valley. It has therefore been plausibly suggested that the Mizpah in which Gedaliah was made governor is to be located at Nebi Samwil. This location would make best sense of the geographical references in Jeremiah 40–41.

For close on 50 years Jerusalem remained in ruins, although it is possible that offerings were made to God at the site of the temple (Jeremiah 41:4–5). In 540 the Persian ruler Cyrus issued an edict permitting the Jews to return to Jerusalem to rebuild the temple (Ezra 1:1–4). The interpretation of Ezra 1–6 presents certain difficulties which lead many experts to conclude that some of the material in chapters 4–5, especially the letters of 4:11–16 and 17–22, comes not from the time of the return from exile, but from the middle of the following century. A surface reading of Ezra 1–6 implies that on their return the exiles, led by Sheshbazzar, began work on the rebuilding of the temple, that the work on the temple and the walls was stopped when representations were made to the Persian king, and that the work resumed with royal permission when the decree of Cyrus was appealed to and confirmed. The temple was completed by Zerubbabel and dedicated in 516 BC (Ezra 6:15).

Nothing is known of the fortunes of Jerusalem from this date to the arrival of Ezra in 458 BC and Nehemiah in 445 BC. The relationship and date of the work of these two men are long-standing problems of biblical scholarship. When Nehemiah reached Jerusalem from the Persian capital Susa, he inspected Jerusalem by night, secretly, and reported what he found as follows: "I went out by night by the Valley Gate to the Jackal's Well and to the Dung Gate, and I inspected the walls of Jerusalem which were broken down and its gates which had been destroyed by fire. Then I went to the Fountain Gate and to the King's Pool; but there was no place for the beast that was under me to pass. Then I went up in the night by the valley and inspected the wall; and I turned back and entered by the Valley Gate, and so returned" (Nehemiah 2:13–15). This description, together with the account of the rebuilding works in Nehemiah 3, enables a rough picture of Jerusalem in the 5th century BC to be drawn. The city of David was still occupied, although archaeological investigations have shown that its eastern walls were on the summit, not on the slope, making the area much smaller. To the north, the city spread westwards to the hills opposite the temple mount. The rebuilding of the walls by Nehemiah in the face of opposition from Sanballat, governor of Samaria, the proclamation of the law by Ezra, and the consolidation of the Jewish religion and worship in Jerusalem laid firm foundations for the future.

The Jerusalem of Ezra and Nehemiah was in some respects quite different from that which existed in New Testament times. The first stage in the alteration occurred in about 175 BC. The face of the ancient world had been changed by the conquests of Alexander the Great from 334 to 323 BC. These conquests included the former territories of Judah and Israel, which from about 332 were subject to various types of Greek rule. In about 175 BC a group of Jews in Jerusalem who wished to embrace Greek culture built a stadium for Greek sports. This encouraged Antiochus IV to install a high priest who supported the further introduction

THE JERUSALEM HILLS

of Greek manners and customs. The end of the tragic train of events was that Antiochus defiled the temple in 167 BC, turning it into a Greek shrine. Also during this period a Greek city was built on the western hill overlooking the city of David. The location of the citadel (the Acra), built to protect the Greek sympathizers, is hotly debated. For the next 26 years the sons of the priest Mattathias, usually known as the Maccabees, waged war on their Greek rulers and the Jewish Hellenizers. Although the temple was reclaimed and rededicated in 164 BC, it was not until 141 BC that the hated citadel protecting the Greek city was finally captured and pulled down. The walls built by the Maccabees after 141 went a long way to giving the city the appearance that it had in New Testament times.

The temple of Herod

The great architect of Jerusalem as Jesus knew it was Herod the Great. He extended the platform on which the temple stood to dimensions which have persisted until the present day. He rebuilt the temple itself, a fact alluded to in John 2:20 when Jesus' statement that he would rebuild the temple in three days if it were destroyed was questioned: "It has taken forty-six years to build this temple, and will you raise it up in three days?" Herod also built a royal palace on the western end of the western hill overlooking the city of David, and a fortress at the northwest corner of the temple, which he named "Antonia" for Mark Antony. He greatly improved the water supplies to the city, thus allowing the potential population to rise to perhaps 70 000.

The temple appears at the beginning of Luke's gospel narrative, in the account of the angelic vision which Zachariah experienced in the temple. Herod's temple stood in massive surroundings, and was entered from its great courtyard by one of 13 gates which led upstairs to a terrace, from which three gates led to the Court of Women. From this court, steps led up to the Nicanor or Beautiful Gate and into the Court of the Israelites, a narrow area which a layman could enter if he was bringing a sacrifice. Beyond the Court of the Israelites was the Court of the Priests where stood the altar; behind this was the building which contained the Holy Place and the Holy of Holies. The Holy of Holies was divided from the Holy Place by the veil.

In the narrative of Luke 1:5–22 Zachariah had drawn the lot which would enable him for the only time in his life to enter the Holy Place, and there to offer and burn incense on the altar of incense. It was while he was preparing to do this that he had the vision of the angel Gabriel, who promised that he and Elizabeth would have a son, and that Zachariah would be dumb until the birth and naming of the child. Because the vision delayed Zachariah's reappearance from the Holy Place, the people in the Court of the Women became anxious, and when he emerged he indicated by signs what had happened. The narrative goes on to record a visit of Mary from Nazareth to "a city of Judah" to visit Elizabeth. The traditional birthplace of John the Baptist, and thus the location of Elizabeth's house, is Ain Karem, a small village several miles southwest of Jerusalem. However, the place of the Baptist's birth is not known for certain, and

Above Ain Karem is a village 4.8 km (3 miles) to the west of Jerusalem. It is the traditional site of the birthplace of John the Baptist, and of the visit of Mary to Elizabeth when Mary spoke the words known as the Magnificat.

Right On the site of the church of St John at Ain Karem Byzantine mosaics have been found from previous churches.

Herod's Temple at Jerusalem

Historians often speak of the periods of the first (c.955–587 BC) and second (515 BC–70 AD) temples. In fact from 20 BC Herod the Great began to enlarge the platform on which stood the temple that had been built by Zerubbabel in the late 6th century BC. He also rebuilt the temple itself. Initially Solomon's temple was primarily a royal sanctuary. It celebrated the royal festivals, while the people worshipped at local shrines. Following Josiah's reform in 622/1 BC the temple became more of a national shrine, a process furthered by the changed conditions of the post-exilic period, in which Jerusalem was the single sanctuary for the Jewish people.

Right The details of Solomon's temple in the time of Ezekiel are given at 1 Kings 6:2–38. Although they are not easy to interpret, it appears that the temple had a vestibule flanked by two pillars. This led to the main hall, at the top end of which was the holy place. Chambers rising to three storeys were built on the outside of the temple wall, with initial access by an external staircase. At 1 Kings 7:13–51 the furnishing and vessels of the temple are described.

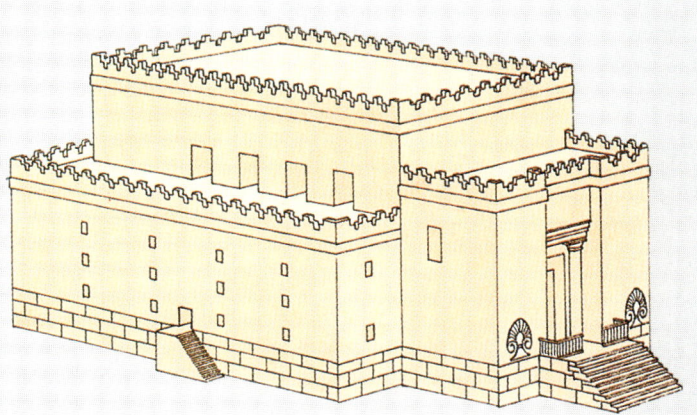

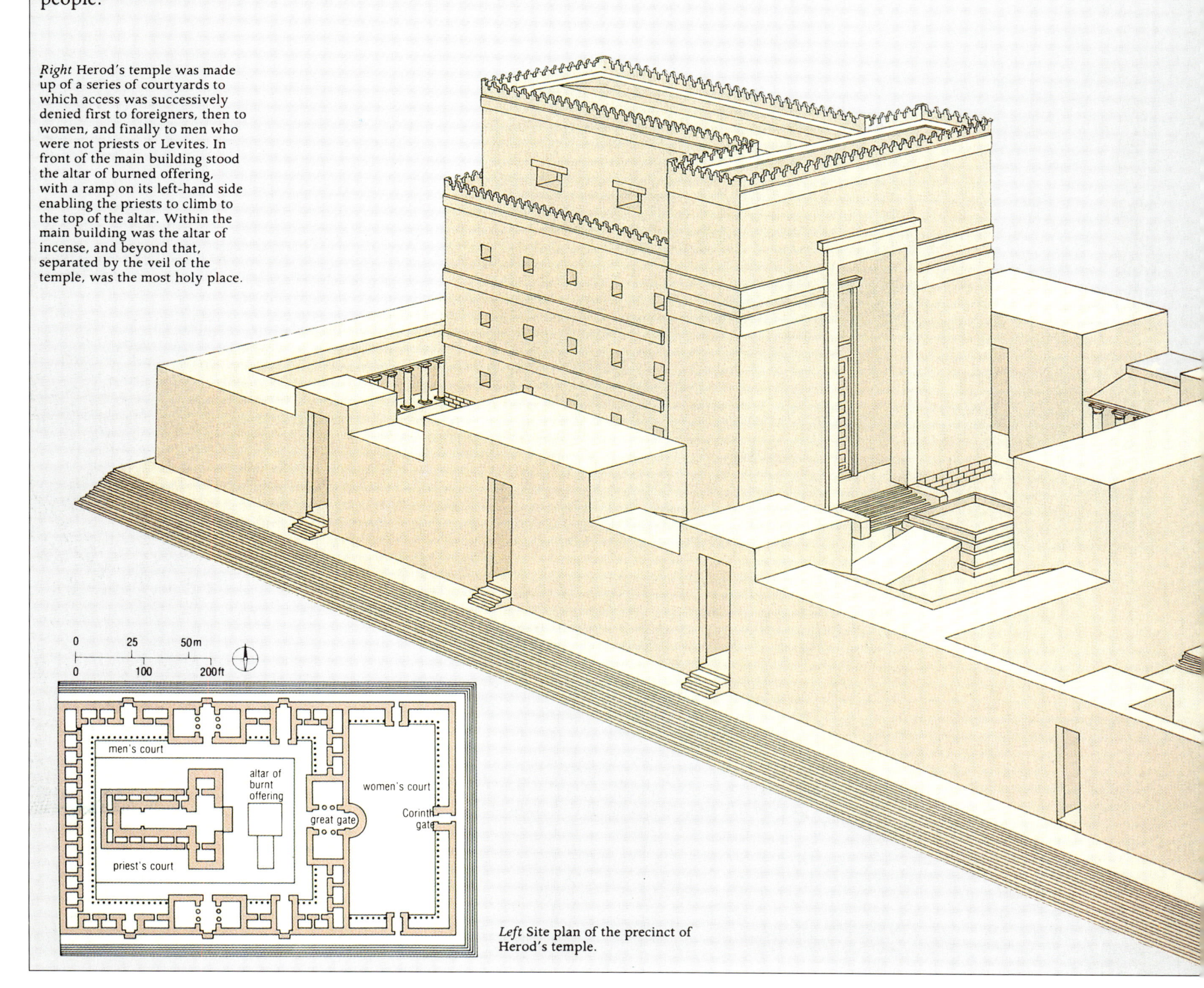

Right Herod's temple was made up of a series of courtyards to which access was successively denied first to foreigners, then to women, and finally to men who were not priests or Levites. In front of the main building stood the altar of burned offering, with a ramp on its left-hand side enabling the priests to climb to the top of the altar. Within the main building was the altar of incense, and beyond that, separated by the veil of the temple, was the most holy place.

Left Site plan of the precinct of Herod's temple.

Below A carving from Capernaum which may have been part of the 4th-century AD synagogue. It portrays the bringing of the Ark of the Covenant to Jerusalem by David. It may attempt to depict the temple, although its date does not encourage the view that it conveys authentic information.

Right On the arch of Titus in Rome is portrayed a procession of prisoners as well as booty, following the capture of Jerusalem in 70 AD. Among the objects depicted is a seven-branched menorah (or lampstand). That such a menorah stood in the temple is agreed, although opinion varies about its exact location there. The menorah that is depicted may be the actual one that was captured by the Romans, or it may be a symbolic representation if it is assumed that the priests concealed the sacred vessels prior to the invasion of the temple.

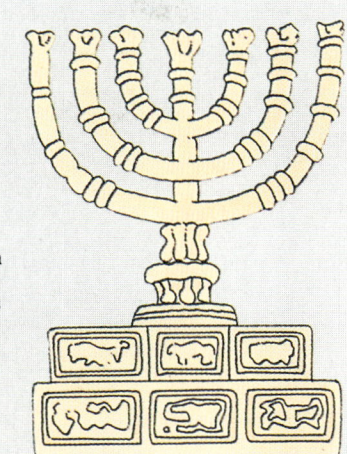

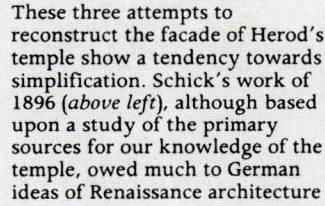

These three attempts to reconstruct the facade of Herod's temple show a tendency towards simplification. Schick's work of 1896 (*above left*), although based upon a study of the primary sources for our knowledge of the temple, owed much to German ideas of Renaissance architecture at the end of the 19th century. Watzinger (1935, *above left*) based his reconstruction upon the details given in the tractate *Middot* ("Measurements"), but had no information about the facade. Vincent and Steve (1956, *above*) present a facade without pillars. This differs from the model of the second temple at the Holyland Hotel in Jerusalem, in which the facade is pillared.

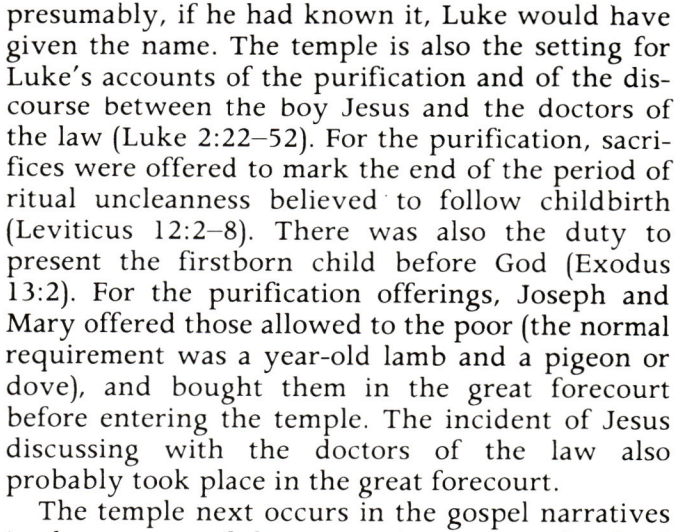

presumably, if he had known it, Luke would have given the name. The temple is also the setting for Luke's accounts of the purification and of the discourse between the boy Jesus and the doctors of the law (Luke 2:22–52). For the purification, sacrifices were offered to mark the end of the period of ritual uncleanness believed to follow childbirth (Leviticus 12:2–8). There was also the duty to present the firstborn child before God (Exodus 13:2). For the purification offerings, Joseph and Mary offered those allowed to the poor (the normal requirement was a year-old lamb and a pigeon or dove), and bought them in the great forecourt before entering the temple. The incident of Jesus discussing with the doctors of the law also probably took place in the great forecourt.

The temple next occurs in the gospel narratives in the account of the temptations, when the devil took Jesus to the holy city, set him on the pinnacle of the temple and said "If you are the Son of God, throw yourself down; for it is written 'He will give his angels charge of you', and 'On their hands they will bear you up, lest you strike your foot against a stone'" (Matthew 4:6, Luke 4:10–11). The highest point of the temple complex would have been the building that housed the Holy Place and Holy of Holies, and the pinnacle may have been one of the sidepieces of the front facade of this building. After the destruction of the temple in 70 AD, the highest point of the temple area remaining was probably the southeast corner, which thus came to be identified as the pinnacle.

Jesus in Jerusalem

In the first three gospels no further event in the life of Jesus is set in the Jerusalem hills until the last week of his life. The gospel of John, on the other hand, records several visits to Jerusalem before the last one of Holy Week. In John 2 is placed the cleansing of the temple, when Jesus drove out the money changers and those who sold sheep and oxen (John 2:13–22). The exact location of these people in the temple or courtyard is not known. Their presence was necessary if the temple was to function normally, otherwise it would be burdensome to votaries to have to purchase privately and bring with them the necessary animals. The money changers were present to enable temple taxes to be paid in the required coinage. No doubt the tradespeople concerned made a reasonable living from these activities, and the temple authorities also took some of the profit. However, we should not make these people out to be bad, and then interpret the cleansing of the temple accordingly. By this action, Jesus was making a radical claim about his own teaching and ministry, that they represented a quite new initiative of God into the world. The advent of Jesus would ultimately have radical consequences for the worship offered in the temple—it would make the sacrifices unnecessary —but his action was not so much to condemn what was taking place in the temple as to show that something new was about to happen. The narrative does not tell us where Jesus resided on the occasion of this visit, nor where he spoke by night with Nicodemus (John 3); but on other occasions he stayed in Bethany (see below).

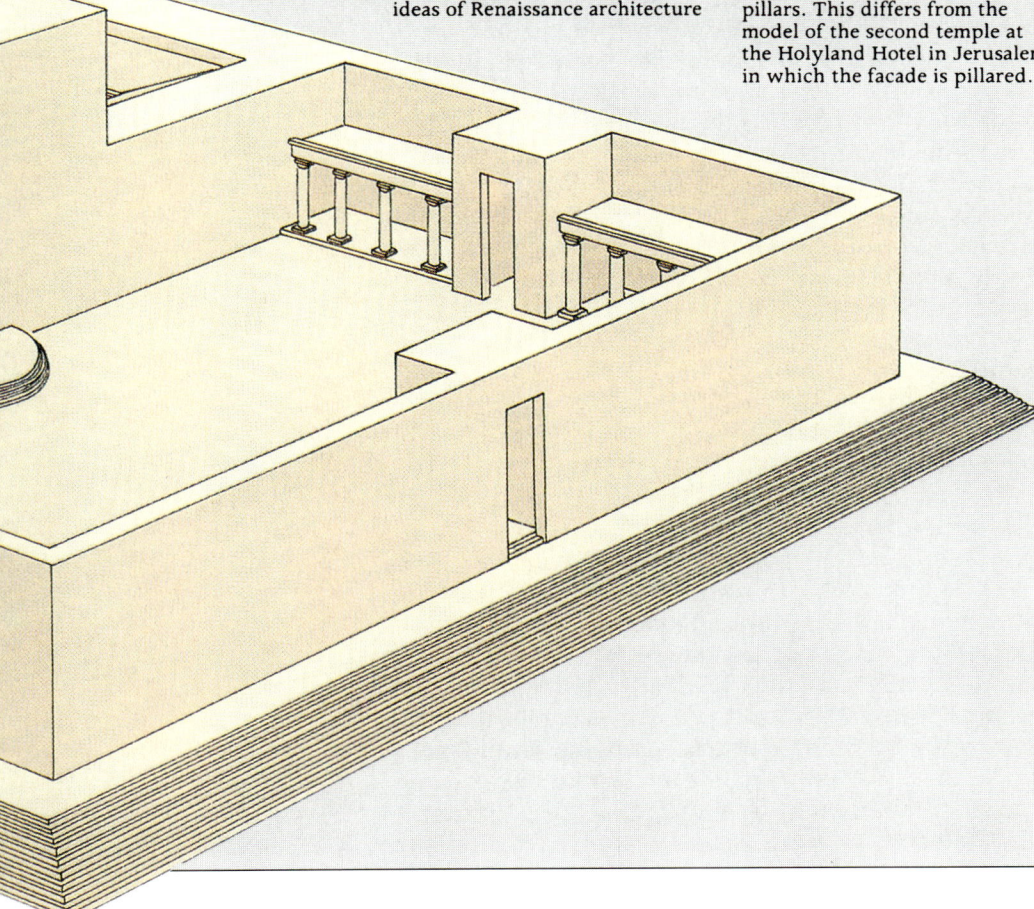

The next visit of Jesus recorded in John's gospel is in chapter 5, and focuses on the healing of the man at the pool of Bethesda. The actual name of the place of the miracle varies greatly in the manuscript tradition between Beth-zatha, Bethsaida and Bethesda. In the copper scroll from Qumran, which lists the locations of hidden treasure, a place is mentioned which some editors read as "Beth-eshdatain"—"place (house) of two outpourings". If this is correct, then Bethesda is confirmed as the likely reading. Unfortunately, the script is not easy to decipher and seems rather to name the location of the treasure as Beth-ha-eshuhain, meaning "house of the two pools". This could be the same place as the site of the miracle, but would give no clue as to which name is correct in the manuscript tradition of John.

The traditional site of the miracle is within the area which belongs to the church of St Anne, just inside the present city walls near St Stephen's Gate. Here two pools have been excavated, together with other locations such as caves. The results indicate that the site was a healing sanctuary after 135 AD. Many details of the story are obscure, however, and it would be unwise to identify the pools themselves as containing the water referred to by the man who was healed by Jesus. His reply was: "Sir, I have no man to put me into the pool when the water is troubled, and while I am going another steps down before me" (John 5:7). From this it is clear that a pool of some sort is envisaged, but it may well have been a pool to the east of the two main pools, in the complex of caves where there is evidence of the continuation of the cult of healing in the 2nd century AD. As presented in the fourth gospel, the incident discloses the radical new element in the ministry of Jesus. The man whom he meets is sick and feeble, he cannot get to the pool when the water is troubled. To do this, he would need the very thing that he seeks through healing—strength and mobility. He is a parable of the human condition, and only when Jesus comes to where he is and grants him the healing power of God does he begin to have any hope.

The next incident located in Jerusalem by John's gospel (apart from Jesus' teaching in the temple) is the healing of the man blind from birth, who was told to go to the pool of Siloam and there wash off the clay with which Jesus had anointed his eyes (John 9:6–7). We have already learned that Hezekiah brought the waters of the Gihon spring to the pool of Siloam when he constructed his tunnel in 701 BC. In the time of Jesus this pool was covered by a roof, open to the sky in the middle, and supported by 16 columns standing in the water. A low wall running just outside the columns possibly divided the inside (cleaner) water from the outside (dirtier) water. However, the pool meant in John 9 may not be this pool, but the so-called lower pool. This pool probably existed before Hezekiah constructed the Siloam tunnel. It was at the southeast foot of the city of David and was fed from the Gihon spring simply by a channel that ran down the valley. For obvious reasons it was of use to an enemy at a time of siege, and was no doubt stopped up by Hezekiah in 701 BC. It was, however, used in the time of Jesus. There is also a reference in Luke 13:4 to a tower in Siloam, which fell upon 18 people and killed them. A tower has been discovered in the Kidron valley, which is probably Maccabean and may well be the one referred to.

The next incident in the fourth gospel involving the Jerusalem area is the account of the raising of Lazarus (John 11). It is set in Bethany, the village that has retained the name of Lazarus in its modern name of el-Azariya. When Jesus heard the news of Lazarus' fatal illness, he was near the river Jordan where John had baptized. When, two days later, he set out for Bethany, Jesus must have followed the road from Jericho to Jerusalem, famous as the setting for the parable of the Good Samaritan (Luke 10:29–37).

The route from Jerusalem to Jericho

From earliest times the route from Jerusalem to Jericho was part of a most important west-to-east route from the coastal plain to the Jordan valley, and was responsible for the strategic importance of Jerusalem. In a matter of 20km (12.4 miles) the route goes from about 720m (2362ft) above to 260m (853ft) below sea level, through the chalk hills to the east of Jerusalem in its higher reaches, and through a band of reddish clays and sandstones in its lower reaches. This reddish feature gave the name Maaleh Adummim ("red ascent") which occurs in the boundary description in Joshua 15:7 and 18:17 as the "ascent of Adummim". Of the 19th-century descriptions of this route, one of the most vivid is that of H.B. Tristram, far too long to be quoted in full. Of the upper part of the route he wrote, "we left the miserable village of modern Bethany on our left, and rapidly descended, but on foot, the rocky staircase which for several hundred feet serves as a road... For three hours we wound down the valleys—if valleys they can be called: depressions of winter torrents, which rake the sides of innumerable round-topped hills, crowded one behind another—of the wilderness of Judea." In the lower part of the journey, the scenery changed. "Instead of limping among the gravels and boulders of winter torrents... we skirted the tremendous gorge of the Wady Kelt, which we could occasionally see by peering down the giddy height, with its banks fringed by strips of cane and oleander... The gorge opens suddenly at a turn of the path about two miles before reaching the plain, where the traveller finds himself in front of a precipice perhaps 500 feet high, pierced by many inaccessible anchorite caverns, and with a steep rugged hill above... When we reached the face of the hill down which the road winds from the top of the gorge, we enjoyed one of the finest views in Southern Palestine. At our feet lay stretched a bright green forest. Beyond it a long brown expanse—the desolate plain which divides it from the Jordan, whose course we could just trace by the depression marked by a dark green line of trees."

This is the terrain in which is set the parable whose opening words so simply describe a situation well known to the hearers of Jesus: "A man was going down from Jerusalem to Jericho, and he fell among robbers" (Luke 10:30). Jesus himself, then, came up this road on his way to Bethany to go to the house of Martha, Mary and Lazarus. On the upper course he did not, however, follow the route described by Tristram, for he would have turned left as he neared the Mount of Olives to go to Bethany, whereas Tristram, going in the opposite direction, passed Bethany behind on the left.

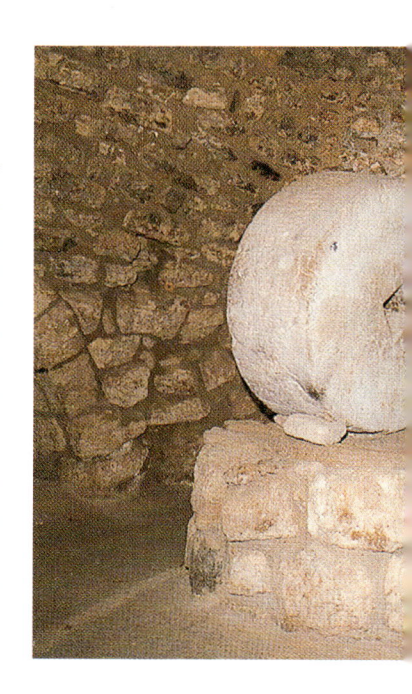

Right The old village of Bethany. In New Testament times it was the home of Mary and Martha and their brother Lazarus whom Jesus raised from the dead.

Above An ancient olive press from Bethany. The rolling stone would go round the groove that is visible on the near side. In the background is a wooden bar of the sort that would be inserted into the hole in the rolling stone, on the outside face of the stone. The bar would be propelled by an animal or a man.

The visitor to el-Azariya today can visit "the tomb of Lazarus". The tomb is in that part of the village that certainly existed in New Testament times, but obviously there is no way of identifying it for certain as that in which Lazarus was laid.

The last days of the life of Jesus are placed by all four gospels in Jerusalem. During his last visit for the Passover of 30 AD Jesus stayed at Bethany (Mark 11:11; John 12:1). John states that Jesus went to Bethany six days before the Passover; the other gospels give the impression, but do not demand the view, that Jesus entered Jerusalem riding on a donkey in the course of an unbroken journey from Jericho to Jerusalem. In support of the assumption that on his journey from Jericho Jesus stayed for some days in Bethany before the triumphal entry into Jerusalem is the consideration that he can hardly otherwise have arranged for the donkey to be available. At the time of Passover the boundaries of Jerusalem were theoretically extended to include Bethany, so that pilgrims there would be living "in Jerusalem" for the festival.

John 12:1–8 places in the house of Mary and Martha the incident of Jesus' anointing by Mary. In Mark 14:3–9 an unnamed woman anoints Jesus in Bethany at the house of Simon the Leper. John's story is before, Mark's after, the triumphal entry.

The triumphal entry itself began from Bethphage, according to Matthew 21:1, although the details are less clear in Mark 11:1 and Luke 19:29 who mention Bethany along with Bethphage, while John 12:12 gives no location, but must imply that Jesus set off from Bethany. Precisely where Bethphage was is not known, but it is probable that the procession passed through the modern village of et-Tur on the summit of the Mount of Olives before coming down into the Kidron valley and climbing up to Jerusalem in the region where St Stephen's Gate is today. The symbolism of the triumphal entry is made clear in Matthew 21:5 and John 12:15 by a quotation from Zechariah 9:9: "Tell the daughter of Zion, Behold your king is coming to you, humble, and mounted on an ass, and on a colt, the foal of an ass."

Jerusalem as Jesus knew it

How much remains of Jerusalem as Jesus knew it? Not a great deal to the naked eye, although the recent recovery and repositioning of pieces of Herodian pavement has strengthened the links with the past. Some of the principal streets in the old city follow the lines of streets in New Testament times, but, by and large, the city known to Jesus has been buried beneath the destructions and rebuildings of the intervening years. The temple area, now adorned by the Dome of the Rock, would have dominated the northeastern part of the city. The city of David would have been within the city walls, and not outside as today. Indeed, the spur of the city of David and the hill to its west would have been more intensely occupied than today, with flights of steps up and down the central valley dividing these hills. However, with proper assistance and a little patience, the modern visitor can probe beneath what the eye sees, and with the help of imagination can experience a little of the Jerusalem of the 1st century AD. Despite its apparent prosperity, with the splendid structures of Herod's building programme only recently completed, it was a city that would not long endure in its present form—as Jesus himself foresaw (Luke 21:20–24). Josephus, who was an eyewitness of the Roman siege barely more than a generation later, gives a powerful description of the ensuing destruction. The Romans razed the entire city, apart from three towers and a stretch of wall on the west, left as protection for the garrison that was to be stationed on the site.

Above In the process of rebuilding the platform on which the temple stood, Herod the Great constructed a massive retaining wall on the southwest side. Today, it is the western or "wailing" wall, the closest point to the temple site that observant Jews will approach.

Right A view of the Damascus Gate from inside the city, taken in the early years of the 20th century. The present gate was built in 1537 though the remains of its 1st-century AD predecessor can be seen at its base. It marks the start of the road to Damascus.

Below The steps shown here are in the grounds of the church of St Peter in Gallicantu, a possible site for the home of the high priest Caiaphas. In the time of Jesus this whole area was much more built up than today. The steps led down from the western hill to the central valley and on to the spur of the city of David. The present steps may date from New Testament times.

Right The plan is based upon archaeological findings, but many uncertainties remain. In particular, the exact position of the northern walls is disputed, and those shown here date from 41–43 AD.

Above Here too we see how levels have altered in Jerusalem since New Testament times. The surface of the pools of Bethesda would have been at the bottom of the excavation in the time of Jesus. Later builders of Byzantine and Crusader churches had to sink the vaulted supports for their buildings deep into the pools.

Right A coin of the reign of Tiberius (14–37 AD).

Above This remarkable picture, taken during recent excavations, shows how a street or courtyard could be laid on top of buildings from an earlier period and how the levels of Jerusalem have risen with time.

Left The pool of Siloam is at the far end of Hezekiah's tunnel from the Gihon spring. In the time of Jesus there was a lower pool, opposite the foot of the spur of the city of David, and an upper pool, shown here.

garden tomb

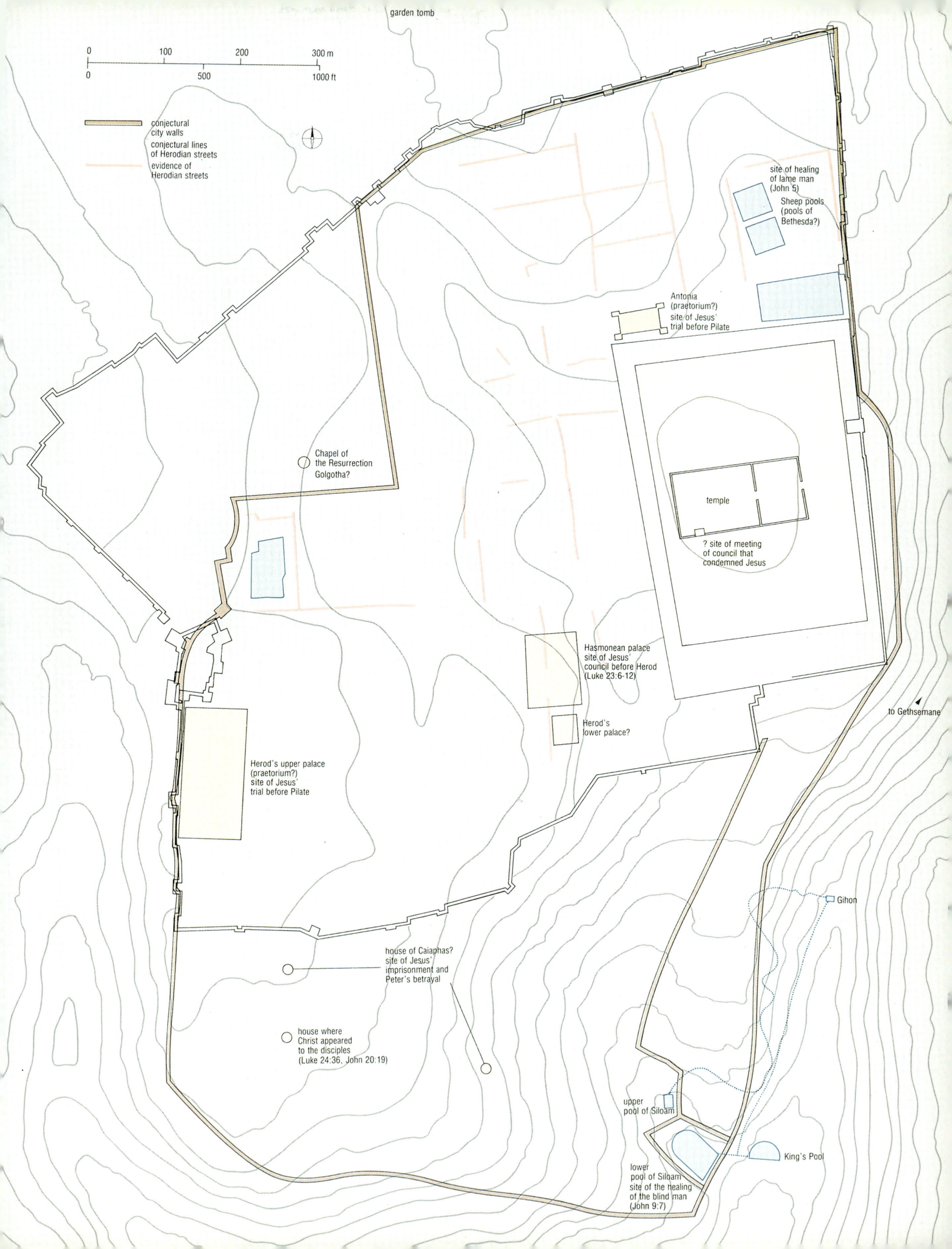

	conjectural city walls
	conjectural lines of Herodian streets
	evidence of Herodian streets

0 — 100 — 200 — 300 m
0 — 500 — 1000 ft

site of healing of lame man (John 5)

Sheep pools (pools of Bethesda?)

Antonia (praetorium?) site of Jesus' trial before Pilate

Chapel of the Resurrection Golgotha?

temple

? site of meeting of council that condemned Jesus

Hasmonean palace site of Jesus' council before Herod (Luke 23:6-12)

Herod's lower palace?

to Gethsemane

Herod's upper palace (praetorium?) site of Jesus' trial before Pilate

Gihon

house of Caiaphas? site of Jesus' imprisonment and Peter's betrayal

house where Christ appeared to the disciples (Luke 24:36, John 20:19)

upper pool of Siloam

King's Pool

lower pool of Siloam site of the healing of the blind man (John 9:7)

The events of Holy Week

For the events of the last week in the life of Jesus, our knowledge of where they took place ranges from the reasonably certain to the highly speculative. In the reasonably certain category we can place the teaching of Jesus in the temple, his teaching on the Mount of Olives concerning the destruction of Jerusalem and the last things (Mark 13), and the withdrawal to the Garden of Gethsemane and Jesus' arrest there. We do not know exactly where Jesus taught in the temple (or its courtyard), nor exactly where he sat on the Mount of Olives as he spoke of the last things, nor the exact location of the Garden of Gethsemane; but we know the general areas of these incidents. On the other hand, we can only speculate about the location of the upper room where the Last Supper was eaten, the venue of the meeting of the council at the high priest's residence, and the place of the Crucifixion and Resurrection. Visitors to Jerusalem today will almost certainly visit the traditional site of the Last Supper at the Cenacle on what is mistakenly called Mount Sion, the Garden of Gethsemane at the foot of the Mount of Olives, the church of St Peter in Gallicantu (a possible site of the meeting place of the council), and the traditional Via Dolorosa (Way of the Cross) from the site of the Antonia to the church of the Holy Sepulchre. In this way they will retrace the events of the life of Jesus from the Last Supper to his death and Resurrection. Along the way they will see much that is worthwhile. For example, in the church of St Peter in Gallicantu they will see a superb example of a cistern that could have been used as a prison; this is worth seeing, whether or not it is the place of Jesus' imprisonment before or after he appeared before the council.

The traditional "Way of the Cross" is based on the assumption that Pilate was residing in the Antonia fortress at the northwest corner of the temple courtyard. Recent writers, however, are agreed that Pilate is much more likely to have resided in Herod's palace in the upper city, at the site of what is today the citadel near the Jaffa Gate. If this is correct, and if the church of the Holy Sepulchre marks the general area of Crucifixion and Resurrection, then the traditional "Way of the Cross" is 90 degrees in the wrong direction! It needs also to be questioned whether the church of the Holy Sepulchre does indeed mark the general area of Crucifixion and Resurrection. The tradition linking the tomb of the Resurrection in the church of the Holy Sepulchre with the tomb from which Jesus rose is very formidable. It goes back to the "discovery" of the tomb in the reign of Constantine in 325 AD, and may have been believed to be the site of the Resurrection as early as before 135 AD. Also it was a tomb area at the time of Jesus' death and Resurrection.

The uncertainties surrounding the traditional location can be set out as follows. First, there remains a slight question about the position of the second north wall at the time of the Crucifixion, although the overwhelming opinion is that it was to the south of where the church of the Holy Sepulchre now stands; in other words the traditional site was indeed *outside* the city walls. The second question concerns the distance between the place of Crucifixion and the tomb in which Jesus was placed. John 19:41 states that "in the place where he was crucified there was a garden, and in the garden a new tomb where no one had ever been laid." The other gospels say nothing about the distance from the tomb to the place of Crucifixion. In the church of the Holy Sepulchre the distance between the tomb and Calvary is a mere 38m (125ft). It has to be asked, assuming John's account to be correct, whether a garden, tended by a gardener (John 20:15) and containing a new tomb, would have been so close to a place of public execution. Some have argued that there is no reason to suppose that Jesus and the two crucified with him were put to death in a usual place of public execution. We are faced here with arguments from silence, but it would be odd if the Romans did not have a place for public executions, and if, having one, they made an exception in the case of Jesus. Another reply would be that the tradition of linking the place of execution with the site of Calvary in the church of the Holy Sepulchre is much less strong than the tradition for identifying the tomb. This is a fair point, and it seems that the site of Calvary was not known to one or two of the early visitors to Constantine's church after 325 AD. Although these arguments are inconclusive at the end of the day, they may indicate that if the tomb of the Resurrection in the church of the Holy Sepulchre is the closest that we shall ever get to authenticity, the same may not be true for the chapel of Calvary.

Of the rival site for the tomb of the Resurrection, the garden tomb in Nablus Road, nothing will be said here with regard to its claims to authenticity. It is, however, well worth a visit, as are the so-called Herod family tomb near the King David Hotel, and the tomb of Queen Helena of Adiabene (the "Tombs of the Kings") near St George's cathedral. These enable visitors to see what sort of tombs and rolling stones were in use in the 1st century AD.

The place in Jerusalem where the disciples stayed from the time of the Crucifixion to the day of Pentecost is traditionally located on the site of the church of the Dormition. Here the risen Christ appeared to his disciples, and the Holy Spirit came upon them on the day of the Pentecost. An interesting problem is that of the location of Emmaus, to which two disciples walked on the first Easter day, accompanied by the risen Christ, whom they did not recognize until he broke bread (Luke 24:13–35). The two disciples then immediately returned to Jerusalem to tell the others what had happened.

The earliest identification of Emmaus, going back to the 4th century, was with Nicopolis, today the abandoned village of Imwas, 31km (19·3 miles) from Jerusalem. However, it seems unlikely that, having reached their destination and having said to Jesus "stay with us, for it is toward evening and the day is now far spent" (Luke 24:29), the disciples would have been able to return the 31km to Jerusalem and still have found the other disciples up and gathered together. The same may also be said for el-Qubeibeh and Abu Ghosh, sites identified with Emmaus since the time of the Crusaders, which are a little over 11km (6·8 miles) from Jerusalem in accordance with the usually accepted reading of Luke 24:13 that Emmaus was 60 stadia

The Golden Gate dominates the 16th-century walls of east Jerusalem, overlooking the Kidron valley. As can be seen from the outside, it is a double gate, consisting of the Gate of Mercy and the Gate of Repentance. This painting shows how the idea of the two gates is continued into the interior, the division being marked by the central columns. Light enters through slits where the gates have been walled up for many centuries. In their present form, they contain blocks of Herodian masonry and Byzantine decoration, as well as later work.

from Jerusalem. The present writer walked the route from el-Qubeibeh with the most athletic of his students, and to the surprise of all it took nearly three hours. A site preferred by some is the modern Motza on the main road from Jerusalem to the coastal plain, site of ancient Motza. The Hebrew name may have been put into Greek as Ammaous, and it is within easy walking distance of Jerusalem, a little over 6km (3·7 miles). However, its distance from Jerusalem does not correspond with the information of Luke 24:13.

The last recorded incident in the life of Jesus, the Ascension, is traditionally located on the Mount of Olives. However, Luke 24:50 states that Jesus "parted from them" at Bethany; and Acts 1:9–12 does not say from where the Ascension took place, except that "they returned to Jerusalem from the mount called Olivet, which is near Jerusalem." Certainly, reading the two passages together (usually held to be by the same author), one would most naturally conclude that Jesus parted from his disciples at Bethany, and that they returned via the Mount of Olives.

In the Acts of the Apostles Jerusalem is the setting for the earliest preaching of Christianity, although in some cases the precise details are obscure. For example, we are told of the location of the disciples on the day of Pentecost only that "they were all together in one place" (Acts 2:1), and we are not told where it was that the visitors to Jerusalem heard the disciples speaking in their languages, nor where Peter addressed the amazed crowd. Some of the earliest preaching (Acts 3:1–4:4) was done in the temple area, or before the council (Acts 4:5–22, 6:9–7:53), and some of the disciples were put in prison (Acts 4:1–4, 5:17–20), but the locations are not known for certain. The site of the stoning of Stephen was located in Byzantine times to the north of the Damascus Gate, which was St Stephen's church. The persecution that followed Stephen's stoning dispersed the disciples to some extent from Jerusalem. Peter is found at Jaffa (Joppa) in Acts 9:36–10:8, but reported back to Jerusalem in Acts 11 to explain why he had gone to preach to non-Jews. In Jerusalem Peter was imprisoned by Herod Antipas (Acts 12:1–17), and the Church met to consider what obligations of the Jewish law should be laid upon non-Jews who became Christians (Acts 15).

The last reference to the city of Jerusalem comes from Acts 21:17–23:35. Paul, arriving in Jerusalem from his third missionary journey, went to the temple to discharge obligations for himself and four others regarding vows that they had made. On one occasion his presence in the temple caused an uproar, because it was alleged that Paul had brought non-Jews with him to the temple (Acts 21:27–29). Paul was extricated by the prompt action of a Roman officer, who was surprised to learn that Paul was a Roman citizen. Paul addressed both the crowd that tried to lynch him and, on the following day, the council, all to no avail. Paul was saved from assassination when his nephew discovered a plot against Paul's life and disclosed it to the Romans. Paul was now taken by night, and with a heavy escort, to the governor's residence at Caesarea.

The Topography of the Passion

The exact location of the events of the Passion and Resurrection of Jesus is a subject of importance to all Christians. The destruction of Jerusalem in 70 AD and the establishing of the Roman colony of Aelia Capitolina on its ruins about 65 years later effectively erased the city Jesus knew, but after the conversion of Constantine early in the 4th century AD efforts began to be made to identify the places mentioned in the New Testament narratives. Constantine's mother Helena, who visited the Holy Land in 326, initiated the first programme for building churches at pilgrim sites. The location of the tomb of the Resurrection at what came to be called the church of the Holy Sepulchre provided a fixed point for the culmination of the Passion; over the centuries, however, the identification of where the incidents of the Passion took place, and where the religious observances were practised, varied to some extent. The way of the cross that is followed by modern pilgrims to Jerusalem goes back to the late 13th century, and is based upon the assumption that Jesus was condemned before Pontius Pilate at or near the Antonia fortress. The present 14 stations of the cross that go from the Franciscan chapel of the Flagellation to the church of the Holy Sepulchre date from the mid-19th century, although stations had been observed along this route since the late 13th century. The prevailing view now is that Jesus was condemned by Pilate at the site of Herod's upper palace. This would make the way of the cross much shorter, assuming that Jesus was crucified near the site of the church of the Holy Sepulchre. There is reasonable knowledge of the location of the Garden of Gethsemane and the meeting place of the Jewish Council. Other places, such as the site of the upper room where the Last Supper was eaten or of Caiaphas' house, are a matter for debate.

Right The red line indicates the way of the cross, the route that Jesus would have taken from the place of his condemnation to Calvary, assuming that Pilate condemned him at the Antonia. The blue line indicates the route preferred by many modern scholars, who believe that Pilate condemned Jesus while residing at Herod's upper palace. The green line suggests a route taken by Jesus following his arrest in the Garden of Gethsemane, when he was taken to the house of Caiaphas.

Below left A rooftop view of the beginning of the (modern) traditional route from the Praetorium to Calvary. To the right of the arch in the center is the convent of the Sisters of Zion. It was near here that Pilate said of Jesus "Behold the man" ("Ecce homo"), according to the modern devotional way of the cross.

Below Under the convent of the Sisters of Zion is a Roman pavement, which has been identified as the pavement mentioned in John 19:13 where Pilate judged Jesus.

THE TOPOGRAPHY OF THE PASSION

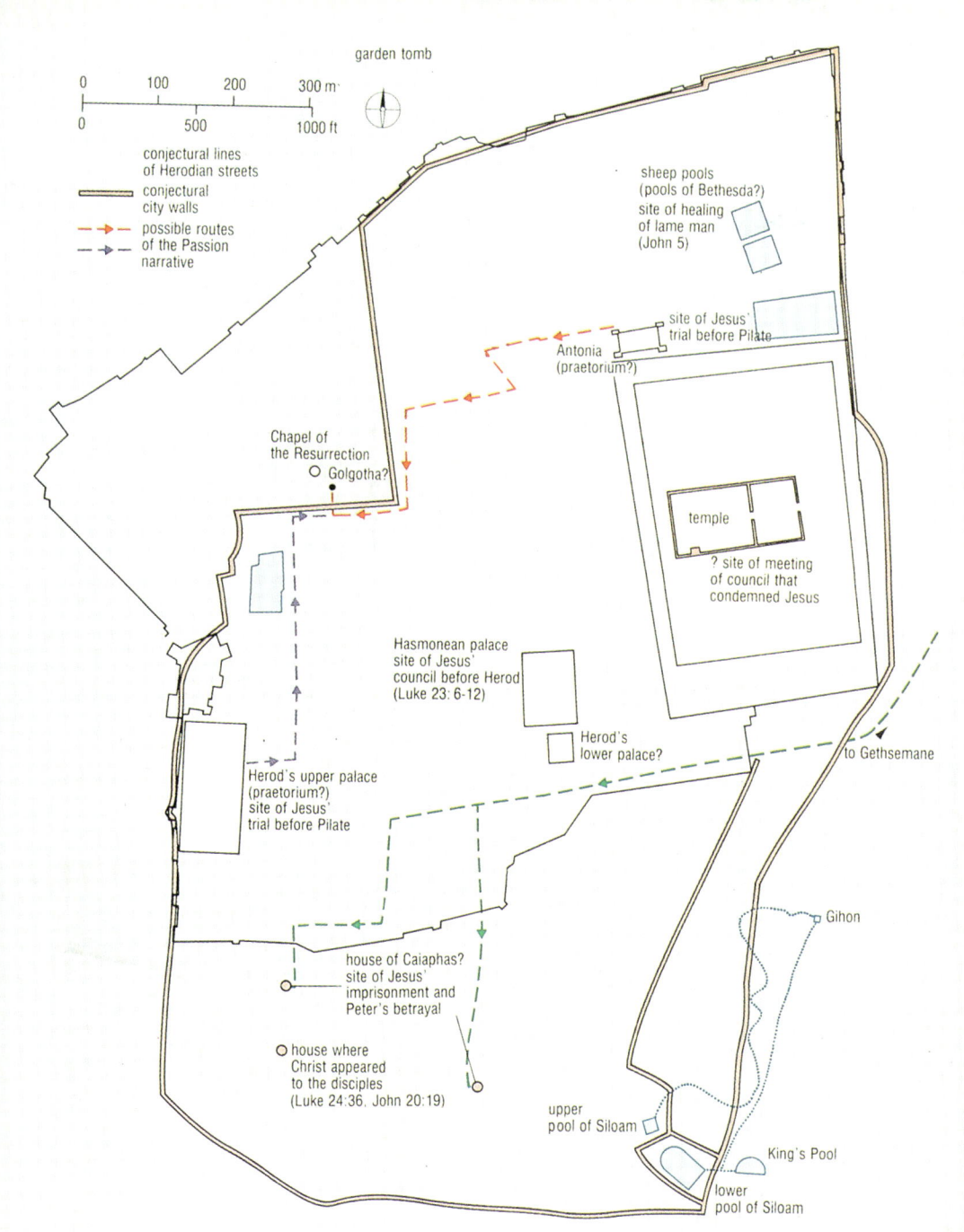

Map legend:
- conjectural lines of Herodian streets
- conjectural city walls
- possible routes of the Passion narrative

Map labels:
- garden tomb
- sheep pools (pools of Bethesda?) site of healing of lame man (John 5)
- site of Jesus' trial before Pilate
- Antonia (praetorium?)
- Chapel of the Resurrection / Golgotha?
- temple
- ? site of meeting of council that condemned Jesus
- Hasmonean palace site of Jesus' council before Herod (Luke 23: 6-12)
- Herod's lower palace?
- to Gethsemane
- Herod's upper palace (praetorium?) site of Jesus' trial before Pilate
- Gihon
- house of Caiaphas? site of Jesus' imprisonment and Peter's betrayal
- house where Christ appeared to the disciples (Luke 24:36, John 20:19)
- upper pool of Siloam
- King's Pool
- lower pool of Siloam

Below The third station of the cross is located in Valley Road, to the left of the entrance to the Armenian Catholic Patriarchate. It records the first of three occasions on which Jesus fell, although on the other two he is helped to bear the cross by Simon of Cyrene. The biblical account does not mention that Jesus fell, although this is a reasonable inference from the fact that Simon was compelled to take the cross.

Left The exterior of the church of the Holy Sepulchre has changed little since David Roberts drew it in 1839, except that the surrounding area is much more built up. The present exterior dates from 1810, following a disastrous fire in 1808.

Right The traditional site of the Garden of Gethsemane contains olive trees a thousand years old. Today part of the garden contains the Church of All Nations, commemorating the agony of Jesus in the garden.

Above right There remain in and around Jerusalem several examples of the kind of tomb in which the body of Jesus may have been placed. In this example we can see the type of rolling stone that probably closed the tomb.

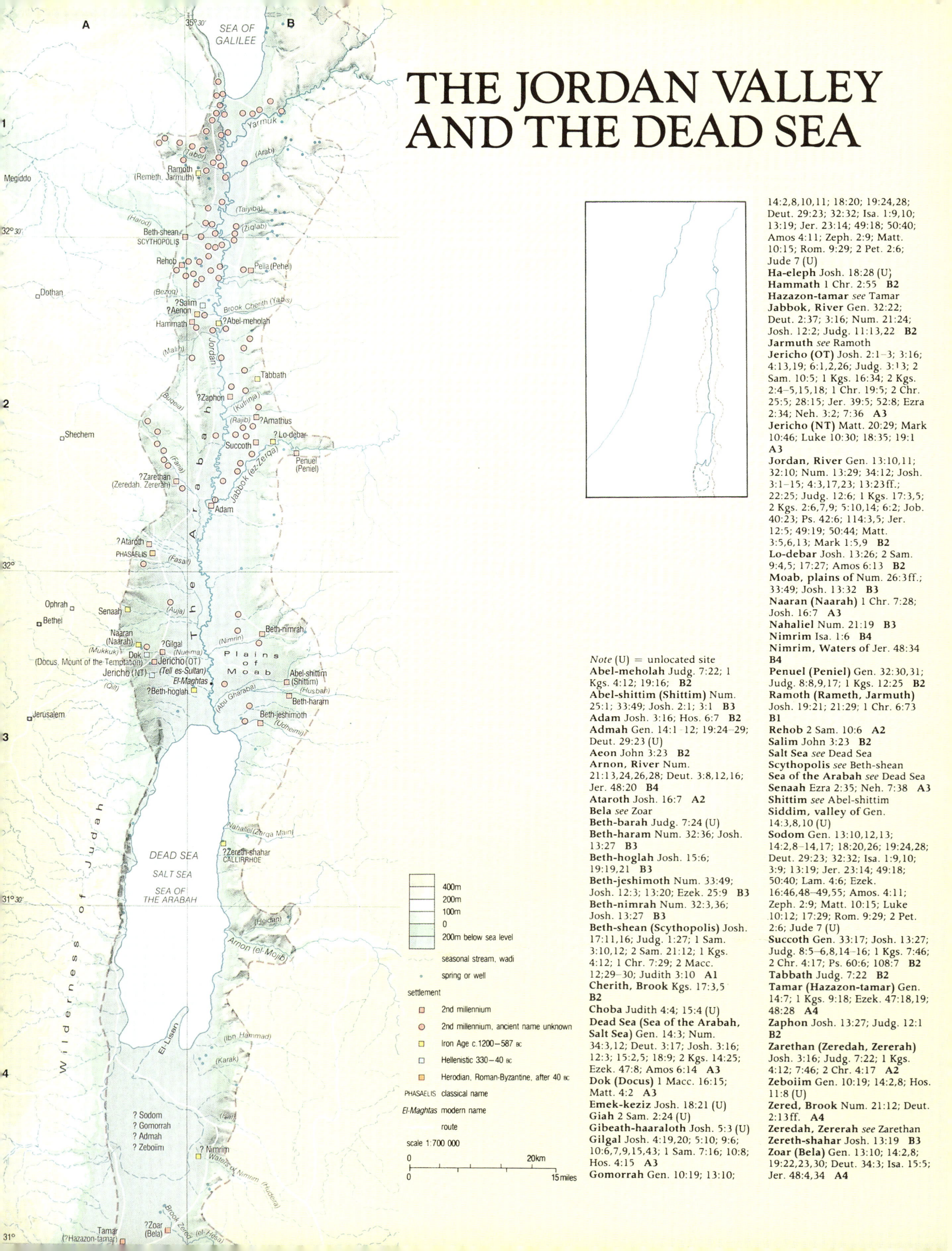

THE JORDAN VALLEY AND THE DEAD SEA

Note (U) = unlocated site

Abel-meholah Judg. 7:22; 1 Kgs. 4:12; 19:16; **B2**
Abel-shittim (Shittim) Num. 25:1; 33:49; Josh. 2:1; 3:1 **B3**
Adam Josh. 3:16; Hos. 6:7 **B2**
Admah Gen. 14:1-12; 19:24-29; Deut. 29:23 (U)
Aeon John 3:23 **B2**
Arnon, River Num. 21:13,24,26,28; Deut. 3:8,12,16; Jer. 48:20 **B4**
Ataroth Josh. 16:7 **A2**
Bela *see* Zoar
Beth-barah Judg. 7:24 (U)
Beth-haram Num. 32:36; Josh. 13:27 **B3**
Beth-hoglah Josh. 15:6; 19:19,21 **B3**
Beth-jeshimoth Num. 33:49; Josh. 12:3; 13:20; Ezek. 25:9 **B3**
Beth-nimrah Num. 32:3,36; Josh. 13:27 **B3**
Beth-shean (Scythopolis) Josh. 17:11,16; Judg. 1:27; 1 Sam. 3:10,12; 2 Sam. 21:12; 1 Kgs. 4:12; 1 Chr. 7:29; 2 Macc. 12:29-30; Judith 3:10 **A1**
Cherith, Brook Kgs. 17:3,5 **B2**
Choba Judith 4:4; 15:4 (U)
Dead Sea (Sea of the Arabah, Salt Sea) Gen. 14:3; Num. 34:3,12; Deut. 3:17; Josh. 3:16; 12:3; 15:2,5; 18:9; 2 Kgs. 14:25; Ezek. 47:8; Amos 6:14 **A3**
Dok (Docus) 1 Macc. 16:15; Matt. 4:2 **A3**
Emek-keziz Josh. 18:21 (U)
Giah 2 Sam. 2:24 (U)
Gibeath-haaraloth Josh. 5:3 (U)
Gilgal Josh. 4:19,20; 5:10; 9:6; 10:6,7,9,15,43; 1 Sam. 7:16; 10:8; Hos. 4:15 **A3**
Gomorrah Gen. 10:19; 13:10; 14:2,8,10,11; 18:20; 19:24,28; Deut. 29:23; 32:32; Isa. 1:9,10; 13:19; Jer. 23:14; 49:18; 50:40; Amos 4:11; Zeph. 2:9; Matt. 10:15; Rom. 9:29; 2 Pet. 2:6; Jude 7 (U)
Ha-eleph Josh. 18:28 (U)
Hammath 1 Chr. 2:55 **B2**
Hazazon-tamar *see* Tamar
Jabbok, River Gen. 32:22; Deut. 2:37; 3:16; Num. 21:24; Josh. 12:2; Judg. 11:13,22 **B2**
Jarmuth *see* Ramoth
Jericho (OT) Josh. 2:1-3; 3:16; 4:13,19; 6:1,2,26; Judg. 3:13; 2 Sam. 10:5; 1 Kgs. 16:34; 2 Kgs. 2:4-5,15,18; 1 Chr. 19:5; 2 Chr. 25:5; 28:15; Jer. 39:5; 52:8; Ezra 2:34; Neh. 3:2; 7:36 **A3**
Jericho (NT) Matt. 20:29; Mark 10:46; Luke 10:30; 18:35; 19:1 **A3**
Jordan, River Gen. 13:10,11; 32:10; Num. 13:29; 34:12; Josh. 3:1-15; 4:3,17,23; 13:23ff.; 22:25; Judg. 12:6; 1 Kgs. 17:3,5; 2 Kgs. 2:6,7,9; 5:10,14; 6:2; Job. 40:23; Ps. 42:6; 114:3,5; Jer. 12:5; 49:19; 50:44; Matt. 3:5,6,13; Mark 1:5,9 **B2**
Lo-debar Josh. 13:26; 2 Sam. 9:4,5; 17:27; Amos 6:13 **B2**
Moab, plains of Num. 26:3ff.; 33:49; Josh. 13:32 **B3**
Naaran (Naarah) 1 Chr. 7:28; Josh. 16:7 **A3**
Nahaliel Num. 21:19 **B3**
Nimrim Isa. 1:6 **B4**
Nimrim, Waters of Jer. 48:34 **B4**
Penuel (Peniel) Gen. 32:30,31; Judg. 8:8,9,17; 1 Kgs. 12:25 **B2**
Ramoth (Remeth, Jarmuth) Josh. 19:21; 21:29; 1 Chr. 6:73 **B1**
Rehob 2 Sam. 10:6 **A2**
Salim John 3:23 **B2**
Salt Sea *see* Dead Sea
Scythopolis *see* Beth-shean
Sea of the Arabah *see* Dead Sea
Senaah Ezra 2:35; Neh. 7:38 **A3**
Shittim *see* Abel-shittim
Siddim, valley of Gen. 14:3,8,10 (U)
Sodom Gen. 13:10,12,13; 14:2,8-14,17; 18:20,26; 19:24,26; Deut. 29:23; 32:32; Isa. 1:9,10; 3:9; 13:19; Jer. 23:14; 49:18; 50:40; Lam. 4:6; Ezek. 16:46,48-49,55; Amos 4:11; Zeph. 2:9; Matt. 10:15; Luke 10:12; 17:29; Rom. 9:29; 2 Pet. 2:6; Jude 7 (U)
Succoth Gen. 33:17; Josh. 13:27; Judg. 8:5-6,8,14-16; 1 Kgs. 7:46; 2 Chr. 4:17; Ps. 60:6; 108:7 **B2**
Tabbath Judg. 7:22 **B2**
Tamar (Hazazon-tamar) Gen. 14:7; 1 Kgs. 9:18; Ezek. 47:18,19; 48:28 **A4**
Zaphon Josh. 13:27; Judg. 12:1 **B2**
Zarethan (Zeredah, Zererah) Josh. 3:16; Judg. 7:22; 1 Kgs. 4:12; 7:46; 2 Chr. 4:17 **A2**
Zeboiim Gen. 10:19; 14:2,8; Hos. 11:8 (U)
Zered, Brook Num. 21:12; Deut. 2:13ff. **A4**
Zeredah, Zererah *see* Zarethan
Zereth-shahar Josh. 13:19 **B3**
Zoar (Bela) Gen. 13:10; 14:2,8; 19:22,23,30; Deut. 34:3; Isa. 15:5; Jer. 48:4,34 **A4**

THE JORDAN VALLEY AND THE DEAD SEA

Description of the region

At the southern end of the Sea of Galilee, slightly to the west, the river Jordan resumes its course along the rift valley down to the Dead Sea. Apparently, the older outlet of the river was about 1km (0·6 miles) to the north of the present outlet. The distance from the exit of the Jordan from the Sea of Galilee to its entry into the Dead Sea is about 105km (65·2 miles) as the crow flies, but such is the tortuous path of the river that its own length between these points is about 322km (200 miles). Although the valley through which the river flows varies in width from about 5 to 22·5km (3·1 to 14 miles), the Jordan itself is generally no wider than 31m (102ft) nor deeper than about 3m (9·8ft), although fluctuations can occur, depending on rainfall. The Negro spiritual hymn's claim that the river Jordan is deep and wide does not accord with reality.

Immediately to the south of the Sea of Galilee a rough triangle is formed between the sea, the river Jordan, and the river Yarmuk which flows in a northwesterly direction and joins the Jordan about 7km (4·4 miles) south of the Sea of Galilee. Of all the parts of the Jordan valley this triangle has altered the most radically since biblical times, all the alterations coming in the present century. At the confluence of the Jordan and the Yarmuk a hydroelectric power station was built between 1927 and 1932, necessitating the construction of dams and reservoirs. On the western side of the triangle were founded agricultural settlements, of which the most famous are the kibutzim Deganya A (founded 1909) and Deganya B (1921), which have made the area look like a miniature paradise.

Above The Jordan valley from the air.

Right Nebi Musa (which means the Prophet Moses) is in the Jordan valley, some 6km (3.7 miles) south of Jericho. Whereas the Old Testament locates the grave of Moses on the eastern side of the Jordan, Muslim tradition holds that he travelled under the ground to a grave in the promised land. In the foreground can be seen the Muslim shrine of pilgrimage to the grave of Moses dating from the 15th century. In the background are the Dead Sea and the hills of Moab.

Left This is a most remarkable region, entirely below sea level, with a curious landscape caused by erosion, and with the river Jordan taking a tortured and serpentine route from the Sea of Galilee to the Dead Sea. It was always a well-settled area and an important route from north to south.

THE JORDAN VALLEY AND THE DEAD SEA

A plotting of the main patterns of settlement in the 2nd millennium indicates that the Jordan–Yarmuk triangle was suitable for agriculture at that time. To the south of the triangle, however, settlement was possible only where major valleys brought water into the Jordan valley from the hills to the west and the east. Of these valleys the most important was the Beth-shean valley, not only on account of its width, but also because it gave access to the valley of Jezreel. The number of settlements in the Beth-shean valley and to its south is quite striking. From the Wadi Malih southwards there are no significant settlements on the west side of the Jordan until the valley of the Wadi Faria is reached. On the eastern side, in contrast, we find a cluster of settlements where the Nahr ez-Zerqa (Jabbok) enters the valley. The Wadi Faria provided an important east–west route from the Jordan valley to the hill country of Samaria. It is surprising that it was not more intensively settled, but it seems to have produced a combination of saline swamps near its entry to the Jordan and a badly eroded channel higher up its own broad valley.

It is noticeable that on both banks of the Jordan south of the Wadi Faria the settlements are few and far between. This is partly because average rainfall falls to 100mm (3·9in) per year at the Dead Sea, and because rainfall on the Judean hills is lower than that further to the north. The most famous city in the southernmost part of the Jordan valley, Jericho, owed its existence to the spring known in Arabic as Ein es-Sultan. Popularly it is called Elisha's spring, because of the story related in 2 Kings 2:19–22. After the ascension of Elijah (2 Kings 2:1–12), Elisha retrieved Elijah's mantle, and demonstrated that he was Elijah's heir as leader of the prophetic groups by using the mantle to enable him to cross the river Jordan. The men of Jericho were quick to enlist the powers of the new prophetic leader to cure the waters of the city. This Elisha did by throwing salt into the spring, declaring "Thus says the Lord, I have made this water wholesome; henceforth neither death nor miscarriage shall come from it."

The Jordan ends its tortuous journey by entering the Dead Sea, or, to give it its biblical name, the Salt Sea (Genesis 14:3). In its present form the Dead Sea is about 80km (49·7 miles) long and 17·5km (10·9 miles) wide. On its surface it is about 400m (1312ft) below sea level. There is no outlet from the Dead Sea, and the inflow from the Jordan and other rivers is offset by the high rate of evaporation of the water in temperatures whose average maximum is more than 40°C (104°F) in July and August, and 20°C (68°F) in the winter months. The high level of evaporation, together with the geological conditions of the area, produces a salinity of the waters of over 26 per cent, compared with the average salinity of oceans which is 3·5 per cent. This makes it impossible for anything to live in the Dead Sea. It is also impossible to swim in it, and modern tourists who try to get from a floating position on their back to a swimming position on their front not only find this very difficult, but run the danger of getting the water in their eyes, with very painful consequences.

Two-thirds of the way down the Dead Sea, a piece of land juts into it from the eastern side. This is known as el-Lisan (the tongue), and it is a significant fact that to its north the depth of the Dead Sea is about 400m (1312ft) while to its south the depth is only 6m (19·7ft) or so. The present Atlas assumes that in biblical times the area to the south of the tongue was dry, and that the cities of the plain, including Sodom, were located in the eastern part of this dry area.

The biblical record

The biblical incidents located in the Jordan valley and Dead Sea area begin, in fact, with the cities of the plain. Genesis 10:19 mentions four of the cities, Sodom, Gomorrah, Admah and Zeboiim, in describing the extent of the territory of the Canaanites. When Lot was given first choice by Abraham as to how they would divide the land between them, Lot "saw that the Jordan valley was well watered everywhere like the garden of the Lord, like the land of Egypt, in the direction of Zoar" (Genesis

The Wadi Qilt is named after one of three springs that in Hellenistic and Herodian times supplied Jericho with water. It is also a large catchment area for rains that fall on the eastern side of the watershed. Its eastern end opens into the Jordan valley through a spectacular gorge. Some 2km (1.2 miles) along the wadi from the Jordan valley is the monastery of St George, founded at the end of the 5th century AD and one of three survivors of the many monastic institutions that flourished in the area in the Byzantine period.

The Dead Sea is most commonly called the Salt Sea in the Old Testament. In ancient times it was famed not only for its provision of salt, but as a source of asphalt, and so it was also called the Asphalt Sea. The name Dead Sea, which is also ancient, derives probably from the fact that nothing can live in the sea on account of its very high salt content, caused by the evaporation of the water and the minerals in the ground. Here salt clusters are shown at the southern end of the sea.

13:10). Zoar is the fifth of the five cities of the plain. Seeing the exceedingly fertile land, Lot moved his tent as far as Sodom (Genesis 13:12).

The area in the region of Sodom today hardly merits description as a "garden of the Lord", and it is not surprising that the cities of the plain have been sought to the north of the Dead Sea, where the oasis of Jericho makes the picture of abundant fertility more credible. However, it appears that the eastern shore of the Dead Sea south of the tongue is well supplied with watercourses, and in some parts with springs, and the majority view of scholars is that the cities of the plain were somewhere in this area, and not north of the Dead Sea. Lot's presence in Sodom, and his being taken captive by the four kings who fought against the cities of the plain, form the background to Abraham's expedition to Dan and beyond Damascus in order to rescue Lot and to defeat the four kings (Genesis 14:1–16).

The best-known incident set south of the Dead Sea is the destruction of Sodom and Gomorrah (Genesis 19). Two of the three messengers who visited Abraham in Hebron (Genesis 18) come on to Sodom where they are entertained by Lot. The wicked men of Sodom, hearing of the presence of the strangers, demand of Lot that he produce them so that they may abuse them sexually. The visitors defend themselves by striking their would-be molesters with blindness. In the morning Lot and his family are given the chance to escape before Sodom (and Gomorrah) is destroyed by fire and brimstone. This they do, except that Lot's wife looks back, and is turned into a pillar of salt.

There have been many attempts to explain the story of the destruction of Sodom and Gomorrah which draw on the strikingly weird nature of the landscape at the southern end of the Dead Sea. One explanation envisages the lowering of the land south of the tongue, and the consequent flooding

THE JORDAN VALLEY AND THE DEAD SEA

of the area. Unfortunately, the story itself says nothing about the cities being destroyed by flooding, and there is reason to believe that the area was dry until the time of the Crusades. If one wishes for a natural explanation for the incident, it may be safest to look to a massive geological movement that possibly separated Mount Sodom from the tongue. If this happened in historical time and in circumstances in which the event was observed and narrated, it could be the basis for the imagery of the Sodom story, even if the time of Abraham and Lot was much later.

Whatever the origins of the story in Genesis 19, it became in the Old Testament a powerful symbol for God's judgment upon wickedness. Amos, in the 8th century, described some of the misfortunes that had come upon Samaria in the words

> I overthrew some of you,
> as when God overthrew Sodom and Gomorrah
> (Amos 4:11),

while Isaiah addresses the rulers in Jerusalem as though they were the rulers of the wicked cities:

> Hear the word of the Lord,
> you rulers of Sodom!
> Give ear to the teaching of our God,
> you people of Gomorrah! (Isaiah 1:10)

Jesus referred to Sodom when he condemned Capernaum, the town chosen for the headquarters of his ministry, for its unbelief: "And you, Capernaum, will you be exalted to heaven? You shall be brought down to Hades. For if the mighty works done in you had been done in Sodom, it would have remained until this day. But I tell you that it shall be more tolerable on the day of judgment for the land of Sodom than for you" (Matthew 11:23–24).

Jericho

About 13km (8.1 miles) to the northeast of the Dead Sea is the lush oasis of Jericho, also called in the Old Testament the city of palms (Judges 3:13). Old Testament Jericho, Tell es-Sultan, was occupied for thousands of years before the time of Joshua, and visitors to the site can see a pre-pottery Neolithic stone tower built about 7000 BC. Exactly where the city, whose capture by Joshua is related in Joshua 6, was located, is not known. It has not so far been discovered in the excavations that have been conducted. There is also uncertainty about the location of Gilgal, which, according to the book of Joshua, served as the base for the Israelite armies that invaded the land of Canaan and was where 12 stones were set up after the Israelites crossed the Jordan (Joshua 4:19–24). It is often provisionally located at Khirbet el-Mafjar, which fits the detail given at Joshua 4:19 that Gilgal was on the east border of Jericho. Old Testament Jericho and the suggested site of Gilgal were close to the Wadi Makkuk, from which there is a route from the Jordan valley to the Bethel hills, and to the town of Ai, which the Israelites were initially unable to defeat because Achan had disobeyed the instruction that nothing of the spoil of Jericho was to be kept for personal benefit.

In the division of the land Jericho was included

Jericho

There are two ancient Jerichos, not one. Old Testament Jericho, Tell es-Sultan, goes back to the 10th millennium BC, with evidence of permanent settlement from the 8th millennium BC. At the foot of the Tell is a copious spring, known today as Elisha's well after the incident recorded in 2 Kings 2:19-22. By the time that the Israelites arrived to attack Jericho in about 1250 BC the city had existed for over 6000 years. Archaeological investigation of the tell yielded a detailed record of the successive settlements on the site, but the level corresponding with the city destroyed by Joshua is not definitely established. New Testament Jericho is a separate site to the south of Tell es-Sultan, where the Wadi Qilt enters the Jordan valley. It was originally a fort built in Hasmonean times to guard the route to Jerusalem along the Wadi Qilt. It was rebuilt on grand lines by Herod the Great.

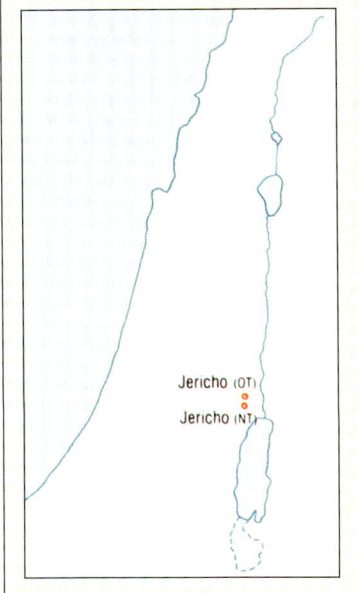

Right Aerial view from the north of Tulul Abu el-Alaiq, site of New Testament Jericho. The Wadi Qilt runs from a little below centre on the left-hand edge to above the centre on the right-hand edge. Where it curves sharply, a small water channel can be seen running along the side of the cliffs. In the foreground the mound to the right of centre is part of the Hasmonean complex of buildings that made up the original winter palace. To its left can be seen the deep excavations of the swimming pool. Herod the Great built over this Hasmonean palace, perhaps to provide his private villa. At the left-hand edge just below the wadi bed is the northern wing of Herod's later palace. The palace continued on the opposite side of the wadi, and a small mound is visible slightly to the right where there was a hall or bath houses. The Dead Sea is out of the picture, beyond the upper left-hand side.

THE JORDAN VALLEY AND THE DEAD SEA

Below One of the remarkable features of Jericho is the pre-pottery Neolithic tower which was built in the 8th millennium BC. The tower is 8.5m (27.9 ft) in diameter and its remains are nearly 8m (26.2 ft) high. It had a door and an internal staircase. It is outside the walls of the city of the period, and was probably a watchtower.

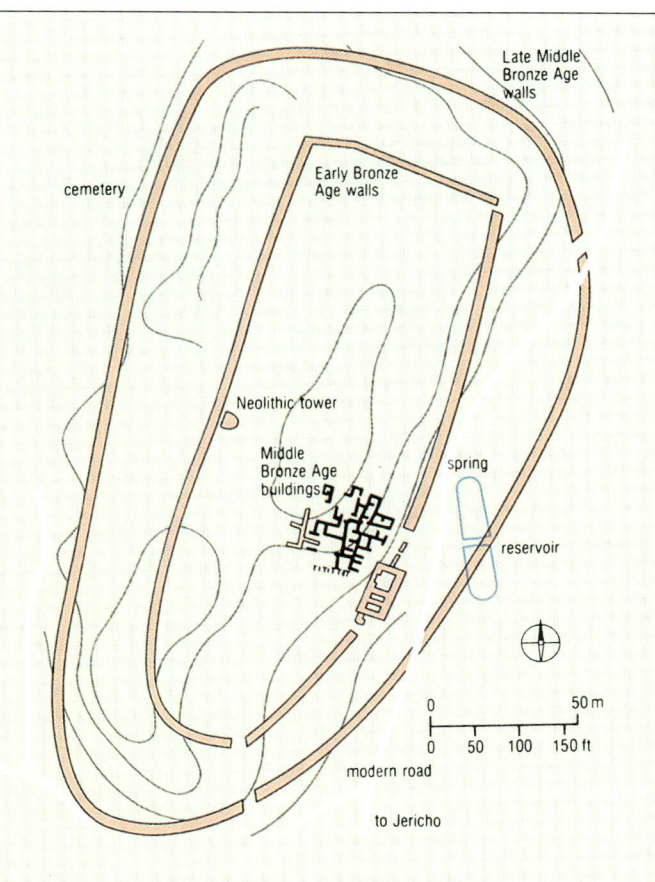

Left Site plan of Tell es-Sultan, Old Testament Jericho. The modern road cuts through the eastern edge of the Tell. The pre-pottery Neolithic tower is marked. It is possible to see the growth of the city from the relative positions of the Early Bronze and the Late Middle Bronze Age walls.

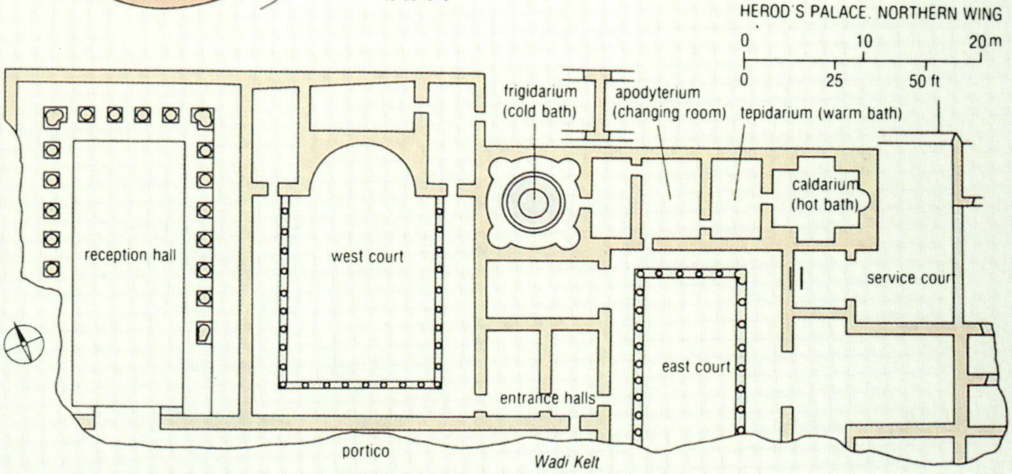

Above The north wing of Herod's palace at New Testament Jericho.

Left An urn in the shape of a head, recovered from a burial at Jericho, c. 18th–16th century BC.

in the area of the tribe of Benjamin (Joshua 18:21). Under its name "city of palms" it served as the point of departure for the Kenites as they accompanied the people of Judah into the southern part of the Judean wilderness (Judges 1:16). In the period of the Judges the "city of palms" was captured by the Moabite king Eglon (Judges 3:12–13). Eglon's defeat by Ehud has already been described (see p.167).

The story of David contains a reference to Jericho as the place where David told his insulted servants to remain. They had been insulted by having half of their beards shaved off and pieces cut from their clothes when David sent them to carry condolences to Hanun, king of the Ammonites, on the death of his father (2 Samuel 10:1-5). The text says that David went to meet them, presumably in Jericho, which still has to be passed if one drives from Jerusalem to Amman, the site of the ancient Ammonite capital. This act of sensitivity on the part of David says much for his loyalty to his servants, and indicates how strongly he felt the insult. Mention has already been made of Jericho as the area from which Elijah was taken up to heaven. At 2 Kings 2 we read how Elijah and Elisha proceeded from Gilgal (presumably a town in the hills, and not the Gilgal close to Jericho) to Bethel and thence to Jericho. They then went to the Jordan and crossed it by means of the power of Elijah's mantle. As they continued on, the fiery horses and chariots took Elijah away, leaving only his mantle behind.

When Joshua captured Jericho and destroyed it, he laid a curse on anyone who rebuilt it: "Cursed before the Lord be the man that rises up and rebuilds this city, Jericho. At the cost of his first-born shall he lay its foundation, and at the cost of his youngest son shall he set up its gates" (Joshua 6:26). If the passages from Judges 3 and 2 Samuel 10 referred to above are correct, then Jericho was soon rebuilt and was occupied by Israelites. At 1 Kings 16:34 the curse of Joshua is taken up: "In his days [the days of Ahab, c. 873–852 BC] Hiel of Bethel built Jericho; he laid its foundation at the cost of Abiram his first-born, and set up its gates at the cost of his youngest son Segub, according to the word of the Lord, which he spoke by Joshua the son of Nun." The point is sometimes made that some of the very early inhabitants of Jericho buried their dead under their houses, and that the biblical passages quoted may be reminiscences of the practice. It is more likely that Hiel's action was a revival of a type of paganism that was encouraged in the reign of Ahab, whereby child sacrifices were made when foundations were laid. Apart from mentioning that "the men of Jericho" helped Nehemiah to rebuild the walls and gates of Jerusalem around 445 BC, the only other main reference to Jericho in the Old Testament informs us that King Zedekiah was captured in the plains of Jericho as he tried to escape from Nebuchadnezzar in 587 BC (2 Kings 25:4–7). In spite of the Babylonian siege, Zedekiah and his guards were able to slip out of Jerusalem at night, only to be overtaken in the plains of Jericho.

The Jericho of New Testament times was not located at Tell es-Sultan, but further to the south, where the Wadi Qilt enters the Jordan valley. In the form in which Jesus knew it, Jericho had been built by Herod the Great (partly on Hasmonean foundations) and by the Roman governors. It was a popular winter residence because of its warm temperatures. The first three gospels, which relate only one visit of Jesus to Jerusalem during his public ministry, include a reference to Jericho during the journey from Galilee along the Jordan valley. Mark relates that, as he was leaving Jericho, Jesus healed the blind beggar Bartimaeus (Mark 10:46–52). Luke puts the healing in the context of Jesus drawing near to the city, not leaving it (Luke 18:35–43). Matthew (20:29–34) agrees with Mark that Jesus healed on his way out of Jericho, but records that two blind men were given their sight. Luke alone has the charming story of the chief tax collector named Zacchaeus, who was too short to see over the heads of the crowds watching Jesus pass through Jericho, and probably too unpopular to dare to mingle with them (Luke 19:1–10). His desire to see Jesus led him to climb a sycamore tree—presumably an undignified thing for a rich chief tax collector to do. In his unconventional way Jesus recognized in Zacchaeus' determination to glimpse him a quality that indicated a sincere desire to live a new life. He invited himself to visit Zacchaeus, to the evident annoyance of the onlookers. But the judgment of Jesus was not at fault. Zacchaeus declared that he would compensate all those he had defrauded, and that he was giving half his wealth to the poor. Jericho was thus the scene of Jesus being able to declare "Today salvation has come to this house, since he also is a son of Abraham. For the Son of man came to seek and to save the lost."

The Jericho area is also traditionally associated with the ministry of John the Baptist, the temptations of Jesus and the baptism of Jesus. The first three gospels give no precise location for John's baptizing ministry. Mark mentions simply "the wilderness" and the "river Jordan" (Mark 1:4–5), while Matthew (3:1) identifies the wilderness as the wilderness of Judea. In John 1:28 a location is given—Bethany beyond the Jordan—but Origen in the first half of the 3rd century AD was unable to find this Bethany. That John conducted his ministry in the Jericho area is indicated by the fact that crowds came to him from Judea and Jerusalem (Mark 1:5). We have seen elsewhere (p.184) that the main route from Jerusalem to the Jordan valley ended at Jericho, and John the Baptist is unlikely to have chosen a spot inconveniently to the north.

The traditional site where John baptized Jesus is at el-Maghtas, about 9km (5·6 miles) east-southeast of Jericho. In the earliest period of Christian veneration of the site, the place of the baptism was on the east side of the Jordan; later veneration moved it to the west side to avoid the inconvenience of crossing the river. Together with the baptism of Jesus, the crossing of the Jordan by the Israelites in the time of Joshua and the ascension of Elijah were also venerated at this spot. The linking of Elijah, the Elijah-like John the Baptist (cf. Matthew 11:14, but against this John 1:21) and Jesus at this spot produced a powerful combination of symbols. The gospel of John informs us that, immediately prior to the raising of Lazarus, Jesus remained for some time at "the place where John at first baptized. . . and many came to him" (John 10:40–41).

From Tell es-Sultan, Old Testament Jericho, there is an excellent view of the Mount of the Temptation. This photograph, taken from the east, shows to the right of centre the path leading to the 19th-century monastic buildings. On the summit a modern wall encloses various Byzantine remains. The

THE JORDAN VALLEY AND THE DEAD SEA

mountain was occupied by many monks and hermits from the 4th century AD until the Persian invasion of 614 AD, after which time it was more sparsely inhabited until the building of the monastery. The tradition associating the site with the temptations of Jesus goes back to the 7th century.

At his baptism by John, Jesus chose to identify himself with those who had come to be baptized as a sign of their repentance. As presented in the gospels, the baptism of Jesus was not a turning from sin, but a turning towards the ministry that he was called to exercise. He received an inner confirmation of God's blessing and calling, after which he was led by the Spirit into the wilderness, there to be tempted for the conventional period of 40 days (Mark 1:12–13). The desert area near Jericho, not far from the place of baptism, is the traditional setting for the temptations, and visitors to Tell es-Sultan (Old Testament Jericho) today get an excellent view of the traditional Mount of the Temptation, on the top of which Jesus was offered all the kingdoms of the world if he would but worship Satan (Matthew 4:8–10). An Arabic name for the mountain, Jebel Quruntul, is apparently derived, via the Crusaders, from the French word *quarante* ("forty"), indicating the 40 days of the temptation.

The Jordan valley

Leaving the Jericho region and looking further to the north, we come to the town of Succoth (today Tell Deir Alla), on the eastern side of the Jordan, and at the mouth of the Nahr ez-Zerqa valley, mentioned in Judges 8:4–9 and 13–16. Following his successful assault on the Midianites in the Harod valley (p.152), Gideon pursued his enemies down the Jordan valley until he and his men reached Succoth. His request to the officials of the city that they should provide food for his men because he was pursuing the Midianite kings was refused. "Are Zebah and Zalmunna already in your hand, that we should give bread to your army?" was the wording of the refusal. Perhaps the officials feared that Gideon's mission would fail and that the Midianite kings would punish Succoth for provisioning Gideon's army. Gideon for his part threatened, and later carried out that threat, to flog the officials with whips made from thorns and briars when he returned successfully from his mission.

The other part of the Jordan valley mentioned in the Bible is where it is joined by the Beth-shean valley. Here, controlling the most accessible route from the valley of Jezreel to the Jordan valley, was the magnificent city mound of Beth-shean (Beisan). It is mentioned in a passage already quoted (p.151) in which the tribe of Joseph complains that its territory is too forested and that "all the Canaanites who dwell in the plain have chariots of iron, both those in Beth-shean and its villages, and those in the Valley of Jezreel" (Joshua 17:16). The natural manner in which to control access to the Jordan and Jezreel valleys was for Beth-shean and the towns surrounding it (its "villages") to deploy horses and chariots. The comparatively open country of the valleys was most suitable for this. The Israelites would have no means of matching this type of military force, and it is no surprise to learn that in the period of the Judges "Manasseh did not drive out the inhabitants of Beth-shean and its villages" (Judges 1:27). In the reign of Saul the Philistines either controlled Beth-shean or had an alliance with its Canaanite inhabitants. After Saul's defeat and death on the slopes of Mount Gilboa (1 Samuel 31) the Philistines fastened Saul's body to the wall of Beth-shean (1 Samuel 31:10). At 2 Samuel 21:12 we read that the bodies of Saul and Jonathan were hung up in the public square of Beth-shean. The remains of these brave men were saved from further insult when the men of Jabesh-gilead, whom Saul had delivered from the Ammonite king Nahash (1 Samuel 11), stole the bodies from Beth-shean by night and buried them in Jabesh. David completed the formalities of burial, when he removed the remains finally to the family tomb of Saul in the territory of Benjamin (2 Samuel 21:13–14). By the time of the reign of Solomon, Beth-shean was in Israelite hands and was included in the 12 administrative districts (1 Kings 4:12).

In Old Testament times the jungle which characterized the banks of the Jordan was inhabited by lions. Jeremiah (49:18f.), prophesying against Edom, brings together the images of Sodom and Gomorrah, and the jungle of the Jordan with its lions: "As when Sodom and Gomorrah and their neighbour cities were overthrown, says the Lord, no man shall dwell there, no man shall sojourn in her. Behold, like a lion coming up from the jungle of the Jordan against a strong sheepfold, I will suddenly make them run away from her." In the Old Testament images can be reversed. Zechariah 11:3 depicts judgment thus:

Hark, the roar of the lions,
for the jungle of the Jordan is laid waste!

In contrast to the image of the Jordan jungle being desolated, Ezekiel 47 depicts future blessing in terms of the waters of the Dead Sea being made fresh by means of the life-giving river which flows from the temple. The Jordan valley and the Dead Sea, although they do not figure prominently in the Bible geographically, contributed to the biblical imagery for judgment and blessing, and formed the context in which Jesus began his public ministry and in solitude reflected on the course it should take.

Below Bronze "standard" covered in gold foil found at Beth-shean, dating from 1500–1200 BC.

Right Aerial view of Beth-shean from the northeast. In the foreground is the Roman amphitheatre of Scythopolis. Beyond it is the tell, whose fine natural features are clearly seen. In the far distance is the Jordan valley and on the skyline the hills of Transjordan. Beth-shean stood at the start of an important east–west route from the Jordan valley via the Harod valley to the valley of Jezreel.

THE JORDAN VALLEY AND THE DEAD SEA

TRANSJORDAN

Transjordan is best thought of as a stretch of land running north to south, divided into sections by the rivers that flow from east to west into the river Jordan or the Dead Sea. These rivers often had considerable influence upon the political divisions. On the other hand, the region is not easy to describe, as the present text makes clear, and contains significant differences. Thus the area to the east of the Sea of Galilee was largely wooded, whereas east of the Dead Sea were the plateaux of Moab, famous for their sheep farming.

Description of the region

To deal with the whole of Transjordan in one section is to give the impression that, compared with the land west of the Jordan, that on the eastern side is unimportant. In order to correct such an impression, it is necessary to say at once that, although Transjordan has not been as intensively excavated as the western side, its place in the general history of Near Eastern culture and religion is not to be underrated. From the point of view of an Atlas of the Bible, its importance can be summarized briefly. First, Transjordan was the home of the small nations—Syria, Ammon, Edom and Moab—which from time to time impinged upon the life of Israel, and which were frequently referred to in prophetic utterances about the nations who were Israel's neighbours. Secondly, from the time of the Israelite settlement to the 8th century BC, there was an Israelite presence in Transjordan, most noticeably in the hilly and wooded region between the Nahr ez-Zerqa (river Jabbok) and the Nahr el-Yarmuk (river Yarmuk). Thirdly, the last stage of the wilderness wanderings as described in the Old Testament and the first phase of the conquest took place in Transjordan. Fourthly, in New Testament times Transjordan contained important Jewish and Hellenistic areas that feature in the gospel narratives.

Above right Aerial view of the Seil el-Mojib (Arnon) looking east. The Arnon is a spectacular gorge that debouches into the eastern side of the Dead Sea. In ancient times it served as the natural northern border of Moab, although an energetic Moabite king such as Mesha could extend Moabite territory to the north of the gorge.

- 2000m
- 1500m
- 1000m
- 500m
- 200m
- 0
- 200m below sea level

seasonal stream, wadi
settlement
- 2nd millennium
- Iron Age c.1200–587 BC
- Persian 587–330 BC
- Hellenistic 330–40 BC
- Herodian, Roman-Byzantine, after 40 BC

?Sela₂ alternative position for named settlement
HIPPOS classical name
route

scale 1:1 500 000

TRANSJORDAN

Note (U) = unlocated site

Abel-keramim Judg. 11:33 C2 C3
Alema see Helam
Almon-diblathaim (Beth-diblathaim) Num. 33:46–47; Jer. 48:22 C3
Ammon Gen. 19:38; Deut. 3:16; Judg. 10:7ff.; 2 Sam. 10:1ff.; 11:1ff.; Amos 1:13 C2 D2
Aphek 1 Kgs. 20:26ff.; 2 Kgs. 13:17 C2
Ar Num. 21:28; Deut. 2:9; Isa. 15:1 C3
Aroer Num. 32:34; Deut. 2:36; 3:12; 4:48; Josh. 12:2; 13:9,16; 2 Sam. 24:5; Jer. 48:19; 1 Chr. 5:8 C3
Aroer Josh. 13:25; Judg. 11:33 C3
Ashtaroth (Be-eshterah) Deut. 1:4; Josh. 9:10; 12:4; 13:12,31; 21:27; 1 Chr. 6:71 D2
Ashteroth-Karnaim see Carnaim
Ataroth Num. 32:3,34 C3
Atroth-shophan Num. 32:35 (U)
Avith Gen. 36:35; 1 Chr. 1:46 (U)
Baal-gad Josh. 11:17; 12:7; 13:5 C1
Baal-peor see Beth-peor
Bamoth-baal Num. 21:19,20; 22:41; Josh. 13:17 C3
Bashan (region) Num. 21:33–35; Josh. 13:29; Isa. 2:13; Ezek. 27:6; 39:18 C2 D2
Baskama 1 Macc. 13:23 C2
Beer (Beer-elim) Num. 21:16 (U)
Be-eshterah see Ashtaroth
Beon see Beth-baal-meon
Beth-arbel Hos. 10:14 C2
Beth-baal-meon (Beon) Num. 32:31,38; Josh. 13:17; 1 Chr. 5:8; Jer. 48:23 C3
Beth-gamul Jer. 48:23 C3
Beth-diblathaim see Almon-diblathaim
eth-peor (Baal-peor) Num. 25:3,5; Deut. 3:29; 4:3,46; 34:6; Josh. 13:20; Ps. 106:28; Hos. 9:10 C3
Beth-shittah Judg. 7:22 (U)
Betonim Josh. 13:26 C3
Bezer (Bozrah) Deut. 4:43; Josh. 20:8; 21:36; 1 Chr. 6:78; Jer. 48:24 C3
Bosor 1 Macc. 5:26,36 D2
Bozrah see Bezer
Bozrah Gen. 36:33; 1 Chr. 1:44; Isa. 34:6; 63:1; Jer. 49:13,22; Amos 1:12 D2
Bozrah 1 Macc. 5:26,28 C4
Caesarea Philippi (Paneas) Matt. 16:13; Mark 8:27 C1
Carnaim (Carnion, Ashteroth-karnaim) Gen. 14:5; 1 Macc. 5:26,43–44 D2
Casphor (Caspin, Chaspho) 1 Macc. 5:26,36; 2 Macc. 12:13 C2
Charax 2 Macc. 12:17 (U)
Chaspho see Casphor
Damascus Gen. 14:15; 15:2; 2 Sam. 8:5,6; 1 Kgs. 11:24; 15:18; 19:5,15; 20:34; 2 Kgs. 8:7,9; 16:9–12; 1 Chr. 18:5,6; 2 Chr. 16:2; 24:23; 28:5,23; Isa. 7:8; 8:4; 10:9; 17:1,3; Jer. 9:27; 49:24; Amos 1:3,5; Acts 9:2,3,10,19; 22:5,6–11; 26:12,20; 2 Cor. 11:32; Gal. 1:17 D1
Dathema (Diathema) 1 Macc. 5:9 D2
Dibon Num. 21:30; 32:3; 32:34; 33:45,46; Josh. 13:9,17; Isa. 15:2,9; Jer. 48:18,22 C3
Dinhabah Gen. 36:32; 1 Chr. 1:43 (U)
Dizahab (Mezahab) Gen. 36:39; 1 Chr. 1:50; Deut. 1:1 (U)
Edom (region) Exod. 15:15; Num. 20:14ff.; 24:18; Deut. 2:13ff.; Josh. 15:1,21; 1 Sam. 14:47; 2 Sam. 8:12,14; 1 Kgs. 9:26; 11:14ff.; 22:47; 2 Kgs. 3:8ff.; 8:20; 14:10; 16:6; 1 Chr. 18:13; 2 Chr. 25:20; Ps. 60:8,9; 83:6; 108:9,10; 137:7; Isa. 11:14; 34:5ff.; Jer. 9:26; 25:21; 49:7; Ezek. 25:12,14; 32:29; Joel 3:19; Amos 1:6,9; 2:1; Obad. 1ff., 8 C4
Edrei Deut. 1:4; Josh. 13:31; Num. 21:33 D2
Eglaim Isa. 15:8 C3
Eglath-skelishiyah Isa. 15:15; Jer. 48:34 (U)
Elealeh Num. 32:3,37; Isa. 15:4; 16:9; Jer. 48:34 C3
Ephron 1 Macc. 5:46; 2 Macc. 12:27 C2
Gadara Matt. 8:28 C2
Gerasa Mark 5:1; Luke 8:26 C2
Gergesa Matt. 8:28; Mark 5:1; Luke 8:26,37 C2
Gilead Gen. 31:23,25; Num. 32:1,39–40; Deut. 3:12–13,15; 34:1; Josh. 12:2,5; 17:1; 22:13; Judg. 10:7,17; 11:1–12,7; 20:1; 2 Sam. 2:9; 17:26; 1 Kgs. 4:13,19; 17:1; 2 Kgs. 10:33; 15:29; Ps. 60:7; 108:8; S. of S. 4:1; 6:5; Jer. 8:22; 22:6; 50:19; Hos. 6:8; 12:11; Amos 1:3,13; Obad. 19; Zec. 10:10 C2
Golan Deut. 4:43; Josh. 20:8; 21:27; 1 Chr. 6:71 C2
Ham Gen. 14:5 C2
Hazar-enan (Hazar-enon) Num. 34:9; Ezek. 47:18; 48:1 (U)
Helam (Alema) 2 Sam. 10:16–17; 1 Macc. 5:26,35 D2
Heshbon Num. 21:25–34; 32:3,37; Deut. 1:4; 2:24,26,30; 3:2,6; 4:46; 29:7; Josh. 9:10; 12:2,5; 13:10,17,21,26; 21:39; Judg. 11:19,26; 1 Chr. 6:81; Neh. 9:22; Isa. 15:4; 16:8,9; Jer. 4:2,34,45; 49:3; S. of S. 7:4 C3
Holon Jer. 48:21 (U)
Horonaim Isa. 15:5; Jer. 48:3,5,34 C3
Ijon 1 Kgs. 15:20; 2 Chr. 16:4 (U)
Iye-abarim Num. 21:11;
33:44,45 C3
Jabesh-gilead Judg. 21:8–14; 1 Sam. 11:1–10; 1 Sam. 31:11–13; 2 Sam. 2:4,5; 21:12; 1 Chr. 10:11,12 C2
Jahaz Num. 21:23; Deut. 2:32; Josh. 13:18; 21:36; Judg. 11:20; 1 Chr. 6:78; Isa. 15:4; Jer. 48:34 C3
Jazer Num. 21:24,32; 32:1,3,35; Josh. 13:25; 21:39; 1 Chr. 6:81; 26:31; Isa. 16:8–9; Jer. 18:32 C3
Jogbehah Num. 32:35; Judg. 8:11 C2
Kamon Judg. 10:5 C2
Kedemoth Deut. 2:26; Josh. 13:18; 21:37; 1 Chr. 6:79 C3
Kenath (Nobah) Num. 32:42; 1 Chr. 2:23 D2
Kerioth Jer. 48:24; Amos 2:2 C3
Kir-hareseth (Kir) 2 Kgs. 3:25; 6:9; Isa. 15:1; 16:7,11; Jer. 48:31,36 C3
Kiriathaim Num. 3:2,37; Josh. 13:19; Jer. 48:1,23; Ezek. 35:9 C3
Kiriath-huzoth Num. 22:39 (U)
Lo-debar 2 Sam. 9:4; 11:27; Amos 6:13 C2
Madmen Jer. 48:2 C3
Mahanaim Gen. 32:2; Josh. 13:26,30; 21:38; 2 Sam. 2:8,12,29; 17:24; 19:32; 1 Kgs. 2:8; 4:14; 1 Chr. 6:80 C2
Maked 1 Macc. 5:26,36 D2
Masrekah Gen. 36:36; 1 Chr. 1:47 (U)
Mattanah Num. 21:18,19 C3
Medeba Num. 21:30; Josh. 13:9,16; 1 Chr. 19:7; Isa. 15:2 C3
Mepha-ath Josh. 13:18; 21:37; 1 Chr. 6:79; Jer. 48:21 C3
Mezahab see Dizahab
Minnith Judg. 11:33 C3
Mizpah Gen. 31:49; Judg. 10:17; 11:11,29,34 C2
Moab (city) Num. 22:36; Deut. 2:36; Josh. 13:9,16 D3
Moab (region) Exod. 15:15; Num. 21:13,15; 22:3ff.; Josh. 24:9; Judg. 3:12–30; Ruth 1:1,4ff.; 2 Sam. 8:2; 2 Kgs. 3:4ff.; Isa. 15:1–16; Jer. 48:1ff.; Amos 2:1ff. C3
Nabadath 1 Macc. 9:37 C3
Nebo Num. 32:3,38; 1 Chr. 5:8; Isa. 15:2; Jer. 48:1,22 C3
Nobah see Kenath
Paneas see Caesarea Philippi
Oboth Num. 21:10–11; 33:43–44 (U)
Pai (Pau) Gen. 36:39; 1 Chr. 1:50 (U)
Rabbah (Rabbath-ammon) Deut. 3:11; Ezek. 21:20; Josh. 13:25; 2 Sam. 11:1,12,26ff.; 1 Chr. 20:1; Jer. 49:2,3; Amos 1:14 C3
Ramath-mizpeh Josh. 13:26 C3
Ramoth-gilead Deut. 4:43; Josh. 20:8; 21:38; 1 Sam. 30:27; 1 Kgs. 22:3,4,6,12,15,20,29; 2 Kgs. 8:28–29; 9:1,4,14; 1 Chr. 6:80; 2 Chr. 18:2,3,5,11,14,19,28; 22:5,6 C2
Raphon 1 Macc. 5:37 D2
Rehob Num. 13:21 C2
Rogelim 2 Sam. 17:27; 19:31 C2
Salecah Deut. 3:10; Josh. 12:5; 1 Chr. 5:11 D2
Sela 2 Kgs. 14:7 C4
Sibmah (Selsam) Num. 32:3,38; Josh. 13:19; Isa. 16:8–9; Jer. 48:32 C3
Teman Jer. 49:7,20; Ezek. 25:13; Amos 1:12; Obad. 1:12 C4
Tishbe 1 Kgs. 17:1; 1 Kgs. 17:1; 21:17,28; 2 Kgs. 1:3,8; 9:36 C2
Tob Judg. 11:3; 2 Sam. 10:6,8 D2
Zair 2 Kgs. 8:21 (U)
Zalmonah Num. 33:41,42 C4

TRANSJORDAN

Left The Mount Hermon range of hills reaches a maximum height of about 3030m (9232ft). They are visible from many parts of northern Israel, and are especially remarkable for remaining snow-capped even in summer. The lower melting snows add to the waters that make up the river Jordan. In the present Atlas the view is taken that the Transfiguration of Jesus took place in this region.

Transjordan can be divided roughly into five areas from north to south. North of the Nahr el-Yarmuk is a broad high plateau which runs in a northeasterly direction to Damascus. This is bounded on its western side by the Mount Hermon range which also runs along a southwest–northeast axis. The area immediately to the north of the Nahr el-Yarmuk is called Bashan in the Old Testament, and it was famed for its fertility. It is usually referred to in the Old Testament as *the* Bashan, possibly meaning "the smooth [and thus fertile] land". In addition to references to the area itself, Bashan features as a term denoting that which is well fed, luxurious or strong. The Psalmist describes the human or impersonal enemies that surround him as "strong bulls of Bashan" (Psalm 22:12), while Amos applies the phrase "cows of Bashan" to the rich women who idle in luxury in the city of Samaria (Amos 4:1).

The second area runs from the Nahr el-Yarmuk to the Nahr ez-Zerqa (river Jabbok) and can be named Gilead, although the name Gilead has several designations and is sometimes used in the Old Testament to indicate territory to the north of the Nahr el-Yarmuk and to the south of Nahr ez-Zerqa as far as Seil el-Mojib (Arnon). A restricted usage is preferred here in the interests of clarity. As defined narrowly, Gilead was similar to the wooded hill country west of the Jordan, and for this reason the Israelites who were settled there were able to maintain their occupation, when others who had settled to the north or south found it hard to resist the pressure of the surrounding nations. Even so, Ramoth-gilead, a town located in less undulating country to the east of the main Gilead mountains, was a bone of contention between Israel and Syria (Damascus) in the 9th century, and at least two battles were fought there (1 Kings 22:1–3; 2 Kings 8:28).

The third area is from the Nahr ez-Zerqa to Seil el-Mojib (Arnon) and can be roughly designated as Ammon. Here again, this is a simplification, because there were periods when Ammon's western border was the northbound Nahr ez-Zerqa before it turns west to flow into the Jordan valley. Again, the area was at one time occupied by the tribe of Reuben, and before that by Sihon, king of the Amorites, whom Israel defeated under the leadership of Moses (Numbers 21:21–30). Although the Seil el-Mojib (Arnon) was the nominal northern border of Moab, an energetic and powerful king such as Mesha (9th century BC) could extend his territory to the north. Thus boundaries were fluid, and a confusing number of different names have over the centuries been given to the areas between Nahr ez-Zerqa and Seil el-Mojib (Arnon). The area of Ammon, as defined here, consisted partly of rugged cliffs and gullies, but also, in its central region, of a plateau which was very fertile.

From the Seil el-Mojib (Arnon) southwards to the Wadi el-Hesa (Brook Zered) is the territory of Moab, as defined strictly. It is dominated by a plateau which is roughly 1000m (3281ft) above sea level, and is about 56k (34·8 miles) long and about 40km (24·9 miles) wide. It is well watered internally by shallow wadis, and was so fertile that, when its king was a vassal of the king of Israel in the 9th century, the annual tribute payable was "a hundred thousand lambs, and the wool of a hundred thousand rams" (2 Kings 3:4) (or, the wool of 100 000 lambs and 100 000 rams). In the story of Ruth the famine in the region of Bethlehem drove Elimelech and his family to seek food in Moab (Ruth 1:1–2). Although further to the east than the Bethlehem and Hebron hills, Moab, in common with the rest of Transjordan, is cooler with snow and frosts in winter, and with summer mists and clouds.

To the south of Wadi el-Hesa and extending towards the gulf of Akaba is the territory of Edom, whose central mountain range reaches at times to over 1700m (5577ft) above sea level. On the eastern side of this range is a plateau some 1000–1100m (3281–3609ft) above sea level where the winter is very cold, with snow and frosts lasting until mid-March or even early April. G.A. Smith notes the comments of those who have been struck by the similarity between parts of the landscape of the plateau and that of Europe. Thus he quotes from Doughty "the limestone moorland of so great altitude resembles Europe, there are hollow, park-like grounds with ever-green oak." It can be seen from the vegetation map (p. 63) that, whereas on the western side of the Jordan the area of naturally occurring Mediterranean forest ends some miles north of Beer-sheba, on the eastern side it extends on the Edom plateau some 150km (93 miles) south of a point level with Beer-sheba.

Right A shepherd's life in Transjordan is largely unchanged since biblical times.

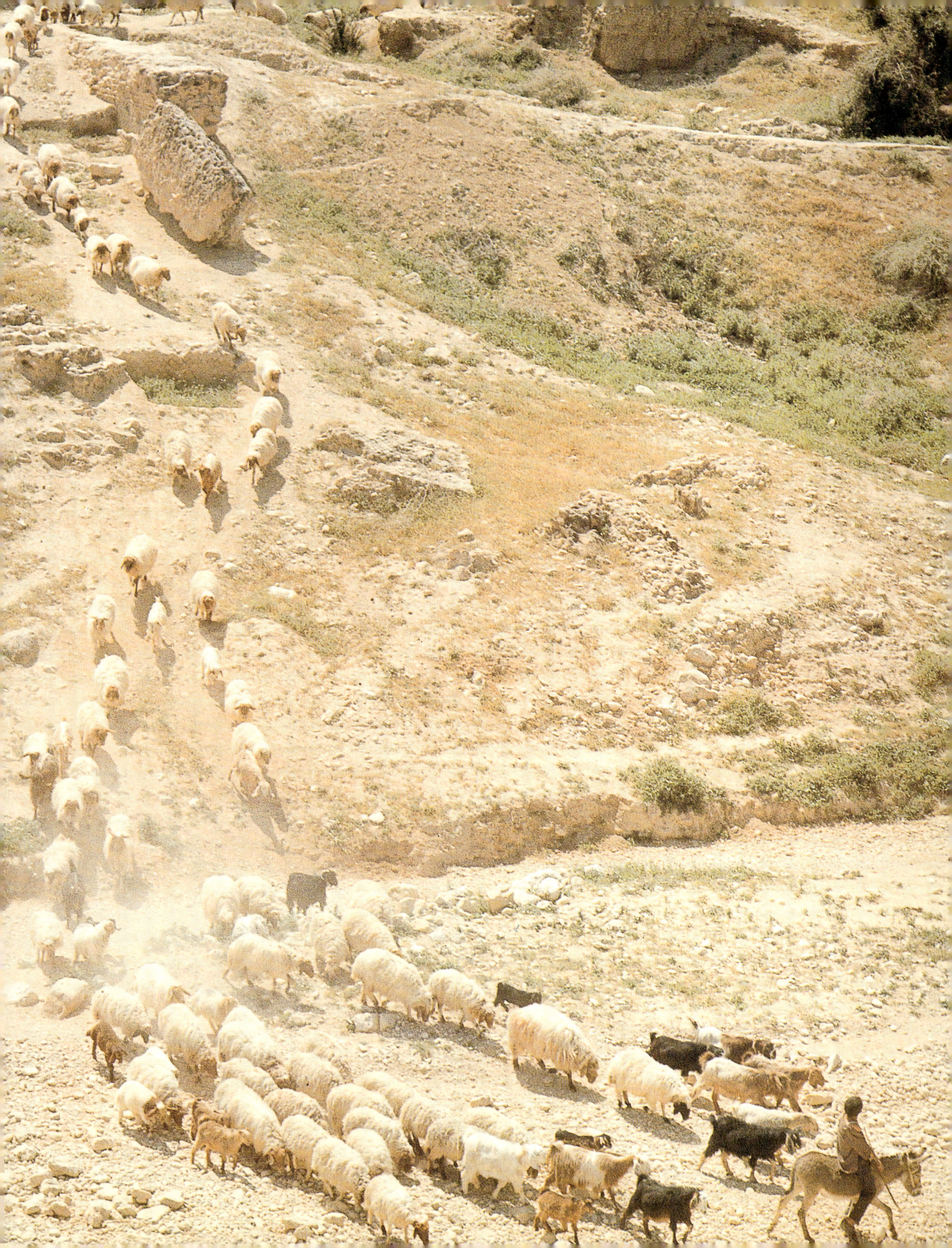

TRANSJORDAN

The biblical record

Transjordan features in the Old Testament first in the story of Jacob and Esau. Esau was to become the founder of Edom (Genesis 36:6–8) according to the Old Testament view of origins, and when Jacob returned to Canaan after his sojourn with Laban in Haran (Genesis 29–31) he journeyed down through Transjordan, possibly to effect a reconciliation with Esau who was in Edom. For the first part of his journey Jacob was fleeing from Laban, his father-in-law. He was overtaken in the hill country of Gilead, presumably between the Yarmuk and Nahr ez-Zarqa (Jabbok), where a pact was made between the two men (Genesis 31:43–54). Jacob now continued southwards, and at the Jabbok experienced the strange encounter with the wrestling angel as a result of which his name was changed from Jacob to Israel (Genesis 32:22–32). Read consecutively, the narrative implies that Jacob's reconciliation with Esau took place soon after he crossed the Jabbok, for Jacob's first destination after the reconciliation was Succoth, where the Jabbok enters the Jordan valley (Genesis 33:17). Jacob next arrived in Shechem (Genesis 33:18), which would be reached by crossing the Jordan and proceeding up the Wadi Faria.

The next substantial reference to Transjordan is in the latter part of Numbers. From Kadesh Moses sent messengers to the king of Edom asking for passage through that land along the route known as the King's Highway (Numbers 20:17). This was refused, and eventually the Israelites made a detour around the southern end of Edom, and then journeyed northwards, keeping to the east of the line of fortified posts which protected the eastern (desert) frontier of Edom (Numbers 21:4, 10–13).

A summary of the itinerary of the Israelites in Numbers 33:41–49 implies that they journeyed unhindered through Edom. This itinerary may, as some scholars suggest, describe the route of an earlier wave of Israelites who entered Transjordan prior to the 13th century when Edom and Moab may have been largely uninhabited; or it may be a pilgrim itinerary from a period when travel through Moab and Edom was permitted. The view that the kingdoms of Edom and Moab, as described in the Bible, were not established until the 13th century BC seems to be asserted less confidently today than was the case 20 years ago. The Israelites, led by Moses, reached "the valley lying in the region of Moab by the top of Pisgah which looks down upon the desert" (Numbers 21:20). From here a message was sent to Sihon, king of the Amorites (Amorite here is perhaps a general term equivalent to Canaanite), for Israel to be allowed to pass through his territory along the King's Highway. This request too was refused, Sihon gathered his army at Jahaz, and Israel defeated him and occupied his territory from the Seil el-Mojib (Arnon) to the Nahr ez-Zarqa (Jabbok). The location of Jahaz is not known, and there is much uncertainty about the geographical setting of the whole incident. Many atlases place Pisgah on the western side of what we have earlier called Ammon, to the northwest of Medeba. On the other hand, Jahaz is often located in the region of Dibon which is 25km (15·5 miles) south of Medeba. The Israelite threat to Sihon is far more likely to have come from the east than the west. The problems

Limestone statue of a Moabite king, found in Amman, 10th–9th century BC.

can only be noted here, with no attempt to try to solve them. Following the victory over Sihon, the Israelites journeyed far to the north and defeated Og, king of Bashan (Numbers 21:33–35). These two victories became fairly rooted in subsequent commemorations of the victories that God had achieved for his people. Thus Psalm 135:10–11 recalls that God

> smote many nations
> and slew mighty kings,
> Sihon, king of the Amorites,
> and Og, king of Bashan.

Israel now camped in what Numbers 22:1 calls the plains of Moab—probably in the Jordan valley opposite to Jericho. The presence of Israel there was of great concern to Balak, the Moabite king, so much so that he sent to the north to hire the prophet Balaam to come and curse Israel. From the topographical point of view, we note that the Israelites were nearly 40km (24·9 miles) north of Balak's northern border, the Arnon (cf. Numbers 22:36). The story of Balaam's journey to Moab, and of his talking ass, has long been a central passage in the discussion among rival schools of how supernatural happenings are to be interpreted in the Bible. On his arrival Balaam proved to be a great disappointment to his employer. Instead of cursing the Israelites he blessed them:

> how fair are your tents, O Jacob, your encampments, O Israel!
> Like valleys that stretch afar,
> like gardens beside a river,
> like aloes that the Lord has planted,
> like cedar trees beside the waters (Numbers 24:5–6).

To add insult to injury, Balaam rounded off his work by cursing Moab and by promising that Israel would dominate Moab and Edom (Numbers 24:17–18).

On the face of it, Balaam was a good prophet, speaking only the words of the God of Israel; but Numbers 25:1–5 records that the Israelites began to practise harlotry with Moabite women, and to turn to the god Baal of Peor. A later passage (Numbers 31:16) held Balaam responsible: "these caused the people of Israel, by the counsel of Balaam, to act treacherously against the Lord in the matter of Peor. . ." Later tradition took very seriously Israel's apostasy at Baal-peor. Thus Psalm 106:28–29 recalls that

> they attached themselves to the Baal of Peor,
> and ate sacrifices offered to the dead;
> they provoked the Lord to anger with their doings,
> and a plague broke out among them.

In the New Testament, as also in Jewish literature, Balaam is consistently represented in a bad light. At 2 Peter 2:15 false prophets are condemned, and those who follow them: "Forsaking the right way they have gone astray; they have followed the way of Balaam. . .who loved gain from wrongdoing. . ." Thus stories set in the plains of Moab opposite Jericho provided a powerful set of symbols for Israel's worship and for Christian admonition. It was in this same region that Moses, from Mount Nebo, saw the promised land which he was not to enter (Deuteronomy 34:1–4). He was buried "in the valley in the land of Moab opposite Beth-peor" (Deuteronomy 34:6). In the apportionment of the land, although the details of Joshua 13 are not easy to interpret, half of the tribe of Manasseh received what has been defined earlier as Gilead and Bashan. Reuben and Gad shared the territory between the Arnon and the Jabbok, with Reuben being in the south. However, it must be noted that Joshua 13:27 puts the northern boundary of Gad at the "lower end of the Sea of Chinnereth". It is to be presumed that Reuben and Gad found it difficult to resist the pressure of the surrounding nations. An ancient poem on the fortunes of the tribes says that

> Raiders shall raid Gad,
> but he shall raid at their heels (Genesis 49:19)

and another such poem prays

> Let Reuben live and not die,
> nor let his men be few (Deuteronomy 33:6).

It was above all in what has been defined in this Atlas as Gilead that the Israelite presence was maintained.

This area produced one of the major Judges in the person of Jephthah, whose exploits are recalled in Judges 11:1–12:6. He is described as a Gileadite, and he had been banished to the land of Tob, to the northeast of Transjordan, where he became a freebooter. When the Ammonites attacked Gilead, Jephthah was called in to help, which he agreed to do if he was made head over the people. He also later made a fateful vow to sacrifice to God the first person he met on his return from battle, if he was victorious. That first person would be his only child, a daughter. Jephthah's diplomatic communication with the king of Ammon recalled how the Israelites had defeated Sihon, king of the Amorites, while the Ammonite king considered himself wronged because Israel took his land from the Arnon to the Jabbok. In the ensuing battle Jephthah not only defeated the Ammonites, but also pursued a vendetta against members of the tribe of Ephraim who had settled in Gilead and who had not been called upon to fight. The exact causes of this incident are obscure.

In the reign of Saul the Ammonites again tried to expand at the expense of Israelites in Transjordan, when King Nahash threatened the men of Jabesh-gilead (1 Samuel 11). This city is usually identified with Tell el-Maqlub on the Wadi el-Yabis, (brook Cherith). Its distance north of the Jabbok, and its position in the heartland of Gilead, suggest either that Nahash had already occupied the southern part of Gilead, or that he had taken his army up the Jordan valley and had penetrated along the Wadi el-Yabis with a view to breaking out from there into the Gilead heartland. Saul's brilliant deliverance of Jabesh-gilead earned him the eternal gratitude of its inhabitants. When Saul's body was triumphantly displayed by the Philistines in Beth-shean, the men of Jabesh-gilead crossed the Jordan to Beth-shean and removed his body to save it from further insult (1 Samuel 31:11–13).

It was to the Israelite part of Transjordan that Abner, Saul's commander, withdrew after Saul's death and defeat by the Philistines. In Mahanaim, for which there are two suggested locations, one on and one near the Jabbok, Abner proclaimed Saul's son Ish-baal as king "over Gilead and the Ashurites and Jezreel and Ephraim and Benjamin and all Israel" (2 Samuel 2:9). No doubt the claims to kingship over the western territories were *de jure* rather than *de facto*. The reign of Ish-baal ended in his assassination after Abner had been killed in Hebron by Joab (see p.99). When David finally broke the power of the Philistines, he brought under his control the whole of Transjordan from Damascus in the north of Edom in the south; but, like Ish-baal, he was forced to flee to Mahanaim when his son Absalom rebelled against him. Presumably, David was counting on the loyalty of the Israelites in Transjordan to whom he had given security by his defeats of their foreign neighbours. The decisive battle between Absalom and David's forces was waged in the forest of Ephraim, a location we would expect to find on the western side of the Jordan. However, all the details of the story require an east-Jordan location for the forest, and it is most likely that it received its name from the Ephraimites who had migrated to Gilead, and who found themselves at odds with Jephthah.

The reign of Solomon saw the breakup of David's empire, with revolts of Edom and Damascus (1 Kings 11:14–25). After the division of the kingdom Damascus made an alliance with Judah and invaded northern Galilee (p. 136). In the reigns of Omri and Ahab, however, in the first part of the 9th century BC, the Israelite domination was maintained, and re-established over Moab. This is known to us from the famous inscription of Mesha, which was discovered in Diban (biblical Dibon, Numbers 21:30 etc.) in 1868. It informs us that Omri, king of Israel, afflicted Moab many days (i.e. years) because Chemosh (the Moabite god—cf. Judges 11:24) was angry with his land. This agrees with the information in 2 Kings 3:4 that Mesha, king of Moab, paid tribute to the king of Israel in the form of wool, or wool and lambs. Mesha claims to have rebelled successfully against Ahab, and to have destroyed the Israelite towns of Ataroth and Nebo. The inscription confirms, by the way, that the tribe of Gad had settled in territory to the north of the Arnon: "And the men of Gad had dwelt in the land of Ataroth from of old." The expedition of Ahab's son Joram (Jehoram) against Mesha was probably an attempt to restore what had been lost in Ahab's reign. It is instructive topographically (2 Kings 3:4–27). The king of Israel took with him the kings of Judah and Edom, as well as the prophet Elisha, and made a long detour so as to come upon the Moabites from the east. The eastern frontier was, of course, fortified, but, unlike the northern and southern boundaries which were additionally protected by the deep valleys of the Arnon and Wadi el-Hesa (Zered), the eastern frontier had no natural protection against an incursion from the desert. When the expedition ran out of water, Elisha somewhat reluctantly told the king to dig trenches, so that these would be filled with water. When this occurred in the morning, the eastern sun reflecting on the waters looked like blood, and the Moabites were convinced that feuding and bloodshed had broken out in the invading armies. The Moabites hurried to the Israelite camp to take the spoil, only to find the opposing armies intact. The Moabites were driven back, their king was surrounded in Kir-hareseth, and disaster was averted only when in desperation he offered his eldest son as a burned offering upon the city wall. Fearful of the consequences that would accrue to them from this action, the Israelites returned across the Jordan.

The reigns of Ahab and his son Joram (Jehoram) were much involved with Transjordan. Gilead was the home of Ahab's opponent, the prophet Elijah (1 Kings 17:1), and the brook Cherith, where he was fed by ravens during the drought, was east of the Jordan. Ahab's reign was also much concerned with wars against Damascus, especially over the ownership of Ramoth-gilead, which was probably located on the eastern side of central Gilead (as defined in this Atlas). Indeed, Ahab was killed in battle at Ramoth-gilead (1 Kings 22). His son Joram was also wounded in battle fighting the Syrians at Ramoth-gilead, but seems to have won back the city. While Joram was recovering from his wounds at Jezreel, one of Elisha's prophets journeyed to Ramoth-gilead carrying a flask of oil, with which he anointed Joram's commander Jehu king, thus beginning a revolution in which the house of Omri and Ahab was completely destroyed.

Among various other references to Transjordan during the remainder of the divided monarchy is the notice that the king of Judah, Amaziah, "killed ten thousand Edomites in the Valley of Salt and took Sela by storm, and called it Joktheel, which is its name to this day" (2 Kings 14:7). The identification of Sela with es-Sela, Petra, has been affirmed and denied. The names Sela and Petra both mean "rock", and the statement that Amaziah took it by storm (although the Hebrew is literally "in war") would fit the fact that access to the city is along a narrow gorge called the Siq, and that its capture would be a feat worthy of mention. The version of the event in 2 Chronicles 25:12, however, simply says that the Judahites took 10 000 Edomites to the top of a rock and threw them down. The location of Sela at Petra is plausible, even if it is not demonstrable, and permits a glimpse of this most remarkable of cities. In the form that it is seen today, it is dominated by facades cut into the soft red sandstone, whose styles date from the 4th century BC to the 2nd century AD. Petra served in the 1st century AD as the capital of Nabatea, in which kingdom Paul spent some years of his life.

Both Israel and Judah enjoyed a prosperous time for several decades in the early 8th century BC, in which some of their earlier control in Transjordan was reasserted. The Ammonites paid tribute to Uzziah, king of Judah (2 Chronicles 26:8), while Jeroboam II controlled Damascus and beyond (2 Kings 14:23–25, 28). However, the second half of the 8th century saw the rise of Assyrian might, and in 733/2 Gilead, together with Galilee, was annexed by Tiglath-pileser III. When Nebuchadnezzar advanced against Judah in 588 BC, a number of Jews fled to other lands, including Ammon, Moab and Edom (Jeremiah 40:11). After the fall of Jerusalem they returned to Judah to support the governor Gedaliah. However, the governorship of

The Khazneh, or treasury, at Petra. The approach to Petra is along a mile-long winding gorge, at the end of which the visitor comes into the open and is confronted by the Khazneh. It is called the treasury because of the "urn" which is in the middle at the top of the monument. According to legend, a pharaoh deposited his treasure there. In fact the monument is probably a temple dating from the 1st century BC. Beyond the entrance there is a central chamber, as well as two rooms to right and left.

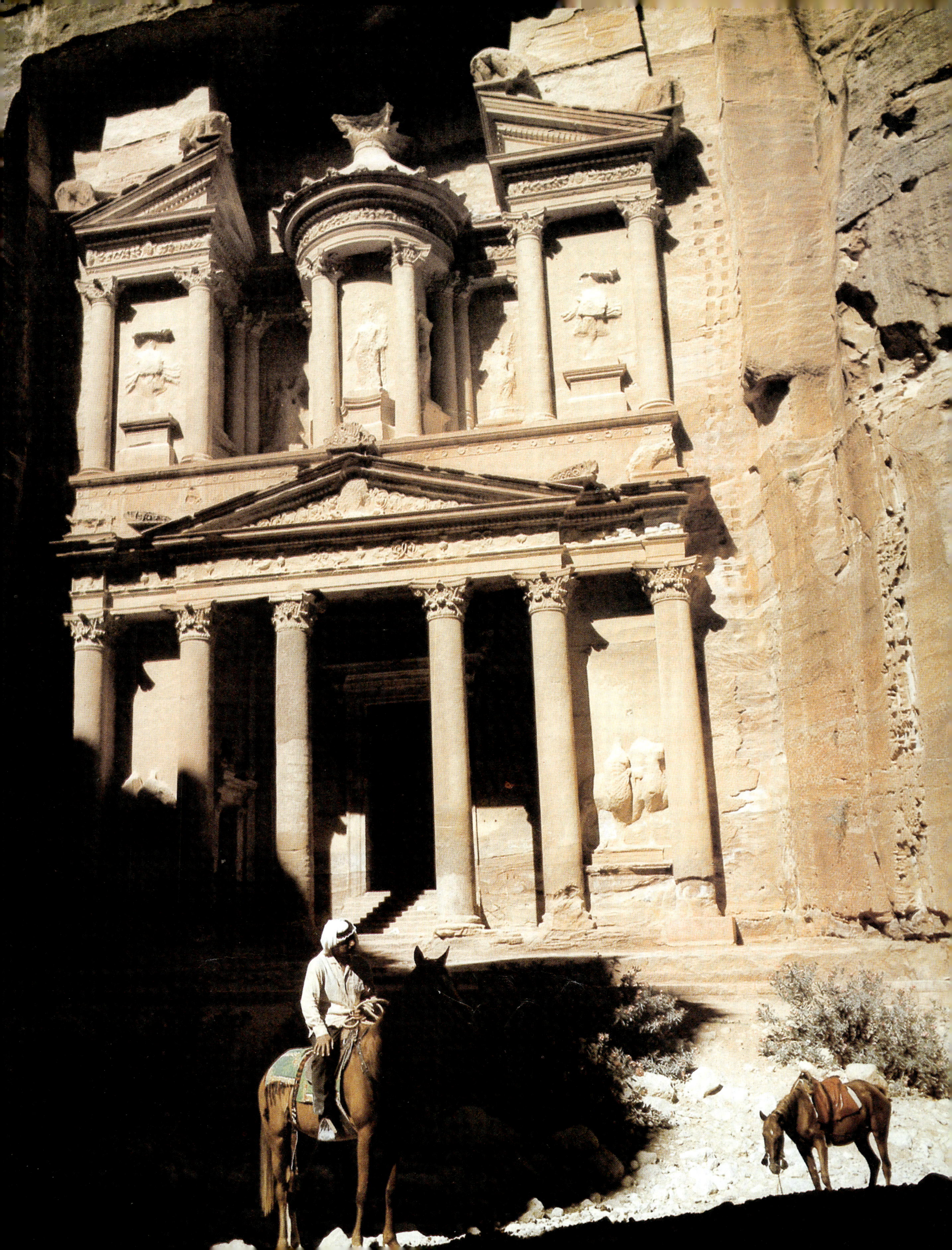

Gedaliah was cut short when he was assassinated, apparently on the orders of Baalis, king of the Ammonites (Jeremiah 40:14). Further, the Edomites took advantage of the fall of Judah, and seized possession of some of the lands of the nation that had so often afflicted them. Their kingdom in the south of Judah, to be called Idumea, was forcibly converted to Judaism by John Hyrcanus (135–104 BC). It was from a forcibly converted Idumean family that Herod the Great was descended.

Transjordan in the time of Jesus

The situation of Transjordan in the time of Jesus was as follows. From the Arnon northwards to the Jabbok, and possibly as far as the Yarmuk, was the region known as Perea, a name derived from the Greek *peran* meaning "beyond". In its southern part it had a predominantly Jewish population which possibly dated back several hundred years to the settlement by the Tobiad family. Although on the eastern side of the Jordan, Perea was a Jewish link between Galilee and Judea, and those who wished to travel from Galilee to Jerusalem without entering non-Jewish territory could do so by crossing the Jordan and going along the eastern side of the valley through Perea.

In its northern section Perea mingled with the Decapolis, a league originally of 10 cities (Greek *deka poleis* means "10 cities"), the earliest of which had been founded in the late 4th century BC. The best known of these are Philadelphia (on the site of Rabbath-ammon, the Ammonite capital, and the modern Amman, capital of Jordan), Gerasa (modern Jerash, with spectacular Roman remains), Pella (the city to which Christians fled before the destruction of Jerusalem in 70 AD), Gadara (which possibly features in the healing of the man called "Legion") and Scythopolis (biblical Beth-shean, and the only member of the Decapolis on the western side of the Jordan). Damascus was also one of the 10 cities. Much of the region which they occupied had been conquered by the Maccabean rulers of Jerusalem in the 2nd and 1st centuries BC, but the Romans restored their independence in 63 BC, and again after the death of Herod the Great in 4 BC. The cities were cosmopolitan in character and some contained Jewish communities; but their ethos and official religion were Hellenistic.

North of the Yarmuk were the regions governed from 4 BC to 34 AD by the tetrarch Philip, with the exception of the area surrounding the cities of Gadara and Hippos, which became part of the

Above The forum at Jerash, ancient Gerasa, one of the cities of the Decapolis. The site was occupied from as early as 2500 BC, but the founding of Gerasa probably took place in the 2nd century BC. It stood on a trade route and was most prosperous from the 1st century BC to the 3rd century AD. Many of its surviving buildings date from the 2nd century AD. The forum, probably built in the 1st century AD, is at the southwest edge of the city. It is an irregular ovoid shape, and from it the street of columns runs for some 600m (656 yd) to the north gate.

province of Syria. Important for our purposes is the fact that included in the territory was the town of Caesarea Philippi, called by Philip's own name in order to distinguish it from the Caesarea on the Mediterranean coast. The town was the site of one of the sources of the Jordan and from the time of its foundation it contained a grotto dedicated to "Pan and the Nymphs". Before it was called Caesarea Philippi, it was called Paneas, together with its district, a name that eventually survived into the modern name Baniyas. To the east of Perea, Decapolis and the territory of Philip, and stretching down into Edom and possibly as far north as Damascus, was the territory of the Nabateans. This people from the desert had begun to move into Edom, apparently as early as the 6th century BC. Under their king Aretas IV (9 BC–40 AD) they enjoyed great power in Transjordan.

According to the strict sequence of events, Transjordan featured first in the New Testament not in the ministry of Jesus, but in that of John the Baptist. Mark 1:14 dates the beginning of the preaching of Jesus from the time of John's imprisonment. The gospels do not say where John was imprisoned, but we learn from Josephus that he was held at Machaerus, a fortress and palace fortified by Herod and said to be second only to Masada. It is located on the western edge of the mountains, about 14km (8·7 miles) north of the Arnon overlooking the Dead Sea, and on a clear day views of the Mount of Olives and part of Jerusalem are possible. The famous incident of Salome dancing before Herod Antipas, after which she requested John the Baptist's head (Mark 6:14–29—the name Salome does not occur in the gospels), seems on the face of it to be set in Galilee, for whose courtiers, officers and leading men Herod made a banquet (Mark 6:21). Either Herod Antipas, who ruled both Galilee and Perea, invited his guests to Machaerus or we must suppose that John's head was brought to wherever in Galilee (Tiberias?) Herod was giving the banquet.

The first incident in the ministry of Jesus to be located in Transjordan (apart from the reference in Matthew 4:25 that "great crowds followed him from... the Decapolis") is the healing of the man "Legion" who was possessed by many demons. The exact location is uncertain. Matthew 8:28 places the encounter in the country of the Gadarenes (and has two demoniacs, not one), while Mark 5:1 and Luke 8:26 have "country of the Gerasenes". The latter place is not known, while Gadara is 10km (6·2 miles) south of the Sea of Galilee beyond the Yarmuk. However, the location of

Right The site of the ancient shrine to Pan at modern-day Baniyas, known in the New Testament as Caesarea Philippi. The modern name preserves the association with Pan. Here Peter made his "great confession" in which he declared Jesus to be the Messiah.

Overleaf Aerial view of Machaerus, the Masada of the eastern side of the Jordan. It was first fortified by Alexander Jannaeus (103–76 BC), but rebuilt by Herod the Great as a great fortress. It commands a view across the Jordan valley to the Jerusalem and Hebron hills. According to the 1st-century AD Jewish historian Josephus, John the Baptist was imprisoned here by Herod Antipas. In the first Jewish Revolt of 67–73 AD it was a stronghold for the rebels, as Masada was, but it was subdued by the Romans, whose camp is just visible.

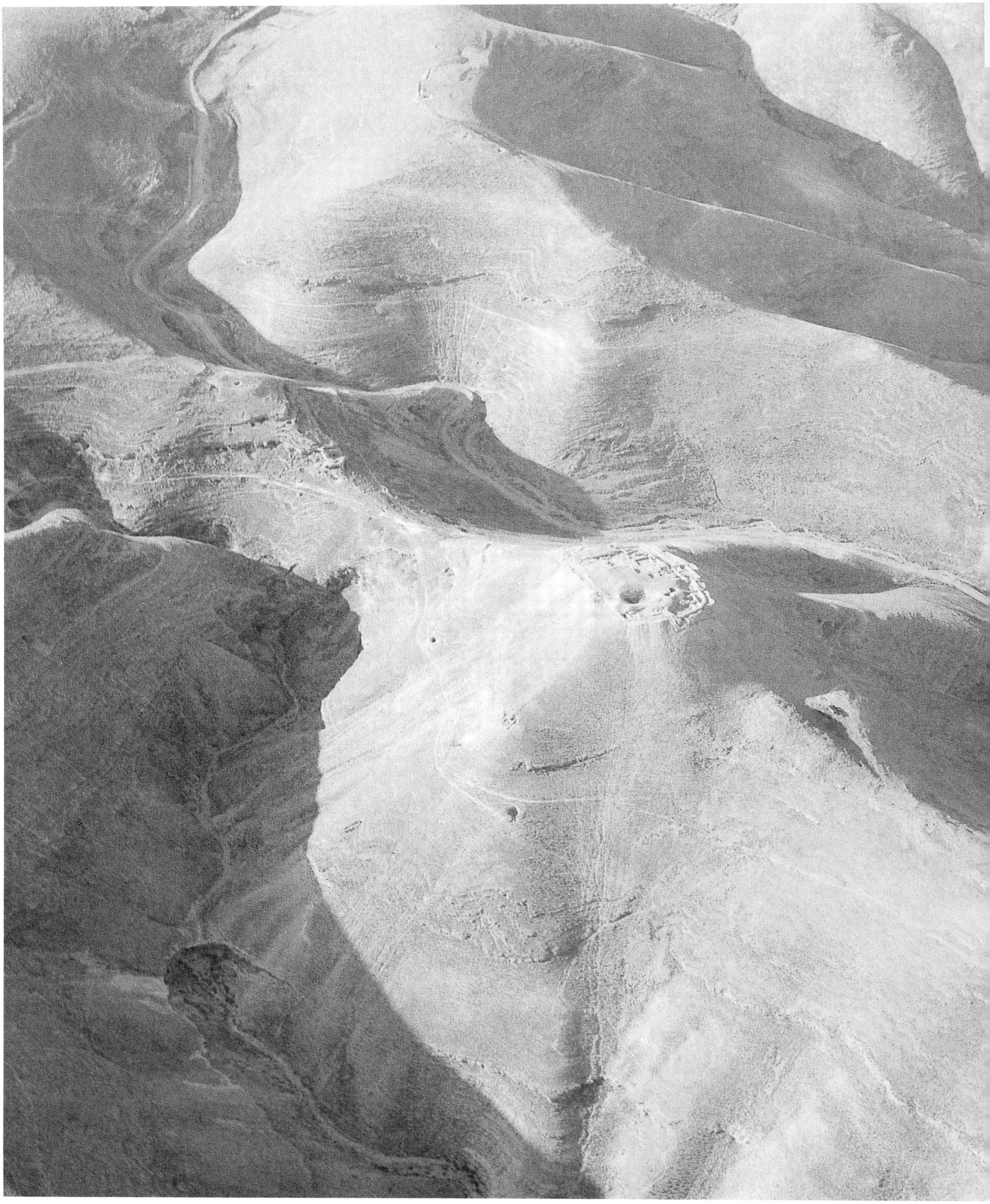

the incident in the Decapolis region seems to be established by the fact that, after the man had been freed from possession by demons, "he went away and began to proclaim in the Decapolis how much Jesus had done for him" (Mark 5:20). That the place of the healing was non-Jewish is suggested by the presence of the herd of pigs into which the unclean spirits entered, pigs being forbidden to Jews.

Although no precise details of location are given, it is to be inferred from Mark 7:31–37 that it was in the Decapolis region that Jesus restored hearing to a deaf man. Taking him aside and touching the man's ears and tongue, Jesus commanded the defective organs to be opened.

One of the momentous events of the ministry of Jesus took place at Caesarea Philippi. Here, surrounded by his disciples, Jesus put to them the question "Who do men say that I am?" (Mark 8:27). The disciples produced the standard replies: John the Baptist, Elijah, one of the prophets. Jesus then asked, " Who do you say that I am?" Peter replied, "You are the Christ", but Jesus charged his disciples to tell no one, and began to speak about the suffering and death that lay ahead of him. As he journeyed towards Jerusalem for the climax of his ministry, he entered the region "beyond the Jordan" (Mark 10:1), a reference to teaching in Perea.

Arguably the most significant event in the life of the Church after the day of Pentecost was the conversion of Saul of Tarsus, better known as Paul. The vision which blinded him, and altered the course of his own life and that of the Church, occurred as he approached Damascus (Acts 9:3). The purpose of his journey to Damascus was to extradite and punish any Jews that he found in Damascus who had accepted faith in Jesus. He was now led to Damascus, sightless, and remained in this condition until a believer in Damascus named Ananias went to where he was and welcomed him into the Christian community with the words "Brother Saul, the Lord Jesus who appeared to you on the road by which you came, has sent me that you may regain your sight and be filled with the Holy Spirit" (Acts 9:17). Saul's Christian preaching in Damascus now confounded those who had known him only as an arch persecutor of Christians. Threats were made against his life, and he escaped from Damascus by being let down over the wall in a basket (Acts 9:25). In 2 Corinthians 11:32–33 there is an account of the same, or a later, event, in Paul's own words: "At Damascus, the governor under King Aretas guarded the city of Damascus in order to seize me, but I was let down in a basket through a window in the wall, and escaped his hands." If this describes a later event, it happened on his return to Damascus after he had gone to Arabia following his conversion (Galatians 1:17).

By Arabia we are probably to understand the Nabatean kingdom, lying east and south of the Dead Sea. Paul perhaps wished to meditate in solitude on what had happened to him. Perhaps he also preached to Jews in the Nabatean kingdom, thus annoying King Aretas, who arranged for his representative (the status of the governor and the extent of Aretas' power in Damascus are matters of debate) to apprehend Saul, but without achieving success.

THE EMPIRES SURROUNDING ISRAEL

Note (U) = unlocated site

Achaia (region) Acts 18:12,27; Rom. 15:26; 2 Cor. 1:1; 9:2; 1 Thess. 1:7,8 D3
Addon Ezra 2:59; Neh. 7:61 (U)
Adramyttium Acts 27:2 E3
Adria, Sea of Acts 27:27 C2
Alexandria Acts 18:24; 27:6; 28:11 E4
Amphipolis Acts 17:1 D2
Antioch 1 Macc. 6:63; Acts 19:19ff.; 13:1; 14:26; Gal. 2:11 G3
Antioch Acts 13:14; 14:19,21; 2 Tim. 3:11 F3
Aphek Josh. 13:4 G4
Apollonia Acts 17:1 D2
Appius, Forum of (Appii Forum) Acts 28:15 B2
Ararat (region) Gen. 8:4; 2 Kgs. 19:37; Isa. 37:38; Jer. 51:27 H3
Arpad 2 Kgs. 18:34; Isa. 10:9; Jer. 49:23 G3
Arvad Ezek. 27:8,11 G4
Asshur Ezek. 27:23 H3
Assos Acts 20:13,14 E3
Athens Acts 17:15 D3
Attalia Acts 14:25 F3
Avva (Ivvah) 2 Kgs. 17:24; 18:34; 19:13; Isa. 37:13 (U)
Baal-zephon Exod. 14:2,9; Num. 33:7 F4
Babylon (Babel) Gen. 10:10; 11:9; 2 Kgs. 17:24,30; 24:1ff.; 25:1ff.; 25:27; Ezra 1:11; 2:1; 5:12–17; 6:1–5; 7:6,9; Ezek. 12:13; 17:16; Ps. 137:1,8; Matt. 1:11,12,17; Acts 7:43; Rev. 16:19; 18:2,10,21 H4
Beroea Acts 17:10,13; 20:4 D2
Beroea 2 Macc. 13:14 G3
Berothah (Berothai, Cun) Ezek. 47:16; 1 Chr. 18:8; 2 Sam. 8:8 (U)
Betah (Tibhath) 2 Sam. 8:8; 1 Chr. 18:8 (U)
Beth-eden (Eden) (region) 2 Kgs. 19:12; Isa. 37:12; Ezek. 27:23; Amos. 1:5 G3
Bithynia (region) Acts 16:7; 1 Pet. 1:1 F2
Buz (region) Jer. 25:23 G5
Calah see Nimrud
Calno (Calneh, Canneh) Isa. 10:9; Ezek. 27:23; Amos 6:2 G3

Caphtor (Crete) Acts 27:7,12–13,21; Titus 1:5 D3 E3
Cappadocia (region) Acts 2:9; 1 Pet. 1:1 G3
Carchemish 2 Chr. 35:20; Isa. 10:9; Jer. 46:2 G3
Caria (region) 1 Macc. 15:23 E3
Casiphia Ezra 8:17 (U)
Cauda (Gaudos) Acts 27:16 D4
Cenchreae Acts 18:18; Rom. 16:1 D3
Chebar, River Ezek. 1:1–3; 3:15,23; 10:15,20,22; 43:3 I4
Cherub Ezra 2:59; Neh. 7:61 (U)
Chilmad Ezek. 27:23 (U)
Chios Acts 20:15 E3
Cilicia (region) Acts 6:9; 15:23,41; 21:39; 22:3; 27:5; Gal. 1:21 F3
Cnidus Acts 27:7 E3
Coele-Syria (region) 1 Esd. 4:48; 7:1; 2 Macc. 8:8 G4
Colossae Col. 1:2 E3
Corinth Acts 18:1–18; 1 Cor. 1:2; 16:5–6; 2 Cor. 1:1,23. 12:14; 13:1; 2 Tim. 4:20 D3
Cos Acts 21:1 E3
Cun see Berothah
Cush (region) Gen. 2:13; 10:6–8; 1 Chr. 1:8–10; Ezek. 38:5 F6
Cuthah 2 Kgs. 17:24 H4
Cyrene Matt. 27:31; Mark 15:21; Luke 23:26; Acts 2:10; 11:20; 13:1 D4
Dalmatia see Illyricum
Daphne 2 Macc. 4:33 G3
Dedan Gen. 10:7; 1 Chr. 1:9; Jer. 49:8; Ezek. 25:13; 27:20 G5
Derbe Acts 14:6,20; 16:1; 20:4 F3
Dumah Gen. 25:14; 1 Chr. 1:30; Isa. 21:11 G5

Ecbatana Ezra 6:2; 2 Macc. 9:3 I4
Eden Ezek. 27:23 I8
Eden (region) see Beth-eden
Elam (Susiana) (region) Gen. 10:22; 14:9; Isa. 21:2; Jer. 25:25; 49:34–39; Ezek. 32:4; Dan. 8:2; Acts 2:9 I4
Ephah Isa. 60:6 G5
Ephesus Acts 18:19–21,24–27; 19:1; 20:1; 1 Cor. 15:32; 16:8; Rev. 1:11; 2:1; Eph. 1:1 E3
Erech Gen. 10:10; Ezra 4:9,10 I4
Etam Judg. 15:8,11 (U)
Etham Exod. 13:20; Num. 33:7 (U)
Euphrates, River Gen. 2:14; 31:21; Josh. 24:2; 1 Kgs. 4:24; 2 Chr. 35:20; Jer. 13:4; 46:2,10; Rev. 9:14; 16:10 H4
Fair Havens Acts 27:8 D3
Galatia (region) Acts 13:14–14:23; 16:1–6; Gal. 1:2; 3:1; 1 Cor. 16:1; Pet. 1:1 F3
Galatian Phrygia (region) Acts 16:61; 18:23 F3
Gaudos see Cauda
Gebal 1 Kgs. 5:18; Ezek. 27:9 G4
Gortyna 1 Macc. 15:23 E3
Goshen (region) Gen. 45:10; 46:28,29; 47:1–6,27; Exod. 8:22 F4
Gozan 2 Kgs. 17:6; 19:12; 1 Chr. 5:26 G3
Hahiroth see Pi-hahiroth
Halah 2 Kgs. 17:6; 1 Chr. 5:26 (U)
Halicarnassus 1 Macc. 15:23
Hamath 1 Sam. 8:9; 2 Kgs. 14:28; 17:24; 18:34; 23:33; Isa. 11:9; Amos 6:2; Zech. 9:2 G4

Hanes Isa. 30:4 (U)
Haran Gen. 11:31; 27:43; 28:10; 2 Kgs. 19:12; Ezek. 27:23 G3
Hauran (region) Ezek. 47:16,18 G4
Hazarmaveth (region) Gen. 10:26; 1 Chr. 1:20 I8
Heliopolis (On) Jer. 43:13 F4
Helbon Ezek. 27:18 G4
Hierapolis Col. 4:13 E3
Iconium Acts 13:51; 14:1,19,21; 16:2; 2 Tim. 3:11 F3
Idumea (region) 1 Macc. 4:61; 5:3; Mark 3:8 F4 G4
Illyricum (Dalmatia) (region) Rom. 15:19; 2 Tim. 4:10 C2
Immer Ezra 2:59; Neh. 7:61 (U)
Ivvah see Avva
Javan (region) Gen. 10:2,4; Isa. 66:19; Ezek. 27:13 E3
Joktan (region) Gen. 10:25 H6
Kadesh 2 Sam. 24:6 G4
Karkor Judg. 8:10 (U)
Kedar (region) Gen. 25:13; Isa. 21:16–17; 60:7; Jer. 2:10; 49:28; Ezek. 27:21 G4
Kir (region) Isa. 22:6; Amos 9:7; 2 Kgs. 16:9 (U)
Kittim (Cyprus) Gen. 10:4; Num. 24:24; Dan. 11:30 F3 F4
Kue (region) 1 Kgs. 10:28; 2 Chr. 1:16 G3
Lacedaemon see Sparta
Laodicea Col. 4:13ff.; Rev. 1:11; 3:14 E3
Lasea Acts 27:8 D3
Lud(u) see Lydia
Luz Judg. 1:26 (U)
Lycaonia (region) Acts 14:6 F3
Lycia (region) Acts 27:5 E3 F3
Lydia (Lud, Ludu) (region) Gen. 10:22; Isa. 66:19; Jer. 46:9; Ezek. 27:10; 30:5 E3

Lystra Acts 14:6–21; 16:1–2; 1 Tim. 3:11 F3
Macedonia (region) Acts 16:9ff.; 20:3; 1 Cor. 16:5; 2 Cor. 1:16; Philem. 4:15; 1 Thess. 1:7 D2
Mallus 2 Macc. 4:30 (U)
Malta Acts 28:1 B3
Memphis (Noph) Hos. 9:6; Isa. 19:13; Jer. 2:16; 44:1; Ezek. 30:13 F5
Meshech (Mushki) (region) Gen. 10:2; Ezek. 27:13 F3
Mesopotamia (Paddan-aram) (region) Gen. 24:10; Judg. 3:8; 1 Chr. 19:6; Acts 2:9; 7:2 H3
Midian (region) Gen. 25:1,4; 36:35; Exod. 2:15ff.; Num. 22:4,7; 25:17; 31:3ff.; Judg. 6:1ff.; 8:28; 1 Kgs. 11:18; Isa. 60:6; Hab. 3:7 G5
Migdol Jer. 44:1; Ezek. 29:10 F4
Miletus Acts 20:15,17; 2 Tim. 4:20 E3
Mitylene Acts 20:14 E3
Mushki see Meshech
Musri (region) 1 Kgs. 10:28 G3
Myndos 1 Macc. 15:23 (U)
Myra Acts 27:5 E3
Mysia (region) Acts 16:7–8 E3
Nahor Gen. 24:10; 29:5 (U)
Neapolis Acts 16:1 D2
Nebaioth (region) Gen. 25:13–16; Isa. 60:7 G4
Nicopolis Titus 3:2 D3
Nile, River Gen. 41:1ff.; Exod. 7:17ff.; Isa. 19:5ff.; Jer. 46:7ff.; Ezek. 29:3 F5
Nimrud (Calah) Gen. 10:11,12 H3
Nineveh Gen. 10:11; 2 Kgs. 19:36; Jonah 1:2ff.; Nahum 1:1; Zeph. 2:13 H3
No (No-amon) see Thebes
Noph see Memphis
On see Heliopolis
Ophir (region) 1 Kgs. 9:28; 10:11; 22:48; Job 22:24; Isa. 13:12 G7 H7
Paddan-aram see Mesopotamia
Palmyra see Tadmor
Pamphylia (region) Acts 2:10; 13:13; 14:24; 15:38 F3
Paphos Acts 13:6–13 F4
Patara Acts 21:1 E3
Pathros (region) Isa. 11:11; Jer. 44:1,15; Ezek. 29:14; 30:14 F5
Patmos Rev. 1:9 E3
Pekod (Puqudu) (region) Jer. 50:21; Ezek. 23:23 I4
Pelusium Ezek. 30:15,16 F4
Perga Acts 13:13; 14:14,25 F3
Pergamum Rev. 1:11; 2:13ff. E3
Perepolis 2 Macc. 9:2 J5
Pethor Num. 22:5; Deut. 23:4 G3
Phaselis 1 Macc. 15:23 F3
Philadelphia Rev. 1:11; 3:7ff. E3
Philippi Acts 16:21ff.; 20:6; 1 Thess. 2:2; Philem. 1:1ff.; 4:15 D2
Phoenix Acts 27:12 D3
Phrygia (region) Acts 3:10; 16:6; 18:23 F3
Pibeseth Ezek. 30:17 F4
Pi-hahiroth (Hahiroth) Exod. 14:2,9; Num. 33:7,8 (U)
Pisidia (region) Acts 13:14; 14:24 F3
Pithom Exod. 1:11 F4
Pontus Acts 2:9; 18:2; 1 Pet. 1:1 G2
Puqudu see Pekod
Put (region) Gen. 10:6; 1 Chr. 1:8; Jer. 46:9; Ezek. 27:10; 30:5; Nahum. 3:9 D4
Puteoli Acts 28:13 B2
Raamses (Zoan) Exod. 1:11; 12:37; Num. 33:3,5 F4
Rages see Rhagae

Red Sea Exod. 10:19; 13:18; 15:4,22; 23:31; Num. 21:14; 33:10,11; Deut. 1:1,40; 2:1; 11:4; Josh. 2:10; 4:23; 24:6; Judg. 11:16; 1 Kgs. 9:26; Neh. 9:9; Ps. 106:7,9,22; 136:13–15; Jer. 49:21; Acts 7:36; Heb. 11:29 G6
Rezeph 2 Kgs. 19:12; Isa. 37:12 G3
Rhagae (Rages) Tobit 1:14; 4:1,20; 5:5; 6:10,12; 9:2 J3
Rhegium Acts 28:13 C3
Rhodes Ezek. 27:15; Acts 21:1 E3
Riblah Ezek. 6:14; 2 Kgs. 23:33; 25:6,20; Jer. 39:5; 52:9,26 G4
Rome Acts 2:10; 18:2; 19:1; 28:14ff.; Rom. 1:7,15; 2 Tim. 1:17 B2
Saba see Sheba
Salamis Acts 13:5 F3
Salmone (Sammanion) Acts 27:7 E3
Samos Acts 20:15 E3
Samothrace Acts 16:11 E2
Sampsames 1 Macc. 15:23 (U)
Sardis Rev. 1:11; 3:1ff. E3
Seleucia Pieria Acts 13:4 G3
Sepharvaim (Sibraim) 2 Kgs. 17:24; 18:34; 19:13; Isa. 36:19; 37:13 (U)
Sheba (Saba) (region) 1 Kgs. 10:1; Ps. 72:15; Jer. 6:20; Ezek. 27:22; 38:13 H8
Shur (region) Gen. 16:7; 20:1; 25:18; Exod. 15:22; 1 Sam. 15:7; 27:8 F4
Sibraim see Sepharvaim
Sicyon 1 Macc. 15:23 D3
Sidon Judg. 1:31; 1 Kgs. 17:9; Isa. 23:2,4,12; Joel 3:4–8; Matt. 11:21; Acts 27:3; Josh. 11:8; 19:28 G4
Smyrna Rev. 1:11; 2:8ff. E3
Sparta (Lacedaemon) 1 Macc. 12:2,5–23 D3
Succoth Gen. 33:17; Josh. 13:27; Judg. 8:4ff.; 1 Kgs. 7:46; Ps. 60:6 F4
Susa Ezra 4:9; Neh. 1:1; Esth. 1:2ff.; Dan. 8:2 I4
Susiana see Elam
Syene Ezek. 29:10; 30:6 F6
Syracuse Acts 28:12 C3
Tadmor (Palmyra) 2 Chr. 8:4 G4
Tahpanhes Jer. 2:16; 43:7ff.; 44:1; 46:14 F4
Tarshish 1 Kgs. 10:22; 22:48; 2 Chr. 9:21; 20:36; Ps.72:10; Jer. 10:9; Ezek. 27:12,25; 38:13 (U)
Tarsus Acts 9:11,30; 11:25; 21:39; 22:3 F3
Tema Gen. 25:14; Job. 6:19; Isa. 21:14; Jer. 25:23 G5
Thebes (No, No-amon) Jer. 46:25; Ezek. 30:14–16; Nahum 3:8 F5
Thessalonica Acts 17:1–3; 27:2; Philem. 4:16; 1 Thess. 1:1; 2 Thess. 1:1; 2 Tim. 4:10 D2
Three Taverns Acts 28:15 B2
Thyatira Acts 16:4; Rom. 1:11; Rev. 2:18,24 E3
Tibhath see Betah
Tigris, River Gen. 2:14; Dan. 10:4 H4
Timna Gen. 36:12,22,40 I8
Tiphsah 1 Kgs. 4:24 G3
Togarmah Gen. 10:3; 1 Chr. 1:6 G3
Troas Acts 16:8,11; 20:5,6; 2 Cor. 2:12; 2 Tim. 4:13 E3
Tubal (region) Gen. 10:2; Isa. 66:19; Ezek. 27:13; 32:26; 38:2; 39:1 G3
Ur Gen. 11:28,31; 15:7; Neh. 9:7 I4
Uzal 1 Chr. 1:21; Gen. 10:27 H7
Zedad Num. 34:8; Ezek. 47:15 (U)
Zoan see Raamses
Zobah (region) 1 Sam. 14:47; 2 Sam. 8:3ff.; 1 Kgs. 11:23 G4

215

THE EMPIRES SURROUNDING ISRAEL

The history of Israel in biblical times was deeply affected by the mighty empires that lay to the south and to the northeast. In the south, Egypt was an ever-present factor, sometimes friend, sometimes foe. The uncertain nature of the relationship between Israel and Egypt is nowhere better illustrated than in the story of the descent to Egypt and the Exodus. The story of Joseph (Genesis 37, 39–49) relates how he was sold into slavery in Egypt by his brothers and became a ruler of the land, with the result that his family was received into Egypt with great acclaim. The story of the Exodus (Exodus 1–14) relates how the Israelites, descended from the family of Joseph, were forced into slavery, from which they cried out to be delivered. Again, in the reign of Solomon, Egypt both made an alliance with Solomon by marriage and sheltered his opponents (1 Kings 9:16; 11:17–22, 40). The changes of dynasty in Egypt did not fundamentally affect relationships with Israel. Whether Egypt was ruled by Egyptians, Ethiopians or the family of Ptolemy (the general of Alexander the Great), Egypt dominated Israel whenever the opportunity arose, and was always ready to support Israel if it was threatened by the northern empires, fearing that the collapse of Israel would put Egypt next in the firing line.

In the northeast, the empire that dominated affairs from the time of the monarchy down to 605 BC was Assyria. Especially in the 9th and 8th centuries Assyria was perceived as the home of terrifying armies that would show no mercy to their enemies. In the 8th century Assyria developed the policy of deporting the notable people of conquered territories, and of replacing them with citizens loyal to Assyria. This policy enabled Assyria to end the independent life of the northern kingdom of Israel in 721 BC.

The displacement of the Assyrians by the Babylonians in 612–609 BC made little difference from Israel's point of view. Although the Babylonians may have seemed to be a little more humane than the Assyrians, they would not tolerate rebellion on the part of client nations, and they exiled the notable people from Jerusalem and Judah in 597 and 587. There was a marked change, however, with the victory of the Persians in 540. The victorious Cyrus decreed that the exiles should be allowed to return to Jerusalem (Ezra 1:1–4), and in the following century Ezra and Nehemiah were given royal support in their attempts to consolidate the life of the Jewish community in Judah (Ezra 7; Nehemiah 2:1–8).

The conquests of Alexander the Great in 333 BC also brought Judah under the control of a regime that set out not to be oppressive, but to respect the customs of the various peoples. Unfortunately, Alexander's successors were not able to live up to these ideals in practice. The Roman empire, which dominated the scene in the New Testament era, did not, of course, originate from the land masses either to the south or to the northeast of Israel; but in New Testament times Rome had come to dominate Egypt and some of the territory to the north of Israel, and the threat of invasion either from the south or from the north had become a thing of the past.

It would be expected in a Bible Atlas that there would be maps of Egypt, Mesopotamia and the

Top A sketch made by David Roberts in November 1838 of the Great Temple at Abu Simbel and its four statues of Ramesses II (1290–1224 BC), flanked by much smaller statues of members of the royal family. The larger statues are about 21m (69ft) high. It is generally accepted that Ramesses II was either the Pharaoh in whose reign the Hebrews left Egypt at the time of the Exodus, or the Pharaoh preceding the Exodus, who oppressed the Hebrews. Between 1964 and 1968 the statues were removed to a new location because the construction of the Aswan dam threatened their original site.

Above Elephantine Island, near the first cataract of the Nile, housed a Jewish colony in the 5th century BC. They were employed by the Persian rulers of Egypt of that time as frontier soldiers. We possess Aramaic documents written by these Jews which indicate, among other things, that they had built a temple and that they celebrated the Passover.

Right The picture of boats on the Nile is a reminder of the importance of that river for the life of Egypt. The Israelites, who had no comparable river to facilitate their travel, regarded the Nile and its boats as a hallmark of Egyptian life.

Greco-Roman world, to show the nature of the lands of these empires that impinged so vitally upon those who lived in the land of the Bible. Such maps are indeed provided (see pp. 34 and 35 and 214). However, if we are to gain a fuller understanding of the biblical text by examining what the land meant to the biblical writers and readers, it is clear that we shall not be helped merely by seeing modern maps of these areas. Travel in the ancient world, until the establishment of the Roman empire, was slow and dangerous. Few Israelites could have had any real idea of what Egypt and Mesopotamia were like, that is, until they began to be deported and dispersed from their homeland. In what follows, attempts will be made to build up a picture of what the empires were like on the basis of what is said about them in the biblical text itself. This will be a way of making explicit what readers would have shared when they thought of these regions.

Egypt

Egypt was a more fertile land than Israel. This can be deduced from the occasions when famines in Israel forced Israelites to go down to Egypt, either to stay there or to buy grain. Thus Abraham is depicted as going to Egypt because of famine (Genesis 12:10), and the whole climax of the story of Joseph depends on the fact that the famine in Israel forced Joseph's brothers to buy grain in Egypt, where Joseph had become a great ruler. Israelites were aware that Egypt's fertility depended on the river Nile. In the dream of Pharaoh, which Joseph interpreted, the fat and the lean cows came up out of the Nile, thus symbolizing the dependence of fertility upon the river. The annual flooding of the Nile could also be used by Jeremiah (46:7–8) as a symbol for the summoning of Egypt to battle:

Who is this, rising like the Nile,
like rivers whose waters surge?
Egypt rises like the Nile,
like rivers whose waters surge.
He said, I will rise, I will cover the earth,
I will destroy cities and their inhabitants.

That the Nile was used for navigation, and that papyrus boats were to be seen upon its waters, is clear from a passage in Isaiah 18:1–2, which envisages the meeting of Judahite and Ethiopian representatives, united in the face of a common enemy from the north:

Ah, land of whirring wings
which is beyond the rivers of Ethiopia;
which sends ambassadors by the Nile,
in vessels of papyrus upon the waters!
Go, you swift messengers,
to a nation, tall and smooth,
to a people feared near and far,
a nation mighty and conquering,
whose land the rivers divide.

In actual references to places in Egypt, quite a few important towns are mentioned, and the division into Upper and Lower Egypt is known. A passage in Ezekiel 30:13–19 mentions no fewer than eight cities, including Thebes, Memphis, Pelusium and Heliopolis.

Egypt's unreliability as an ally is asserted in the Bible on several occasions. The most striking summary is put into the mouth of the Assyrian commander who besieged Jerusalem in 701 BC. He taunts Hezekiah for "relying now on Egypt, that broken reed of a staff, which will pierce the hand of any man who leans on it" (2 Kings 18:21). A verse in Isaiah 30:7 asserts that "Egypt's help is worthless and empty, therefore I have called her 'Rahab who sits still'." But if Egypt was an unreliable ally, her wisdom and skill in administration were acknowledged. When Solomon's wisdom is praised, it is because it exceeded the wisdom of Egypt. It is also likely that David looked to Egyptian expertise when he needed to assume control of the empire that his conquests brought him. Recent scholarship has emphasized the similarities between parts of the wisdom literature of the Old Testament (for example, the book of Proverbs) and Egyptian wisdom literature; and the Wisdom of Amen-en-ope is strikingly similar to chapters 22–23 of Proverbs. Egypt, then, for the readers and writers of the Bible, was an ambivalent symbol. It was a rich, fertile and powerful land, possessing wisdom and knowledge, stretching along its great river. Israel owed its very origin to events that had taken place there at the time of the Exodus, and it was always a place from which help could be sought, even if in vain, and to which people fled for refuge. Its culture was exotic, especially when contact was established with Ethiopians, the tallness of whose stature and the blackness of whose

THE EMPIRES SURROUNDING ISRAEL

skins were a matter for wonder. Yet for the Prophets, Egypt was constantly an object of condemnation, and no language expressed judgment more powerfully than when Ezekiel proclaimed (30:12): "I will dry up the Nile, and will sell the land into the hand of evil men."

Assyria
In comparison with Egypt, Assyria is mentioned less frequently in the Old Testament, and there is little to indicate that readers of the Bible had any idea of what the territory might look like. This is all the more surprising in view of the traditions that indicate that the forebears of the Hebrews came from northern Mesopotamia (Genesis 11:27–30). That Mesopotamia was dominated by the great rivers Tigris and Euphrates was clear, but otherwise few places are named, and the prophetic books do not contain oracles of condemnation of Assyria on a scale comparable with Egypt and Babylon. Two of the smaller prophetic books are concerned with Nineveh, one of the great Assyrian cities, although it is far from clear whether the writers had actually been to the city. In the book of Jonah, whose theme is the repentance of Nineveh when the Prophet warned of its imminent destruction, there are no details other than that it was "an exceeding great city, three days' journey in breadth" (Jonah 3:3). At Jonah 4:11 the city's population is given as 120 000 persons.

The book of Nahum, which similarly concerns itself with Nineveh, is also uninformative. Phrases such as "The chariots rage in the streets, they rush to and fro through the squares...The officers are summoned, they stumble as they go, they hasten to the wall..." (Nahum 2:4–5) do not demand a

Above Slaves were used by the Assyrians to move timber. This relief comes from the palace of King Sargon II at Khorsabad. Sargon claimed to have finally defeated Samaria, the capital of the northern kingdom of Israel, in 722/1 BC.

Right Ashurbanipal (699–629 BC), whose exploits in hunting lions are commemorated here, was the last or last-but-one king of the Assyrian empire. During his reign he was preoccupied with rebellions, and after his death Josiah, king of Judah (640–609 BC), took advantage of Assyria's growing weakness to establish his independence.

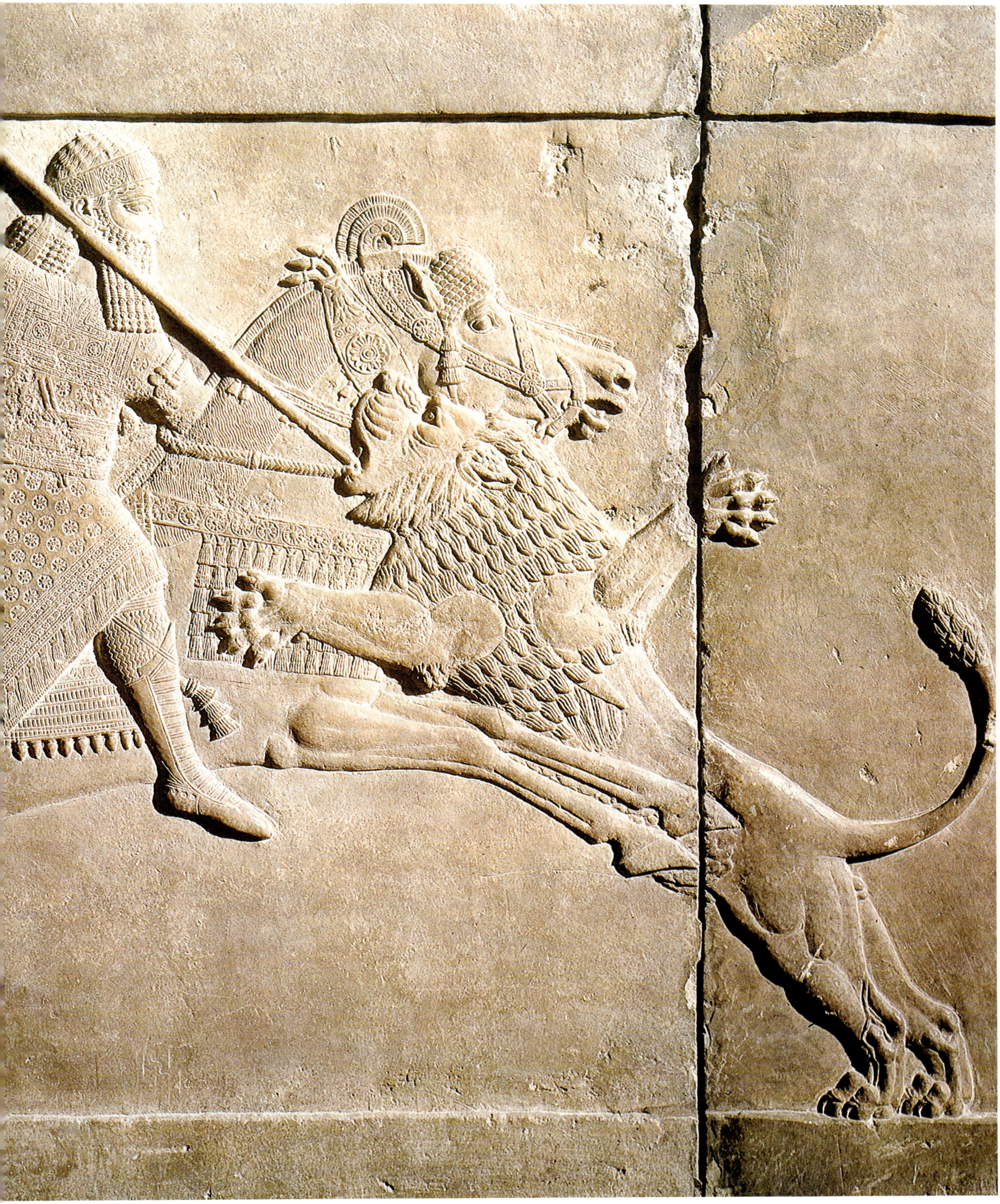

THE EMPIRES SURROUNDING ISRAEL

knowledge of the city, on the part of either writer or reader. Where Nahum is more explicit, it is by way of describing Assyrian methods of warfare. If the passage in Isaiah 5:27–29 is a description of Assyria, it is a chilling picture of what readers felt when they heard that name:

> None is weary, none stumbles,
> none slumbers or sleeps,
> not a waistcloth is loose,
> not a sandal-thong broken;
> their arrows are sharp,
> all their bows bent,
> their horses' hoofs seem like flint,
> and their wheels like the whirlwind.
> Their roaring is like a lion,
> like young lions they roar;
> they growl and seize their prey,
> they carry it off, and none can rescue.

Babylon

Given that in 597 and 587 BC inhabitants of Judah were exiled to Babylon, and that some of their descendants later returned to Judah, we would expect to find many references to Babylon. In fact, there are far fewer references to Babylon than to Egypt, and although some details about places and the way of life in Babylon are to be found, they do not amount to more than a general picture that could have been appropriate to other places as well as to Babylon. The passage about Babylon that will be most familiar to readers comes from the beginning of Psalm 137:

> By the waters of Babylon,
> there we sat down and wept,
> when we remembered Zion.
> On the willows there
> we hung up our lyres.

The waters referred to are the canals and rivers, either of the city of Babylon itself or of the country of Babylon. However, the point is made that rivers and canals were important both for irrigation and for transport. At one of the canals, called the river Chebar (Ezekiel 1:1), the great inaugural vision of Ezekiel occurred, when the presence and glory of God with his people in exile were disclosed to the Prophet.

The narratives are more informative about the city of Babylon itself than about the land, yet even here some explanation of the narratives must have been necessary for the allusions to be fully understood. Today we know that the annual procession of the gods was one of the highlights of the religious year in Babylon, as the images representing the gods were taken through the city on carriages drawn by animals. In Isaiah 46:1–2, however, the allusion to this event is full of irony, as the Prophet compares the idols, that need to be pulled by animals, with the God of Israel, who has sustained his chosen people:

> Bel bows down, Nebo stoops,
> their idols are on beasts and cattle;
> these things you carry are loaded
> as burdens on weary beasts.

Again, a reader needs some help to understand the allusion to the gates and walls of the city of Babylon when Isaiah 45:2b declares

> I will break in pieces the doors of bronze
> and cut asunder the bars of iron.

The first five chapters of the book of Daniel are set in Babylon, but few if any details are given about the city itself in the stories.

It is, perhaps, not surprising that there should be little information about Babylon. When the exiles first reached their new homes, they must have been dazzled by what they saw. Babylon itself at the beginning of the 6th century was one of the wonders of the ancient world, and it is

Nimrud was a town on the river Tigris, south of present-day Mosul. In the Old Testament it is called Calah (Genesis 10:11). From the first half of the 9th century BC it was a royal residence. In the 1830s, when sketched by Sir Robert Ker Porter (*left*), it was thought to be the Tower of Babel. Excavations from 1845 by A.H. Layard disclosed its secrets. His reconstruction of the palace is shown *above*.

Right The river Euphrates, the other major river of Mesopotamia, has changed its course more than once over the millennia. In Old Testament times Babylon stood on one of the main channels of the Euphrates. Today the main channel is some 20km (12·4 miles) to the west.

possible today to appreciate some of its magnificence thanks to the marvellous reconstructions of the processional way and the Ishtar Gate in the Vorderasiatisches Museum in East Berlin. If ordinary Israelites were impressed by the magnificence of Babylon, the prophetic writers were not. Babylon is constantly criticized for its idolatry, its reliance on astrologers and its treasures. A remarkable shift can be discerned in the book of Jeremiah with regard to Babylon. The nation raised up by God to punish the chosen people becomes the object of rebuke, and all that is great about the city is threatened with destruction. The condemnation found in Jeremiah 50:36–38 lists the chief characteristics that biblical readers would have associated with Babylon, only to declare judgment against them:

> A sword upon the diviners,
> that they may become fools!
> A sword upon her warriors,
> that they may be destroyed!
> A sword upon her horses and upon her chariots,
> and upon all the foreign troops in her midst,
> that they may become women!
> A sword upon all her treasures,
> that they may be plundered!
> A drought upon her waters,
> that they may be dried up!
> For it is a land of images,
> and they are mad over idols.

Persia

The Jews were under the domination of the Persians from 540 to 333 BC, and the books that most strongly reflect the Persian period are Ezra, Nehemiah and Esther. The last book is set in the capital of Susa, but tells us little about the city other than that it had a square and that in the garden of the king's palace were "white cotton curtains and blue

Above A reconstruction of the Ishtar Gate at Babylon built by Nebuchadnezzar in about 580 BC.

Left Relief of a bull from the Ishtar Gate, made from coloured enamelled bricks.

THE EMPIRES SURROUNDING ISRAEL

Right The tomb of Cyrus the Great at Pasargadae in present-day Iran. Cyrus, king of the Medes and Persians, conquered Babylon in 540 BC and permitted the Jews to return to Jerusalem, although only a few did so.

Right Relief of a Persian soldier from the palace of Darius at Susa, c. 500 BC. The Persians adopted from the Babylonians the technique of producing coloured enamelled brick.

hangings caught up with cords of fine linen and purple to silver rings and marble pillars, and also couches of gold and silver on a mosaic pavement of porphyry, marble, mother-of-pearl and precious stones"(Esther 1:16).

If any picture of Persia comes over in the biblical narratives, it concerns the administration of the country rather than its physical features. The impression created is that of a vast territory ruled over by many officials. Esther 9 speaks of letters being sent to 127 provinces, and the previous chapter even implies that these 127 provinces covered territory from India to Ethiopia, ruled over by satraps, princes and governors. Effective means of communication are implied, with the use of mounted couriers using swift horses that were specially bred from the royal stud. In Ezra various Persian official letters that are recorded imply a concern in the capital for small details of government and administration even in far-flung corners of the territory.

Greece and Rome

Apart from the book of Daniel, there is little or no reference in the Old Testament to the aftermath of the conquest of Syria, Palestine and Egypt by Alexander the Great following the battle of Issus in 333 BC. Veiled references to Alexander's rise, to the division of his kingdom after his death among his generals, and to the struggles between their descendants, are contained in Daniel 11. The rise of Antiochus IV and his persecution of the Jews are behind the symbolism of Daniel 7. However, no attempt is made, nor is any attempt required to be made, to describe parts of the Greek empire.

It is in the New Testament that reference is made to Greek cities, particularly in the Acts of the Apostles and in the book of Revelation. Among the most famous of these Greek cities are numbered Antioch, the main base of missionary outreach to Gentiles, Ephesus with its famous temple dedicated to Artemis (Diana), Athens where Paul preached on the Areopagus, and Corinth where Paul stayed for 18 months.

The most explicit references to Greek cities come in the first three chapters of the book of Revelation, where a knowledge of the situations and

Far left A mosaic of Paul from old St Peter's in Rome. According to tradition, Paul was beheaded in Rome after his appeal to be tried there as a Roman citizen.

Left The city of Corinth is prominent in the New Testament as the home of the church to which Paul wrote several letters. In ancient times the city had a temple dedicated to Apollo.

characteristics of some of the seven cities is necessary in order for the allusions to be appreciated. For example, it has been suggested that the promise to the Church at Philadelphia that a victor will be made a pillar in the temple of God is a promise made in deliberate contrast to the earthquakes that frequently devastate the area. Recent photographs taken at an interval of only a few years from exactly the same spot reveal how the landscape can be devastated by an earthquake, and how the figure of being a pillar in a temple, a symbol for security, can be fitting in the circumstances. Again, the charge against Laodicea, that it should be either hot or cold but not lukewarm, has been illustrated on the basis of the hot and cold springs at the source of the city's water supply.

The city of Rome itself is described only in the closing part of the Acts of the Apostles, the two places in it explicitly mentioned being the Forum of Appius and the Three Taverns (Acts 28:15). However, the Roman empire itself was a constant part of daily life in New Testament times. Jews in Judea were familiar with Roman soldiers, they had to pay taxes to Caesar, and they had to handle Roman coinage. Communications by road within the empire were as quick and safe as they had ever been, and even a Jew such as Saul of Tarsus could enjoy the benefits of Roman citizenship. As in the case of some of the other empires mentioned above, the attitude to Rome in the New Testament is ambivalent. When Paul advised the Romans to be subject to the ruling authorities because those in authority had been appointed by God (Romans 13:1), he no doubt had in mind the power of the Roman empire to enforce law and order and to maintain justice. A very different attitude to Rome is found in the book of Revelation. Here, the persecution of Christians leads to its portrayal as demonic, and it is interesting that the code name for the Roman empire is Babylon.

These last remarks enable a conclusion to be drawn. Throughout the Bible, lands serve as powerful theological symbols. The land of the Bible itself was a symbol of God's provision and of the people's rejection of that provision. God gave his people a land of their own, but they turned to other gods and cast off their dependence upon him. Loss of the promised land at the exile was one of the most effective ways in which both the sovereignty and the providence of God could be demonstrated. It is no accident that the return to the promised land after the exile is described in language borrowed from the description of the original journey through the wilderness to the promised land. As for the lands that surrounded Israel, they too were powerful symbols. The fact that they did not recognize the God of Israel and that they often threatened the very existence of the chosen people made them apt subjects for descriptions of the sovereignty of God. He could use them to chastize his people, and in turn he controlled the destinies of the nations such that he could also punish those nations he used. Thus a geographical understanding of the biblical world does not exhaust the meaning of the world in which Israel existed. In the Bible, geography shades into theology.

Below left Ephesus was a city in which Paul lived and worked for two years. The success of his mission began to threaten the livelihood of those who made shrines of the goddess Artemis (Acts 19). The picture shows the road along which the procession passed on the occasion of the festival of Artemis.

Below A statue of Artemis from Ephesus, dating from the 2nd century AD.

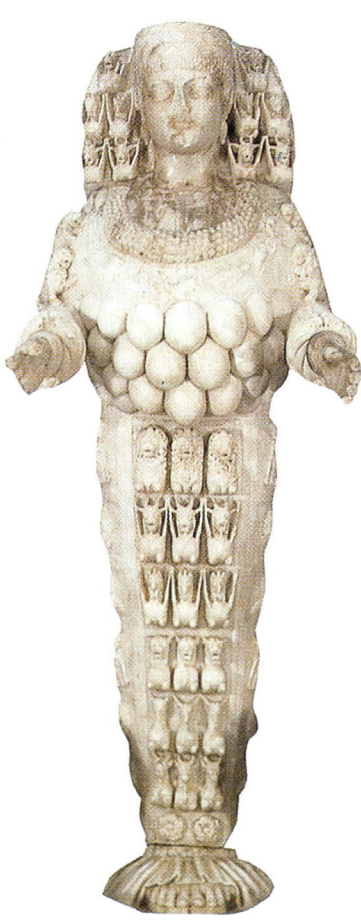

LIST OF ILLUSTRATIONS

Site plans by John Brennan, Oxford; Inkwell Studios, Oxford.

Abbreviations: t = top, tl = top left, tr = top right, c = centre, b = bottom etc.
PA = Pictorial Archive, Jerusalem; BM = British Museum, London; WB = Werner Braun, Jerusalem; DH = David Harris, Jerusalem; SH = Sonia Halliday, Weston Turville, Bucks.; RK = Rolf Kneller, Jerusalem; GN = Garo Nalbandian, Jerusalem; RN = Richard Nowitz, Jerusalem; ZR = Zev Radovan, Jerusalem; JF = John Fuller, Cambridge; DB = Dick Barnard, Milverton, Somerset; JB = John Brennan, Oxford.

Endpapers. Jerusalem, from Bernhard von Breitenbach's Map of the Holy Land, 1483: British Library, London (Photo Fotomas Index, London).

page
2 6. Relief carvings of prophets, the Annunciation and apostles, from Bamberg cathedral (photo Bildarchiv Foto Marburg, Marburg).
8–9. JF.
13. Scribe Eadwine writing, miniature from the Canterbury copy of the Utrecht Psalter: Master and Fellows of Trinity College, Cambridge MS R.17.1, f.283v.
14. Books of the Bible: DB.
15. St. John the Evangelist and Wedric, Abbot of Liessies; leaf from a French MS of 1146, illuminated by an English artist: Musée de la Société Archéologique, Avesnes-sur-Helpe.
16bl. Early scripts: JB.
16br. The scribes of Sennacherib, Assyrian relief: BM (photo Michael Holford).
17tl. Administrative tablet from Jamdat Nasr c.2900 BC: BM (photo Michael Holford).
17c. The Cyrus Cylinder: BM inv. no. 90920.
17tr. Roman glass inkwell, Second Temple period: Israel Museum, Jerusalem.
17bc. Fragment of the Septuagint, 2nd century AD: John Rylands University Library, Manchester, Papyrus Rylands GK 458.
17b. Inscription from Temple Mount: Dept. of Antiquities, Jerusalem (photo ZR).
18t. C. Tischendorf, lithograph by Schneller: BM.
18c. Codex Sinaiticus: BM MS Add 43725.
18bl. Codex Sinaiticus, end of St. John's gospel: BM ibid. f.260.
18br. The library at St. Catherine's monastery, Sinai: Jerusalem Publishing House.
19. St. Catherine's monastery, Sinai: WB.
20b. The Nag Hammadi library: Institute for Antiquity and Christianity, Claremont, California.
20r. First page of St. Thomas's gospel: ibid.
20cl. Fragment of St. John's gospel, first half of second century: John Rylands University Library, Manchester, Papyrus Rylands GK 457.
21. Initial page of St. Matthew, Lindisfarne Gospels: British Library, MS Cott. Nero Div. f.27.
22tr. Luther by Cranach the Elder: Uffizi, Florence (photo Mansell Collection, London).
22cr. Papal bull against Luther, from *Contra Errores Martini Lutheri et Sequacium*, 1520.
22c. Titlepage of the first complete German Bible, 1534: Universitätsbibliotek, Karl-Marx-Universität, Leipzig.
22l. Titlepage of the English Great Bible, 1539: British Library c.18 d.1.
23. Moses on Mt. Sinai, the Paris Psalter f.422: Bibliothèque Nationale, Paris.
43. The Ascension; stained glass, Le Mans cathedral: SH.
44tl. Moses on Mt. Sinai: British Library MS. Add 54180 f.5b.
44bl. Lot's wife turned into a pillar of salt, from Sarajevo Haggadah, Sarajevo Museum.
44–45. Israel in Egypt by Sir Edward Poynter: Guildhall Art Gallery, London (photo The Bridgeman Art Library).
44–45b. Joseph receives his brethren, from the 6th-century Vienna Genesis: Osterreichishe Nationalbibliothek, Vienna, E.1176 C cod.theo.graec. 31 f.45.
45br. The Sacrifice of Isaac; etching by Rembrandt: BM H.283.
46–47. Scenes from the story of Samson; from the Maciejowski Bible, French 13th century: Pierpont Morgan Library, New York, MS 638 ff. 14v, 15v, 15r.
48cl. Jael and Sisera, after the Master of Flémalle: Herzog–Anton–Ulrich Museum, Brunswick.
48t. David and Goliath by Lorenzo Ghiberti: detail from bronze relief from the Baptistery doors, Florence (photo Phaidon Archives, Oxford).
49t. Jonah and the Whale, Hebrew MS from Corunna, Spain: British Library, MS Kennicott 1, f.305.
48–49b. The Queen of Sheba visits Solomon; fresco by Piero della Francesca: Church of San Francesco, Arezzo (photo Scala, Florence).
49tr. Judith by Botticelli: Uffizi, Florence (photo Scala, Florence).
50l. The Annunciation and Nativity; limewood panel by the Ottobeuren Master: Klostermuseum, Ottobeuren.
50t. The Prodigal Son; etching by Rembrandt; BM H.147.
50b. The Good Samaritan; etching by Rembrandt: BM H.101.
51t. The entry of Christ into Jerusalem by Pietro Lorenzetti: Lower Church, San Francesco, Assisi (photo Scala, Florence).
51b. The mocking of Christ; fresco by Fra Angelico: San Marco, Florence (photo Scala, Florence).
52–53. The Maestà by Duccio: Museo dell'Opera del Duomo, Siena (photo Scala, Florence).
54–55. The Deposition by van der Weyden: Prado, Madrid (photo Scala, Florence).
55r. The Penitent Magdalene; woodcarving by Donatello: The Baptistery, Florence (photo Scala, Florence).
56tl. Peter's sorrow from 17th-century Ethiopic MS of Octateuch: British Library, Oriental MS 481 f. 104b.
56r. Descent of the Holy Ghost by El Greco: Prado, Madrid (photo Scala, Florence).
56c. The story of St. Paul, from a Carolingian MS, 9th century: Phaidon Archives, Oxford.
57. Madaba mosaic, from Elsevier *Atlas of Israel*, 1970, Jerusalem.
64cl. Neo–Babylonian clay tablet showing map of the world: BM.
64bl. Madaba Map, Jordan: Custodia Terra Sancta, Studium Biblicum Franciscanum Museum, Jerusalem.
64–65. Ebstorf world map. c.1235: Equinox Archive, Oxford.
65tr. Map of the Holy Land by Matthew Paris: British Library Cotton MS. Nero DV.
65br. Palestine Exploration Fund map, from Elsevier *Atlas of Israel*, 1970, Jerusalem.
66tr. Peacock: Bodleian Library, Oxford, MS Ashmole 1511 f.72.
66cr. Three dogs: Ibid.
66cl. Birds: Ibid., MS Bodley 764 f.73v.
66bc. Lions: Ibid., MS Ashmole 1511 f.10v.
66br. Hyrcus the he-goat: Ibid., MS Bodley 764 f.36v.
67l. God creating the animals: Ibid., MS Ashmole 1511 f.6v.
67tr. Bear and cubs: Ibid., MS Bodley 764 f.22v.
67cr. Badgers: Ibid., f.50v.
67b. Bees: Ibid., MS Ashmole 1511 f.75v.
67br. Bull: Ibid., MS Bodley 130 f.84.
68–69. Plants of the Bible: Crown copyright; reproduced with the permission of the Controller of Her Majesty's Stationery Office and of the Director, Royal Botanic Gardens, Kew.
70–71. Fisherman, Galilee: SH.
72t. Acre; lithograph by David Roberts: Fotomas Index, London.
72b. Haifa; lithograph by David Roberts.
72c. Terracotta figurine of pregnant woman, Achzib 8–6th century BC: Israel Museum (photo DH).
74t. Phoenician marble anthropoid sarcophagus: Ny Carlsberg Glyptothek, Copenhagen.
74c. Roman ruins, Tyre: ZR.
75r. Sarcophagus of King Tabnit of Sidon: JF.
75c. General view of Tyre: French Archaeological Institute, Beirut.
75tl. Melkart bowl: JP.
76. Caesarea marshes: PA.
78l. Dor: WB.
78c. Head of Hellenistic figurine: ZR.
80. Philistine figurine from Ashdod, 12th century BC: Israel Museum (photo DH).
81t. Gaza: Bible Scene, Barnet.
81b. Joppa: SH.
82–83. Aqueduct: SH.
83br. Aerial view of Caesarea: WB.
83tl. Coins: JF.
83c. Arches, Caesarea: RK.
83tc. Masonry on coast of Caesarea: RN.
84. Zorah and Eshtaol: DH.
86. Shephelah: Bible Scene, Barnet.
88ct. Duck's head from Fosse Temple, Lachish: Israel Museum.
88cb. Assyrian ramp, Lachish: University of Tel Aviv (photo Weinberg).
89b. Lachish: Bible Scene, Barnet.
89t. Pots from Lachish: Lachish Expeditions, University of Tel Aviv (photo A. Hay).
89cr. Lachish letters: Equinox Archive, Oxford.
90–91. Reconstruction of Lachish: DB.
90. Siege of Lachish, after A. H. Layard.
91. The tribute, after A. H. Layard.
92–93. Illustrations from A. H. Layard's engravings after Assyrian reliefs.
94. Judean hills: DH.
96. Flowers in the desert: RN.
98c. Ploughing near Hebron: ZR.
98b. Ein Sinia village, Hebron: DH.
99. Tomb of the Patriarchs, Hebron: WB.
100–01b. Bethlehem by W. Holman Hunt: private collection, U.K.
100cl. Church of the Holy Nativity, Bethlehem: SH.
101r. Bethlehem: GN.
101tc. Bethlehem streets: SH.
102. Herodium: GN.
103. Herodium from above: Zefa Picture Library, London (photo WB).
104b. Judean desert: ZR.
104tl. Riders in Judean desert: GN.
106–07. Rainstorm: PA.
108. Palm trees, En-gedi: Jamie Simpson, Brookwood.
109tr. Sheep grazing: RN.
109tl. Hoard from the Cave of Treasure: Israel Museum (photo DH).
109c. Waterfall: Prof. J. Rogerson, Sheffield.
110–11. Aerial view of Masada: SH.
110b. Synagogue after excavation, Masada: from Y. Yadin, *Masada*.
111. Frescoes, Masada: Ibid.
111c. Ballista, Masada: Linda Proud, Oxford.
111b and br. Sandals, basket, pan and jug: JF.
112–13c. View from caves of Qumran: Palphot, Jerusalem.
113cr. Jars, Qumran, 1st century AD: Israel Museum (photo DH).
113br. Scroll of Isaiah, 1st century AD: Israel Museum.
115. Mount Sinai: RK.
116t. Desert scene: DH.
116–17. Sinai desert from cave: RN.
118c. Ostracon inscribed "House of Yahweh": from the Arad Excavation Report.
118cb. Fragment of pot, Arad: JF.
118b. Seal, Arad: JF.
119t. Tel Arad: WB.
119br. Holy of Holies, Arad, 9th century BC: Israel Museum (photo DH).
119bl. Model of Arad: Israel Museum, Jerusalem.
120–21. Tell Beer-sheba: PA.
121c. Market scene: RK.
121b. Figurine from Beer-sheba: Prof. Herzog, University of Tel Aviv.
122–23. Kadesh-barnea: PA.
124t. Wilderness of Zin: ZR.
124b. Ezion-geber: DH.
125c. Copper snake, Timna: Dr. Beno Rothenburg, Tel Aviv.
125c. Fragment of Hathor, Timna: Ibid.
125br. Timna: DH.
125bl. Copper mines, Timna: WB.
126–27. Sinai desert: WB.
127r. Jebel Musa: ZR.
128l. Dan: GN.
131. Lower Galilee: PA.
132–33. Tiberias; lithograph by David Roberts: Fotomas Index, London.
134b. Tell Hazor: PA.
135t. Lion orthostat: Israel Museum (photo DH).
135tr. Hazor mask: Ibid.

225

LIST OF ILLUSTRATIONS

135br. Mask in situ at Hazor excavation: Prof. Y. Yadin.
137. Nazareth: GN.
138c. Aerial view of Capernaum: RN.
138b. Ark of the Covenant: GN.
139bl. Olive press: SH.
139br. Grinders: DH.
140. Mount Tabor: RK.
141t. Tabgha mosaic: GN.
141c. Chorazin: WB.
142b. Threshing, Galilee: ZR.
142t. Winnowing: WB.
143bl. Ploughing in olive grove: GN.
143tr. Shepherd: GN.
143br. Taboon (bread oven): ZR.
144tl. Oil press: DH.
144tr. Oil lamp, Hellenistic period: ZR.
144cl. Entrance to tomb: SH.
144cr. Ossuaries, 50BC–70AD: Israel Museum (photo DH).
144b. Bone dice, Roman period, Jerusalem: Hebrew University, Jerusalem (photo ZR).
145tl. Coin mould, Roman period, Jerusalem: Dept. of Antiquities, Jerusalem (photo ZR).
145tc. Cosmetic equipment, clay, stone and bone, Roman period, Masada: Hebrew University (photo ZR).
145tr. Clay beer jug, Philistine period, Tel Qasila: Dept. of Antiquities, Jerusalem (photo ZR).
145cl. Judean denarius: Custodia Terra Sancta, Studium Biblicum Franciscanum, Jerusalem.
145c. Stone weights: DH.
145cr. Frying pan from Lachish: JF.
145bl. Figurine of woman bathing, Canaanite period: Dept. of Antiquities, Jerusalem (photo DH).
146. Valley of Jezreel: RK.
150t. Wadi Faria: PA.
150b. Entry to Nablus; lithograph by David Roberts: Equinox Archives, Oxford.
153. Head of figurine, Canaanite period: ZR.
154–155t. Samaria: ZR.
155tr. Sphinx in lotus thicket; 9th century BC Samarian ivory from Ahab's palace: Israel Museum, Jerusalem.
155b. Beitin: RK.
156. Horned altar: DH.
157cl. Triumph of a king after a victorious expedition; ivory: Dept. of Antiquities, Jerusalem (photo DH).
157cr. Seal, Megiddo: ZR.
157b. Megiddo: PA.
157br. Ram and monkey: ZR.
157cr. Megiddo tunnel: GN.
159. Samaritans: WB.
160ct. Incense stand: ZR.
160bc. Stelae, Gezer: ZR.
160tr. Bull: Israel Museum (photo DH).

160br. Shrine of the stelae, Hazor: Israel Museum (photo DH).
161l. Gold dagger, Canaanite period, Gezer: Dept. of Antiquities, Jerusalem (photo ZR).
161tr. Fertility goddess: DH.
161bc. Philistine anthropoid sarcophagus: Dept. of Antiquities, Jerusalem (photo GN).
161br. Demon: JF.
164–65. Jerusalem from the Mount of Olives by Edward Lear, 1859: Christies, London (photo The Bridgeman Art Library).
166–67. Gibeon: PA.
170–71. Wadi Suwenit: PA.
172–73. The Old City of Jerusalem: RN.
174–75. Aerial view of the City of David, Jerusalem: PA.
174tr. Tomb of King David: WB.
174cl. Heads: ZR.
174bl. Pots, Roman period, City of David: ZR.
176. Absalom's tomb: ZR.
178–79t. Anata: ZR.
178–79c. Siloam inscription: Dept. of Antiquities, Jerusalem (photo ZR).
179b. Hezekiah's tunnel: SH.
181t. Ain Karem: GN.
181b. Mosaic, Ain Karem: Custodia Terra Sancta, Studium Biblicum Franciscanum Museum, Jerusalem.
182–83. Herod's temple: DB.
184–85t. Olive press, Bethany: SH.
185tr. Bethany: Custodia Terra Sancta, Studium Biblicum Franciscanum Museum, Jerusalem.
186tc. Wailing Wall: Camerapix–Hutchison, London.
186tr. Stepped road, Jerusalem: SH.
186cr. Damascus Gate; from a 19th-century lantern slide in collection of Prof. J. Rogerson.
186bc. Pool of Siloam: SH.
186br. Excavations in the City of David: Israel Exploration Society (photo Prof. Avigad).
186bl. Pool of Bethesda: SH.
186b. Coin: ZR.
189. Golden Gate, Jerusalem; from a watercolour by H. G. Gray from *Jerusalem: The City Plan* 1948.
190cr. The lithostratos: GN.
190bl. Via Dolorosa: SH.
190–91bc. The Church of the Holy Sepulchre; lithograph by David Roberts.
191tr. Station of the Cross: Jerusalem Publishing House.
191cr. Tomb with a rolling stone: SH.
191br. Garden of Gethsemane: SH.
193b. Nebi Musa: WB.
193t. Aerial view of River Jordan: GN.
194. Wadi Qilt: ZR.
195. Salt deposits at the Dead Sea: WB.

196–97. Abu el-Alaiq: PA.
197tl. Neolithic tower, Jericho: DH.
197br. Head, 16th century BC, Jericho: DH.
198–99. Monastery on the Mount of Temptation: SH.
200. Hathor, bronze and gold foil, 1500–1200 BC: Israel Museum.
200–01. Tell Beth-shean: PA.
203. Seil el-Mojib: PA.
204. Mount Hermon: SH.
205. Shepherd and flock: ZR.
206. Clay figurine of a king of Moab: Custodia Terra Sancta, Studium Biblicum Franciscanum Museum.
209. Petra: Zefa Picture Library, London.
210. Gerash: Ibid.
211. Caesarea Philippi: SH.
212–13. Machaerus: PA.
214. Assyrian King Sargon; relief from Khorsabad: Louvre, Paris (photo Scala, Florence).
216–17t. King Ramesses II, Abu Simbel, from *Sketches in Egypt and Nubia* by David Roberts, 1838.
216c. Elephantine Island: A. A. M. van der Heyden, Amsterdam.
217. Boats on the Nile: Ibid.
218. Slaves of Sargon; relief from Khorsabad: Louvre, Paris (photo Scala, Florence).
218–19. Lion hunt of Ashurbanipal: British Museum, London.
220t. Palace of Nimrud; from *Monuments of Nineveh* by A. H. Layard (photo Ashmolean Museum, Oxford).
220b. View of Nimrud by Sir Robert Ker Porter: British Library, London.
221. The Euphrates River at Babylon: Robert Harding Picture Library, London.
222t. Ishtar Gate, Babylon: State Museum, East Berlin.
222b. Bull, relief: Ibid.
223t. Tomb of Cyrus the Great: E. Bohm, Mainz.
223l. Persian soldier, relief: State Museum, East Berlin.
224tl. Mosaic of St. Paul in the crypt of St. Peter's, Rome: Scala, Florence.
224tr. Temple of Apollo, Corinth: SH.
224bl. Road to the Magnesian Gate, Ephesus: W. Wilkinson, London.
224br. Statue of Artemis from Ephesus: SH.

Acknowledgments
We would like to thank the following for their assistance in Israel: Father Michele Piccirillo of the Studium Biblicum Franciscanum, Jerusalem, Yosh Gafni of the Jerusalem Publishing House, Harold Harris of Zefa Ltd., and the Dean, Warden and Staff of St. George's cathedral, Jerusalem.

BIBLIOGRAPHY

The bibliography refers to works cited directly in the main text of the Atlas and to other works that may be of interest to non-specialists.

Other atlases of the Bible
L. H. Grollenberg, *Atlas of the Bible* (London & Edinburgh 1956). Probably the best Bible atlas ever produced, this was translated from the original Dutch. Its maps and diagrams are superb, and it is only a pity that its photographs are printed in black and white.
Y. Aharoni and M. Avi-Yonah, *The Macmillan Bible Atlas* (rev. edn., New York 1972). Drawing on material previously published in several of the Carta (Jerusalem) atlases, this indispensable work illustrates the topography of all major biblical incidents, as well as other incidents that affected biblical history. Its thrust is primarily historical.
J. H. Negenman, *New Atlas of the Bible* (London 1969). This follow-up to Grollenberg was able to use colour photography. However, it did not succeed in matching Grollenberg's standards of cartography and elucidation.
Oxford Bible Atlas, ed. Herbert G. May (2nd end., Oxford 1974). The *OBA* has long been the best Bible atlas at the inexpensive end of the market, especially valuable for students who could not afford Grollenberg. A new edition, revised by Dr. J. Day, was not published in time to be consulted for the present work.
Reader's Digest Atlas of the Bible. An Illustrated Guide to the Holy Land (Pleasantville, New York, 1981). A beautifully illustrated book whose highlights include reconstructions of Caesarea, Herodian Jerusalem and Masada. Its thrust is historical rather than geographical.
Student Map Manual. Historical Geography of the Bible Lands (Jerusalem 1979). This map manual is meant to be used in conjunction with Pictorial Archive colour slides and very large Student Maps. Nonetheless, it is a very useful book in its own right, it coordinates maps with relevant biblical texts, and its Index of Main Names indicates periods of occupation of sites. Its east-west orientation is not easy to get used to.
G. E. Wright and F. V. Filson, *The Westminster Historical Atlas to the Bible* (rev. edn., Philadelphia 1956). This has been to North American students what the *Oxford Bible Atlas* has been to British students, and is an excellent student manual with an essentially historical approach.

General works on geography and historical geography of the Bible
Y. Aharoni, *The Land of the Bible. A Historical Geography* (London 1967). First published in Hebrew in 1962, this sets the history of ancient Israel in its geographical and archaeological context. The author was one of Israel's leading archaeologists.
D. Baly, *The Geography of the Bible* (rev. edn., London 1974). Probably the best work in English on the geography of Israel as related specifically to the Bible. It is regionally and geographically orientated, with many diagrams and illustrations.
D. Baly, *Geographical Companion to the Bible* (London 1963). A valuable account of many features of the land as they affect and illumine biblical narratives.
Y. Karmon, *Israel, a Regional Geography* (London 1971). Probably the most useful book for specialists and non-specialists alike, it discusses physical geography, population and land use, setting all these in an historical perspective.
O. Keel, M. Küchler, C. Uehlinger, *Orte und Landschaften der Bibel* (Zürich and Göttingen 1982 (vol. 2), 1984 (vol. 1)). This projected 4-volume work is intended as a travel guide for visitors to the Holy Land. Vol. 1 deals with historical geography and vol. 2 with Judea, part of the Jordan valley and the south coastal plain, the Negev and Sinai. Vol. 3 will cover Samaria and Galilee, and vol. 4 will be devoted to Jerusalem. This is a monumental work, based upon many years of travelling in the Holy Land, and the most painstaking study of the technical literature. It is indispensable for any serious study of the Holy Land.
G. Dalman, *Sacred Sites and Ways: Studies in the Topography of the Gospels* (London 1935). This is a translation of *Orte und Wege Jesu* (3rd edn., Gütersloh 1924). One of the most extensive studies of the topography of the ministry of Jesus ever written, this is still a valuable work in spite of its age.
E. Orni and E. Efrat, *Geography of Israel* (Jerusalem 1964). More technical than Karmon, this is a valuable work, but probably less readable than Karmon for non-specialists.
Encyclopaedia Biblica (Jerusalem 1964–82) 8 vols. (in Hebrew). An indispensable work of reference, with articles on all major aspects of the history, geography, archaeology and topography of ancient Israel.
H. Shanks, *The City of David. A Guide to biblical Jerusalem* (Washington, D.C., 1973). A delightfully written scholarly guide for those who wish to explore in depth what remains of the city of David.
T. L. Thompson, *The Settlement of Sinai and the Negev in the Bronze Age* (Beihefte zum Tübinger Atlas des vorderen Orients, Reihe B Nr. 8, Wiesbaden 1975); *The Settlement of Palestine in the Bronze Age* (Beihefte zum Tübinger Atlas des vorderen Orients, Reihe B Nr. 34, Wiesbaden 1979). These two books are, in fact, compendiums of all known sites in the Bronze Age, together with brief descriptions of the findings and their source of information. In the present Atlas, I have worked through these invaluable volumes in plotting what I have loosely called settlements in the 2nd millennium.
M. Zohary, *Plants of the Bible* (Cambridge 1982). The late Professor Zohary was the doyen of studies in this area, whose last book presented in popular form a lifetime of research and publication.
Y. Ben-Arieh, *The Rediscovery of the Holy Land in the Nineteenth Century* (Jerusalem and Detroit 1979). A richly illustrated account of exploration and discovery, which puts the work of Thomson, Tristram and many others into historical perspective.

Descriptions of the Holy Land in earlier centuries
H. Donner, *Pilgerfahrt ins Heilige Land. Die ältesten Berichte Christlicher Palästinapilger (4–7. Jahrhundert)* (Stuttgart 1979). Accounts of eight pilgrims to the Holy Land between 333 and 680 AD are translated into German, together with very extensive information about the lands of the Bible during this period.
J. P. Peters, *Early Hebrew Story. Its Historical Background* (London 1908). By modern standards, this is an old-fashioned account of the origin of Hebrew traditions. However, it contains a memorable description of Bethel, cited in this Atlas.
G. A. Smith, *The Historical Geography of the Holy Land*, (26th edn., London 1935). Probably the greatest of the classics in English, this first appeared in 1894, and was last completely revised in 1931. Although still indispensable for serious study, non-specialists will find it harder going than Thomson.
W. M. Thomson, *The Land and the Book; or, Biblical Illustrations drawn from the Manners and Customs, the Scenes and Scenery of The Holy Land* (London 1859). This account of Thomson's journey from Beirut to Jerusalem between January and May 1857 became one of the most celebrated and frequently quoted books in British biblical scholarship of the 19th century. It draws upon Thomson's many visits to the sites over a period of 25 years, is rich in illustrations, and gives a vivid picture of landscapes some of which have since altered out of all recognition.
H. B. Tristram, *The Land of Israel: a Journal of Travels in Palestine, undertaken with special reference to its Physical Character* (3rd edn., London 1876). As the title suggests, Tristram's book is more technical than that of Thomson. It is the fruit of 10 months of exploration in 1863–64, has some fine engravings, and is deservedly a classic.
C. Wilson and C. Warren, *The Recovery of Jerusalem. A Narrative of Exploration and Discovery in the City and the Holy Land*, 2 vols. (London 1871). This is a collection of papers dating from 1864–65 to 1868, contributed by early scientific explorers of Jerusalem, the Sea of Galilee, the Hauran and Sinai. The narratives describe vividly the difficulties encountered, and the account of the passage through Hezekiah's tunnel is memorable.
F. J. Bliss (with plan and illustrations by A. C. Dickie), *Excavations at Jerusalem 1894–1897* (London 1898). A book still often referred to in spite of its age, it provided the basis for much subsequent research.
S. Runciman, *A History of the Crusades*, 2 vols. (Cambridge 1951–52). Contains many references to the state of the land in Palestine in the 11th–12th centuries.

Treatment of particular areas
Y. Ben-Arieh, *The Changing Landscape of the Central Jordan Valley* (Scripta Hierosolymitana, vol. 15, Studies in Geography, Pamphlet no. 3, Jerusalem 1968). A monograph rather than a pamphlet, this valuable study of the Jordan–Yarmuk triangle south of the Sea of Galilee traces its history and land use from palaeolithic to modern times.
N. Glueck, *The Other Side of the Jordan* (New Haven, 1945); *The River Jordan, Being an Illustrated Account of Earth's Most Storied River* (Philadelphia 1946). These studies, although now somewhat overtaken by subsequent research, remain classics of the areas they describe.
K. M. Kenyon, *Jerusalem. Excavating 3,000 Years of History* (London 1967). A record of the important excavations in the area of the city of David in the 1960s.
E. Otto, *Jerusalem – die Geschichte der Heiligen Stadt* (Kohlhammer/Urban-Taschenbücher No. 308, Stuttgart 1980). Deals with the history of Jerusalem from earliest times to the Latin (Crusader) kingdom of Jerusalem, based upon exhaustive knowledge of the technical literature, especially that dealing with recent excavations.
J. Wilkinson, *Jerusalem as Jesus knew it* (London 1978). An admirable and lucid account, with many helpful illustrations, of the relationship between the Jerusalem of the New Testament period and Jerusalem as the modern visitor sees it today.

Guides to Biblical History
J. Bright, *A History of Israel* (London 1981). Probably still the best large Old Testament history for beginners. The picture presented is fairly traditional, but is set in the context of archaeological and other modern discoveries.
S. Herrmann, *A History of Israel in Old Testament Times* (rev. edn., London 1981). Similar to Bright in size, this is a valuable contribution from the German side
M. Noth, *The History of Israel* (rev. edn., London 1960) Definitely not a work for beginners, this great book summed up Noth's life work in the areas of tradition history and archaeology and topography of ancient Israel. Its earlier chapters are now a little dated, but for the time of Solomon onwards this remains indispensable.
F. F. Bruce, *New Testament History* (rev. edn., London 1971). This has become the standard work in English on the history implied in the gospels, Acts and the epistles.

GAZETTEER

All locatable places mentioned in the Bible are listed below. The figures and letters in bold type give an initial grid reference for the site on the topographical maps in Part Three. The subsequent numbers refer to other pages with maps on which the site appears. Alternative name forms are also included.

Abarim, mountains of **202 C1**; 59
Abdon (Ebron) **73 B3**; 29
Abel-beth-maacah **129 D1**; 33
Abel-keramim **202 C2 C3**; 30
Abel-meholah **192 B2**; 30, 32, 33
Abel-shittim **192 B3**; 28
Abilene (region) **202 C1**
Abronah **114 B4**
Accaron see Ekron
Acco (Ptolemais) **73 B4**; 28, 32, 36, 38, 40, 59, 63
Achor, vale of **105 B1**; 59
Achshaph **129 A3 A4**; 28
Achzib (coastal plain) **73 B3**; 29, 59
Achzib (Chezib) (Shephelah) **85 C3**; 28, 29
Acraba (Akrabatta, Akrabattene) **148 D3**; 37, 38
Adadah see Aroer
Adam **192 B2**; 30
Adamah **129 D3**; 29
Adamah see Madon
Adami-nekeb **129 C4**; 29
Adasa **162 D2**
Adida see Hadid
Adithaim **148 B4**
Adora see Adoraim
Adoraim (Adora) **95 C2**; 37, 38
Adramyttium **214 E3**
Adria, Sea of **214 C2**
Adullam **85 D3**; 28, 30
Aenon **192 B2**
Ahlab (Mahalah) **73 C2**; 28, 29
Ai (Aija) **148 C4**; 25, 28
Aialon see Aiath
Aith (Aialon, Avvim) **148 C4**
Aija see Ai
Aijalon (Elon) **85 D1**; 28, 29, 30, 32, 33, 59
Aijalon, valley of **85 C1 D1**; 59
Aila see Elath
Ain see En-rimmon
Ain-rimmon see En-rimmon
Akrabatta see Acraba
Akrabattene see Acraba
Alema see Helam
Alemeth see Almon
Alexandria **214 E4**; 36, 40
Almon (Alemeth) **163 E3**
Almon-diblathaim (Beth-diblathaim) **202 C3**
Amathus 37, 38
Ammathus see Hammath
Ammon (region) **202 C2 D2**; 29, 32, 33, 34, 59
Amphipolis **214 D2**; 40
Anab **95 B3**; 28, 29
Anaharath **129 C5**
Ananiah see Bethany
Anathoth **163 E3**; 33
Anim **95 C3**; 29, 32, 59
Antioch (Pisidia) **214 F3**; 40
Antioch (Syria) **214 G3**; 40
Antipatris see Aphek
Aphairema see Ophra
Aphek (Antipatris) (coastal plain) **79 D1**; 28, 30, 38, 59, 63
Aphek (Aphik) (Asher) **73 B4**; 28, 29, 32
Aphek (Transjordan) **202 C2**; 33
Aphek (Phoenicia) **212 G4**
Aphek see Eben-ezer
Aphekah **95 C2 C3**
Aphik see Aphek
Apollonia (coastal plain) **77 A4**; 37, 38
Apollonia (Greece) **214 D2**; 40
Appius, Forum of **214 B2**; 40
Ar **202 C3**
Arab **95 C3**
Arabah **114 C3**; **192 B2**; 26, 59
Arabia (region) **214 H5 I5**; 24, 34, 35, 36, 40
Arad **114 C1**; 26, 28, 33, 38
Aram see Syria
Ararat (Urartu) (region) **214 H3**; 34, 35
Arbatta (region) **77 B2 C2**
Arbela **129 C4**; 37, 38
Argob (region) **202 D2**; 32
Arimathea (Ramah, Ramathaim-zophim, Rathamin) **148 B3**; 30, 37
Arnon (river) **192 B4**; 59
Aroer (Adadah) (Negev) **114 B1**; 29
Aroer (Gilead) **202 C3**; 29, 30, 32, 59
Aroer (Moab) **202 C3**; 29
Arpad **214 G3**
Arubboth **77 C3**; 32
Arumah **148 C3**; 30
Arvad **214 G4**; 34

Ascalon see Ashkelon
Ashan **114 B1**
Ashod (Azotus) **79 B3**; 28, 29, 30, 32, 33, 34, 37, 38, 40, 59, 63
Asher (tribe) 29, 30, 32
Ashkelon (Ascalon) **79 B4**; 28, 30, 34, 35, 37, 38, 59, 63
Ashnah (Shephelah) **85 C3**
Ashnah (Shephelah) **85 D2**
Ashtaroth (Be-eshterah) **202 D2**; 29, 59
Ashteroth-karnaim see Carnaim
Asia (region) **214 E3**; 40
Asor (Azor) **79 C1**
Asshur **214 H3**; 24, 34, 35
Assos **214 E3**; 40
Assyria (region) **214 H3**; 24, 34, 35
Ataroth (Valley of Jezreel) **147 B5**; 29
Ataroth (Jordan valley) **192 A2**
Ataroth (Moab) **202 C3**
Ataroth-addar **163 D2**
Athens **214 D3**; 40
Athlit (Atlit) **79 B1**
Atlit see Athlit
Attalia **214 F3**; 40
Avvim see Aiath
Azekah **85 C2**; 28, 30, 35
Azmaveth (Beth-azmaveth, Bethasmoth) **163 E2**
Azmon **114 A2**
Aznoth-tabor **129 C4**
Azor see Asor
Azotus see Ashdod
Azzah **148 C2**

Baalah, Mount **79 C2**
Baalah see Kiriath-jearim
Baalath **79 C2**; 32
Baal-gad **202 C1**; 28
Baal-hazor **148 C4**
Baal-peor see Beth-peor
Baal-perazim **162 D4**; 30
Baal-shalisha **148 B3**; 30
Baal-zephon (Mons Casius) **214 F4**; 26
Babel see Babylon
Babylon (Babel) **214 H4**; 24, 25, 34, 35, 36
Babylonia (Chaldea) (region) **214 H4 I4**; 34, 35, 36
Bahurim **163 E3**
Bamoth-baal **202 C3**; 29
Bascama see Baskama
Bashan (region) **202 C2 D2**; 29, 32, 33, 59
Baskama (Bascama) **202 C2**
Beer (Shephelah) **85 C2**
Beer (Lower Galilee) **129 D5**; 30
Beeroth (Benjamin) **162 D3**
Beeroth (Berea) (Benjamin) **162 D2**; 28
Beeroth (Bene-jaakan) (Negev) **114 A2**
Beer-sheba **114 B1**; 25, 26, 29, 30, 32, 33, 37, 38, 59, 63
Beerzeth **148 C4**
Be-eshterah see Ashtaroth
Bela see Zoar
Belus see Kedron
Bene-berak **79 C1**
Bene-jaakan see Beeroth
Benjamin (tribe) 29, 30, 32
Beon see Beth-baal-meon
Berach, vale of **105 B2 B3**; 59
Berea see Beeroth
Beroea (Greece) **214 D2**; 40
Beroea (Syria) **214 G3**
Besor, Brook of **114 B1**; 59
Beten **129 A4**; 29
Beth-anath **129 B3 C1 C4**; 28
Beth-anoth **95 C2**; 29
Bethany (Ananiah) **163 E3**
Beth-arabah **105 D1**; 29
Beth-arbel **202 C2**
Bethasmoth see Azmaveth
Beth-aven **163 E2**; 29, 30
Beth-aven see Bethel
Beth-azmaveth see Azmaveth
Beth-baal-meon (Beon) **202 C3**; 29
Beth-basi **95 D1**
Beth-dagon (coastal plain) **79 C2**; 29
Beth-dagon (Galilee) **129 C3**
Beth-diblathaim see Almon-diblathaim
Beth-eden (Eden) (region) **214 G3**; 34
Beth-eked **147 B4**
Bethel (Beth-aven, Luz) **148 C4**; 25, 28, 29, 30, 33, 59
Beth-emek **73 B4**
Beth-ezel **95 B3**
Beth-gamul **202 C3**
Beth-haccherem **162 C3 D4**
Beth-haggan (En-gannim, Ginae) **147 C4**; 38
Beth-hanan **162 C2**; 32
Beth-haram **192 B3**; 29
Beth-hoglah **192 B3**; 29
Beth-horon (lower) **148 B4**; 29, 32
Beth-horon (upper) **148 B4**; 29, 33
Bethir **162 C4**
Beth-jeshimoth **192 B3**; 29

Bethlehem (Ephrath, Ephrathah) (hill country of Judah) **95 D1**; 25, 30, 38, 59
Bethlehem (Galilee) **129 B4**; 29, 30
Beth-marcaboth see Madmannah
Beth-nimrah **192 B3**; 29
Beth-peor (Baal-peor) **202 C3**
Beth-pelet **114 B1**
Bethphage **162 D3**
Beth-rehob (region) **202 C1**
Bethsaida (Julias) **129 D3**; 38
Bethesda, Pool of 186, 190
Beth-shean (Scythopolis) **192 A1**; 28, 29, 30, 32, 33, 37, 38, 59, 63
Beth-shemesh (Har-heres, Ir-shemesh) (Shephelah) **85 C2**; 29, 30, 32, 33, 59
Beth-shemesh (Galilee) **129 B2 D4**; 28, 29
Beth-shittah **147 D3**
Bethsura see Beth-zur
Beth-tappuah **95 C2**
Bethuel see Bethul
Bethul (Bethuel) **95 B4 C3**
Beth-zaith (Beth-zita, Bezeth) **95 C2**
Beth-zechariah **95 C2**
Bezeth see Beth-zaith
Beth-zita see Beth-zaith
Beth-zur (Bethsura) **95 C2**; 37
Betonim **202 C3**
Bezek (mountains of Gilboa) **147 D4**; 30
Bezek (Benjamin) **148 A4**
Bezer (Bozrah) **202 C3**; 29, 32, 59
Bileam see Ibleam
Bithynia (region) **214 F2**; 40
Bosor **202 D2**
Bozkath **85 C3**
Bozrah (Edom) **202 C4**
Bozrah (Syria) **202 D2**
Bozrah see Bezer
Buz (region) **214 G5**

Cabbon **85 C3**
Cabul **73 C4**; 29, 32
Cabul, land of 32
Cadasa see Kedesh
Caesarea (Strato's Tower) **77 B3**; 37, 38, 40
Caesarea Philippi (Paneas) **202 C1**; 38
Calah see Nimrud
Callirrhoe see Zareth-shahar
Calneh see Calno
Calno (Calneh, Canneh) **214 G3**
Cana **129 B4 C4**
Canaan (region) 26
Canneh see Calno
Capernaum **129 D3**; 38
Capharsalama **162 D2**
Caphtor (Crete) **214 D3 E3**
Cappadocia (region) **214 G3**; 40
Carchemish **214 G3**; 34, 35
Caria (region) **214 E3**
Carmel **95 C3**; 29, 30, 59
Carmel, Mount **147 B2**; 33, 38, 59
Carnaim (Carnion, Ashteroth-karnaim, Karnaim) **202 D2**; 33
Carnion see Carnaim
Casphor (Caspin, Chaspho) **202 C2**
Caspin see Casphor
Cauda (Gaudos) **214 D4**; 40
Cenchreae **214 D3**; 40
Chaldea see Babylonia
Chaspho see Casphor
Chebar (river) **214 I4**
Chephar-ammoni **148 C4**; 35
Chephirah **162 C3**; 28
Cherith, Brook **192 B2**; 59
Chesalon **162 B3**
Chesulloth (Chisloth-tabor) **129 B4**; 29
Chezib see Achzib
Chinnereth (Chinneroth, Gennesaret) **129 D3**; 28, 29, 33
Chinneroth see Chinnereth
Chios **214 E3**
Chisloth-tabor see Chesulloth
Chitlish **85 B3**; 29
Chorazin **129 D3**
Cilicia (region) **214 F3**; 34, 35, 36, 40
Cnidus **214 E3**; 40
Coele-Syria (region) **214 G4**
Colonia Amasa **162 C3**
Colossae **214 E3**; 40
Corinth **214 D3**; 40
Cos **214 E3**; 40
Cozeba **95 C2**
Cush (Ethiopia) (region) **214 F6**
Cuthah **214 H4**; 34
Cyrene **214 D4**; 36, 40

Dabbesheth **147 B3**
Daberath **129 C4**; 29
Dalmanutha see Taricheae
Dalmatia see Illyricum
Damascus **202 D1**; 24, 25, 26, 32, 33, 34, 35, 36, 38, 40
Dan (Laish, Leshem) **129 D1**; 25, 29, 30, 32, 33, 59

Dan (tribe) 29, 30
Dannah **95 C3**
Daphne **214 G3**
Dathema (Diathema) **202 D2**
Dead Sea (Sea of the Arabah, Salt Sea) **192 A3**
Debir (Shephelah) **85 C4 D4**
Debir (Kiriath-sannah, Kiriath-sepher) (hill country of Judah) **95 B3 C3**; 28, 29, 30, 59
Decapolis (region) 38
Dedan **214 G5**
Derbe **214 F3**; 40
Diathema see Dathema
Dibon **202 C3**; 26, 29, 32, 59
Dilean **85 B3**; 29
Dimnah see Rimmon
Dimonah **114 C1**; 29, 59
Diocaesarea see Sepphoris
Diospolis see Lod
Doberus **214 D2**
Docus see Dok
Dok (Docus, Mount of the Temptation) **192 A3**; 37
Dophkah **115 A2**; 26
Dor (Dora, Tantura) **77 B2**; 28, 29, 32, 33, 37, 38, 59
Dothan **147 C4**; 33, 59
Dumah (hill country of Judah) **95 B3**; 29
Dumah (Arabia) **214 G5**

Ebal, Mount **148 C2**; 28, 59
Eben-ezer (Aphek) **79 D1**; 30
Eben-ezer see Jeshanah
Ebron see Abdon
Ecbatana **214 I4**; 34, 35, 36
Eden see Beth-eden
Eden **214 I8**
Edom (region) **202 C4**; 25, 26, 32, 33, 34, 35, 59
Edrei **202 D2**; 59
Eglaim **202 C3**; 37
Eglon **85 B3 C4**; 28
Egypt (region) **214 F5**; 24, 25, 32, 34, 35, 36, 40
Egypt, Brook of **115 A1 B1**; 34, 35
Ekron (Accaron) **79 D3**; 28, 29, 30, 34, 37
Elah, valley of **79 C3 D3**; 59
Elam (Susiana) (region) **214 I4**; 34, 35
Elam **85 C3**
Elasa **148 B4**
Elath (Aila) **114 C4**; 32, 34
Elealeh **202 C3**
Elon **85 C2**
Elon see Aijalon
Elteke see Eltekeh
Eltekeh (Elteke) **79 D2**; 34
Emmaus (Nicopolis) **85 C1**; 37, 38
Emmaus **162 A2 C2 C3**
En-dor **129 C5**; 28, 29
En-eglaim **105 C1**
En-gannim **85 C2**
En-gannim see Beth-haggan
En-gedi (Hazazon-tamar) **105 C3**; 29, 30, 37, 38, 59
En-haddah **129 C4**
En-hazor **129 C2**; 29
Enmishpat see Kadesh-barnea
En-rimmon (Ain, Ain-rimmon) **95 B3**; 29
En-rogel **162 D3**; 32
En-shemesh **163 E3**
Ephah **214 G5**
Ephesus **214 E3**; 34, 35, 36, 40
Ephraim see Ophra
Ephraim (tribe) 29, 30, 32
Ephrath see Bethlehem
Ephrathah see Bethlehem
Ephron **202 C2**
Ephron see Ophra
Erech (Uruk) **214 I4**; 26, 34, 35
Esdraelon, plain of see Jezreel, valley of
Eshan **95 B3**
Eshtaol **85 D2**; 30
Eshtemoa **95 C3**; 29
Etam **95 D1**
Etham **214 F4**; 26
Ether **85 C3**
Ethiopia see Cush
Euphrates (river) **214 H4**; 24, 34, 35
Ezem **114 B1**; 29
Ezion-geber **114 B4**; 26

Fair Havens **214 D3**

Gaash **148 B4**
Gabatha **129 B4**
Gad (tribe) 29, 30
Gadara (Perea) **202 C2**; 37, 38
Gadara (Decapolis) **202 C2**; 37, 38
Galatia (region) **214 F3**; 40
Galatian Phrygia (region) **214 F3**
Galilee (region) **129 C2 C4**; 34, 37, 38, 59
Galilee, Sea of (Kinneret, Lake of

229

GAZETTEER

Gennesaret, Sea of (Chinnereth, Sea of Tiberias) 129 D4
Gallim 162 D3
Gamala 202 C2; 37, 38
Gath (Metheg-ammah) 79 D3; 28, 30, 32, 59
Gath see Gittaim
Gath-hepher 129 B4
Gath-rimmon 79 C1; 29
Gaudos see Cauda
Gaulanitis (region) 38
Gaza 79 B4; 24, 28, 29, 30, 32, 33, 34, 35, 36, 37, 38, 59, 63
Gazara see Gezer
Geba (Manasseh) 147 C5
Geba (Gibeah, Gibeath-elohim) (Benjamin) 163 E2; 29, 30, 33
Geba (Ephraim) 148 C3
Gebal 214 G4; 34
Gederah (Jerusalem hills) 162 C2
Gederah (Gederoth) (Shephelah) 85 C2; 29
Gederoth see Gederah
Gederothaim 85 C2
Gedor 95 C2; 29
Gennesaret see Chinnereth
Gerar 114 B1; 25, 37
Gerasa 202 C2; 37, 38
Gergesa 202 C2
Gerizim, Mount 148 C2; 28, 30, 37, 59
Geshur (region) 28, 29
Gezer (Gazara) 85 C1; 28, 29, 30, 32, 33, 37, 59
Gibbethon 79 C2; 29
Gibe-ah 95 C1
Gibeah 162 D3; 30, 33
Gibeah see Geba
Gibeath-elohim see Geba
Gibeon 162 D2; 28, 29, 30, 32, 59
Gihon (spring) 186, 190
Gilboa 147 D4; 30
Gilead 202 C2; 30
Gilead (region) 202 C2; 25, 29, 30, 33, 34, 35, 37, 59
Gilgal (coastal plain) 79 D1
Gilgal (Ephraim) 148 C3; 33
Gilgal (Jordan valley) 192 A3; 28, 30
Gimzo 79 D2
Ginae see Beth-haggan
Gischala 129 C2; 36, 38
Gittaim (Gath) 79 D2
Golan 202 C2
Golgotha 186, 190
Gophna (Ophni) 148 C4; 38
Gortyna 214 E3
Goshen 95 B3
Goshen (region) 214 F4; 26
Gozan 214 G3; 34
Greece (region) 214 D3
Gurbaal see Jagur

Hadid (Adida) 79 D2; 37
Haifa 73 A5
Halhul 95 C2
Halicarnassus 214 E3
Ham 202 C2
Hamath 214 G4; 30, 34, 35
Hammath (Jordan valley) 192 B2
Hammath (Ammathus) (Galilee) 129 D4; 29
Hammon 73 B3; 29
Hannathon 129 B4; 29
Hapharaim 147 B3
Haran 214 G3; 24, 25, 34, 35
Har-heres see Beth-shemesh
Harim 85 C3
Harod (valley of Jezreel) 147 D3
Harod (Benjamin) 163 E4
Harosheth-ha-goiim 147 B2; 30
Hauran (region) 214 G4; 33
Havvoth-jair (region) 202 C2; 30, 32
Hazar-addar 114 B2
Hazarmaveth (region) 214 I8
Hazar-shual 114 B1
Hazazon-tamar see En-gedi
Hazazon-tamar see Tamar
Hazeroth 148 C2
Hazor (Galilee) 129 D2; 25, 28, 29, 30, 32, 33, 34, 59, 63
Hazor (Benjamin) 162 D3
Hazor, Plain of 129 D2
Hebron (Kiriath-arba) 95 C2; 25, 26, 28, 29, 30, 32, 33, 34, 35, 37, 38, 59, 63
Helam (Alema) 202 D2
Heleph 129 C4; 29
Heliopolis (On) 214 F4; 24, 26, 35
Helkath 129 A4; 29
Hepher 77 B3; 28, 32
Heptapegon (Tabgha) 129 D3
Hereth 95 C2
Hermon, Mount (Senir, Sirion) 202 C3 C4; 28, 59
Herodium 38
Heshbon 202 C3; 26, 29, 30
Hierapolis 214 E3; 40

Hilen see Holon
Hippos (Susitha) 202 C2; 37, 38
Holon (Hilen) 95 C2; 29
Hor, Mount 114 A2 B2 C2; 26
Horeb see Sinai, Mount
Horem 129 C2; 29
Horesh 95 C3; 30
Hormah (Zephath) 114 B1 C1; 26, 28
Horonaim 202 C3
Hosah (Uzu) 73 C2; 29
Hukkok 129 C3; 29
Hushah 162 C4

Ibleam (Bileam) 147 C4; 28, 29, 32, 59
Iconium 214 F3; 40
Idalah 129 B4
Idumea (region) 214 F4 G4; 37, 38
Illyricum (Dalmatia) (region) 214 C2; 40
Iphtah (Tricomias) 85 D3; 29
Iphtah-el 129 B4
Irpeel 162 D2
Ir-shemesh see Beth-shemesh
Israel (region) 214 G4; 32, 33, 34
Issachar (tribe) 29, 30, 32
Itabyrium see Tabor, Mount
Italy (region) 214 B2; 36
Ithlah 162 B3
Ituraea see Jetur
Iye-abarim 202 C3; 26

Jabbok (river) 192 B2
Jabesh-gilead 202 C2; 30
Jabneel (Jamnia) (coastal plain) 79 C2; 29
Jabneel (Galilee) 129 B4
Jacob's well 148 C2
Jagur (Gurbaal) 95 B4
Jahaz 202 C3; 29, 30
Jamnia 79 C2; 37, 38
Jamnia see Jabneel
Janim 95 C2
Janoah (Galilee) 129 B1 B3 D1
Janoah (Ephraim) 148 D3; 29
Japhia 129 B4
Jarmuth 85 C2; 28, 29
Jarmuth see Ramoth
Jashub 77 C3
Jattir 95 C3; 29
Javan (region) 214 E3
Jazer 202 C3; 29
Jebus see Jerusalem
Jehud 79 D1; 29
Jekabzeel (Kabzeel) 95 B4; 29
Jericho 192 A3; 26, 28, 29, 30, 32, 33, 35, 37, 38, 59, 63
Jeruel, Wilderness of 105 B2 B3
Jerusalem (Salem, Jebus, Aelia Capitolina) 163 D3; 24, 25, 28, 30, 32, 33, 34, 35, 37, 38, 40, 59, 63
Jeshanah (Eben-ezer) 148 C4; 33
Jeshua 95 B4
Jetur (Ituraea) 202 C1
Jezreel (hill country of Judah) 95 C3
Jezreel (valley of Jezreel) 147 C3; 29, 32, 33, 59
Jezreel, valley of (Great Plain, plain of Esdraelon, plain of Megiddo) 147 C3; 59
Jogbehah 202 C2; 30
Jokdeam 95 C3; 29
Jokmeam see Jokneam
Jokneam (Jokmeam) 147 B3; 28, 32
Joktan (region) 214 H6
Joppa 79 C1; 29, 30, 32, 33, 37, 38, 40, 59, 63
Jordan (river) 192 B2
Jotapata see Jotbah
Jotbah (Jotapata) 129 B4
Judah, Wilderness of 105 B1 B3
Judah (region, tribe) 29, 30, 32, 33, 34, 35
Judea (region) 37, 38
Julias see Bethsaida
Juttah 95 C3; 29

Kabzeel see Jekabzeel
Kadesh 214 G4
Kadesh-barnea (Enmishpat, Massah, Meribah) 114 A2 B2; 26
Kain 95 C3
Kamon 202 C3; 30
Kanah 129 B1; 29
Kanah, Brook of 79 D1; 59
Karnaim see Carnaim
Kartan (Kiriathaim) 129 C2
Kattath see Kitron
Kedar (region) 214 G4
Kedemoth 202 C2; 29
Kedesh (Cadasa) (Galilee) 129 D2; 28, 29, 30, 32, 38, 59
Kedesh (Ziddim) (Galilee) 129 D4; 29
Kedron 79 C3
Kedron (Belus) (river) 79 C2
Keilah 85 D3; 30
Kenath (Nobah) 202 D2
Kerioth 202 C3

Kerioth-hezron 95 C3
Khume see Kue
Kidron, Brook 163 E4
Kir see Kir-hareseth
Kir-hareseth (Kir) 202 C3; 33, 59
Kiriathaim 202 C3; 29
Kiriathaim see Kartan
Kiriath-arba see Hebron
Kiriath-jearim (Baalah, Mahaneh-dan) 162 C3; 28, 29, 30, 33
Kiriath-sannah see Debir
Kiriath-sepher see Debir
Kishon 129 C5
Kishon (river) 47 C3; 59
Kitron (Kattath) 129 A4; 28
Kittim (Cyprus) 214 F3
Kue (Khume) (region) 214 G3; 34, 35

Lachish 85 C3; 24, 25, 32, 33, 34, 35, 59
Lacedaemon see Sparta
Lahmam 85 C3
Laish see Dan
Laishah 162 D3
Lakkum 129 D4; 29
Laodicea 214 E3; 40
Lasea 214 D3; 40
Lebanon, Mountains of 202 C1; 35
Lebanon, valley of 202 C1
Lebonah 148 C3; 30
Lehi 162 B4; 30
Leja (region) 202 D2
Leshem see Dan
Libnah 85 C3; 28, 29
Libya (Lubim) (region) 214 E4; 35, 40
Lod (Lydda, Diospolis) 79 D2; 37, 38, 40, 59, 63
Lo-debar (Jordan valley) 192 B2; 29
Lo-debar (Transjordan) 202 C2
Lubim see Libya
Lud see Lydia
Ludu see Lydia
Luz see Bethel
Lycaonia (region) 214 F3
Lycia (region) 214 E3 F3; 40
Lydda see Lod
Lydia (Lud, Ludu) (region) 214 E3; 35
Lystra 214 F3; 40

Maan 202 C4
Maarath (Maroth) 95 C2
Macedonia (region) 214 D2; 36, 41
Machaerus 202 C3; 37, 38
Madai (Media, Medes) (region) 214 I3 J3; 24, 34, 35, 36
Madmannah (Beth-marcaboth) 95 B3
Madmen 202 C3
Madon (Adamah) 129 C4; 28
Magbish 85 C3
Magdala see Taricheae
Mahalab see Ahlab
Mahanaim 202 C2; 25, 29, 32, 33, 59
Makaz 85 C2; 32
Maked 202 D2
Makkedah 85 C3; 28
Malatha 37, 38
Malta 214 B3; 40
Mamre (Terebinthus) 95 C2; 25
Manahath 162 D3
Manasseh (tribe) 29, 30
Maon 95 C3; 29, 30
Mareshah (Marisa) 85 C3; 37
Marisa see Mareshah
Maroth see Maarath
Masada 105 C4; 30, 37, 38
Mashal see Mishal
Massah see Kadesh-barnea
Mattanah 202 C3; 26
Medeba 202 C3; 29, 32, 37, 59
Medai see Madai
Medes see Madai
Megiddo 147 C3; 24, 28, 29, 30, 32, 33, 34, 35, 59, 63
Me-jarkon 79 C1
Memphis (Noph) 214 F5; 24, 26, 34, 35, 36
Mepha-ath 202 C3
Meribah see Kadesh-barnea
Merom 129 C3 D2
Merom, waters of 129 C3 D2; 28
Meshech (Mushki) (region) 214 F3
Mesopotamia (Paddan-aram) (region) 214 H3; 24
Metheg-ammah see Gath
Michmash 163 E2; 30
Michmethath 148 C2; 29
Middin 105 C1
Midian (region) 214 G5; 26
Migdal-el 129 D2
Migdal-gad 85 C3; 29
Migdol 214 F4; 26, 35
Migron 163 E2
Miletus 214 E3; 35, 40
Minnith 202 C3
Mishal (Mashal) 73 B4; 29

Misrephoth-maim 73 B3; 28
Mitylene 214 E3
Mizpah (hill country of Judah) 162 D2; 28, 30, 33, 35
Mizpah (Transjordan) 202 C2; 30
Mizpeh, valley of 202 C1; 28
Moab, city of 202 D3; 59
Moab, plains of 192 B3; 26, 59
Moab (region) 202 C3; 29, 30, 32, 33, 34, 35, 59
Modein see Modin
Modin (Modein) 148 B4
Moladah 114 B1; 29
Mons Casius see Baal-zephon
Moreh, hill of 129 C5; 30
Moresheth-gath 85 C3
Motza (Colonia Amasa, ? Emmaus) 162 C3
Mount of the Temptation see Dok
Mushki see Meshech
Musri (region) 214 G3
Myra 214 E3; 40
Mysia (region) 214 E3

Naarah see Naaran
Naaran (Naarah) 192 A3; 29
Nabadath 202 C3
Nabateans (tribe) 34, 37, 38
Nahaliel 192 B3
Nahalol (Nahalal) 129 A4 B4; 28
Nahash 85 C3
Nain 129 C5
Naphtali (region) 129 C3; 29, 30, 32, 33, 59
Naphath-dor (region) 77 C2; 32
Nazareth 129 B4
Neapolis (Macedonia) 214 D2; 40
Neapolis (Palestine) 148 C2; 38
Nebaioth (region) 214 G4
Neballat 79 D2
Nebo (hill country of Judah) 95 C2
Nebo (Transjordan) 202 C3
Nebo, Mount 202 C3; 26, 59
Negeb (region) 25, 26, 59
Neiel 73 C4; 29
Nephtoah 163 D3
Netophah 95 D1
Nezib 85 D3
Nibshan 105 C1 C2; 29
Nicopolis 214 D3
Nicopolis see Emmaus
Nile (river) 214 F3
Nimrim 192 B4
Nimrim, Waters of 192 B4; 59
Nimrud (Calah) 214 H3; 34
Nineveh 214 H3; 24, 34, 35
No see Thebes
No-amon see Thebes
Nob 162 D3; 30
Nobah see Kenath
Noph see Memphis

Oboth 114 C2; 26
On see Heliopolis
Ono 79 D1
Ophir (region) 214 G7 H7
Ophni see Gophna
Ophrah (coastal plain) 77 C4
Ophrah (valley of Jezreel) 147 C3 D3; 30
Ophrah (Aphairema, Ephron, Ephraim) (Benjamin) 148 C4; 30, 33, 37, 38

Paddan-aram see Mesopotamia
Palmyra see Tadmor
Pamphylia (region) 214 F3; 40
Paneas see Caesarea Philippi
Paphos 214 F4; 40
Parah 163 E2; 29
Paran, Wilderness of 114 B3; 26
Patara 214 E3; 40
Pathros (region) 214 F5; 35
Patmos 214 E3
Pekod (Puqudu) (region) 214 I4
Pella 202 C2; 37, 38, 40, 59
Pelusium (Sin) 214 F4; 26, 36
Peniel see Penuel
Penuel (Peniel) 192 B2; 25, 30, 33
Perea (region) 37, 38
Perga 214 F3; 40
Pergamum 214 E3; 40
Persepolis 214 J5; 35, 36
Persia (Persis) (region) 214 J5; 35, 36
Persis see Persia
Pethor 214 G3
Petra 202 C4
Pharathon see Pirathon
Pharpar (river) 202 D1; 59
Phasaelis 214 F3; 38
Philadelphia (Asia) 214 E3; 40
Philadelphia (Transjordan) 202 C3
Philippi 214 D2; 40
Philistia (region) 30, 33
Phoenicia (region) 37, 40
Phoenix 214 D3
Phrygia (region) 214 F3; 34, 35, 36, 40

GAZETTEER

Pibeseth 214 F4
Pinon *see* Punon
Pirathon (Pharathon) 148 C2; 30
Pisgah, Mount 202 C3; 59
Pisidia (region) 214 F3; 40
Pithom 214 F4; 26
Pontus (region) 214 G2; 40
Ptolemais *see* Acco
Punon (Pinon) 114 C2; 26
Puqudu *see* Pekod
Put (region) 214 D4
Puteoli 214 B2; 40

Raamses (Tanis, Zoan) 214 F4; 26
Rabbah (Jerusalem hills) 162 C3; 29
Rabbah (Rabbath-ammon, Rabbath-bene-ammon, Philadelphia) (Ammon) 202 C3; 24, 30, 32, 33, 37, 38, 59
Rabbath-ammon *see* Rabbah
Rabbath-bene-ammon *see* Rabbah
Rabbath-moab 202 C3
Rabbith 147 D4
Rages *see* Rhagae
Rakkath 129 D4; 29
Rakkon 79 C1; 29
Rama 129 C3
Ramah (Galilee) 129 B2
Ramah (Jerusalem hills) 162 D2; 30, 33
Ramah *see* Arimathea
Ramathaim-zophim *see* Arimathea
Ramath-mizpeh 202 C3; 29
Ramoth (Remeth, Jarmuth) 192 B1; 29
Ramoth-gilead 202 C2; 29, 32, 33, 59
Raphia 114 A1; 34, 37, 38
Raphon 202 D2
Rathamin *see* Arimathea
Red Sea 115 B3; 24, 26
Rehob (coastal plain) 73 B4
Rehob (Galilee) 129 B2; 28, 29
Rehob (Jordan valley) 192 A2
Rehob (Transjordan) 202 C2
Rehoboth 114 B1
Remeth *see* Ramoth
Rephaim, valley of 162 C4
Reuben (tribe) 29, 30
Rezeph 214 G3
Rhagae (Rages) 214 J3; 36
Rhegium 214 C3; 40
Rhodes 214 E3; 35, 36, 40
Riblah 214 G4; 35
Rimmon (Dimnah, Rimmono) 129 B4; 29
Rimmon *see* En-rimmon
Rimmono *see* Rimmon
Rogelim 202 C2
Rome 214 B2; 40
Rumah 129 B4

Saba *see* Sheba
Salamis 214 F3; 40
Salecah 202 D2
Salem 148 C2
Salem *see* Jerusalem
Salim 192 B2
Salmone (Sammanion) 214 E3
Salt, City of 105 C1 C2; 29
Salt, valley of 114 B1; 59
Samaria (Sebaste) 147 C5; 33, 34, 37, 38, 40, 59, 63
Samaria (region) 33, 35, 37, 38
Sammanion *see* Salmone
Samos 214 E3; 40
Samothrace 214 E2
Sansannah 95 B2
Sardis (Sardes) 214 E3; 35, 36, 40
Sarepta *see* Zarephath
Sarid 129 B5; 29
Scythopolis *see* Beth-shean
Sebaste *see* Samaria
Secacah 105 C1; 29
Sela 202 C4
Seleucia Pieria 214 G3; 40
Selsam *see* Sibmah
Senaah 192 A3
Senir, Sirion *see* Hermon, Mount
Sepphoris (Diocaesarea) 129 B4; 37, 38
Shaalabin *see* Shaalbim
Shaalbim (Shaalabin, Shaalbon) 148 B4; 28, 29, 32
Shaalbon *see* Shaalbim
Shaaraim *see* Sharuhen
Shahazumah 129 C5
Shamir (hill country of Judah) 95 B3
Shamir (Ephraim) 148 C3; 30
Sharon, plain of 77 B3 B4; 59
Sharuhen (Shaaraim, Shilhim) 114 A1; 29, 33
Sheba (Saba) (region) 214 H8
Shechem 148 C3; 25, 28, 29, 30, 32, 33, 37, 59, 63
Shema 114 B1; 29
Shihor-libnath (river) 77 B4; 59
Shikkeron 79 C3
Shilhim *see* Sharuhen
Shiloh 148 C3; 28, 29, 30, 32, 59
Shimron (Simonias) 129 B4; 28, 29
Shion 129 C4
Shittim *see* Abel-shittim
Shunem 129 C5; 29, 33
Shur, Wilderness of 115 A1; 25, 26
Sibmah (Selsam) 202 C3; 29
Sicyon 214 D3
Sidon 214 G4; 33, 34, 35, 36, 40
Siloam, Pool of 186, 190

Simeon (tribe) 29, 30
Simonias *see* Shimron
Sin *see* Pelusium
Sinai, Mount (Horeb) 115 A1 A2; 26
Smyrna 214 E3; 40
Soco (Socoh) (coastal plain) 77 C3; 32, 33
Soco (Socoh) (Shephelah) 85 C2; 30
Soco (Socoh) (hill country of Judah) 95 C3
Sorek, valley of 85 C2
Sparta (Lacedaemon) 214 D3; 36
Strato's Tower *see* Caesarea
Succoth (Jordan valley) 192 B2; 25, 29, 30, 32, 59
Succoth (Egypt) 214 F4; 26
Susa 214 I4; 24, 34, 35, 36
Susiana *see* Elam
Susitha *see* Hippos
Sychar 148 C2
Syene 214 F6; 35, 36
Syracuse 214 C3; 40
Syria (Aram) (region) 202 D1; 33, 34, 35, 40

Taanach 147 C3; 28, 29, 30, 32, 33, 59
Taanath-shiloh 148 D2; 29
Tabbath 192 B2; 30
Tabgha *see* Heptapegon
Tabor, Mount (Itabyrium) 129 C4; 29, 30, 37, 59
Tadmor (Palmyra) 214 G4; 24, 32
Tahpanhes 214 F4; 26, 35
Tamar (Hazazon-tamar) 192 A4; 26, 32
Tantura *see* Dor
Tappuah (Tephon) 148 B3; 28, 29
Taralah 162 D2
Taricheae (Dalmanutha, Magdala) 129 D4; 37, 38
Tarsus 214 F3; 36, 40
Tekoa 95 D2; 33
Tema 214 G5
Teman 202 C4
Tephon *see* Tappuah
Terebinthus *see* Mamre
Thamna *see* Timnath-serah
Thebes (No, No-amon) 214 F5; 34, 35, 36
Thebez 147 D5; 30
Thessalonica 214 D2; 40
Three Taverns 214 B2; 40
Thyatira 214 E3; 40
Tiberias 129 D4; 38
Tigris (river) 214 H4; 24
Timna (Negev) 114 B4
Timna (Arabia) 214 I8
Timnah (Shephelah) 85 C2; 29, 30
Timnah (Jerusalem hills) 162 B4; 29
Timnath *see* Timnath-serah
Timnath-heres *see* Timnath-serah

Timnath-serah (Thamna, Timnath, Timnath-heres) 148 B3; 38
Tiphsah 214 G3; 32
Tirzah 147 D5; 28, 33, 59
Tishbe 202 C2; 33
Tob 202 D2
Togarmah 214 G3
Trachonitis (region) 202 D1; 38
Tricomias *see* Iphtah
Troas 214 E3; 40
Tubal (region) 214 G3
Tyre (Tyrus) 73 C2; 24, 29, 32, 33, 34, 35, 36, 37, 38, 40, 59, 63
Tyre of Tobiah 202 C3
Tyrus *see* Tyre

Ur 214 I4; 24, 25, 35
Urartu *see* Ararat
Uzal 214 H7
Uzu *see* Hosah
Uzzen-sheerah 114 B4

Yiron 129 C2; 29

Zaanannim 129 C4
Zair *see* Zior
Zalmonah 202 C4; 26
Zanoah (Shephelah) 85 D2
Zanoah (hill country of Judah) 95 C3; 29
Zaphon 192 B2; 29, 30
Zarephath (Sarepta) 73 C1; 33
Zarethan (Zeredah, Zererah) 192 A2; 30, 32
Zebulun, valley of 73 A4; 59
Zebulun (tribe) 29, 30, 32
Zela 162 D3
Zelzah 162 D2; 30
Zemaraim 148 C4; 33
Zenan 85 B3
Zephath *see* Hormah
Zephathah, vale of 79 C3 C4
Zered, Brook 192 A4; 59
Zeredah 114 B3
Zeredah *see* Zarethan
Zererah *see* Zarethan
Zereth-shahar 192 B3; 29
Ziddim *see* Kedesh
Ziklag 114 B1; 29, 30
Zin, Wilderness of 114 B2 C2; 26
Zior (Zair) 95 C2
Ziph (hill country of Judah) 95 C3; 29, 30
Ziph (Negev) 114 B1
Ziph, Wilderness of 95 C3
Zoan *see* Raamses
Zoar (Bela) 192 A4; 25, 37
Zobah (region) 214 G4
Zorah 85 C2; 30

INDEX

Page numbers in italics refer to illustrations or their captions. The Arabic particle "el-" has been disregarded in alphabetization.

Aaron 123
Abel-beth-maacah 130, 136, 177
Abiathar 171, 179
Abijam, king of Judah 178
Abimelech, king of Gerar 118–119
Abimelech (son of Gideon) 152
Abiram 123
Abishai 103, 177
Abner 31, 99, 172, 208
Abraham 194, 195; dates of 17, 24; called by God to promised land 24; travels of 25, 119, 217; heir born to 25; fights Canaanite coalitions 24, 134, 195; at Beer-sheba 120; at Bethel 153; at Hebron 98–99, *98*; at Shechem 24, 151, 153
Absalom 31, *32*, 151, 177, 208
Abu Ghosh (Emmaus?) 188
Abu Simbel: temple at *216*
Acco (Ptolemais) 58, 72, *72*, 74, 75
Achan 196
Achish, king of Gath 31, 119
Achzib *72*, 74
Acts, book of 18, 21, 42; cited 41, 42, 51, 56, 75, 82, 88, 159, 189, 213, 223, 224, *224*
Adad-nirari III, king of Assyria 137
Adam 68
'Admah 194
Admon, Mount 130
Adonijah 177, 179
Adullam 86, 87, 88, 109, 173; cave of 87, 109
Adummim see Maaleh Adummim
Afula 152
agriculture 60, 62, 72, 78; ancient 74, 80, 98, 194; —, difficult in Galilee 130; —, limited in Judah 149; modern 60, *63*, 78, 134, 193; unchanged techniques in 98, *142*, *142*, *143*; see also pastoralism
Ahab, king of Israel 33, *34*, 134, 158, 208; in conflict with prophets 33, 75, 127, 136, 154, 155, 156; fights Syrians 33, 136, 155; death of 92, 155–156
Ahaz, king of Judah 35, 88, 124, 178
Ahaziah, king of Judah 156, 158
Ahijah 33, 153, 178
Ahimaaz 177
Ahimelech 171
Ahlab 74, 75
Ai (Khirbet et-Tell) 27, 153, 164, 196
Aijalon 87, 88, 178; valley of 58, 84, 86, 164, 171
Ain Karem 181–183, *181*
Akaba, Gulf of 117, 123
Alexander the Great 36, *36*, 74, 180, 216, 223
Alexander II of Russia 18
Alexander Jannaeus 39, 112, *211*
Alexandria 21
Allonim hills 130, 136
altars *118*, *156*, 176
Amalekites 119, 121, 152
Amasa 177
Amaziah, king of Judah 87–88, 208
Amaziah (priest of Bethel) 154
Amen-en-ope, Wisdom of 217
Amman 198, 210; statue from *206*
Ammon 202, 204, 206, 208; founded by son of Lot 25; settled by Israelites 25; Israelite rule extended to 31, 208
Ammonites 180, 207; and Jabesh-gilead 29, see also Nahash; defeated by Jephthah 207
Amorites: equated with Canaanites 206
Amos 35, 98, 103, 116, 154; book of, cited 98, 116, 154, 156, 196, 204
Ananias (of Damascus) 213
Anathoth (Anata) 179, *179*, 180
Andrew, St 140
Anim 94
animals: domestic 66, 66–67, 98, *142*, *143*, 213; wild 42, 62, 66, *66–67*, 103, 134, 164; identification of biblical 66; in art 66, *66–67*, 88, *109*, *125*, *126*, *135*, *154*, *157*, *160*, *222*

Annunciation *50*
Antioch (in Pisidia) 42
Antioch (in Syria) 21, 41, 42, 223
Antiochus IV (Seleucid king) 37, 180–181, 223
Aphek (Aphik) 74, 81; Philistine victory at 29, 82, 153; Syrian defeat at 155
Apocrypha 18
Apollos 42
Aquila 42
Arabah see under rift valley
Arabia: equated with Nabatean kingdom 42, 213
Arad 118, *118–119*, 120, 121; basin 119, 120, 121
Aramaic *216*; script *16*
Arbatta 134
Archelaus 39
archers *92*, *93*
architecture, domestic *98*, *138*
Aretas IV, king of the Nabateans 211, 213
Aristobulus I, prince of Judea 37–39, 134, 137
Ark of the Covenant 82, 126, 138; at Bethel 152, 154; at Kiriath-jearim 172; at Jerusalem 176, *183*; captured by Philistines 153
Arnon, river (Seil el-Mojib) 202, 204, 206, 207, 208, 210
Aroer 121
art: Bible in 43, *44–56*
Artemis *see* Diana
Arumah (Khirbet el-Urma) 152
Asa, king of Judah 119, 136, 178
Asahel 172
Ashdod 81, *81*, 82
Asher, tribe of 152; territory of 74, 136
Ashkelon 81; Samson at 82
Ashurbanipal *218*
Asia 42
Askar 159
asses 66, 185, 207
Assyria 33, 92, 158, 208, 216, 218–221; part of fertile crescent 24; empire of *34*, 216; defeats Damascus *34*, 35; defeated by Babylonians 35, 36; and Israel 33, *34*, 134, 178; and Judah 34, 88, 217; army of *93*, see also under Lachish
Astarte: figurines of *161*
Ataroth 208
Athaliah 33–35
Athens 42, 223
Athlit 78, 80
Attalia 42
Attara-Rama basin 150
Augustus Caesar (Octavian) *38*, 39, 137, 158
Authorized (King James) Version 21, 173
el-Azariya 184, 185
Azekah 86, 87, 88, *89*

Baal 33; prophets of and Elijah 150, 154
Baal-hanan 86
Baalis, king of the Ammonites 210
Baal-peor 207
Baal-shalisha 168
Baasha, king of Israel 136, 178
Babel, Tower of *221*
Babylon 36, 92, 216, 221–222, *221*, 224; empire of 35, *65*, 216; defeats Assyria 35, 36; attacks cities of Judah 35, 88, *89*, 180, 208; Jews exiled to 17, 36, 112, 116, 180, 216, 221; defeated by Persia 35, 36, 223; Ishtar Gate of, reconstructed *222*, *222*; witchcraft in *161*; as symbol 222, 224
Babylonia: part of fertile crescent 24
Bahurim 177
baking *143*
Balaam 207
Balak, king of Moab 207
Balata 159
Baniyas 211, *211*; *see also* Caesarea Philippi
Barak 29, 152
Barnabas, St 42; "Epistle of" 18
Bartimaeus 198
Baruch 17

basalt: common in Galilee 137, *138*, 140, *141*; grinders made from 137, *139*
Bashan 204, 207; cattle of 67, 156, 204; mountain of 164
bears 62, 66, 103, 134, 164
Beatitudes, Mount 141
bedouin *104*, *121*, 142; *see also* pastoralism
Beer-lahai-roi 119
Beer-sheba 98, 118, 119, 120, 126, 153; Patriarchs at 24, 119, 120, *121*; as southernmost point of promised land 120; post-exilic resettlement of 120–121; figurine from *121*; ancient tell of 120, 121, *121*; basin 94, 119, 121; —, settlement in 119—120
Beitin *154*, *see also* Bethel
Bel *17*, 221
Bene-berak 87
Ben-hadad, king of Syria 136, 155, 178
Benjamin, tribe of 29, 152; territory of 165, 168, 178, 198; and Levite's concubine 168; seizes wives at Shiloh 153; attacked by Philistines 29; part of kingdom of Judah 33, 98, 149, 178
Bernice 82
Beroea 42
Beth-anath 136
Bethany: Jesus at 39, 184, 185, 189
Bethany "beyond the Jordan" 198
Beth-arabah 112
Beth-aven 154
Bethel (Beitin) 153, *154*, 168; Patriarchs at 24, 25, 153, *154*, *160*, 164; shrine at 33, 136, 152, 153, 154, *154*, *160*
Bethel hills 27, 29, 33, 58, 60, 149, *149*, *163*, 164
Beth-haggan (Jenin) 149, 156
Beth-horon 178
Bethlehem 58, 94, 98, 100, *100*, *101*, 103, 104, 168; equated with Ephrath 168–169; birthplace of David and Jesus 39, 100, 103; Philistines at 87; children slaughtered at 39, 103; church of the Nativity at *100*, *101*; Rachel's tomb near 168
Beth-phage 185
Bethsaida 140, 141
Beth-shean *200*, 207; standard from *200*; valley of 151, 152, 154, 158, 194, 200
Beth-shemesh 86, 87, 88, 136
Bible: composition of 14–18; content of 14; manuscript texts of 18–21, 113; and oral tradition 17, 18; printed texts of 21; sales of 14; variant readings of 18, 21; Hebrew version of 16, *16*, 17–18, 21; Greek version of *17*, 18; Latin version of 21; Samaritan version of 18; German version of 22, *22*; English versions of 21; in art 43, *44–56*, *see also* manuscripts, illuminated
el-Bireh 158
Bishop's Bible 21
Bithynia 42
Bitter Lakes 27
Boaz 100
Botticelli *49*
brazen serpent 117, 123, *125*, 126
bread *143*, 171

Caesarea 21, 42, 76, 78, 82, *83*, 189; principal city of Judea 39, 82; harbour at 82, *83*; aqueducts at 82, *83*; Peter at 41, 42, 82
Caesarea Philippi (Baniyas) 39, 141, 211, *211*, 213
Caiaphas: house of *186*, 190
Calah see Nimrud
Caleb 87, 99, 123
camels *121*, 142
Cana of Galilee (Kafr Kanna) 141
Canaan 25, *25*, 26, 28, 60, 62, 99; land of promised to Abraham 24, 151; Israelites' conquest of see under Joshua
Canaanites *121*, *153*, 200; coalitions of 136, 152, 164
Capernaum *138*, *138–139*, 141, 196; as

base for Jesus' ministry 39, 140–141; buildings at *138*, 140; synagogue at *138*, 140; —, carving from *183*
Carmel (southeast of Hebron) 98, 103
Carmel (range) 74, *147*, 149, 150–151; divides coastal plain 58, 72, 76; coast of 76; ancient settlement in 150, 151; routes through *146*, 150–151, 157; vegetation of 60
Carmel, Mount 72, *72*, 75, 81, 154; Elisha at 155; horn of 150, 154; springs on 82, *83*
cattle 66; *see also under* Bashan
chariots 88, *92*, *93*, 157; Canaanite 81, 136, 151, 200; of Jehu 156
Chebar, river 36, 221
Chemosh 208
Cherith, brook 207; Elijah at 208
Chinneroth 130, 136
Chorazin 141; synagogue at *141*
Christ *see* Jesus
Christianity 36; origins of 39; spread of 40, 41; and Jewish converts 41; and Gentile converts 40, 42
Chronicles, books of 17; 1 Chronicles, cited 86; 2 Chronicles, cited 81, 82, 88, 103, 108, 119, 178, 179, 208
cities of the plain 194–196; *see also* Gomorrah; Sodom
"city of palms" *see under* Jericho
City of Salt 112
Claudius 42
coastal plain 58, 178; divided by Mount Carmel 58; north of Mount Carmel 72–75, *73*; south of Mount Carmel 76–83, *77*, *79*; ancient settlement in 74, 80–81; and communications 81, 120, 151, 155; vegetation of 60
Codex Bezae 21
Codex Sinaiticus 18, *18*, 20
Codex Vaticanus 18, 20
coins *83*, *145*, *186*, 224
communications 58, 60, 81, 150–151, 224; *see also under individual regions*
Constantine 100, 190
copper: mined at Timna 124, 125, *125*; sceptre of *109*; snake of 126
Corinth 42, 223, *224*
Corinthians, epistles to: 1 Corinthians, cited 40, 42, 116–117, *143*; 2 Corinthians, cited 42, 112, 213
Cornelius (Roman centurion) 41, 42
Coverdale, Miles 21, 22, *22*
Cranach, Lukas 22, *22*
Cranmer, Thomas 22
Cromwell, Thomas 22
Crucifixion: site of 188
Crusades 64, 164, 178–179
cuneiform script *16*
Cyprus 42
Cyrus, king of Persia *17*, 35, 36, 180, 216, *223*; Cylinder of *17*

Damascus 31, 58, 208, 210; alliance with Judah 33, 136, 208; at war with Israel 33, *33*, 136, 137, 208; defeated by Assyrians *34*, 35, 137; St Paul at 42, 213; *see also* Syria
Dan, tribe of 136; harassed by Philistines 29, *29*, 87; migration of 165–168; territory of 81, *84*, 87
Dan (city) *128*, 134–136; as northernmost point of promised land 120, 130; shrine at 33, 136, *160*
Daniel, book of 17, 117, 221, 223
Darius: relief from palace of *223*
Dathan 123
David, king of Israel and Judah 31, 33, 86, 100, 103, 121, *138*, 157; and Goliath 29, 43, *48*, 87; and Philistines 31, *31*, 81, 82, 92, 103, 119, 164, 172, 173; and Saul 87, 103, 108–109, 171, 200; and Jonathan 103; becomes king 31, 99, 103, 153; moves capital to Jerusalem *see under* Jerusalem; and Ish-baal 172, 208; empire of *32*; and woman bathing (Bathsheba) *145*; servants of insulted 198; revolts against *32*, 136, 151, 177,

233

INDEX

178, 208; tomb of *174*
Dead Sea (Salt Sea) 58, 60, 104, *109*, *110*, 177, *192*, *193*, 194, *195*, *203*; rainfall at 194; salinity of 194, *195*
Dead Sea scrolls 18, *112*, 113, *113*; copper scroll 184; Isaiah scroll *113*; see also Qumran
Debir 86, 87
Deborah 29, 152
Decapolis 39, 210, 211, 213
Deganya A 193
Deganya B 193
Deir Sharaf basin 150, 154, *155*
Delilah 87
Demetrius II 37
Derbe 42
Deuteronomy, book of: cited 116, 117, 123, 124, 126, *145*, 151, *161*, 207; list of tribes in 26, *29*
Diana (Artemis) 42, 223, *224*
Dibon (Diban) 206, 208
dice *144*
Dimona 121
Dinah 151
dogs 66, 156
domestic utensils *17*, *89*, *111*, *118*, *145*
Donatello 55
Dor (Tantura) 78, *78*, 81, 82
Dothan 98; Elisha at 156; valley of (Sahel Arrabeh) 149, 150, *151*, 155
Doughty, C.M.: quoted 204
Duccio 51, *52*–*53*

Ebal, Mount (Jebel Islamiyeh) 150, 151
Ecclesiastes, book of 17
Edom 26, 123–124, 127, 152, 200, 202, 208; climate of 204; founded by Esau 25, 206; Moses requests passage through 123, 206; Israelites rule over 31, 208; Nabateans in 211
Edomites 87, 103, 124; and Judah 208, 210
Eglon, king of Moab 165, 198
Eglon 86, 87
Egypt 92, 126, 134, 216, 217–218, 223; part of fertile crescent *24*; Jewish communities in 18, 36, *216*; biblical manuscripts from 20, *20*; Patriarchs and 24, 25, *25*, 119, 120, 153, 217; Hebrews' bondage in 26, *44*; Jesus' flight to 39; in Madaba mosaic 65; and Palestinian art *153*, *154*, *156*; as symbol 217, 218
Ehud 165
Ein el-Ghuweir 112
Ein Qedeis 123
Ein el-Qudeirat 123, *123*
Ein et-Turaba 112
Ekron 81, 82, 87
Elath 117, 124
Elephantine Island 36, *216*
Eli 153
Eliashib *118*
Eliezer 24
Elijah 33, 75, 126, 127; opposes house of Omri 136, *154*, *155*, *156*; challenges prophets of Baal 150, 154; ascension of 194, 198
Elimelech 103, 204
Elisha 33, 198, 208; opposes house of Omri 136, 155, 156; and Syrians 156; curses insolent boys 164; restores Shunammite's son 141, *155*; and Jericho well 194, 196
Elizabeth 181, *181*
Elohim: term discussed 33
Emek ha-Mikhmetat see Sahel Mahneh
Emmaus 188–189
En-gedi 98, 108, *109*, 112; David at 108, *109*
En Harod 152
Ephes-dammim 87
Ephesians, epistle to 112, 176
Ephesus 42, 223, *224*
Ephraim, tribe of 26, *29*, 149, 152, 207; territory of 81, 151, 168; attacked by Philistines 29; "forest of" 151, 208
Ephron 165
Epistle of Barnabas 18
epistles 18, *20*; see also Corinthians; Ephesians; etc.
erosion 60, 62, *121*, *123*, *124*, *193*

Esau: founds Edom 25, 206; and Jacob 120, 206
Eshtaol *84*, 87
Eshtemoa 94
Essenes 112, 113
Esther, book of 17, 222–223, *223*
Ethiopians 216, 217–218
Euphrates, river *24*, 218, *221*
Eve 68
Exodus 25, 126, 127, 215, *216*; routes of 26–27, *27*, *115*, 117, 126; book of 17; —, cited *44*, 116, *116*, 126, 127, *160*, 216
Ezekiel 36; vision of 176; book of 36, 75, *75*; —, cited 67, *143*, 200, 217, 218, *221*
Ezion-geber 121, 123–124, *124*
Ezra 35, 36, 180, 216; book of, cited 17, 82, 158, 180, 216, 222, 223

Felix 82
fertile crescent *24*
fertility cults see under paganism
Festus 82
fish 72, 74, 134, 137, 141, *141*
Flémalle, Master of *48*
Former Prophets 17
Forum of Appius 224
Fra Angelico *51*
Francesca, Piero della *48*
frankincense 69

Gabara 141
Gabriel 181
Gad (prophet) 109, 112
Gad, tribe of *29*; territory of 207, 208
Gadara 210, 211
Galatia 42
Galatians, epistle to 42, 213
Galilee 38, 39, *39*, 40, 60, *128*–*129*, 130–141; physical features of 58, *128*, 130; geology of 130; rainfall in 130; lower *128*, 130, *130*, *146*; upper *128*, 130; —, difficult to settle in *128*, 130; vegetation of *128*; meaning of name 130; apportioned between tribes 136; menaced by Syria 33, 136, 137; conquered by Assyrians 35, 134, 137, 208; significance of Maccabean revolt for 37, 134; Jesus' ministry in 39, 140–141
Galilee, Sea of 39, 58, 60, 130, *130*, *132*–*133*, 140, 141, 193, *193*; many names for 130; population near 130; basalt manufactures from *139*; as centre of Jesus' ministry 140
Gallio 42
Gath 81, 82, 87
Gath-rimmon 87
Gaza 58, 78, 81, *81*, 88, 152; Samson at *46*, *81*, 82, 86
Geba (Gibeath-elohim) 169, *170*–*171*, *172*, 178
Gedaliah 36, 153, 180, 208–210
Gederah 88
Genesis, book of 17; as geographical text-book *64*–*65*; tribal lists in *29*, 98; cited 25, 26, *44*, 45, 67, 98, 99, 118–119, 120, 123, 134, 151, 153, *160*, 164, 168, 194, 194–195, 206, 207, 216, 217, 218, *221*
Geneva Bible 21
Gerar 118–119
Gerasa (Jerash) 210, *210*
Gerizim, Mount (Jebel et-Tur) 18, 150, 151, 152; sacred to Samaritans 158, 159, *159*
Gethsemane, Garden of 40, 188, 190, *191*
Geus, C.H.J. de 123
Gevat 130
Gezer 81, 86, 178; dagger from *161*; sacred stones at *160*
Ghiberti, Lorenzo *48*
Gibeah (Tell el-Ful) 168, 169, 171; Saul rules from 171, 172
Gibeath-elohim see Geba
Gibeon 87, *163*, 164, *165*, *166*–*167*, 172, 174, 177, 178; alliance with Joshua 28, 86, 164, 171; Saul and 171–172; as holy place 176; pool of 172, 180; great stone of 177
Gideon 152, 200
Gilboa (range) 149, 150, 151

Gilboa, Mount 31, 119, 200
Gilead 25, 204, 206, 207, 208
Gilgal (near Jericho) 152, 168, 169, 196, 198
Gilgal (in Jerusalem hills) 168, 169, 198
Givat Ha-more 141, 152
goats 66, *66*, 98, 120, see also pastoralism
golden calf see under idolatry
Goliath 29, 43, *48*, 82, 87
Gomorrah 98, 194, 195–196; as symbol for wickedness 196, 200
Good Samaritan 50, 158, 184
Goshen 26, 27
gospels 18, *20*, see also under John; Luke; Mark; Matthew
Great Bible 21, *22*
Greek: New Testament written in 36; version of Bible in 17, 18
Greeks: in Decapolis 210; at Dor 78; empire of 223, see also Alexander the Great; influence Jewish culture 36, 180–181

Haifa 72, 74, 75, 76; bay of 58, 72, *72*, *73*, 74
Hananiah 180
Hannah 152
Hanukkah: commemorates rededication of temple 37
Hanun, king of Ammon 198
Haran *24*, 120, 158; battle of 36
Harod, valley of 151, 152, 154, 158
Harosheth-ha-goiim 136
Hasmoneans 37, 38, 39, 78, 112
Hathor 125, *125*
Hazael, king of Syria 33, 35, 137
Hazor 28, 130, 134, *135*, 136; stelae at *160*
Hebrew: script, ancient forms of 16, *16*, 17; Bible in 16, 17–18, 21; see also Dead Sea Scrolls
Hebrews (Israelites, Jews): "people of the book" 14; oral traditions of 17; first appearance of in history 24; passim
Hebrews, epistle to 123, 137, 177
Hebron 98, 103, 153; Patriarchs at 24, 25, 98, *98*, 99, 103, 164; and Israelite invasion 87, 98, 99; Samson brings gates of Gaza to *46*, 82, 86; David king at 31, 99, 100, 103, 172, 173; Absalom at 103, 177; villages of 99; glassware from *98*
Hebron hills 94, *94*, 98, 103, 117, 119, 120, 121, 149, *163*, 164; rainfall of 94; vegetation of 94; and communications 98, 120; ceded to Edomites 103
Helbah 74
Helena, Empress 190
Helena of Adiabene, Queen: tomb of 188
Heliopolis 217
Henry VIII 22
Hereth, forest of 109, 112
Hermon (range) 204; as scene of Transfiguration? 39, 141, *204*
Herod Agrippa I 42
Herod Agrippa II 82
Herod Antipas 39, *39*, 137, 140, 189, 211, *211*
Herod family: tomb of 188
Herodium *102*–*103*
Herod the Great 38, 39, *39*, 98, 103, 137, 210; massacres infants 39; builds Caesarea 82; builds Herodium 103; builds at Jericho 196, *196*, *197*, 198; builds at Jerusalem 186, see also under Jerusalem, temple; rebuilds Machaerus 211; rebuilds Masada 112; rebuilds Samaria *154*
Hezekiah 35, 81, 88, 178, 217; and defence of Jerusalem against Assyrians 178–179, 184; tunnel of 178–179, *178*
Hiel of Bethel 198
Hiram, king of Tyre 74–75, *75*, 130
Holofernes *49*
Holy Land see Israel
Holy Spirit: descent of 56
Holy Week: events of 39–40, 188
Hor, Mount 123
Horbat Sevi (Khirbet el-Hureibeh)

136
Horeb, Mount see Sinai, Mount
Horesh 103
Hormah 121
horses; in warfare see chariots
Hosea 35; book of, cited 154, 156
Hoshea, king of Israel 35
Huleh valley 130, 134, 136
Hunt, W. Holman *100*

Iconium 42
idolatry: in Babylon 222; in Israel 33, 156; in Judah 36, 179; (worship of) golden calves 33, 44, 117, 127, *160*–*161*; punished by God 29
Idumea 38, *39*, *39*, 103, 210
Ijon 136
Imaret el-Khoreisha 123
Imwas 188
ink 17
Iphtah (Tarqumiya) *84*
Ira, Mount 121
Iron hills 151
Isaac 17, 24, *25*; at Beer-sheba 120; at Gerar 118–119; tomb of 99; sacrifice of *45*
Isaiah 35, 137; book of, cited 66, 69, 76, 112, 116, 130, 137, *142*, *145*, 152, *161*, 176, 178, 196, 217, 221
Ish-baal 31, 172, 208
Ishmael (assassin of Gedaliah) 36, 180
Israel, land of: use of term explained 12; part of fertile crescent *24*; and its neighbours 25, 216–224; physical geography of 58–60, *58*–*59*, see also individual regions; geology of 60; climate of 60, *60*; landscape of ancient 60; vegetation of 60–62, *63*, 204; ancient settlement patterns in 62; life in ancient and modern compared 25, 142; mapping of 64, *64*–*65*; as symbol 224
Israel, (northern) kingdom of 33, *33*, 87, 92, 134, 153; heartland of 149; boundaries of extended 136, 137; and Judah 33, *33*, 178; harassed by Shishak 33, *33*, 121, 153, 178; obliterated by Assyrians *33*, *34*, 35, 149; repopulated with non-Jews 156, 158
Issachar, tribe of 29, 152
Issus, battle of 36, 223
ivories 154, 156

Jabbok, brook (Nahr ez-Zerqa) 194, 200, 202, 204, 206, 207, 208, 210
Jabesh-gilead 168; delivered by Saul 29, 169, 200, 207
Jabin, king of Hazor 136, 152
Jabneh 81
Jacob 17, 24, *25*, 120, 151; and Esau 120, 206; at Bethel 153, *160*; tomb of 99; sons of 25, 98
Jacob's well 159
Jael *48*, 136
Jaffa see Joppa
Jahaz 206
Jamdat Nasr: tablet from *16*
James, St 41, 158
James, St (brother of Jesus) 42
Janoah 130
Jarmuth 86, 88
Jeba (Geba) *170*–*171*, 172
Jebel Helal 26
Jebel Islamiyeh see Ebal, Mount
Jebel Musa see Sinai, Mount
Jebel Quruntul see Temptation, Mount of the
Jebel es-Sabha 123
Jebel Serbal 126–127
Jebel et-Tih *127*
Jebel et-Tur see Gerizim, Mount
Jebus: equated with Jerusalem 165
Jebusites 31, 165, 173
Jehoahaz, king of Israel 33, 137
Jehoash (Joash), king of Judah 35, 87–88, 120, 137
Jehoiachin, king of Judah 36, 180
Jehoram see Joram
Jehoshaphat, king of Judah 124, 155
Jehu, king of Israel 33, 136, 156, 158, 208
Jenin see Beth-haggan
Jephthah 207
Jerahmeelites: Negeb of 117

INDEX

Jerash see Gerasa
Jeremiah 17, 36, 179, 180; book of 18, 88, 179–180; —, cited 66, 116, 153, 158, 160, 179, 200, 208, 210, 217, 222
Jericho 194, 196–198, 199; Joshua and 27, 153, 196, 198; Old Testament city of 196, 197, 198, 198, 199; John the Baptist in vicinity of 112, 140, 198; Jesus at 198; New Testament city of 196; called "city of palms" 165, 196, 198; springs at 194, 194, 196; tower at 197; urn from 197; monasteries near 194, 198–199; route from to Jerusalem 184
Jeroboam (I), king of Israel 33, 136, 153, 154, 160–161, 178
Jeroboam II, king of Israel 33, 35, 137, 208
Jerome, St: translates Bible 21
Jerusalem 172–191; as Jebusite city 86, 99, 164, 165; David's capital at 31, 32, 33, 100, 153, 164, 172, 174, 176, 177, see also Jerusalem, city of David; established as religious centre 138, 176, 183, see also Jerusalem, temple; threatened by Shishak 33, 87, 178; attacked by Joash 88; attacked by Assyrians 35, 88, see also under Hezekiah; attacked by Babylonians 35, 36, 88, 180; exiles' hopes of return to expressed 116; in post-exilic period 36, 158, 180, 198, 216; resented by Samaritans 158; rebuilt by Herod 39, 181, Jesus at 39, 40, 158, 183, 185; early Christian community at 41, 42, 189; John Mark 42; apostles persecuted at 41, 42, 159, 189; Council of 42, 189; destroyed by Romans 39, 186, 190; besieged by Crusaders 164, 178–179
—, site of 164, 172–173, 174; water supply of 173, 178–179, 181; equated with Salem? 164; equated with Jebus 165; on early maps 64, 64–65; view of 165; modern development around 60; route from to Beer-sheba 98; route from to Jericho 184
—, Antonia fortress 181, 188, 190; chapel of the Flagellation 190; church of St Anne 184; church of the Dormition 173, 188; church of the Holy Sepulchre 188, 191; church of St Peter in Gallicantu 186; church of the Resurrection 65; citadel (Herod's palace) 173, 188, 190; city of David 31, 172–173, 174, 174, 186; convent of the Sisters of Zion 190; Dome of the Rock 174, 186; gates of 185, 186, 189; house of Caiaphas 186; "Millo" 173; necropolis 174; pool of Bethesda 184, 186; pool of Siloam 178, 178, 179, 184, 186; spring of En-rogel 176, 177; spring of Gihon 173, 176, 177, 178, 179, 184, 186; temple 118, 118, 174, 176, 180; —, Solomon's (first) 31, 33, 177, 182, 182; —, destroyed by Babylonians 35, 36; —, post-exilic 17, 36, 37, 158, 180; —, defiled by Greeks 37, 181; —, Herod's 39, 181, 182, 182, 183, 186; —, destroyed by Romans 39, 183, 183; —, structure of 181, 182, 183; —, analogies with Arad shrine 118, 118; —, furnishings of 178, 182, 183; —, Jesus and 181, 183; tomb of Absalom 178; tomb of David 174; tomb of Jehoshaphat 178; tower of Siloam 84; walls of 173, 178, 179, 181; Way of the Cross 188, 190, 191; Zion (Mount) 176; —, as symbol 176, 177
Jerusalem hills (or saddle) 28, 58, 60, 94, 98, 149, 162–163, 178; settlement in 163, 164; vegetation of 164; communications through 163, 164, 184; as Judah/Israel border 33
Jesus 18, 38, 51–54, 100, 112, 176; childhood of 134; baptism of 39, 198, 199; temptation of 198,

198–199, 199–200; ministry of 39–40, 138, 183–184, 198, 211–213; miracles of 75, 138, 138, 140, 141, 141, 184, 198, 211; and Jerusalem 51, 158, 183, 186, 186; and temple 183, 184, 188; and Essenes 112; Transfiguration of 127, 140, 141; Passion of 40, 51 137, 188, 190, 190, 191; —, early accounts of 18; tomb of 188, 190, 191; Resurrection of 188, 190; Ascension of 189; kingship of 177; sent to non-Jews? 42
Jethro 125, 126
Jezebel 33, 75, 126, 136, 154, 156
Jezreel 154–155, 156
Jezreel, valley (or plain) of 58, 60, 130, 136, 146, 149, 149, 150, 151, 154, 155, 158, 178, 200; scene of Israelite-Canaanite battles 136, 151, 152; on communications route 149, 151, 194, 200; settlement in 151
el-Jib 165, 166–167
Joab 74, 99, 136, 172, 177
Joash see Jehoash
Job, book of 17
Joel, book of: cited 69
Johanan 180
John, St 15, 158, 159; gospel of 15, 18, 20, 20, 112; —, cited 54, 55, 117, 130, 140, 141, 158, 159, 181, 183 184, 185, 188, 198
John the Baptist 39, 112, 140, 181; ministry of 39, 198; as fulfilment of Isaiah's prophecy 112; and Essenes 112; imprisonment and death of 211, 211
John Hyrcanus 37, 103, 112, 158, 210
John Mark 42
Jokneam 150, 153
Jonah 82; and the whale 49; book of, cited 49, 82, 218
Jonathan (son of Saul) 103, 169–171, 200
Jonathan (David's spy) 177
Jonathan Maccabeus 37, 112
Joppa (Jaffa) 81, 81, 82; Peter at 41, 189
Joram (Jehoram) 33, 156, 208
Jordan, river 58, 193–194, 200, 203, 204; sources of 128; course of 130, 134, 193, 193; Israelites' crossing of 196, 198; John the Baptist by 39, 198
Jordan, valley of 94, 130, 152, 178, 192, 193, 194; topography of 193; rainfall in 194; settlement in 193, 194; "jungle" in 200
Joseph 24, 25, 26, 98, 99; in Egypt 120, 216, 217; and his brethren 45
Joseph, St 39, 183
Josephus 110, 113, 186, 211, 211
Joshua 123, 151; conquest of Canaan by 27–28, 28, 88, 92, 99, 151, 153, 196; book of, cited 26, 27–28, 28, 29, 32, 74, 81, 86–87, 88, 99, 108, 112, 113, 119, 121, 130, 134, 136, 151, 153, 158, 164, 165, 172, 184, 196, 198, 200, 207
Josiah, king of Judah 36, 120, 156, 218; prophecy concerning 153; religious reforms of 177, 179, 180, 182; death of 153
Jotham 152
Judah, tribe of 26, 29, 98, 109, 112, 119; territory of 81, 98, 108, 112, 121, 164–165; Negeb of 117; harassed by Philistines 29, 81, 87
Judah, (southern) kingdom of 33, 33, 33–35, 88, 92, 124, 172, 178; nature of territory of 149; Jerusalem as capital of 103; and Israel 33, 178; attacked by Shishak 33, 33, 87, 121, 178; and Assyria 34, 35, 35, 36, 88, 178, 179; defeated by Babylonians 35, 208
Judas Maccabeus 37, 103
Judea 38, 39, 39, 82, 110, 134, 158, 224
Judean desert 94, 94, 96–97, 98, 103, 104–112, 104, 105, 149, 163, 164; rainfall in 95, 104, 105, 108, 109; landscape of 95, 104, 104; settlement in 105, 108, 112; John the Baptist in 198
Judean hills 28, 60, 94–103, 94, 95;

settlement in 98; communications in 98; see also Hebron hills
Judean plain 76
Judges: period of the 29, 30, 152–153, 200; book of 17, 29, 30, 86, 87; —, cited 46, 47, 48, 67, 74, 81, 82, 127, 136, 140, 152, 158, 165, 168, 169, 198, 200, 207, 208
Judith 49; book of, cited 49
Julius Caesar 38, 39
Justinian 19

Kadesh-barnea 123, 123; and site of Mount Sinai 126
Kafr Kanna see Cana of Galilee
Kanah, brook see Wadi Qana
Karmon, Y.: quoted 99, 137
Kedesh 130, 136
Kedesh-naphtali 136
Keilah 86, 87
Kenaan, Mount 130
Kenites 198; Negeb of 117
Ker Porter, Sir Robert 221
Kirbet el-Hureibeh see Horbat Sevi
Khirbet el-Mafjar 196
Khorsabad: reliefs at 218
Kidron valley 174, 177, 178, 185; tower in 184
King James Bible see Authorized Version
Kings, books of 154; 1 Kings 33, 75, 87, 92; —, cited 33, 48, 66, 86, 118, 121, 123, 124, 126, 127, 130, 136, 153, 154, 155, 156, 160–161, 164, 176, 177, 178, 179, 182, 204, 208, 216; 2 Kings 87; —, cited 81, 88, 124, 130, 136–137, 141, 144, 145, 154, 155, 156, 164, 168, 177, 194, 196, 198, 200, 204, 208, 217
kingship: Gideon refuses 152; Saul and 29, 31; of Christ 177; sacred status of 21
Kir-hareseth 208
Kiriath-arba see Hebron
Kiriath-jearim 29, 165, 168, 178; meaning of 164; Ark of the Covenant at 172
Kishon see Nahal Kishon
Kitchener, H.H. (Lord Kitchener) 65
Korah 123
kurkar ridges 76, 80

Laban 206
Lachish 86, 87, 88, 88, 89, 118, 164; conquered by Joshua 86, 88; conquered by Assyrians 86, 88, 91, 92, 178; conquered by Babylonians 88; letters 88, 89; reliefs of siege of 88, 90, 92; reconstruction of 90–91
Laish: Dan at 87, 136
Laodicea 224
Last Supper 188, 190; different gospel accounts of 21; and Passover 40; see also Holy Week
Latter Prophets 17
Law (Torah) 17, 17, 25; whether applicable to Gentile converts to Christianity 40, 42
Layard, A.H. 90, 91, 221
Lazarus 184
Lear, Edward 165
Lebanon 88, 130
Lehi 87
leopards 62, 134
Lepsius, Richard: quoted 126–127
Levi 151
Levites 151; concubine of 168
Leviticus, book of: cited 183
Libnah 86
Lindisfarne Gospels 20
lions 46, 66, 103, 155, 156, 200, 218
el-Lisan 194
Litani, river 130
Lod 78; basin 78, 80, 81, 84, 87
Lord's Prayer: different gospel versions of 21
Lorenzetti, Pietro 51
Lot 98, 134, 153, 194 195; wife of 44, 195; sons of 25
Luke, St, gospel of 21; cited 21, 39, 40, 50, 103, 112, 127, 130, 137, 138, 140, 141, 144, 158, 181, 183, 184, 185, 188, 189, 198, 211
Luther, Martin 22, 22
Lystra 42

Maaleh Adummim 184
Maccabees 112; revolt of 37, 37, 181; book of, cited 103, 134
Machaerus 211, 211, 212–213
Machpelah, cave of 98
Madaba: mosaic from 65
Madon 136
Magdala see Taricheae
el-Maghtas 198
Magi 103
Magnificat 181
Mahanaim 172, 208
Mahaneh-dan 168
Malachi, book of: cited 127
Manasseh, tribe of 26, 29, 152, 158, 200; territory of 81, 151, 207
Manasseh, king of Judah 36, 179
manuscripts, illuminated 15, 20, 45, 46–47, 49, 56
Maon 98, 103, 112
Mareshah 86, 87, 88
Mari 134
Marj Sanur 149, 150
Mark, St, gospel of 21; —, cited 56, 66, 75, 112, 127, 130, 137, 138, 140, 141, 171, 177, 185, 188, 198, 199, 211, 213
Mark Antony 38, 39; Antonia fortress called after 181
Mary, the Virgin 39, 181, 181; purification of 183
Mary Magdalene, St 55, 141, 185
Masada 39, 105, 110, 110, 111, 112; David at? 108–112
Massah 116, 123
Mattathias 37, 181
Matthew, St 140; gospel of 20, 21; —, cited 39, 40, 51, 68, 69, 71, 75, 103, 112, 140, 140–141, 141, 143, 145, 183, 185, 198, 200, 211
"Matthew's" Bible 21
Medeba 206
Megiddo 146, 151, 156, 157, 157, 158, 164; Ahab's forces at 155; Josiah killed at 36, 158; Assyrian province of 137
Melchizedek 177
Melkart 75, 136
Memphis 217
Menashe hills 146, 150, 151, 158
menorah 183
Menzaleh, Lake 27
Meribah 116, 123
Merneptah 26–27
Merom 136; "waters of" 136
Meron, mountains 130
Mesad Rahel 123
Mesha, king of Moab 202, 204; inscription of 208
Mesopotamia 216, 217, 218; Patriarchs' links with 24, 25, 218
Micah, book of: cited 88, 100, 103, 144, 156, 169, 176
Micaiah ben Imlah 156
Michmash 169, 169–171, 172
Middin 112
Midian 126
Midianites 125, 152; routed by Gideon 152, 200; shrine of at Timna 125, 125, 126
Miletus 42
Mizpah 168, 169, 178; administration at 36, 153, 158, 180
Moab 26, 103, 136, 152, 202, 202, 203, 204, 206, 208; founded by son of Lot 25; under Israelite rule 31, 33, 208; at war with Israel 165, 207, 208; David's parents in 109; plains of 207; sheep farming in 203, 204
Moreh, hill of 151
Moreh, oak of 151
Moresheth-gath 86, 88
mosaics 65, 141, 181, 224
Moses 44, 116, 117, 123, 127, 151, 204, 206; Midianite connections of 125, 126; sees promised land 207
Motza 189
Muhraqa 150
Mukhmas 172
Muslims 142, 174

Nabal 98, 103
Nabateans 42, 211, 213
Nablus 58, 151, 159; formerly Neapolis 158

INDEX

Naboth: vineyard of 156
Nag Hammadi 20
Nahal Aijalon 76
Nahal Alexander 80
Nahal Ammud 130
Nahal Aroer 121
Nahal Beer Sheva 94, 119, *121*
Nahal Besor 119
Nahal Beth Horon 86
Nahal David 108
Nahal Dishon 136
Nahal Ezyona 87
Nahal ha-Elah 87
Nahal Hadera 80
Nahal Hillazon 72
Nahal Iron 150–151, 157
Nahal Kesalon 164
Nahal Kishon 72, *72*, 74, 75, 136, 150, 151, 152, 154
Nahal Lachish 76, 86, 87, 98
Nahal Meir 86
Nahal Mishmar *109*
Nahal Naaman 72
Nahal Nahshon 76, 86
Nahal Oren 150
Nahal Poleg 80
Nahal Refaim 88
Nahal Shechem 150
Nahal Shiqmah 76, 84, 118
Nahal Sorek 80, 81, 86, 87, 164–165
Nahal Tabor 130
Nahal Tanninim 58, 76
Nahal Tut 150
Nahal Yarkon 76, 80, 81, 87
Nahal Yoqneam 150
Nahal Zin 117, 123
Nahariyya 72
Nahash, king of Ammon 169, 200, 207
Nahr el-Yarmuk *see* Yarmuk, river
Nahr ez-Zerqa *see* Jabbok, brook
Nahum, book of: cited 218–221
Nain 141
Naomi 103
Naphtali, tribe of 152; territory of 130, 136; —, overrun by Syrians 136
Nathan 177
Nathaniel 137
Nazareth 39, *136–137*, 137, 138, 141, 181; Jesus rejected at 137, 140; church of the Annunciation *136*
Neapolis *see* Nablus
Neapolis (in Greece) 42
Nebi Musa *193*
Nebi Samwil 172, 176, 180
Nebo (god) *17*, 221
Nebo (town) 208
Nebo, Mount 207
Nebuchadnezzar, king of Babylon 36, 88, 158, 198, 208
Neco (Pharaoh Necho II) 36, 158
Negeb *see* Negev
Negev 76, *114*, 116–126, 152, 178; meaning of 84, 117; geology of 118, 121, *121*–123; rainfall in 118, 120; ancient settlements in *115*; communications in 118, 120, 121; alternative Exodus routes through *115*
Nehemiah 35, 36, 158, 180, 198, 216; book of, cited 88, 103, 121, 180, 216, 222
Netanya 78, 80
New English Bible 169, 173
Nibshan 112
Nicodemus 183
Nile, river 216, 217
Nimrud (Calah) *221*
Nineveh 218–221
Nob 17
Numbers, book of: cited 26, 98, 99, 116, 117, 118, 121, 123, *125*, 130, 206

Oboth 123
Octavian *see* Augustus Caesar
Og, king of Bashan 207
olives 68, 86, 137; presses for *139*, *144*, *185*
Olives, Mount of *165*, *173*, 177, 185, 188, 189
Omer *121*
Omri, king of Israel 33, *33*, 134, 136, 154, 155, 156, 158, 208
On 123

Onias III 112
Ophrah 152
Oreb 152
Origen 198
ossuaries *144*
Ottobeuren Master *50*

paganism 36, 37, *89*, 156, 160, 161, 179, 207; promoted by Jezebel 75, 136; cult of the dead 160; fertility cults 72, 160, *160*; witchcraft 160, *161*; *see also* idolatry
Palestine *see* Israel
Palestine Exploration Fund 65
Palm Sunday 39
Pan: shrine of at Caesarea Philippi 211
Paran, wilderness of 123
Paris, Matthew 65
Parthians *38*, 199
Passion *see under* Jesus
Passover 26, 185; Samaritan celebration of *159*; and Last Supper 40
pastoralism: ancient 98, 100, 149, *203*; modern *104*, *105*, *109*, *143*, *154*, *204–205*; *see also* goats; sheep
Patriarchs 24–25, *25*, 65, 118; *see also* Abraham; Isaac; Jacob
Paul, St 168, 116, 117, 189, 224, *224*; conversion of 56, 213; journeys of 40, 41–42, 74, 82, 213, 223
Pella (in Decapolis) 210
Pelusium 217
Penptah 75
Penuel: capital of Israel moved to 33, 153
Perea *38*, 39, *39*, 210, 213
Persia 35, 36, 216; empire of 216, 222–223
Peter, St 42, 140, 189; confesses Jesus the Messiah 39, 141, *211*, 213; denies Jesus 56; and missionary work 41, 42, 159, *159*; house of at Capernaum 138, *138*, 140
2 Peter (epistle): cited 207
Peters, J.P.: quoted 153
Petra 208, *208–209*
Pharisees 113
Philadelphia 210, 224
Philip, St 41, 82, 159
Philip (son of Herod the Great) 39, 138, 140, 210
Philippi 42
Philistines 33, 81, 88, 119, 157, 172; arrival of 29, *81*, 119; harass tribe of Dan 29, *29*; and Samson 82, 87; and Samuel 168; capture Ark 153; and Saul 31, *31*, 99, 103, 164, 200; and David 31, *31*, 81, 87, 92, 99, 164, 172, 173; fertility cult of *161*; burial rites of *161*
Phoenicia 74; script of *16*; —, inscription in 75; influence of on Palestinian art 72; sarcophagus from 74; *see also* Sidon; Tyre
Phrygia 42
pigs 213; wild 66, 134
pilgrimage 27, 64, 65, 68, 138, 190
Pisgah, Mount 206
Pithom 26
plants 68, *68*; fruiting 68, 69, 72, 134, 137; *see also* trees
ploughing 98, *143*
Pompey *38*, 39, 78
Pontius Pilate 39, 82, 137, 190
pottery *135*, 137
Poynter, Edward 44
Priscilla 42
Prodigal Son 43, *50*
Prophets 17
Proverbs, book of 17, 217; cited 66
Psalms, book of 17; cited 66, 67, 116, 123, 127, *142*, 152, 164, 176, 177, 204, 207, 221
Ptolemais *see* Acco
Ptolemy, dynasty of 36, 216

Qarqar, battle of *34*
el-Qubeibeh 188–189
Quirinius 39
Qumran 18, *105*, 112, 113, *113*; identified with City of Salt? 112, 113; identified with Secacah? 112, 113

Raamses 26
Rabbath-Ammon 210
Rachel: tomb of 168–169
Ramah 168, 169, 171, 178, 180
Ramallah 94
Ramathaim-zophim 168
Ramesses II 26, *216*
Ramoth-gilead 204, 208; Ahab killed at 33, 155; Jehu anointed at 156
Rebekah 25, 120
Rechabites 116
Red Sea 27, 126
Reformation: and Bible 21, 22
Rehob 74
Rehoboam 33, 121, 136; fortifies cities of Judah 87, *90*, 103; and northern tribes 153, 178
Rembrandt 45, *50*
Rephaim, valley of 164, 173
Reuben *29*; territory of 204, 207
Revelation, book of 223, 223–224, 224
Revised Standard Version 21, 169, 173
Revised Version 18, 21
rift valley 58, *58*, 60, 120, 123, 130, 149, 151; southern part of (*Arabah*) 117, 123–126; *see also* Jordan, valley of
Roberts, David 72, *151*, *191*, 216
Rogers, John 22, *22*
Romans *38*, 39, 74, 92, 186; empire of 216, 217; Jewish revolts against 39, 110, *211*; *see also* Masada
Romans, epistle to: cited 224
Rome 224; mosaic from *224*
Rosh ha-Niqra 72, 74, 75
Rujm el-Bahr 112
Runciman, Steven: quoted 164, 178–179
Ruth 100, 103; book of, cited 100, 204
Rylands fragment 17, 20, *20*

Sadducees 113
Sahel Arrabeh *see* Dothan, valley of
Sahel Kafr Istuneh *see* Shiloh, valley of
Sahel Mahneh (Emek ha-Mikhmetat) 150, 151
St. Catherine's monastery (Mount Sinai) 18, *18*, *19*, 20
Salem: equated with Jerusalem? 164
Salome 21
Salome Alexandra 39
Salt Sea *see* Dead Sea
Samaria (Sebaste) 153, *154*, 156, 158; capital of Israel at 33, 88, 134, 154; Ahab's council of war at 155–156; besieged by Syrians 155, 156; conquered by Assyrians 35, 154, 156, *218*; corruption and idolatry of 156; rebuilt by Herod the Great 154, 158; ivories from *154*
Samaria (region) 39, *39*, 158, *159*; population of deported 156; annexed to Judea 158; shunned by Jews 158, 159; Christianity spreads to 41, 159
Samarian hills 58, 60, 134, *146*, 149–150, *149*, 178; character of 149; ancient settlement in 150; routes through 149
Samaritans: as separate religious community 18, 158, *159*; and ministry of Jesus 158–159; shunned by Jews 158, 159; hostility of towards Jerusalem 158; *see also* Good Samaritan
Samson *81*, 82, *84*, 86, *86*, 87; scenes from story of *46–47*
Samuel 29, 152–153, 168; and Philistines 168; and Saul 168, 169; anoints David king 103; sons of 120
1 Samuel 17: cited 29–31, *48*, 82, 87, 98, 103, 108, 109, 112, 117, 119, 120, 121, 152–153, 164, 168, 169, 169–171, 172, 200, 207, 208
2 Samuel: cited 67, 74, 87, 99, 103, 109, 136, *145*, 151, 171, 172, 173, 176, 177, 198, 200
Sanballat 158, 180
Sarah 25, 98
Sarepta *see* Zarephath
Sargon II, king of Assyria 218
Sasa 130

Saul, king of Israel and Judah 29–31, 168, 169, 207–208; chosen as king 29–31, 168, 169; and Gibeonites 171–172; and Philistines 31, *31*, 99, 119, 164, 169; seeks to kill David 82, 87, 103, 108, 112; death of 31, 200
Saul of Tarsus *see* Paul, St
Scopus, Mount *173*
sculpture 72, 78, *81*, 88, *90*, *121*, *135*, *157*, *161*, *174*, *206*, *216*, *218*, *224*
Scythopolis *200*, 210; *see also* Beth-shean
Sebaste *see* Samaria
Secacah 112
Sede Boqer 121
Seilun *see* Shiloh
Seir, Mount 126
Sela (es-Sela): equated with Petra? 208
Seleucids, dynasty of 37
Sennacherib, king of Assyria 88, 120, 178; captures Lachish 86, 88, *91*, 178; scribes of *16*
Sepphoris 137, 141
Sergius Paulus 42
Sermon on the Mount 141
Sethos I 26
Shaalim, land of 168
Shalisha, land of 168
Sharon, plain of 76, 80
Sheba (son of Bichri) 136
Sheba, queen of *48*
Shechem (Tell Balata) 98, 152, 153, 158; Patriarchs at 24, 25, *25*, 151, 164, 206; capital of Israel at 33, 153; Abimelech and 152; destroyed 158; rebuilt as Neapolis 158
Shechem prince of Shechem 151
Shechemite Dodecalogue 151
sheep 66, 98, 103, 104, *104*, 108, *109*, *143*, 154; parable of the one lost 112
"Shema, servant of Jeroboam": seal of *156*
Shephelah 28, 58, *58*, 60, 84–88, *84–85*, 94, 98, 149; meaning of 84; geology of 84; climate of 84–86; settlement in 86; vegetation of 86; landscape of 86; communications 86, 120; defensibility of 88
"Shepherd" of Hermas 18
Sheshbazzar 180
Shiloh (Seilun) 152–153, 158, 168; destroyed by Philistines 29, 153; sanctuary and festival at 152, 168; valley of (Sahel Kafr Istuneh) 149, 152
Shimei 177
Shimron 136
Shishak (Pharaoh Shoshenq I) 33, *33*, 87, 120, 121
Shunem 141
Shur, wilderness of 116
Sidon 39, 74, *74*, 75, *75*, 136
siege engines *90*, *93*, *111*
Sihon, king of Amorites 204, 206, 207
Silas 42
Simeon 151; tribe of 26, *29*
Simon of Cyrene *191*
Simon Maccabeus 37, 112, 134
Simon Magus 159
Sinai peninsula *115*, 117, 126–127, *127*
Sinai, Mount (Horeb, Mount) *19*, 27, *115*, 117, 126–127, 176; Moses on 25, *44*, *115*, 117; equated with Jebel Musa 117, 126–127, *127*
Sirbonis, Lake 27
Sisera 29, *48*, 136, 152
Smith, G.A. 78, 84, 108, 204
Soco 87, 88
Sodom 98, 138, 194; location of 194, 195; destruction of 195–196; as symbol for wickedness 196, 200
Solomon 31, *81*, 86, 103, 120, 121, 123, *124*, 130, 134, 158, 164, 216; wins succession struggle 177, 179; empire of 31, 123–124; administrative districts of 32, 78, 157, 178, 200; wisdom of 176, 217; visited by queen of Sheba *48*; and northern tribes 153; builds temple 31, 74, 75, 177; *see also* Jerusalem, temple; apostasy of 33, 179

Song of Songs (Song of Solomon) 17, 108
Stephen, St 41, 159, 189
Succoth 200, 206
Suez, gulf of: Exodus route along 27
Susa 180, 222–223, *223*
Sychar 159
Syria 92, 202, 223; part of fertile crescent *24;* Acco and *72;* and Ramoth-gilead 204; Roman province of 210–211; *see also* Damascus

Tabgha: site of feeding of five thousand *141*
Tabnit, king of Sidon 75
Tabor, Mount 130, 136, *140*, 141; traditional site of Transfiguration *140*, 141
Tahpanes 36
Taricheae (Magdala) 141
Tarqumiya *see* Iphtah
Tarsus 42
Tekoa 98, 103
Tel Aviv 78
Tel Halif 119
Tel Hannaton 130
Tell Balata *see* Shechem
Tell el-Farah *see* Tirzah
Tell el-Ful *see* Gibeah
Tell el-Kheleifa 123, 124
Tell en-Nasbeh 180
Tel Malhata 118, 120
Tel Masos 120, 121
Tel Sera 119
Temptation, Mount of the *198*, 199–200
tent shrine 125, 126, 176
Thebes (in Egypt) 217
Thebez 152
Thessalonica 42
Thomas, St: gospel of *20*
Thomson, W.M.: quoted 76–78, 78, 134, 151
Three Taverns 224
threshing *142*
Thutmore III *153*
Tiberias *130*, *132–133*, 137, 141
Tiberius: coin of *186*
Tiglath-pileser III, king of Assyria 35, 88, 130, 134, 137, 208
Tigris, river *24*, 218
Timna 124, 125, *125;* Hathor temple at 124, 125, *125*, 126
Timnah 88; Samson at *46*, 87
Timsah, Lake 27
Tirzah (Tell el-Farah) 152, 154
Tischendorf, Constantin 18, *18*
Titus: arch of *183*
Tob, land of 207
tombs *144*, *178*, 188, *191*
Torah: translated into Greek 17
Trajanus Decius: coin of *83*
Transfiguration 39, 127, *140*, 141, *204*
Transjordan 25, 136, 141, 202, *203*, *204*, 206–213; climate of 60; mountains of *130;* Israelites in 202; conquered by Assyrians 35; Greek cities in 36–37, *see also* Decapolis; *see also individual regions:* Ammon; Edom; Moab; Syria; *etc.*
trees 68, *69*, 78, 151; loss of since biblical times 60–62, *62*, *63*, 80, 98, 164, *165;* replanted *62, 84;* balsam 164, 173; carob 58, 86; cedar 86; —, fable of thistle and 88; oak, deciduous (Tabor oak) 58, 60, 80, 130, 151; —, evergreen 60, *63*, 74. 86, 94, *94*, *128*, 130, 151; palms *108;* sycamore (sycamore fig) 86, 98
tribes of Israel, the twelve 26, *29,32;* founded by sons of Jacob 25; political (dis)unity of *30*, 33, 168; divide into ten northern and two southern 33, *see also* Israel, kingdom of *and* Judah, kingdom of; territory apportioned between 152, 207, *see also under individual tribes*
Tristram, H.B.: quoted 184
Troas 42
Tubas 150, 152
et-Tur 185
Tyndale, William 21, 22, 22
Tyre 39. 42, 74, 75, *75*, 82, 136; cities ceded to by Solomon 31, 74–75, 130; besieged by Nebuchadnezzar 75; St Paul at *74;* "ladder of" 75; coin of *145*

Ur 24
Uzziah, king of Judah 35, 81, 124, 208

Vespasian 158
Via Dolorosa *see* Jerusalem, Way of the Cross
vines (grapevines) 68, 86, 98, 137; confined to Christian areas 142

Wadi Deir Ballut 149
Wadi Faria 150, *151*, 156, 194, 206
Wadi Fasail 152
Wadi el-Ghar 98
Wadi el-Halil 98
Wadi el-Hesa *see* Zered, brook
Wadi el-Humr 152
Wadi el-Kub 149
Wadi Makkuk 196
Wadi Malih 194
Wadi Nablus 150, *151*, 154
Wadi Qana 82; equated with brook Kanah? 81
Wadi Qilt (Wady Kelt) 184, *194*, 196, *196*, 198
Wadi el-Qudeirat *123*
Wadi Seilun 149
Wadi Sereda 94
Wadi Suwenit 169, *170–171*, *172*

Wadi el-Yabis 207
Way of the Cross *see under* Jerusalem
"Way of the Sea" 150–151
Wedric, abbot of Liessies *15*
weights and measures *145*
Weyden, Roger van der *54*
wilderness: as symbol 112, 116–117, *116*
wisdom literature 217
witchcraft 160
writing: invention of 14–17; different systems of 16, *16;* utensils *17*

Yarkon, river *see* Nahal Yarkon
Yarmuk: river (Nahr el-Yarmuk) 202, 204, 206, 210; triangle 193

Zacchaeus 198
Zachariah 181
Zadok 177
Zalmunna 152, 200
Zanoah 88
Zarephath (Sarepta) 75
Zebah 152, 200
Zeboiim 194
Zebulun, tribe of 136, 152
Zebulun, valley of 74
Zechariah, book of: cited 185, 200
Zedekiah, king of Judah 35, 36, 180, 198
Zeeb 152
Zelzah: site of Rachel's tomb 169
Zerah the Ethiopian 119
Zered, brook (Wadi el-Hesa) 204, 208
Zerubbabel 158, 180, 182
Zeus Olympios: cult of 37
Ziklag 119; David at 31, 119
Zin, wilderness of *124*
Zin, Mount 123
Zion, Mount *see under* Jerusalem
Ziph 103
Zoar 195
Zorah *84*, 87, 88
Zuph, land of 168